Business
Plans
Handbook

Highlights

Business Plans Handbook, Volume 5 (BPH-5) is a collection of actual business plans compiled by entrepreneurs seeking funding for small businesses throughout North America. For those looking for examples of how to approach, structure, and compose their own business plans, *BPH-5* presents 25 sample plans, including plans for the following businesses:

- Bagel Shop
- Bread Bakery
- Car Wash
- Cigar Shop
- Climbing Outfitter
- Computer Reseller
- Detective Agency

- Freight Expediting
- Gift Store
- Internet Cafe
- Marketing Consultancy
- Metal Shop
- Pasta Franchise
- Taxi Service

FEATURES AND BENEFITS

BPH-5 offers many features not provided by other business planning references including:

○ Twenty-five business plans, with a focus on the uses and effects of the Internet and various online services within the small business sector. Each of these real business plans represents an owner's successful attempt at clarifying (for themselves and others) the reasons that the business should exist or expand and why a lender should fund the enterprise.

○ Two fictional plans that are used by business counselors at a prominent small business development organization as examples for their clients. (You will find these in the Business Plan Template Appendix.)

○ An expanded directory section that includes: listings for venture capital and finance companies, which specialize in funding start-up and second-stage small business ventures, and a comprehensive listing of Service Corps of Retired Executives (SCORE) offices. In addition, the Appendix also contains updated listings of all Small Business Development Centers (SBDCs); associations of interest to entrepreneurs; Small Business Administration (SBA) Regional Offices; and consultants specializing in small business planning and advice. It is strongly advised that you consult supporting organizations while planning your business, as they can provide a wealth of useful information.

○ A Small Business Term Glossary to help you decipher the sometimes confusing terminology used by lenders and others in the financial and small business communities.

○ An expanded bibliography, arranged by subject, containing citations from over 1,500 small business reference publications and trade periodicals.

○ A Business Plan Template which serves as a model to help you construct your own business plan. This generic outline lists all the essential elements of a complete business plan and their components, including the Summary, Business History and Industry Outlook, Market Examination, Competition, Marketing, Administration and Management, Financial Information, and other key sections. Use this guide as a starting point for compiling your plan.

○ Extensive financial documentation required to solicit funding from small business lenders. *BPH-5* contains the most comprehensive financial data within the series to date. You will find examples of: Cash Flows, Balance Sheets, Income Projections, and other financial information included with the textual portions of the plan.

Business Plans Handbook

A COMPILATION OF ACTUAL BUSINESS PLANS DEVELOPED BY SMALL BUSINESSES THROUGHOUT NORTH AMERICA

VOLUME

5

Kristin Kahrs,
Paul R. Kahrs,
Editors

GALE

DETROIT · LONDON

Editors: Kristin and Paul Kahrs

Contributing Desktop Specialist: Shelley Andrews

Project Manager: William Harmer

Contributing Editors: Eva M. Davis and Jennifer Arnold Mast
Assistant Editor: Ellen Sciba

Technical Training Specialist: Gwen Turecki-Luczycka

Managing Editor: Deborah M. Burek

Production Director: Mary Beth Trimper
Assistant Production Manager: Evi Seoud
Production Assistant: Deborah Milliken

Product Design Manager: Cynthia Baldwin

Data Entry Services Manager: Eleanor Allison
Senior Data Entry Associate: Beverly Jendrowski
Data Entry Associate: Timothy Alexander

While every effort has been made to ensure the reliability of the information presented in this publication, Gale Research does not guarantee the accuracy of the data contained herein. Gale accepts no payment for listing; and inclusion in the publication of any organization, agency, database product, publication, or individual does not imply endorsement by the editor or publisher.

Errors brought to the attention of the publisher and verified to the satisfaction of the publisher will be corrected in future editions.

3 2280 00608 6672

ISBN 0-7876-1263-4
ISSN 1084-4473

Printed in the United States of America

10 9 8 7 6 5 4 3 2 1

Contents

Appendixes

Introduction

Perhaps the most important aspect of business planning is simply *doing* it. More and more business owners are beginning to compile business plans even if they don't need a bank loan. Others discover the value of planning when they *must* provide a business plan for the bank. The sheer act of putting thoughts on paper seems to clarify priorities and provide focus. Sometimes business owners completely change strategies when compiling their plan, deciding on a different product mix or advertising scheme after finding that their assumptions were incorrect. This kind of healthy thinking and re-thinking via business planning is becoming the norm. The editors of *Business Plans Handbook, Volume 5 (BPH-5)* sincerely hope that this latest addition to the series is a helpful tool in the successful completion of your business plan, no matter what the reason for creating it.

This fifth volume, like each volume in the series, offers genuine business plans used by real people. *BPH-5* provides 25 business plans used by actual entrepreneurs to gain funding support for their new businesses. The business and personal names and addresses and general locations have been changed to protect the privacy of the plan authors.

NEW BUSINESS OPPORTUNITIES

As in other volumes in the series, *BPH-5* finds entrepreneurs engaged in a wide variety of creative endeavors. For instance, business plans that discuss capitalizing on new trends include those for a rock climbing equipment outfitter that takes advantage of nearby climbing terrain; an upscale bread-only bakery; a cigar, coffee *and* wine emporium, which is one entrepreneur's effort to ride the crest of more than one trend; and an Internet Cafe, providing both Internet access and the coffee that Internet savvy customers seem to enjoy. Another Internet-related business is discussed in the *OpExNeT* business plan. This is an example of a revolutionary approach to bidding and contracting that takes advantage of Internet technololgy. The franchise business plans included in this volume will offer an excellent introduction to this alternative way of starting a business. Franchises highlighted in *BPH-5* include a take-out fresh pasta restaurant, a postal services center, and an office furniture retailer. Popular and traditional businesses are featured in *BPH-5* as well. Among them are a taxi service seeking to make inroads in an underserviced area, a detective agency seeking start-up funding, a gift shop exploiting the lucrative summer tourist trade, a retailer of party supplies and accessories, and a gag and costume store located in a prominent downtown area. The omnipresent nature of computers gives rise to numerous businesses related to them. Also included in this volume are two very different business plans for computer resellers that provide hardware, software, and support.

Comprehensive financial documentation has become increasingly important as today's entrepreneurs compete for the finite resources of business lenders. Our plans illustrate the financial data generally required of loan applicants, including Income Statements, Financial Projections, Cash Flows, and Balance Sheets.

ENHANCED APPENDIXES

In an effort to provide the most relevant and valuable information for our readers, we have updated the coverage of small business resources. For instance, you will find: a directory section, which includes listings of all of the Service Corps of Retired Executives (SCORE) offices; an informative glossary, which includes small business terms; and a bibliography, which includes reference titles essential to starting and operating a business venture in all 50 states. In addition we have updated the list of Small Business Development Centers (SBDCs); Small Business Administration Regional Offices; venture capital and finance companies, which specialize in funding start-up and second-stage small business enterprises; associations of interest to entrepreneurs; and consultants, specializing in small business advice and planning. For your reference, we have also reprinted the business plan template, which provides a comprehensive overview of the essential components of a business plan and two fictional plans used by small business counselors.

SERIES INFORMATION

If you already have the first four volumes of *BPH*, with this fifth volume, you will now have a collection of 131 real business plans (not including the one updated plan in the second volume, whose original appeared in the first, or the two fictional plans in the Business Plan Template Appendix section of the second, third, fourth, and fifth volumes); contact information for hundreds of organizations and agencies offering business expertise; a helpful business plan template; a foreword providing advice and instruction to entrepreneurs on how to begin their research; more than 1,500 citations to valuable small business development material; and a comprehensive glossary of terms to help the business planner navigate the sometimes confusing language of entrepreneurship.

ACKNOWLEDGEMENTS

The Editors wish to thank William Harmer of the Small Business Resources and Technology team for his diligence in coordinating this title.

The Editors also wish to sincerely thank Palo Alto Software, makers of Business Plan Pro, the premier business planning software tool, for providing the use of several business plans in this volume.

Thanks are also in order for the many contributors to *BPH-5*, whose business plans will serve as examples to future generations of entrepreneurs, as well as the users of the title who called with their helpful suggestions. Your help was greatly appreciated.

COMMENTS WELCOME

Your comments on *BPH-5* are appreciated. Please direct all correspondence, suggestions for future volumes of *BPH*, and other recommendations to the following:

Business Plans Handbook, Volume 5
(Address until September 15, 1998)
Gale Research
835 Penobscot Bldg.
645 Griswold St.
Detroit MI 48226-4094

(Address after September 15, 1998)
Gale Research
27500 Drake Rd.
Farmington, MI 48331-3535

Phone: (313)961-2242
Fax: 800-339-3374
Toll-Free: 800-347-GALE
Telex: 810 221 7087
E-mail: William.Harmer@gale.com

Business
Plans
Handbook

Bagel Shop

BUSINESS PLAN

USA BAGELS

5535 Winston Blvd.
Troy, MI 43846

This business plan is an example of a niche food service operation that capitalizes on the ever-growing popularity of bagels. The store offers affordable and fresh products attempting to cater to those who wish to eat in a more healthful way. It also hopes to ride the crest of another very complementary trend: gourmet coffee consumption.

- MARKET ANALYSIS

- KEY POINTS

- EXPANSION

- DISTRIBUTION SITE

- PROMOTION OPTIONS

- COMPETITION

- USA BAGELS COMPARISON

- LOAN SUMMARY STATEMENT

- BREAKDOWN OF COSTS

- MANAGEMENT

- CONSOLIDATED BALANCE SHEET

BAGEL SHOP
BUSINESS PLAN

MARKET ANALYSIS

We believe that the metropolitan area is a great place to develop our bagel shops. For one, there are no other bagel-specific shops in the area. The closest one competition wise, would be Blackwells Bagel in Westland, and the Bagel Bakery potentially in Livonia. The lack of bagel shops in the metropolitan area definitely presents a need for our business. In our area specifically, the only competition would be that of the donut-type or the bakery-type morning-oriented business. We believe that the bagel business is different and specific enough to meet the needs of a different calling, specifically the call to eating healthier. Fresh baked bagels will be served all day. We will keep well stocked so as not to run out of customers favorite varieties. Bagels are a healthy alternative to the morning donut or pastry.

Our business fits well demographically, as 40% of the households fall into the $50,000.00 plus per year income level. The area also contains over 250,000 people residing in a 5-mile radius from which draw business.

The bagel shop consumer comes from all income levels of the market. Bagels are a relatively inexpensive luxury, costing as little or less than a donut or muffin. Almost anyone could afford a stop at our shop from time to time. Ninety-four percent of the metropolitan area are Caucasian, another strong demographic indicator of consumers that frequent our type of establishment. This is not to say that people of other ethnic backgrounds don't consume our product or wouldn't be welcome in our establishment, this is just a demographic indicator.

People are eating with a more health conscious emphasis. Not only will we be able to meet the needs of the "breakfast on the go" individual, we will also be able to meet the needs of the person looking for a quick lunch, who would rather have a healthy alternative to the fattening fast food. Our store will be equipped with a drive-thru for quick pick-up of a deli-bagel sandwich made from a wide selection of deli meats or vegetarian toppings.

KEY POINTS

Concept: From-scratch bagel baker and gourmet coffee house under one roof.

Direction: Developed and operated by people who have been franchisees and understand the need for teamwork and support.

Market Approach: Repeat sales of...
- Bagels by the dozen
- Cream cheese by the pound
- Gourmet coffee and espresso beverages by the drink
- Whole bean coffee by the pound
- Fresh baked treats

Products:

- Large 5 oz. steamed Bagel
- From scratch and baked fresh daily
- Versatile for sandwiches as well as bulk sales
- Method of preparation lends itself to production and promotion of novelty bagels
- Blended flavors of cream cheeses prepared on the premise
- Mountain Coffees roasted to peak of flavor and sold as: bulk varietal and blended whole beans, individually prepared gourmet coffee and espresso beverages
- Jonesy's Fresh cookies, muffins, cinnamon rolls and brownies baked daily in store

Direct purchase of core products: cream cheese and bagel ingredients. Satellites: up to two satellites can be serviced by a single production store. Wholesale opportunities: hospitals, schools, corporate and special events. Dual-Branding, Mountain Coffee, Jonesy's Bakery Items and USA Bagels.

Tools for Growth

USA relies on the production and bulk sales of their top of the line bagel recipe, along with their homemade cream cheeses, deli meats, and delicious Mountain coffee to position themselves in one of the fastest growing industries in the country.

EXPANSION

Between 1984 and 1993, yearly bagel consumption has grown an incredible 169%. Bagel sales exceed 2.5 billion dollars yearly, and are growing 20% annually.

The specialty or gourmet coffee segment in this country is now earning 7 billion dollars annually. While many may participate in this market, no single franchise organization dominates the market place. We would definitely like to be part of this growing industry.

Although USA franchises are located throughout the U.S. and up into Canada, the number of actual stores is not great (approximately 135). However, USA is still in its early stages of franchising and in approximately four years has established 135 privately held franchised stores.

Name recognition is growing daily. There are currently USA franchises in Redford, Bloomfield Hills, and Troy. Troy and Milford territories have just been assigned, and with our development of the metropolitan area puts the last piece of the puzzle into place for USA to be recognized as a leading force in the bagel business in the metropolitan area.

Great potential exists, not only in retail sales, but also in corporate/delivery orders, and event delivery sales. The key factor will be getting the in-store sales generated through advertising exposure, and then approximately 3-6 months later, venture into outside sales.

With the expansion into outside sales, comes greater community awareness. We feel this will in turn increase in-store sales via wider awareness of our operations, our great product and service.

Eventually we will expanding into a three-store operation. This business plan deals specifically with our first operation. We'll deal more with the expansion once our first operation is running sound.

For our initial store we will approximately 2200 sq. Ft. of operating space. The actual site has not yet been selected, however we are working with Jack Reaves, of Coleman Realty, to find a location and expedite the process. We will need a location that offers ample parking, easy in and out access for the morning and afternoon rush times, and high visibility from the road.

DISTRIBUTION SITE

√Local newspapers
√Radio spots
√Yellow Pages
√Ad spots
√On-location event sponsoring

PROMOTION OPTIONS

Bagel Baker, Livonia MI
Blackwells Bagels, Westland, MI

COMPETITION

Strengths

Already up and running. In speaking with Bagel Bakery & Blackwells' management, business seems steady. Blackwells use a different method of production. Their bagels are boiled, baked, and then steamed.

Weaknesses

Their bagel baking proceess tends to make their bagels hard and crusty. Their shelf life is very short, as they start out with a partially hardened product. We have tried their bagels and they do not compare to the quality of bagel we will produce. They don't use the amount of fresh ingredients we do, and they can't. Often their product is not made fresh in the store, rather, it is shipped frozen.

USA BAGELS COMPARISON

We offer a difference! Bagels made fresh every day. Cream cheeses made fresh everyday. All made from fresh ingredients everyday. Our bagels are not boiled, so they don't end up hard and crusty. A softer bagel makes a tastier & pleasing product.

LOAN SUMMARY STATEMENT

In the purchase of the USA franchise, we are seeking a small business loan from the SBA, due to the fact that their rates tend to be a little better. The loan would be in the amount of $200,000.00. This would be for the purchase or lease of equipment, inventory, the leasehold improvements of a current lease site, cash reserves for three months, and enough working capital to successfully launch a production/retail delivery operation. This loan together with an equity investment of $40,000.00 and $45,000.00 in personal mutual funds as collateral, would be sufficient to finance the business so it can operate as a viable/profitable enterprise.

BREAKDOWN OF COSTS

Prepaid Expenses		
Franchise Fee	$30,000.00	
Grand Opening Fee	2,500.00	
Total Prepaid Expenses		32,500.00
Other Expenses		
Training	$2,500.00	
Leasehold Improvements	75,000.00	
Furniture/Fixtures	90,000.00	
Open Inventory	6,000.00	
First Months Rent + deposit	7,500.00	
Yellow Pages Ad	1,200.00	
Insurance	6,000.00	
Pre-Paid Deposits	4,500.00	
Additional Funds 3 months	14,000.00	
Total Other Expenses		$196,000.00

Dan Beecham - Director

Beecham has been a Director of USA Bagels since January of 1993. He was President of USA and its affiliates from the date of their inception until February of 1996, at which time he became a Consultant to USA and its affiliates. Mr. Beecham opened the first USA Bagels store in Boston, MA in 1986. Since 1986 he has been the President of USA Bagels, Inc., which currently operates 3 stores in the western suburbs of Boston, pursuant to a license agreement with USA.

Evan Smith - President, Chief Executive Officer and Director

Mr. Smith has been Chief Executive Officer and Director of USA. In February of 1996 he became President of USA and its affiliates. From December of 1986 to December 1993, he was Chief Executive of Boston Personnel Services of Boston, MA.

Consolidated
Balance Sheet

	Month 1	Month 2	Month 3	Month 4	Month 5	Month 6
Sales	$39,000.00	$42,900.00	$47,000.00	$49,000.00	$52,000.00	$52,000.00
Cost of Goods Sold						
Food & Pkg.	11,700.00	12,870.00	14,100.00	14,700.00	15,600.00	15,600.00
Labor	9,750.00	10,725.00	11,750.00	12,250.00	13,000.00	13,00.00
Total Cost of Goods Sold	21,450.00	23,595.00	25,850.00	26,950.00	28,600.00	28,600.00
Gross Profit	$17,550.00	$19,305.00	$21,150.00	$22,050.00	$23,400.00	$23,400.00
Controllable Expenses						
Uniforms	125.00	125.00	125.00	125.00	125.00	125.00
Repair & Maintenance	100.00	100.00	100.00	100.00	100.00	100.00
Payroll Taxes	1,300.00	1,300.00	1,300.00	1,300.00	1,300.00	1,300.00
Supplies	520.00	520.00	520.00	520.00	520.00	520.00
Telephone	200.00	200.00	200.00	200.00	200.00	200.00
Utilities	700.00	700.00	700.00	700.00	700.00	700.00
Management Salary	2,000.00	2,000.00	2,000.00	2,000.00	2,000.00	2,000.00
Total Controllable Expenses	$4,945.00	$4,945.00	$4,945.00	$4,945.00	$4,945.00	$4,945.00
Other Operating Expenses						
General Insurance	125.00	125.00	125.00	125.00	125.00	125.00
Workers Comp Insurance	205.00	205.00	205.00	205.00	205.00	205.00
Health Insurance	425.00	425.00	425.00	425.00	425.00	425.00
Rent	2,520.00	2,520.00	2,520.00	2,520.00	2,520.00	2,520.00
Common Area Maintenance	200.00	200.00	200.00	200.00	200.00	200.00
Royalties	1,950.00	2,145.00	2,350.00	2,450.00	2,600.00	2,600.00
Taxes & Licenses	500.00	500.00	500.00	500.00	500.00	500.00
Interest Expense (Start-up Loan)	2,620.00	2,620.00	2,620.00	2,620.00	2,620.00	2,620.00
Total Other Operating Expenses	$8,545.00	$8,740.00	$8,945.00	$9,045.00	$9,195.00	$9,195.00
Franchise	1,040.00	1,040.00	1,040.00	1,040.00	1,040.00	1,040.00
All Other	2,080.00	2,080.00	2,080.00	2,080.00	2,080.00	2,080.00
Total Advertising	$3,120.00	$3,120.00	$3,120.00	$3,120.00	$3,120.00	$3,120.00
Total Operating Expenses	$38,060.00	$40,400.00	$42,860.00	$44,060.00	$45,860.00	$45,860.00
Net Income	$940.00	$2,500.00	$4,140.00	$4,940.00	$6,140.00	$6,140.00

Month 7	Month 8	Month 9	Month 10	Month 11	Month 2	Year 1 Total
$52,000.00	$52,000.00	$52,000.00	$52,000.00	$52,000.00	$52,000.00	$593,900.00
15,600.00	15,600.00	15,600.00	15,600.00	15,600.00	15,600.00	178,170.00
13,000.00	13,000.00	13,000.00	13,000.00	13,000.00	13,000.00	148,475.00
28,600.00	28,600.00	28,600.00	28,600.00	28,600.00	28,600.00	326,645.00
$23,400.00	$23,400.00	$23,400.00	$23,400.00	$23,400.00	$23,400.00	$267,255.00
125.00	125.00	125.00	125.00	125.00	125.00	1,500.00
100.00	100.00	100.00	100.00	100.00	100.00	1,200.00
1,300.00	1,300.00	1,300.00	1,300.00	1,300.00	1,300.00	15,600.00
520.00	520.00	520.00	520.00	520.00	520.00	6,240.00
200.00	200.00	200.00	200.00	200.00	200.00	2,400.00
700.00	700.00	700.00	700.00	700.00	700.00	8,400.00
2,000.00	2,000.00	2,000.00	2,000.00	2,000.00	2,000.00	24,000.00
$4,945.00	$4,945.00	$4,945.00	$4,945.00	$4,945.00	$4,945.00	$59,340.00
125.00	125.00	125.00	125.00	125.00	125.00	1,500.00
205.00	205.00	205.00	205.00	205.00	205.00	2,460.00
425.00	425.00	425.00	425.00	425.00	425.00	5,100.00
2,520.00	2,520.00	2,520.00	2,520.00	2,520.00	2,520.00	30,240.00
200.00	200.00	200.00	200.00	200.00	200.00	2,400.00
2,600.00	2,600.00	2,600.00	2,600.00	2,600.00	2,600.00	29,695.00
500.00	500.00	500.00	500.00	500.00	500.00	6,000.00
2,620.00	2,620.00	2,620.00	2,620.00	2,620.00	2,620.00	31,440.00
$9,195.00	$9,195.00	$9,195.00	$9,195.00	$9,195.00	$9,195.00	$108,835.00
1,040.00	1,040.00	1,040.00	1,040.00	1,040.00	1,040.00	12,480.00
2,080.00	2,080.00	2,080.00	2,080.00	2,080.00	2,080.00	24,960.00
$3,120.00	$3,120.00	$3,120.00	$3,120.00	$3,120.00	$3,120.00	$37,440.00
$45,860.00	$45,860.00	$45,860.00	$45,860.00	$45,860.00	$45,860.00	$532,260.00
$6,140.00	$6,140.00	$6,140.00	$6,140.00	$6,140.00	$6,140.00	$61,640.00

Bread Bakery

BREADCRAFTER

8900 Green Lake Road
Port Hanover, Michigan, 49333

This business plan is a tightly constructed, succinct consideration of all factors relevant to launching this bakery. From rent charges to competition and seasonal changes to costs per loaf, this plan hasn't left anything out...all without being overly verbose. This exemplary plan is very focused and complete, which will help the business stay on course.

- EXECUTIVE SUMMARY

- THE COMPANY

- PRODUCTS

- PRODUCTION

- MARKET

- MARKETING

- RISKS

- FINANCES

BREAD BAKERY
BUSINESS PLAN

EXECUTIVE SUMMARY

Awareness of high quality baked goods is on the rise. Good bread is a rare combination of nutrition, convenience, and luxury. Today's consumer has less time to create wholesome, handmade bread, but increasingly appreciates the nutritional and sensory benefits it provides. Good bread provides fiber and carbohydrates in a convenient, low fat form that is portable and delicious. Good bread never goes out of style.

Breadcrafter will produce and sell high quality, handmade breads to the residents and tourists of Port Hanover and Freeman County. The Company will focus on European Style; naturally leavened breads and baguettes made with high quality ingredients. Breads will be baked and sold at a storefront facility using a 4 deck, steam injected bread oven. Labor saving devices will allow the proprietor to run the entire operation with the help of two part time, seasonal employees.

Breadcrafter's main competition includes a health food store, three pastry shops and three supermarkets in the Port Hanover area. Its advantage lies in the high quality of its products due to specialization and artisan manufacturing. The main marketing focus will be an eye catching sign, the scent of fresh bread wafting out of the storefront, and periodic printed advertisements. The company will sample its products liberally.

After establishing the operation, the company will explore the possibility of making takeout sandwiches. Delivering wholesale bread and baked goods to area restaurants and specialty retailers will also be considered.

The company is being founded by Kevin Richards, an artisan baker currently baking breads and pastries for Toothsome Foods Company in Port Hanover, Michigan. Kevin has spent the last two years building the TFC program from the ground up. His wife Renee Richars is also a bread baker, having baked for one year at the Grainery Food Co-op, Breadcrafter's chief competitor. Together they bring a wealth of practical experience and a realistic market sense to the company.

Breadcrafter is currently seeking $70,000 in loans to get the business underway. Major costs include equipment purchases, shop rent, ingredient purchases, site modifications, and marketing, which total $61,000. Projected sales for the first three months, based on market and competition studies, will total $41,087. Total operating expenses and cost of sales will leave an average profit of $4,740 per month.

Opening day is scheduled for July 1st, 1996. While Breadcrafter has the potential for high growth, the first three years will be spent establishing company financial stability and increasing market share.

THE COMPANY

Breadcrafter will be created to serve the Port Hanover community by exploiting the need for a good bread bakery. It will offer a variety of high quality, European and American style artisan breads, baked fresh in its storefront bakery.

The company's immediate goals are to achieve start up by July 1st, 1996, in time to capitalize on the lucrative summer tourist season. It will start with the proprietor, Kevin Richards, as baker and manager with the help of two part time employees. The company should gross over $100,000 in its first year. Long term goals include the addition of a takeout sandwich store to the storefront and wholesale bread sales within one year.

Kevin Richards, the proprietor and baker, is the creator of Breadcrafter. For four years, he has been employed at Toothsome Foods Company, a specialty foods manufacturer in Port Hanover, Michigan. His experience as a Production Supervisor and as a Research & Development Cook bring a sense of production realities and technical savvy to the company. As the driving force behind TFC's current Handmade Bread program, Kevin has two years practical experience with sourdough breads. He holds a BA in English Literature from the University of Michigan.

Renee Richards, Kevin's wife, also has bread baking experience. She baked bread at the Grainery Food Co-op in Port Hanover, Michigan for one year, and she contributes a keen sense of the bread market. She also contributes retail sales experience accrued through several retail jobs around Port Hanover.

The company is in the process of securing $70,000 in start up financing.

PRODUCTS

Breadcrafter's breads will stand out from the competition due to their uniqueness and outstanding quality. Most of the breads are European in style, including Sourdough, Miche (a traditional French whole wheat bread), and Sourdough Rye. These breads are made by the sourdough method which uses no added yeast. This method imparts a rich flavor, which can be tangy or mild, as well as a toothsome inner crumb and a crackly crust. By using this method, a skilled baker can create truly delicious breads without added fats or sugars, making many of Breadcrafter's products 100% fat free. Sourdough breads also have an extended shelf life, remaining fresh for days without the use of preservatives. Breadcrafter will also offer specialty breads, which will be made in the sourdough way with the addition of such luxurious ingredients as Parmagian cheese with fresh ground pepper and dried Michigan cherries with roasted pecans. Spent Grain Bread, made with barley leftover from beer brewing, is another unique product that Breadcrafter will offer. Two varieties of French style baguettes will be offered fresh daily, a high demand product that is available nowhere else in the area. Breadcrafter will also produce White and Wheat Sandwich Breads with soft crust and a tender crumb for traditional American Style sandwiches. As the needs of the customer change, so will the lineup of Breadcrafter's products. The bakery equipment is chosen with versatility in mind.

After establishing the business, Breadcrafter will research the possibility of producing sandwiches to increase revenues. This investment would require approximately $1500.00 for the purchase of equipment and ingredients. The company will also pursue wholesale contracts. Toothsome Foods Company has indicated interest in a contract to produce two Christmas products on a per loaf basis, Cherry Chocolate Fruitcake and Midwest Christmas Stollen. These products can help generate revenues in the slower Autumn months. The proprietor will also consider producing some of Toothsome Foods' current lineup of Handmade Breads on a wholesale basis.

A self serve beverage cooler filled with soft drinks will also help increase revenues, as will the sale of fresh brewed coffee.

PRODUCTION

Production of sellable breads is projected to begin on July 1st 1996. Raw ingredients will be ordered for twice a month delivery from North Farm Co-op and Sysco Inc., at which time a two week production schedule will be drawn up by Kevin Richards, the proprietor/baker. Ingredients will be stored in a dry storage area and in a walk in cooler (already on the proposed premises). Rent of the facility will be $1,050 per month with utility costs running approximately $725/month.

Scheduling will begin with three large bakes per week (MWF) and two small bakes (T,TH). Due to the extended shelf life of sourdough breads, product can be sold for two days before staling. Each bake day the baker will bake breads in a deck oven. The oven provides intense, even heat and a controllable amount of steam injection, allowing tremendous control of crust crispness. Everything from soft white sandwich breads to thick crusted, dense savory breads to sweet baked goods can be perfectly baked in this oven. While breads are baking, the baker will begin mixing the long fermenting doughs to be baked off the next day. Labor saving equipment including a dough divider and a bread moulder makes this possible. Hot breads will begin coming out of theoven by 7:00 AM, and all baking will be finished by 10:00 AM.

The storefront will open at 9:00 AM and close at 6:00 PM Monday through Friday. Saturday hours will be 9:00 AM to 4:00 PM for sales only. Part time employees will work the counter and assist with store maintenance during peak hours while the baker is baking. A beverage cooler and coffee machine will encourage convenience sales at the register.

Breadcrafter will economize on bookkeeping costs by handling its payroll duties in house. Year end bookkeeping will be handled by a professional accountant.

MARKET

The specialty bread market is about to experience enormous growth. Throughout the country small bakeries are appearing at an increasing rate. Chain stores, such as Great Harvest Bread Company, are experiencing tremendous growth by capitalizing on the wholesome appeal of fresh baked loaves. According to the Bread Baker's Guild of America, a trade organization, membership increased 40% between 1994 and 1995. As people become more aware of its healthy nutritional profile, good bread becomes even more attractive.

There is currently only one source for artisan breads in Port Hanover, Toothsome Foods Company, where the proprietor learned to bake. Market tests performed in the summer of 1995 by Toothsome Foods Company showed strong demand for the product, no price resistance and the need for a more frequent and visible presence. As a pilot program with no promotion in the summer of 1995, Toothsome Foods Company was able to sell all available loaves (20 30 per bake, two bakes per week) all summer long. Even without the benefit of window signage or a consistent delivery schedule, Kevin Richards and TFC have developed a loyal following of regular buyers that continues to grow.

The Millwright Bakery in Maple, MI., a similar operation to Breadcrafter, currently bakes 200-700 loaves a day for wholesale in the Connor City Area. This bakery has been open since November 1995 and has not yet experienced a summer tourist influx. It has stopped taking on new accounts for fear of exceeding its production capacity during that season. Millwright finds the Port Hanover area very attractive, but delivery from Maple is impractical. This summer season will bring Millwright a large influx of cash, and they will almost certainly consider establishing a bakery in Port Hanover if none yet exists.

Breadcrafter will set up its storefront bakery in the Green Lake Shopping Center. The center is conveniently located on one of the busiest arteries to and from Port Hanover. It has plenty of parking and is easily accessible from the road. The shopping center currently contains a successful, higher end grocery store, a successful liquor convenience store, and a donut bakery that also sells country clutter handicrafts. The shopping center is currently a destination for people seeking gourmet foods. These people will appreciate Breadcrafter's products. There is very little market overlap between Breadcrafter and the donut shop, and the two could exist in synergy.

Pricing of artisan type breads around Port Hanover currently ranges from $2.50 per loaf (GraineryWhole Wheat) to $5.95 per loaf (Toothsome Foods Pesto Bread). Breadcrafter's products will range in price from $2.25 (Sourdough Baguette) to $4.95 (Pepper Parmesan Loaf).

Grainery Food Co-op

Breadcrafter's primary competitor. The Grainery currently has a customer base that regularly buys whole grain breads. These customers are interested in healthy foods, and they will appreciate the attractive nutritional profile of our products. Due to undercapitalization, the Grainery will have trouble responding to the quality advantage our equipment and methods provides. Many potential customers are reluctant to patronize the Grainery, perceiving its patrons and employees as "too liberal". True or not, these customers may feel more comfortable at Breadcrafter. Renee Richards, the proprietor's wife, was formerly a Grainery bread baker. She knows their business well.

Helmut's Pastry Shop

An established bakery specializing in pastries and doughnuts. They have a capable facility. Due to heavy investment in pastry equipment and relatively small bread sales, they are unlikely to react strongly to our presence.

Twin's Bakery

Very similar to Helmut's.

The Coffee Mug

Specializing in donuts, pastries, and country clutter handicrafts. They sell some lower quality breads. Major risk is their location, right next door to Breadcrafter's prospective site. This risk could also be an asset, bringing bakery customers in search of better bread to Breadcrafter.

Fred's Markets

Large supermarket with in store bakery. Fred's offers nonscratch, relatively low quality breads and pastries at very low prices. Their largest advantage, other than price, is the convenience of one stop shopping. There is some possibility of future wholesale distribution of our products.

Daley's Supermarkets

Very similar to Fred's

Taylor's

Similar to Fred's and Daley's, but smaller. Higher possibility of future wholesale distribution.

Toothsome Foods Company

Downtown specialty foods retailer. Current employer of Breadcrafter's proprietor. TFC has a small, undercapitalized bread program Due to the absence of the baker, they are unlikely to compete. Proprietor will offer to buy some of the bakery equipment. Future wholesale distribution of contract products is a strong possibility.

Breadcrafter's production capacity will be an advantage over the specialty stores. Product specialization will be an advantage over the pastry shops and supermarkets. Breadcrafter's product quality will be an advantage over all local competitors.

MARKETING

Breadcrafter will sell its products to new and repeat customers from its storefront in the Green Lake Shopping Center, located on the busy stretch of M-17 between Port Hanover and Crescent Heights, Michigan. A large, tasteful, storefront sign will catch the attention of passing motorists. The smell of bread as it comes from the oven will bring customers in from the parking lot. Breadcrafter will offer a sample of fresh baked bread to anyone who comes into the store.

Breadcrafter's products will be truly unique in the marketplace. The look, feel and taste of its breads, when compared with the competition, will underscore their quality and value. Many of the products, such as Pepper Parmesan Bread and Sourdough Baguettes, will not be available anywhere else. Breadcrafter will also actively encourage customer satisfaction. Our product line will react to the needs and desires of the customer, thereby encouraging repeat and word of mouth sales. As a small hands on facility Breadcrafter will have the freedom to react quickly and accurately to changes in the market. Due to its uniqueness and convenient location, Breadcrafter will become a destination for food lovers.

Printed advertisements, which will run opening week, will highlight bread as an everyday product, to be purchased fresh on a weekly or daily basis. More printed advertisements will run Labor Day weekend and during the Christmas season. Costs for these advertisements will be approximately $200 each.

RISKS

The major risk to any Port Hanover area retail operation is the seasonality of the customer base. Breadcrafter will address this problem by opening at the height of the lucrative summer season. This will give the company a good supply of working capital to help with the startup period. The company will market itself primarily to the year round population. Contract products prepared for Toothsome Foods Company will bring in cash during the slow fall season. Unless strong demand shows a need, labor will be eliminated in the slower seasons and advertising will be minimal. Depending on available cash after Christmas, Breadcrafter will contemplate adding a sandwich bar to serve local shoppers and employees.

Breadcrafter will budget $9,800 in cash reserves as a cushion to help weather the startup period.

FINANCES

(Personal Income Statement removed for privacy.)

Start Up Costs

Equipment	$46,000
Materials	$4,500
Rent (2 Months)	$2,100
Site Modification	$5,000
Signage, Stationary, etc.	$1,000
Consultation	$1,000
Supplies	$600
Cash Reserves	$9,800
Total Start Up Costs	$70,000

The compnay is in the process of securing financing for startup. The proprietor currently has $20,000 from private sources and is seeking $50,000 in additional bank loans.

Two part time employees will be hired to start working on opening day. They will be retained until Labor Day weekend unless strong sales show a further need for them. In the fall, winter and spring, the proprietor and his wife will be the only staff required. Employees will be paid $5.50 per hour, and will work a combined total of 30 hours per week. Wage expenditures will be $707.00 a month with additional payroll taxes running $71.00, for a total expenditure of $778.00.

Payroll

The Green Lake storefront currently under consideration rents for $1050 a month.

Rent

Heat and Electric bills for Jordan Galleria, a downtown storefront of approximately the same dimensions required by Breadcrafter, pays $225.00 at the height of the winter heat season. Taking into account walk in and reach in cooler use, a figure of $350.00 is a reasonable estimated monthly average.

Utilities

The bread oven will be run four hours per day on busy bake days. Conversations with other bakery owners have indicated that a 4 deck oven consumes $4 of gas per hour, for a total of $343.00 per month at maximum capacity.

A total figure of $725.00 per month is a reasonable estimated monthly average.

Breadcrafter will run an advertisement in the Port Hanover News Review during opening week. Another advertisement will run Labor Day weekend. Total advertisement expenditures will run $200 per month. The News Review is known to do spotlight stories on new Port Hanover businesses and Breadcrafter will take advantage of this publicity.

Advertising

Advertising expenditures will be kept to a minimum in the fall, winter and spring. The company will rely on community service functions, liberal sampling, and word of mouth to reach new customers.

The estimated maintenance cost for the first month is $500.00. From there it gradually diminishes to $200 a month for the remainder of the year. After the first of the year maintenance estimates are reduced to $100 a month.

**Repair and
Maintenance**

A Business Owner's Policy, covering contents, liability, and some loss of income, will cost $400 $500 a year for Breadcrafter, as quoted by Sam Williams of Port Hanover Insurance. Worker's Comp will run $2.25 for every $100 paid. Breadcrafter has budgeted $50 a month in general insurance and $20 a month in Worker's Comp. Health Insurance premiums for the proprietor and his family will run $250 per month.

Insurance

The company has budgeted $150 a month on miscellaneous taxes and licenses.

Taxes and Licenses

General Supplies

General supplies will consist mainly of bread bags which cost $.05 each for paper and $.03 each for plastic. Bag material, which affects the quality of the crust in storage, will be chosen by the customer. These prices have been included in the cost of sale of each loaf. Cleaning and maintenance supplies will total no more than $50 per month. Breadcrafter has budgeted $125 per month as a conservative figure.

Professional Fees

Professional fees after startup will be kept to a minimum. The proprietor will perform all the necessary filing and bookkeeping chores required except year end tax filing and calculation of depreciation. The company has budgeted $325 in January and

$325 in March to cover these needs.

Miscellaneous

Breadcrafter has budgeted $120 per month to cover miscellaneous expenses.

Proposed Baking Materials Requirements

Ingredients	Amount	$/unit	Total
GW Flour	1000.0	0.40	880.00
Unbl Wht Four	3000.0	0.55	660.00
Dried Cherries	80.0	5.50	440.00
Beverages	0.42	1200	504.00
Parmagian Cheese	80.0	5.00	400.00
WW Flour Daily	800.0	0.49	392.00
Pecan Halves	30.0	5.50	165.00
Coffee	20	8	160.00
Yeast	50.0	1.88	94.00
Powdered Milk	50	1.66	83.00
Fennel Seeds	24.0	2.68	64.32
Lecithin	10	5	50.00
Rye Flour	100.0	0.49	49.00
Canola Oil	70	0.67	46.90
Flax Seeds	20.0	1.99	39.80
Sunflower Seeds	50.0	0.78	39.00
Sesame Seeds	12.0	2.42	29.04
All Purpose	1000.0	0.46	23.00
Sugar	50	0.45	22.50
Pepper	5	4.3	21.50
Sea Salt	100.0	0.21	21.00
Cracked Wheat	25.0	0.46	11.50
Baking Powder	5.0	1.21	6.05
Half n Half	2	2	4.00
Total			$4205.61

	Quantity	Price Each	Total
Oven, Snorr	1	18000	18000
Divider, Snorr	1	4000	4000
Mixer, ASF	1	4000	4000
Moulder, Snorr	1	2400	2400
Bannetons, FBM	60	30	1800
Loader, Snorr	1	1500	0
Loaf Pans	100	10	1000
Bread Slicer, used	1	950	950
Pan Racks, Snorr	6	140	840
Cooling Racks, Snorr	2	600	1200
Software, Computer upgrades	1	500	850
Triple sink, Louie	1	400	560
Heavy Scale, McMaster-Carr	1	400	400
Maple bench, materials	1	400	600
Small Loaf Pans	100	4	400
Countertop Mixer	1	390	1200
Flour Bins	3	127	381
Sheet Pans	40	9	175
Food Processor	1	250	250
Cash Register	1	250	250
Coffee Maker	1	250	250
Books			50
Bread Boards	40	5	200
Baskets	100	2	200
Chest Freezer, used	1	200	200
Coffee Mill	1	200	200
Baker's Canvas,MTR,FBM	3	9.8	196
Oven Peels	2	75	150
Garbage Disposal	1	150	150
15" Skillet	1	120	120
Garbage Cans	3	40	120
Handsink, Louie's	1	100	80
Gm/Oz Scale	1	150	150
Faucetts	2	50	100
Used range	1	100	100
Counter, Used	1	100	100
File Cabinet, 4 drawer	1	100	100
7qt Saucepan	1	85	85
Bread Knives	4	20	80
Mop Bucket, MacMaster	1	80	80
Timer	2	35	70
Dough Tubs	5	10	50
Oven Thermometer	1	40	40
1 qt Saucepan	1	40	40
Mopheads	10	3	30
Coffee Pots	6	5	30
Whisks	4	6	24
Lames	2	12	24
Thermometers	2	10	20
Wooden Spoons	5	4	20

Proposed Equipment Requirements

**Proposed
Equipment
Requirements**

Measuring Cups	5	4	20
Dough Knives	3	6	18
Oven Mits	4	4	16
Spoonulas	3	5	15
Sieve	1	15	15
Dough Scrapers	3	4	12
Ladles	3	4	12
Pastry Brushes	2	5	10
Brooms	1	10	10
Dustpans	1	10	10
Mop	1	10	10
Pastry Brush 1 1/2"	2	3	6
Sifter	1	4	4
Measuring spoons	1	3	3
Total			$43321

**Miscellaneous
Requirements**

Supplies	Amount	$/#	unit	Toatl
Paper Bags	4000	$0.05	ea.	$200.00
Plastic Bags	2000	$0.02	ea.	$40.00
Register Tape	1	$20.00	cs	$20.00
Bleach	6	$1.30	$7.80	
Handsoap	4	$5.75	Cartridge	$23.00
Floorsoap	45	$0.42	packet	$18.90
Kitchen Soap	4	$8.71	5-qut	$34.84
Plastic Film	2	$20.67	roll	$41.34
Aluminum Foil	1	$71.27	roll	$71.27
Stationary	1	$50.00	cs	$50.00
Purchase orders	1	$20.00	cs	$20.00
Receipt Pads	1	$20.00	cs	$20.00
File Folders	1	$20.00	cs	$20.00
Garbage Bags	312	$0.31	ea.	$96.72
Paper Cups	1000	$0.03	ea.	$15.00
Total				$671.07

Sourdought Loaf: Scale at 24 oz   20 Breads

Unbleached White	$0.49	15.15 lb	$7.42	47.34%
Water	$0.01	12.75 lb	$0.13	39.83%
Gold & White Flour	$0.40	3.79 lb	$1.52	11.85%
Salt	$0.14	0.31 lb	$0.04	0.98%
		32.00	$9.11	100.00%

ingredient total	$9.11
Yield	20
Unit cost	$0.46
Bag	$0.05
retail	$3.95
net	$3.44

Whole Wheat: Scale at 24 oz   30 Breads

Water	$0.01	18.26 lb	$0.18	38.85%
Gold & White Flour	$0.40	14.17 lb	$5.67	30.15%
Whole Wheat Flour	$0.46	14.17 lb	$6.52	30.15%
Salt	$0.14	0.40 lb	$0.06	0.86%
		47.00	$12.43	100.00%

ingredient total	$12.43
Yield	30
Unit cost	$0.41
Bag	$0.05
retail	$3.95
net	$3.49

Sourdough Baguette: Scale at 12 Oz   30 Breads

Unbleached White	$0.49	10.65 lb	$5.22	47.34%
Water	$0.01	8.96 lb	$0.09	39.83%
Gold & White Flour	$0.40	2.67 lb	$1.07	11.85%
Salt	$0.14	0.22 lb	$0.03	0.98%
		22.50	$6.41	100.00%

ingredient total	$6.41
Yield	30
Unit cost	$0.21
Bag	$0.05
retail	$2.25
net	$1.99

Seed Baguette: Scale at 24 oz   30 Breads

Gold & White Flour	$0.40	9.58 lb	$3.83	41.59%
Water	$0.01	8.08 lb	$0.08	35.06%
Whole Wheat Flour	$0.46	3.22 lb	$1.48	13.99%
Sunflower Seeds	$1.19	1.20 lb	$1.43	5.21%
Sesame Seeds	$2.75	0.37 lb	$1.03	1.62%
Fennel Seeds	$2.36	0.19 lb	$0.44	0.82%
Salt	$0.14	0.18 lb	$0.03	0.78%
Dark Ses Oil	$1.71	0.11 lb	$1.19	0.48%
Poppy Seeds	$4.25	0.10 lb	$0.45	0.46%
		23.04	$8.96	100.00%

Bread Cost/Profit Analysis

...continued

ingredient total			$8.96	
Yield			30	
Unit cost			$0.30	
Bag			$0.04	
retail			$2.50	
net			$2.16	

Pepper Parmesan:	Scale at 24 Oz	20 Breads		
Unbleached White	$0.49	12.84 lb	6.29	40.13%
Water	$0.01	10.81 lb	0.11	33.77%
Parmesan	$3.00	4.24 lb	12.72	13.25%
Gold & White Flour	$0.40	3.21 lb	1.29	10.04%
Pepper	$4.20	0.64 lb	2.67	1.99%
Salt	$0.14	0.26 lb	0.04	0.82%
		32.00	23.11	100.00%

ingredient total			$23.11	
Yield			20	
Unit cost			$1.16	
Bag			$0.05	
retail			$4.95	
net			$3.74	

Sourdough Rye:	Scale at 24 Oz	20 Breads		
Water	$0.01	12.43 lb	$0.12	38.88%
Gold & White Flour	$0.40	11.57 lb	$4.63	36.20%
Rye Flour	$0.49	5.79 lb	$2.84	18.10%
Whole Wheat Flour	$0.46	1.91 lb	$0.88	5.96%
Salt	$0.14	0.28 lb	$0.04	0.86%
		31.97	$8.50	100.00%

ingredient total			$8.50	
Yield			20	
Unit cost			$0.43	
Bag			$0.05	
retail			$3.95	
net			$3.47	

Beverage Cost/ Profit Analysis

	cost	retail	profit
Coke classic	$0.35	$0.90	$0.55
Sprite	$0.35	$0.90	$0.55
Diet Coke	$0.35	$0.90	$0.55
Minute Maid	$0.35	$0.90	$0.55
Naya	$0.52	$1.25	$0.73
Fruitopia	$0.64	$1.25	$0.61
tea	$0.35	$0.90	$0.55
Avg	$0.42	$1.00	$0.58

	$/#
Frontier Organic Coffee, incl shipping	
Mexican Altura	$7.05
Decaf	$9.00

Production Schedule

July	Retail	Raw	m	t	w	th	f-sat	Revenue	Cost
Sour	3.95	0.55	20	20		30		276.50	38.50
Miche	3.95	0.50	20	20		30		276.50	35.00
Sour Rye	3.95	0.50	10	30				158.00	20.00
white	3.50	0.55	20	20	20	20	30	385.00	60.50
wheat	3.50	0.55	20	20	20	20	30	385.00	60.50
Cherry Peca	4.95	1.25	10	20				148.50	37.50
Pepper Par	4.95	1.50	10	20				148.50	45.00
Spent Grain	3.95	1.00	10	30				158.00	40.00
Baguette	2.25	0.25	30	30	30	30	40	360.00	40.00
Seed Bag	2.50	0.35	30	30	30	30	40	400.00	56.00
			180	100	140	100	300	2696.00	433.00
Beverages	1.00	0.42	60	40	40	40	120	300.00	126.00
Other								0.00	0.00

average daily units							Bread	11554	1855.71
Bread	137					monthly	Bev	1286	540
Beverage	50						Other	0	0.00
Other	0						Total	12840	2395.71

August	Retail	Raw	m	t	w	th	f-sat	Revenue	Cost
Sour	3.95	0.55	20	20		30		276.50	38.50
Miche	3.95	0.50	20	20		30		276.50	35.00
Sour Rye	3.95	0.50	10	30				158.00	20.00
white	3.50	0.55	20	20	20	20	30	385.00	60.50
wheat	3.50	0.55	20	20	20	20	30	385.00	60.50
Cherry Peca	4.95	1.25	10	20				148.50	37.50
Pepper Par	4.95	1.50	10	20				148.50	45.00
Spent Grain	3.95	1.00	10	30				158.00	40.00
Baguette	2.25	0.25	30	30	30	30	40	360.00	40.00
Seed Bag	2.50	0.35	30	30	30	30	40	400.00	56.00
			180	100	140	100	300	2696.00	433.00
Beverages	1.00	0.42	60	40	40	40	120	300.00	126.00
Other								0.00	0.00

average daily units	Bread							11554.3	1855.71
Bread	137					monthly	Bev	1285.71	540
Beverage	50						Other	0.00	0.00
Other	0						Total	12840	2395.71

Production Schedule
...continued

September	Retail	Raw	m	t	w	th	f-sat	Revenue	Cost
Sour	3.95	0.55	20				20	158.00	22.00
Miche	3.95	0.50	20				20	158.00	20.00
Sour Rye	3.95	0.50						0.00	0.00
white	3.50	0.55	20		20		30	245.00	38.50
wheat	3.50	0.55	20		20		30	245.00	38.50
Cherry Peca	4.95	1.25	10				10	99.00	25.00
Pepper Par	4.95	1.50	10				10	99.00	30.00
Spent Grain	3.95	1.00	10				20	118.50	30.00
Baguette	2.25	0.25	20	20	20	20	30	247.50	27.50
Seed Bag	2.50	0.35	20	20	20	20	30	275.00	38.50
			150	40	80	40	200	1645.00	270.00
Beverages	1.00	0.42	30	20	20	20	60	150.00	63.00
Other	4.50	3.00		200		200		1800.00	1200.00

average daily units							Bread	7050.00	1157.14
Bread	85					monthly	Bev	642.86	270.00
Beverage	25						Other	0.00	0.00
Other	67		TFC Fruitcake				Total	15407.1	6570.00

October	Retail	Raw	m	t	w	th	f-sat	Revenue	Cost
Sour	3.95	0.55	20				20	158.00	22.00
Miche	3.95	0.50	20				20	158.00	20.00
Sour Rye	3.95	0.50						0.00	0.00
white	3.50	0.55	20		20		30	245.00	38.50
wheat	3.50	0.55	20		20		30	245.00	38.50
Cherry Peca	4.95	1.25	10				10	99.00	25.00
Pepper Par	4.95	1.50	10				10	99.00	30.00
Spent Grain	3.95	1.00	10				20	118.50	30.00
Baguette	2.25	0.25	20	20	20	20	30	247.50	27.50
Seed Bag	2.50	0.35	20	20	20	20	30	275.00	38.50
			150	40	80	40	200	1645.00	270.00
Beverages	1.00	0.42	30	20	20	20	60	150.00	63.00
Other				5.00	2.70	75	75	750.00	405.00

average daily units							Bread	7050.00	1157.14
Bread	85					monthly	Bev	642.86	270.00
Beverage	25						Other	3214.29	1735.71
Other	25		TFC Stollen				Total	10907.1	3162.86

Car Wash

BUSINESS PLAN

J&J VENTURES, INC.,
T/A EAST CHINA AUTO WASH

100 Elizabeth Road
Trenton, NJ 19030

J&J Ventures, Inc. seeks financing to build and operate a state-of-the-art car wash in a small, but growing, community outlying several urban areas as well as a major metropolitan area. The car wash is expected to attract the increasing local population in addition to commuter traffic. The company plans to offer self serve car washing and an automatic wash facility, plus numerous additional products and services, such as vending machines and carpet shampooing.

- EXECUTIVE SUMMARY

- NATURE OF VENTURE

- MARKET DESCRIPTION AND ANALYSIS

- DESCRIPTION OF PRODUCTS AND SERVICES

- BUILDING AND EQUIPMENT

- MANAGEMENT TEAM AND OWNERSHIP

- BUSINESS STRATEGIES

- FINANCIAL DATA

- EXHIBITS

Company: J&J Ventures, Inc., T/A East China Auto Wash
100 Elizabeth Road
Trenton, NJ 19030
Tel: (610) 698-4000
Fax: (610) 698-4001

Contacts: Scott Jones, Co-Owner
Larry Jones, Co-Owner

Business Type: Self Serve Car Wash

Company Summary: J&J Ventures, Inc. (J&J) was formed to own and operate a self service car wash consisting of five self service bays and one automatic bay. The business will be located on King Road in East China Township, Delaware County, NJ. Delaware County is the tenth-largest county in the state and East China Township is the fastest growing township in the county. J&J will develop a well equipped, attractive, low maintenance, customer friendly car wash facility. The car wash will service the local community in an effort to develop a loyal base of repeat customers as well as draw new customers from the surrounding communities and attract the area's growing local and commuter traffic.

Management

Scott Jones, Co-Owner

Scott Jones will be responsible for operational and financial management, sales, marketing and promotion. Mr. Jones has been a corporate lender for Citicorp serving as Vice President in the middle market lending area for the past 11 years. He brings extensive knowledge and experience in the field of banking, finance, sales and marketing. Mr. Jones graduated from New York University in 1983 with a B.S. in Business Administration—Marketing. In May, 1994, he received a Masters of Business Administration—Finance from Georgetown University.

Larry Jones, Co-Owner

Larry Jones will be responsible for mechanical and electrical operations and materials procurement. After receiving his B.S. in Mechanical Engineering from Boston University, Mr. Jones accepted a position as Project Manager for Blackwell and Meldrum, Inc., a premier national engineering and construction firm. Mr. Jones later formed Jones Works, Inc., a commercial/industrial electrical construction firm, which grew to $1.2 million in sales with a workforce of 17 employees. Mr. Jones later joined Stelton, Inc. as a Project Manager. Mr. Jones was project manager for the $20 million electrical construction project at the New Jersey Convention Center. More recently he has been assigned as project manager of the $15 million electrical construction project at the new Civic Arena. As a result, Mr. Jones brings extensive knowledge and experience in the areas of project/program management, electrical and mechanical engineering and construction, contract administration, materials procurement and labor management.

Market: The company's target market will consist primarily of local residential customers. Research indicates that 90% of self serve business comes from a three-mile radius. The population of East China Township is approximately 4,791 (estimated 1995) and has grown 92% since 1990, making it Delaware County's fastest growing township. The population demographics consist of a mix of newer single-family homes and townhouse developments, older residential areas, scattered mobile home parks and apartment dwellings.

J&J will also target local businesses and will attract customers from surrounding communities and commuter traffic. According to a 1993 New Jersey Department of Transportation traffic survey, the traffic count on King Road west toward Bella Rd. averaged 9,673 vehicles and 8,533 vehicles east toward Wainledge Rd.

Product and Services: The company will provide state-of-the-art, reliable, customer friendly products and services, including a seven-selection wash control station in each self service bay, seven vacuums, two fragrance machines and several accessory product and food/drink vending machines. For the customers' convenience, the automatic bay will provide a complete, detailed wash and wax.

Competition: J&J's competition within a ten-mile radius consists primarily of several local, established, self serve washes. The Simcoe Car Wash is located within the town of Simcoe on Wainledge Rd., south approximately 2.5 miles from the J&J location. The Downtown Tillion Car Wash is located in the town of Tillion on Wainledge Rd., north approximately 8 miles from the J&J location. Both competitors maintain only four-bay self service washes with no automatic tunnel. The Simcoe facility is a well-maintained corrugated steel structure, but has no front access and is on a small lot with only two vacuums. The Downtown Tillion wash is well maintained and has good front access, but has limited vending facilities and only three vacuums.

Uniqueness: Several factors will make the J&J car wash unique. The company will offer a modern, easily accessible, high quality car wash facility featuring a variety of income producing services, including vacuums, fragrance machines, carpet shampooers and vending machines. Management will actively promote the company's service through local advertisements, cross-couponing with local merchants, direct mail promotions and promotional giveaways (coffee mugs, key chains, golf balls, etc.).

Project Cost: The total project cost is estimated to be $460M. A breakdown of these costs is as follows:

Lot Purchase Price (including permits)	$110M
Building and Turnkey Equipment System	300M
Site Work and Paving	50M
Total	$46OM

Funds Sought: J&J is seeking to finance $332M, or 70% of the $46OM proposed project cost, through a local financial institution. The company will seek to obtain either conventional mortgage/equipment financing or an SBA guaranteed mortgage loan at a fixed rate amortizing over 15 to 20 years, and a fixed rate equipment loan amortizing over five to seven years. The remaining balance of the required funds will be provided through a $60M seller note and from J&J's equity contribution of approximately $78M for project costs and $73M for start-up costs and working capital.

Use of Proceeds: The company intends to use the proceeds of the bank loans to finance building construction, equipment purchases and installation and site development costs.

	1996	1997	1998	1999	2000	
						Summary of Financial Projections
Sales	106,800	136,800	171,600	189,600	207,600	
Operating Expenses	77,400	85,500	94,600	102,200	108,100	
Pretax Profit	(5,700)	18,000	45,700	58,300	72,700	
Total Assets	493,200	473,400	466,000	473,500	486,600	
Total Liabilities	382,000	367,900	349,700	329,800	307,900	
Net Worth	111,200	105,500	116,300	143,700	178,700	

**NATURE OF
VENTURE**

Background

The self serve car wash industry is an established industry although it continues to grow within the Northeast at a rate of 5-8% annually. Engineering and design improvements have contributed to the industry's growth and have enhanced profit potential.

**Products and
Services**

J&J will develop an attractive, low maintenance, fully equipped and customer friendly car wash designed to draw a wide customer base. The car wash will feature state-of-the-art equipment designed for quality, reliability and easy usage. Each self service bay will contain an eight-selection wash control system featuring wheel and tire shampoos, pre-soap wash, foam brush, spot-free rinse, wax and final rinse, with an LED money and time countdown display and a last minute horn-alert function. Face plate instructions and function descriptions will make the system customer friendly. Each short barrel trigger gun will provide a high pressure wash, enabling customers to get to hard-to-reach places easily and quickly. Conveniently located within each self serve bay will be a soft, but durable, foaming brush for quick, easy and thorough cleaning. Surrounding the wash bay area will be seven coin operated, high powered vacuums with conveniently located floor mat hangers. In addition, there will be a centrally located carpet shampoo machine, two fragrance machines and bill changers, along with a vending area that will feature accessory items such as drying towels, tire cleaner and food and drink items.

**Location of
Venture**

East China Auto Wash will be located on King Road in the borough of Simcoe, East China Township, Delaware County, NJ. The site is approximately two miles west of the town of Simcoe (Wainledge Rd.) and five miles east of the town of Bedford (Bella Rd.). The City of Trenton is approximately 10 miles from the site.

The site is zoned for commercial development and has been approved by the East China Planning Commission for the development of a self serve car wash. The subject property is adjoined by seven additional land parcels that are zoned for commercial development. This includes a proposed convenience store and 40-unit storage facility scheduled to open in Spring, 1996. The remaining lots are expected to be developed within the next year and include a small retail shopping area.

According to East China Township authorities, the surrounding area is expected to continue to grow in conjunction with the construction of a 100-unit apartment complex within a quarter-mile of the site, as well as additional townhouse, single-family and semi-detached housing developments.

According to the New Jersey Department of Transportation, a 1995 traffic survey for King Road, Wainledge Rd. and Bella Rd. determined the average daily traffic counts to be as follows:

King Road
Eastbound = 9,673 vehicles
Westbound = 8,533 vehicles

Bella Rd. and King Road
Eastbound = 8,321 vehicles
Westbound = 6,500 vehicles

Wainledge Rd. and King Road
Northbound = 10,848 vehicles
Southbound = 8,735 vehicles

J&J will target the local residents and businesses of East China and Plymouth Townships in order to develop a loyal base of repeat customers as well as draw new customers from the surrounding communities. In addition, the company will seek to attract the area's growing commuter traffic.

J&J's target market will consist of local residential customers, local businesses and commuter traffic. Research indicates that up to 90% of self serve business comes from within a three-mile radius. Consequently, the company will focus on attracting and developing a loyal customer base from the surrounding community. The business will be situated on the main thoroughfare between Simcoe and Bedford and intersects both Wainledge Rd. to the east and Bella Rd. to the west. J&J expects to capture commuter traffic traveling to Camden, Passaic and Trenton.

Market Trends

Delaware County is an urban county of 343,130 persons (estimate 1992) situated in western New Jersey. The county seat, the City of Trenton, is near Philadelphia and is one of the leading industrial and trade complexes in the nation.

Demographic and Economic Trends

Delaware County is one of the leading agricultural counties within the state, with approximately 50 percent of its land area devoted to agricultural uses. Delaware is also an important industrial area, with emphasis in the production of textiles, metals and food products. The City of Trenton is the county's most populous municipality and its center of industry and commerce.

East China Township is located approximately 10 miles northeast of Trenton, and Plymouth Township is several miles closer. East China is Delaware County's fastest growing township, growing by 41.0% from 1990 to 1995. The township consists of 13.2 square miles of land with a population of 4,791 (1995 estimate) of which 59.1% of the population is between the ages of 18 and 59. Approximately 93.8% are married couples with a median household income of $39,550. Approximately 82.1% of housing units in the township are owner-occupied.

Plymouth Township consists of 8.6 square miles of land and borders East China Township to the south. The 1995 population is estimated at 1,370, of which 61.4% of the population is between the ages of 18 and 59. Approximately 87.4% are married couples with a median household income of $35,670. Approximately 68.6% of housing units within the township are owner-occupied.

A change in economic conditions can influence the area demographics and consumer spending habits. The region continues to expand modestly due to increased capital investment, productivity gains and low labor costs resulting in a relatively low inflation rate of 2.3%. This low inflation rate and interest rate environment has spurred the region's manufacturing, finance, insurance, real estate and service industries. The health of the local economy is important since many of the local East China and Plymouth Township residents commute to work in Trenton, Passaic and Camden.

Current Competitors and Competitive Products and Services

J&J's principal competition will come from two local, self serve washes within a ten-mile radius.

Simcoe Car Wash is located in the town of Simcoe, approximately two and one-half miles east on Wainledge Rd., and is well established in the area. However, the facility is outdated, maintaining only four self serve bays with no automatic tunnel. The wash area is small with no front access. In addition, there are only two vacuum stations and minimal vending facilities.

The Downtown Tillion Car Wash is located within the town of Tillion on Wainledge Rd., approximately eight miles southeast of the J&J location. The business is well established with good visibility from the highway and good access. However, the facility has not been modernized and maintains only four self serve bays with no automatic tunnel. There are only three vacuums and minimal vending facilities.

DESCRIPTION OF PRODUCTS AND SERVICES

Uniqueness of the Products and Services

The East China Auto Wash will be unlike any of its surrounding competitors due to several factors. The company will offer a modern, easily accessible, high quality car wash system featuring a variety of convenient, income producing services, such as vacuums, fragrance machines, carpet shampooer and vending machines. J&J will have a modern and professional look and will feature an automatic bay, which will provide a complete, detailed wash and wax.

Management will actively promote the company's services through local advertisements, cross couponing with local merchants, direct mail promotions and through promotional giveaways.

Advantages Over Competition

J&J's principal competitive advantages will stem from its ability to offer a modern, professional car wash utilizing a state-of-the-art, self serve car washing system, including a convenient automatic wash. Moreover, J&J will utilize cost effective and targeted advertising and promotion to become the preferred car wash in the area.

BUILDING AND EQUIPMENT

The building will consist of five self service bays, one automatic bay, an equipment room and office/storage area containing approximately 4,025 square feet. The building will be constructed of 8" concrete block, except exterior walls, which will be split face block and brick veneer atop a 5" concrete floor and concrete foundation. All interior walls in the bays and equipment room are to be covered with "Kalite white textured fiberglass paneling .090" in thickness. The roof will consist of 2 x 4 pre-engineered steel beams with a pre-finished ribbed metal roof.

Vacuums will be mounted on 30" x 4" concrete pads, each containing a 10' light pole and 4' fluorescent fixture.

A breakdown of equipment needs is as follows:

Quantity	Description
1	5-bay High Pressure system, 5 HP, 3 phase motors and starters, dual belt drive, "CAT" 310 ceramic plunger pumps, 100 VA rated 24 volt transformers, solid state timers, trigger controls w/US paraplate unloader/regulator valves, glycerin filled pressure gauges, Master menu sign package plus 4 additional signs per bay, booms with rebuildable swivels. Deluxe System includes stainless steel equipment chassis, stainless steel tanks w/lids, hour meters and function indicator lights, momentary push button test features, hot/cold rinse selector switch, coin boxes w/8 position rotary switch, meter heater, countdown timers with last coin alert, Slugbuster II coin and token accepter and 1 D-5 vault per bay with medico locks, all stainless steel wand holders and one pair mat hangers per bay.
1	5-bay Low Pressure, all stainless steel Foaming Brush and antifreeze Combination Super System, with stainless steel 180 degree booms.
1	5-bay Low Pressure, all stainless steel Foaming White Wall Cleaning System.
1	5-bay Low Pressure all stainless steel Presoak System.
1	5-bay RayPak Floor Heat System, -10 degree, with 403,000 BTU gas fired heater, manifolds, manifold boxes, tubing, fittings & wire ties, plus engineering layout. Includes installation of tubing to Customers prepared slab. (Does not include copper plumbing, materials or labor.)
1	5-bay RayPak 514,000 BTU Wash Water Heater with circulating pump and motor, pressure and temperature relief valves, thermostat and flow wash.
4	IVS stainless steel mirror finish, solid state 2" Vac with lighted domes, installed.

2	IVS stainless steel mirror finish, solid state 2" Gemini Air Vac with lighted dome, installed.
2	Hamilton Model RNS rear load $1.00, $5.00, $10.00 and $20.00 Bill Changer w/bill stacker.
6	Stainless steel drop shelf vendors, adjustable $.25 to $1.00.
1	Air Compressor, 5 HP, 80 gallon tank, stationary with starter, 2 stage, 3 phase, galvanized tank.
1	Hako "Flipper" lot sweeper.
1	Fragrance Scent dispenser w/H bracket.
1	Valley Sales 9F1248T Twin Water Softener. (Based on 10 GPG hardness.)
1	Pro Syncro Model 1500 Spot Free Rinse System with 1000 gallon underground poly tank & Repressurization System.
12	United containers 10 gallon trash receptacles w/liners.
1	Ambi-Rad s.s. infrared heater for automatic bay.
1	Panther 2 Automatic Rollover Wash System with 2 LAMMSCLOTH Flex Wrap-A-Rounds and 42 curtain strips, consisting of:
	Red/Green light entry/exit system.
	Pre-soak air hose activation system.
	Free standing bi-directional pre-soak application arch.
	Machine treadle activation system.
	Dual overhead, oscillating, LAMMSCLOTH top mitten.
	LAMMSCLOTH flex-a-round front, side and rear cleaning system.
	Free standing final rinse application arch.
	Umbilical boom and supply lines.
	Motor control stations and central computer (UL approved).
	Forward and reverse jog switch.
	29-foot travel track system with rolling curb rail system.
	Polished aluminum framework.
	Panther protective covering.
1	"Clear Fold" air operated plastic strip door for automatic bay.
1	"Air Lift" air operated solid panel door for automatic bay.
1	Continental Water Reclaim Unit Model MRS 15/30.
1	Hamilton ACW-4 Auto Cashier for automatic bay.

MANAGEMENT TEAM AND OWNERSHIP

J&J's management team will consist of Scott Jones and Larry Jones, who together will be co-owners maintaining a majority ownership interest in the company. Scott and Larry are highly focused, hard working, energetic and broadly experienced individuals whose combined talents provide a strong and qualified management team. Scott Jones provides the needed experience in the areas of business administration, finance, sales and marketing. His extensive business background and academic credentials compliment the strengths and talents of Larry Jones. Larry Jones provides strong technical and engineering expertise and will be responsible for mechanical and electrical operations and materials procurement. Resumes on the management team are included in the Exhibits section.

BUSINESS STRATEGIES

J&J will employ a differentiation strategy that will create value for the customer beyond that available from existing competition. The company will focus on providing a modern, professional, high quality car washing environment that features state-of-the-art, reliable, customer friendly products and services.

Marketing Plan and Supporting Strategies

J&J will support its differentiation strategy by effective execution of its marketing plan, which contains several integral supporting strategies, including product/service, promotional/sales and pricing.

J&J's product/service strategy will be to provide state-of-the-art, reliable, high quality and customer friendly products and services. Each self service bay will feature an eight-selection wash control system with an LED money and time countdown display and a last minute horn-alert function. Face plate instructions and function descriptions will make the system customer friendly. Surrounding the wash bay area will be eight conveniently located, high powered vacuums and one carpet shampooer. In addition, there will be two centrally located fragrance machines and bill changers, along with a vending area that will feature accessory items, such as drying towels, tire cleaners and food/drink items. The vacuums, carpet shampooer and accessory items will be in constant demand and provide a strong source of additional income.

J&J will utilize multiple, constant, but limited advertising and promotional sources. These sources will be selected to maximize the return on allocated advertising/promotional dollars. The local community residents and businesses will be attracted through the Yellow Pages, local newspaper advertisements, flyers, coupons and periodic direct mail programs. J&J will highlight its modern and professional facilities and specific products and services, such as its automatic bay, carpet shampooer and car accessory items.

J&J will offer certain promotional giveaway items, such as car window shades, key chains, calendars and coffee mugs, which will all include the distinctive East China logo. In addition, special offers will include free vacuuming and carpet shampooing on certain weekdays.

The company will also join certain industry associations, such as the International Carwash Association (ICA) and the local chamber of commerce. These associations provide valuable business tips, allow the business owner to develop industry contacts and build community relations.

J&J will utilize a combination of competitor based and prestige pricing. This will ensure pricing is in line with local competitors for products and services where little value can be added, such as in the case of vending machine products. However, prestige pricing will be employed in areas such as the automatic bay and self serve bays, where J&J can offer higher quality, reliability and convenience. The company's strategy will be to position itself among the leading competitors and compete on quality, reliability, convenience, customer service and, lastly, on price. By developing a high quality image and reputation J&J can maintain premium pricing and still become the preferred car wash in the area.

The average customer is expected to spend between $1.75 and $5.00 per visit. The industry standard for a four-minute self serve wash is between $1.50 to $2.00 per cycle, and for an automatic wash, $5.00 to $5.50 per cycle. The industry average for vacuums is $0.75 to $1.00 per four-minute cycle. J&J will charge $1.75 per cycle for self serve, $5.00 per automatic wash and $1.00 per cycle for vacuum.

Financial Strategy

J&J will be owned and operated by Scott and Larry Jones, who will retain financial and managerial control. The principals will together own 100% of the company's capital stock.

J&J will seek to finance $322M of the total project cost of $460M through a local financial institution. The company will seek to obtain either conventional mortgage/equipment financing or an SBA guaranteed mortgage loan at a fixed rate amortizing over 15 to 20 years, and a fixed rate equipment loan amortizing over five to seven years. The remaining balance of the required funding will be provided through a $60M seller note to be repaid over 15 years, bearing interest at 8 1/4% fixed per annum. J&J's cash contribution will be approximately $151M, of which $78M will be for project costs and the remainder for start-up costs and working capital purposes.

J&J expects to realize strong consistent sales and earnings growth in year one, which will increase significantly by year five. This growth will be principally attributable to the increase in local population as a result of continued expansion of residential housing developments and from the establishment of local businesses within the immediate area. A 100-unit residential apartment complex, as well as a new office building complex, is planned to be constructed along King Road. J&J expects the other surrounding land parcels will be sold for commercial development, including a storage facility and possibly a convenience store by Spring, 1996. The company expects to develop additional loyal customers through execution of its advertising/promotional programs. In addition, J&J expects to grow sales as a result of the area's growing commuter traffic. Sales will also be favorably impacted from the sale of high-margin accessory products and services. Through the five-year period, management will effectively control purchases and overhead to maximize operating efficiency and profitability. In addition, operating expenditures will be carefully managed to ensure incremental revenue growth, resulting in increased bottom-line profitability.

Overall Growth Strategy

FINANCIAL DATA

Financial Statements

For the purposes of this projection it is assumed the company began operations on 12/31/95. A brief analysis of the 1995 financial statement is as follows:

1995 Income Statement

Sales

Since 12/31/95 is assumed to be the company's start date, no sales were recorded in 1995.

Operating Expenses

Includes primarily start-up expenditures consisting of EDU fees, utility connection/permit expenses, legal costs, bank loan costs and initial advertising/promotional expenses.

1995 Balance Sheet

Paid-In-Capital

There will be approximately $151M in equity investments as of the company's inception date.

Cash

This figure represents management's desired minimum cash balance available for working capital purposes.

Fixed Assets

This will include real estate and equipment. Real estate will be depreciated over 20 years and equipment over seven years, assuming straight line depreciation.

Long-Term Debt

This represents the long-term portion of an original $195M bank mortgage loan at 10% fixed amortizing over 20 years and a $127M equipment loan at 9% fixed amortizing over 7 years. Also included is the long-term portion of a $60M seller note at 8.25% fixed amortizing over 15 years.

Estimated Start-Up Costs

Desired Minimum Cash Balance	20,000
Initial Expenditures	
EDU Fees24,000	
Utility Connection Fees/Permits	5,000
Prepaid Insurance	3,200
Prepaid Real Estate Taxes	5,000
Deposits	5,000
Bank Loan Costs	8,200
Advertising and Promotion	2,000
Legal and Accounting	500
Total Initial Expenditures	52,900
Real Estate and Equipment	
Building	119,000
Equipment	181,000
Site Improvements	50,000
Land	110,000
Total Real Estate and Equipment	460,000
Total Start Up Costs	532,900
Financing Requirements	
Seller Note	60,000
Mortgage Financing	322,00
Equity Investment	150,900
Total Financing Requirements	**$532,900**

	12/31/95	12/31/96	12/31/97	12/31/98	12/31/99	12/31/00
ASSETS						
Cash	20,000	38,600	69,400	115,700	167,600	225,900
Accounts Receivable						
Inventory						
Current Assets	20,000	38,600	69,400	115,700	167,600	225,900
Gross Fixed	460,000	460,000	460,000	460,000	460,000	460,000
Accumulated Depreciation	0	39,800	79,600	119,400	159,200	199,000
Net Fixed Assets	460,000	420,200	380,400	340,600	300,800	261,000
Prepaid	8,200	9,600	11,200	12,200	13,200	14,200
Other Current Assets/Deposits	5,000	5,000	5,000	5,000	5,000	5,000
Total Assets	**493,200**	**473,400**	**466,000**	**473,500**	**486,600**	**506,100**
LIABILITIES						
Accounts Payable	0	3,100	3,700	4,500	5,200	5,600
Current Long Term Debt - Bank	16,900	18,500	20,300	22,200	24,300	26,700
Curr. Port Long Term Debt - Seller	2,100	2,300	2,500	2,700	2,900	3,200
Current Liabilities						
Long Term Debt - Bank	305,100	288,200	269,700	249,400	227,200	202,900
Long Term Debt - Seller	57,900	55,800	53,500	51,000	48,300	45,400
Total Liabilities	**382,000**	**367,900**	**349,700**	**329,800**	**307,900**	**283,800**
NET WORTH						
Paid in Capital	150,900	150,900	150,900	150,900	150,900	150,900
Retained Earnings	(39,700)	(45,400)	(34,600)	(7,200)	27,800	71,400
Total Net Worth	**111,200**	**105,500**	**116,300**	**143,700**	**178,700**	**222,300**
Total Liabilities & Net Worth	**493,200**	**473,400**	**466,100**	**473,560**	**486,600**	**506,100**

**Annual Projections:
Balance Sheet**

Annual Projections: Income Statement

	12/31/95	12/31/96	12/31/97	12/31/98	12/31/99	12/31/00
SALES						
5 Self Service Bays	0	72,000	96,000	108,000	120,000	132,000
1 Automatic Bay	0	18,000	24,000	30,000	36,000	42,000
7 Vacuums	0	16,800	25,200	33,600	33,600	33,600
Total Annual Revenue	0	106,800	136,800	171,600	189,600	206,700
OPERATING EXPENSES						
Chemical and Vending	0	5,300	6,800	8,600	9,500	10,400
Gas and Electric	0	6,400	8,200	10,300	11,400	12,500
EDU Fees	24,000	0	0	0	0	0
Water & Sewer	0	3,200	4,100	5,200	5,700	6,300
Utility Connections/Permits	5,000	0	0	0	0	0
Telephone	0	250	250	300	350	400
Trash Removal	0	1,100	1,400	1,700	1,900	2,100
Insurance	0	3,200	4,100	5,200	5,700	6,200
Real Estate Taxes	0	5,000	5,500	6,000	6,500	7,000
Accounting & Legal	500	300	500	600	700	800
Repairs & Maintenance	0	2,100	2,700	3,400	5,700	6,200
Labor	0	8,000	9,400	10,700	12,100	13,500
Depreciation	0	39,800	39,800	39,800	39,800	39,800
Bank Charges	0	250	250	300	350	400
Bank Loan Costs	8,200	0	0	0	0	0
Advertising and Promotion	2,000	2,300	2,500	2,500	2,500	2,500
Total Operating Expenses	39,700	72,400	85,500	94,600	102,200	108,100
Operating Profit/Loss	(39,700)	29,400	51,300	77,000	87,400	99,500
Interest Expense	0	35,100	33,300	31,300	29,100	26,800
Pre-Tax Loss/Income	(39,700)	(5,700)	18,000	45,700	58,300	72,700
Taxes	0	0	7,200	18,300	23,300	29,100
NET INCOME(LOSS)	(39,700)	(5,700)	10,800	27,400	35,000	43,600

	12/31/95	12/31/96	12/31/97	12/31/98	12/31/99	12/31/00
CASH FLOW FROM OPERATING ACTIVITIES						
Net Income (Loss)	(39,700)	(5,700)	10,800	27,400	35,000	43,600
Depreciation	0	39,800	39,800	39,800	39,800	39,800
Increase/(Decrease) in Accounts Payable	0	3,100	600	800	700	400
(Increase)/Decrease in Other Assets	(13,200)	(1,400)	(1,600)	(1,000)	(1,000)	(1,000)
Net Cash in Operating Activities	(52,900)	35,800	49,600	67,000	74,500	82,800
CASH FLOW FROM INVESTMENT ACTIVITIES						
Purchase of Equip. & Real Estate	(460,000)	0	0	0	0	0
Net Cash in Investment Activities	(460,000)	0	0	0	0	0
CASH FLOW FROM FINANCING ACTIVITIES						
Increase/(Decrease) in CPLTD	19,000	1,800	2,000	2,100	2,300	2,700
Incr/(Decr) in Long Term Debt	363,000	(19,000)	(20,800)	(22,800)	(24,900)	(27,200)
Increase - Paid in Capital	150,900	0	0	0	0	0
Net Cash from Financing Activities	532,900	(17,200)	(18,800)	(20,700)	(22,600)	(24,500)
Net Change in Cash	20,000	18,600	30,800	46,300	51,900	58,300
Beginning Cash	0	20,000	38,600	69,400	115,700	167,600
Ending Cash	20,000	38,600	69,400	115,700	167,600	225,900

**Annual Projections:
Cash Flow Analysis**

**Five-Year
Financial
Projections and
Assumptions**

These Financial Projections are based on estimates and assumptions set forth therein, and have been delivered for the information and convenience of persons who wish to evaluate the feasibility of the company's strategy and goals. Each such person who has received them realizes that financial projections are inherently speculative. The Financial Projections are based upon the company's assumptions, reflecting conditions it expects to exist or the course of action it expects to take. As the company is in the start-up stage, these projections are based on estimates and not on the company's historical results. Because events and circumstances do not occur as anticipated, there will be differences between the Financial Projections and actual results, and those differences may be material. The Financial Projections are based upon detailed underlying assumptions. Interested parties should consult their own professional advisors regarding the validity and reasonableness of the assumptions contained herein.

Income Statement

Sales

Sales are projected to reach $106,800 in 1996 and increase by 28% in 1997, 25% in 1998, 10% in 1999 and 9% in 2000. Sales through the projection period will be fueled by the increase in local population as a result of continued expansion of residential housing developments and from the establishment of new local businesses within the immediate area. J&J will attract and develop these new customers through execution of its advertising/promotional programs.

J&J's principal sources of income will be generated through the self serve bays, automatic bay and from vacuum sales. Self serve bay revenue will comprise between 63% and 70% of total annual revenue throughout the projection period. Monthly sales per self serve bay will increase from $1200 to $2200 through the projection period. Automatic bay revenue is expected to be the fastest growing sales category, increasing from $1,200 per month in 1996 to $2,800 per month in 2000. Income generated through vacuum sales is projected to increase substantially from 1996 to 1998, remaining relatively stable thereafter. The aforementioned sales figures are based on industry averages and assume average daily traffic of 8000 to 10,000 vehicles.

Operating Expenses

Due to significant sales growth through the projection period, expenses are forecasted to increase yet decline as a percentage of sales while remaining within industry averages. Operating expenses are projected to decline from 72% in 1996 to 52% in 2000 as a result of effective management and control of expenses.

Taxes

The effective tax rate is projected to be 40%. For the purposes of this projection, available tax losses are not carried forward, but are available to be used in future periods to reduce taxable income.

Balance Sheet

Fixed Assets

Fixed assets include principally real estate and equipment to be depreciated over 20 years and 7 years respectively, assuming straight line depreciation.

Accounts Payable

The majority of suppliers are expected to extend 30-day terms and J&J will pay within those terms.

Long-Term Debt

Long-term debt will consist of the remaining principal balance of bank real estate and equipment loans. Also included will be the remaining principal balance of the seller note.

Net Worth

J&J expects to achieve profitability in 1997 and thereafter. The company plans to finance growth through cash flow from operations. No additional equity will be required after 1995. Net worth is expected to improve from 1996 and thereafter, comprising a greater percentage of total capitalization.

The resumes of the owners are included as Exhibits. Several other Exhibits are available upon request:
- Site Overview showing the layout of roads and land parcels in the immediate area.
- Map of housing developments in East China Township.
- Table listing the numbers of occupied and available single-family homes, semi-detached homes, townhouses and apartments in East China and Plymouth Townships. Also lists proposed housing developments.

SCOTT JONES
478 Parker
Lemuel, NJ 19307
(610) 578-7405

OBJECTIVE

The opportunity to perform as an Executive Bank Manager with a long-range goal of becoming a Senior Manager.

PROFILE

Seasoned financial executive with over ten years of experience in financial management, financial analysis, consultative sales negotiation, cash management and business development. Recognized as an effective problem-solver and decision-maker; a self-directed and motivated individual with sound judgment; a strong sense of teamwork and a proven leader.

EDUCATION

> **Georgetown University**
> Master of Business Administration—May 1994
> Finance—GPA 3.6/4.0

> **New York University**
> Bachelor of Science Degree—May 1983
> Business Administration/Marketing

PROFESSIONAL EXPERIENCE

> **Citicorp, Camden, NJ— March 1987 to Present**
> **Vice President/Team Leader/Relationship Manager**

Responsibilities include corporate lending, portfolio management, cash management sales and business development for regional middle market companies in two counties.
- Manage all facets of banking relations for 45 clients with aggregate commitments of $40 million and aggregate outstandings of $25 million.
- Developed $5 million in new loan outstandings and loan fees of $60,000 in 1994, including five new client relationships.
- Surpassed performance goals and objectives each year as evidenced by performance rating of quality to exceptional since 1987. Qualified for corporate bonus program each year since the program's inception in 1990.
- Expertise in arranging financing for six corporations involved in the federal government contracting industry.
- Developed corporate direct mail program including promotional brochure, database management and telemarketing program.
- Team leader for two relationship managers, four credit analysts and one administrative staff member. Responsible for performance evaluations, salary and bonus recommendations, in-house training and mentoring.
- Due diligence analysis as part of the Citicorp Due Diligence Team in connection with potential bank acquisition/merger candidates.
- Sponsor and mentor for a trainee in the Wholesale Bank Training Program.

Citicorp, Camden, NJ
Senior Credit Analyst—March 1985 to 1987

Wholesale Bank Training Program Graduate: Supported relationship managers through financial analysis, administrative support, sales presentations and preparation of loan documentation and approval reports in the following divisions: Regional Middle Market, Northeast Corporate, Cash Management and Real Estate Finance.

Eastman Kodak Chemicals Div., Hartford, CT—October 1983 to March 1985
Sales Representative

Responsibilities included locating and developing new accounts; development and servicing of existing accounts in three counties.

CONTINUING EDUCATION/PROFESSIONAL COURSE WORK

Richardson Group Consultative Negotiation Skills Course
Richardson Group Consultative Selling: Prospecting and Retention Frank Ward Relationship Management Course
Phoenix-Hecht Professional Sales Course
Graduate Financial Accounting and Corporate Finance (Wharton Business School)
Proficient in Quattro-Pro, Lotus, Wordperfect, FAMAS and FAST

AFFILIATIONS

New Jersey Business Network—Board Member
Adult Volleyball Management Committee

ACTIVITIES

Football referee, softball, golf, weight lifting.

REFERENCES

Available upon request.

Resume of Larry Jones

LARRY JONES
45612 Winchester
Snelling, New Jersey 19096
(610) 623-0912

EDUCATION

Boston University
Bachelor of Science Degree, May, 1982
Field of Concentration—Mechanical Engineering

BACKGROUND

Thirteen years of comprehensive general management and project/program leadership experience...Problem solving, results oriented leader who exercised full P & L and operational responsibility...Designed, estimated, negotiated and administered diverse contracts...Decisive manager with a record of completing projects on time, generating strong profit margins and earning customer/contractor respect.

EXPERIENCE

February 1991 to Present
Stelton, Inc., Passaic, New Jersey
Project Manager—Civic Arena
Management of $15 million electrical construction project. Project is GMP fee based stadium construction project. Responsibilities include contract administration, labor management, materials procurement, engineering, contractor interface and overall P & L responsibility.

Project Manager-New Jersey Convention Center
Management of $20 million electrical construction project including base electrical construction, fire and security systems as well as building automation system. Supervised foreman, scheduled subcontractors, initiated change orders and negotiated through settlement, established and incorporated extensive computerized cost and labor tracking system. Generated change orders in excess of 25% of base contract value. Assisted in development of project claim. Project was completed on time and generated revenues far in excess of projected goals.

March 1984 to February 1991
Jones Works, Inc., Snelling, New Jersey
President/General Manager
Established and built commercial/industrial electrical construction firm from inception to $1.2 million in sales with a workforce of up to 17 employees in five years. Exercised complete operational and P & L responsibility including design, estimating, budgeting and project management.

June 1982 to March 1984
Blackwell and Meldrum, Inc., Barton, New Jersey
Project Engineer—Corrosion Engineer
Designed and installed cathodic protection system for a nuclear plant cooling tower. Managed $1.2 million project, supervised 33 union personnel, generated 14% profit margin and completed job ahead of schedule.

Assisted in design of and subsequently installed a cathodic protection system at an aquarium at Seaworld. Supervised construction, administered contract, materials procurement and subsequent testing.

Conducted corrosion studies on gas and oil pipelines as well as fossil fuel storage tank facilities throughout the United States.

REFERENCES
Will be furnished upon request.

Cigar Shop

BUSINESS PLAN

HOLY SMOKES

399 Tobacco Rd.
Rock Valley, MI 58223

This premium retailer of cigars, fine wines, and gourmet coffee has made an effort to capitalize on several complementary niche markets. The plan's contention is that a consumer who enjoys a fine cigar will also enjoy premium wines as well, thus enabling the the products to sell each other. This is the old idea of diversifying your product mix to cater to the most people, but with a trendy twist.

- EXECUTIVE SUMMARY

- OBJECTIVES

- MISSION

- KEYS TO SUCCESS

- COMPANY SUMMARY

- PRODUCTS

- COMPETITIVE COMPARISON

- SOURCING

- MARKET ANALYSIS SUMMARY

- COMPETITION

- STRATEGY AND IMPLEMENTATION SUMMARY

- MANAGEMENT SUMMARY

- FINANCIAL PLANNING

EXECUTIVE SUMMARY

Holy Smokes will be an upscale retail establishment, located near the border of Haverhill Heights and Pine Hill Shores, that carries the following:

- Premium Tobacco (i.e. cigars and pipe tobacco)
- Fine Wines
- Exotic Beers
- Gourmet Coffees
- Various accessories

Holy Smokes will cater to the people who enjoy some of life's finer pleasures. With the heart of the boating community on one side of Holy Smokes and the most affluent area of Pine Hill on the other, it should do very well.

The primary factors in making Holy Smokes a success will be---positioning, service and satisfaction.

With a solid positioning strategy, service that is second to none and a "smart" inventory, successwill be eminent.

With all of these factors into play, we expect the sales to grow at a rate of 10-15% per month. The tobacco will be the revenue-maker in the beginning, but the wine, beer and coffee should balance out the revenue within 18-24 months. Thus, making Holy Smokes the premiere tobacconist and retailer of fine wet goods in the area.

OBJECTIVES

1. To become the premier retailer of tobacco products and fine wet goods in the area.
2. To have a 10-15% growth rate per month during the first year.

MISSION

Holy Smokes will be an establishment that offers a few of life's pleasures and unparalleled service. Holy Smokes will cater to those who enjoy a nice bottle of wine, a good cigar or both, and it will be inviting to those who may not be familiar with such things but want to learn about them. Holy Smokes will be for young and old, men and women and a wide variety of budgets.

We intend to take full advantage of the positioning strategy still available in the area of Holy Smokes. We will be the only establishment to carry such items under one roof and offer the knowledge and service to accompany these products. Once the positioning strategy is well in hand at Holy Smokes profit margins should steadily increase. Thus, making certain that all of our commitments, made prior to opening, will be fulfilled without difficulty.

KEYS TO SUCCESS

1. Location: Holy Smokes is right next to the heart of one of the largest boating populations in the country. It is also neighboring the wealthy city of Pine Hill Shores

2. Image: As stated earlier, Holy Smokes will be an establishment that caters to specific tastes. However, in order to attract such tastes Holy Smokes must offer an environment conducive to the selling of such items. Holy Smokes will have the aesthetic atmosphere that the specific tastes are after when buying these items.

3. Service: Once we have attracted customers to our establishment with our image, we will keep them coming back with our knowledgeable and accommodating service.

4. Selection: Although we will cater to those who enjoy finer things does not mean we will include only the wealthy. With a solid selection, Holy Smokes will be able to please a wide variety of budgets and tastes.

Holy Smokes will be a retail establishment that sells the following: **Products**

- Premium Cigars and Accessories
- Pipe Tobacco and Accessories
- Fine Wines
- Exotic Beers (i.e. Microbrews)
- Gourmet Coffees

At Holy Smokes, we will not simply carry these items to sell, but they will be sold in a manner that is both tasteful and tactful. A true appreciation for such items, to please the experienced buyer, will be displayed. While at the same time, keeping the environment friendly for the inexperienced buyer to learn.

Holy Smokes will be a privately held corporation in Michigan. John Jacobs, Holy Smokes   **Company Ownership**
owner/operator, will be the majority owner.

The legal and professional personnel, to make Holy Smokes a corporation, is forthcoming.

The attached start-up table will give insight to expenses needed for the start of the business.   **Startup Summary**
The table is detailed and should be self explanatory.

Startup Expenses

Legal	TBA
Occupancy (Rent & Loan)	$2,000
Brochures	$100
Consultants	$1,000
Insurance	$600
Utilities	$300
Research and development	$200
Advertising (opening)	$1,000
Loan Payoffs	$13,500
Licenses and Permits	$300
Other	$2,000
Total Start-up Expense	$21,000

Startup Summary
...continued

Start-up Assets Needed

Cash requirements	$29,000
Start-up inventory	$30,000
Other Short-term Assets	$13,000
Total Short-term Assets	$72,000
Long-term Assets	
Capital Assets	
Total Assets	$72,000
Total Startup Requirements	$93,000
Left to finance:	$13,000

Start-up Funding Plan

Investment	
Investor 1	$0
Investor 2	$0
Other	$0
Total investment	$0
Short-term borrowing	
Unpaid expenses	$0
Short-term loans	$80,000
Interest-free short-term loans	$0
Subtotal Short-term Borrowing	$80,000
Long-term Borrowing	
Total Borrowing	$80,000
Loss at start-up	($8,000)
Total Equity	($8,000)
Total Debt and Equity	$72,000
Checkline	$0

Company Products

The products at Holy Smokes will sell based on a mixture of existing marketing needs:

The increased demand for pleasures like cigar & pipe smoking, fine wines, import & microbrews and gourmet coffee.

Along with the increasing demand people are becoming more knowledgeable about such items. Thus, people are not only looking for said items but the knowledge that goes along with them.

The product line at Holy Smokes includes premium tobacco, fine wine, exotic brews and gourmet coffee.

Company Locations and Facilities

Holy Smokes will be located in the City of Haverhill Heights off Woodlawn just South of Two Mile Road.

It borders the Nautical Mile, on Woodlawn from Two to Three Mile Rd., in Haverhill Heights and the City of Pine Hill Shores. It occupies a free standing commercial building that measures 1500square feet and has on-sight parking for approximately 10-12 cars.

The building will be purchased outright by John Jacobs.

PRODUCTS

Holy Smokes will be an upscale retail establishment that will carry fine wet goods and premium tobacco. By offering a solid selection in a "fitting" environment, Holy Smokes will be able to satisfy a number of tastes and budgets for the growing number of people who enjoy such pleasures.

Product Description

Holy Smokes will sell the following:

Premium cigars, pipe tobacco and accessories

With the increasing popularity and demand of premium tobacco, the market is need of a place where tobacco cannot only be purchased, but people can receive pertinent information regarding the various tobaccos (i.e. storage, tastes and various brands). Holy Smokes will be that place, and once a person has had the opportunity to experience Holy Smokes, there will be no looking back!

Fine Wines, Exotic Beers and Gourmet Coffees

With the recent surge in cigar smoking, a greater appreciation for things associated has also emerged. People no longer look for a cigar only. They are beginning to look for a fine wine, an import beer or a gourmet java to accompany their cigar.

COMPETITIVE COMPARISON

Holy Smokes will be a unique retail experience. There is no current establishment like Holy Smokes. The places that are trying either, over-price with limited stock and knowledge or over-stock and over-price with limited knowledge.

However, at Holy Smokes, one will be able to get a Fine Wine and a true Premium Cigar.

Both items will be properly cared for and displayed, in an environment conducive for purchasing said items. We will also be a place that will accommodate a wide variety of tastes and budgets. Of course there will be cigars, wines and things associated, that will cost a good sum of money. However, not all of them will. There will be good wines and good cigars that are not as expensive.

Holy Smokes will be the place that provides the service and the know-how to assist with purchasing these items. It will be the place that truly respects such pleasures.

Sales Literature

In one year alone, from 1995 to 1996, imported premium cigar sales have jumped 63% to almost 300 million.* And the top executives within the industry see the trend continuing for years to come.

Michigan ranks 8th in premium cigar sales.**

The Detroit Metro Market (Defined as the counties of Lapeer, Macomb, Monroe, Oakland, St. Clair and Wayne)***

      Ranks 6th in the country in Total Retail Sales***
      Ranks 8th in Total Effective Buying Income (EBI)***
      Ranks 12th EBI of households of $150,000 or more***

Source: Cigar Insider, December 1996, Page 18
Source: Norman Sharp, President Cigar Assoc. of America, April 1996
Source: Sales and Marketing Management, 1996 Survey of Buying Power

(EBI)" A measurement of income developed by Sales and Marketing Management. . . .EBI is defined as money income less personal tax and non-tax payments. . . .often referred to as "disposable" or "after-tax" income."

SOURCING/ OPERATING MARGINS

A. Premium Cigars

1. Per Box Markup
a. 90% if bought from exclusive distributor or factory direct, will include following costs:

    16% State Tobacco Tax
    Operating Costs -- Estimated $300 per day

b. when purchased through a local middle man percentage will vary, usually a 10-20% loss. The price one has to pay when supply is low and customers need to be satisfied.

2. Per cigar Markup 100%

B. Premium Wine

1. Markup: 30-50% depending on market competition and wholesale buying practices
2. will include overhead costs also

C Premium Beer Markup (Same schedule as wine)

D. Gourmet Coffee Markup (Estimated) 50%: specific information concerning this matter will be provided as soon as it becomes available.

MARKET ANALYSIS SUMMARY

The clientele for Holy Smokes will be up-scale, mostly of older men. However, the interest is on the rise in the younger men and women.

Market Segmentation

Market Segmentation on cigars has been obtained through the Cigar Association of America and is as follows:

- Mostly men
- On the rise with women and young people
- Increased concentration in 40-60 year olds
- Educated
- 2% are women
- 10-12 million occasional smokers in the U.S.

The specifics on the Wine, Beer and Coffee have yet to be obtained. However, one must keep in mind that a relatively small business, such as Holy Smokes, will have to concentrate on pleasing the cigar, wine and beer enthusiasts as a whole, regardless of age, sex,etc. If a place has positioned itself as "the place" for wine enthusiasts, cigar aficionados or both, it has then built sustenance for the long haul. Holy Smokes will be "the place". It will be for the person who isintrigued by the growing appreciation for cigar smoking, pipes, wines, etc.. And it will also attract the experienced enthusiast by offering great selection and service that is second to none.

Product is distributed in a variety of ways: **Distribution Patterns**

Tobacco

  Regional distributors
  Direct sales
  Manufacturers who support their own distribution

Beer and Wine

  Beer and Wine distribution is regional, mostly on-site business.

Coffee

  Coffee distribution information is limited at this time. As more becomes available it will be added to this plan.

Competition is strong, especially with tobacco. A lot of it is price and availability. Who has   **COMPETITION**
what? How much? However with the growing appreciation for cigars, wine, beer and coffee people are now seeking places that not only offer said items but also good service and reasonable prices. Very few places have the knowledge base with items like these.

Folger's Humidor: Sheffield, MI.   **Main Competitors**
Harry Folger(owner) is an icon when it comes to tobacco. However, he is out of Holy Smokes's immediate market area and he does not carry the premium wet goods. He carries luggage along with the tobacco. A very important distinguishing feature.

Westminster's: Haverhill Heights, Grevely Heights, Sheffield, and various other locations in the mid-west.
They are in my market area and a lot bigger than Humidor One,but they are really high priced and they, too, do not carry the wet goods.

Reinhold Tobacco: Sheffield, MI (There are other locations in the East along with a large mail order circuit)
Gus Bommarito another industry icon. However, he is also out of my area and does not carry the wet goods. He carries colognes.

Fine Wine Emporium: Pine Hill Woods, MI
They are big on the wine, as the name suggests, and they carry cigars as well. However, selection is extremely limited and they seem to cater strictly to the wine enthusiast.

Wine Merchants, Inc.: Sheffield and Whitman Hills, MI
They too cater strictly to the wine enthusiast.

There is some very good competition in the area, but they all seem to sway one way or the other. There is room for an establishment, like Holy Smokes, to come in and position itself as the place that offers some of the finer pleasures in life. It will be able to accomplish this task by having a suitable atmosphere, fair prices and unparalleled customer service.

STRATEGY AND IMPLEMENTATION SUMMARY

Our strategy will be to serve people who either, truly enjoy or are intrigued with the pleasures that will be offered.

This will be done by offering the following:

- Great selection
- Fair prices
- Knowledgeable service to assist with buying when needed.
- Creating an environment that makes these pleasures much more appreciable

Marketing Strategy

Our primary focus: Premium Cigars
This will be the big draw and, once in, people will be able to buy a beverage that suits their smoke and mood. Again, Holy Smokes will be an establishment that is conducive to selling such pleasures and this, too, will be a big draw.

Target Markets and Market Segments

Holy Smokes will focus on the tobacco market to get started, with interest growing in the wines, beers, and coffees.

Holy Smokes will be the ONLY place in the area that will offer reasonably priced items such as these in an upscale environment. If you want a rare wine and a premium cigar, Holy Smokes is the place to go. In fact, it will be the only place to go.

Pricing Strategy

A detailed price list will be made available as soon is as it is complete . The pricing markup was discussed earlier and will be applied accordingly.

Promotion Strategy

Advertising will be used a lot for the opening, nothing real elaborate or expensive. I plan to advertise in most of the local community papers like the Pine Hill News, Sentinel, and the Macomb Daily. A lot of advertising will be done through friends -- word of mouth. I have already begun to inform people that a store like Holy Smokes is definitely on the horizon. There will also be a consideration for local radio spots. Specific advertising figures have yet to be obtained, andas soon as they are they will be included in this plan.

Distribution Strategy

Product that is obtained to sell will come through various channels. And product sold will mainly be through the retail outlet. Mail order and special order items will be available upon request.

Our advantage comes with the way in which our retail outlet looks and is run. As stated earlier, Holy Smokes will be a place where patrons, with various levels of expertise, will enjoy doing business.

Business Plans Handbook, Volume 5

CIGAR SHOP

The sales forecast estimates sales by months for the first year and is divided into categories.

Sales	FY1998
Tobacco	$112,928
Wine	$20,269
Beer	$0
Coffee	$0
Other	$6,380
Total Sales	$139,577

Cost of sales	FY1998
Tobacco	$51,123
Wine	$14,842
Beer	$14,842
Coffee	$6,394
Other	$3,208
Subtotal Cost of Sales	$90,409

One plan for Holy Smokes is to become part of the Retail Tobacco Dealers of America (RTDA). The RTDA is an association that offers the following privileges to its members:

Access to the Tobacco Convention they arrange: The convention is 4 days and most people will do most of their buying for the year in these four days. Anyone involved with tobacco will be part of this convention.

- A yearly almanac that includes all of the tobacco dealers in the industry
- Tobacco Legislation
- Trade Magazines
- News Bulletins
- Service and Support

One of the keys to success for Holy Smokes will be service, and it will be added into the cost of the product. People are going to get the service and environment desired with a very competitive price.

John Jacobs will be the owner and operator. there will be no employees to start.

I have run a small cigar business out of my home office for the past year. Sales are steady and slowly growing for the time put into selling. However, days are numbered in such a capacity. The industry will not continue to let such a business exist successfully. With Holy Smokes, I willbe able to establish a position in the market that will maintain over the long haul.

Management Team Gaps

Fine Wine - However, a lot of effort is being put into learning more about the subject. Holy Smokes provides the time and effort needed to become knowledgeable with all it sells, not just simply tag it and put it on the shelf.

Coffee - It is being done similar to that of the wine.

FINANCIAL PLAN

With the tobacco, business growth should be steady. The tobacco, coupled with the proper positioning strategy, will be sufficient enough to bring in the customers for the fine wine, premium beer and gourmet coffee. With a steady growth in all areas and a good inventory turnover rate, Holy Smokes will be able to finance any growths with cash flow.

General Assumptions

	FY1998	FY1999	FY2000
Short Term Interest Rate	11.00%	11.00%	11.00%
Long Term Interest Rate	11.00%	11.00%	11.00%
Payment days	30	30	30
Collection days	30	30	30
Inventory Turnover	4	4	4
Tax Rate Percent	25.00%	25.00%	25.00%
Expenses in Cash	50.00%	50.00%	50.00%
Sales on credit	30.00%	30.00%	30.00%
Personnel Burden %	10.00%	10.00%	10.00%

Note: Ratios on assumptions are used as estimators and may therefore have different values than ratios calculated in the ratios section.

	FY1998	FY1999	FY2000
Sales	$139,577	$0	$0
Direct Cost of Sales	$90,409	$0	$0
Other	$0	$0	$0
Total Cost of Sales	$90,409	$0	$0
Gross margin	$49,168	$0	$0
Gross margin percent	35.23%	0.00%	0.00%
Operating expenses:			
Advertising/Promotion	$7,000	$0	$0
Travel	$0	$0	$0
Miscellaneous	$12,000	$0	$0
Other	$6,000	$0	$0
Payroll expense	$0	$0	$0
Leased Equipment	$0	$0	$0
Utilities	$7,200	$0	$0
Insurance	$0	$0	$0
Rent	$42,000	$0	$0
Depreciation	$0	$0	$0
Payroll Burden	$0	$0	$0
Other	$0	$0	$0
Contract/Consultants	$0	$0	$0
Other	$0	$0	$0
Total Operating Expenses	$74,200	$0	$0
Profit Before Interest and Taxes	($25,032)	$0	$0
Interest Expense ST	$10,230	$11,440	$11,440
Interest Expense LT	$1,073	$1,980	$1,980
Taxes Incurred	($9,084)	($3,355)	($3,355)
Net Profit	($27,251)	($10,065)	($10,065)
Net Profit/Sales	19.52%	0.00%	0.00%

**Projected
Profit & Loass**

Projected Cash Flow

	FY1998	FY1999	FY2000
Net Profit:	($27,251)	($10,065)	($10,065)
Plus:			
Depreciation	$0	$0	$0
Change in Accounts Payable	$8,426	($8,426)	$0
Current Borrowing (repayment)	$24,000	$0	$0
Increase (decrease) Other Liabilities	$0	$0	$0
Long-term Borrowing (repayment)	$18,000	$0	$0
Capital Input	$0	$0	$0
Subtotal	$23,175	($18,491)	($10,065)
	FY1998	FY1999	FY2000
Less:			
Change in Accounts Receivable	$5,210	($5,210)	$0
Change in Inventory	$5,139	($35,139)	$0
Change in Other ST Assets	$0	$0	$0
Capital Expenditure	$0	$0	$0
Dividends	$0	$0	$0
Subtotal	$10,349	($40,349)	$0
Net Cash Flow	$12,826	$21,859	($10,065)
Cash balance	$41,826	$63,684	$53,619

Projected Balance Sheet

	FY1998	FY1999	FY2000
Short-term Assets			
Cash	$41,826	$63,684	$53,619
Accounts receivable	$5,210	$0	$0
Inventory	$35,139	$0	$0
Other Short-term Assets	$13,000	$13,000	$13,000
Total Short-term Assets	$95,175	$76,684	$66,619
Long-term Assets			
Capital Assets	$0	$0	$0
Accumulated Depreciation	$0	$0	$0
Total Long-term Assets	$0	$0	$0
Total Assets	$95,175	$76,684	$66,619
Debt and Equity			
Accounts Payable	$8,426	$0	$0
Short-term Notes	$104,000	$104,000	$104,000
Other ST Liabilities	$0	$0	$0
Subtotal Short-term Liabilities	$112,426	$104,000	$104,000
Long-term Liabilities	$18,000	$18,000	$18,000
Total Liabilities	$130,426	$122,000	$122,000
Paid in Capital	$0	$0	$0
Retained Earnings	($8,000)	($35,251)	($45,316)
Earnings	($27,251)	($10,065)	($10,065)
Total Equity	($35,251)	($45,316)	($55,381)
Total Debt and Equity	$95,175	$76,684	$66,619
Net Worth	($35,251)	($45,316)	($55,381)

Profitability Ratios	FY1998	FY1999	FY2000
Gross margin	35.23%	0.00%	0.00%
Net profit margin	-19.52%	0.00%	0.00%
Return on Assets	-28.63%	-13.13%	-15.11%
Return on Equity	0.00%	0.00%	0.00%

Activity Ratios			
AR Turnover	8.04	0.00	0.00
Collection days	23	0	0
Inventory Turnover	2.78	0.00	0.00
Accts payable turnover	9.77	0.00	0.00
Total asset turnover	1.47	0.00	0.00

Debt Ratios:	FY1998	FY1999	FY2000
Debt to net Worth	0.00	0.00	0.00
Short-term Debt to Liab.	0.86	0.85	0.85

Liquidity ratios			
Current Ratio	0.85	0.74	0.64
Quick Ratio	0.53	0.74	0.64
Net Working Capital	($17,251)	($27,316)	($37,381)
Interest Coverage	-2.21	0.00	0.00

Additional ratios	FY1998	FY1999	FY2000
Assets to sales	0.68	n.a.	n.a.
Debt/Assets	137%	159%	183%
Current debt/Total Assets	118%	136%	156%
Acid test	0.49	0.74	0.64
Asset Turnover	1.47	0.00	0.00
Sales/Net Worth	0.00	0.00	0.00

Projected
Balance Sheet

	May-97	Jun-97	Jul-97	Aug-97	Sep-97	Oct-97	Nov-97	$35,765
Short-term Assets								
Cash	$35,000	$38,662	$43,522	$46,118	$44,575	$42,907	$41,010	$39,132
Accounts receivable	$1,479	$1,849	$2,127	$2,480	$2,852	$3,279	$3,770	$4,338
Inventory	$26,550	$22,558	$17,961	$15,861	$18,243	$20,979	$24,120	$27,735
Other Short-term Assets	$13,000	$13,000	$13,000	$13,000	$13,000	$13,000	$13,000	$13,000
Total Short-term Assets	$76,029	$76,069	$76,610	$77,459	$78,669	$80,165	$81,900	$84,206
Long-term Assets								
Capital Assets	$0	$0	$0	$0	$0	$0	$0	$0
Accumulated Depreciation	$0	$0	$0	$0	$0	$0	$0	$0
Total Long-term Assets	$0	$0	$0	$0	$0	$0	$0	$0
Total Assets	$76,029	$76,069	$76,610	$77,459	$78,669	$80,165	$81,900	$84,206

Debt and Equity

	May-97	Jun-97	Jul-97	Aug-97	Sep-97	Oct-97	Nov-97	$35,765
Accounts Payable	$4,891	$4,911	$5,206	$5,542	$5,928	$6,615	$7,125	$7,711
Short-term Notes	$82,000	$84,000	$86,000	$88,000	$90,000	$92,000	$94,000	$96,000
Other ST Liabilities	$0	$0	$0	$0	$0	$0	$0	$0
Subtotal Short-term Liabilities	$86,891	$88,911	$91,206	$93,542	$95,928	$98,615	$101,125	$103,711
Long-term Liabilities	$1,500	$3,000	$4,500	$6,000	$7,500	$9,000	$10,500	$12,000
Total Liabilities	$88,391	$91,911	$95,706	$99,542	$103,428	$107,615	$111,625	$115,711
Paid in Capital	$0	$0	$0	$0	$0	$0	$0	$0
Retained Earnings	($8,000)	($8,000)	($8,000)	($8,000)	($8,000)	($8,000)	($8,000)	($8,000)
Earnings	($4,362)	($7,842)	($11,096)	($14,082)	($16,759)	($19,450)	($21,725)	($23,506)
Total Equity	($12,362)	($15,842)	($19,096)	($22,082)	($24,759)	($27,450)	($29,725)	($31,506)
Total Debt and Equity	$76,029	$76,069	$76,610	$77,459	$78,669	$80,165	$81,900	$84,206
Net Worth	($12,362)	($15,842)	($19,096)	($22,082)	($24,759)	($27,450)	($29,725)	($31,506)

Projected Cash Flow

	May-97	Jun-97	Jul-97	Aug-97	Sep-97	Oct-97	Nov-97	Dec-97
Net Profit:	($4,362)	($3,480)	($3,254)	($2,986)	($2,677)	($2,692)	($2,275)	($1,781)
Plus:								
Depreciation	$0	$0	$0	$0	$0	$0	$0	$0
Change in Accounts Payable	$4,891	$20	$294	$336	$386	$687	$510	$586
Current Borrowing (repayment)	$2,000	$2,000	$2,000	$2,000	$2,000	$2,000	$2,000	$2,000
Increase (decrease) Other Liabilities	$0	$0	$0	$0	$0	$0	$0	$0
Long-term Borrowing (repayment)	$1,500	$1,500	$1,500	$1,500	$1,500	$1,500	$1,500	$1,500
Capital Input	$0	$0	$0	$0	$0	$0	$0	$0
Subtotal	$4,029	$40	$540	$850	$1,210	$1,496	$1,735	$2,306
Less:	May	Jun	Jul	Aug	Sep	Oct	Nov	Dec
Change in Accounts Receivable	$1,479	$370	$278	$353	$372	$427	$491	$569
Change in Inventory	($3,450)	($3,992)	($4,597)	($2,100)	$2,382	$2,736	$3,141	$3,615
Change in Other ST Assets	$0	$0	$0	$0	$0	$0	$0	$0
Capital Expenditure	$0	$0	$0	$0	$0	$0	$0	$0
Dividends	$0	$0	$0	$0	$0	$0	$0	$0
Subtotal	($1,971)	($3,622)	($4,319)	($1,747)	$2,754	$3,163	$3,632	$4,184
Net Cash Flow	$6,000	$3,662	$4,860	$2,596	($1,544)	($1,668)	($1,897)	($1,878)
Cash balance	$35,000	$38,662	$43,522	$46,118	$44,575	$42,907	$41,010	$39,132

General Assumptions

	May-97	Jun-97	Jul-97	Aug-97	Sep-97	Oct-97	Nov-97	Dec-97
ST Interest Rate	11.00%	11.00%	11.00%	11.00%	11.00%	11.00%	11.00%	11.00%
LT Interest Rate	11.00%	11.00%	11.00%	11.00%	11.00%	11.00%	11.00%	11.00%
Payment days	30	30	30	30	30	30	30	30
Collection days	30	30	30	30	30	30	30	30
Inventory Turnover	4.00	4.00	4.00	4.00	4.00	4.00	4.00	4.00
Tax Rate Percent	25.00%	25.00%	25.00%	25.00%	25.00%	25.00%	25.00%	25.00%
Expenses in cash %	50.00%	50.00%	50.00%	50.00%	50.00%	50.00%	50.00%	50.00%
Sales on credit	30.00%	30.00%	30.00%	30.00%	30.00%	30.00%	30.00%	30.00%
Personnel Burden %	10.00%	10.00%	10.00%	10.00%	10.00%	10.00%	10.00%	10.00%

Sales Forecast

	May-97	Jun-97	Jul-97	Aug-97	Sep-97	Oct-97	Nov-97	Dec-97	Jan-98
Sales									
Tobacco	$4,000	$5,100	$5,865	$6,745	$7,756	$8,920	$10,250	$11,797	$11,797
Wine	$750	$862	$992	$1,141	$1,312	$1,510	$1,736	$1,997	$1,997
Beer	$0	$0	$0	$0	$0	$0	$0	$0	$0
Coffee	$0	$0	$0	$0	$0	$0	$0	$0	$0
Other	$250	$287	$331	$381	$438	$500	$579	$667	$667
Total Sales	$5,000	$6,249	$7,188	$8,267	$9,506	$10,930	$12,565	$14,461	$14,461

Cost of Sales	May-97	Jun-97	Jul-97	Aug-97	Sep-97	Oct-97	Nov-97	Dec-97	Jan-98
Tobacco	$2,000	$2,300	$2,645	$3,042	$3,498	$4,023	$4,626	$5,319	$5,319
Wine	$550	$630	$727	$836	$962	$1,106	$1,271	$1,462	$1,462
Beer	$550	$630	$727	$836	$962	$1,106	$1,271	$1,462	$1,462
Coffee	$250	$287	$331	$381	$438	$503	$579	$665	$665
Other	$100	$145	$167	$192	$221	$255	$293	$337	$337
Subtotal Cost of Sales	$3,450	$3,992	$4,597	$5,287	$6,081	$6,993	$8,040	$9,245	$9,245

**Projected
Profit & Loss**

	May-97	Jun-97	Jul-97	Aug-97	Sep-97	Oct-97	Nov-97	Dec-97
Sales	$5,000	$6,249	$7,188	$8,267	$9,506	$10,930	$12,565	$14,461
Direct Cost of Sales	$3,450	$3,992	$4,597	$5,287	$6,081	$6,993	$8,040	$9,245
Other	$0	$0	$0	$0	$0	$0	$0	$0
Total Cost of Sales	$3,450	$3,992	$4,597	$5,287	$6,081	$6,993	$8,040	$9,245
Gross margin	$1,550	$2,257	$2,591	$2,980	$3,425	$3,937	$4,525	$5,216
Gross margin percent	31.00%	36.12%	36.05%	36.05%	36.03%	36.02%	36.01%	36.07%
Operating expenses:								
Advertising & Promotion	$1,000	$500	$500	$500	$500	$1,000	$1,000	$1,000
Travel	$0	$0	$0	$0	$0	$0	$0	$0
Miscellaneous	$1,000	$1,000	$1,000	$1,000	$1,000	$1,000	$1,000	$1,000
Other	$500	$500	$500	$500	$500	$500	$500	$500
Payroll expense	$0	$0	$0	$0	$0	$0	$0	$0
Leased Equipment	$0	$0	$0	$0	$0	$0	$0	$0
Utilities	$600	$600	$600	$600	$600	$600	$600	$600
Insurance	$0	$0	$0	$0	$0	$0	$0	$0
Rent	$3,500	$3,500	$3,500	$3,500	$3,500	$3,500	$3,500	$3,500
Depreciation	$0	$0	$0	$0	$0	$0	$0	$0
Payroll Burden	$0	$0	$0	$0	$0	$0	$0	$0
Other	$0	$0	$0	$0	$0	$0	$0	$0
Contract/Consultants	$0	$0	$0	$0	$0	$0	$0	$0
Other	$0	$0	$0	$0	$0	$0	$0	$0
Total Operating Expenses	$6,600	$6,100	$6,100	$6,100	$6,100	$6,600	$6,600	$6,600
Profit Before Interest & Taxes	($5,050)	($3,843)	($3,509)	($3,120)	($2,675)	($2,663)	($2,075)	($1,384)
ST Interest Expense	$752	$770	$788	$807	$825	$843	$862	$880
LT Interest Expense	$14	$28	$41	$55	$69	$83	$96	$110
Taxes Incurred	($1,454)	($1,160)	($1,085)	($995)	($892)	($897)	($758)	($594)
Net Profit	($4,362)	($3,480)	($3,254)	($2,986)	($2,677)	($2,692)	($2,275)	($1,781)
Net Profit/Sales	87.23%	55.69%	45.27%	36.12%	28.16%	24.63%	18.10%	12.31%

Climbing Outfitter

BUSINESS PLAN

ROCKHOUND OUTFITTERS

2268 Eagle Rock Dr.
Greenfield, WY 76551

This business plan is an excellent example of a business in a field with high growth potential. Capitalizing on current leisure and sport trends, Rockhound Outfitters is located in an area that takes particular advantage of nearby climbing opportunities and isolates it from the competition. Market analysis and promotional strategies are well-thought-out. This business plan was compiled using Business Plan Pro, by Palo Alto Software ©.

- EXECUTIVE SUMMARY

- COMPANY SUMMARY

- PRODUCTS

- MARKET ANALYSIS SUMMARY

- STRATEGY AND IMPLEMENTATION SUMMARY

- MANAGEMENT SUMMARY

- FINANCIAL PLAN

CLIMBING OUTFITTER
BUSINESS PLAN

EXECUTIVE SUMMARY

Rockhound Outfitters will sell the best rockclimbing gear and Northwest coffee. The store is located one mile from Eagle Rock State Park in the Central Wyoming desert. This is the company's permanent residence.

75% of Profits will go to the owner and employees and 25% to Eagle Rock Park restoration projects. This plan introduces the rewards, community and financial, of investment in Rockhound Outfitters.

Objectives

1. To make Rockhound Outfitters the number one destination for rockclimbing equipment customers in Wyoming, and to achieve the largest market share in the region for rockclimbing gear.

2. To be an active and vocal member of the community, and to provide continual re-investment through participation in community activities and financial contributions.

3. To achieve a 65% profit margin within the first year.

4. To achieve a net profit of $30,000 by year two.

Mission

Rockhound Outfitters is an equipment store specializing in rockclimbing gear and coffee/espresso drinks. We encourage rockclimbers to be safe and fun. We also understand that rockclimbers need a healthy dose of the newest, coolest gear and raw caffeine; we provide them with the best of both.

Our goal is to be the embarkment point for rockclimbers throughout Central Wyoming.

We believe it is important to remain an active member of the community, and to impact our customer's lives in more ways than the selling of merchandise:
Providing safety instruction and travel tips that make our sport safe and fun; re-investing in the community and the wilderness destinations that allow our sport to exist: local, state, and national parks.

Keys to Success

To succeed in this business we must:

• Sell products that are of the highest reliability and quality.
• Provide for the satisfaction of 100% of our customers.
• Be an active member of the community: i.e., host sportclimbing and rockclimbing events.
• Encourage the two most important values in climbing: safety and fun.

COMPANY SUMMARY

Rockhound Outfitters sells quality products and provides excellent customer service for rockclimbers and coffee-lovers. We have purchased a retail store that we use to market and merchandise our products. It is located one mile from Eagle Rock State park, five miles from Greenfield. The company was incorporated on January 1, 1996.

Rockhound Outfitters is a privately held corporation. Ownership: 60%, Ethan Reilley; 40%, Sarah Robinson.

• 93% of startup costs will go to assets.
• The building will be purchased with a down payment of $8,000 on a twenty year mortgage.
• The espresso machine will cost $4500(straight-line depreciation, 3 years).
• Startup costs will be financed through a combination of owner investment, short-term loans, and long term borrowing. The startup chart shows the distribution of financing.
• Other miscellaneous expenses include: Marketing/advertising consultancy fees of $1,000 for our company logo and assistance in designing our grand-opening ads and brochures.
• Legal fees for corporate organization filings ($300).
• Retail merchandising/designing consultancy fees of $3,500 for store layout and fixture purchasing consulting.

Start-up Plan

Start-up Expenses	
Legal	$300
Marketing consultants	$1,000
Business and liability insurance	$600
1st month's pmt+deposit	$2,500
Design costs	$3,500
Other	$0
Total Start-up Expense	$7,900

Start-up Assets Needed	
Cash requirements	$7,000
Start-up inventory	$16,000
Other Short-term Assets	$1,000
Total Short-term Assets	$24,000
Long-term Assets	$140,000
Total Assets	$164,000
Total Start-up Requirements:	$171,900
Left to finance:	$0

Start-up Funding Plan

Investment	
Ethan Reilley	$10,900
Sarah Robinson	$2,900
Other	$0
Total investment	$13,800

...continued

Startup Summary

...continued

Short-term borrowing	
Unpaid expenses	$0
Short-term loans	$10,000
Interest-free short-term loans	$1,000
Subtotal Short-term Borrowing	$11,000
Long-term Borrowing	$148,000
Total Borrowing	$159,000
Loss at start-up	($8,800)
Total Equity	$5,000
Total Debt and Equity	$164,000
Checkline	$0

COMPANY PRODUCTS

Rockhound Outfitters sells high-quality rockclimbing gear to serious climbers. The gear is checked by knowledgeable employees who use and recommend equipment tocustomers and management.

The gear is purchased from well-known manufacturers like Black Diamond, Boreal, and Petzl. Management will rely on employees and customers to shorten the feedback loop in product and service offerings. Climbing gear is delivered every Thursday.

Straight espresso bean rebuys arrive on Mondays and Thursdays, ensuring the freshest beans possible. Modified rebuys are done by Sam Williamston on the first of each month. Sam is very demanding and will always get the freshest beans.

Company Locations and Facilities

The company office is located in the owner's residence, 5566 Russet Drive, Ford Valley, WY 76550.

The office is about 700 square feet and has ample space for the first three years of growth.

Deliveries and shipments are serviced through the store located at 2268 Eagle Rock Drive, Greenfield, WY 76551.

The 5000 square foot retail building is owned by Rockhound Outfitters and there is no excess storage capacity.

Products

Espresso is the big money-maker for Rockhound Outfitters, with coffee peripherals coming in a close second. The rockclimbing gear is a long-term sales project that will rely on future catalog and "Word-of-Mouth" sales.

Product Description

Rockhound Outfitters sells the entire raft of coffee-drinks: lattes, mochas, cappuccino, espresso, and a delicious house blend.

Rockhound Outfitters also sells carabiners, nuts, ropes, webbing, shoes, and harnesses; our product mix is sufficient to satisfy even the most hard-core enthusiast.

All products are quality-checked when they arrive and quality-checked before the customer takes them home.

Rockhound Outfitters has several advantages over its leading competitor.

1. Newer inventory and more modern interior fixtures.
2. Espresso drinks are made available to consumers while they shop, increasing marketing message impact.
3. Rockhound Outfitters is a fun, spacious store catering to both the climbing "Pro"'s and the inexperienced. Our competitor, The Rock Lobster, is an exclusive "Pro" shop that we believe discourages newcomers to the sport. Our positioning encourages those just getting started, a one-stop destination for equipment advice and purchasing opportunities, technique and safety instruction, and conversation with other enthusiasts.
4. We expect a high degree of expertise and enthusiasm from our employees and we compensate them accordingly.

Rockhound Outfitters will use advertising and sales programs to get the word out to customers.

2000 four-color brochures to be distributed throughout Ford Valley and area facilities: outdoor clothing shops, hotels, ranger stations, chambers of commerce, tourism council offices, area eateries, and other tourist-frequented spots one month before the grand opening in July.

Half -page newspaper advertisements in Wyoming regional newspapers, advertising the following sales promotion: introductory rockclimbing classes, two days for $100 per person. Copy: magazine and newspaper advertisements.

Sourcing is critical for any enterprise, especially a retail operation. The Bean People are to be our coffee vendors, and will handle many in-store merchandising issues for their line coffee products. Operational supplies for the coffee bar will be purchased from the regional supply wholesaler, who will handle special merchandising issues, such as point-of-sale materials. The sport and recreation inventory will be sourced directly from the manufacturers like Black Diamond, Boreal, and Petzl.

Advertising costs are outsourced to Hamilton Marketing. Most sales promotion and public relations work is handled in-house by Ethan Reilley.

Future seminars and climbing-clinics will be handled either by Ethan or several certified and experienced tour and adventure professionals.

We use off-the-shelf, PC-based software for accounting purposes, including AR/AP, inventory, purchasing, sales, and returns.

Our business plan is generated on an annual basis using Business Plan Pro from Palo Alto Software, and reviewed quarterly for evaluation. Further functionality is provided by Palo Alto Software's companion package, Marketing Plus, that allows us to make the most use of our marketing dollars by focusing our communications with our target markets and enhancing our marketing-tracking capability.

We are currently studying the costs, benefits, and feasibility of creating and maintaining an Internet presence on the World Wide Web. A possible Web site would allow enhancedcommunication with our target markets and the community at large. On-line commerce is becoming an increasingly attractive option due to the relatively low cost-of-goods, the global reach of the medium, and the increasing security. Our business model could quite conceivably expand to include a form of Internet commerce in a variety of adventure equipment.

Future Products

Future expansion may allow for a horizontal increase of our product line by offering additional product categories: water sport gear, camping gear, and mountain biking accessories.

MARKET ANALYSIS SUMMARY

Consumer expenditures for rockclimbing equipment rose to $2,000,000 in Central Wyoming in 1995. We expect sales to increase steadily as Wyoming's population grows and the rockclimbing industry becomes increasingly popular.

The presence of several large universities located in Western Wyoming helps fuel our business, as does the status of Eagle Rock as a international destination spot for rockclimbing enthusiasts. Individuals from as far away as Japan, Europe, South America, and Australia seek out Eagle Rock as a beautiful and challenging sport- and rockclimbing destination. We count worldwide readers of such publications as Rock & Ice magazine and Outdoor Adventure among our target audience.

Market Segmentation

The weekend warriors purchase during weekends. When these climbers are on a rock wall, they want to look COOL.

Hardcore climbers are very fickle about the gear they use. This segment is very brand loyal and provides the company with powerful WOM marketing.

Curious Georges that want to stop in for a gander on their way to their campsites or hotel rooms.

Industry Analysis

The rockclimbing industry is dispersing faster than ever. Although the gear is expensive, people buy it because it provides them with long term fun.

High profit margins on coffee sales and low overhead costs lead to high profit margins in the espresso industry.

Industry Participants

The rockclimbing gear industry is still fairly young. Climbing stores are generally small in size and community oriented. These stores seek to attract the most knowledgeable $6-8/hour employees.

Distribution Patterns

Generally, traditional distribution channels are followed. The products are bought from wholesalers who have little say in how products are marketed, beyond the occasional sales promotion display provided via the manufacturer. This is beneficial in keeping the marketing and product costs low, while maintaining profit margins of 60% or more.

Customers are very brand oriented and effects the distribution patterns(rebuys) on the retail end.

Climbers demand knowledgeable employees in a convenient location.

Comparison: REI has placed its stores in urban industrial areas. Costco, a wholesaler, implements a similar strategy that draws the suburban dweller out of the house, this strategy keeps these customers isolated from the competition.

Products and services are the most important factors when selling rockclimbing gear. Brand name products sell well in stores that maintain a good selection, good location, and knowledgeable, friendly employees.

Espresso shops need to be fast, efficient, and friendly. Fortunately, there are no espresso shops in close proximity to Rockhound Outfitters.

Our nearest competitor is Kelly's Gear. Our next closest competitor is The Rock Lobster, located near Greenfield. Neither of these retailers offer espresso to their customers.

Kelly's sells limited gear (clothes), they do not promote, and they do not market their products extensively. On the positive side, they sell ice cream and carry more GenX apparel than Rockhound Outfitters. We see their products as complementary to ours; Ice Cream/Espresso. Their biggest weakness is a small store size.

The Rock Lobster will be our toughest competitor, for they have already established themselves in the rockclimbing community, they have a very experienced and knowledgeable staff of expert climbers working for them, and they are located on the highway that leads directly to Eagle Rock. They sell 75-80% of the same gear that we carry.

The market analysis shows potential customers and the company's target markets. Weekend Warriors make up the largest market segment, we expect this market to grow at a rate of 4% per year. This market constitutes the bulk of climbers, those that spend their weekends at Eagle Rock. Curious Georges constitute the second largest market. The last market segment is the smallest, the Hardcore climbers. A combination of students, climbing instructors, and climbing juggernauts make up this market sector.

Market Analysis

Potential Customers	Customers	Growth rate
Weekend warriors	40,000	3%
Hard-Core Climbers	2,300	4%
Curious Georges	30,000	4%
Other	0	0%
Total	72,300	3.45%

STRATEGY AND IMPLEMENTATION SUMMARY

Rockhound Outfitters uses a strategy of total market service.

Assumptions:
1. Every person is a potential customer and all potential markets experience growth.
2. Marketing to one segment of the population will lead to an expansion in overall market growth.

Marketing Strategy

Our marketing strategy will focus on three segments. Those three segments are described in the following subtopics.

The plan will benchmark our objectives for sales promotion, mass selling, and personal selling.

We are focusing our marketing effort on the weekend warriors and the hard-core climbing community. We will implement a strategy that treats these customers as a community. This means our marketing resources will be centered around both sales promotions(events, displays) and personal sales(customer service, friendly atmosphere).

The marketing budget will not exceed $7,000 per year.

Marketing promotions will be consistent with the Mission Statement.

Pricing Strategy

We are a store that is positioned for impulse buying therefore it is important that we maintain a flexible pricing strategy.

Our pricing strategy will be based on competitive parity guidelines. We will not exceed competitors' prices by more than 10%, and if a customer sees a price elsewhere for less we will give it to them for that price.

Price says a lot about a product. The products that are innovative and not available elsewhere in the region will be marked up to meet the demand curve.

Promotion Strategy

Rockhound Outfitters will implement a strong sales promotion strategy, advertising will be secondary.

Hamilton Marketing will be paid up to $2000 to determine the impact of promotionary campaigns on the surrounding populous(cousin jed and uncle bill).

Promotionary campaigns will be partially outsourced to Hamilton Marketing.

Advertising will be consistent with Hamilton Marketing.

Sales promotions and Public Relation strategies will work together to inform customers of new products, to encourage an image of community involvement for Rockhound Outfitters, and to limit environmental impact.

Hamilton Marketing is creating a billboard program that will integrate rockclimber interests with Rockhound Outfitters image of community, fun, and expertise.

Advertising

Ethan Reilley will host numerous climbing events.

Sales Promotion

Sales compensation is based on a % of profits.

Sales Strategy

All potential sales will be attended to in a timely fashion and long-term salesperson-customer relationships will take precedence over sales closure.

The following information gives a run-down on forecasted sales. We expect Sales to increase at a rate of 1% per month for each product in the first few months.

Sales Forecast

November through January, we expect zero sales, Rockhound Outfitters will be closed. February through March we expect 1% sales growth once again, becoming 2% growth as we round to the second summer. In 1998 and 1999, we expect solid 20% sales growth as Rockhound Outfitters claims a larger market share. Seven percent decreasing costs due to lower agency and efficiency costs are included in the 1998-1999 figures.

Note: For company purchases, the per unit price of inventory purchases includes cost of shipping.

Sales	FY1998	FY1999	FY2000
Carabiners	$32,279	$38,735	$48,419
Ropes	$6,276	$7,532	$9,415
Books and Magazines	$1,210	$1,453	$1,816
Cookies	$1,009	$1,210	$1,513
Espresso regulars	$65,903	$79,084	$98,855
Espresso shakes	$6,052	$7,263	$9,078
Other	$0	$0	$0
Total Sales	$112,730	$135,276	$169,095

Cost of sales	FY1998	FY1999	FY2000
Carabiners	$14,122	$15,958	$18,032
Ropes	$2,914	$3,293	$3,721
Books and Magazines	$605	$684	$773
Cookies	$403	$456	$515
Espresso regulars	$11,298	$12,766	$14,426
Espresso shakes	$1,345	$1,520	$1,717
Line 7	$0	$0	$0
Other	$0	$0	$0
Subtotal Cost of Sales	$30,687	$34,677	$39,185

Sales Programs

Sales programs will include sales awards for highest sales and customer service awards for those employees who best exemplify Rockhound Outfitters's commitment to customers.

Service and Support

Customer service issues are handled on the spot based a policy that faulty merchandise is returnable. Costs will be absorbed and accounted towards Goodwill.

Milestones

The milestone table shows purchasing, sales, and marketing goals. Sam will conduct straight rebuys while touching base with the The Bean People Inc. distributor in Port Parson, WY. We have paid a deposit of $700 (06/28/97) to set up a thirty day grace period on all purchases from The Bean People Inc. There is no franchise fee and The Bean People will donate advertising, consulting, and literature provided that all sales $ from Bean People mugs, cups, and T-shirts go directly to The Bean People Inc.

Business Plan Milestones

Milestone	Mngr	Date	Dept.	Budget	Act date	Act $	Date P-A	$ P-A
Coffee beans	SW	6/30/96	Purchasing	$700	6/28/96	$1,123	2	($423)
Meet with rep	ER	6/25/96	Sales	$400	6/28/96	$473	(3)	($73)
Complete advertising	ER	6/26/96	Marketing	$500	6/26/96	$500	0	$0
June rebuy/ beans & cookies	SW	7/30/96	Purchasing	$705	7/28/96	$0	2	$705
Jordan Rock Festival	ER	8/23/96	Marketing	$650	8/23/96	$650	0	$0
Straight rebuy	SW	8/30/96	Purchasing	$712	8/30/96	$712	0	$0
Straight rebuy	SW	9/30/96	Purchasing	$720	9/30/96	$720	0	$0
Straight rebuy	SW	10/30/96	Purchasing	$726	10/30/96	$726	0	$0
Straight rebuy	SW	11/30/96	Purchasing	$726	11/30/96	$726	0	$0
Straight rebuy	SW	12/30/96	Purchasing	$726	12/30/96	$726	0	$0
Straight rebuy	SW	1/30/97	Purchasing	$726	1/30/97	$726	0	$0
Other	SW	2/28/97	Purchasing	$726	2/28/97	$726	0	$0
Totals						$8,017		

MANAGEMENT SUMMARY

The CEO of Rockhound Outfitters believes very strongly that relationships should be forthright, work should be structured with enough room for creativity, and pay should be commensurate with the amount and quality of work completed.

No person is better than another; except in ability, knowledge, and experience.

Organizational Structure

Rockhound Outfitters is not departmentalized. The owner, Ethan Reilley, is also the CEO, CFO, and lead manager. The company makes all decisions in accordance with the company mission. Employees are given specific tasks based upon their creativity, knowledge, and social ability.

Every three months, the CEO assess the results of these tasks and the personality of the employee involved to determine promotion and/or salary issues.

Ethan Reilley: Manager, CEO, and founder. Ethan spent four years selling shoes and apparel for Nordstrom, Inc. He graduated from the University of Wyoming in 1987 with a degree in Finance. In 1990 Ethan went to work for Boeing as an accounts manager and was quickly promoted to head of investments for the regional division. MBA, University of Pennsylvania. BA, University of Wyoming. 35 years old, married, 1 child.

Sam Williamston: Assistant manager. Sam is an avid rockclimber, diver, river rafter, mountain climber, and tour guide. He graduated from the University of Wyoming in 1989 with a degree in leisure studies. He spent 5 years with Hilton hotels as a service analyst.

Management Team

Sam knows climbing and he knows people, but he has no experience in marketing and inventory control.

Ethan Reilley will be unable to delegate much responsibility through the first three to fourmonths of operation, leading to time constraints and priority leakage.

Management Gaps

The personnel plan is included in the following table. It shows the owner's salary (Other) followed by two part-time salaries for espresso servers/gear experts. Sam Williamston is being given $1,500 per month + 25% of company profit. This means that when the company is not profitable, Sam's wages fall accordingly (25%*Profit decrease). Part-time employees will not be included in the profit sharing program.

Personnel Plan

Personnel Plan

Job title	FY1998	FY1999	FY2000
Sam Williamston	$13,900	$14,595	$15,325
Part-time emp.	$4,000	$4,200	$4,410
Other	$36,000	$37,800	$39,690
Subtotal	$53,900	$56,595	$59,425

Growth will be moderate, cash flows steady.

Marketing will remain below 15% of sales.

The company will invest residual profits into financial markets and not company expansion(unless absolutely necessary).

Future cash investments will use NPV projections to achieve maximum return with limited risk.

FINANCIAL PLAN

We do not sell anything on credit. The personnel burden is very low because benefits are not paid to part-timers. And the short-term interest rate is extraordinarily low because of Mr. Reilley's long-standing relationship with Alamo Federal.

Important Assumptions

**Important
Assumptions**

General Assumptions

	FY1998	FY1999	FY2000
Short Term Interest Rate	6.00%	6.00%	6.00%
Long Term Interest Rate	7.50%	7.50%	7.50%
Payment days	30	30	30
Inventory Turnover	9	9.00	9.00
Tax Rate Percent	30.00%	30.00%	30.00%
Expenses in cash%	0.00%	0.00%	0.00%
Sales on credit	0.00%	0.00%	0.00%
Personnel Burden %	4.13%	4.13%	4.13%

Note: Ratios in assumptions are used as estimators and may therefore have different values than ratios calculated in the ratios section.

**Key Financial
Indicators**

**Break-even
Analysis**

A break-even analysis table has been completed on the basis of average costs/prices.

Break Even Analysis

Monthly Units Break-even	909
Monthly Sales Break-even	$21,000

Assumptions

Average Unit Sale	$23.10
Average Per-Unit Cost	$12.10
Fixed Cost	$10,000

**Projected Profit
and Loss**

We predict advertising costs and consulting costs will go down in the next three years. This will give Rockhound Outfitters a profit to sales ratio of nearly 10% by the year 2000. Normally, a startup concern will operate with negative profits through the first two years. We will avoid that kind of operating loss by knowing our competitors and our target markets.

Pro-forma Income Statement

	FY1998	FY1999	FY2000
Sales	$112,730	$135,276	$169,095
Direct Cost of Sales	$30,687	$34,677	$39,185
Other	$0	$0	$0
Total Cost of Sales	$30,687	$34,677	$39,185
Gross margin	$82,043	$100,599	$129,910
Gross margin percent	72.78%	74.37%	76.83%
Operating expenses:			
Advertising/Promotion	$4,500	$5,500	$5,200
Travel	$300	$0	$0
Payroll expense	$53,900	$56,595	$59,425
Leased Equipment	$0	$0	$0
Utilities	$1,089	$1,122	$1,155
Insurance	$780	$803	$828
Mortgage Payment	$13,500	$13,905	$14,322
Depreciation	$1,200	$1,236	$1,273
Payroll Burden	$2,470	$2,335	$2,451
Contract/Consultants	$2,000	$2,000	$1,800
Total Operating Expenses	$79,739	$83,496	$86,454
Profit Before Interest and Taxes	$2,304	$17,103	$43,456
Interest Expense ST	$278	$0	$0
Interest Expense LT	$10,983	$16,110	$15,786
Taxes Incurred	($2,687)	$298	$8,301
Net Profit	($6,270)	$695	$19,369
Net Profit/Sales	-5.56%	0.51%	11.45%

We are positioning ourselves in the market as a medium risk concern with steady cash flows. Accounts payable is paid at the end of each month while sales are in cash, giving Rockhound Outfitters an excellent cash structure. Solid NWC and intelligent marketing will secure a cash balance of $29,000 by January 1, 2001. Fifty percent of cash above $10,000 will be invested into semi-liquid stock portfolios to decrease the opportunity cost of cash held.

Projected Cash Flow

Projected Cash Flow

...continued

Pro-Forma Cash Flow

	FY1998	FY1999	FY2000
Net Profit:	($6,270)	$695	$19,369
Plus:			
Depreciation	$1,200	$1,236	$1,273
Change in Accounts Payable	$5,659	$543	$473
Current Borrowing (repayment)	($10,000)	$0	$0
Increase (decrease) Other Liabilities	($1,000)	$0	$0
Long-term Borrowing (repayment)	($2,880)	($2,880)	($2,880)
Capital Input	$0	$0	$0
Subtotal	($13,291)	($406)	$18,235
Less:	FY1998	FY1999	FY2000
Change in Accounts Receivable	$0	$0	$0
Change in Inventory	($11,206)	$623	$704
Change in Other ST Assets	$0	$0	$0
Capital Expenditure	$0	$0	$0
Dividends	$0	$0	$4,000
Subtotal	($11,206)	$623	$4,704
Net Cash Flow	($2,085)	($1,029)	$13,531
Cash balance	$4,915	$3,886	$17,417

Projected Balance Sheet

All of our tables will be updated monthly to reflect past performance and future assumptions. Future assumptions will not be based on past performance but rather economic cycle activity, regional industry strength, and future cash flow possibilities. We expect solid growth in Net Worth beyond the year 2000.

Pro-forma Balance Sheet

	Starting Balances	FY1998	FY1999	FY2000
Short-term Assets				
Cash	$7,000	$4,915	$3,886	$17,417
Accounts receivable	$0	$0	$0	$0
Inventory	$16,000	$4,794	$5,417	$6,122
Other Short-term Assets	$1,000	$1,000	$1,000	$1,000
Total Short-term Assets	$24,000	$10,709	$10,303	$24,538
Long-term Assets				
Capital Assets	$140,000	$140,000	$140,000	$140,000
Accumulated Depreciation	$0	$1,200	$2,436	$3,709
Total Long-term Assets	$140,000	$138,800	$137,564	$136,291
Total Assets	$164,000	$149,509	$147,867	$160,829

Debt and Equity

	FY1998	FY1999	FY2000
Accounts Payable	$0	$5,659	$6,202	$6,675
Short-term Notes	$10,000	$0	$0	$0
Other ST Liabilities	$1,000	($0)	($0)	($0)
Subtotal Short-term Liabilities	$11,000	$5,659	$6,202	$6,675
Long-term Liabilities	$148,000	$145,120	$142,240	$139,360
Total Liabilities	$159,000	$150,779	$148,442	$146,035
Paid in Capital	$13,800	$13,800	$13,800	$13,800
Retained Earnings	($8,800)	($8,800)	($15,070)	($18,374)
Earnings	$0	($6,270)	$695	$19,369
Total Equity	$5,000	($1,270)	($574)	$14,795
Total Debt and Equity	$164,000	$149,509	$147,867	$160,829
Net Worth	$5,000	($1,270)	($574)	$14,795

We expect our net profit margin, gross margin, and ROA to increase steadily over the three year period. ROE will decrease due to lower equity needs and higher cash inflows. Our net working capital will increase to almost $34000 by year 3, proving that we have the cash flows to remain a going concern. The following table shows these important financial ratios.

Ratio Analysis

Profitability Ratios:	FY1998	FY1999	FY2000	RMA
Gross margin	72.78%	74.37%	76.83%	0
Net profit margin	-5.56%	0.51%	11.45%	0
Return on Assets	-4.19%	0.47%	12.04%	0
Return on Equity	0.00%	0.00%	130.92%	0

Activity Ratios				
AR Turnover	0.00	0.00	0.00	0
Collection days	0	0	0	0
Inventory Turnover	2.95	6.79	6.79	0
Accts payable turnover	9.55	9.55	9.55	0
Total asset turnover	0.75	0.91	1.05	0

Debt Ratios:	FY1998	FY1999	FY2000	RMA
Debt to net Worth	0.00	0.00	9.87	0
Short-term Debt to Liab.	0.04	0.04	0.05	0

Liquidity ratios				
Current Ratio	1.89	1.66	3.68	0
Quick Ratio	1.05	0.79	2.76	0
Net Working Capital	$5,050	$4,102	$17,864	0
Interest Coverage	0.20	1.06	2.75	0

Additional ratios	FY1998	FY1999	FY2000	RMA
Assets to sales	1.33	1.09	0.95	0
Debt/Assets	101%	100%	91%	0
Current debt/Total Assets	4%	4%	4%	0
Acid Test	1.05	0.79	2.76	0
Asset Turnover	0.75	0.91	1.05	0
Sales/Net Worth	0.00	0.00	11.43	0

Appendix:
Projected Balance
Sheet

Pro-forma Balance Sheet

	Starting Balances	May-97	Jun-97	Jul-97	Aug-97	Sep-97	Oct-97
Short-term Assets							
Cash	$7,000	$15,263	$18,652	$22,269	$22,568	$22,205	$20,347
Accounts receivable	$0	$0	$0	$0	$0	$0	$0
Inventory	$16,000	$12,578	$9,087	$5,491	$4,842	$4,600	$3,450
Other Short-term Assets	$1,000	$1,000	$1,000	$1,000	$1,000	$1,000	$1,000
Total Short-term Assets	$24,000	$28,840	$28,739	$28,760	$28,410	$27,805	$24,797
Long-term Assets							
Capital Assets	$140,000	$140,000	$140,000	$140,000	$140,000	$140,000	$140,000
Accumulated Depreciation	$0	$100	$200	$300	$400	$500	$600
Total Long-term Assets	$140,000	$139,900	$139,800	$139,700	$139,600	$139,500	$139,400
Total Assets	$164,000	$168,740	$168,539	$168,460	$168,010	$167,305	$164,197

Debt and Equity

		May-97	Jun-97	Jul-97	Aug-97	Sep-97	Oct-97
Accounts Payable	$0	$5,195	$5,457	$5,852	$5,595	$5,419	$4,384
Short-term Notes	$10,000	$9,175	$8,350	$7,525	$6,700	$5,875	$5,050
Other ST Liabilities	$1,000	$917	$833	$750	$667	$583	$500
Subtotal Short-term Liabilities	$11,000	$15,287	$14,640	$14,127	$12,962	$11,877	$9,934
Long-term Liabilities	$148,000	$147,760	$147,520	$147,280	$147,040	$146,800	$146,560
	$145,360	$145,120	$145,120	$142,240	$139,360		
Total Liabilities	$159,000	$163,047	$162,160	$161,407	$160,002	$158,677	$156,494
Paid in Capital	$13,800	$13,800	$13,800	$13,800	$13,800	$13,800	$13,800
Retained Earnings	($8,800)	($8,800)	($8,800)	($8,800)	($8,800)	($8,800)	($8,800)
Earnings	$0	$693	$1,378	$2,053	$3,008	$3,627	$2,703
Total Equity	$5,000	$5,693	$6,378	$7,053	$8,008	$8,627	$7,703
Total Debt and Equity	$164,000	$168,740	$168,539	$168,460	$168,010	$167,305	$164,197
Net Worth	$5,000	$5,693	$6,378	$7,053	$8,008	$8,627	$7,703

	Nov-97	Dec-97	Jan-98	Feb-98	Mar-98	Apr-98	FY1998	FY1999	FY2000
	$14,317	$9,625	$4,727	$5,816	$5,325	$4,915	$4,915	$3,886	$17,417
	$0	$0	$0	$0	$0	$0	$0	$0	$0
	$400	$400	$400	$4,563	$4,655	$4,794	$4,794	$5,417	$6,122
	$1,000	$1,000	$1,000	$1,000	$1,000	$1,000	$1,000	$1,000	$1,000
	$15,717	$11,025	$6,127	$11,379	$10,980	$10,709	$10,709	$10,303	$24,538
	$140,000	$140,000	$140,000	$140,000	$140,000	$140,000	$140,000	$140,000	$140,000
	$700	$800	$900	$1,000	$1,100	$1,200	$1,200	$2,436	$3,709
	$139,300	$139,200	$139,100	$139,000	$138,900	$138,800	$138,800	$137,564	$136,291
	$155,017	$150,225	$145,227	$150,379	$149,880	$149,509	$149,509	$147,867	$160,829

	Nov-97	Dec-97	Jan-98	Feb-98	Mar-98	Apr-98	FY1998	FY1999	FY2000
	$0	$0	$0	$5,482	$5,557	$5,659	$5,659	$6,202	$6,675
	$4,225	$3,400	$2,575	$1,750	$925	$0	$0	$0	$0
	$417	$333	$250	$167	$83	($0)	($0)	($0)	($0)
	$4,642	$3,733	$2,825	$7,399	$6,565	$5,659	$5,659	$6,202	$6,675
	$146,320	$146,080	$145,840	$145,600					
	$150,962	$149,813	$148,665	$152,999	$151,925	$150,779	$150,779	$148,442	$146,035
	$13,800	$13,800	$13,800	$13,800	$13,800	$13,800	$13,800	$13,800	$13,800
	($8,800)	($8,800)	($8,800)	($8,800)	($8,800)	($8,800)	($8,800)	($15,070)	($18,374)
	($945)	($4,588)	($8,438)	($7,620)	($7,045)	($6,270)	($6,270)	$695	$19,369
	$4,055	$412	($3,438)	($2,620)	($2,045)	($1,270)	($1,270)	($574)	$14,795
	$155,017	$150,225	$145,227	$150,379	$149,880	$149,509	$149,509	$147,867	$160,829
	$4,055	$412	($3,438)	($2,620)	($2,045)	($1,270)	($1,270)	($574)	$14,795

Appendix:
Important
Assumptions

Pro-Forma Cash Flow

	May-97	Jun-97	Jul-97	Aug-97	Sep-97	Oct-97
Net Profit:	$693	$685	$675	$955	$619	($925)
Plus:						
Depreciation	$100	$100	$100	$100	$100	$100
Change in Accounts Payable	$5,195	$262	$395	($256)	($176)	($1,035)
Current Borrowing (repayment)	($825)	($825)	($825)	($825)	($825)	($825)
Increase (decrease) Other Liabilities	($83)	($83)	($83)	($83)	($83)	($83)
Long-term Borrowing (repayment)	($240)	($240)	($240)	($240)	($240)	($240)
Capital Input	$0	$0	$0	$0	$0	$0
Subtotal	$4,840	($101)	$21	($349)	($605)	($3,008)
Less:	May	Jun	Jul	Aug	Sep	Oct
Change in Accounts Receivable	$0	$0	$0	$0	$0	$0
Change in Inventory	($3,423)	($3,491)	($3,596)	($649)	($242)	($1,150)
Change in Other ST Assets	$0	$0	$0	$0	$0	$0
Capital Expenditure	$0	$0	$0	$0	$0	$0
Dividends	$0	$0	$0	$0	$0	$0
Subtotal	($3,423)	($3,491)	($3,596)	($649)	($242)	($1,150)
Net Cash Flow	$8,263	$3,390	$3,616	$299	($363)	($1,858)
Cash balance	$15,263	$18,652	$22,269	$22,568	$22,205	$20,347

Appendix:
Projected
Cash Flow

General Assumptions

	May-97	Jun-97	Jul-97	Aug-97	Sep-97	Oct-97
Short Term Interest Rate	6.00%	6.00%	6.00%	6.00%	6.00%	6.00%
Long Term Interest Rate	7.50%	7.50%	7.50%	7.50%	7.50%	7.50%
Payment days	30	30	30	30	30	30
Inventory Turnover	9.00	9.00	9.00	9.00	9.00	9.00
Tax Rate Percent	30.00%	30.00%	30.00%	30.00%	30.00%	30.00%
Expenses in cash%	0.00%	0.00%	0.00%	0.00%	0.00%	0.00%
Sales on credit	0.00%	0.00%	0.00%	0.00%	0.00%	0.00%
Personnel Burden %	5.50%	5.50%	5.50%	5.50%	5.50%	5.50%

Note: Ratios in assumptions are used as estimators and may therefore have different values than ratios calculated in the ratios section.

Nov-97	Dec-97	Jan-98	Feb-98	Mar-98	Apr-98	FY1998	FY1999	FY2000
($3,647)	($3,644)	($3,850)	$818	$575	$775	($6,270)	$695	$19,369
$100	$100	$100	$100	$100	$100	$1,200	$1,236	$1,273
($4,384)	$0	$0	$5,482	$74	$102	$5,659	$543	$473
($825)	($825)	($825)	($825)	($825)	($925)	($10,000)	$0	$0
($83)	($83)	($83)	($83)	($83)	($83)	($1,000)	$0	$0
($240)	($240)	($240)	($240)	($240)	($240)	($2,880)	($2,880)	($2,880)
$0	$0	$0	$0	$0	$0	$0	$0	$0
($9,080)	($4,692)	($4,898)	$5,252	($399)	($271)	($13,291)	($406)	$18,235
Nov	Dec	Jan	Feb	Mar	Apr	FY1998	FY1999	FY2000
$0	$0	$0	$0	$0	$0	$0	$0	$0
($3,050)	$0	$0	$4,163	$91	$140	($11,206)	$623	$704
$0	$0	$0	$0	$0	$0	$0	$0	$0
$0	$0	$0	$0	$0	$0	$0	$0	$0
$0	$0	$0	$0	$0	$0	$0	$0	$4,000
($3,050)	$0	$0	$4,163	$91	$140	($11,206)	$623	$4,704
($6,030)	($4,692)	($4,898)	$1,088	($490)	($411)	($2,085)	($1,029)	$13,531
$14,317	$9,625	$4,727	$5,816	$5,325	$4,915	$4,915	$3,886	$17,417

Nov-97	Dec-97	Jan-98	Feb-98	Mar-98	Apr-98	FY1998	FY1999	FY2000
6.00%	6.00%	6.00%	6.00%	6.00%	6.00%	6.00%	6.00%	6.00%
7.50%	7.50%	7.50%	7.50%	7.50%	7.50%	7.50%	7.50%	7.50%
30	30	30	30	30	30	30	30	30
9.00	9.00	9.00	9.00	9.00	9.00	9	9.00	9.00
30.00%	30.00%	30.00%	30.00%	30.00%	30.00%	30.00%	30.00%	30.00%
0.00%	0.00%	0.00%	0.00%	0.00%	0.00%	0.00%	0.00%	0.00%
0.00%	0.00%	0.00%	0.00%	0.00%	0.00%	0.00%	0.00%	0.00%
0.00%	0.00%	0.00%	5.50%	5.50%	5.50%	4.13%	4.13%	4.13%

Appendix:
Personnel Plan

Personnel Plan

Job title	May-97	Jun-97	Jul-97	Aug-97	Sep-97	Oct-97
Sam Williamston	$1,500	$1,500	$1,500	$1,500	$1,500	$1,600
Part-time emp.	$500	$500	$500	$500	$500	$500
Other	$3,000	$3,000	$3,000	$3,000	$3,000	$3,000
Subtotal	$5,000	$5,000	$5,000	$5,000	$5,000	$5,100

Appendix:
Projected Profit
and Loss

Pro-forma Income Statement

	May-97	Jun-97	Jul-97	Aug-97	Sep-97	Oct-97
Sales	$12,573	$12,824	$13,209	$13,341	$12,674	$9,505
Direct Cost of Sales	$3,423	$3,491	$3,596	$3,632	$3,450	$2,588
Total Cost of Sales	$3,423	$3,491	$3,596	$3,632	$3,450	$2,588
Gross margin	$9,150	$9,333	$9,613	$9,709	$9,224	$6,918
Gross margin percent	72.78%	72.78%	72.78%	72.78%	72.78%	72.78%
Operating expenses:						
Advertising/Promotion	$500	$500	$500	$500	$500	$500
Travel	$0	$0	$300	$0	$0	$0
Payroll expense	$5,000	$5,000	$5,000	$5,000	$5,000	$5,100
Leased Equipment	$0	$0	$0	$0	$0	$0
Utilities	$120	$121	$121	$122	$122	$122
Insurance	$70	$70	$70	$70	$70	$70
Mortgage Payment	$1,125	$1,125	$1,125	$1,125	$1,125	$1,125
Depreciation	$100	$100	$100	$100	$100	$100
Payroll Burden	$275	$275	$275	$275	$275	$281
Contract/Consultants	$0	$200	$200	$200	$200	$0
Total Operating Expenses	$7,190	$7,391	$7,691	$7,392	$7,392	$7,298
Profit Before Interest and Taxes	$1,960	$1,942	$1,922	$2,317	$1,831	($380)
Interest Expense ST	$46	$42	$38	$34	$29	$25
Interest Expense LT	$924	$922	$921	$919	$918	$916
Taxes Incurred	$297	$294	$289	$409	$265	($396)
Net Profit	$693	$685	$675	$955	$619	($925)
Net Profit/Sales	5.52%	5.34%	5.11%	7.16%	4.88%	-9.73%

Nov-97	Dec-97	Jan-98	Feb-98	Mar-98	Apr-98	FY1998	FY1999	FY2000
$0	$0	$0	$1,600	$1,600	$1,600	$13,900	$14,595	$15,325
$0	$0	$0	$0	$500	$500	$4,000	$4,200	$4,410
$3,000	$3,000	$3,000	$3,000	$3,000	$3,000	$36,000	$37,800	$39,690
$3,000	$3,000	$3,000	$4,600	$5,100	$5,100	$53,900	$56,595	$59,425

Nov-97	Dec-97	Jan-98	Feb-98	Mar-98	Apr-98	FY1998	FY1999	FY2000
$0	$0	$0	$12,573	$12,824	$13,209	$112,730	$135,276	$169,095
$0	$0	$0	$3,423	$3,491	$3,596	$30,687	$34,677	$39,185
$0	$0	$0	$3,423	$3,491	$3,596	$30,687	$34,677	$39,185
$0	$0	$0	$9,150	$9,333	$9,613	$82,043	$100,599	$129,910
0.00%	0.00%	0.00%	72.78%	72.78%	72.78%	72.78%	74.37%	76.83%
$0	$0	$0	$500	$500	$500	$4,500	$5,500	$5,200
$0	$0	$0	$0	$0	$0	$300	$0	$0
$3,000	$3,000	$3,000	$4,600	$5,100	$5,100	$53,900	$56,595	$59,425
$0	$0	$0	$0	$0	$0	$0	$0	$0
$0	$0	$0	$115	$123	$123	$1,089	$1,122	$1,155
$50	$50	$50	$70	$70	$70	$780	$803	$828
$1,125	$1,125	$1,125	$1,125	$1,125	$1,125	$13,500	$13,905	$14,322
$100	$100	$100	$100	$100	$100	$1,200	$1,236	$1,273
$0	$0	$0	$253	$281	$281	$2,470	$2,335	$2,451
$0	$0	$300	$300	$300	$300	$2,000	$2,000	$1,800
$4,275	$4,275	$4,575	$7,063	$7,599	$7,599	$79,739	$83,496	$86,454
($4,275)	($4,275)	($4,575)	$2,087	$1,735	$2,014	$2,304	$17,103	$43,456
$21	$17	$13	$9	$5	$0	$278	$0	$0
$915	$913	$912	$910	$909	$907	$10,983	$16,110	$15,786
($1,563)	($1,562)	($1,650)	$350	$246	$332	($2,687)	$298	$8,301
($3,647)	($3,644)	($3,850)	$818	$575	$775	($6,270)	$695	$19,369
0.00%	0.00%	0.00%	6.50%	4.48%	5.87%	-5.56%	0.51%	11.45%

Appendix:
Sales Forecast

Sales	May-97	Jun-97	Jul-97	Aug-97	Sep-97	Oct-97
Carabiners	$3,600	$3,672	$3,782	$3,820	$3,629	$2,722
Ropes	$700	$714	$735	$743	$706	$529
Books and Magazines	$135	$138	$142	$143	$136	$102
Cookies	$113	$115	$118	$119	$113	$85
Espresso regulars	$7,350	$7,497	$7,722	$7,799	$7,409	$5,557
Espresso shakes	$675	$689	$709	$716	$680	$510
Other	$0	$0	$0	$0	$0	$0
Total Sales	$12,573	$12,824	$13,209	$13,341	$12,674	$9,505

Cost of sales	May-97	Jun-97	Jul-97	Aug-97	Sep-97	Oct-97
Carabiners	$1,575	$1,607	$1,655	$1,671	$1,588	$1,191
Ropes	$325	$332	$341	$345	$328	$246
Books and Magazines	$68	$69	$71	$72	$68	$51
Cookies	$45	$46	$47	$48	$45	$34
Espresso regulars	$1,260	$1,285	$1,324	$1,337	$1,270	$953
Espresso shakes	$150	$153	$158	$159	$151	$113
Line 7						
Other	$0	$0	$0	$0	$0	$0
Subtotal Cost of Sales	$3,423	$3,491	$3,596	$3,632	$3,450	$2,588

Nov-97	Dec-97	Jan-98	Feb-98	Mar-98	Apr-98	FY1998	FY1999	FY2000
$0	$0	$0	$3,600	$3,672	$3,782	$32,279	$38,735	$48,419
$0	$0	$0	$700	$714	$735	$6,276	$7,532	$9,415
$0	$0	$0	$135	$138	$142	$1,210	$1,453	$1,816
$0	$0	$0	$113	$115	$118	$1,009	$1,210	$1,513
$0	$0	$0	$7,350	$7,497	$7,722	$65,903	$79,084	$98,855
$0	$0	$0	$675	$689	$709	$6,052	$7,263	$9,078
$0	$0	$0	$0	$0	$0	$0	$0	$0
$0	$0	$0	$12,573	$12,824	$13,209	$112,730	$135,276	$169,095

Nov-97	Dec-97	Jan-98	Feb-98	Mar-98	Apr-98	FY1998	FY1999	FY2000
$0	$0	$0	$1,575	$1,607	$1,655	$14,122	$15,958	$18,032
$0	$0	$0	$325	$332	$341	$2,914	$3,293	$3,721
$0	$0	$0	$68	$69	$71	$605	$684	$773
$0	$0	$0	$45	$46	$47	$403	$456	$515
$0	$0	$0	$1,260	$1,285	$1,324	$11,298	$12,766	$14,426
$0	$0	$0	$150	$153	$158	$1,345	$1,520	$1,717
						$0	$0	$0
$0	$0	$0	$0	$0	$0	$0	$0	$0
$0	$0	$0	$3,423	$3,491	$3,596	$30,687	$34,677	$39,185

Computer Reseller

BUSINESS PLAN

COMPUTECH MANAGEMENT

14853 Holyfield Ave.
Denver, CO 96774

This plan for revamping an aging computer reseller reflects the changes that any mature company needs to make to compete in a changing business climate. Capital infusion will allow the company to expand its service capacity and carve out a more secure place for itself in a highly competitive field. Note the increased emphasis on promotional efforts to help the company re-launch itself. This business plan was compiled using Business Plan Pro, by Palo Alto Software ©.

- EXECUTIVE SUMMARY

- COMPANY SUMMARY

- PRODUCTS

- MARKET ANALYSIS SUMMARY

- STRATEGY AND IMPLEMENTATION SUMMARY

- MANAGEMENT SUMMARY

- FINANCIAL PLAN

COMPUTER RESELLER
BUSINESS PLAN

EXECUTIVE SUMMARY

By focusing on its strengths, its key customers, and the underlying values they need, CompuTech Management (CTM) will increase sales to more than $10 million in three years, while also improving the gross margin on sales and cash management and working capital.

This business plan leads the way. It renews our vision and strategic focus: adding value to our target market segments, the small business and high-end home office users, in our local market. It also provides the step-by-step plan for improving our sales, gross margin, and profitability.

This plan includes this summary, and chapters on the company, products and services, market focus, action plans and forecasts, management team, and financial plan.

Objectives

1. Sales increasing to more than $10 million by the third year.
2. Bring gross margin back up to above 25%, and maintain that level.
3. Sell $2 million of service, support, and training by 1998.
4. Improve inventory turnover to 6 turns next year, 7 in 1996, and 8 in 1997.

Mission

CTM is built on the assumption that the management of information technology for business is like legal advice, accounting, graphic arts, and other bodies of knowledge, in that it is not inherently a do-it-yourself prospect. Smart business people who aren't computer hobbyists need to find quality vendors of reliable hardware, software, service, and support. They need to use these quality vendors as they use their other professional service suppliers, as trusted allies.

CTM is such a vendor. It serves its clients as a trusted ally, providing them with the loyalty of a business partner and the economics of an outside vendor. We make sure that our clients have what they need to run their businesses as well as possible, with maximum efficiency and reliability. Many of our information applications are mission critical, so we give our clients the assurance that we will be there when they need us.

Keys to Success

1. Differentiate from box-pushing, price-oriented businesses by offering and delivering service and support — and charging for it.

2. Increase gross margin to more than 25%.

3. Increase our non-hardware sales to 20% of the total sales by the third year.

COMPANY SUMMARY

CTM is a 10-year-old computer reseller with sales of $7 million per year, declining margins, and market pressure. It has a good reputation, excellent people, and a steady position in the local market, but has been having trouble maintaining healthy financials.

Company Ownership

CTM is a privately-held C corporation owned in majority by its founder and president, Eugene Foley. There are six part owners, including four investors and two past employees. The largest of these (in percent of ownership) are Dean Radcliff, our attorney, and Steve Holcomb, our public relations consultant. Neither owns more than 15%, but both are active participants in management decisions.

CTM has been caught in the vice grip of margin squeezes that have affected computer resellers worldwide. The detailed numbers below include other indicators of some concern:

Company History

- The gross margin % has been declining steadily.
- Inventory turnover is getting steadily worse.

These concerns are part of the general trend affecting computer resellers. The margin squeeze is happening throughout the computer industry worldwide.

Past Performance

	1994	1995	1996
Sales	$3,773,889	$4,661,902	$5,301,059
Gross	$1,189,495	$1,269,261	$1,127,568
Gross % (calculated)	31.52%	27.23%	21.27%
Operating Expenses	$752,083	$902,500	$1,052,917
Collection period (days)	35	40	45
Inventory turnover	7	6	5
Balance Sheet			1996
Short-term Assets			
Cash			$55,432
Accounts receivable			$395,107
Inventory			$651,012
Other Short-term Assets			$25,000
Total Short-term Assets			$1,126,551
Long-term Assets			
Capital Assets			$350,000
Accumulated Depreciation			$50,000
Total Long-term Assets			$300,000
Total Assets			$1,426,551
Debt and Equity			
Accounts Payable			$223,897
Short-term Notes			$90,000
Other ST Liabilities			$15,000
Subtotal Short-term Liabilities			$328,897
Long-term Liabilities			$284,862
Total Liabilities			$613,759
Paid in Capital			$500,000
Retained Earnings			$238,140
Earnings	$437,411	$366,761	$74,652
Total Equity			$812,792
Total Debt and Equity			$1,426,551
Other Inputs			1996
Payment days			30
Sales on credit			$3,445,688
Receivables turnover			8.72

Company Locations and Facilities

We have one location, a 7,000 square foot store in a suburban shopping center located conveniently close to the downtown area. It includes a training area, service department, offices, and showroom area.

PRODUCTS

Competitive Comparison

The only way we can hope to differentiate well is to define the vision of the company to be an information technology ally to our clients. We will not be able to compete in any effective way with the chains using boxes or products as appliances. We need to offer a real alliance.

The benefits we sell include many intangibles: confidence, reliability, knowing that somebody will be there to answer questions and help at the important times.

These are complex products, products that require serious knowledge and experience to use, and our competitors sell only the products themselves.

Unfortunately, we cannot sell the products at a higher price just because we offer services; the market has shown that it will not support that concept. We have to also sell the service and charge for it separately.

Sales Literature

Copies of our brochure and advertisements are available upon request. Of course one of our first tasks will be to change the message of our literature to make sure we are selling the company, rather than the product.

Sourcing

Our costs are part of the margin squeeze. As competition on price increases, the squeeze between manufacturer's price into channels and end-users ultimate buying price continues.

With the hardware lines, our margins are declining steadily. Our margins are being squeezed from the 25% of five years ago to more like 13-15% at present. In the main-line peripherals a similar trend shows, with prices for printers and monitors declining steadily. We are also starting to see that same trend with software

In order to hold costs down as much as possible, we concentrate our purchasing with Martinson, which offers 30-day net terms and overnight shipping from the warehouse in Denver. We need to concentrate on making sure our volume gives us negotiating strength.

In accessories and add-ons we can still get decent margins, 25% to 40%.

Technology

We have for years supported both Windows and Macintosh technology for CPUs, although we've switched vendors many times for the Windows (and previously DOS) lines. We are also supporting Novell, Banyon, and Microsoft networking, Xbase database software, and Claris application products.

MARKET ANALYSIS SUMMARY

CTM focuses on local markets, small business and home office, with special focus on the high-end home office and the 5-20 unit small business office.

The segmentation allows some room for estimates and nonspecific definitions. We focus on a small-medium level of small business, and it is hard to find information to make an exact classification. Our target companies are large enough to need the high-quality information technology management we offer, but too small to have a separate computer management staff such as an MIS department. We say that our target markct has 10-50 employees, and needs 5-20 workstations tied together in a local area network; the definition is flexible.

Defining the high-end home office is even more difficult. We generally know the characteristics of our target market, but we can't find easy classifications that fit into available demographics. The high-end home office business is a business, not a hobby. It generates enough money to merit the owner's paying real attention to the quality of information technology management, meaning that there is both budget and concerns that warrant working with our level of quality service and support. We can assume that we aren't talking about home offices used only part-time by people who work elsewhere during the day, and that our target market home office wants to have powerful technology and a lot of links between computing, telecommunications, and video.

Market Segmentation

We are part of the computer reselling business, which includes several kinds of businesses:

Industry Analysis

1. Computer dealers: storefront computer resellers, usually less than 5,000 square feet, often focused on a few main brands of hardware, usually offering only a minimum of software, and variable amounts of service and support. These are usually old-fashioned (1980s-style) computer stores and they usually offer relatively few reasons for buyers to shop with them. Their service and support is not usually very good and their prices are usually higher than the larger stores.

2. Chain stores and computer superstores: these include major chains such as CompUSA, Computer City, Future Shop, etc. They are almost always more than 10,000 square feet of space, usually offer decent walk-in service, and are often warehouse-like locations where people go to find products in boxes with very aggressive pricing, and little support.

3. Mail order: the market is served increasingly by mail order businesses that offer aggressivepricing of boxed product. For the purely price-driven buyer, who buys boxes and expects no service, these are very good options.

4. Others: there are many other channels through which people buy their computers, usually variations of the main three types above.

The national chains are a growing presence. CompUSA, Computer City, Incredible Universe, Babbages, Egghead, and others. They benefit from national advertising, economies of scale, volume buying, and a general trend toward name-brand loyalty for buying in the channels as well as for products.

Industry Participants

Local computer stores are threatened. These tend to be small businesses, owned by people who started them because they liked computers. They are under-capitalized and under-managed. Margins are squeezed as they compete against the chains, in a competition based on price more than on service and support.

Distribution Patterns

Small Business buyers are accustomed to buying from vendors who visit their offices. They expect the copy machine vendors, office products vendors, and office furniture vendors, as well as the local graphic artists, freelance writers, or whomever, to visit their office to make their sales.

There is usually a lot of leakage in ad-hoc purchasing through local chain stores and mail order. Often the administrators try to discourage this, but are only partially successful.

Unfortunately our Home Office target buyers may not expect to buy from us. Many of them turn immediately to the superstores (office equipment, office supplies, and electronics) and mail order to look for the best price, without realizing that there is a better option for them at only a little bit more.

Competition and Buying Patterns

The small business buyers understand the concept of service and support, and are much more likely to pay for it when the offering is clearly stated.

There is no doubt that we compete much more against all the box pushers than against other service providers. We need to effectively compete against the idea that businesses should buy computers as plug-in appliances that don't need ongoing service, support, and training.

Our focus group sessions indicated that our target Home Offices think about price but would buy based on quality service if the offering were properly presented. They think about price because that's all they ever see. We have very good indications that many would rather pay 10-20% morefor a relationship with a long-term vendor providing back-up and quality service and support; they end up in the box-pusher channels because they aren't aware of the alternatives.

Availability is also very important. The Home Office buyers tend to want immediate, local solutions to problems.

Main Competitors

Chain stores

We have Store 1 and Store 2 already within the valley, and Store 3 is expected by the end of next year. If our strategy works, we will have differentiated ourselves sufficiently to not have to compete against these stores.

Strengths: national image, high volume, aggressive pricing, economies of scale

Weaknesses: lack of product, service and support knowledge, lack of personal attention.

Other local computer stores

Store 4 and Store 5 are both in the downtown area. They are both competing against the chains in an attempt to match prices. When asked, the owners will complain that margins are squeezed by the chains and customers buy on price only. They say they tried offering services and that buyers didn't care, instead preferring lower prices. We think the problem is also that they didn't really offer good service, and also that they didn't differentiate from the chains.

MARKET ANALYSIS SUMMARY

The home offices in Denver are an important growing market segment. Nationally, there are approximately 30 million home offices, and the number is growing at 10% per year. Our estimate in this plan for the home offices in our market service area is based on an analysis published four months ago in the local newspaper.

Home offices include several types. The most important, for our plan's focus, are the home offices that are the only offices of real businesses, from which people make their primary living. These are likely to be professional services such as graphic artists, writers, and consultants, some accountants and the occasional lawyer, doctor, or dentist. There are also part-time home offices with people who are employed during the day but work at home at night, people who work at home to provide themselves with a part-time income, or people who maintain home offices relating to their hobbies; we will not be focusing on this segment.

Small business within our market includes virtually any business with a retail, office, professional, or industrial location outside of someone's home, and fewer than 30 employees. We estimate 45,000 such businesses in our market area.

The 30-employee cutoff is arbitrary. We find that the larger companies turn to other vendors, but we can sell to departments of larger companies, and we shouldn't be giving up leads when we get them.

Market Analysis

Potential Customers	Total Customers	Growth rate
Consumer	12,000	2%
Small Business	15,000	5%
Large Business	33,000	8%
Government	36,000	-2%
Other	19,000	0%
Total	115,000	2.78%

1. Emphasize service and support.

We must differentiate ourselves from the box pushers. We need to establish our business offering as a clear and viable alternative for our target market, to the price-only kind of buying.

2. Build a relationship-oriented business.

Build long-term relationships with clients, not single-transaction deals with customers. Become their computer department, not just a vendor. Make them understand the value of the relationship.

3. Focus on target markets.

We need to focus our offerings on small business as the key market segment we should own. This means the 5-20 unit system, tied together in a local area network, in a company with 5-50 employees. Our values (training, installation, service, support, knowledge) are more cleanly differentiated in this segment.

As a corollary, the high end of the home office market is also appropriate. We do not want to compete for the buyers who go to the chain stores or mail order, but we definitely want to be able to sell individual systems to the smart home office buyers who want a reliable, full-service vendor.

4. Differentiate and fulfill the promise.

We can't just market and sell service and support, we must actually deliver as well. We need

STRATEGY AND IMPLEMENTATION SUMMARY

to make sure we have the knowledge-intensive business and service-intensive business we claim to have.

Marketing Strategy

The marketing strategy is the core of the main strategy:

1. Emphasize service and support
2. Build a relationship business
3. Focus on small business and high-end home office as key target markets

Pricing Strategy

We must charge appropriately for the high-end, high-quality service and support we offer. Our revenue structure has to match our cost structure, so the salaries we pay to assure good service and support must be balanced by the revenue we charge.

We cannot build the service and support revenue into the price of products. The market can't bear the higher prices and the buyer feels ill-used when they see the same product priced lower at the chains. Despite the logic behind this, the market doesn't support this concept.

Therefore, we must make sure that we deliver and charge for service and support. Training, service, installation, networking support— all of this must be readily available and priced to sell and deliver revenue.

Promotion Strategy

We depend on newspaper advertising as our main way to reach new buyers. As we change strategies, however, we need to change the way we promote ourselves:

1. Advertising

We'll be developing our core positioning message: "24 Hour On-Site Service - 365 Days a Year With No Extra Charges" to differentiate our service from the competition. We will be using local newspaper advertising, radio and cable TV to launch the initial campaign.

2. Sales Brochure

Our collaterals have to sell the store, and visiting the store, not the specific book or discount pricing.

3. We must radically improve our direct mail efforts, reaching our established customers with training, support services, upgrades, and seminars.

4. It's time to work more closely with the local media. We could offer the local radio a regular talk show on technology for small business, as one example.

Sales Strategy

1. We need to sell the company, not the product. We sell CTM, not Apple, IBM, Hewlett-Packard, or Compaq, or any of our software brand names.

2. We have to sell our service and support. The hardware is like the razor, and the support, service, software services, training, and seminars are the razor blades. We need to serve our customers with what they really need.

The important elements of the sales forecast are shown in the Total Sales by Month in Year 1 table. The non-hardware sales increase to about $2 million total in the third year.

Sales Forecast

Unit Sales	1997	1998	1999
Systems	1,666	1,750	1,850
Service	4,975	6,000	7,500
Software	3,725	5,000	6,500
Training	2,230	4,000	8,000
Other	4,575	5,000	5,500
Total Unit Sales	17,171	21,750	29,350

Unit Prices	1997	1998	1999
Systems	$1,977	$1,984	$1,977
Service	$73	$84	$87
Software	$215	$195	$180
Training	$47	$72	$79
Other	$300	$300	$300

Total Sales	1997	1998	1999
Systems	$3,293,500	$3,472,868	$3,657,248
Service	$365,000	$504,000	$652,500
Software	$799,250	$975,000	$1,170,000
Training	$103,865	$288,000	$632,000
Other	$1,372,500	$1,500,000	$1,650,000
Total Sales	$5,934,115	$6,739,868	$7,761,748

Unit Direct Costs	1997	1998	1999
Systems	$1,000	$992	$988
Service	$60	$67	$70
Software	$100	$98	$90
Training	$22	$43	$47
Other	$150	$150	$150

Direct Costs	1997	1998	1999
Systems	$1,666,000	$1,736,434	$1,828,624
Service	$298,500	$403,200	$522,000
Software	$372,500	$487,500	$585,000
Training	$49,506	$172,800	$379,200
Other	$686,250	$750,000	$825,000
Subtotal Direct Costs	$3,072,756	$3,549,934	$4,139,824

Our strategy hinges on providing excellent service and support. This is critical. We need to differentiate on service and support, and to therefore deliver as well.

Service and Support

1. Training: details would be essential in a real business plan, but not in this sample plan.
2. Upgrade offers: details would be essential in a real business plan, but not in this sample plan.
3. Our own internal training: details would be essential in a real business plan, but not in this sample plan.
4. Installation services: details would be essential in a real business plan, but not in this sample plan.

5. Custom software services: details would be essential in a real business plan, but not in this sample plan.

6. Network configuration services: details would be essential in a real business plan, but not in this sample plan.

Milestones

Our important milestones are shown on the table below.

Business Plan Milestones

Milestone	Mngr	Date	Dept.	Budget	Act date	Act $	Date P-A	$ P-A
Corporate Identity	TJ	12/17/95	Marketing	$10,000	1/15/96	$12,004	(29)	($2,004)
Seminar implementation	IR	1/10/96	Sales	$1,000	12/27/95	$5,000	14	($4,000)
Business Plan Review	RJ	1/10/96	GM	$0	1/23/96	$500	(13)	($500)
Upgrade mailer	IR	1/16/96	Sales	$5,000	2/12/96	$12,500	(27)	($7,500)
New corporate brochure	TJ	1/16/96	Marketing	$5,000	1/15/96	$5,000	1	$0
Delivery vans	SD	1/25/96	Service	$12,500	2/26/96	$3,500	(32)	$9,000
Direct mail	IR	2/16/96	Marketing	$3,500	2/25/96	$2,500	(9)	$1,000
Advertising	RJ	2/16/96	GM	$115,000	3/6/96	$100,000	(19)	$15,000
X4 Prototype	SG	2/25/96	Product	$2,500	2/25/96	$0	0	$2,500
Service revamp	SD	2/25/96	Product	$2,500	2/25/96	$2,500	0	$0
6 Presentations	IR	2/25/96	Sales	$0	1/10/96	$1,000	46	($1,000)
X4 Testing	SG	3/6/96	Product	$1,000	1/16/96	$0	50	$1,000
3 Accounts	SD	3/17/96	Sales	$0	3/17/96	$2,500	0	($2,500)
L30 Prototype	PR	3/26/96	Product	$2,500	4/11/96	$15,000	(16)	($12,500)
Tech95 Expo	TB	4/12/96	Marketing	$15,000	1/25/96	$1,000	78	$14,000
VP S&M hired	JK	6/11/96	Sales	$1,000	7/25/96	$5,000	(44)	($4,000)
Mailing system	SD	7/25/96	Service	$5,000	7/14/96	$7,654	11	($2,654)
Other							0	$0
Totals				$181,500		$175,658	11	$5,842

MANAGEMENT SUMMARY

Our management philosophy is based on responsibility and mutual respect. People who work at CTM want to work at CTM because we have an environment that encourages creativity and achievement. The team includes 22 employees, under a president and four managers.

Organizational Structure

The team includes 22 employees, under a president and four managers.

Our main management divisions are sales, marketing, service, and administration. Service handles service, support, training, and development.

Management Team

Eugene Foley, President: 46 years old, founded CTM in 1984 to focus on reselling high-powered personal computers to small business. Degree in computer science, 15 years with Large Computer Company, Inc. in positions ending with project manager. Eugene has been attending courses at the local Small Business Development Center for more than six years now, steadily adding business skills and business training to his technical background.

Janice Carly, VP Marketing: 36 years old, joined us last year following a very successful career with Continental Computers. Her hiring was the culmination of a long recruiting search. WithContinental she managed the VAR marketing division. She is committed to re-engineering CTM to be a service and support business that sells computers, not vice-versa. MBA, undergraduate degree in history.

Max Webber, VP Service and Support: 48 years old, 18 years with Large Computers, Inc. in programming and service-related positions, 7 years with CTM. MS in computer science and BS in electrical engineering.

Annette Yezbick, VP Sales: 32, former teacher, joined CTM part-time in 1991 and went full-time in 1992. Very high people skills, BA in elementary education. She has taken several sales management courses at the local SBDC.

Mark Saul, Director of Administration: 43, started with CTM as a part-time bookkeeper in 1987, and has become full-time administrative and financial backbone of the company.

At present we believe we have a good team for covering the main points of the business plan. The addition of Janice Carly was important as a way to cement our fundamental re-positioning and re-engineering.

Management Team Gaps

At present, we are weakest in the area of technical capabilities to manage the database marketing programs and upgraded service and support, particularly with cross-platform networks. We also need to find a training manager.

The Personnel Plan reflects the need to bolster our capabilities to match our positioning. Our total headcount should increase to 22 this first year, and to 30 by the third year. Detailed monthly projections are included in the appendices.

Personnel Plan

Personnel Plan			

Production	1997	1998	1999
Manager	$12,000	$13,000	$14,000
Assistant	$36,000	$40,000	$40,000
Technical	$12,500	$35,000	$35,000
Technical	$12,500	$35,000	$35,000
Technical	$24,000	$27,500	$27,500
Fulfillment	$24,000	$30,000	$60,000
Fulfillment	$18,000	$22,000	$50,000
Other		$0	$0
Subtotal	$139,000	$202,500	$261,500

Sales and Marketing	1997	1998	1999
Manager	$72,000	$76,000	$80,000
Technical sales	$60,000	$63,000	$85,000
Technical sales	$45,500	$46,000	$46,000
Salesperson	$40,500	$55,000	$64,000
Salesperson	$40,500	$50,000	$55,000
Salesperson	$33,500	$34,000	$45,000
Salesperson	$31,000	$38,000	$45,000
Salesperson	$21,000	$30,000	$33,000
Salesperson	$0	$30,000	$33,000
Other	$0		$0
Subtotal	$344,000	$422,000	$486,000

Personnel Plan

...continued

Administration	1997	1998	1999
President	$66,000	$69,000	$95,000
Finance	$28,000	$29,000	$30,000
Admin Assistant	$24,000	$26,000	$28,000
Bookkeeping	$18,000	$25,000	$30,000
Clerical	$12,000	$15,000	$18,000
Clerical	$7,000	$15,000	$18,000
Clerical	$0	$0	$15,000
Other	$0	$0	$0
Subtotal	$155,000	$179,000	$234,000

Other	1997	1998	1999
Programming	$36,000	$40,000	$44,000
Other technical	$0	$30,000	$33,000
Other	$0	$0	$0
Subtotal	$36,000	$70,000	$77,000

Total Headcount	22	25	30
Total Payroll	$674,000	$873,500	$1,058,500
Payroll Burden	$107,840	$139,760	$169,360
Total Payroll Expenditures	$781,840	$1,013,260	$1,227,860

Other Management Considerations

Our attorney, Dean Radcliff, is also a co-founder. He invested significantly in the company over a period of time during the 1980s. He remains a good friend of Eugene and has been a steady source of excellent legal and business advice.

Steve Holcomb, public relations consultant, is also a co-founder and co-owner. Like Radcliff, he invested in the early stages and remains a trusted confidant and vendor of public relations and advertising services.

FINANCIAL PLAN

The most important element in the financial plan is the critical need for improving several of the key factors that impact cash flow:

1. We must at any cost stop the slide in inventory turnover and develop better inventory management to bring the turnover back up to 8 turns by the third year. This should also be a function of the shift in focus towards service revenues to add to the hardware revenues.

2. We must also bring the gross margin back up to 25%. This too is related to improving the mix between hardware and service revenues, because the service revenues offer much better margins.

3. We plan to borrow another $150,000 long-term this year. The amount seems in line with the balance sheet capabilities.

Important Assumptions

On our General Assumptions table, the most ambitious and also the most questionable assumption is our projected improvement in inventory turnover, from 5 turns last year to 6, 7, and then 8. This is critical to healthy cash flow, but will also be difficult.

	1997	1998	1999	General Assumptions
Short Term Interest Rate	8.00%	8.00%	8.00%	
Long Term Interest Rate	8.50%	8.50%	8.50%	
Payment days	35	35	35	
Collection days	45	45	45	
Inventory Turnover	6.00	5.00	5.00	
Tax Rate Percent	20.00%	20.00%	20.00%	
Expenses in cash%	14.00%	14.00%	14.00%	
Sales on credit	70.00%	75.00%	80.00%	
Personnel Burden %	16.00%	16.00%	16.00%	

Note: Ratios in assumptions are used as estimators and may therefore have different values than ratios calculated in the ratios section.

Break-even Analysis

Key Financial Indicators

For our break-even analysis, we assume running costs of approximately $94,000 per month, which includes our full payroll, rent, and utilities, and an estimation of other running costs. Payroll alone, at our present run rate, is only about $55,000.

Margins are harder to assume. Our overall average of $343/248 is based on past sales. We hope to attain a margin that high in the future.

The chart shows that we need to sell about $340,000 per month to break even, according to theseassumptions. This is about half of our planned 1995 sales level, and significantly below our last year's sales level, so we believe we can maintain it.

Break Even Analysis:

Monthly Units Break-even	620
Monthly Sales Break-even	$214,232

Assumptions:

Average Unit Sale	$345.59
Average Per-Unit Cot	$178.95
Fixed Cost	$103,300

The most important assumption in the Projected Profit and Loss statement is the gross margin, which is supposed to increase to 25%. This is up from barely 21% in the last year. The increase in gross margin is based on changing our sales mix, and it is critical.

Projected Profit and Loss

Month-by-month assumptions for profit and loss are included in the appendices.

Projected Profit and Loss

Pro-forma Income Statement

	1997	1998	1999
Sales	$5,934,115	$6,739,868	$7,761,748
Direct Cost of Sales	$3,072,756	$3,549,934	$4,139,824
Production payroll	$139,000	$202,500	$261,500
Other	$6,000	$6,600	$7,260
Total Cost of Sales	$3,217,756	$3,759,034	$4,408,584
Gross margin	$2,716,359	$2,980,834	$3,353,164
Gross margin percent	45.78%	44.23%	43.20%
Operating expenses:			
Sales and marketing expenses			
Sales/Marketing Salaries	$344,000	$422,000	$486,000
Ads	$150,000	$316,733	$332,570
Catalog	$25,000	$19,039	$19,991
Mailing	$113,300	$0	$0
Promo	$16,000	$0	$0
Shows	$20,200	$0	$0
Literature	$7,000	$0	$0
PR	$1,000	$0	$0
Seminar	$31,000	$0	$0
Service	$10,250	$0	$0
Training	$60,000	$0	$0
Total Sales and Marketing Expense	$777,750	$757,772	$838,561
Sales and Marketing Percent	13.11%	11.24%	10.80%
General & Administrative Expenses			
G&A Salaries	$155,000	$179,000	$234,000
Leased Equipment	$30,000	$31,500	$33,075
Utilities	$9,000	$9,450	$9,923
Insurance	$6,000	$6,300	$6,615
Rent	$84,000	$88,200	$92,610
Depreciation	$12,681	$13,315	$13,981
Payroll Burden	$107,840	$139,760	$169,360
Other	$6,331	$6,648	$6,980
Total General and Administrative Expense	$410,852	$474,173	$566,544
General and Administrative Percent	6.92%	7.04%	7.30%

Other Operating Expenses

**Projected Profit and
Loss**
...continued

Other Salaries	$36,000	$70,000	$77,000
Contract/Consultants	$12,000	$30,000	$30,000
Other	$3,000	$3,150	$3,308

Total Other Operating			
Expenses	$51,000	$103,150	$110,308
Percent of Sales	0.86%	1.53%	1.42%

Total Operating			
Expenses	$1,239,602	$1,335,095	$1,515,413
Profit Before			
Interest and Taxes	$1,476,757	$1,645,739	$1,837,751
Interest Expense ST	$8,133	$6,000	$6,000
Interest Expense LT	$22,545	$19,395	$15,849
Taxes Incurred	$289,216	$324,069	$363,180
Net Profit	$1,156,863	$1,296,275	$1,452,722
Net Profit/Sales	19.50%	19.23%	18.72%

The cash flow depends on assumptions for inventory turnover, payment days, and accounts receivable management. Our projected 45-day collection days is critical, and it is also reasonable. We need $150,000 in new financing in March to get through a cash flow dip as we build up for mid-year sales.

Projected Cash Flow

Pro-Forma Cash Flow

	1997	1998	1999
Net Profit:	$1,156,863	$1,296,275	$1,452,722
Plus:			
Depreciation	$12,681	$13,315	$13,981
Change in Accounts Payable	$127,271	$47,683	$60,473
Current Borrowing (repayment)	($15,000)	$0	$0
Increase (decrease) Other Liabilities	$0	$0	$0
Long-term Borrowing (repayment)	($36,708)	($39,953)	($43,484)
Capital Input	$0	$0	$0
Subtotal	$1,245,106	$1,317,320	$1,483,691
Less:	1997	1998	1999
Change in Accounts Receivable	$304,718	$151,799	$194,504
Change in Inventory	$15,868	$267,992	$161,543
Change in Other ST Assets	$0	$0	$0
Capital Expenditure	$300,000	$200,000	$400,000
Dividends	$0	$0	$0
Subtotal	$620,586	$619,791	$756,047
Net Cash Flow	$624,520	$697,529	$727,644
Cash balance	$679,952	$1,377,481	$2,105,125

Projected Balance Sheet

The Projected Balance Sheet is quite solid. We do not project any real trouble meeting our debt obligations — as long as we can achieve our specific objectives.

Pro-forma Balance Sheet

Short-term Assets	Starting Balances	1997	1998	1999
Cash	$55,432	$679,952	$1,377,481	$2,105,125
Accounts receivable	$395,107	$699,825	$851,624	$1,046,128
Inventory	$651,012	$666,880	$934,872	$1,096,415
Other Short-term Assets	$25,000	$25,000	$25,000	$25,000
Total Short-term Assets	$1,126,551	$2,071,657	$3,188,978	$4,272,668
Long-term Assets				
Capital Assets	$350,000	$650,000	$850,000	$1,250,000
Accumulated Depreciation	$50,000	$62,681	$75,996	$89,977
Total Long-term Assets	$300,000	$587,319	$774,004	$1,160,023
Total Assets	$1,426,551	$2,658,976	$3,962,982	$5,432,691

Debt and Equity		1997	1998	1999
Accounts Payable	$223,897	$351,168	$398,850	$459,323
Short-term Notes	$90,000	$75,000	$75,000	$75,000
Other ST Liabilities	$15,000	$15,000	$15,000	$15,000
Subtotal				
Short-term Liabilities	$328,897	$441,168	$488,850	$549,323
Long-term Liabilities	$284,862	$248,154	$208,201	$164,717
Total Liabilities	$613,759	$689,322	$697,051	$714,040
Paid in Capital	$500,000	$500,000	$500,000	$500,000
Retained Earnings	$238,140	$312,792	$1,469,655	$2,765,930
Earnings	$74,652	$1,156,863	$1,296,275	$1,452,722
Total Equity	$812,792	$1,969,655	$3,265,930	$4,718,652
Total Debt and Equity	$1,426,551	$2,658,976	$3,962,982	$5,432,691
Net Worth	$812,792	$1,969,655	$3,265,930	$4,718,652

The table follows with our main business ratios. We do intend to improve gross margin, collection days, and inventory turnover.

Ratio Analysis

Profitability Ratios:	1997	1998	1999	RMA
Gross margin	45.78%	44.23%	43.20%	0
Net profit margin	19.50%	19.23%	18.72%	0
Return on Assets	43.51%	32.71%	26.74%	0
Return on Equity	58.73%	39.69%	30.79%	0

Activity Ratios	1997	1998	1999	RMA
AR Turnover	5.94	5.94	5.94	0
Collection days	48	56	56	0
Inventory Turnover	4.88	4.69	4.34	0
Accts payable turnover	9.00	8.80	8.79	0
Total asset turnover	2.23	1.70	1.43	0

Debt Ratios:	1997	1998	1999	RMA
Debt to net Worth	0.35	0.21	0.15	0
Short-term Debt to Liab.	0.64	0.70	0.77	0

Liquidity ratios				
Current Ratio	4.70	6.52	7.78	0
Quick Ratio	3.18	4.61	5.78	0
Net Working Capital	$1,630,490	$2,700,127	$3,723,346	0
Interest Coverage	48.14	64.81	84.11	0

Additional ratios	1997	1998	1999	RMA
Assets to sales	0.45	0.59	0.70	0
Debt/Assets	26%	18%	13%	0
Current debt/Total Assets	17%	12%	10%	0
Acid Test	1.60	2.87	3.88	0
Asset Turnover	2.23	1.70	1.43	0
Sales/Net Worth	3.01	2.06	1.64	0

Appendix:
Projected
Balance Sheet   Pro-forma Balance Sheet

		Jan-97	Feb-97	Mar-97	Apr-97	May-97	Jun-97
Short-term Assets	Starting Balances						
Cash	$55,432	$206,949	$162,514	$143,335	$227,142	$219,347	$342,392
Accounts receivable	$395,107	$456,049	$484,668	$599,622	$552,650	$479,500	$423,850
Inventory	$651,012	$470,438	$505,882	$618,326	$570,548	$486,990	$433,480
Other Short-term Assets	$25,000	$25,000	$25,000	$25,000	$25,000	$175,000	$175,000
Total Short-term Assets	$1,126,551	$1,158,437	$1,178,065	$1,386,283	$1,375,340	$1,360,837	$1,374,722
Long-term Assets							
Capital Assets	$350,000	$450,000	$550,000	$600,000	$600,000	$650,000	$650,000
Accumulated Depreciation	$50,000	$51,000	$52,010	$53,030	$54,060	$55,100	$56,150
Total Long-term Assets	$300,000	$399,000	$497,990	$546,970	$545,940	$594,900	$593,850
Total Assets	$1,426,551	$1,557,437	$1,676,055	$1,933,253	$1,921,280	$1,955,737	$1,968,572

Debt and Equity							
		Jan-97	Feb-97	Mar-97	Apr-97	May-97	Jun-97
Accounts Payable	$223,897	$264,437	$296,635	$335,167	$319,953	$284,561	$246,225
Short-term Notes	$90,000	$90,000	$90,000	$165,000	$75,000	$75,000	$75,000
Other ST Liabilities	$15,000	$15,000	$15,000	$15,000	$15,000	$15,000	$15,000
Subtotal Short-term Liabilities	$328,897	$369,437	$401,635	$515,167	$409,953	$374,561	$336,225
Long-term Liabilities	$284,862	$281,920	$278,958	$275,974	$272,970	$269,944	$266,897
Total Liabilities	$613,759	$651,357	$680,593	$791,141	$682,923	$644,505	$603,121
Paid in Capital	$500,000	$500,000	$500,000	$500,000	$500,000	$500,000	$500,000
Retained Earnings	$238,140	$312,792	$312,792	$312,792	$312,792	$312,792	$312,792
Earnings	$74,652	$93,287	$182,670	$329,319	$425,565	$498,440	$552,659
Total Equity	$812,792	$906,079	$995,462	$1,142,111	$1,238,357	$1,311,232	$1,365,451
Total Debt and Equity	$1,426,551	$1,557,437	$1,676,055	$1,933,253	$1,921,280	$1,955,737	$1,968,572
Net Worth	$812,792	$906,079	$995,462	$1,142,111	$1,238,357	$1,311,232	$1,365,451

	Jul-97	Aug-97	Sep-97	Oct-97	Nov-97	Dec-97	1997	1998	1999
	$217,918	$263,815	$292,826	$428,300	$483,679	$679,952	$679,952	$1,377,481	$2,105,125
	$327,250	$278,775	$401,625	$691,075	$800,362	$699,825	$699,825	851,624	$1,046,128
	$303,260	$300,760	$469,480	$792,768	$816,700	$666,880	$666,880	$934,872	$1,096,415
	$475,000	$475,000	$325,000	$25,000	$25,000	$25,000	$25,000	$25,000	$25,000
	$1,323,428	$1,318,350	$1,488,931	$1,937,143	$2,125,742	$2,071,657	$2,071,657	$3,188,978	$4,272,668
	$650,000	$650,000	$650,000	$650,000	$650,000	$650,000	$650,000	$850,000	$1,250,000
	$57,211	$58,283	$59,366	$60,460	$61,565	$62,681	$62,681	$75,996	$89,977
	$592,789	$591,717	$590,634	$589,540	$588,435	$587,319	$587,319	$774,004	$1,160,023
	$1,916,217	$1,910,067	$2,079,565	$2,526,683	$2,714,177	$2,658,976	$2,658,976	$3,962,982	$5,432,691

	Jul-97	Aug-97	Sep-97	Oct-97	Nov-97	Dec-97	1997	1998	1999
	$183,985	$174,650	$284,866	$442,369	$453,237	$351,168	$351,168	$398,850	$459,323
	$75,000	$75,000	$75,000	$175,000	$175,000	$75,000	$75,000	$75,000	$75,000
	$15,000	$15,000	$15,000	$15,000	$15,000	$15,000	$15,000	$15,000	$15,000
	$273,985	$264,650	$374,866	$632,369	$643,237	$441,168	$441,168	$488,850	$549,323
	$263,828	$260,737	$257,624	$254,490	$251,333	$248,154	$248,154	$208,201	$164,717
	$537,813	$525,387	$632,491	$886,859	$894,570	$689,322	$689,322	$697,051	$714,040
	$500,000	$500,000	$500,000	$500,000	$500,000	$500,000	$500,000	$500,000	$500,000
	$312,792	$312,792	$312,792	$312,792	$312,792	$312,792	$312,792	$1,469,655	$2,765,930
	$565,611	$571,888	$634,282	$827,032	$1,006,815	$1,156,863	$1,156,863	$1,296,275	$1,452,722
	$1,378,403	$1,384,680	$1,447,074	$1,639,824	$1,819,607	$1,969,655	$1,969,655	$3,265,930	$4,718,652
	$1,916,217	$1,910,067	$2,079,565	$2,526,683	$2,714,177	$2,658,976	$2,658,976	$3,962,982	$5,432,691
	$1,378,403	$1,384,680	$1,447,074	$1,639,824	$1,819,607	$1,969,655	$1,969,655	$3,265,930	$4,718,652

Appendix:
Projected Cash
Flow   **Pro Forma Cash Flow**

	Jan-97	Feb-97	Mar-97	Apr-97	May-97	Jun-97
Net Profit:	$93,287	$89,382	$146,650	$96,246	$72,874	$54,220
Plus:						
Depreciation	$1,000	$1,010	$1,020	$1,030	$1,040	$1,050
Change in Accounts Payable	$40,540	$32,198	$38,532	($15,214)	($35,392)	($38,337)
Current Borrowing (repayment)	$0	$0	$75,000	($90,000)	$0	$0
Increase (decrease) Other Liabilities	$0	$0	$0	$0	$0	$0
Long-term Borrowing (repayment)	($2,942)	($2,962)	($2,983)	($3,005)	($3,026)	($3,047)
Capital Input	$0	$0		$0	$0	$0
Subtotal	$131,886	$119,628	$258,218	($10,943)	$35,497	$13,886
Less:	Jan	Feb	Mar	Apr	May	Jun
Change in Accounts Receivable	$60,942	$28,619	$114,953	($46,972)	($73,150)	($55,650)
Change in Inventory	($180,574)	$35,444	$112,444	($47,778)	($83,558)	($53,510)($130,220)
Change in Other ST Assets	$0	$0	$0	$0	$150,000	$0
Capital Expenditure	$100,000	$100,000	$50,000	$0	$50,000	$0
Dividends	$0	$0	$0	$0	$0	$0
Subtotal	($19,632)	$164,063	$277,397	($94,750)	$43,292	($109,160)
Net Cash Flow	$151,517	($44,435)	($19,180)	$83,807	($7,795)	$123,046
Cash balance	$206,949	$162,514	$143,335	$227,142	$219,347	$342,392

Appendix:
Important
Assumptions   General Assumptions

	Jan-97	Feb-97	Mar-97	Apr-97	May-97	Jun-97
Short Term Interest Rate	8.00%	8.00%	8.00%	8.00%	8.00%	8.00%
Long Term Interest Rate	8.50%	8.50%	8.50%	8.50%	8.50%	8.50%
Payment days	35	35	35	35	35	35
Collection days	45	45	45	45	45	45
Inventory Turnover	6.00	6.00	6.00	6.00	6.00	6.00
Tax Rate Percent	20.00%	20.00%	20.00%	20.00%	20.00%	20.00%
Expenses in cash%	14.00%	14.00%	14.00%	14.00%	14.00%	14.00%
Sales on credit	70.00%	70.00%	70.00%	70.00%	70.00%	70.00%
Personnel Burden %	16.00%	16.00%	16.00%	16.00%	16.00%	16.00%

	Jul-97	Aug-97	Sep-97	Oct-97	Nov-97	Dec-97	1997	1998	1999
	$12,952	$6,277	$62,394	$192,750	$179,782	$150,048	$1,156,863	$1,296,275	$1,452,722
	$1,061	$1,072	$1,083	$1,094	$1,105	$1,116	$12,681	$13,315	$13,981
	($62,239)	($9,336)	$110,216	$157,503	$10,868	($102,069)	$127,271	$47,683	$60,473
	$0	$0	$0	$100,000	$0	($100,000)	($15,000)	$0	$0
	$0	$0	$0	$0	$0	$0	$0	$0	$0
	($3,069)	($3,091)	($3,113)	($3,135)	($3,157)	($3,179)	($36,708)	($39,953)	($43,484)
	$0	$0	$0	$0	$0	$0	$0	$0	$0
	($51,295)	($5,078)	$170,581	$448,213	$188,598	($54,084)	$1,245,106	$1,317,320	$1,483,691

	Jul	Aug	Sep	Oct	Nov	Dec	1997	1998	1999
	($96,600)	($48,475)	$122,850	$289,450	$109,287	($100,537)	$304,718	$151,799	194,504
	($2,500)	$168,720	$323,288	$23,932	($149,820)	$15,868	$267,992	$161,543	
	$300,000	$0	($150,000)	($300,000)	$0	$0	$0	$0	$0
	$0	$0	$0	$0	$0	$0	$300,000	$200,000	$400,000
	$0	$0	$0	$0	$0	$0	$0	$0	$0
	$73,180	($50,975)	$141,570	$312,738	$133,219	($250,357)	$620,586	$619,791	$756,047
	($124,475)	$45,897	$29,011	$135,475	$55,379	$196,273	$624,520	$697,529	$727,644
	$217,918	$263,815	$292,826	$428,300	$483,679	$679,952	$679,952	$1,377,481	$2,105,125

	Jul-97	Aug-97	Sep-97	Oct-97	Nov-97	Dec-97	1997	1998	1999
	8.00%	8.00%	8.00%	8.00%	8.00%	8.00%	8.00%	8.00%	8.00%
	8.50%	8.50%	8.50%	8.50%	8.50%	8.50%	8.50%	8.50%	8.50%
	35	35	35	35	35	35	35	35	35
	45	45	45	45	45	45	45	45	45
	6.00	6.00	6.00	6.00	6.00	6.00	6.00	5.00	5.00
	20.00%	20.00%	20.00%	20.00%	20.00%	20.00%	20.00%	20.00%	20.00%
	14.00%	14.00%	14.00%	14.00%	14.00%	14.00%	14.00%	14.00%	14.00%
	70.00%	70.00%	70.00%	70.00%	70.00%	70.00%	70.00%	75.00%	80.00%
	16.00%	16.00%	16.00%	16.00%	16.00%	16.00%	16.00%	16.00%	16.00%

Appendix:
Personnel Plan

Production	Jan-97	Feb-97	Mar-97	Apr-97	May-97	Jun-97
Manager	$1,000	$1,000	$1,000	$1,000	$1,000	$1,000
Assistant	$3,000	$3,000	$3,000	$3,000	$3,000	$3,000
Technical	$0	$0	$0	$0	$0	$0
Technical	$0	$0	$0	$0	$0	$0
Technical	$2,000	$2,000	$2,000	$2,000	$2,000	$2,000
Fulfillment	$2,000	$2,000	$2,000	$2,000	$2,000	$2,000
Fulfillment	$1,500	$1,500	$1,500	$1,500	$1,500	$1,500
Other						
		$0	$0			
Subtotal	$9,500	$9,500	$9,500	$9,500	$9,500	$9,500

Sales and Marketing	Jan-97	Feb-97	Mar-97	Apr-97	May-97	Jun-97
Manager	$6,000	$6,000	$6,000	$6,000	$6,000	$6,000
Technical sales	$5,000	$5,000	$5,000	$5,000	$5,000	$5,000
Technical sales	$3,500	$3,500	$3,500	$3,500	$3,500	$4,000
Salesperson	$2,500	$2,500	$2,500	$2,500	$2,500	$4,000
Salesperson	$2,500	$2,500	$2,500	$2,500	$2,500	$4,000
Salesperson	$2,500	$2,500	$2,500	$2,500	$2,500	$3,000
Salesperson	$2,000	$2,000	$2,000	$2,000	$2,000	$3,000
Salesperson	$0	$0	$0	$0	$0	$3,000
Salesperson	$0	$0	$0	$0	$0	$0
Other	$0	$0	$0	$0	$0	$0
Subtotal	$24,000	$24,000	$24,000	$24,000	$24,000	$32,000

Administration	Jan-97	Feb-97	Mar-97	Apr-97	May-97	Jun-97
President	$5,500	$5,500	$5,500	$5,500	$5,500	$5,500
Finance	$0	$0	$0	$0	$0	$4,000
Admin Assistant	$2,000	$2,000	$2,000	$2,000	$2,000	$2,000
Bookkeeping	$1,500	$1,500	$1,500	$1,500	$1,500	$1,500
Clerical	$1,000	$1,000	$1,000	$1,000	$1,000	$1,000
Clerical	$0	$0	$0	$0	$0	$1,000
Clerical	$0	$0	$0	$0	$0	$0
Other	$0	$0	$0	$0	$0	$0
Subtotal	$10,000	$10,000	$10,000	$10,000	$10,000	$15,000

Other	Jan-97	Feb-97	Mar-97	Apr-97	May-97	Jun-97
Programming	$3,000	$3,000	$3,000	$3,000	$3,000	$3,000
Other technical	$0	$0	$0	$0	$0	$0
Other	$0	$0	$0	$0	$0	$0
Subtotal	$3,000	$3,000	$3,000	$3,000	$3,000	$3,000

Total Headcount	0	0	0	0	0	0
Total Payroll	$46,500	$46,500	$46,500	$46,500	$46,500	$59,500
Payroll Burden	$7,440	$7,440	$7,440	$7,440	$7,440	$9,520
Total Payroll Expenditures	$53,940	$53,940	$53,940	$53,940	$53,940	$69,020

Note: Ratios in assumptions are used as estimators and may therefore have different values than ratios calculated in the ratios section.

Jul-97	Aug-97	Sep-97	Oct-97	Nov-97	Dec-97	1997	1998	1999
$1,000	$1,000	$1,000	$1,000	$1,000	$1,000	$12,000	$13,000	$14,000
$3,000	$3,000	$3,000	$3,000	$3,000	$3,000	$36,000	$40,000	$40,000
$0	$2,500	$2,500	$2,500	$2,500	$2,500	$12,500	$35,000	$35,000
$0	$2,500	$2,500	$2,500	$2,500	$2,500	$12,500	$35,000	$35,000
$2,000	$2,000	$2,000	$2,000	$2,000	$2,000	$24,000	$27,500	$27,500
$2,000	$2,000	$2,000	$2,000	$2,000	$2,000	$24,000	$30,000	$60,000
$1,500	$1,500	$1,500	$1,500	$1,500	$1,500	$18,000	$22,000	$50,000
$9,500	$14,500	$14,500	$14,500	$14,500	$14,500	$139,000	$202,500	$261,500

Jul-97	Aug-97	Sep-97	Oct-97	Nov-97	Dec-97	1997	1998	1999
$6,000	$6,000	$6,000	$6,000	$6,000	$6,000	$72,000	$76,000	$80,000
$5,000	$5,000	$5,000	$5,000	$5,000	$5,000	$60,000	$63,000	$85,000
$4,000	$4,000	$4,000	$4,000	$4,000	$4,000	$45,500	$46,000	$46,000
$4,000	$4,000	$4,000	$4,000	$4,000	$4,000	$40,500	$55,000	$64,000
$4,000	$4,000	$4,000	$4,000	$4,000	$4,000	$40,500	$50,000	$55,000
$3,000	$3,000	$3,000	$3,000	$3,000	$3,000	$33,500	$34,000	$45,000
$3,000	$3,000	$3,000	$3,000	$3,000	$3,000	$31,000	$38,000	$45,000
$3,000	$3,000	$3,000	$3,000	$3,000	$3,000	$21,000	$30,000	$33,000
$0	$0	$0	$0	$0	$0	$0	$30,000	$33,000
$0	$0	$0	$0	$0	$0	$0		$0
$32,000	$32,000	$32,000	$32,000	$32,000	$32,000	$344,000	$422,000	$486,000

Jul-97	Aug-97	Sep-97	Oct-97	Nov-97	Dec-97	1997	1998	1999
$5,500	$5,500	$5,500	$5,500	$5,500	$5,500	$66,000	$69,000	$95,000
$4,000	$4,000	$4,000	$4,000	$4,000	$4,000	$28,000	$29,000	$30,000
$2,000	$2,000	$2,000	$2,000	$2,000	$2,000	$24,000	$26,000	$28,000
$1,500	$1,500	$1,500	$1,500	$1,500	$1,500	$18,000	$25,000	$30,000
$1,000	$1,000	$1,000	$1,000	$1,000	$1,000	$12,000	$15,000	$18,000
$1,000	$1,000	$1,000	$1,000	$1,000	$1,000	$7,000	$15,000	$18,000
$0	$0	$0	$0	$0	$0	$0	$0	$15,000
$0	$0	$0	$0	$0	$0	$0	$0	$0
$15,000	$15,000	$15,000	$15,000	$15,000	$15,000	$155,000	$179,000	$234,000

Jul-97	Aug-97	Sep-97	Oct-97	Nov-97	Dec-97	1997	1998	1999
$3,000	$3,000	$3,000	$3,000	$3,000	$3,000	$36,000	$40,000	$44,000
$0	$0	$0	$0	$0	$0	$0	$30,000	$33,000
$0	$0	$0	$0	$0	$0	$0	$0	$0
$3,000	$3,000	$3,000	$3,000	$3,000	$3,000	$36,000	$70,000	$77,000
0	0	0	0	0	22	22	25	30
$59,500	$64,500	$64,500	$64,500	$64,500	$64,500	$674,000	$873,500	$1,058,500
$9,520	$10,320	$10,320	$10,320	$10,320	$10,320	$107,840	$139,760	$169,360
$69,020	$74,820	$74,820	$74,820	$74,820	$74,820	$781,840	$1,013,260	$1,227,860

Appendix: Projected Pro-forma Income Statement
Profit and Loss

	Jan-97	Feb-97	Mar-97	Apr-97	May-97	Jun-97
Sales	$440,365	$468,000	$579,000	$500,000	$435,000	$388,000
Direct Cost of Sales	$225,219	$242,941	$299,163	$275,274	$233,495	$206,740
Production payroll	$9,500	$9,500	$9,500	$9,500	$9,500	$9,500
Other	$500	$500	$500	$500	$500	$500
Total Cost of Sales	$235,219	$252,941	$309,163	$285,274	$243,495	$216,740
Gross margin	$205,146	$215,059	$269,837	$214,726	$191,505	$171,260
Gross margin percent	46.59%	45.95%	46.60%	42.95%	44.02%	44.14%
Operating expenses:						
Sales and marketing expenses						
Sales/Marketing Salaries	$24,000	$24,000	$24,000	$24,000	$24,000	$32,000
Ads	$15,000	$15,000	$12,000	$10,000	$15,000	$10,000
Catalog	$2,000	$3,000	$2,000	$2,000	$2,000	$2,000
Mailing	$3,000	$11,800	$5,500	$10,500	$10,500	$5,500
Promo	$0	$0	$0	$0	$0	$0
Shows	$0	$0	$0	$0	$0	$0
Literature	$0	$7,000	$0	$0	$0	$0
PR	$0	$0	$0	$1,000	$0	$0
Seminar	$1,000	$0	$0	$5,000	$5,000	$5,000
Service	$2,000	$1,000	$1,000	$500	$2,500	$500
Training	$5,000	$5,000	$5,000	$5,000	$5,000	$5,000
Total Sales and Marketing Expense	$52,000	$66,800	$49,500	$58,000	$64,000	$60,000
Sales and Marketing Percent	11.81%	14.27%	8.55%	11.60%	14.71%	15.46%
General & Administrative Expenses						
G&A Salaries	$10,000	$10,000	$10,000	$10,000	$10,000	$15,000
Leased Equipment	$2,500	$2,500	$2,500	$2,500	$2,500	$2,500
Utilities	$750	$750	$750	$750	$750	$750
Insurance	$500	$500	$500	$500	$500	$500
Rent	$7,000	$7,000	$7,000	$7,000	$7,000	$7,000
Depreciation	$1,000	$1,010	$1,020	$1,030	$1,040	$1,050
Payroll Burden	$7,440	$7,440	$7,440	$7,440	$7,440	$9,520
Other	$500	$505	$510	$515	$520	$525
Total General and Administrative Expense	$29,690	$29,705	$29,720	$29,735	$29,750	$36,845
General and Administrative Percent	6.74%	6.35%	5.13%	5.95%	6.84%	9.50%
Other Operating Expenses						
Other Salaries	$3,000	$3,000	$3,000	$3,000	$3,000	$3,000
Contract/Consultants	$1,000	$1,000	$1,000	$1,000	$1,000	$1,000
Other	$250	$250	$250	$250	$250	$250
Total Other Operating Expenses	$4,250	$4,250	$4,250	$4,250	$4,250	$4,250
Percent of Sales	0.97%	0.91%	0.73%	0.85%	0.98%	1.10%
Total Operating Expenses	$85,940	$100,755	$83,470	$91,985	$98,000	$101,095
Profit Before Interest and Taxes	$119,206	$114,304	$186,367	$122,741	$93,505	$70,165
Interest Expense ST	$600	$600	$1,100	$500	$500	$500
Interest Expense LT	$1,997	$1,976	$1,955	$1,934	$1,912	$1,891
Taxes Incurred	$23,322	$22,346	$36,662	$24,061	$18,219	$13,555
Net Profit	$93,287	$89,382	$146,650	$96,246	$72,874	$54,220
Net Profit/Sales	21.18%	19.10%	25.33%	19.25%	16.75%	13.97%

Jul-97	Aug-97	Sep-97	Oct-97	Nov-97	Dec-97	1997	1998	1999
$273,500	$261,500	$443,000	$765,750	$760,500	$619,500	$5,934,115	$6,739,868	$7,761,748
$141,630	$135,380	$219,740	$381,384	$393,350	$318,440	$3,072,756	$3,549,934	$4,139,824
$9,500	$14,500	$14,500	$14,500	$14,500	$14,500	$139,000	$202,500	$261,500
$500	$500	$500	$500	$500	$500	$6,000	$6,600	$7,260
$151,630	$150,380	$234,740	$396,384	$408,350	$333,440	$3,217,756	$3,759,034	$4,408,584
$121,870	$111,120	$208,260	$369,366	$352,150	$286,060	$2,716,359	$2,980,834	$3,353,164
44.56%	42.49%	47.01%	48.24%	46.31%	46.18%	45.78%	44.23%	43.20%
$32,000	$32,000	$32,000	$32,000	$32,000	$32,000	$344,000	$422,000	$486,000
$4,000	$4,000	$20,000	$15,000	$20,000	$10,000	$150,000	$316,733	$332,570
$2,000	$2,000	$2,000	$2,000	$2,000	$2,000	$25,000	$19,039	$19,991
$10,500	$10,500	$10,500	$22,000	$8,000	$5,000	$113,300	$0	$0
$0	$0	$1,000	$0	$15,000	$0	$16,000	$0	$0
$3,200	$0	$10,000	$7,000	$0	$0	$20,200	$0	$0
$0	$0	$0	$0	$0	$0	$7,000	$0	$0
$0	$0	$0	$0	$0	$0	$1,000	$0	$0
$5,000	$5,000	$5,000	$0	$0	$0	$31,000	$0	$0
$500	$500	$500	$500	$500	$250	$10,250	$0	$0
$5,000	$5,000	$5,000	$5,000	$5,000	$5,000	$60,000	$0	$0
$62,200	$59,000	$86,000	$83,500	$82,500	$54,250	$777,750	$757,772	$838,561
22.74%	22.56%	19.41%	10.90%	10.85%	8.76%	13.11%	11.24%	10.80%
$15,000	$15,000	$15,000	$15,000	$15,000	$15,000	$155,000	$179,000	$234,000
$2,500	$2,500	$2,500	$2,500	$2,500	$2,500	$30,000	$31,500	$33,075
$750	$750	$750	$750	$750	$750	$9,000	$9,450	$9,923
$500	$500	$500	$500	$500	$500	$6,000	$6,300	$6,615
$7,000	$7,000	$7,000	$7,000	$7,000	$7,000	$84,000	$88,200	$92,610
$1,061	$1,072	$1,083	$1,094	$1,105	$1,116	$12,681	$13,315	$13,981
$9,520	$10,320	$10,320	$10,320	$10,320	$10,320	$107,840	$139,760	$169,360
$530	$535	$540	$545	$550	$556	$6,331	$6,648	$6,980
$36,861	$37,677	$37,693	$37,709	$37,725	$37,742	$410,852	$474,173	$566,544
13.48%	14.41%	8.51%	4.92%	4.96%	6.09%	6.92%	7.04%	7.30%
$3,000	$3,000	$3,000	$3,000	$3,000	$3,000	$36,000	$70,000	$77,000
$1,000	$1,000	$1,000	$1,000	$1,000	$1,000	$12,000	$30,000	$30,000
$250	$250	$250	$250	$250	$250	$3,000	$3,150	$3,308
$4,250	$4,250	$4,250	$4,250	$4,250	$4,250	$51,000	$103,150	$110,308
1.55%	1.63%	0.96%	0.56%	0.56%	0.69%	0.86%	1.53%	1.42%
$103,311	$100,927	$127,943	$125,459	$124,475	$96,242	$1,239,602	$1,335,095	$1,515,413
$18,559	$10,193	$80,317	$243,907	$227,675	$189,818	$1,476,757	$1,645,739	$1,837,751
$500	$500	$500	$1,167	$1,167	$500	$8,133	$6,000	$6,000
$1,869	$1,847	$1,825	$1,803	$1,780	$1,758	$22,545	$19,395	$15,849
$3,238	$1,569	$15,598	$48,188	$44,946	$37,512	$289,216	$324,069	$363,180
$12,952	$6,277	$62,394	$192,750	$179,782	$150,048	$1,156,863	$1,296,275	$1,452,722
4.74%	2.40%	14.08%	25.17%	23.64%	24.22%	19.50%	19.23%	18.72%

Sales Forecast

Unit Sales	Jan-97	Feb-97	Mar-97	Apr-97	May-97	Jun-97	Jul-97
Systems		45	50	75	152	160	133
Service		200	325	300	325	350	375
Software		150	200	225	250	325	318
Training		145	155	165	170	225	200
Other		1,000	1,000	1,200	500	100	100
Total Unit Sales	1,540	1,730	1,965	1,397	1,160	1,126	959

Unit Prices	Jan-97	Feb-97	Mar-97	Apr-97	May-97	Jun-97	Jul-97
Systems		$2,000	$2,000	$2,000	$1,829	$1,891	$1,966
Service		$75	$69	$58	$46	$50	$47
Software		$200	$200	$200	$200	$223	$217
Training		$37	$35	$39	$41	$56	$50
Other		$300	$300	$300	$300	$300	$300

Total Sales	Jan-97	Feb-97	Mar-97	Apr-97	May-97	Jun-97	Jul-97
Systems		$90,000	$100,000	$150,000	$278,000	$302,500	$261,500
Service		$15,000	$22,500	$17,500	$15,000	$17,500	$17,500
Software		$30,000	$40,000	$45,000	$50,000	$72,500	$69,000
Training		$5,365	$5,500	$6,500	$7,000	$12,500	$10,000
Other		$300,000	$300,000	$360,000	$150,000	$30,000	$30,000
Total Sales	$440,365	$468,000	$579,000	$500,000	$435,000	$388,000	$273,500

Unit Direct Costs	Jan-97	Feb-97	Mar-97	Apr-97	May-97	Jun-97	Jul-97
Systems		$1,000	$1,000	$1,000	$1,000	$1,000	$1,000
Service		$60	$60	$60	$60	$60	$60
Software		$100	$100	$100	$100	$100	$100
Training		$22	$22	$22	$22	$22	$22
Other		$150	$150	$150	$150	$150	$150

Direct Costs	Jan-97	Feb-97	Mar-97	Apr-97	May-97	Jun-97	Jul-97
Systems		$45,000	$50,000	$75,000	$152,000	$160,000	$133,000
Service		$12,000	$19,500	$18,000	$19,500	$21,000	$22,500
Software		$15,000	$20,000	$22,500	$25,000	$32,500	$31,800
Training		$3,219	$3,441	$3,663	$3,774	$4,995	$4,440
Other		$150,000	$150,000	$180,000	$75,000	$15,000	$15,000
Subtotal Direct Costs		$225,219	$242,941	$299,163	$275,274	$233,495	$206,740

Aug-97	Sep-97	Oct-97	Nov-97	Dec-97	1997	1998	1999	
76	65	120	253	279	258	1,666	1,750	1,850
400	400	550	850	600	300	4,975	6,000	7,500
233	243	428	575	548	230	3,725	5,000	6,500
150	150	200	220	250	200	2,230	4,000	8,000
100	125	130	100	120	100	4,575	5,000	5,500
983	1,428	1,998	1,797	1,088	17,171	21,750	29,350	

Aug-97	Sep-97	Oct-97	Nov-97	Dec-97	1997	1998	1999	
$2,132	$2,115	$2,083	$1,966	$1,980	$1,984	$1,977	$1,984	$1,977
$50	$50	$91	$124	$75	$67	$73	$84	$87
$242	$253	$220	$211	$204	$207	$215	$195	$180
$33	$33	$50	$55	$60	$50	$47	$72	$79
$300	$300	$300	$300	$300	$300	$300	$300	$300

Aug-97	Sep-97	Oct-97	Nov-97	Dec-97	1997	1998	1999	
$162,000	$137,500	$250,000	$497,500	$552,500	$512,000	$3,293,500	$3,472,868	$3,657,248
$20,000	$20,000	$50,000	$105,000	$45,000	$20,000	$365,000	$504,000	$652,500
$56,500	$61,500	$94,000	$121,250	$112,000	$47,500	$799,250	$975,000	$1,170,000
$5,000	$5,000	$10,000	$12,000	$15,000	$10,000	$103,865	$288,000	$632,000
$30,000	$37,500	$39,000	$30,000	$36,000	$30,000	$1,372,500	$1,500,000	$1,650,000
$261,500	$443,000	$765,750	$760,500	$619,500	$5,934,115	$6,739,868	$7,761,748	

Aug-97	Sep-97	Oct-97	Nov-97	Dec-97	1997	1998	1999	
$1,000	$1,000	$1,000	$1,000	$1,000	$1,000	$1,000	$992	$988
$60	$60	$60	$60	$60	$60	$60	$67	$70
$100	$100	$100	$100	$100	$100	$100	$98	$90
$22	$22	$22	$22	$22	$22	$22	$43	$47
$150	$150	$150	$150	$150	$150	$150	$150	$150

Aug-97	Sep-97	Oct-97	Nov-97	Dec-97	1997	1998	1999	
$76,000	$65,000	$120,000	$253,000	$279,000	$258,000	$1,666,000	$1,736,434	$1,828,624
$24,000	$24,000	$33,000	$51,000	$36,000	$18,000	$298,500	$403,200	$522,000
$23,300	$24,300	$42,800	$57,500	$54,800	$23,000	$372,500	$487,500	$585,000
$3,330	$3,330	$4,440	$4,884	$5,550	$4,440	$49,506	$172,800	$379,200
$15,000	$18,750	$19,500	$15,000	$18,000	$15,000	$686,250	$750,000	$825,000
$141,630	$135,380	$219,740	$381,384	$393,350	$318,440	$3,072,756	$3,549,934	$4,139,824

Computer Reseller

BUSINESS PLAN

ELLIPSE TECHNOLOGIES, INC.

1500 North River Street
Kalamazoo, MI 48221

This business plan demonstrates that in order to enter an industry where there are already several successful dominant players, a business has to cater to a small segment of the marketplace or offer unique services. Ellipse does both. As a reseller of computer equipment and software, Ellipse is very aware of its position in this competitive arena, and plans to successfully address this challenge.

- EXECUTIVE SUMMARY

- COMPANY OVERVIEW

- PRODUCT STRATEGY

- MARKET ANALYSIS

- MARKETING PLAN

- FINANCIAL PLAN

- CONCLUSION

- CASH FLOW PROJECTION

EXECUTIVE SUMMARY

Ellipse Technologies' mission is to supply clients with state-of-the-art computers and computer related products, along with a plan for integration of computer technologies into clients' day-to-day business operations.

Ellipse Technologies' core business activity consists of value-added reselling of computers and computer products, including various kinds of system, network system, voice recognition, and image processing. Additionally, Ellipse Technologies provides custom training, and maintains support contracts with certain clients to insure stability in their computer operations and information systems.

The largest volume product sold by Ellipse Technologies is a family of voice recognition software from Dragon Systems, Inc. The voice recognition software consists of large vocabulary speech products that accepts voice input to a Microsoft Windows-
based personal computer to run commands and produce text.

The principals of Ellipse Technologies have built a solid base of voice recognition clients in the fields of physical rehabilitation, healthcare, and law. During this time, as advances in both computer hardware and the voice recognition software have occurred, sales of voice recognition technologies have grown steadily. This growth hasoccurred with minimal investment in advertising and marketing.

Ellipse Technologies plans to significantly expand its sales and client base by increased marketing and advertising.

COMPANY OVERVIEW

Legal Business Description

The legal name of Ellipse Technologies is Ellipse Technologies, Inc.

The legal form of Ellipse Technologies is a Subchapter S Corporation, incorporated in the state of Michigan.

The business location of Ellipse Technologies is 1500 North River Street, Kalamazoo, Michigan, 48221.

Management Team

Our management team consists of 3 individuals whose backgrounds consist of years of in-depth experience in computer system development, sales, healthcare, and marketing with corporations and institutions throughout Michigan and the U.S.

In-House Management

- Matt Williams, President
- Darlene VanMarkus, Vice President of Marketing
- Maria Williams, OTR, CHT, Corporate Secretary, Operations Director

Outside Management Support [hourly/project basis]

- Don Hoffman, Accountant/CPA
- Joanna Crenshaw, Corporate Attorney
- Sam Hillman, Financial and Business Consultant

Dragon Systems, Inc. (Ellipse Technologies is a Premier Reseller of products)

Infotel, Inc. (Ellipse Technologies is a reseller of computer hardware)
FOSA Computer (Ellipse Technologies is a reseller of notebook computers)

Strategic Alliances

Ellipse Technologies currently offers several main products and services:

- DragonDictate for Windows - Personal Edition (Resell software from Dragon Systems, Inc.)
- DragonDictate for Windows - Classic Edition (Resell software from Dragon Systems, Inc.)
- DragonDictate for Windows - Power Edition (Resell software from Dragon Systems, Inc.)
- DragonPro Medical Vocabulary - (Resell software from Dragon Systems, Inc.)
- DragonPro Legal Vocabulary - (Resell software from Dragon Systems, Inc.)
- DragonPro Business Vocabulary - (Resell software from Dragon Systems, Inc.)
- Dragon Naturally Speaking, Continuous Dictation software- (Resell software from Dragon Systems, Inc.)
- Dragon Xtools Development System - (Resell software from Dragon Systems, Inc.)
- Custom configured desktop Voice Recognition computer systems (Resell software, Resell hardware, system integration)
- Custom configured portable Voice Recognition computer systems (Resell software, Resell hardware, system integration)
- Custom configured desktop and portable business computer systems (Resell hardware, system Integration)
- Consulting, training, and installation of voice recognition products (Services)
- Custom configured networked computer systems (Resell hardware, system configuration)
- Networked computer system installation, support, and training (Services)

PRODUCT STRATEGY: CURRENT PRODUCT

MARKET ANALYSIS

The voice recognition market is growing at a rapid rate. The market for these products amounted to 20.6 million units sold world-wide in 1994, and 45.3 million in 1995.

Market Definition

Unit sales figures were over 145 million in 1996. Projections are for over 1,700 million in 1997, and 4.2 billion units in 1998, based on data supplied by FSG Associates, a national market research firm.

The traditional market for voice recognition sales has been for individuals with physical disabilities. With today's and tomorrow's computer hardware combined with improvements in the performance of the voice recognition software, the market is shifting to professionals who need to (inexpensively) produce large quantities of documentation.

Customer Profile

Ellipse Technologies' target market includes physical rehabilitation, healthcare, and law. The most typical customer of our products is someone who needs to operate a computer and (especially) produce textual material, but cannot (or chooses not to) use the computer keyboard. This often includes individuals with physical disabilities, physicians and other healthcare professionals, or those in the legal profession, who produce large volumes of documentation.

Competition

Companies that compete in this market are IBM (and representatives), and Kurzweil Applied Intelligence (and representatives), along with other Dragon resellers (to a lesser extent within the state of Michigan). All companies charge competitive prices:

- DragonDictate for Windows 30,000 word vocabulary $695
- Kurzweil Voice for Windows 30,000-60,000 word vocabulary $595
- IBM VoiceType - 50,000 word vocabulary $795

Dragon Systems has clear advantages over other competitors in the voice recognition market. Dragon was the first company to introduce voice recognition software for personal computers, it holds patents in many sectors of this technology, and its software is reputed to be the easiest to use, compared with competing products.

Additionally, Dragon Systems will be releasing a new product this summer called Naturally Speaking. Naturally Speaking is a continuous speech product that allows the user to talk at speeds of over 100 words per minute with a high degree of accuracy. This product is expected to cause sales of voice recognition software to dramatically increase.

Ellipse Technologies has competitive advantages over other resellers in this industry. Its management team entered the market of voice recognition early and has already established a network of clients at major hospitals and rehabilitation agencies throughout the state of Michigan. Ellipse Technologies maintains a status with Dragon Systems known as a Premier Reseller of Dragon software. As a Premier Reseller, it works directly with Dragon Systems to develop marketing plans and provide support and training for all Dragon products in exchange for a regular supply of leads, referrals, and sales consulting.

Risk

The top business risks that Ellipse Technologies faces as it begins to expand in the voice recognition market are: (1) Other, larger companies will enter the market; and (2) that voice recognition technology will become "mainstream" and be bundled with complete computer system packages.

These risks are minimized by the fact that: (1) The investment in money, personnel, and "know-how" are significant. Ellipse Technologies' staff has over 2 years experience in installing, configuring, and supporting voice recognition products, and therefore a major lead from all other competitors, (2) Even though voice recognition technology is likely to be part of most computer systems in the future, it will take quite a while before professional assistance is not required. This is evidenced by the fact that there is still a large need for word processor consulting, training, and support even though word processing software has been sold and marketed for over 15 years.

Ellipse Technologies' marketing strategy is to enhance, promote and support the fact that our products are cost-effective solutions for anyone who produces volumes of text using a computer. We can also demonstrate our products' cost-effective nature for use in rehabilitation, since it is Americans with Disability Act (ADA)-compliant, bringing many Workman's Compensation claim individuals back into the marketplace.

MARKETING PLAN

Because of Ellipse Technologies' special market relationship with Dragon Systems within the state of Michigan, our sales strategy includes telephone follow-up with daily leads submitted by Dragon Systems, processing credit card purchases made by telemarketing staff at Dragon Systems, and selling hardware and custom training for customers of voice recognition systems.

Sales Strategy

Additionally, Ellipse Technologies plans to undertake direct sales activity to institutions and large business organizations. Likely customers include hospitals, schools, clinics, banks, insurance companies, and law firms. On a regular basis Ellipse Technologies plans to attend or sponsor seminars or conferences for purposes of exhibiting voice recognition and other state-of-the-art computer technologies.

A partial list of Ellipse Technologies' major current customers includes:

- Middleton Medical Center
- Michigan Jobs Commission
- Jordan Clinic of Petoskey
- Kalamazoo Rehabilitation Center
- Detroit Medical Center
- Michigan Rehabilitation Services
- Donald Sutherland, MD, PC
- Littleton & Littleton, PC
- Pharmacia Upjohn
- Benjamin County Central Schools
- Randolph-Milton, PC
- Michigan Land Use Institute
- Kalamazoo Area Public Schools
- Watertown Public Schools

Our advertising and promotion strategy is to position Ellipse Technologies as the leading voice recognition system dealer in the state of Michigan. Additionally, we wish to achieve name recognition as a supplier of high-tech, state-of-the-art computer systems and components that emphasize voice recognition. Our slogan, "Taking business to new horizons," is intended to signify a company that provides forward-looking office solutions.

Advertising and Promotion

We will utilize the following media and methods to allow our message to reach our customers: (1) Advertisements in tradejournals and industry newsletters; (2) Direct sales contacts to institutions, providing them with on-site seminars and trials of the products; (3) Direct mail of literature and videocassettes demonstrating the power of our products; and (4) Sponsorship and attendance at published seminars and conferences to exhibit our products.

For the next 12 months, advertising, marketing, and promotion will require approximately $12,000. Much of this cost will come from ongoing sales revenues, however Ellipse Technologies is seeking part of this money to begin its market thrust.

On an ongoing basis beyond that period, we will budget our advertising investment as 5% to 10% of total sales.

Public Relations

During 1997 Ellipse Technologies will focus on the following publicity strategies: (1) Direct mail of literature and videocassettes to large legal and healthcare organizations; and (2) Direct mail of invitations to seminars held in various cities to demonstrate the capabilities of the technologies.

We will track, wherever possible, the incremental revenue generated from our publicity efforts. We anticipate at least 40 percent of total sales will be generated directly from our publicity, journal advertising, and name recognition, 20 percent from follow-up of direct referrals from Dragon Systems, 20 percent from "cold calls" of target organizations, and 20 percent of sales from indirect referrals and "word-of-mouth" referrals.

FINANCIAL PLAN

Our objective, at this time, is to propel the company into a prominent market position in the areas of voice recognition and high-tech office solutions. We feel that within 3 years Ellipse Technologies will be in a suitable position for further expansion or profitable acquisition.

Assumptions

The cash flow analysis shown in Appendix A shows revenues based on the first 4 months of operation. It also delineates revenues from a network maintenance contract with Benjamin County Central Schools that includes contractually specified service revenue and a moderate amount of hardware sales revenues.

After the first few months of administrative setup, sales are expected to increase, and then grow at a rate of approximately 5% per month for hardware and 10% per month for the software. This is expected due to greatly increased expenditures for advertising and promotion, coupled with national expectations of the growth of certain technologies.

Capital Requirements

According to the opportunities and requirements for Ellipse Technologies described in this business plan, and based on what we feel are sound business assumptions, our first year outside capital requirements are for $16,000.

The loan will be used to purchase a high-end demonstration computer, and to finance an initial thrust in advertising, marketing, and promotion beyond levels spent in the past.

Exit/Payback

The increase in profits generated by Ellipse Technologies sales will allow us to have the funds to repay the loan in 24 months.

CONCLUSION

Ellipse Technologies enjoys an established track-record of excellent sales, support, and service for our customers. Their expressions of satisfaction, encouragement, and testimonials are numerous, and we intend to continue our advances in the voice recognition marketplace with even more unique and effective products and services.

This page intentionally left blank to accomodate tabular material on the following page...

...continued

Cash Flow Analysis

	Nov	Dec	Jan	Feb	Mar	Apr
Cash On Hand	$8,000	$7,375	$7,171	$7,113	$6,979	$7,116
Income						
Dragon Hardware Sales	$7,000	$7,700	$8,085	$8,489	$8,914	$9,359
Dragon Software Sales	$4,755	$4,993	$5,242	$5,505	$5,780	$6,069
Training	$950	$999	$1,048	$1,101	$1,156	$1,214
Other Hardware Sales*	$1,800	$1,800	$1,890	$1,985	$2,084	$2,188
Support Contract	$3,000	$3,000	$3,000	$3,000	$3,000	$3,000
Total Income	$17,505	$18,491	$19,266	$20,079	$20,933	$21,830
Cost of Goods Sold						
Dragon Hardware Sales	$5,460	$6,006	$6,306	$6,622	$6,953	$7,300
Dragon Software Sales	$2,853	$2,996	$3,145	$3,303	$3,468	$3,641
Other Hardware Sales*	$1,566	$1,566	$1,644	$1,727	$1,813	$1,903
Total Cost of Goods Sold	$9,879	$10,568	$11,096	$11,651	$12,233	$12,845
Gross Profit	$7,626	$7,924	$8,170	$8,428	$8,700	$8,985
Expenses						
Advertising	$200	$200	$200	$220	$220	$220
Bank Serv. Charges	$25	$25	$25	$25	$25	$25
Electricity/Utilities	$100	$150	$150	$150	$150	$150
Equipment	$500	$600	$700	$700	$700	$700
Insurance	$100	$100	$100	$100	$100	$100
Interest Expense	$150	$150	$150	$150	$150	$150
Internet Setup & Charge	$100	$100	$100	$100	$100	$100
Licenses & Permits	$20	$20	$20	$20	$20	$20
Marketing	$200	$200	$220	$220	$220	$250
Meals	$150	$150	$150	$180	$180	$180
Miscellaneous	$100	$100	$100	$100	$100	$100
Office Furniture	$150	$150	$150	$150	$150	$150
Office Supplies	$100	$50	$50	$50	$50	$50
Pagers	$100	$100	$100	$100	$100	$100
Gross Wages	$4,000	$4,000	$4,000	$4,200	$4,200	$4,200
Payroll Taxes	$0					
FICA	$248	$248	$248	$260	$260	$260
FUTA	$2	$2	$2	$2	$2	$2
Medicare	$56	$56	$56	$59	$59	$59
Postage & Delivery	$200	$200	$200	$200	$200	$200
Professional Fees						
Accounting	$100	$100	$100	$100	$100	$100
Legal	$200	$200	$200	$200	$200	$200
Rent	$1,300	$750	$750	$750	$750	$750
Software	$0	$0	$0			
Telephone	$350	$150	$150	$150	$150	$150
Travel	$250	$250	$250	$300	$300	$300
Unemployment Contrib.		$76	$76	$76	$76	$76
TOTAL EXPENSES	$8,251	$8,128	$8,228	$8,563	$8,563	$8,563
NET PROFIT	($625)	($204)	($58)	($135)	$137	$422
Remaining Cash	$7,375	$7,171	$7,113	$6,979	$7,116	$7,538

May	June	July	Aug	Sep	Oct	
$7,538	$6,056	$4,888	$4,050	$3,258	$2,831	
$9,827	$10,319	$10,835	$11,376	$11,945	$12,542	$116,392
$6,372	$6,691	$7,025	$7,377	$7,745	$8,133	$75,686
$1,274	$1,338	$1,405	$1,475	$1,549	$1,627	$15,136
$2,297	$2,412	$2,533	$2,659	$2,792	$2,932	$27,372
$3,000	$3,000	$3,000	$3,000	$3,000	$3,000	$36,000
$22,771	$23,760	$24,798	$25,888	$27,032	$28,234	$270,587
$7,665	$8,049	$8,451	$8,874	$9,317	$9,783	$90,786
$3,823	$4,014	$4,215	$4,426	$4,647	$4,880	$45,412
$1,999	$2,099	$2,204	$2,314	$2,429	$2,551	$23,814
$13,487	$14,162	$14,870	$15,613	$16,394	$17,214	$160,011
$9,284	$9,598	$9,928	$10,274	$10,638	$11,020	$110,575
$250	$250	$250	$250	$250	$250	$2,760
$25	$25	$25	$25	$25	$25	$300
$150	$150	$150	$150	$150	$150	$1,750
$700	$700	$700	$700	$700	$700	$8,100
$100	$100	$100	$100	$100	$100	$1,200
$150	$150	$150	$150	$150	$1,650	
$100	$100	$100	$100	$100	$1,100	
$20	$20	$20	$20	$20	$20	$240
$250	$250	$250	$250	$250	$2,560	
$220	$220	$220	$220	$220	$220	$2,310
$100	$100	$100	$100	$100	$100	$1,200
$150	$150	$150	$150	$150	$150	$1,800
$50	$50	$50	$50	$50	$50	$650
$100	$100	$100	$100	$100	$100	$1,200
$6,200	$6,200	$6,200	$6,200	$6,200	$6,200	$61,800
$384	$384	$384	$384	$384	$384	$3,832
$3	$3	$3	$3	$3	$3	$33
$87	$87	$87	$87	$87	$87	$865
$200	$200	$200	$200	$200	$200	$2,400
$100	$100	$100	$100	$100	$100	$1,200
$100	$100	$100	$100	$100	$100	$1,800
$750	$750	$750	$1,050	$1,050	$1,050	$10,450
$150	$150	$150	$150	$150	$150	$2,000
$350	$350	$350	$350	$350	$350	$3,750
$76	$76	$76	$76	$76	$76	$841
$10,766	$10,766	$10,766	$11,066	$11,066	$11,066	$115,790
($1,482)	($1,168)	($838)	($791)	($428)	($46)	($5,215)
$6,056	$4,888	$4,050	$3,258	$2,831	$2,785	

Detective Agency

BUSINESS PLAN

BARR DETECTIVE AGENCY

PO Box 2001
Grand Haven, MI 45533

This business plan offers an excellent consideration of factors involved in starting an investigative practice. Unlike many other entrepreneurial ventures, this field needs to keep abreast of the changing legal climate. Changing regulations reform the marketplace, making it necessary for investigators to be aware of each new peice of legislation that impacts their clients and industry practices.

- BACKGROUND OF BUSINESS

- BACKGROUND OF OWNER

- MISSION AND STRATEGY

- REGULATORY CONSIDERATIONS AND INSURANCE

- LICENSING AND MARKET EXCLUSIVITY

- GENERAL COMPETITIVE ANALYSIS

- SPECIFIC COMPETITIVE ANALYSIS

- SERVICE OVERVIEW AND MARKET CONSIDERATIONS

- STRENGTHS AND WEAKNESSES OF SERVICES OFFERED

- APPROACH TO THE MARKET

- ADVERTISING

- BUSINESS LOGISTICS

- NOTES ON FINANCIAL INFORMATION

- THIRD QUARTER AND YEAR END STATEMENTS

DETECTIVE AGENCY
BUSINESS PLAN

BACKGROUND OF BUSINESS

Barr Detective Agency has been in business in various formats since October of 1990. The business name has changed several times to reflect the incorporation of the business and its partners The name reverted back to Barr Detective Agency in 1995 and is currently operated as a sole proprietorship with the exclusive owner of the business being Glenn A Barr. The business has been largely inactive for the last couple of years and is DOW undergoing retooling of its sales efforts in order to become more active and profitable.

BACKGROUND OF OWNER

The current owner of Barr Detective Agency is Glenn A Barr. Mr. Barr is licensed as both a private investigator and security guard director in the State of Michigan. His background includes two years as a U.S. Army Military Police officer, three years as a practice investigator and district manager for Pinkerton's, Inc. and eight years of private practice investigation. His education includes graduating with honors from Central Michigan University and extensive graduate level training in both psychology and legal studies.

MISSION AND STRATEGY

The mission of Barr Detective Agency is to offer first class corporate investigative and security services to the private sector in accordance with all applicable provisions of state law and the licensure authority of the Michigan State Police. The business is currently licensed and licensure itself is a valuable commodity within the state. The strategy of Barr Detective Agency will be to outsell its investigative counterparts through an innovative sales process that will be revealed in the marketing section of this plan.

REGULATORY CONSIDERATIONS AND INSURANCE

In addition to the thorough screening that is required of all potential applicants, each business is required by statute to be bonded. The bonding for Barr Detective Agency currently exceeds the state mandated minimum and is set at $10,000.00 a piece. Liability insurance is also easily obtainable and affordable for this business because of the low exposure to litigation in the industry. Them is one exception to this rule; however, and that is in loss prevention. Physically detaining shoplifters carries a high degree of risk and injury and lawsuits are more common in this one investigative service than in all others combined. Invasion of privacy lawsuits are minimal and are usually easily defeated if the investigator stays within prescribed guidelines The granting of weapons permits is a significant factor in driving up the costs of liability insurance cod should be avoided except for the most outstanding and reliable personnel in the organization. Even then, weapons training and restricted use will prevent a large number of liability problems down the road. Armed accounts only account for a small fraction of the investigative market and therefore should not be considered a significant weighting factor in terns of coverage.

LICENSING AND MARKET EXCLUSIVITY

The competition among licensed private investigators is less than in many other businesses. The rigorous licensing and approval process is slow and arduous. Therefore, a dearth of wouldbe private investigators are kept from the market. Only the more serious individuals stand a realistic chance of surviving the screening process, which focuses heavily on provable experience dealing with the investigative laws in this state. The Private Investigator Licensing Act of 1963 erects a formidable barrier to licensing by requiring that each individual is separately licensed for either security or investigations, and not both. That means that each process is separate from the other and requires a completely different set of qualifications and experience. The man prerequisite for becoming a licensed private investigator is to have three years of investigative experience in the field prior to application. The same prerequisite applies to the security process as well. After this is accomplished, a thorough background check is performed on the individual seeking to become licensed. Very high standards al applied. In fact, the process is so stringent that a majority of licensed private investigators are exlaw enforcement officers of varying degrees. This is an advantage that I shall address more fully in the next section.

The competitive advantage alluded to in the previous section is simple. Since so many applicants and licensees in this state are exlaw enforcement officers, there is an utter lack of experienced business personnel in this field. Most law enforcement training is not geared towards business and the amount of inexperience in this aspect of the field is shocking. Since my skills were learned in a business environment, there is a decided edge in my favor in regard to business planning and development. Another distinct advantage is that because so much of the competition has already served in a career capacity, many of the investigators in the field are only parttime at best and do not take either the cases or the business seriously. There are other investigators in the field who come from either a loss prevention or private security background, and these competitors are more difficult to challenge.

GENERAL COMPETITIVE ANALYSIS

The Knoll Group of New York City and Business Risk International the two premier investigative companies in the United States. Other national companies such as Pinkerton and Burns International provide investigative services to their manufacturing clients, but mostly on an ad hoc basis and not with investigative services being the beneficiary, but more as a peripheral service that helps them sell security services. There is surprisingly little in the way of national competition because the laws are so complex and difficult to apply on a broad scope. Further, there is the notion that the field of private investigation should be a small one, similar to a law firm. As such, most companies tend to be local and regional, covering three or fewer states. Here in Grand Haven, there are currently 52 agencies licensed to do business. Although that number appears quite high, there are very few agencies doing high volume work. With the exception of one agency, none of the other agencies are noteworthy. The one agency that is noteworthy is Fatmans. He has a well-run agency with an international reputation. He specializes primarily in marital investigations and is not considered a keen competitor.

SPECIFIC COMPETITIVE ANALYSIS

Any private investigative company will usually offer a mix of services. Developing a portfolio of different services is especially helpful when laws change and enhance or eliminate the need for certain types of investigations. The field of private investigation offers a large array of possible services, which are explained in detail in the section that follows.

SERVICE OVERVIEW AND MARKET CONSIDERATIONS

STRENGTHS AND WEAKNESSES OF SERVICE OFFERED

The bread and butter of investigators throughout the United States. Barr Detective Agency is no exception. Worker's Compensation fraud referrals are the most common form of investigation that insurance companies request; however, there is still a great need for liability, fire and accident reinvestigation cases as well. My agency is most experienced in the injury fraud type of case and it is so commonly requested that it should be considered a specialization.

Insurance Investigations

Background Investgations

Commonly only requested by corporations looking to hire applicants without a strong sense of who they are besides what is listed on their resume, background investigations can be lucrative assignments if obtained in volume. They are virtually useless sources of revenue as stand alone cases. The reason for this is that a background check has a natural component of cost. To do a national criminal search requires an up front cost as well as several other forms of credential verification. For this reason, only large background volume will produce decent net profile. The companies using background checks, to a large degree, also perform them inhouse via their human resources department.

Loss Prevention

Commonly known as store detective work. Many companies hire their own inhouse investigator to perform this task, but there are still large chains that subcontract out this type of work From the client's view, this is an advantageous relationship because the liability for a false arrest can be significantly shifted to a properly insured vendor private investigation company. The work tends to be on an hourly basis, therefore earnings are limited. A large account, however, can generate sufficient revenue to allow for decent profit margins.

Personal Protection

These accounts are accounts of opportunity. When developed, these are high paying accounts that can make up a significant portion of revenue in a short period of time. What is so appealing is that the person being protected needs a high degree of protection usually around the clock. Therefore, the rate of pay is high and is continuous as long as the individual needs protection. Some positions are fulltime, as with a celebrity, but most often personal protection assignments are short lived and deal with a specific threat by some individual that provides a period of uncertainty that the target must endure. After the threat has been ended or minimized, the assignment is usually ended or phased out and the revenue stream is terminated. Sometimes, the perpetrator is apprehended immediately and no significant revenue is obtained. In either situation personal protection accounts are lucrative, but inherently unstable and it is best to avoid this type of assignment as a source for long term gain. However, in the short term, they are highly profitable.

Store Testing

Also known as "mystery shopping." An excellent service comparable to background checks. Testing is performed by an operative working undercover as a normal customer. The store and its operations are reported on and a score affixed to determine the comparative value of the store. Testing must be performed in volume if it is to be profitable in any meaningful sense. Large accounts are known to exist in this field; however, they are difficult accounts to obtain by anything less than a national corporation.

Domestics

This term refers to the type of cases that cover a broad array of individually ordered, noncommercial, type of investigations. Also known as marital or spousal investigations, these are occasional sources of intermittent revenue. They have fallen out of favor in Michigan for a couple of reasons. One, because they are noncommercial, domestics are often simple information gathering, but sometimes clients wish the investigator to perform surveillance in an unlawful manner, such as tapping phones or harassing the individual. Because of this, liability exposure is greatly enhanced, in addition to the added threat posed by a hostile spouse who may act irrationally. Secondly, the laws of this state preclude using evidence gathered in a divorce case because Michigan has no fault divorce laws. In those states that still have partial fault divorce laws, the domestic market is seen as a key market. Michigan has a change of divorce laws pending in the state legislature, but so far, no legislative action has been approved. Until or unless the legal climate changes in Michigan, domestic cases should not be considered a strong source of revenue.

Is an excellent side business with enormous profit potential. Here, the largest problem stems from the fact that a great deal of equipment is needed to perform this kind of hightech. electronic work. A spectrum frequency analyzer, a wall sweep unit, and a phone line tracer system are just some of the pieces of equipment needed to do a thorough job in this field. Some investigators have been known to buy a few gadgets and try to pass themselves off as electronic counter-measures specialists, but with limited success. This is an elite field and difficult to break into; average equipment costs approach $50,000. The one key factor which makes this field so attractive is the fact that billing for this type of service is in the $5,000 to $10,000 range per assignment and assignments are usually completed in a matter of two to three days.

Electronic Countermeasures and Debugging

Process serving involves tracking down and giving individuals notice of court actions that are pending against them. They can be either very time-consuming or quick and easy, depending on the subject being served. These cases can be a profitable portion of any company's repertoire of investigative services. However, this service requires tremendous volume to be profitable and assignments have to be procured on an individual law firm basis. There are no national accounts for process serving anywhere in the country at the present time. Laws for each state are different and hence process serving is a local type of account, limiting the revenue, which is capable of being generated.

Process Serving

Usually performed for large manufacturing companies that have internal drug or theft problems. As a source of revenue, these type of cases can be considered profitable; however, the true worth of a manufacturing client is not the revenue derived from this one form of limited investigation, but from the steady stream of other investigations that can springboard from a strong client relationship. Manufacturing companies need background checks, employee honesty determinations and host of smaller investigative services. Further, the manufacturing client is an ideal market for security services.

Internal Surveys/ Undercover Investigations

Usually performed for litigators in large law firms. These types of investigations usually involve reconstructing accident scenes, as with insurance companies, or finding evidence to refute the opposing counsel's legal strategy. Evidence may be in the form of written statements or in the form of actual proof subject to chain of evidence requirements. These cases are usually profitable, but difficult to come by. They are cases of opportunity like some of the other cases mentioned here and that limits their usefulness.

Legal Investigations

Considering all of the aforementioned market opportunities, it should be clear that the best approach to the market is through selling insurance investigative services. Therefore, the concentration of effort will take place in that market. The most common manner of approaching insurance agents is through direct sales. Sales letters followed up with phone contact serve as the best method of contacting those companies most likely to need investigative services. The S.I.U. unit of an insurance company is the ideal contact source and those companies, which are most prone to use vendor private investigators, can be located through the insurance underwriter's handbook. Direct sales will account for most of the sales effort of Barr Detective Agency.

APPROACH TO THE MARKET

The advertising budget for Barr Detective Agency is small compared to some other service businesses for a good reason. Investigative clients are clients of opportunity. Normal retail advertising is not a solid approach, because most clients are gotten through word-of-mouth

ADVERTISING

and only when they have a problem. Similar to the legal profession, the best cases are derived through the referral system. There are a couple of exceptions to this rule, and those exceptions are legal and insurance clientele. Insurance companies and law firms have a pressing need for investigative services on a regular basis. In fact, they are the only groups of commercial clients in the business. Therefore, any advertising strategy has to incorporate this factor as the main principle for advertising. Targeting law firms and insurance companies through trade publications provides an inherent advantage in strategic advertising because it allows the focus to be on two select groups and nowhere else. All other investigative accounts can have minimal advertising efforts directed at them without a significant impact on revenue.

BUSINESS LOGISTICS

Location

Barr Detective Agency can be run from a home office located in Grand Haven, Michigan. The office will be large enough to accommodate all the needs for running a medium size investigative firm.

Benefit

The advantages to working out of a home office is enormous. Without the expenditure of rent for office space, the business has a greatly improved chance for success.

Minimal Overhead

Besides phone usage and other minor costs, overhead can be kept to an absolute minimum. There is no reason for any significant expenditure of revenue except for the cost of occasional equipment updates.

Benefit

Having minimal overhead maximizes the chance for success.

Equipment

All necessary equipment has been purchased and is available for use. The one equipment deficit would be in the area of surveillance camera equipment. The equipment on hand could be upgraded to utilize better technology that is now available.

Benefit

A significant capital outlay can be avoided because the necessary equipment has already been procured.

NOTES ON FINANCIAL INFORMATION PRESENTED

Introduction

The following financial information is accurate as of fiscal year 1995. The information presented was prepared by an accounting firm using standard accounting principles. These figures have not been audited, but do represent the best information available at the time that it was gathered. Barr Dectective Agency makes no other representations as to its value.

Balance Sheet

The balance sheet statement is based on the third quarter performance of 1995 and includes the year ending statement as well.

The P and L statement is based on the third quarter performance of 1995 and includes the year ending statement as well.

CURRENT ASSETS:
Cash in Bank - Checking	$2,149.29	
Cash in Bank - Payroll	803.77	
Cash in Bank - Savings	0.04	
Total Current Assets		$4,696.56

PROPERTY AND EQUIPMENT:
Equipment	$4,661.13	
Accum. Deprec - Equipment	3,141.93	
Furniture & Fixtures	429.44	
Accum. Deprec - Furn. & Fix.	429.44	
Vehicles	10,000.00	
Accum. Deprec. - Vehicles	3,995.00	
Total Property and Equipment		$7,524.20

OTHER ASSETS:
Photographic Equipment	$780.33	
Total Other Assets		$780.33
Total Assets		$13,001.09

CURRENT LIABILITIES:
American Express	$947.10	
Payroll Taxes Payable	3,950.82	
Total Current Liabilities		$4,897.92

NON_CURRENT LIABILITIES:
Note Payable - Beneficial Nat'l	403.03	
Note Payable - Whirlpool Fin.	237.65	
Note Payable - First of America	351.92	
Note Payable - Officer	230	
Total Non-Current Liabilities		$1,222.60

EQUITY:
Capital	$3,216.90	
Additional PIC - Barr	5,517.54	
Additional PIC - Kearney	2,104.63	
Net Income (Loss)	6,684.56	
Total Equity		6,880.57
Total Liabilities and Equity		$13,001.09

**Balance Sheet--
Third Quarter
August**

CURRENT ASSETS:		
Cash In Bank - Checking	$92.91	
Cash In Bank - Payroll	3,720.90	
Cash In Bank - Savings	0.04	
Employee Advances	3,351.00	
Total Current Assets		$7,164.85
PROPERTY AND EQUIPMENT:		
Equipment	$4,919.13	
Accum. Deprec. - Equipment	3,141.93	
Furniture & Fixtures	429.44	
Accum. Deprec. - Furn. & Fix.	429.44	
Vehicles	10,000.00	
Accum. Deprec. - Vehicles	3,995.00	
Total Property and Equipment		$7,782.20
OTHER ASSETS:		
Photographic Equipment	$780.33	
Total Other Assets	$780.33	
Total Assets		$15,727.38
CURRENT LIABILITIES:		
American Express	$947.10	
Payroll Taxes Payable	5,008.11	
Total Current Liabilities		$5,955.21
NON-CURRENT LIABILITIES:		
Note Payable-Beneficial Nat'l	$403.03	
Note Payable-Whirlpool Fin.	185.65	
Note Payable-First of America	351.92	
Note Payable - Officer	230	
Total Non-Current Liabilities		$1,170.60
EQUITY:		
Capital	$(3,216.90)	
Additional PIC - Barr	5,517.54	
Additional PIC - Kearney	(2,104.63)	
NET INCOME (LOSS)	8,405.56	
TOTAL EQUITY		$8,601.57
TOTAL LIABILITIES & EQUITY		$15,727.38

CURRENT ASSETS:

Cash In Bank - Checking	$88.10	
Cash In Bank - Payroll	128.6	
Cash In Bank - Savings	0.04	
Employee Advances	3,351.00	
Total Current Assets		$3,567.74

PROPERTY AND EQUIPMENT:

Equipment	$4,919.12	
Accum. Deprec. - Equipment	3,141.93	
Furniture & Fixtures	429.44	
Accum. Deprec. - Furn. & Fix.	429.44	
Vehicles	10,000.00	
Accum. Deprec. - Vehicles	3,995.00	
Total Property and Equipme		$7,782.20

OTHER ASSETS

Photographic Equipment	$780.33	
Total Other Assets		$780.33
Total Assets		$12,130.27

CURRENT LIABILITIES:

American Express	$947.10	
Payroll Taxes Payable	4,858.43	
Total Current Liabilities		$5,805.53

NON_CURRENT LIABILITIES:

Note Payable - Beneficial Nat'l	403.03	
Note Payable - Whirlpool Fin.	(14.35)	
Note Payable - First of America	351.92	
Note Payable - Officer	230	
Total Non-Current Liabilities		$970.60

EQUITY:

Capital	($3,216.90)	
Additional PIC - Barr	5,879.54	
Additional PIC - Kearney	(2,104.63)	
Net Income (Loss)	4,796.13	
Total Equity		5,354.14
Total Liabilities and Equity		$12,130.27

Profit & Loss Statement--Third Quarter July

	Current Period		Year To Date	
SALES:				
Sales	$11,994.91	100.00%	$68,922.18	100.00%
Total Sales	11,994.91	100	68,922.18	100
SELLING EXPENSES:				
Licenses, Fees, & Permits	35	0.3	280.26	0.4
Surveillance Expense	2,090.45	17.4	9,732.51	14.1
Total Selling Expenses	2,125.45	17.7	10,012.77	14.5
GENERAL & ADMINISTRATIVE:				
Wages	3,284.70	27.4	$14,650.43	21.3
Auto Expense	2,340.00	19.5	7,058.67	10.2
Bank Charges	118.66	1	314.66	0.5
Advertising	0	0	906.82	1.3
Dues & Subscriptions	0	0	106	0.2
Equipment Rental	300	2.5	1,716.55	2.5
Lease Payments	0	0	40	0.1
Insurance - Workmans Comp	325.25	2.7	919.25	1.3
Insurance - General	176	1.5	1,370.85	2
Insurance - Auto	0	0	602.04	0.9
Legal & Accounting	165	1.4	1,675.58	2.4
Miscellaneous Expense	309.22	2.6	1,258.82	1.8
Office	64.79	0.5	1,346.37	2
Contract Labor	3,184.17	26.5	6,599.51	9.6
Postage	0	0	164.83	0.2
Uniforms	302.44	2.5	998.22	1.4
Rent	0	0	817.5	1.2
Repairs & Maintenance	0	0	403.67	0.6
Supplies	249.8	2.1	1,239.06	1.8
Taxes - FICA & Medicare	251.3	2.1	1,117.90	1.6
Taxes - MESC	88.69	0.7	395.59	0.6
Taxes - FUTA	26.28	0.2	117.19	0.2
Telephone	645.32	5.4	6,126.18	8.9
Answering Service	0	0	148.2	0.2
Travel	0	0	1,630.29	2.4
Meals	0	0	426.51	0.6
Total General & Admin.	11,832.12	98.6	52,150.69	75.7
Net Operating Income (Loss)	1,962.66	16.4	6,758.72	9.8
OTHER (INCOME) AND EXPENSES:				
Fines & Penalties	0	0	74.2	0.1
Interest Income	$0.00	0.00%	$(0.04)	(0.0)
TOTAL OTHER (INCOME) AND EXP	0.0	0.0	74.16	0.1
NET INCOME (LOSS)				
BEFORE TAX	(1,962.66)	(16.4)	6,684.56	9.7
NET INCOME (LOSS)	(1,962.66)	(16.4)	$6,684.56	9.70%

	Current Period		Year To Date		**Profit & Loss Statement--Third Quarter August**
SALES:					
Sales	$13,990.80	100.00%	$82,912.98	100.00%	
Total Sales	13,990.80	100	82,912.98	100	
SELLING EXPENSES:					
Licenses, Fees, & Permits	20	0.1	300.26	0.4	
Surveillance Expense	1,844.47	13.2	11,576.98	14	
Total Selling Expenses	1864.47	13.3	11,877.24	14.3	
GENERAL & ADMINISTRATIVE:					
Wages	3,552.00	25.4	18,202.43	22	
Auto Expense	946.35	6.8	8,005.02	9.7	
Bank Charges	31.38	0.2	346.04	0.4	
Advertising	100	0.7	1,006.82	1.2	
Dues & Subscriptions	0	0	106	0.1	
Equipment Rental	74	0.5	1,790.55	2.2	
Lease Payments	0	0	40	0	
Insurance - Workmans Comp	0	0	919.25	1.1	
Insurance - General	175.88	1.3	1,546.73	1.9	
Insurnace - Auto	0	0	602.04	0.7	
Legal & Accounting	725	5.2	2,400.58	2.9	
Miscellaneous Expense	815.71	5.8	2,074.53	2.5	
Office	192.96	1.4	1,539.33	1.9	
Contract Labor	1,563	11.2	8,162.51	9.8	
Postage	29.7	0.2	194.53	0.2	
Uniforms	460	3.3	1,458.22	1.8	
Rent	0	0	817.5	1	
Repairs & Maintenance	0	0	403.67	0.5	
Supplies	74.66	0.5	1,313.72	1.6	
Taxes - FICA & Medicare	271.75	1.9	1,389.65	1.7	
Taxes - MESC	95.9	0.7	491.49	0.6	
Taxes - FUTA	28.4	0.2	145.59	0.2	
Telephone	853.26	6.1	6,979.44	8.4	
Answering Service	0	0	148.2	0.2	
Travel	0	0	1,630.29	2	
Meals	0	0	426.51	0.5	
Total General & Admin.	9,989.95	71.4	62,140.64	74.9	
Net Operating Income (Loss)	2,136.38	15.3	8,895.10	10.7	
OTHER (INCOME) AND EXPENSES:					
Fines & Penalties	415.38	3	489.58	0.6	
Interest Income	$0.00	0.00%	$(0.04)	(0)	
TOTAL OTHER (INCOME) AND EXPENSE	415.38	3	489.54	0.6	
NET INCOME (LOSS) BEFORE TAX	1,721.00	12.3	8,405.56	10.1	
NET INCOME (LOSS)	$1,721.00	12.30%	$8,405.56	10.10%	

Profit & Loss Statement--Third Quarter September

	Current Period		Year To Date	
SALES:				
Sales	$9,219.23	100.00%	92,132.21	100.00%
Total Sales	9,219.23	100	92,132.21	100
SELLING EXPENSES:				
Licenses, Fees, & Permits	0	0	300.26.2	0.3
Surveillance Expense	2,637.85	28.6	14,214.83	15.4
Total Selling Expenses	2,637.85	28.6	14,515.09	15.8
GENERAL & ADMINISTRATIVE:				
Wages	3,093.75	33.6	21,296.18	23.1
Auto Expense	694.45	7.5	8,699.47	9.4
Bank Charges	67.61	0.7	413.65	0.4
Advertising	0	0	1,006.82	1.1
Dues & Subscriptions	0	0	106	0.1
Equipment Rental	144.25	1.6	1,934.80	2.1
Lease Payments	0	0	40	0
Insurance - Workmans Comp	663.25	7.2	1,582.50	1.7
Insurance - General	176	1.9	1,722.73	1.9
Insurance - Auto	0	0	602.04	0.7
Legal & Accounting	119.15	1.3	2,519.73	2.7
Miscellaneous Expense	481.7	5.2	2,556.23	2.8
Office	179.98	2	1,719.31	1.9
Contract Labor	887.70	9.6	9,050.21	9.8
Postage	50.27	0.5	244.8	0.3
Uniforms	60.69	0.7	1,518.91	1.6
Rent	0	0	817.5	0.9
Repairs & Maintenance	0	0	403.67	0.4
Supplies	147.03	1.6	1,460.75	1.6
Taxes - FICA & Medicare	236.67	2.6	1,626.32	1.8
Taxes - MESC	83.53	0.9	575.02	0.6
Taxes - FUTA	24.75	0.3	170.34	0.2
Telephone	1,599.31	17.3	8,578.75	9.3
Answering Service	0	0	148.2	0.2
Travel	318.13	3.5	1,948.42	2.1
Meals	38.07	0.4	464.58	0.5
Total General & Admin.	9,066.29	98.3	71,206.93	77.3
Net Operating Income (Loss)	2,484.91	27	6,410.19	7
OTHER (INCOME) AND EXPENSES:				
Fines & Penalties	1,124.52	12.2	1,614.10	1.8
Interest Income	$0.00	0.00%	$(0.04)	(0)
TOTAL OTHER (INCOME)				
AND EXP	1,124.52	12.2	1,614.06	1.8
NET INCOME (LOSS)				
BEFORE TAX	(3,609.43)	(39.2)	4,796.13	5.2
NET INCOME (LOSS)	(3,609.43)	(39.20)%	3,609.43	5.20%

CURRENT ASSETS:
Cash in Bank - Checking $32.94
Cash in Bank - Payroll 389.14
Cash in Bank - Savings 0.04
Employee Advances 3,351.00
TOTAL CURRENT ASSETS 3,773.12

PROPERTY AND EQUIPMENT:
Equipment $4,919.13
Accum. Deprec - Equipment 3,141.93
Furniture & Fixtures 429.44
Accum. Deprec - Furn. & Fix. 429.44
Vehicles 10,000.00
Accum. Deprec. - Vehicles 3,995.00
Total Property and Equipme $7,782.20

OTHER ASSETS:
Notes Receivable-Kearney $3,571.94
Suspense $780.33
Total Other Assets $4,352.27

Total Assets $15,907.59

LIABILITIES AND EQUITY

CURRENT LIABILITIES:
American Express $947.10
Payroll Taxes Payable 7,085.68
Total Current Liabilities $8,032.78

NON_CURRENT LIABILITIES:
Note Payable - Beneficial Nat'l 403.03
Note Payable - Whirlpool Fin. (122.35)
Note Payable - First of America 351.92
Note Payable - Officer 10,530.00
Total Non-Current Liabilities $11,162.60

EQUITY:
Capital ($3,216.90)
Additional PIC - Barr 6,031.44
Additional PIC - Kearney 1,467.31
Net Income (Loss) (7,569.64)
Total Equity (3,287.79)

Total Liabilities and Equity $15,907.59

**Profit & Loss
Year Ending**

	Current Period		Year To Date	
SALES:				
Sales	$9,317.65	100.00%	107,239.16	100.00%
Total Sales	9,317.65	100	107,239.16	100
SELLING EXPENSES:				
Licenses, Fees, & Permits	10.35	0.1	482.16	0.4
Surveillance Expense	3,189.25	34.2	22,107.58	20.6
Total Selling Expenses	3,199.60	34.3	22,589.74	21.1
GENERAL & ADMINISTRATIVE:				
Wages	0.00	0	28,307.21	26.4
Auto Expense	740.00	7.9	10,319.47	9.6
Bank Charges	77.5	0.8	517.51	0.5
Advertising	0	0	1,159.02	1.1
Dues & Subscriptions	0	0	106	0.1
Equipment Rental	0	0	2,000.80	1.9
Lease Payments	0	0	40	0
Insurance - Workmans Comp	0	0	1,582.50	1.5
Insurance - General	0	0	1,727.37	1.6
Insurance - Auto	0	0	602.04	0.6
Legal & Accounting	0	0	2,719.73	2.5
Miscellaneous Expense	129	0.3	2,813.03	2.6
Office	289.98	3.1	2,292.21	2.1
Contract Labor	1,860.47	20	14,554.19	13.6
Postage	13.37	0.1	278.07	0.3
Uniforms	146.08	1.6	1,806.99	1.7
Rent	0	0	817.5	0.8
Repairs & Maintenance	0	0	507.67	0.5
Supplies	0	0	1,786.32	1.7
Taxes - FICA & Medicare	0	0	1,955.48	1.8
Taxes - MESC	0	0	764.32	0.7
Taxes - FUTA	0	0	645.17	0.6
Telephone	653.04	7	10,654.36	9.9
Answering Service	0	0	148.2	0.1
Travel	0	0	2,341.59	2.2
Meals	27.4	0.3	576.98	0.5
Total General & Admin.	3,836.84	41.2	91,202.65	85
Net Operating Income (Loss)	2,281.21	24.5	(6,553.23)	(6.1)
OTHER (INCOME) AND EXPENSES:				
Fines & Penalties	0	0	1,016.45	0.9
Interest Income	$0.00	0.00%	$(0.04)	(0)
TOTAL OTHER (INCOME)				
AND EXP	0	0	1,016.41	0.9
NET INCOME (LOSS)				
BEFORE TAX	2,281.21	24.5	(7,569.64)	(7.1)
NET INCOME (LOSS)	2,281.21	24.50%	$(7,569.64)	(7.10)%

Fire Equipment Retailer

BUSINESS PLAN

GALLAGHER'S FIRE SERVICE

432 Janeway Blvd.
Collier, VA 26650

This plan for a fire equipment retailer reveals how paying attention to needs in your community can pay off when it comes to planning your business. Often overlooked, city services, like the fire department, represent a niche market of sorts and can be a source of income as well as the general populace.

- EXECUTIVE SUMMARY

- DESCRIPTION OF THE BUSINESS AND INDUSTRY

- MARKET ANALYSIS

- COMPETITOR ANALYSIS

- STRATEGIC PLAN

- ORGANIZATION

- FINANCIAL PLAN AND FINANCIAL REQUEST

- SUMMARY AND CONCLUSIONS

- APPENDICES

EXECUTIVE SUMMARY

Mission Statement

To improve and promote safety in the home and at the workplace.

Business Objective(s)

We would like to turn it into a full-time family operated business within the next five years.

Competitive Advantage

Our business is a family owned small business that will attract the local community. It is a small area where marketing strategy relies on the promotion of word of mouth advertising.

Market Strategy

Word of mouth advertising and the implementation of safety seminars and product demonstrations.

The Management Team

Steve J. Gallagher, Jr. is the owner and operator. He takes care of all the refurbishing, public relations, and distribution. Dawn D. Gallagher takes care of ordering, marketing, and accounts receivable and accounts payable.

The Product

We will sell new and used extinguishers, hydrants, hoses, signs, smoke detectors, and equipment for several fire departments. Along with selling the products, we will refurbish and refill old extinguishers to make them look and operate like new equipment.

This is a unique business, in that we take old extinguishers that are no longer usable, break them down, completely refurbish the mechanical components, refill with a dry chemical, paint, and reapply stickers.

DESCRIPTION OF THE BUSINESS AND INDUSTRY

The Company

Our company was established out of a market demand. We were offered our first job in February of 1995. We had not even bought all of our equipment and supplies to complete a job of this size. This was what encouraged us to begin our business. We saw the need for the business in the area and the profit that could be made.

The business is very time consuming and a dirty job, but it also allows us to control the growth. It is something that you can work as much or as little as you want to. We also are very conscious about the environment. By refilling and putting to use the old fire extinguishers, they do not take up space in a landfill somewhere.

Our products have taken to the market very well. Some of the business owners didn't realize that there were laws as to how many extinguishers they needed and the distance between them that was allowed.

Competition is always a concern. They may not exist today but you can never verify their non-existence tomorrow. At the present time, the closest business that offers similar services is more than one hour away.

The development of OSHA brought about laws that every business will have at least one extinguisher every 75 feet, and the commercial vehicles will have at least one extinguisher when they are on the highways.

The Industry

The industry will probably level off in the next three to five years, to a sustained rate that will provide us with a comfortable living. Once the demand has been met, we will check into carrying over into someone else's territory.

Fire safety equipment is used for prevention of a fire or to aid in the containing of a fire. The equipment must be in proper functioning condition to work when it is needed.

The Product

MARKET ANALYSIS

Description of the Customer

We decided on our business because of the customer's needs. We heard of a company's need for our business and that other local companies were also looking for this type of business. With the laws, these services are something that all businesses should have for their legal protection. We also read all of the OSHA rules and regulations to find out what most of our customers legally need.

Most of our customers are small businesses. We set up a monthly service contract, which kept our customers buying products and using our services. As a business would grow or expand or a new business opened, their needs would change. Our expectations are that our services will continue to be needed and as new laws and regulations change, we will learn them and pass them on to our customers. Our most effective media is word of mouth.

Target Market Description

Our customer's real criterion to purchase is the law. They want us to come back and make sure their equipment is still able to function properly if they should need it. They like being able to purchase our product or services from their own business, or in some cases, their own homes. We believe this is a service that our customers really like.

Summer is the best season for our market. Construction sites are very profitable for our business. They often have small fires that need to be extinguished, so they use their equipment. This in turn produces a need for us to come out and pick up their product with loaner equipment available until their products are returned.

Price really wouldn't affect our customer's purchases. This is a product that they have to purchase, and we are the only business that sells these types of products. They will pay for better quality. We only get our products from top name supplier. They better brand names really speak for themselves.

Competition has not moved into our territory yet. That was a big factor in our starting this type of business.

Market Influences	OSHA laws and other regulations.
Competitive Advantage(s)	We will keep the customer satisfied with our prices and customer service. We will only purchase the top of the line products to pass on to our customers and also offer a warranty on our services. We make it convenient to the customers by going to them. We keep up with the market changes. Our friendly incomparable services will keep our customers happy.

COMPETITOR ANALYSIS

Existing Competitors	We have no local competitors in the area. In our geographic segment our products and services are provided by no other company.
Potential Competitors	The market at this time is really to small.

STRATEGIC PLAN

Market Strategy	Short-term, provide in existing market, and long-term, to expand products, territory and market share.
Promotion	We use public relations for our promotions. We set up booths at different local events and direct marketing. We also use the newspaper and yellow pages as means of advertisement. This has been very effective.
Suppliers	Our major suppliers are Walter Kiddie, Amick, and Water Works. Their terms are all net 30 days. We try to keep as much on hand as we can, but delivery is less than one week. We try to schedule IIT Inventory, less overhead.
Distribution	Our product will be distributed by ourselves. We deliver our own products to our customers. This gives us a personal relationship with our customers.
Customer Service	On site, and the same business day if material is in stock.

New competition, new OSHA laws (good and bad).

ORGANIZATION

To provide the best equipment for the cheapest money.

Management Philosophy

This is a sole proprictorship. We were required to purchase a business license from the Department of Tax and Revenue in Chuckton, Virginia.

Business Organization

Death of someone, or to hand down to the children.

Succession Plan

Our attorney is Garth C. Blake. We bank locally at the Bank of Thomasville. We carry our insurance through Glenby County Insurance Agency, and our advertising agency is the Citizen's News.

Identification of Firms Assisting the Company

We currently employ two employees. They both are pursuing their college degrees. We have no plans to hire anyone else at the present time. We hope to take the business full-time with our current employees.

Steve will continue taking any classes offered through the local university that will help him to better understand the laws and regulations for the safety equipment.

Staffing Plan

Keep away from too much overhead, and to keep low prices as to not allow competition.

Risk Management Strategies

FINANCIAL PLAN AND FINANCIAL REQUEST

We chose equity financing. This was another reason to chose this type of business. It has a very low start up cost. We invested very little money from our savings to purchase our equipment and supplies we needed.

Financial Request

The cash accounting method best suited our needs. We worked on an as need basis for awhile with products. We would order them on credit and then when we were paid, we would pay our supplier.

Financial Practices

SUMMARY AND CONCLUSION

I believe that my business will prevail, not only for my service, but for the safety my service provides.

Current and Projected Profit and Loss Statement

	Year 1	Year 2	Year 3	Year 4	Year 5
Revenues	32,000	55,000	50,000	62,000	70,000
Less: Cost of Sales	26,000	40,000	35,000	43,000	47,000
Gross Profit	6,000	15,000	15,000	19,000	23,000
Less:					
Salary Expense					
Payroll Expense					
Other Services					
Office Supplies	500	750	750	900	1,050
Maintenance & Repairs	500	500	500	600	
	700				
Advertising	200	500	1,000	1,000	1,000
Automobile	1,000	1,500	1,500	2,000	2,000
Travel & Entertainment					
Consulting Services					
Rent					
Telephone	200	400	400	450	500
Utilities					
Insurance	300	300	300	300	350
Taxes					
Interest	200	500	500	550	600
Depreciation	500	500	500	500	700
Other Expenses					
Total Expenses	3,400	4,950	5,450	6,300	6,900
Operating Profit	2,600	10,050	9,550	12,700	16,100
Add: Other Income					
Less: Other Expenses					
Pretax Profit	2,600	10,050	9,550	12,700	16,100
Income Tax Provision	650	2,512	2,387	3,175	4,025
Net Income after Taxes	1,950	7,538	7,163	9,525	12,075

	Current	Projected
Assets		
Current Assets:		
Cash and equivalents	46,500	60,000
Accounts receivable	3,000	6,000
Inventory (net)	12,000	15,000
Office supplies	500	750
Prepaid items	1,000	1,000
Other current assets	5,000	5,000
Total Current Assets	68,000	87,750
Fixed Assets (net):		
Furniture and fixtures	1,500	1,500
Leasehold improvements		
Machinery and equipment		
Total Fixed Assets		
Other Assets	2,000	4,000
Total Assets	71,500	93,250
Liabilities and net worth:		
Current Liabilities:		
Accounts payable	6,000	12,000
Taxes payable	3,000	5,000
Interest payable		
Current portion of		
long-term debt		
Short-term debt	15,000	30,000
Miscellaneous payables		
Total Current Liabilities	24,000	47,000
Long-term Liabilities		
Long-term debt (net)		
Convertible debentures		
Total Long-Term Liabilities	24,000	47,000
Net Worth:		
Capital stock	71,500	93,250
Paid-in surplus		
Retained earnings		
Total Net Worth	71,500	93,250

Current and Projected Balance Sheet

Franchise Postal Service

BUSINESS PLAN

EXPRESS POSTAL CENTER

8820 Bellevue St.
Anniston, MI 63439

This plan is a good example of a well-chosen franchise. The owners have considered many important factors, such as population growth, demographics, competition, franchise track record, and location. This business is well-positioned in every respect.

- EXECUTIVE SUMMARY

- BUSINESS DESCRIPTION

- LOCATION

- MARKETING

- MANAGEMENT

- FINANCIAL FORECAST

- APPENDIXES

- SOURCE OF FUNDS SCHEDULE

FRANCHISE POSTAL SERVICE
BUSINESS PLAN

EXECUTIVE SUMMARY

Express Postal Center (EPC) is an exciting franchise opportunity with a strong potential for growth. EPC is Postal/Shipping center that will bring a wealth of services to the Anniston area. The overwhelming support and guidance offered through a franchise assures us of a strong foothold in the business community.

American businesses are quickly growing in a direction of small offices I home of offices. individuals are utilizing the home office structure, however they have nether the space nor financial resources to fully equip and operate productively. Every day more and more business people are traveling. working out of hotel rooms, etc. This industry provides support services that business people need and have some to rely on in an office atmosphere. To the private consumer, the Center also offers the same quality services as are offered to the business person, as well as enjoying the specialized attention and assistance provided in this one-stop shipping store.

In recent years, many Fortune companies have undergone aggressive down-sizing programs. In doing so, the disbursement of the virtual office has considerable increased the need for services of offered though businesses such as the EPC Centers.

Franchising combines the initiative and dedication of individuals, along with the economies and scale of a national chain. With the current failure rate of new business in the marketplace, the percentage of success stories lies within franchising. As an EPC Franchise Owner, we can enjoy the best of both worlds: We will be part of a cutting-edge industry and be teamed with the most experienced and powerful company in the industry.

Express Postal Center is a service franchise with locations throughout the United States and internationally. There are currently 3,000 centers worldwide. It is an industry leader in providing private postal/shipping, and business communication services.

EPC was founded in 1980, began franchising in 1980, and became a public company in 1986. EPC is traded on NASDAQ. On average EPC opens one new franchise center each business day. They were ranked in the top quartile in the Businesss Gold 100 as of 1994. The future growth patterns have been aggressively set while continuing to maintain a top-rated standard of excellence and providing overwhelmingly good service.

Express Postal Center is five times larger than their nearest competitor and is one of the fastest growing franchise companies in the world. Because of the network size, they can provide overwhelming support and participation in national programs chat ore not a available to independent businesses or other smaller franchise companies.

One of the most important aspects of this Center is the convenience of the one-stop shipping source. While it may be slightly less expensive to go to the local UPS office or Post office, it has been proven that the average individual will spend a little more money for the conveniences provided in one location. Business hours for the Center will be Monday through Friday from a 8:00am to 6:00pm, and Saturday from 9:00am to 5:00pm with extended hours during the holiday season. These hours will he adjusted as the community dictates a need. People with very busy lives will utilize a full- service postal center rather than make several trips to venous locations, standing in lines, funding parking etc., in order to accomplish the same tasks.

A business person can run their business from the Center. Every business need can be accomplished through the Center. Time is money and the more time a business person can spend doing his/her job efficiently, the more money he/she stands to make.

After looking at many different franchise opportunities, we decided to pursue an EPC franchise for many different reasons. It is a strong, service-oriented business with an extensive support organization backing it. This support is based not only on Corporate but also on the support of all the other stores through state of the art networking. We were also impressed with past growth, future projections, and the overall success rate of the EPCs around the country. All this information was gathered through many phone conversations with different EPC store within Colorado and Michigan. This is overwhelming support from the EPC franchise headquarters and other EPC owners throughout the Country.

The services offered will be promoted through a comprehensive national television advertising program provided through the franchise organization, additional local cable t.v., community newspapers, six local radio stations, two local phone directories, inexpensive circulars circulars with coupons, and visibility of a prime location and signage.

The business venture itself will be organized under a Limited Liability Corporation to incorporate the tax advantages. Possible expansion to m multiple Center locations will be scheduled to take place during year four in The Northern Michigan region. Jack Hall will serve as President of theEPC and Gayle Hall will serve as Vice President. Jack has overt 20 years experience as a Service Engineer for Xerox Corporation, and Gayle has 18 years experience as a Word Processing Manager/Operator.

Initial projections for this EPC indicate that the break even point will be reached between twelve and fifteen months after operations commence, and an adequate cash flow will be maintained thereafter.

BUSINESS DESCRIPTION

The Business venture will be organized as a Limited Liability Corporation. Jack will serve as President of the EPC and Gayle will serve as Vice President. Projected opening date for this store is April 1, 1997. This date was specifically chosen in order to take advantage of advertising programs prior to the highly increased volume of business during the summer tourist season. It also allows for essential and valuable hands-on experience prior to this busy season. This business is not seasonal, but operates on a consistent year-round basis with hectic holiday peaks, such as a retail outlet. There is a slight slow down during the months of February and March, but overall it is consistently busy. Business hours for the Center will be Monday through Friday from 8:00am to 6:00pm, and Saturday from 9:00am to 5:00pm, with extended hours during the holiday season. These hours will adjusted as the community dictates a Deed.

To business customers, this EPC is their copy center, private mail room, shipping department, support staff, office supply store, print shop and communications headquarters. The EPC National Accounts Network offers customer referrals to the EPC from companies such as Xerox, Panasonic, Ricoh and many others. To the consumer, the Center offers the convenience of expert packing and shipping (US Mail, UPS, Federal Express, Western Union, etc.), private mailboxe$, quality photocopying, facsimile machines, binding services, passport photos' lamination, money orders, word processing and dictation transcription services, and on-site computer services. Available industry data indicates a strong need for these services.

The principal products and services available to the consumer include expert packing and shipping, reliable overnight delivery, a full-service copy center, private mailboxes, facsimile transmission/reception, word processing and personal computers, dictation transcription, office/mailing supplies, passport photos, laminating and binding, and fast efficient postal services.

These services will cater to all individuals; no one is excluded. The local merchant needing to package and ship expensive merchandise across the country, to a family member sending grandparents homemade cookies. The ability to have professionally trained people package and ship literally any item across the country offers great comfort, especially in an area like Anniston. This area in Northern Michigan has a strong populous of permanent summer residents. These individuals often require venous services ranging from keeping in close contact with out of state/ country business ventures to shipping personal household items from one location to another on an annual basis.

Labor costs are to be kept at a minimum. One of the owners will be in the Center at all times. Initial labor will be obtained through Greenbriar Temporary Services, keeping taxes and benefits at a minimum.

LOCATION

The site selected for this EPC is 8820 Bellevue Street in Anniston, Michigan (previously the DeeDee's Donuts building) serving Greenbriar, Charleston, and Braynor Counties. Location being of utmost importance, this is an easily accessible location with very strong visibility from both directions on Bellevue Street. The parking area consists of one entrance/exit off Bellevue Street and one alternate entrance/exit off an adjacent street. There arc 25 parking spaces (13 in the front of the building and an additional 12 in the rear of the building), with additional parking available on the street. This site is centrally located in the heart of the Anniston, bordered on both the south and the north side by a shopping centers. In addition, a college is located within 2 miles of the Center. The most recently available traffic count going directly past the Center as recorded, by the State of Michigan shows 28,000 vehicles in 1994, 24,000 vehicles in 1996, with an average of 3 passengers per vehicle. This location is within four blocks from downtown Anniston on the major thoroughfare. The location affords convenient access to residential neighborhoods and provides alternate routes for the consumer. We are very excited about this location and the incredible potential it presents.

MARKETING

On-site evaluate on and the most recent census data provided by the Anniston Regional of Commerce portrays Greenbriar County is a predominantly white, middle to upper middle class community with tourism being a major economic force. The county is a four-season vacation area offering numerous attractions as well as long-standing permanent summer residents. The Anniston/Point Freeman area boasts a wealthy permanent summer community that will be an ongoing financial benefit to the Center. Greenbriar County is a diversified economic development that includes industry, specialty shopping, health care, education, and other services.

The area being includes Greenbriar, Charleston and Braynor counties. According to the most recent census Greenbriar and Charleston counties have a combined population of 52,871. where 38,737 is over the age of 18. The educational level in this two county area is comprised of 80.5% of the population having a high school education or above. The median Household Income for these two counties is $29,016.

The targeted customers are likely to utilize the Center because of the numerous professional services offered and the outstanding quality of service received. One of our main goals is to supply absolutely the highest quality, most accommodating service money can buy. The return customer is of utmost importance and in a service business. Service is what a customer should expect and will receive.

Competition in the area consist of the local UPS office located on M12. This UPS office is approximately 6 miles from Anniston and has very limited business hours (Mon-Fri 3:00pm to 5:00pm). The U.S. Post Office is located at 455 University Street in Anniston.

The Post Office has very limited on street parking and is difficult to get to through downtown traffic. Theonly other competition in town is the Postal Connection located at 4403 East Bellevue Street. This is considered competitive only for rural traffic. In addition, the Postal Connection does not have the extensive services offered through the EPC. The location of this store is on the outskirts of town and offers very limited services (UPS and US mail). The lack of competition for the EPC has been a major contributing factor to locating this Center in Anniston.

The greatest advantage the Center will have over any Competition is the network of the franchise organization. There is overwhelming support received from not only the franchise organization itself, but the professional, committed owners of other Centers, all networked via state of the art computer programs, hardware and software. The training received through the franchise organization includes operating procedures, profit center development, advertising, marketing and management. As a franchise owner, we will benefit from a national network television advertising program designed to increase awareness of the EPC name and services that helps drive business into the Center. For local marketing, we will be using the Yellow Pages as well as being supplied with professional print, radio and television advertising to be used at the local level. All of this, combined with extended hours of operation, location, and the professional staff that will be employed will maximize the earning potential of this business venture

The combined experience and personalities of Jack and Gayle Hall are a perfect fit for this business. Jack is a very dedicated, self-motivated, professional with over 20 years experience dealing with Xerox customers. He combines an outgoing personality with the professional persona needed to gain confidence with both the business customer and the local consumer. In addition, Jack brings a wealth of knowledge about business machine service and mainte-nance. Gayle's experience as a Word Processing Manager within a very large insurance brokerage firm allows her the professional experience needed to coordinate tasks and successfully manage employees. She also has-a very outgoing personality with the warmth of a small town atmosphere. Gayle's skills of typing 120 words per minute coupled with imagination and creativity will be an asset to the customer requiring word processing and on-site computer services.

MANAGEMENT

...continued

Balance Sheet (Forecast)

	1-Aug-96	31-Jul-97	31-Jul-98	31-Jul-99
Assets				
Current Assets:				
Cash and cash equivalents	$30,000.00	$37,665.00	$123,428.00	$239,423.00
Supplies	3,000	3,000	3,000	3,000
Total Current Assets	33,000	40,665	126,428	242,423
Equipment:				
Office Equipment	13,020	13,020	13,020	13,020
Leasehold improvements	21,250	21,250	21,250	21,250
Vehicles	5,000	5,000	5,000	5,000
	39,270	32,630	25,990	19,350
Less accumulated depreciation	0	6,640	13,280	19,920
Total Equip. Net of Accum.				
Depreciation	39,270	32,630	25,990	19,350
Intangibles:				
Organization costs	3,750	3,437	3,124	2,811
Franchise fees	24,950	23,287	21,624	19,961
Total Intangibles	28,700	26,724	24,748	22,772
Total Assets	100,970	100,019	177,166	284,545
Liabilities and Proprietors Capital				
Current maturities of				
long term debt	2,274	2,512	2,775	3,065
Long term debt net of				
current maturities	72,726	70,214	67,439	64,374
Proprietors capital	25,970	27,293	106,952	217,106
Total Liabilities and				
Proprietor's Capital	$100,970.00	$100,019.00	$177,166.00	$284,545.00

Asset	Cost	Source of Funds	
			Source of Funds Schedule
Initial Franchise Fee	$24,950.00	Savings	
Training Fee	$2,100.00	Savings	
Traveling & Living Expenses while Training	$3,600.00	Savings	
Design Fee	$750.00	Savings	
Real Property:			
Mo. Rental Payment	$1,348.00	Savings	
Triple-Net	$245.00	Savings	
Leasehold Improvements: Costs;Sinage; Furniture & Décor Items	$21,250.00	Loan	
Computer Hardware: IBM PC	$4,900.00	Loan	
MBE Software	$3,000.00	Savings	
Equipment	$7,700.00	Loan	
Mailboxes (Minimum 10 Modules)			
Fax Machine (Thermal)			
Cash Register			
Copiers			
Passport Camera			
Finishing Package			
(includes Laminator, Comb Binder, Velobind, Starter Supplies)			
Yellow Pages	$500.00	Savings	
Start-Up Supplies	$5,000.00	Loan	
Security Deposits/Utility Deposits	$3,200.00	Savings	
Insurance	$1,200.00	Savings	
Grand Opening Marketing Fund	$3,500.00	Savings	
Additional Funds	$30,000.00	Loan	
TOTAL	$113,243.00		

Cash Flow:
Scenario One
Year One

Year One		Month 1	Month 2	Month 3	Month 4	Month 5	Month 6
Revenues		$5,000	$5,500	$6,050	$6,655	$7,321	$8,053
Expenses (Variable)							
Advertising		400	440	484	532	586	600
Cost of Goods	(.35)	1,750	1,925	2,118	2,329	2,562	2,819
Misc.	(.01)	50	55	61	67	73	81
Salaries		2,100	2,100	2,100	2,100	2,100	2,100
Supplies	(.01)	50	55	61	67	73	81
Taxes/Ben	(.20)	420	420	420	420	420	420
Telephone		100	100	100	100	100	100
Utilities		200	200	200	200	200	200
Expenses (Fixed)							
Equipment		600	600	600	600	600	600
Insurance		100	100	100	100	100	100
Janitorial		100	100	100	100	100	100
Lease		1,500	1,500	1,500	1,500	1,500	1,500
Loan		1,000	1,000	1,000	1,000	1,000	1,000
Prof. Services		150	150	150	150	150	150
Triple-Net		0	0	0	0	0	0
Total Expenditure		8,520	8,745	8,994	9,265	9,564	9,851
Co-Op Adv.	(.01)	50	55	61	67	73	81
Franchise Royalty		250	275	303	333	366	403
Nat. Media Fund	(.025)	125	138	151	166	183	201
Net Profits		3,945	3,713	3,459	3,176	2,865	2,483
Cash Flow		3,945	7,658	11,117	14,293	17,158	19,641

(10% Increase per/mo 1-9…5% Increase per/mo 10-18…1% Increase per/mo 19-36)

Month 7	Month 8	Month 9	Month 10	Month 11	Month 12	TOTAL
$8,858	$9,743	$10,717	$11,253	$11,815	$12,406	$103,371
600	600	600	600	600	600	6,642
3,100	3,410	3,751	3,939	4,135	4,342	36,180
89	97	107	113	118	124	1,035
2,100	2,100	2,100	2,100	2,100	2,100	25,200
89	97	107	113	118	124	1,035
420	420	420	420	420	420	5,040
100	100	100	100	100	100	1,200
200	200	200	200	200	200	2,400
600	600	600	600	600	600	7,200
100	100	100	100	100	100	1,200
100	100	100	100	100	100	1,200
1,500	1,500	1,500	1,500	1,500	1,500	18,000
1,000	1,000	1,000	1,000	1,000	1,000	12,000
150	150	150	150	150	150	1,800
0	0	0	0	0	0	0
10,148	10,474	10,835	11,035	11,241	11,460	120,132
89	97	107	113	118	124	1,035
443	487	536	563	591	620	5,170
221	244	268	281	295	310	2,583
2,043	1,559	1,029	739	430	108	108
21,684	23,243	24,272	25,011	25,441	25,549	25,549

Cash Flow:
Scenario One
Year Two

Year Two		Month 13	Month 14	Month 15	Month 16	Month 17	Month 18
Revenues		$13,026	$13,678	$14,361	$15,080	$15,834	$16,625
Expenses (Variable)							
Advertising		600	600	600	600	600	600
Cost of Goods	(.35)	4,459	4,788	5,026	5,278	5,542	5,819
Misc.	(.01)	130	137	144	151	158	166
Salaries		3,000	3,000	3,000	3,000	3,000	3,000
Supplies	(.02)	130	137	144	151	158	166
Taxes/Ben	(.20)	600	600	600	600	600	600
Telephone		100	100	100	100	100	100
Utilities		200	200	200	200	200	200
Expenses (Fixed)							
Equipment		600	600	600	600	600	600
Insurance		100	100	100	100	100	100
Janitorial		100	100	100	100	100	100
Lease		1,560	1,560	1,560	1,560	1,560	1,560
Loan		1,000	1,000	1,000	1,000	1,000	1,000
Prof. Services		150	150	150	150	150	150
Triple-Net		0	0	0	0	0	0
Total Expenses		12,729	13,072	13,324	13,590	13,868	14,161
Co-Op Adv.	(,01)	130	137	144	151	158	166
Franchise Royalty	(.05)	651	684	718	754	792	831
Nat. Media Fund	(.025)	330	342	359	377	396	416
Net Profits		814	557	184	208	620	1,051
Cash Flow		26,363	26,920	27,104	26,896	26,276	25,225

(10% Increase per/mo 1-9...5% Increase per/mo 10-18...1% Increase per/mo 19-36)

Month 19	Month 20	Month 21	Month 22	Month 23	Month 24	TOTAL
$16,791	$16,959	$17,129	$17,300	$17,473	$17,648	$191,904
600	600	600	600	600	600	7,200
5,877	5,936	6,055	6,116	6,177	67,068	83,449
168	170	171	173	175	176	1,919
3,000	3,000	3,000	3,000	3,000	3,000	36,000
168	170	171	173	175	176	1,919
600	600	600	600	600	600	7,200
100	100	100	100	100	100	1,200
200	200	200	200	200	200	2,400
600	600	600	600	600	600	7,200
100	100	100	100	100	100	1,200
100	100	100	100	100	100	1,200
1,560	1,560	1,560	1,560	1,560	1,560	18,720
1,000	1,000	1,000	1,000	1,000	1,000	12,000
150	150	150	150	150	150	1,800
0	0	0	0	0	0	0
14,023	14,286	14,347	14,411	14,476	14,539	167,026
168	170	171	173	175	176	1,919
840	848	856	865	874	882	9,595
420	424	428	433	437	441	4,803
1,140	1,231	1,327	1,418	1,511	1,610	37,829
24,085	22,854	21,527	20,109	18,598	16,988	16,988

Cash Flow:
Scenario One
Year Three

Year Three	Month 25, 26, 27	Month 28, 29, 30	Month 31, 32, 33	Month 34, 35, 36	**TOTAL**
Revenues	$17,824.00	$18,364.00	$18,921.00	$19,495.00	$74,604.00
	18,003	18,548	19,111	19,690	75,352
	18,183	18,734	19,302	19,887	76,106
	54,010	55,646	57,334	59,072	226,062
Expenses (Variable)					
Advertising	1,800	1,800	1,800	1,800	7,200
Cost of Goods (.35)	18,904	19,476	20,067	20,676	79,123
Misc. (.01)	540	556	573	591	2,260
Salaries	9,000	9,000	9,000	9,000	36,000
Supplies (.02)	540	556	573	591	2,260
Taxes/Ben	1,800	1,800	1,800	1,800	7,200
Telephone	300	300	300	300	1,200
Utilities	600	600	600	600	2,400
Expenses (Fixed)					
Equipment	1,800	1,800	1,800	1,800	7,200
Insurance	300	300	300	300	1,200
Janitorial	300	300	300	300	1,200
Lease	4,866	4,866	4,050	4,050	19,464
Loan	3,000	3,000	3,000	3,000	12,000
Prof. Services	450	450	450	450	1,800
Triple-Net	0	0	0	0	0
Total Expenses	44,200	44,804	45,429	46,074	180,507
Co-Op Adv. (.01)	784	808	832	857	2,260
Franchise Royalty (.05)	3,920	4,039	4,161	4,287	11,303
Nat Media Fund (.025)	1,351	1,391	1,434	1,476	5,652
Net Profits	5,219	6,113	7,031	7,977	26,340
Cash Flow	11,769	5,656	1,375	9,352	9,352

(10% Increase per/mo 1-9...5% Increase per/mo 10-18... 1% Increase per/mo 19-36)

This page left intentionally blank to accomodate tabular material following.

Cash Flow:
Scenario Two
Year One

Year One		Month 1	Month 2	Month 3	Month 4	Month 5	Month 6
Revenues		$5,000	$5,500	$6,050	$6,655	$7,321	$8,053
Expenses (Variable)							
Advertising		400	440	484	532	586	600
Cost of Goods	(.35)	1,750	1,925	2,118	2,329	2,562	2,819
Misc.	(.01)	50	55	61	67	73	81
Salaries		3,000	3,000	3,000	3,000	3,000	3,000
Supplies	(.02)	100	110	122	134	146	162
Taxes/Ben	(.20)	600	600	600	600	600	600
Telephone		100	100	100	100	100	100
Utilities		200	200	200	200	200	200
Expenses (Fixed)							
Equipment		600	600	600	600	600	600
Insurance		100	100	100	100	100	100
Janitorial		100	100	100	100	100	100
Lease		1,350	1,350	1,350	1,350	1,350	1,350
Prof. Services		150	150	150	150	150	150
Loan Payment		700	700	700	700	700	700
Total Expenses		9,200	9,430	9,685	9,962	10,267	10,562
Co-Op Adv.	(,01)	50	55	61	67	73	81
Franchise Royalty	(.05)	250	275	303	333	366	403
Nat. Media Fund	(.025)	125	138	151	166	183	201
Net Profits		4,625	4,398	4,150	3,873	3,568	3,194
Cash Flow		4,625	9,023	13,173	17,046	20,614	23,808

(10% Increase per/mo 1-12)

Month 7	Month 8	Month 9	Month 10	Month 11	Month 12	TOTAL
$8,858	$9,743	$10,717	$11,790	$12,969	$14,266	$ 106,922
600	600	600	600	600	600	6,642
3,100	3,410	3,751	4,127	4,539	4,993	37,423
89	97	107	118	130	143	1,071
3,000	3,000	3,000	3,000	3,000	3,000	36,000
178	194	214	236	260	286	2,142
600	600	600	600	600	600	7,200
100	100	100	100	100	100	1,200
200	200	200	200	200	200	2,400
600	600	600	600	600	600	7,200
100	100	100	100	100	100	1,200
100	100	100	100	100	100	1,200
1,350	1,350	1,350	1,350	1,350	1,350	16,200
150	150	150	150	150	150	1,800
700	700	700	700	700	700	8,400
10,867	11,201	11,572	11,981	12,429	12,922	130,078
89	97	107	118	130	143	1,071
443	487	536	590	648	713	5,347
221	244	268	295	324	357	2,673
2,762	2,286	1,766	1,194	562	131	131
26,570	28,856	30,622	32,748	33,748	34,158	32,247

Cash Flow:
Scenario Two Year
Two

Year Two		Month 13	Month 14	Month 15	Month 16	Month 17	Month 18
Revenues		$14,979	$15,728	$16,515	$17,340	$18,207	$19,117
Expenses (Variable)							
Advertising		600	600	600	600	600	600
Cost of Goods	(.35)	5,243	5,505	5,780	6,069	6,372	6,691
Misc.	(.01)	150	157	165	173	182	191
Salaries		3,000	3,000	3,000	3,000	3,000	3,000
Supplies	(.02)	300	314	330	346	364	382
Taxes/Ben	(.20)	600	600	600	600	600	600
Telephone		100	100	100	100	100	100
Utilities		200	200	200	200	200	200
Expenses (Fixed)							
Equipment		600	600	600	600	600	600
Insurance		100	100	100	100	100	100
Janitorial		100	100	100	100	100	100
Lease		1,350	1,350	1,350	1,350	1,350	1,350
Prof. Services		150	150	150	150	150	150
Loan Payment		700	700	700	700	700	700
Total Expenses		13,193	13,476	13,775	14,088	14,418	14,764
Co-Op Adv.	(,01)	150	157	165	173	182	191
Franchise Royalty	(.05)	479	786	826	867	910	956
Nat. Media Fund	(.025)	374	393	413	434	455	478
Net Profits		783	916	1,336	1,778	2,242	2,728
Cash Flow		31,464	30,548	29,212	27,434	25,192	22,464

(5% Increase per/mo 13-24)

Month 19	Month 20	Month 21	Month 22	Month 23	Month 24	TOTAL
$20,073	$21,077	$22,131	$23,237	$24,399	$25,619	$238,422
600	600	600	600	600	600	7,200
7,026	7,377	7,746	8,133	8,540	8,967	83,449
201	211	221	232	244	256	2,383
3,000	3,000	3,000	3,000	3,000	3,000	36,000
402	422	442	464	488	512	4,766
600	600	600	600	600	600	7,200
100	100	100	100	100	100	1,200
200	200	200	200	200	200	2,400
600	600	600	600	600	600	7,200
100	100	100	100	100	100	1,200
100	100	100	100	100	100	1,200
1,350	1,350	1,350	1,350	1,350	1,350	16,200
150	150	150	150	150	150	1,800
700	700	700	700	700	700	8,400
15,129	15,510	15,909	16,329	16,772	17,235	180,598
201	211	221	232	244	256	2,383
1,004	1,054	1,107	1,162	1,220	1,281	11,652
502	527	553	581	610	640	5,960
3,237	3,775	4,341	4,933	5,553	6,207	37,829
19,227	15,452	11,111	6,178	625	5,582	5,582

Cash Flow:
Scenario Two
Year Three

Year Three	Month 25, 26, 27	Month 28, 29, 30	Month 31, 32, 33	Month 34, 35, 36	**TOTAL**
Revenues	$25,875.00	$26,659.00	$27,467.00	$28,299.00	$108,300.00
	26,134	26,926	27,742	28,582	109,384
	26,395	27,195	28,019	28,868	110,477
	78,404	80,780	83,228	85,749	328,161
Expenses (Variable)					
Advertising	1,800	1,800	1,800	1,800	7,200
Cost of Goods (.35)	27,441	28,273	29,130	30,012	14,856
Misc. (.01)	784	808	832	857	3,281
Salaries	9,000	9,000	9,000	9,000	36,000
Supplies (.02)	1,568	1,616	1,664	1,714	6,562
Taxes/Ben	2,400	2,400	2,400	2,400	9,600
Telephone	300	300	300	300	1,200
Utilities	600	600	600	600	2,400
Expenses (Fixed)					
Equipment	1,800	1,800	1,800	1,800	7,200
Insurance	300	300	300	300	1,200
Janitorial	300	300	300	300	1,200
Lease	4,050	4,060	4,050	4,050	16,200
Prof. Services	450	450	450	450	1,800
Total Expenses	50,793	51,697	52,626	53,583	208,699
Co-Op Adv. (.01)	784	808	832	857	3,281
Franchise Royalty (.05)	3,920	4,039	4,161	4,287	16,407
Loan Payment	2,100	2,100	2,100	2,100	8,400
Net Profits	20,807	22,136	23,509	24,922	91,374
Cash Flow	26,389	48,525	72,034	96,956	96,956

(1% per/mo 25-36)

Freight Expediting

BUSINESS PLAN

GAZELLE EXPEDITING INC.

900 St. Clair Blvd.
Chicago, IL 60609

August 1990

Gazelle Expediting seeks to create a nationwide network of air freight forwarding agents. It plans to accomplish this by recruiting independent freight expediters who are being pinched by competition, as well as agents who are dissatisfied with their current network relationship. Gazelle proposes to provide corporate support functions and perquisites to motivate its agents to excel, thus ensuring the growth of Gazelle Expediting.

- INTRODUCTION

- EXECUTIVE SUMMARY

- MANAGEMENT COMPANY DESCRIPTION

- MARKET PLAN

- COMPETITIVE ANALYSIS

- TARGET MARKET

- SPECIFIC MARKET ACTIVITIES

- ACTION PLAN

- FINANCIAL PLAN

- ACCOUNT LIST

FREIGHT EXPEDITING
BUSINESS PLAN

INTRODUCTION

The goal of Gazelle Expediting Inc. is to establish a worldwide air freight forwarding network consisting of independent agent members, operating under one corporate name.

In today's competitive marketplace there exists the opportunity to establish a cohesive group of independent agents. These agents can be successful by working within a well-planned organization offering discounted transportation costs and effective marketing strategies. You can attract well-qualified, motivated, independent agent members by giving them unique opportunities within the corporation, such as:

- a progressive, participatory management structure;
- profit sharing;
- access to group purchase of various insurances and pension plans.

The company will grow based on the acquisition of agents nationwide operating under the Gazelle Expediting corporate identity. Ms. Smith (see executive summary), a current agent member, understands the needs, desires and motivations of her associates. Well respected in the air freight industry, she will use her extensive contacts for the development and growth of Gazelle Expediting.

Agent members who want to not only survive but to be successful and profitable must be aligned with a finely-tuned, streamlined organization. Gazelle Expediting will have progressive "state of the art" techniques and equipment for minimizing costs and maximizing profits, including an IBM computer system designed specifically for the air freight industry. Advanced administrative support systems will be geared to the growth of the individual agents and the corporation as a whole. By custom designing our strategies we will have the flexibility to meet the needs of various marketplaces. Gazelle Expediting will continually strive to acquire only the best available agent members so that all involved will experience exemplary levels of service and commitment to our business.

Based on the acquisition of a minimum of 6 agent members per year, first-year revenues should total $3,200,000. Projected growth should lead to gross revenues of $37,250,000 with 32 established agent members by the fifth year.

EXECUTIVE SUMMARY

Owner and president of Gazelle Expedited, Inc., Jane Q. Smith, will be the president and chief executive officer of Gazelle Expediting Inc. Gazelle Expedited was incorporated in 1988 and is located in Chicago, Illinois. The business has been growing over 200% per annum and has revenues exceeding $60,000 monthly.

Ms. Smith graduated from Illinois State University with a B.S. degree (cum laude). Ms. Smith has over 14 years of air freight experience. Half of those years were spent with the former number-one domestic forwarding company, Burlington Northern Air Freight. The other years were split between an independent agent and an agent member operation. Ms. Smith has experience in various management positions ranging from operations, sales, marketing and administrative duties. Her instincts and abilities have been developed, enabling her to make appropriate management decisions, which are critical in this rapidly changing field. Ms. Smith has established and maintained the significant nationwide business contacts necessary for the superior performance demanded in this field. She has the background and qualities necessary to direct and guide a successful air freight forwarding network.

Gazelle Expediting Inc. is a management company incorporated in the State of Illinois. The primary purpose of Gazelle Expediting is to form and manage a network of agent members under one national banner that will facilitate the movement of freight from point of pick up to its ultimate destination.

Agent members will be responsible for local sales, marketing, pick up, packaging, routing, delivery, freight monitoring, customer service contact and expediting.

Gazelle Expediting will provide the necessary administrative support systems to the agent members. This will include:

- marketing support functions;
- accounts receivable processing;
- collections;
- accounts payable relative to all transportation services;
- transportation negotiations and contracts for worldwide discounts with various vendors;
- strategic planning and direction for maintenance marketing and growth;
- national account coordination;
- operations policies and procedures.

Computer systems will be designed for rapid invoicing of receivables, quick turnaround of all critical documents, and the necessary cash management controls.

An in-depth knowledge of the industry, coupled with creative problem solving and rapid decision making will allow the corporation to both support and motivate agents to excel in performance, paving the way for their substantial growth.

Strong management and advanced support systems will permit agent members to focus their energies on marketing and customer satisfaction, thereby maximizing their market growth opportunities. This will be reflected in the individual growth of the agent members and the total growth of the management organization, Gazelle Expediting Inc.

MANAGEMENT COMPANY DESCRIPTION

Air cargo is an $8 billion a year industry which has experienced a growth of approximately 20% per annum for the past several years. While market growth is expected to slow for the coming 3-5 years, it is still expected to exceed the GNP.

The industry has six significant cargo carriers who own their equipment. These six players handle approximately 75% of the air cargo business, comprised of both direct customer shipments and air freight forwarders' shipments. Identifiable air freight forwarders number between 500 and 600. Their organizations are either wholly owned, agent member, or independents. Local independents are estimated to number approximately 15,000.

Contracting agents for Gazelle Expediting will be drawn from both existing air freight forwarders and independent agents. These agents are generating revenues from $500,000 to $10,000,000 annually with net profits ranging from 5% to 10%. Agents will generally be located within a quarter mile of a major metropolitan airport.

Gazelle Expediting will solicit agent members based upon their reputation for excelling in performance and growth. Integrity and trust are additional selecting factors in this industry, which operates based on verbal direction and quick decision making.

Cash flow and/or the increase in profits and services are the major reasons to align with an agent member corporation. Payables are due within 15 to 30 days and receivables are on a 30- to 90-day float. The major cost factors are the actual transportation charges. These costs are discounted based on escalating volume, allowing the larger networks to be more competitive and putting the smaller organizations at a disadvantage, thereby giving independent agents a strong motivation to join a growth-oriented organization.

MARKET PLAN

A three-year exclusive contract will be established with each agent member, specifying each party's respective responsibilities and defining the commission split. For providing their management and billing services, Gazelle Expediting will retain 40% of the gross net profit (gross revenue minus all related transportation costs). This is equal to approximately 17.4% of the gross revenue.

Following is a conservative growth expectation forecast, upon which the financial projections have been based. The first agent member will be Gazelle Expedited (owned by Ms. Smith). Five more agent members have been pre-selected, with two verbally committed to membership and three expressing extremely strong intentions of joining the organization. These agents have gross revenues ranging from $500,000 to $3,000,000 per year. Agent members will be expected to sell at a minimum gross profit margin of 40%, ensuring profitable margins. A minimum of six new agent members will be added each year.

Advanced administrative systems handling support functions will be in place the first month of operation. Agent members and independents who are experiencing dissatisfaction with their current arrangements and who meet previously stated guidelines will be contacted. Unique incentives for participation will include a Member Advisory Council, profit sharing based on profitability and gross revenues, and opportunities to participate in group insurance and pension plans. Operational and marketing material, designed to attract new business, will be supplied free of charge. Airline and transportation discounts are already in place and escalating discounts will be available as volume increases. National account coordination will be handled through Gazelle Expediting Inc. headquarters.

Marketing efforts will be concentrated in the top one hundred metropolitan areas of the United States and Canada. Market research to locate and target the most suitable agent members and independents will be an ongoing operational task.

Gazelle Expediting will have six agent members generating $3,200,000 the first year of operation. Six additional agent members will be added in Year 2 and seven agent members in Year 3, generating $13,650,000 in revenues. Years 4 and 5 see additional agent member acquisitions totaling 32 members and generating $37,250,000. Emphasis will shift to include both domestic and international growth until an appropriate balance is reached, allowing us to take advantage of the free trade agreement with Canada, the European unification and other opportunities as they become available.

COMPETITIVE ANALYSIS

Major competitors include General, United, All-Purpose, Lineway, Best, First By Air, and other similar air freight management organizations. All are existing agent member network corporations with established market recognition factors. Gross revenues differ per corporation from a low of $5 million to a high of $100 million. Varying degrees of ultimate customer and agent member loyalty exist, based on pricing policies and ability to deliver expected levels of service.

These companies offer differing kinds of transportation discounts, negotiated contractual agreements, printed market materials, accounts receivable and payable processing, and administrative support systems. The contracts with the agent members offer commission splitting of gross net profit (gross invoice minus all transportation costs). The commission split ranges from 50/50 to 35/65, with 35% to the management corporation and 65% to the agent member.

Major market weaknesses include ineffective accounts receivable and payable management, untimely commission payments, lack of organization and direction, and inadequate marketing support systems. While agent members have virtually no say in operational policies and procedures, almost all marketing planning and strategy development is left up to the individual agent member to implement.

Agent member management companies are generally outdated in their management systems and policies, which has resulted in reduced profitably and growth and increased agent member dissatisfaction. Agent members feel thwarted by the various obstacles and, hence, lack motivation to develop and excel.

TARGET MARKET

The target market consists of mid-sized ($500,000 to $10,000,000 per annum) independent and agent member forwarders who are located in the top 100 major metropolitan areas and who aspire to grow in an aggressive, controlled manner.

These agents routinely handle shipments of 70-plus pounds at an average 40%, or better, gross profit. They excel in handling expedited and critical freight movements, providing exemplary service and commitment to their customers. They have demonstrated in their marketplace that values such as trust, integrity and personal involvement are keys to their success.

They have operations, marketing and cash flow considerations, which will be enhanced by aligning themselves with Gazelle Express Service.

Extensive feedback from various agent members indicates a crucial need for a strong management company with which to align.

SPECIFIC MARKET ACTIVITIES

- Informal survey of random and selected air freight forwarders and independents regarding their ideal wants and needs from a management company.
- Confidential discussions with a preferred group of agent members regarding likelihood of changing alliance, and of the potential structure, organization and services of Gazelle Expediting.
- Review of computer systems having the capacity needed for processing the business and providing unique management reports.
- Conceptual design of selected marketing material.
- Review of existing agent contracts.
- Negotiations of contracts with major transportation carriers.
- Investigating group insurance contracts for agent member coverage.
- Reviewing business insurances, e.g., cargo, liability.
- Establishing a contract for the agent members, detailing the respective responsibilities of each party and defining the sales commission.
- Developing an incentive program for the independent owner to participate in profit sharing based on gross sales and profitability.

ACTION PLAN

Pre-Operational

- Incorporate business.
- Negotiate and sign office lease agreement.
- Set up office, equipment, supplies, telephone system, etc.
- Select and order computer system and related software.
- Establish bank relationship.
- Arrange for receivables financing.
- Establish legal and accounting relationships; ensure necessary compliance.
- Finalize standard agent member contract.
- Obtain necessary insurances.
- Affiliate with a Marketing/PR firm.
- Develop an in-depth marketing plan to identify and target potential agent members.
- Sign agreement with Gazelle Expedited Inc. to become the first agent member of Gazelle Expediting.

Month 1
- Sign agreement with second agent member.
- Continue agent member solicitation.
- Finalize marketing materials; print and distribute.
- Set up marketing tracking system.
- Distribute operational policies and procedures.
- Establish accounting procedures and implement.
- Hire secretary/receptionist, administrator and accounting personnel, as needed.
- Continue transportation negotiations.

Month 2
- Sign on third agent member.
- Continue agent member solicitation.
- Monitor and refine operational, accounting and communications procedures.

Months 3 & 4
- Sign on an additional 2 agent members.
- Continue agent member solicitation.
- Initiate PR Plan.
- Hire administrative analyst and A/R person.

Months 5 & 6
- Sign on an additional 2 agent members.
- Continue solicitation activities.
- Continue PR plan.
- Evaluate results to date; implement necessary modifications.

Months 7-12
- Continue solicitation activities.
- Hire additional A/R personnel.
- Continue review/evaluation of progress to date.
- Develop and implement national advertising plan.
- Create Member Advisory Council.
- Identify target markets and accounts.
- Develop second-year Strategic Market Plan and make appropriate operational adjustments.

FINANCIAL PLAN

Attached is the income and cash flow projection for five years. Financing is based on receivables (partial customer list available upon request), borrowing and an initial investment of $50,000. The interest rate used is 12.5%. The cost of sale is 82.6% of gross revenues, based on paying 56.5% for transportation costs and 26.1% for commission. The financial projections follow the market plan previously discussed.

	Year 1	Year 2	Year 3	Year 4	Year 5
Revenue	3,200,000	7,500,000	13,650,000	20,750,000	37,250,000
Cost of Sales	2,643,200	6,195,000	11,274,900	17,139,500	30,768,500
Gross Profit	556,800	1,305,000	2,375,100	3,610,500	6,481,500
Expenses	372,350	598,400	1,051,050	1,463,500	2,462,500
Interest	25,000	37,500	187,500	0	0
	397,350	635,900	1,069,800	1,463,500	2,462,500
Income	**159,450**	**669,100**	**1,305,300**	**2,147,000**	**4,019,000**
Fed Income Tax	54,213	227,494	443,802	729,980	1,366,460
Net Income	105,237	441,606	861,498	1,417,020	2,652,540
Receivables	-533,333	-716,667	-1,025,000	-1,183,333	-2,750,000
Payables	220,267	295,983	423,325	488,717	1,135,750
Cash Available (Used)	207,830	20,923	259,823	722,403	1,038,290
Receivable Loan	200,000	100,000	-300,000	0	0
Investment	50,000	0	0	0	0
Cash Flow	**42,170**	**120,923**	**-40,177**	**722,403**	**1,038,290**

Income and Cash Flow Projection

	Year 1	Year 2	Year 3	Year 4	Year 5
Payroll	135,000	240,000	485,000	690,000	1,250,000
Payroll Taxes	33,750	60,000	121,250	172,500	312,500
Office Expense	20,000	23,000	25,000	30,000	35,000
Computer Expense	50,000	60,000	75,000	85,000	105,000
Communications	24,000	36,000	54,000	81,000	160,000
Insurance	10,000	20,000	35,000	50,000	80,000
Professional	20,000	30,000	45,000	55,000	70,000
Marketing	25,000	40,000	65,000	90,000	120,000
Rent	9,600	14,400	20,000	25,000	35,000
Printing	20,000	40,000	75,800	125,000	225,000
Travel & Ent	25,000	35,000	50,000	60,000	70,000
Total Expenses	**372,350**	**598,400**	**1,051,050**	**1,463,500**	**2,462,500**

Expense Analysis

A partial account list is available upon request. It lists the names, addresses and phone numbers of more than 70 accounts. Most of these are in the metropolitan area, although approximately 10% of them are located throughout the United States and Ontario, Canada.

ACCOUNT LIST

Gift Store

BUSINESS PLAN

CRYSTAL CREEK GIFTS

1329 Thompson Blvd.
Charlevoix, MI 49625

This gift and clothing store is located in a thriving tourist location. The summer season's influx of travelers will make up the bulk of this store's clientele, which has prepared carefully for it's market by choosing affordable and attractive products with wide appeal. This business plan is thorough in it's analysis of patrons and financing.

- STATEMENT OF PURPOSE

- BASIC BUSINESS DEFINITION

- MARKET ANALYSIS

- MARKETING PLAN

- ORGANIZATION AND MANAGEMENT

- MANAGEMENT

- SUMMARY OF SOURCES AND USE OF FUNDS

- CAPITAL EQUIPMENT

- START-UP COSTS

- WORKING CAPITAL

GIFT STORE
BUSINESS PLAN

STATEMENT OF PURPOSE

This business Plan has been developed as a planning, operating, and policy guide for the owners of Crystal Creek and as a financing proposal to submit to local financial institutions.

Mike and Hannah Taylor are requesting a loan of $70,000 and a credit line of $25,000. This sum will be sufficient to purchase capital equipment and beginning inventory to cover start-up costs and to provide adequate working capital to successfully initiate this new business. The legal structure will be set up as a proprietorship. The anticipated opening date is April 1, 1997.

BASIC BUSINESS DEFINITION

The Crystal Creek Gifts is a year-round retail clothing store, located at 1329 Thompson Blvd. in Charlevoix, Michigan. It will service the summer tourist trade (80% of business between May-October). The merchandise carried will be men's sportswear (20%), ladies' sportswear (50%) with accessories at (10%), and gift items (20%). We aim to carry unique products and high quality apparel.

MARKET ANALYSIS

The target market for Crystal Creek is concentrated on the tourist to our area. He/she is a professional, well-educated, up-scale clientele who's taste in clothing and gifts reflect an unique, active, lifestyle. The target market income is $25,000 and higher. Crystal Creek will focus on these individuals during the tourist season, May through October.

Downtown Charlevoix attracts tourists who are walking up and down Thompson looking for items which they don't find at big city malls and an item which will remind them of their trip to Charlevoix.Thompson Boulevard also attracts a local or seasonal resident who enjoys the amenities of downtown. These include personal service, holiday shopping nights, "Friday Night Live," and the friendly atmosphere.

MARKETING PLAN: PRODUCT DIFFERENTIATION STRATEGY

To offer products that are different from competition in ways other than price.

Products and Services

Ladies apparel will consist of "groupings" of clothing which coordinate and sell each other. An example of this would be shorts, tees, and sweaters in sporty colors; cotton and twill bottoms, fun-embroidered sweatshirts. Menswear includes Rugby-stripe golf shirts, cotton sweaters, golf caps, and nautical and golf-embroidered sweatshirts. Brand names will be recognizable for their quality. Gift items will be moderately prices items: flowerpots, calendars, frames, birdhouses, many impulse items which will intrigue customers from the front display window.

Pricing

Crystal Creek will use a 50% mark-up for fashion goods. A 60% mark-up for fleece embroidered goods will compensate for seasonal markdowns. Gift items will be evaluated for quality and priced accordingly.

Promotion

The promotional budget for Crystal Creek is approximately $200 a month in the off-season, which would cover the cost of small newspaper ads. During the season, in addition to newspaper ads, the store plans to run ads in up-scale local magazines, possibly do a postcard mailing to customers.

The advantage for Crystal Creek's to be on Thompson Boulevard is tremendous. Not only does Thompson Boulevard have the best walking traffic, but being in an area of other successful stores attracts people to the area. Other advantages to downtown include participation in the Downtown Development Authority which promotes downtown throughout the year via craft shows, "Friday Night Live," holiday shopping nights, etc.

Attorney: David Stanford, Esq., 410 S. North Street, Charlevoix, MI 49625

Accountant: Linda Persimmons, 346 E. Thompson Boulevard, P.O. Box 2050, Charlevoix, MI 49625

Insurance Agent: Jerry Smith 515 Baylor Street, Charlevoix, MI 49625

Other: Rick Bameldi, Economic Development Contact for Northwest Michigan Council of Governments, P.O. Box 67809, Charlevoix, MI 49625

Mike and Hannah Taylor, the owners of Crystal Creek, will be responsible for ordering inventory, merchandising, maintaining accounting and inventory records, supervising day-to-day records operations and hiring, training, and scheduling employees other than part-time help in the busiest part of the season. Mike and Hannah will be responsible for the majority of working hours.

Mike Taylor has a marketing degree from Ferris State University. He also has 15 years' experiencein merchandising day-to-day operations of a business in addition to experience in hiring, training employees.

Hannah Taylor is a graduate of Michigan State University's merchandising program and has many years experience as a buyer and shop manager at private golf clubs, resorts, and retail stores.

Mike and Hannah Taylor have owned their own shop before. In 1989, they secured a loan from Second National Bank in Newton, Michigan, to operate the ProShop Express at Wanatchee Country Club. The loan was paid back, on time, over the course of the golf season. The following year, 1990, a loan was also taken out and paid back on time.

Sources

Owners' Equity Investment	$7,000
Requested Bank Loan	95,000
Total	$102,000

Uses

Capital Equipment	$13,900
Beginning Inventory	50,000
Start-Up Costs	9,500
Working Capital	28,600
Total	$102,000

Security Collateral:

Business Assets (capital, equipment, inventory)	$63,900
Lien against equity in personal residence	17,100
Common Stock - Bill Knapp	14,000
Total Collateral	$95,000

Summary of Sources and Uses of Funds

Sources:

Owner(s) investment (including cash, equipment, inventory, etc.)	$7,000
Requested bank loan	70,000
Other source: Line of Credit	25,000
Other source:	
Total	$102,000

Uses:

Capital equipment (total from Worksheet 20)	13,900
Beginning inventory (total from Worksheet 21)	50,000
Start-up costs (total from Worksheet 22)	9,500
Working capital (total from Worksheet 23)	28,600
Other: (with inventory)	$102,000

CAPITAL EQUIPMENT

Office furniture, business machines (computer equipment, copier, FAX machine, cashregister, typewriter), store fixtures (display cases, shelves, stands, counters), delivery equipment, air conditioners, production machinery and construction equipment

List of only the equipment needed to start business, not what is already owned:

Equipment Cost

Fixtures	$9,000
Computer	3,000
Copier	600
Fax	500
Cash Register	500
Stereo	500
Television	300
Total	$13,900

BEGINNING INVENTORY

Products Cost	
Merchandise & Gifts	$50,000
Total	$50,000

START-UP COSTS

Start-up costs are one-time expenses that are incurred prior to opening our business. Some of these expense categories, such as professional services and advertising, also may be on-going expenses. Therefore, they may be part of your working capital estimate for the first six months of operation.

Remodeling and decorating	$3,000
Interior and exterior signs	1,000
Installation of fixtures and equipment	1,000
Telephone installation	200
Rent deposit	1,000
Utility company deposits	500
Licenses and permits	500
Legal, accounting and other professional fees (for start-up)	300
Advertising and promotion (for start-up)	1,000
Office supplies (initial inventory)	500
Other supplies (initial inventory)	500
Total	$9,500

Minimum working capital requirements should be estimated by totaling projected expenses for the first six months of Year 1.

Item	Total Estimated Expenses for Months 1 through 6
Advertising	$5,900
Dues and subscriptions	400
Insurance	750
Interest	3,600
Maintenance and repairs	500
Postage and supplies	1,000
Professional services	1,000
Rent	7,800
Salaries/wages	3,000
Taxes	350
Telephone	600
Travel/entertainment	3,150
Utilities	550
Total	$ 28,600

...continued

Projected Income Statement: Detail by Month

	Jan	Feb	March	April	May	June
Gross Sales				10,000	15,000	20,000
Less: Cost of good sold				6,000	8,000	11,000
Gross Profit				4,000	7,000	9,000
Expenses						
Advertising			700	1,200	700	1,300
Credit card service charges				75	75	200
Depreciation			225	225		
Dues and subscriptions			200	200		
Insurance			375			
Interest			700	700	700	700
Maintenance and repairs		80	45	40	40	45
Postage and supplies		225	275	100	200	200
Professional services		150	150	500	100	200
Rent		1,300	1,300	1,300	1,300	1,300
Salaries/wages: Employees						1,000
Taxes						100
Telephone		150	150	100	100	100
Travel and entertainment		2,200	300	100	200	200
Utilities		105	105	80	80	90
Other operating expenses		200	100	100	100	100
Total expenses		4,410	4,250	5,095	3,595	5,535
Profit (or Loss) Before Taxes		(4,410)	(4,250)	(1,095)	3,405	3,465

Projected Income Statement: Detail by Quarter Year 1

	1st qtr	2nd qtr	3rd qtr	4th qtr	Total
Gross Sales		45,000	85,000	60,000	190,000
Less: Cost of goods sold		25,000	50,000	35,000	110,000
Gross Profit		20,000	35,000	25,000	80,000
Expenses					
Advertising	700	3,200	3,100	1,000	8,000
Credit card service charges		350	650	400	1,400
Depreciation	225	225	225	225	900
Dues and subscriptions	200	200	200	200	800
Insurance		375	375	375	1,125
Interest	700	2,100	2,100	2,100	7,000
Maintenance and repairs	125	125	125	125	500
Postage and supplies	500	500	500	500	2,000
Professional services	300	800	600	300	2,000
Rent	2,600	3,900	3,900	3,900	14,300
Salaries/wages: Employees		1,000	5,000		6,000
Taxes		100	600		700
Telephone	300	300	300	300	1,200
Travel and entertainment	2,500	500	500	500	4,000
Utilities	210	250	260	210	930
Other operating expenses	300	300	300	300	1,200
Total expenses	8,660	14,225	18,735	10,435	52,055
Profit (or Loss) Before Taxes	(8,660)	5,775	16,265	14,565	27,945

July	August	Sept.	Oct.	Nov.	Dec.	Total
32,500	30,000	22,500	18,000	16,000	26,000	190,000
19,000	18,000	13,000	11,000	10,000	14,000	110,000
13,500	12,000	9,500	7,000	6,000	12,000	80,000
1,400	1,300	400	400	200	400	8,000
200	250	200	100	100	200	1,400
225			225			900
200			200			800
375			375			1,125
700	700	700	700	700	700	7,000
40	45	40	40	45	40	500
200	200	100	100	100	300	2,000
200	200	200	100	100	100	2,000
1,300	1,300	1,300	1,300	1,300	1,300	14,300
2,000	2,000	1,000				6,000
250	250	100				700
100	100	100	100	100	100	1,200
150	150	200	150	150	200	4,000
90	90	80	70	70	70	930
100	100	100	100	100	100	1,200
7,530	6,685	4,520	3,960	2,965	3,510	52,055
5,970	5,315	4,980	3,040	3,035	8,490	28,945

Projected Income Statement: Detail by Quarter Year 2

	1st qtr	2nd qtr	3rd qtr	4th qtr	Total
Gross Sales	$20,000	50,000	90,000	65,000	225,000
Less: Cost of goods sold	13,000	28,000	53,000	37,000	131,000
Gross Profit	7,000	22,000	37,000	28,000	94,000
Expenses					
Advertising	600	1,800	2,400	1,200	6,000
Credit card service charges	150	400	700	450	1,700
Depreciation	450	450	450	450	1,800
Dues and subscriptions	250	250	250	250	1,000
Insurance	200	200	200	200	800
Interest	1,800	1,800	1,800	1,800	7,200
Maintenance and repairs	125	125	125	125	500
Postage and supplies	500	500	500	500	2,000
Professional services	300	800	600	300	2,000
Rent	4,050	4,050	4,050	4,050	16,200
Salaries/wages: Employees		1,100	5,500		6,600
Taxes		120	730		850
Telephone	300	300	300	300	1,200
Travel and entertainment	2,500	500	500	500	4,000
Utilities	225	240	255	225	945
Other operating expenses	350	350	350	350	1,400
Total Expenses	$11,800	12,985	18,710	10,700	54,195
Profit (or Loss) Before Taxes	($4,800)	9,015	18,290	17,300	39,805

Projected Cash Flow Statement: Detail by Month

	Jan	Feb	March	April	May	June
Beginning Cash			84,090	64,265	15,995	18,000
Add:						
Cash sales				10,000	15,000	20,000
Collection on receivables						
Loan/other cash injection		102,000				
Total Cash Available		102,000	84,090	74,265	30,995	38,000
Deduct:						
Advertising			700	1,200	700	1,300
Bad debts						
Credit card service charges				75	75	200
Dues and subscriptions			200	200		
Insurance			375			
Interest			700	700	700	700
Maintenance and repairs		80	45	40	40	45
Postage and supplies		225	275	100	200	200
Professional services		150	150	500	100	200
Rent		1,300	1,300	1,300	1,300	1,300
Salaries/wages						1,000
Taxes						100
Telephone		150	150	100	100	100
Travel and entertainment		2,200	300	100	200	200
Utilities		105	105	80	80	90
Capital expenditure including start-up		11,000	12,400			
Loan principal payment			800	800	800	800
Owner's draw		2,700	2,700	2,700	2,700	2,700
Purchases (merchandise)				50,000	6,000	8,000
Total Cash Paid Out		17,910	19,825	58,270	12,995	16,935
Net Cash Available		84,090	64,265	15,995	18,000	21,065

July	August	Sept.	Oct.	Nov.	Dec.	Total
21,065	6,860	2,275	(675)	(2,840)	(4,205)	
32,500	30,000	22,500	18,000	16,000	26,000	190,000
						102,000
53,565	36,860	25,275	17,325	13,160	21,795	292,000
1,400	1,300	400	400	200	400	8,000
200	250	200	100	100	200	1,400
200			200			800
375			375			1,125
700	700	700	700	700	700	7,000
40	45	70	70	45	40	500
200	200	100	100	100	300	2,000
200	200	200	100	100	100	2,000
1,300	1,300	1,300	1,300	1,300	1,300	14,300
2,000	2,000	1,000				6,000
250	250	100				700
100	100	100	100	100	100	1,200
150	150	200	150	150	200	4,000
90	90	80	70	70	70	930
						23,400
5,800	5,800	800	800	800	800	18,000
2,700	2,700	2,700	2,700	2,700	2,700	29,700
31,000	19,000	18,000	13,000	11,000	10,000	166,000
46,705	34,085	25,950	20,165	17,365	16,910	287,115
6,860	2,775	(675)	(2,840)	(4,205)	4,885	4,885

Projected Cash Flow: Detail by Quarter Year 1

	1st qtr	2nd qtr	3rd qtr	4th qtr	Total
Beginning Cash		64,265	21,065	(675)	
Add:					
Cash sales		45,000	85,000	60,000	190,000
Collection on receivables					
Loan/other cash injection	102,000				102,000
Total Cash Available		109,265	106,065	59,325	
Deduct:					
Advertising	700	3,200	3,100	1,000	8,000
Bad debts					
Credit card service charges		350	650	400	1,400
Dues and subscriptions	200	200	200	200	800
Insurance		375	375	375	1,125
Interest	700	2,100	2,100	2,100	7,000
Maintenance and repairs	125	125	125	125	500
Postage and supplies	500	500	500	500	2,000
Professional services	300	800	600	300	2,000
Rent	2,600	3,900	3,900	3,900	14,300
Salaries/wages		1,000	5,000		6,000
Taxes		100	600		700
Telephone	300	300	300	300	1,200
Travel and entertainment	2,500	500	500	500	4,000
Utilities	210	250	260	210	930
Capital expenditures	23,400				23,400
Loan principal payment	800	2,400	12,400	2,400	18,000
Owner's draw	5,400	8,100	8,100	8,100	29,700
Purchases (merchandise)		64,000	68,000	34,000	166,000
Total Cash Paid Out	37,735	88,200	106,740	54,440	287,115
Net Cash Available	64,265	21,065	(675)	4,885	4,885

	1st qtr	2nd qtr	3rd qtr	4th qtr	Total
Beginning Cash	$4,885	(2,515)	(3,985)	6,705	
Add:					
Cash sales	20,000	50,000	90,000	65,000	235,000
Collection on receivables					
Loan/other cash injection					
Total Cash Available	24,885	47,600	86,015	71,705	
Deduct:					
Advertising	600	1,800	2,400	1,200	6,000
Bad debts					
Credit card service charges	150	400	700	450	1,700
Dues and subscriptions	250	250	250	250	1,000
Insurance	200	200	200	200	800
Interest	1,800	1,800	1,800	1,800	7,200
Maintenance and repairs	125	125	125	125	500
Postage and supplies	500	500	500	500	2,000
Professional services	300	800	600	300	2,000
Rent	4,050	4,050	4,050	4,050	16,200
Salaries/wages		1,100	5,500		6,600
Taxes		120	730		850
Telephone	300	300	300	300	1,200
Travel and entertainment	2,500	500	500	500	4,000
Utilities	225	240	255	225	945
Capital expenditures					
Loan principal payment	2,400	2,400	2,400	2,400	9,600
Owner's draw	9,000	9,000	9,000	9,000	36,000
Purchases (merchandise)	5,000	28,000	50,000	40,000	123,000
Total Cash Paid Out	27,400	51,585	79,310	61,300	219,595
Net Cash Available	2,515	(3,985)	6,705	10,405	10,405

Projected Cash Flow: Detail by Quarter Year 2

Projected Balance Sheets

		Start-Up	End Yr 1	End Yr 2
Assets				
Current Assets				
Cash		$31,000	$4,885	$10,405
Accounts receivable				
Inventory		50,000	70,000	70,000
Prepaid expenses				
Total Current Assets		81,000	74,885	80,405
Fixed Assets				
Land				
Building				
Equipment		14,000	14,000	14,000
Less accumulated depreciation		0	900	1,800
Net Fixed Assets			13,100	12,200
Total Assets		$95,000	$87,985	$92,605
Liabilities				
Current Liabilities				
Accrued expenses				
Taxes payable				
Short-term notes payable (Credit Line)		25,000	15,000	
Current portion long-term debt				
Total Current Liabilities		25,000	15,000	
Long-term debt		70,000	62,000	54,000
Total Liabilities		95,000	77,000	54,000
Total Equity			10,985	38,605
Total Liabilities and Equity (Net Worth)		$95,000	87,985	92,605

Internet Bid Clearinghouse

BUSINESS PLAN   OPEXNET, LLC

The Operations Expense Network
Atlanta, Georgia

This exemplary business plan, which has not been disguised from the original as the others in this volume have, describes an innovative, unique and revolutionary electronic bid clearinghouse for building and facilities managers. This self-regulating web database will be an organizing force for the many thousands of bids that take place each day. Its power to transform this particular industry is compellingly stated...so much so, that this plan won the Wake Forest University Babcock Entrepreneurs 1998 Business Plan Competition.

- EXECUTIVE SUMMARY

- THE INDUSTRY, OPEXNET, AND OUR PRODUCTS AND SERVICES

- MARKET RESEARCH AND ANALYSIS

- THE ECONOMICS OF BUSINESS

- MARKETING PLAN

- DESIGN AND DEVELOPMENT PLANS

- OPERATIONS PLAN

- THE MANAGEMENT TEAM

- FINANCIAL PLAN

- CRITICAL RISKS AND PROBLEMS

- SUPPLIER LIST

- STRATEGIC ALLIANCES AND ACQUISITIONS

EXECUTIVE SUMMARY

OpExNeT, LLC is a virtual company specializing in providing building managers products and services that:

- Evaluate Vendors
- Reduce Administration Expenses
- Reduce Repair/Maintenance Expenses
- Reduce Utilities Expenses
- Increase Vendor's Added Value
- Create Efficient Marketspace

OpExNeT's core competency is built around a shared Client/Vendor database. This database is a compilation of building manager surveys for vendor information. In return, the building manager has access to the maintenance and service norm charts configured specifically for their equipment/service needs, location and quality expectation level. At that time, the client has the option of purchasing specialized bid products and network services. Our objective is to become the daily stop of everybuilding and facilities manager in North America.

This simple process of bringing building and facilities managers together with the vendors they need, quickly, efficiently and without obligation, is the prelude to the ability to create a market push. Advertising can be directed as narrowly or wide as the advertiser wishes with products appropriately aimed at the client's needs.

The timing of this business start-up is no mistake. Deregulation of the electric industry is two to three years away. Capturing brand equity prior to this time is essential. The sheer volume of transactions required is staggering. Over 200,000 building service and maintenance bids take place every day. A low margin industry by virtue of the excesses of the 1980s, building and facilities managers are forced to find ways to reduce operating expenses on a daily basis.

Initially, our target market will be focused around our first three databases. These are elevator maintenance, generator maintenance and HVAC maintenance. These also happen to be industries in which our team has a great deal of pricing knowledge. The marketing of OpExNeT will be targeted at the stand alone low--rise and mid-rise office building management companies located in urban and suburban areas who own a PC and are connected to the Internet.

The greatest advantage OpExNeT has over its competitors is that no other entity like OpExNeT exists on the Internet today. The closest relations would be systems like Chrysler's SPIN and GE's supplier networks which are Intranet designed to assist the procurement departments of global manufacturing concerns. Still, while these systems provide Internet reach and speed, they are limited to the body of knowledge contained within the corporation. OpExNeT offers an industry-wide view taking full advantage of the Internet's efficiencies.

There are benefits in being first. Establishing OpExNeT as the de facto standard of the building and facility management industry is critical to the task. Once this is accomplished, the management of the OpExNeT systems will begin to resemble more of a customized subscription magazine than a service provider bulletin board. Subscriptions will then be the path to profit.

The beauty of these databases is that they are self updating and low maintenance once a critical mass has been reached. Investment in setting up the standard norms and the Internet website is intensive only in the initial phases of their development. This is why a carefully implemented strategic plan will not only affect the velocity of the concept introduction butwill also be critical to our ability to keep the systems costs low in the long-run, $250,000 in sales revenue in year one will produce little or no after-tax earnings. However, sales are expected to grow to over $5,000,000 by 2002 and produce after-tax earnings of $1,726,000.

The OpExNeT team consists of three individuals with over 40 years in combined experience in the building management industry and corporate management, The team is a mix of entrepreneurial start-
up talent, e-business creation know-how and project management skills that are able to take an Internet business into profit sustaining existence.

Unique to this period in the history of the development of the Internet, OpExNeT believes that it alone has an opportunity to provide the building management industry with needed products and services that have never been offered before. In an effort to obtain a 100% market share worth over $1,000,000 in annual sales revenue by the year 2000 and retain it successfully, OpExNeT is seeking an equity investment of $240,000 to implement plans described herein. The common stock sold for the $240,000 investment will represent about 35% of OpExNeT's outstanding common stock after the offering is completed.

For OpExNeT to become the gatekeeper of building management services, three critical items must happen:

1. The databases created must have value to the building management community and the suppliers who serve them.

2. The deregulation of the utilities industry must proceed in the U.S. market and 50% of the markets must be open by the year 2002.

3. The techniques required to transmit data over power line at 10 times the current speed of datalink transmission are developed and commercialized prior to the deregulation of the utilities industry.

Once all three of these events have taken place, the second stage of OpExNeT strategy can begin. The ability of even the smallest devices to communicate with a host will enable true systems integration. And, at that time we will be contacting you about AVAJ...

THE INDUSTRY, OPEXNET AND OUR PRODUCTS AND SERVICES

Industry Analysis

The building maintenance industry is highly fragmented on the customer side and more oligopolistic on the supplier side. While myriads of building owners and managers exist a all levels 80% of the services provided to this group are dominated by a few multinational manufacturer and service entities. One would expect that if the products provided by the manufacturers are indeed commodities, the services would also follow suit. But they have not. Service providers average margin levels of over 50%. One might argue that this is because the capital require to provide the immense distribution network creates a natural barrier to entry for competition. The truth is that most parts and repairs are readily available. One could assume that the liabilities of the business might place insurance requirements out of reach of a small competitor. The truth is that improvements in equipment quality have substantially driven down liability exposure. One might concur that complex software algorithms have prevented equipment diagnosis by those without specially coded terminals. The truth is that specially coded terminals for most equipment can be purchased over the Internet. One might venture to say that the unions have control over the experienced and trainable service technician pool. The truth is that the union has little real power. The real reason for barrier to new competition is lack of pricing information.

Traditionally, accurate maintenance pricing has been closely guarded by the oligopolistic few. While associations in other industries provide vast arrays of market research, the building maintenance industry associations provide little or no information, Sources such as Means Costing Data are for the most part inaccurate and have little value.

The building maintenance price datum we will be focusing on are:

- HVAC Controls
- Elevators and Material Transfer
- Boilers, Heating Systems
- Roofing and Exterior Face
- Air Handling
- Water Treatment and Plumbing Systems
- Electrical Systems and Lighting
- Building Access Systems
- Parking Access Systems
- Security Systems
- Energy
- Cleaning

OpExNeT

OpExNeT was created to meet the needs of the building management professional. We provide a means for the typical building management professional to access our database, retrieve equipment specific pricing, receive local and national comparison data, and be provided with options for bid documents and services. The opportunity for a new Internet business to enter into this type of business was realized in 1996 after an exhaustive study of the building management industry was conducted by a global elevator manufacturer and service provider. The study identified key accounts, representing almost 17% of the unit volume and 24% of the sales volume, that contributed super normal profits. The study went on to examine the nature of the margin. These accounts did not run any more efficiently or require any less service than most others yet they were priced well above the market norms. The study concluded that these super normal profit levels were due to inefficiencies in market price knowledge. Long-term contracts with price index clauses that more than exceeded inflation had moved the annuities well beyond the market norms. Furthermore, it was assumed, since all elevator maintenance contracts use these indices, that these key accounts existed in the competitors' maintenance bases also and possibly in equal proportions. The recommendations of the study were not to wake the sleeping giant and ride the cash cow for as long as possible.

This positioning by the elevator companies and other building service providers has opened the door to a new gatekeeper. Previously, these companies saw little risk of being exposed. The possible whistleblowers consisted of consultants, who had little interest in driving prices and commissions down, and the associations, whose fragmented membership and tight purses were skillfully lobbied by suppliers.

Accordingly, three executives formed a new company, OpExNeT, LLC. OpExNeT stands for Operations Expense Network. As is evident from the name, OpExNeT is intended to fulfill the gatekeeper role for a number of industries, eventually. The goal is to provide similar benefits of existing supplier-company Intranet, combine the full breadth of industry knowledge and simplify the client's entire operations expense process. OpExNeT's success rests on its ability to seamlessly move from product, customer database, to process, efficient procurement and management systems. To this end, OpExNeT, LLC was formally incorporated in the state of Georgia in 1998, and the principals invested $40,000 of their funds in it.

Our Products and Services

OpExNeT products are two-fold, To the building management professional, we offer Apples2Apples and bid related documentsand services. To the building equipment industry, we offer a complete compendium of competitive pricing and customer data.

Price Comparisons	Free	Advertisement National	$10,000/yr
Contracts	$ 20	Advertisement Local	s 1,000/yr
Bid Service	$100	Database National	$25,000/yr
Subscriptions	$9.95/mo	Database Local	$ 2,500/yr

Market Entry and Growth

Every day, over 200,000 bids take place for maintenance of building equipment. After the year 2000, an additional 5,000 bids per day will be added for Utility services. Each bid represents, at a minimum of 30 -40 man hours, involving the building manager and a clerical person. This team represents an average of $451hr, totaling the administrative expense at about $1,350 to $1,800 if a formal bid is carried out. For this reason, and the associated paperwork headaches, most building management teams do not follow a formal bid process. Our experience in the marketplace is that if the bid processed could be out-sourced at a reasonable price, most would take advantage of it. Given the climate of the Building Management industry, sales relationships with clientele are not as strong as cost concerns. Clearly, the costs of such a service must:

1. Present the Client with all of the pertinent information in a standardized, concise and unambiguous way.

2. Cost less than existing associated Administrative expenses

3. Provide an Operating expense reduction or service enhancement of greater value than the subscription rate.

4. Always allow the Client to make the final decision.

Primary Steps

The first step was to create the website and, then grow the database. Our Initial databases are focused on the Elevator, HVAC Control, and Generator Maintenance pricing and were created using industry models and location CPI indices. The website is designed to automatically draw from the industry models, apply location escalators and calculate present norms. Eventually, once the regional databases reach a critical mass, the website will be referred directly to the ever evolving, self-maintaining pricing datum.

We need to establish OpExNeT as the defacto standard for supplier pricing information. To accomplish this, we are offering maintenance price comparisons to the building management industryfor free as of June 1998. Over 60% of all contracts turn over between July (government contracts) and January (fiscal/calendar years), All advertising and promotions will be directed towards maximizing Client use of the product.

By August 1998, we will stage Utility, Cleaning, Lighting and Security for initial database construction.

Secondary Steps

After the first year of operation, OpExNeT will be prepared to begin sale of its database to the industry suppliers. Information collected will include:

1. Competitive Pricing
2. Contract Renewal Dates
3. Vendor Ratings
4. Client Data
5. Equipment Data

Advertising, location and equipment specific, will be provided as a part the pricing review. Based upon the customers initial entries, the advertising will be targeted and appropriate to the inquirer and, therefore, extremely valuable to the advertiser. A ProCast type of service will be made available for a fee by June 1999.

Eventually OpExNeT will be positioned as an industry consultant for the building management industry. Services will be extended to provide university campuses and school systems comparative data. Electronic bulletin boards for specific equipment types and expenses will be available for shared knowledge.

Bid services will provide a contractors' electronic bulletin board. This service will be subscription fee based and provide a central warehouse for bid information throughout North America. Complete documents and forms will be available for e-mail transmittal of proposal and quotations.

Eventually, this subscription service will include a daily newsletter containing items such as information for budgeting modernization/renovation work. The newsletter content will be Client specific, based upon their building profiles, and focused on the Total Building System Integration Concept.

Our target in the year 2003 is to take Total Building System Integration from concept to reality. Chips present in every electrical consuming device will be able to communicate in concert with any other device. This communication can occur regardless of the protocol with which they were originally designed. Encoders and closed feedback loops can be tapped for diagnosis and preventive maintenance. OpExNeT will be in a unique position to harness this information.

The bottom line is ... the OEM's ability to retain maintenance accounts based upon the use of proprietary codes and passwords will be eliminated. OpExNeT's charter is to enable the independent contractor by providing a central base for remote monitoring, equipment tracking, and diagnostic targeting.

Control over building electrical consumption can be coordinated with utilities vendors in a brokered arrangement to "block" usage time, thereby smoothing out peak cycles without any perceptible environmental change by the building's occupants. Networks of these buildings could offer tremendous gains in energy efficiency.

MARKET RESEARCH AND ANALYSIS

US Office Market Gains Strength

The average Net Operating Income (NOI) for office buildings was $8.57 per square foot in 1996, a 2.5% increase over the previous year, according to the BOMA EE Report. This reversed a four year trend of shrinking NOI in the office buildings industry. The increase in NOI can be attributed to a 4% decline in operating and fixed expenses.

In 1996 constant dollars, Total Expenses were held to a five year low of $9.81 per square foot while for the sixth consecutive year Total Income decreased to $18.38 per square foot.

A detailed look at Office Rent, the major component of Total Income, highlights some important trends (Table 1). In real terms, for the last five years, base rent and additional rent (a combination of pass-throughs and operating cost escalations) have declined. At the same time, there was a drop in the amount of free rent offered to office tenants. This helped offset the same drop in base and additional rent. It is interesting to note over the past four years, the ratio of additional rent to total office rent has remained relatively constant at about 16%. Property owners and managers appear to have made improvements in overall tenant satisfaction and tenant retention as indicated by the first drop in lease cancellations in four years.

Table I - Office Rent Components (US $/Sq. Ft.)

	Base Rent	Additional Rent	Base Rent Escalators	Lease Cancellations	Rent Abatements	Tenant Service Income
1992	$15.27	$3.09	$0.08	$0.03	$0.16	$0.17
1993	$15.09	$2.90	$0.13	$0.05	$0.11	$0.22
1994	$14.69	$2.76	$0.06	$0.08	$0.09	$0.19
1995	$14.21	$2.70	$0.04	$0.06	$0.08	$0.22
1996	$14.06	$2.67	$0.02	$0.05	$0.08	$0.23

Office building owners and managers have been effective at controlling costs. Operating Expenses have remained constant or decreased in real terms over the last six years. The largest decline was observed in Utility expenses, the largest component of overall Operating Expenses. Repairs/Maintenance expenses and Cleaning expenses also fell over that six year period.

The average downtown office building in the U.S. spent $9.03 per square foot in Operating plus Fixed Expenses. Suburban buildings spent an average $6.87 per square foot. Buildings in the Middle Atlantic region had the highest downtown Total Operating plus Fixed Expenses in the country followed by the North Central region and the Pacific Southwest region. These higher regional expenses were driven in large part by the large cities within them, such as New York, Chicago and Los Angeles. The region with the lowest downtown Operating plus Fixed Expenses was the Pacific Northwest.

Reflecting regional trends, four of the five cities with the highest Operating plus Fixed Expenses were located in the Middle Atlantic region (Table 2a). However, only one of the five cities with the lowest Total Operating plus Fixed Expenses was located in the Pacific Northwest region (Table 2b).

Table 2a: Five Highest

City	Average Operating Plus Fixed Expenses
New York, NY	$16.59
Chicago, IL	$12.30
Boston, MA	$12.24
Hartford, CT	$11.15
Washington, DC	$11.02

Table 2b: Five Lowest

City	Average Operating Plus Fixed Expenses
Fort Meyers, FL	$3.32
Oklahoma City, OK	$4.25
Shreveport, LA	$4.35
Portland, ME	$4.52
Billings, MT	$4.56

Canadian Office Market Evolves into Tenant Driven Market

The Canadian office market has gradually shifted from an owner's market in 1991 to tenant's market in 1996. Net Operating Income adjusted for inflation, fell for the sixth consecutive year, The 1996 drop occurred because of a 10% decline in Total Income, which was marginally offset by a 1% drop in total Expenses. Total Income, adjusted for inflation, has fallen 34% over the last six years, Total Expenses increased 2,3% from 1991 to 1993 and has since fallen by 8.4% to its present level of $12.49 per square foot.

The reasons behind the decline in Total Income become more apparent in the analysis of its major component Office Rent (Table 3). Over the last five years, base rent and additional rent have dropped, 24% and 50% respectively. Along similar lines, free rent (rent abatement) has steadily increased since 1993 which is not unusual in a soft market. On the positive side, income from lease cancellations dropped in 1995 and 1996 after and large increase from 1993 to 1994, suggesting fewer tenants are leaving their office space before their leases expire and that tenant retention rates are improving. Tenant service income has remained relatively constant over the last four years.

Table 3: Office Rent Components (Can $/Sq. Ft.)

	Base Rent	Additional Rent	Lease Cancellations	Rent Abatements	Tenant Service Income
1992	$17.10	$9.81	$0.05	$0.24	$0.02
1993	$17.21	$7.74	$0.01	$0.16	$0.05
1994	$15.65	$7.43	$0.11	$0.33	$0.05
1995	$13.76	$6.54	$0.09	$0.35	$0.04
1996	$13.73	$6.48	$0.08	$0.32	$0.05

A detailed look at Total Operating Expenses reveals some interesting trends. Specifically, Utility expenses, adjusted for inflation, dropped for the first time in six years and Cleaning expenses continued their six year downward trend. Roads/grounds and Administrative expenses have dropped in each year of the last five years while Repairs/Maintenance expenses dropped for the fourth year in a row. Security expenses increased by I cent over last year, but were still below the expenditure levels of the 1991 - 1993 period. The drop in Total Operating expenses is of particular importance because they are the only expenses that can be directly controlled by building owners and managers and they help offset the decline in income.

Almost one-third of all operating expenses in Canadian officebuildings is attributed to utility expenses. Conversely, only 1% of all operating expenses goes towards maintaining roads and grounds.

Administrative, Cleaning, Repairs/Maintenance and Security expense components contributed to the highest portion of Total Operating Expenses in downtown locations for 1996, while suburban locations had higher percentages of Roads/Grounds and Utility expense components. In monetary terms, only utility costs are higher in suburban locations than downtown.

The Canadian city with the highest Total Operating Expenses was Toronto and the city with the lowest downtown office rent was Saskatoon.

Overall North American Trends and Statistics

The potential client market is tight but avails itself to a low cost supplier comparison solution. Rising Administrative and Repair/Maintenance expenses in a low inflationary state are separating themselves from real market prices. Continued cost pressure on the building manager is expected.

A tight employment market will add value to the typical service mechanics wages. The opportunity to enter the market as an independent contractor becomes more attractive as large companies fight to hold back labor rate increases. For the first time in 40 years, the lack of cost of living increases creates an atmosphere of stagnation.

Primary Customer Profile

Title: Building Manager	
Average Age:	42
Gender: 37% Female	
Years in Business:	15
Annual Salary:	$38,523
Other Compensation:	$ 5,120
Number of Staff:	4.8
Use PC's:	87%
Use Internet:	38%

Secondary Customer Profile

Title: Building Engineer	
Average Age:	36
Gender: 92% Male	
Years in Business:	14
Annual Salary:	$32,162
Other Compensation:	N/A
Number of Staff.	2.3
Use PC's:	42%
Use Internet:	65%

What we find significant in the Building Manager pool is the percentage of women. BOMA membership is now 25% female, a far cry from the 2% that represented their gender in 1970. More importantly, about 70% of BOMA's education classes are occupied by women this year. This may be due to property management's dependency on strong organizational, managerial and financial skills which are not gender-specific. Perhaps it's the people skills, the listening skills and a degree of patience that attracts women to the field. It should be noted that a large number of these women entered building management from the education field.

The Building Engineer is the second client segment that can be easily identified. This group is more technical in nature. They have hands on experience in most building systems and are more likely to research the nature of mechanical and electrical problems. Of those who use a personal computer, a very high percentage also utilize the Internet.

Market Size and Trends

The market is estimated to contain an average of 200,000 maintenance and service bids per day. This total is subject to seasonal cycles. Bid activity peaks in July, October and January. Due to the shortage of skilled labor in the North American market, the trend to outsource building maintenance activities is expected to grow well into the next millennium. Tightness and volatility in the real estate market further establish the need to keep building personnel at a minimum. The growth of outsourced services as a percentage of total building services has grown from 2 percent 1952, to more than 60 percent today.

Competition

Information Providers

Although there is no existing competition for the markets for which we intend to pursue, there are F. W. Dodge is a division of McGraw-Hill Publishing that focuses on the information needs of the construction market. Dodge Reports are the industry standard for publishing bid information and collecting data regarding Contractor, Architect, Owner/Developer and Supplier statistics. Dodge's core competency revolves around a nationwide distribution system which has permeated even the smallest markets. The service is subscription fee based to owners/developers, architects and suppliers. Fees average $1,800 per bid posting and supplier subscriptions are approximately $2,500 per year regardless of usage. Dodge posts very few maintenance and/or bids. Those that are posted are typically for stare and federal government projects with multiple buildings where vast access to bid information is required by law. Dodge has only recently started posting minimal information on the Internet. They claim that the Internet is not used by enough of its customers to justify the investment. It is apparent, however, that a shift in this type of business to the Internet will obsolete their existing distribution systems as well as their competitive advantage. Regional examples of Dodge Report competition exist, such as CMD in the southeast, with similar products and distribution methods. Other possible contenders are the huge database purveyors like Metromail, Great Universal, and American Business Information. Their strengths are their brand equity, existing databases, data collection methodology and reach. Their weaknesses involve the cost of distribution (primarily mail systems) and inflexibility of database design. As the Internet grows in acceptance, it may become their undoing.

Consultants

Lerch Bates Associates is a large consultant firm offering elevator performance and evaluation services to the owner/developer and building management industry. Lerch Bates works closely with elevator/escalator manufacturers to stay up on the latest research and development trends. Their specifications and reviews are targeted towards the high-end market with specialized services driven towards the unique answer. However, over 80% of their products and processes are "canned". Their existing products are fee based, typically 3 - 10% of the total bid package depending upon whether the service includes just initial specifications or it includes overseeing during the life-cycle of the project. The strength of their presence in each marketplace is dependent upon the abilities of the local consultant and his relationships with the building community. Presently, they offer no Internet services. Each supplier industry has its bevy of functional consultants. Each has a similar approach to the market. However, there also exist a group of facility management consultants, such as Richard Bowers & Co., who offer energy bidding services. They, perhaps, would be more amenable to an alliance. The strengths of the typical consultant are their brand equity, experience, and specification to the task. Their weakness involve high pricing, little market penetration in breadth or depth, and dependence on functional specialty. The middle and low-end markets offer the ideal entry point.

BOMA/BOMI are building industry associations dedicated to furthering the industry needs and its views in the internal and external markets. Prolific lobbyists for laws that benefit their constituency, their greatest threat may come from regulatory obstacles which could be created to constrict OpExNeT's growth into other service sectors. BOMI is also considered the industry's librarian and statistician. While well funded, organizations like these are more likely to adopt OpExNeT rather than attempt to duplicate and compete. Supplier associations like NEII, would be more likely to attempt to stop OpExNeT's entry. Most supplier associations, like their manufacturing base, are not in a position to fund a competitive entity nor do they consider it within their charter. They do have good brand equity among the industry especially in the area of education. It is likely that OpExNeT will have to form an alliance with BOMA to gain a successful and expedient market entry.

Industry Associations

Manufacturers/service providers are the most threatened by OpExNeT's market entry. Improved information among their client base could represent a 15% -20% decrease in critical service margins due to customer churning, reduced contract lengths, increased contract requirements and improved competition. Yet, a manufacturer/service provider alternative would not offer clients the unbiased positioning of a third party concern. We would expect, however, that manufacturers may take a number of approaches to discredit OpExNeT's databases.

**Manufacturers/
Service Providers**

Honeywell and Johnson Controls provide the greatest threat to OpExNeT's long-term strategy. They are well positioned with the utilities having offered performance contracts to most of their mutual customers. Approaching the building management industry from the environmental control side, they have vast technical and economic resources. Even with these resources, however, both have only dabbled in Total Building Systems Integration from a monitoring standpoint. Their competitive advantage is brand equity, established technical sales force in MSNs over 800,000, and a proven methodology. Weaknesses are their high cost structure and, therefore, their high pricing and extensive contract cycles.

Our intent is to obtain 100% of this market and keep it. Being the first to enter this type of business is an advantage that must be translated into sustainable profit. Because growing the market is so important, circulation numbers will be our critical measure. Our sales force will be directed towards obtaining advertising dollars in addition to the networks subscription and service sales on the following schedule:

**Estimated Market
Share and Sales**

	1998 3rd Quarter	1998 4th Quarter	1999	2000	2001	2002
Circulation	5,000	20,000	50,000	100,000	500,000	1,000,000
Sales	$50,000	$200,000	$500,000	$1,000,000	$3,000,000	$5,000,000

Support of this sales forecast will require 2 or 3 additional salespeople in 2000 to achieve national coverage. Recruitment of the sales force will largely come from the print and advertising industries.

The beauty of the OpExNeT system is that the market evaluation and updating is continuous and completely self-maintaining. Every time a client enters a request for pricing information, the databases are updated and the models are re-calibrated with the new pricing information. Validity is automatically gained in the self-reporting style of data collection.

**Ongoing
Market Evaluation**

We will continue to scan the market for signs of any changes in behavior by our potential competitors. Our presence at area trade shows and BOMA/BOMI meetings and conventions will not only aid in establishing our name but also allow us to watch, learn and listen to the needs of clients and suppliers. The role of facilitator could place OpExNeT in a unique position to help both parties work more efficiently and with greater understanding.

In addition, the market is very suitable for multiple segmentations. As our databases become large enough to combine into discernible groups, which we expect to happen very quickly, we will endeavor to customize our offerings and our pitch to achieve maximum penetration of each and every group. The larger the OpExNeT community becomes, the greater the return to the client.

THE ECONOMICS OF BUSINESS

It is our contention that OpExNeT has the opportunity to be one of the first successful business to business Internet enterprises. Given that it is a service business and a virtualbusiness at that, certain economics hold true. Cost of Goods Sold represent less than 20% of Sales Revenue in the earlier stages, however, true to the scalability of most Internet businesses, Costs of Goods Sold will eventually be 3%-5% of Sales when efficiencies are met. It is exactly this scalability that we will exploit. To accomplish this, relatively high levels of Selling and Marketing, and Software Engineering (50% - 100% of Sales) are required to "jump start" the process.

Gross and Operating Margins

As expected, in 1998, we will see Gross Margins of 80% and Operating Margins of -66%. However, the progression of margins and earnings over the first five years is forecasted to improve dramatically. Gross margins will reach more than 90% and Operating margins more than 70%.

Profit Potential and Sustainability

After accumulating $492,000 in losses by the year 2000, the turnaround is dramatic. Net Earnings rise from $959,000 in 2001 to over $4,186,000 in 2003. Profit sustainability is achievable if OpExNeT's reputation has successfully been established and repeated innovation provides building management products that meet the customer value proposition.

Fixed, Variable and Semi-variable Costs

As would be expected, the fixed costs associated with an Internet start-up are low. We estimate that these costs will be only 5% of total revenue. These costs include administrative overhead and Internet systems. Variable costs include labor required to facilitate the bulletin board, technical chat lines and network response services. These costs represent 20% of total revenue but will decrease with respect to the circulation base settling in at 3% - 5%. Semi-variable costs including management and sales staff are expected to keep pace with the growth in revenue at 24%.

Months to Break-Even

In Exhibit 3, we calculate a break-even point at 10 months after inception of the business entity. We do note the seasonality of the business however, which could extend this point 3 months if market entry and velocity does not meet its critical window.

Months to Reach Positive Cash Flow

In Exhibit 4, we calculate that it will take no more than 18 months after inception of the business entity to reach positive cash flow. We do note the seasonality of the business however, which could extend this point 3 months if market entry and velocity does not meet its critical window.

THE MARKETING PLAN

Overall Marketing Strategy

Hit the market fast and hard. OpExNeT plans to sell building management services through the Internet. Close to 100% of all of the Client side sales will be sold through this channel of distribution. Residual sales may come from telephone and mail orders.

This dominant channel, while made available through developments in technology, has become the marketspace due to the existing markets inability to facilitate efficient information exchange. Obviously favorable to small independent contractors, this channel can offer value proposition priced maintenance and service on a localized basis that until now the OEM's have failed to provide.

The approach is simple. Treat the building management as a community for which you have a valuable public service...free maintenance and service pricing evaluation. Create the confidence that none of the profile information will be given to any other building management client. If in receiving this information the Client perceives a gap in her and her suppliers value proposition, have the bid services easily accessible and available for purchase as well as the advertisements of competitive local suppliers for that service. We have drawn the client in and the point of access is within our control environment. The marketed proposition will be appropriately targeted, clear and concise.

Our objective of 5,000 entries in the first three months will be mostly generated from the two trade shows in June. Critical to the task is achieving 10,000 entries by the end of 1998. Given the inequalities existing in the marketplace, word of mouth alone should guarantee our success. However, OpExNeT will participate in national and local trade magazines to help build brand equity. OpExNeT's selling and marketing budget for 1998 is $86,000.

Pricing

In an effort to drive volume, similar to the print industry's circulation drive, pricing will be well under theClient's cost comparison. OpExNeT's pricing structure will not be the reason a potential Client does not try the products.

Advertising and Database products, on the other hand, are priced for what they represent. Complete access to the Building and Facilities Management Industry with unparalleled levels of specificity.

Sales Tactics

Client products will be driven towards subscription sales. An automatic monthly withdrawal from the client's bank account will be our first choice of payment. Visa, MasterCard and Amex direct charges will also be accepted. This means of payment minimizes cancellation and guarantees payment,

Advertising is sold initially to nationally based OEM's who will have a vested interest in having their ad appear when their customers validate pricing. Fear will be the tactic used. More importantly, local independents are given the chance to target their local audience on an equal stance with the large multinational OEM's.

Database sales are not expected to begin until the year 2000 or 100,000 entries, whichever comes first. At that time, the database will reach its first validation stage and client segmentation can begin.

**Service and
Warranty Policies**

Satisfaction in the services rendered is 100% guaranteed. Any Client who is not totally satisfied can contact OpExNeT via e-mail, fax or "800" number and receive a complete refund. This type of no hassles posture will help OpExNeT achieve market penetration. Take away all of the barriers to trying the products and what do you have ... another entry.

**Advertising
and Promotion**

Full page advertising directed at the building manager profile will be posted in the June, July and August issues of Buildings, The Facilities Construction and Management Magazine. The campaign will revolve around the OpExNeT slogan "Putting your building on the highway". The first priority will be OpExNeT's logo design. The logo must contemporary, creative and free flowing yet denote a solid business theme and objectives ... interconnectivity, community and marketspace.

During the year, OpExNeT plans to exhibit at the following conventions and events:

BOMA Convention   June 21-23, 1998   Philadelphia, PA
NeoCon World's Trade Fair   June 08-1 0, 1998   Chicago, IL

Distribution

All advertising and promotion distribution will be through the normal means afforded by the print media and event of choice. At this time, no advertising agency has been selected to oversee advertising and promotion effectiveness although this will be considered in later contexts.

DESIGN AND DEVELOPMENT PLANS

**Development
Status and Tasks**

The following database norms are the following stages of development:

Elevator Maintenance	Stage III	Completed 01 March 1998
HVAC Control Maintenance	Stage III	Completion by June 1998
Generator Maintenance	Stage III	Completion by June 1998
Utility Service	Stage I	Stage II Completion by April 1998
Cleaning Service	Stage II	Stage III Completion by June 1998
Lighting Maintenance	Stage II	Stage III Completion by June 1998
Security Service	Stage I	Stage II Completion by August 1998

**Difficulties
and Risks**

Great care must be taken in developing these norms for the industry. Inaccurate data could invalidate the entire database and substantially hamper market penetration efforts. For all entries by Clients, a two standard deviation test will be in effect. Skewing of the distribution curves by entries will result in a reconfiguring of the norm, Updates will be ongoing and constant.

**Product
Improvement
and New Products**

Initially, the graphical user interface and report layout will be subject to the most visible evolution of the product. Studies being conducted by leading educators on learning curve productivity and individual learning style segmentations will be utilized in design concepts. Targets for further development are database enhancement and accessibility,

In the new product arena, systems integration tools, especially those utilizing power line data transmission and chip enhanced servos/encoders, are our primary focus. Any product that

OpExNeTcan use to enhance market efficiencies for building managers and maintain its gatekeeper position will be fair game. Close relationships with Clients and industry associations will point the way towards the products that will improve building efficiency, reliability and comfort.

Presently, in Exhibit 1, over $300,000 is budgeted for software engineering through the year 2002. $60,000 of these funds are already dedicated development of the OpExNeT website. The balance will be appropriated for product improvement and new products.	**Costs**

Presently, OpExNeT owns no patents on product or process. OpExNeT does have registered names and trademarks that must be vigorously protected. The unhindered development of OpExNeT's brand equity is critical to its success.   **Proprietary Issues**

OPERATIONS PLAN

Geographical Location

Another benefit of an Internet start-up is the total flexibility in locating operations. Our location logistics are limited to access to telephone lines, access to suppliers, cost of living considerations, progressiveness of business atmosphere and access to a major airport. Based upon these logistical issues, Atlanta, Georgia was selected as our corporate headquarters.

Warehousing and Distribution

From the Atlanta Headquarters, distribution will be carried out over the Internet. This is not just limited to the website, access to the database and downloaded maintenance reports. Our Internet distribution system will include maintenance contracts, specifications and a client/supplier connection service. Important to this type of distribution system is the security of two specific channels. First, the means of accessing all databases must include password firewalls. Before new data is included in a database, it will be compared to two standard deviations from the norm. Secondly, encryption must be provided for payment of services rendered.

Our website is hosted by Advanced Website Creations with connections to 15 popular search engines. It will be the responsibility of AWC to provide servers to store Client entriesuntil weekly downloads can be made onto OpExNeT's local client-
server network. Based upon the estimated maximum load of 20,000 hits per month, our allowable storage area of 10mb should be sufficient to accommodate 800 profiles per week. Download time, 56,000 baud, is estimated to take between 30 to 45 minutes depending upon line integrity and server operations.

Strategy and Plans

Our strategy for year one is volume. We must leverage our low-cost structure and the full power of the Internet to obtain maximum exposure in the marketspace. Advertising is directed at building and facilities managers is every magazine and journal, national and local, that they use. Promotions will kick-off this year at the NeoCon 98 World's Trade Fair and continue at Five North American Trade Fairs through December. OpExNeT will also participate in educational seminars aimed at Internet business and "Choosing your Maintenance Team".

Year two is the beginning of OpExNeT's expansion into the Daily News Bulletins and Letters of Interest containing subjects such as product developments, recalls, recommendations, enhancements, regulatory changes and effects, etc. The object is to make OpExNeT the daily stop for the busy building manager and engineer.

Regulatory and Other Approvals/ Environmental Issues

Many states have regulations that, in effect, prohibit the marketing of service contracts other than through manufacturers and dealers. We must be careful not to cross this line until the barriers to entry have been dropped. In the promotion of Internet business, the removal of this type of state regulation will be a focus of our lobbying efforts.

Another issue will be an extension of the moratorium on state sales taxes for services rendered in that state. Continuation of this practice should help OpExNeT keep administrative costs to a minimum.

THE MANAGEMENT TEAM

John F. Ellingson, President
Luis Hernandez, VP Finance
Kevin Spencer, VP Marketing

Key Management Personnel

John F. Ellingson, President

Mr. Ellingson, age 35, has a BBA in Marketing, a BBS in economics, and an MBA from Wake Forest University. His experience includes 12 years of increasing responsibility in sales and marketing management and over one year in general management responsibilities in the design, introduction, and sales of equipment and services over the Internet. This experience was accumulated with Westinghouse Electric, Schindler, and WolTech STT.

In 1989, Mr. Ellingson was responsible for the integration of Schindler Canada into the North America KG. The project was largely automated using an SAP framework and accomplished well within original costs estimates and the 18 month schedule. Mr. Ellingson sold over $29m in elevator equipment and services to the building management industry during his tenure in sales.

In 1997, Mr. Ellingson started a market entry consulting business aimed at European Coating and equipment manufacturers attempting to enter North America. The company is ongoing with 8 clients in various stages of progress.

Luis Hernandez, VP Finance

Mr. Hernandez, age 45, has BS in Industrial Engineering and an MBA from Drew University. His experience includes 23 years in operations and financial management responsibilities in project management, productivity and systems integration. This experience was accumulated with Phillip Morris, Coors, Koppers, Planters and Dean Foods.

In 1997, Mr. Hernandez heads Dean Foods National Productivity Team surveying, recommending and implementing management and systems changes to improve productivity, morale, reliability and speed of over 270 operations across the nation.

Kevin Spencer, VP Marketing

Mr. Spencer, age 37, has a BA in Marketing from Florida State University. His experience includes 14 years in the advertising business including managing and operating his own agency for 8 years. His ad concept, logo design webpage design, catalog and mailing design, press release and marketing plan experience was accumulated with Broach Advertising and Marketing Made Central.

In 1997, Mr. Spencer's list of clients included Joe Boxer, Girbaud, Champion, Cone Mills and other prestigious consumer brands.

Table 2 lists the ownership, the cash investment and the previous salary of each OpExNeT team member. As one can clearlysee, this data represents the commitment and belief of the individuals in OpExNeT's future.

Management Compensation and Ownership

Principals	Shares	Direct Owned	Annual Investment	Previous Salary	Salary Reduction
John F. Ellingson	200,000	$20,000	$60,000	$85,000	24%
Luis Hernandez	150,000	$18,248	$60,000	$72,000	16%
Kevin Spencer	20,000	$ 1,752	$60,000	$70,000	14%
Investment Total		$40,000			

Management is immediately vested in the company upon its inception. Equity is presently being used as the prime incentivising force, however, plans for a more formal incentive structure as well as employee contracts will be addressed prior to new sales force hire.

Incentives, Vesting, Employee Agreements

OpExNeT's bylaws require that a board of directors, between four to six members, be assembled. The present directors are Messrs. Ellingson, Hernandez, Spencer and Groves with two directorships reserved for representation of equity investors.

Board of Directors

OpExNeT is presently represented by Mr. Bill Venema of Venema, Delaschmit and Self as general counsel. The firm of Coopers & Lybrand, LLP have been retained as independent auditors.

Supporting Professional Advisors and Services

...continued

THE FINANCIAL PLAN

Pro forma financial statements are presented as Exhibits 1 through 7.

Exhibit 1: Sales and Earnings Forecasts

Fiscal Years Ended December 31, 1998-2003

(000)	1998	1999	2000	2001	2002	2003
Sales	$250	500	1,000	3,000	5,000	10,000
Cost of Sales						
Material	30	50	100	100	100	100
Labor	20	100	200	200	200	200
Total	50	150	300	300	300	300
Gross Margin	200	350	400	2,400	4,400	9,400
Percent	80.0%	70.0%	40.0%	80.0%	88.0%	94.0%
Selling and Marketing	86	100	100	100	200	500
Software Engineering	100	30	30	50	100	100
Administration & General	180	180	200	500	1,200	1,800
Total	366	310	330	650	1,500	2,400
Earnings before						
Interest and Taxes	(166)	40	70	1,750	2,900	7,000
Interest Expense (income)	24	24	24	24	24	24
Earnings before						
Federal and State Taxes	(190)	16	46	1,726	2,876	6,976
Federal & State Taxes				639	1,150	2,790
Net earnings before						
Extraordinary Item	(190)	16	46	1,087	1,726	4,186
Extraordinary Item	0	(190)	(174)	(128)	0	0
Net Earnings	(190)	(174)	(128)	959	1,726	4,186
Percent Sales before						
Extraordinary Item	(76%)	(35%)	(13%)	36%	35%	42%
Percent Sales after						
Extraordinary Item	(96%)	(45%)	(21%)	32%	35%	42%

1. All operations are performed in a leased facility in Atlanta, GA. Labor rates, line costs, lease rates, etc. used are consistent with the area.

2. All projections are in 1998 dollars.

3. Interest Payments are computed at 1 0% on borrowings. Borrowings will be provided by bank lines of credit.

       Balance sheet assumptions are:

       a) Accounts receivable: 30-day collection through mid-I 999; 45 days thereafter.

       b) Accounts payable: 60-day average through 1 999; 36 - 40 days thereafter.

5. Income taxes include state and federal.

6. Losses for 1998-99 carried forward and deducted in accordance with IRS Code Section 172.

7. Organizational expenses and initial design cost estimated to be $25,000 and $60,000, respectively, have been expensed.

Fiscal Year Ended December 31, 1998

(000)	Jun.	Jul.	Aug.	Sep.	Oct.	Nov.	Dec.	Total
Sales								
Services			5	10	10	10	20	55
Subscriptions			5	5	10	10	50	80
Advertising			5	20	30	30	30	115
Total			15	35	50	50	100	250
Cost of Sales								
Material	10	4	4	3	3	3	3	30
Labor			3	3	4	5	7	20
Total	10	4	7	6	7	8	10	50
Gross Margin			8	29	43	42	90	200
Percent			53%	83%	86%	84%	90%	80%
Selling & Mktg.	30	12	12	8	8	8	8	86
Software Engineering	20	20	20	10	10	10	10	100
Admin. & Gen.	40*	15	25	25	25	25	25	180
Total	90	47	57	43	43	43	43	366
EBIT	(100)	(51)	(49)	(14)	0	(1)	47	(166)
Interest Expense		14	2	2	2	2	2	24
Earnings before Federal & State Taxes	(100)	(65)	(51)	(16)	(2)	(3)	45	(190)
Net Earnings	(100)	(65)	(51)	(16)	(2)	(3)	45	(190)

Note: includes expenses during two months prior to incorporation.

Exhibit 3:
Quarterly Sales
and Earnings
Forecasts

Fiscal Year Ended December 31, 1998-99

(000)			1998					1999
Sales	3Q	4Q.	Total	IQ	2Q	3Q	4Q	Total
Services	15	40	55	15	50	15	20	100
Subscriptions	10	70	80	20	40	20	40	120
Advertising	25	90	115	130	70	40	40	280
Total	50	200	250	165	160	75	100	500
Cost of Sales								
Material	21	9	30	20	10	10	10	50
Labor	5	16	20	16	28	28	28	100
Total	26	25	50	36	38	38	38	150
Gross Margin	24	175	200	129	122	37	62	350
Percent	48%	88%	80%	78%	76%	49%	62%	70%
Selling and Marketing	62	24	86	65	10	15	10	100
Software Engineering	70	30	100	20	10			30
Admin. & General	105	75	180	45	45	45	45	180
Total	237	129	366	130	65	60	55	310
EBIT	(211)	46	(166)	(1)	57	(22)	7	40
Interest Expense	18	6	24	6	6	6	6	24
Earnings before Federal &								
State Taxes	(229)	40	(190)	(7)	51	(28)	1	16
Net Earnings	(229)	40	(190)	(7)	51	(28)	1	16

Fiscal Years Ended December 31, 1998-2003

(000)	1998	1999	2000	2001	2002	2003
Cash Receipts						
Accounts Recvbl.	150	400	800	2,400	4,000	8,000
Notes Receivable						200
Interest				64	86	124
Total	150	400	800	2,464	4,086	8,324
Cash Disbursements						
Purchase of Materials	27	48	95	97	97	97
Service Labor	13	91	193	195	195	195
Operations Overhead	5	7	15	20	20	20
Warranty Expense						
Admin. &, Gen., Selling And Engineering	366	310	330	650	1,500	2,400
Equipment	36	20	50	80	80	80
Federal & State Taxes				311	547	3,326
Interest	24	24	24	24	24	24
Total	471	500	707	1,377	2,463	6,142
Cash provided (drained) by Operations	(321)	(100)	93	1,087	1,623	2,182
Investment in long-term notes recvbl.			70	1,030	1,680	2,250
Bank borrowing (repayment)	60		(10)	(50)	80	80
Sale of common stock	240					
Net increase (decrease) is cash balance	(21)	(100)	13	7	23	12

Exhibit 5: Pro Forma Monthly Cash Flows

Fiscal Year Ended December 31, 1998

(000)	Jun.	Jul.	Aug.	Sep.	Oct.	Nov.	Dec.
Cash Receipts							
Accounts Receivable			15	35	50	50	
Notes Receivable							
Interest							
Total			15	35	50	50	
Cash Disbursements							
Purchase of Materials	10	4	4	3	3	3	
Service Labor			3	3	4	5	
Operations Overhead		1	1	1	1	1	
Warranty Expense							
Administration, General, Selling and Eng.		90	47	57	43	43	
Equipment		20	8	8			
Federal & State Taxes							
Interest		16	2	2	2	2	
Total	10	131	65	74	53	54	
Cash provided (drained) by Op.	(10)	(131)	(50)	(39)	(3)	(4)	
Investment in L/T notes rec.							
Bank borrowing (repayment)							
Sale of common stock	240						
Net increase (dec.) in cash balance	230	(131)	(50)	(39)	(3)	(4)	
Opening cash balance	40	270	139	89	50	47	
Closing cash balance*	270	139	89	50	47		

*Initial cash balance from investments of principals made prior to June 1, 1998. No corporate expenditures prior to June 1, 1998,

Fiscal Years Ended December 31, 1998-99

(000)		1998					1999	
	3Q	4Q	Total	1Q	2Q	3Q	4Q	Total
Cash Receipts								
Accts Receivable	15	135	150	160	175	80	95	510
Notes Receivable								
Interest								
Total	15	135	150	160	175	80	95	510
Cash Disbursements								
Purchase of Mtls	18	9	27	16	10	10	10	46
Service Labor	3	12	15	18	26	26	28	98
Op. Overhead	2	3	5	3	3	3	3	12
Warranty Expense								
Admin & General	137	143	280	198	85	70	55	408
Selling and Eng.								
Equipment	28	8	36	18	2			20
Federal & State Taxes								
Interest	18	6	24	6	6	6	6	24
Total	206	181	387	259	132	115	102	608
Cash provided (drained) by Op.	(191)	(46)	(237)	(99)	43	(35)	(7)	(98)
Bank borrowing (repayment)			60			60		
Sale of common stock		240	240	240				
Net increase (dec.) in cash bal.	49	(46)	3	(39)	43	(35)	(7)	(38)
Opening cash balance	40	89	40	43	4	47	12	43
Closing cash balance*	89	43	43	4	47	12		

Exhibit 7: Pro Forma Balance Sheet

Fiscal Years Ended December 31, 1998-2003

(000)	1998	1999	2000	2001	2002	2003
Current						
Cash	43	82	(8)	5	12	25
Accounts Receivable	150	510	830	2,380	3,920	7,910
Notes Receivable						200
Inventory						
Total	193	532	822	2,385	3,932	8,135
Property, Plant and Equipment	36	20	50	80	80	80
Less: Depreciation	18	10	25	40	40	40
Total Assets	211	622	847	2,425	3,972	8,175
Current Liabilities						
Accounts Payable & Accrued	47	156	303	312	312	312
Expense	340	452	404	1,065	2,151	5,830
Bank Loans Payable		60	50		80	80
Equity						
Capital Stock - common $. 10 par						
720,000 authorized shares	28	40	40	40	40	40
Paid-In Surplus						
Retained Earnings						
	(132)	(46)	90	1,048	1,429	1,953
Total Liabilities and Equity	208	622	847	21425	3,972	8,175

Break-Even Analysis

Break-even is calculated to occur at 30,000 in entries or $300,000 in sales.

Cost Control

As would be expected, the degree of OpExNeT's success will depend on its ability to control costs. To accomplish this, OpExNeT's management will have to rely on its experience in product development, project management and cost control. Software projects are notorious for coming in over budget and late. We find that most delays and additional costs are due to changes in the scope of work and poor planning. We believe that this document lays the groundwork for a definitive yet scalable and flexible product. This will be the key to the speed with which we enter the market and the adaptability that allows us to dominate it.

In further detail, software engineering projects will be benchmarked for progress. Databases are staged in three parts each with significant milestone dates identified. Costs reports from our suppliers will be updated at least every two weeks if not on a real time basis using Primavera Project Management Software and Networking. All subtasks will be identified and a critical path will be established.

After the completion of the website and related databases, ratio analysis of actual costs to estimate will be analyzed to identify any cost elements that caused significant deviation from budget.

OpExNeT, Inc. is incorporated in the state of Georgia and currently has 720,000 shares of $.10 par value common voting stock authorized and 370,000 shares issued as of June 01, 1998. OpExNeT now intends to raise $240,000 through the sale of 240,000 shares of its common voting stock at $1 per share. The common stock sold in this financing will represent about 33% of OpExNeT's outstanding common stock after the offering is completed.

Financing

Table 4 shows the capitalization of OpExNeT before and after the proposed offering.

Capitalization

Stockholders	Shares Owned Pre-Offering	Shares Owned Post-Offering	%Ownership	Investment	Cost/ Share
John F. Ellingson	200,000	200,000	32.8%	$20,000	$0.10
Luis Hernandez	150,000	150,000	24.6%	$18,248	$0.12
Kevin Spencer	20,000	20,000	3.3%	$1,752	$0.09
Investors of Offering		240,000	39.3%	$240yooo	$1.00
Totals	370,000	610,000	100.0%	$280,000	

The money raised in this offering ($240,000) together with the money raised earlier by the sale of stock to OpExNeT's principals and key employees, will be used to design, test and post the website and databases for client access. An additional $60,000 in bank borrowing will occur in the first quarter of 1999 (see Pro Forma Cash Flows and Balance Sheets). By the year 2000, OpExNeT expects to have a $250,000 revolving line of credit through Atlanta banks.

Use of Funds

As with any new venture, there are risks with OpExNeT's plans. Recognition of these risks, evaluation of their severity and proper contingency planning of outcomes must be considered, The following are a list of potential risks, although not all inclusive, which need to be addressed for impact.

CRITICAL RISKS AND PROBLEMS

Risk: Acceptance of the use of the Internet does happen as quickly as we predict.
Evaluation: While we believe this risk to be small, given the client group we are targeting it is a possibility. Additional market research will be conducted to determine exactly what the Internet usage trend is.
Contingency: OpExNeT is prepared to intensify Internet use training through BOMA/BOMI and similar organizations to accelerate use. Furthermore, our pricing comparison information can be obtained via fax or mail with a phone-in survey. The costs to mail this information and the advertising will be substantially higher.

Risk: The OpExNeT databases do not get validation from the client base.
Evaluation: A possible reaction to receiving pricing normssubstantially different from the clients existing contract may require additional reinforcing from client and more likely OEM companies.
Contingency: We are preparing a single page piece of literature explaining the methodology

behind the database norm compilation. We will also keep complete statistical data on the entry content of each grouping and issue warnings for segments where entry data numbers vary greatly from the norm but not in enough numbers to justify a norm shift.

Risk: Clients do not accept confidentiality of the process.
Evaluation: It is possible that building managers will not share there existing contract information for fear of competition gaining critical insight to their operations.
Contingency: Every reinforcement will be made to emphasize the cooperative nature of this service. Each report will contain a pledge that the individual data entered will not be made available to other building management entities.

Risk: The system receives more volume than it can handle.
Evaluation: This is a condition we might relish instead of dread however the consequences can be just as damaging to OpExNeT's brand equity as too little volume.
Contingency: Our account with Advanced Web Creations of 10mb storage can be easily and quickly modified for a higher volume of transactions. AWC presently services account with ten times more volume than our estimates presently indicate we will need.

Risk: Potential competitors impart an interest in the market prior to us reaching our critical mass.
Evaluation: If there is a large enough perceived value to the database we are accumulating, other database companies may proceed into the market to compete for the information.
Contingency: This is the main reason behind our strategy to give the price comparison evaluations away for free. Association with BOMA and industry print would have to be accelerated to gain strategic alliance.

Risk: Delays in website or database design.
Evaluation: Delays for the first set of database are unlikely since they have already been created. Delays in either can be minimized to about $5,000 per month additional cash requirement.
Contingency: Strict project manager and adherence to the critical path requirements should minimize this risk. We should pursue the possibility of having another $10,000 in borrowing available, within debt-equity guidelines, to provide a another two months of room.

SUPPLIER LIST

- Advanced Web Creations
- Marketing Made Central
- WolfTech STT, LLC

STRATEGIC ALLIANCES AND ACQUISITIONS

Associations

BOMA/BOMI	LCSC	ASHE
APPA	NAIOP	AIA
IREM	IFMA	ASIS
NACORE	AFE	IIDA

Publications

- Buildings Magazine
- Facilities Design & Management
- Building Design & Construction
- Building Operations Management
- Today's Facility Manager
- Energy User News
- American School & University
- Health Facilities Management

Internet Café

BUSINESS PLAN

WIRED BEAN

345 Pine St.
Salem, OR 54228

This business plan for an Internet and coffee café is an excellent example of an owner considering all aspects of starting up from competition to financing and investment to promotion. As a well-rounded plan, this one provides a good checklist for other entrepreneurs to use in completing their own plans. Note the clear language, choice of location (low competition), and consideration of all costs. This plan was compiled using Business PlanPro, by Palo Alto Software ©.

- EXECUTIVE SUMMARY

- COMPANY SUMMARY

- SERVICES

- MARKET ANALYSIS SUMMARY

- STRATEGY AND IMPLEMENTATION SUMMARY

- MANAGEMENT SUMMARY

- FINANCIAL PLAN

EXECUTIVE SUMMARY

Wired Bean, unlike most cafes will provide a unique forum for communication and entertainment through the medium of the Internet. Wired Bean, and cafes like it are the answer to an increasing demand. To provide to the general public: (1) access to the methods of communication, and volumes of information now available on the Internet, and (2) access at a cost they can afford and in such a way that they aren't socially, economically, or politically isolated. Wired Bean's goal is to provide the community with a social, educational, entertaining, atmosphere for world wide communication.

This business plan is prepared to obtain financing in the amount of $33,290, to begin work on site preparation and modifications, equipment purchases, and to cover expenses in the first year of operations. The approved financing from the Oregon Economic Development Fund consists of 72% percent of the total borrowing. This debt will be retired within 36 months. They will donate equity of $24,000 that will be cleared at the end of 36 months. Dividends will be paid quarterly on the outstanding equity.

Wired Bean will be incorporated as an LLC corporation. This will shield the owner Peter Jones, and the three outside investors, Jerry Thomas, Jack Simmons, and Gary St. Clair, from issues of personal liability and double taxation. The investors will be treated as shareholders and therefore will not be liable for more than their individual personal investment of $6,000 each. The owner Peter Jones, will contribute $13,000 of his personal savings towards this business venture.

The financing, in addition to the capital contributions from the owner and shareholders, will allow Wired Bean to successfully open and maintain operations through year one. The large initial capital investment will allow Wired Bean to provide it's customers with a fully featured Internet cafe. A unique, upscale, and innovative environment is required to provide the customer with an atmosphere that will spawn socialization. The successful operation of year one will provide Wired Bean with a customer base that will allow it to be self sufficient in year two.

Objectives

Wired Bean's objectives for the first three years of operation include:

- The creation of a unique, upscale, innovative environment that will differentiate Wired Bean from local coffee houses.
- Educating the community on what the Internet has to offer.
- The formation of an environment that will bring people with diverse interests and backgrounds together in a common forum.
- Good coffee and bakery items at a reasonable price.
- Affordable access to the resources of the Internet and other on-line services.

Mission

As the popularity of the Internet continues to grow at an exponential rate, easy and affordable access to the information super highway is quickly becoming a necessity of life. Wired Bean provides communities with the ability to access the Internet. We will provide communities with a place to gather for entertainment, and socialization. People of all ages and backgrounds will come to enjoy the unique, upscale, and innovative environment that Wired Bean provides. Our friendly and resourceful staff educates the community on the benefits of the Internet. Wired Bean also provides the best coffee and bakery items in town.

The Keys to the success for Wired Bean are:

1) The creation of a unique, innovative, upscale atmosphere that will differentiate Wired Bean from other local coffee shops and future Internet cafes.
2) The establishment of Wired Bean as a community hub for socialization and entertainment.
3) The creation of an environment that won't intimidate the novice user. Wired Bean will position itself as an educational resource for individuals wishing to learn about the benefits the Internet has to offer.
4) Great coffee and bakery items.

The risks involved with starting Wired Bean are:

1) Will there be a demand for the services offered by Wired Bean in Salem?
2) Will the popularity of the Internet continue to grow, or is the Internet a fad?
3) Will individuals be willing to pay for the service Wired Bean offers?
4) Will the cost of accessing the Internet from home drop so significantly that there will not be a market for Internet Cafes such as Wired Bean?

Wired Bean, soon to be located in downtown Salem on North River and Pine, will offer the community easy and affordable access to the Internet. Wired Bean will provide full access to E-mail, WWW, FTP, Usenet and other Internet applications such as telnet and gopher. Wired Bean will also provide customers with a unique and innovative environment for enjoying great coffee, specialty beverages, and bakery items..

Wired Bean, will appeal to individuals of all ages and backgrounds. The instructional Internet classes, and the helpful staff that Wired Bean provides, will appeal to the audience that does not associate themselves with the computer age. This educational aspect will attract younger and elder members of the community that are rapidly gaining interest in the unique resources on-line communications have to offer. The downtown location will provide business people with convenient access to their morningcoffee and on-line needs.

Wired Bean is a privately held Oregon Limited Liability Corporation Peter Jones, the founder of Wired Bean, is the majority owner. Jerry Thomas, Jack Simmons, and Gary St. Clair, all hold minority stock positions as private investors.

Wired Bean's start-up costs will cover coffee making, site renovation and modification, capital to cover losses in the first year and the communications equipment necessary to get it's customers on-line.

The communications equipment necessary to provide Wired Bean's customers with a high-speed connection to the Internet and the services it has to offer make up a large portion of the start-up costs. These costs will include the computer terminals and all costs associated with their set-up. Costs will also be designated for the purchase of two laser printers and a scanner.

In addition, costs will be allocated for the purchase of coffee making equipment. One espresso machine, an automatic coffee grinder, and minor additional equipment will be purchased from Allan Brothers.

Start-up Summary
...continued

The site at North River and Pine will require funds for renovation and modification. A single estimated figure will be allocated for this purpose The renovation/modification cost estimate will include the costs associated with preparing the site for opening business.

Start-up Plan

Startup Expenses

Legal	$500
Stationery etc.	$500
Brochures	$500
4-Group Automatic	$10,700
Bean Grinder	$795
Consultants	$2,000
Insurance	$700
Rent	$1,445
Computer Systems(x11)+print	$24,310
Communication Lines Setup	$840
Fixtures	$20,000
Other	$0
Total Start-up Expense	$62,290

Start-up Assets Needed

Cash requirements	$24,000
Start-up inventory	$2,000
Other Short-term Assets	$0
Total Short-term Assets	$26,000
Long-term Assets	
Capital Assets	$0
Total Assets	$26,000
Total Startup Requirements:	$88,290
Left to finance:	$0

Start-up Funding Plan

Investment

Oregon Economic Development Council	$24,000
Peter Jones	$13,000
Investor2	$6,000
Investor3	$6,000
Investor4	$6,000
Other	$0
Total investment	$55,000

Short-term borrowing

Unpaid expenses	$0
Short-term loans	$9,290

Interest-free short-term loans	$0
Subtotal Short-term Borrowing	$9,290
Long-term Borrowing	$24,000
Total Borrowing	$33,290
Loss at start-up	($62,290)
Total Equity	($7,290)
Total Debt and Equity	$26,000
Checkline	$0

Wired Bean will provide full access to E-mail, WWW, FTP, Usenet and other Internet applications such as telnet and gopher. Printing, scanning, and introductory courses to the Internet will also be available to the customer. Wired Bean will also provide customers with a unique and innovative environment for enjoying great coffee, specialty beverages, and bakery items.

Company Products

A site has been chosen at North River and Pine in downtown Salem. This site was chosen for various reasons, including:

Company Locations and Facilities

- Proximity to the downtown business community.

- Proximity to trendy, upscale restaurants such as Hamilton Bistro.

- Proximity to LTD's Salem Station. Parking availability.

- Low cost rent -85c per square foot for 1700 square feet.

- High visibility.

All of these qualities are consistent with Wired Bean's goal of providing a central hub of communication and socialization for the Salem community.

Wired Bean will provide full access to E-mail, WWW, FTP, Usenet and other Internet applications such as telnet and gopher. In addition Wired Bean will provide an Introduction to the Net class for customers that haven't yet discovered the wonders of the Internet. By offering this class for a modest fee, Wired Bean will increase it's customer base by creating customers. Wired Bean will also provide customers with a unique and innovative environment for enjoying great coffee, specialty beverages, and bakery items.

Products

Wired Bean will offer it's customers full access to the Internet, coffee, and bakery items.

Product Description

Wired Bean will be the first Internet cafe in Salem. Wired Bean will differentiate itself from the strictly coffee cafes in Salem by providing it's customers with Internet service. The coffee offered at Wired Bean will come from the Frederickson Supply company.

Competitive Comparison

Sourcing

Wired Bean will obtain computer support and Internet access from Capitol Computers located in Salem. Capitol will provide the Internet connections, network consulting, and the hardware required to run the Wired Beanwork. Frederickson Supply will provide Wired Bean with coffee equipment, bulk coffee, and paper supplies. At this time, a contract for the bakery items has not been completed. Wired Bean is currently negotiating with Wonder Bagel and the Belgian Bakery to fulfill the requirement. For startup purposes, Wired Bean will temporarily make use of Costco's fine bakery department.

Technology

Wired Bean will invest in high-speed computers to provide it's customers with a fast and efficient connection to the Internet. The computers will be reliable and fun to work with. Wired Bean will continue to upgrade and modify the systems to stay current with communications technology. One of the main attractions associated with Internet cafes, is the state of the art equipment available for use. Not everyone has a pentium based PC in their home or office.

Future Products

As Wired Bean grows, more communications systems will be added. The possibility of additional units has been accounted for in the current floor plan. As the demand for Internet connectivity increases, along with the increase in competition, Wired Bean will continue to add new services to keep it's customer base.

MARKET ANALYSIS SUMMARY

Wired Bean is faced with the exciting opportunity of being the first-mover in the Salem cyber-cafe market. The consistent popularity of coffee combined with the growing interest in the Internet has been proven to be a winning concept in other markets and will produce the same results in Salem.

Market Segmentation

Wired Bean's customers can be divided into two groups. The first group is familiar with the Internet and desires a progressive and inviting atmosphere where they can get out of their office or bedroom and enjoy a great cup of coffee. The second group is not familiar with the Internet, yet, is just waiting for the right opportunity to enter the on-line community. Wired Bean's target market falls anywhere between the ages of eighteen and fifty. This extremely wide range of ages is due to the fact that both coffee, and the Internet appeal to a variety of people. In addition to these categories, Wired Bean's target market is the educated and upwardly mobile segment of Salem which resides primarily in the central and eastern portions of the city. The majority of these individuals are students and business people.

Industry Analysis

The retail coffee industry in Salem experienced rapid growth at the beginning of the decade and is now moving into the mature stage of its life-cycle. Many factors contribute to the large demand for good coffee in Salem. The University is a main source of demand for coffee retailers. The climate in Salem is extremely conducive to coffee consumption. Current trends in the Northwest reflect the popularity of fresh, strong, quality coffee and specialty drinks. Salem is a haven for coffee lovers.

The popularity of the Internet is growing exponentially. Those who are familiar with the information superhighway are well aware of how fun and addicting surfing the net can be. Those who have not yet experienced the Internet, need a convenient, relaxed atmosphere where they can feel comfortable learning about and utilizing the current technologies. Wired Bean seeks to provide its customers with affordable Internet access in an innovative and supportive environment.

Do to intense competition, cafe owners must look for ways to differentiate their place of business from others in order to achieve and maintain a competitive advantage. The founder of Wired Bean realizes the need for differentiation and strongly believes that combining a cafe with complete Internet service is the key to success. The fact that no cyber-cafes are established in Salem, presents Wired Bean with a chance to enter the window of opportunity and enter into a profitable niche in the market.

There are approximately sixteen coffee wholesalers in Linn County. These wholesalers distribute coffee and espresso beans to over twenty retailers in the Salem area. Competition in both channels creates an even amount of bargaining power between buyers and suppliers resulting in extremely competitive pricing. Some of these major players in the industry (i.e. Frederickson Supply Co., Inc. and JavaJoint Ltd.) distribute and retail coffee products.

Industry Participants

The number of on-line service providers in Salem is approximately eight and counting. These small, regional service providers use a number of different pricing strategies. Some charge a monthly fee while others charge hourly and/or phone fees. Regardless of the pricing method used, obtaining Internet access through one of these firms can be expensive. Larger Internet servers such as America On-line, Prodigy and CompuServe are also fighting for market share in this rapidly growing industry. These service providers are also rather costly for the average consumer. Consumers who are not convinced they would frequently, and consistently travel the Internet, will not be willing to pay these prices.

The dual product/service nature of Wired Bean's business faces competition on two levels. Wired Bean competes not only with coffee retailers, but also with Internet service providers. The good news is that Wired Bean does not currently face any direct competition from other cyber-cafes in the Salem market. There are a total of three cyber-cafes in the state of Oregon. One located in Portland and two in Ashland.

Distribution Patterns

Heavy competition between coffee retailers in Salem, creates an industry where all firms face the same costs. There is a positive relationship between price and quality of coffee. Some coffees retail at $8/pound while other, more exotic beans may sell for as high as $16/pound. Wholesalers sell beans to retailers at an average of a 50 percent discount. For example, a pound of Sumatran beans wholesales for $6.95 and retails for $13.95. And as in most industries, price decreases as volume increases.

The main competitors in the retail coffee segment are Purgatory Cafe, Mud Hub, JavaJoint and Frederickson Supply These businesses are located in or near the downtown area, and target a similar segment to Wired Bean's (i.e. educated, upwardly mobile students and business people).

Competition and Buying Patterns

Competition from on-line service providers comes from locally owned businesses as well as national firms. There are approximately eight, local, on-line service providers in Salem. This number is expected to grow with the increasing demand for Internet access. Larger, on-line service providers such as AOL and CompuServe are also a competitive threat to Wired Bean. Due to the nature of the Internet, there are no geographical boundaries restricting competition.

Factors such as current trends, addiction and historical sales data ensure that the high demand for coffee will remain constant over the next five years. The rapid growth of the Internet and on-line services that has been witnessed world-wide is only the tip of the iceberg. The potential

Market Analysis

growth of the Internet is enormous, to the point where one day, a computer terminal with on-line connection will be as common and necessary as a telephone. This may be ten or twenty years down the road, but for the next five years, the on-line service provider market is sure to experience tremendous growth. Being the first cyber-cafe in Salem, Wired Bean will enjoy the first-mover advantages of name recognition and customer loyalty. Initially Wired Bean will hold a 100 percent share of the cyber-cafe market in Salem. In the next five years, competitors will enter the market. Wired Bean has set a goal to maintain greater than a 50 percent market share.

Market Analysis

Potential Customers	Customers	Growth rate
Internet Familiar	25,000	4%
Internet Unfamiliar	50,000	3%
Other	0	0%
Total	75,000	3.50%

Market Survey

A market survey was conducted in the Fall of 1996. Key questions were asked of fifty potential customers. Some key finding include:

- Thirty five subjects said they would be willing to pay for access to the internet.

- Five dollars an hour was the most popular hourly internet fee.

- Twenty four subjects use the internet to communicate with others on a regular basis.

STRATEGY AND IMPLEMENTATION SUMMARY

Wired Bean will follow a differentiation strategy to achieve a competitive advantage in the cafe market. By providing Internet service, Wired Bean separates itself from all other cafes in Salem. In addition, Wired Bean provides a comfortable environment with coffee and bakery items, distinguishing itself from other Internet providers in Salem.

Marketing Strategy

Wired Bean will position itself as an upscale coffee house and Internet service provider. It will serve high-quality coffee and espresso specialty drinks at a competitive price. Due to the number of cafes in Salem, it is important that Wired Bean sets fair prices for its coffee. Wired Bean will use advertising as its main source of promotion. Ads placed in The Daily Cyclone, Salem Weekly, and the Jubilee Herald will help build customer awareness. Accompanying the ad, will be a coupon for a free hour of Internet travel. Furthermore, Wired Bean will give away three free hours of Internet use to beginners who sign up for an introduction to the Internet workshop provided by Wired Bean.

Target Markets and Market Segments

Wired Bean intends to cater to people who want a guided tour on their first spin around the information highway and to experienced users eager to indulge their passion for computers in a social setting. Furthermore, Wired Bean will be a magnet for local and traveling professionals who desire to work or check their e-mail messages in a friendly atmosphere. These professionals will either use Wired Bean's PCs, or plug their notebooks into Internet connections. Wired Bean's target market covers a wide range of ages. From members of Generation X who grew up surrounded by computers, to Baby Boomers who have come to the realization that people today, cannot afford to ignore computers.

Wired Bean bases it's prices for coffee and specialty drinks on the "Retail Profit Analysis" provided by our supplier; Frederickson Supply Co., Inc. Frederickson Supply has been in the coffee business for 22 years and has developed a solid pricing strategy.

Determining a fair market, hourly price, for on-line use is more difficult because there is no direct competition from another cyber-cafe in Salem. Therefore, Wired Bean considered three sources to determine the hourly charge rate. First, the cost to use other Internet servers, whether it is a local networking firm or a provider such as America On-line. Internet access providers use different pricing schemes. Some charge a monthly fee, while others charge an hourly fee. In addition, some providers use a strategy with a combination of both pricing schemes. Thus, it can quickly become a high monthly cost for the individual. Second, Wired Bean looked at how cyber-cafes in other markets such as Portland and Ashland went about pricing Internet access. Third, Wired Bean used the market survey conducted in the Fall of 1996. Evaluating these three factors resulted in Wired Bean's hourly price of five dollars.

Wired Bean will implement a pull strategy in order to build consumer awareness and demand. Initially, Wired Bean has budgeted $5,000 for promotional efforts which will include advertising with coupons for a free hour of Internet time in local publications and in-house promotions such as offering customers free Internet time if they pay for an introduction to the Internet workshop taught by Wired Bean's computer technician. Wired Bean realizes that in the future, when competition enters the market, additional revenues must be allocated for promotion in order to maintain market share.

As a retail establishment, Wired Bean employs people to handle sales transactions. Computer literacy is a requirement for Wired Bean employees. If an employee does not possess basic computer skills when they are hired, they are trained by our full-time technician. Our full-time technician is also available for customers in need of assistance. Wired Bean's commitment to friendly, helpful service is one of the key factors that distinguishes Wired Bean from other Internet cafes.

Any customer who runs into trouble working on a terminal can ask Wired Bean's full-time technician for assistance. If the technician is not available, Wired Bean's part-time employees are trained to deal with common problems encountered by novices. Also, if Wired Bean's founder, Peter Jones is around, he is always willing to personally help a customer.

In the event that a customer is unsatisfied with a food or beverage product, Wired Bean will courteously remedy the situation by either replacing the item, or offering a complete refund.

Wired Bean will purchase coffee beans from Frederickson Supply Co., Inc., a coffee wholesaler and retailer based in Corvallis. Frederickson Supply is extremely supportive of its buyers. They sell as well as lease coffee equipment such as grinders and espresso machines. Frederickson Supply provides the following: a one or two year parts and labor limited warranty, installation and testing, on-call service (24hrs/day-7 days/week), training on-site, or at their Corvallis facility, and a start-up kit including syrups, chocolate and other supplies necessary to operate an espresso machine.

Pricing Strategy

Promotion Strategy

Sales Strategy

Service and Support

Strategic Alliances

Timeline

From the time of start-up, Wired Bean has allocated $5,000 for promotional efforts. The majority of these funds will go towards advertising, while the remaining dollars support in-house promotions such as coupons for free Internet access. Wired Bean realizes that direct competition is just around the corner. Therefore, Wired Bean is planning on contributing an additional 2%-5% of revenue toward promotion as it becomes necessary to combat competitive threats. Due to the uncertainty of competition at the present time, Wired Bean is not setting a scheduled plan for implementation of sales promotions.

Management Summary

Wired Bean is owned and operated by Mr. Peter Jones. The company, being small in nature, requires a simple organizational structure. Implementation of this organizational form calls for the owner, Mr. Jones, to make all of the major management decisions in addition to monitoring all other business activities.

Personnel Plan

The staff will consist of six, part-time employees working thirty hours a week at $5.50 per hour. In addition, one full-time technician (who is more technologically oriented to handle minor terminal repairs/inquiries) will be employed to work forty hours a week at $10.00 per hour. The three private investors, Jerry Thomas, Jack Simmons and Gary St. Clair will not be included in management decisions. This simple structure provides a great deal of flexibility and allows communication to disperse quickly and directly. Because of these characteristics, there are few coordination problems seen at Wired Bean that are common within larger organizational chains. This strategy will enable Wired Bean to react quickly to changes in the market. In the future, a full-time manager will be employed.

Personnel Plan

Job title	1996	1997	1998
Owner	$24,000	$36,000	$48,000
Part Time 1	$7,920	$8,158	$8,402
Part Time 2	$7,920	$8,158	$8,402
Part Time 3	$7,920	$8,158	$8,402
Part Time 4	$7,920	$8,158	$8,402
Part Time 5	$7,920	$8,158	$8,402
Part Time 6	$7,920	$8,158	$8,402
Technician	$15,360	$15,821	$16,295
Other	$0	$0	$0
Subtotal	$86,880	$100,766	$114,709

FINANCIAL PLAN

Summary of Financial Statement

Sales: Wired Bean is basing their projected coffee and espresso sales on the financial snapshot information provided to them by Frederickson Supply Co. Internet sales were estimated by calculating the total number of hours each terminal will be active each day and then generating a conservative estimate as to how many hours will be purchased by consumers.

Cost of Goods Sold: The cost of goods sold for coffee related products was determined by the "retail profit analysis" we obtained from Frederickson Supply Co. The cost of bakery items is 20% of the selling price. The cost of Internet access is $660 per month, paid to Capitol Computers for networking fees. The cost of e-mail accounts is 25% of the selling price.

Fixture Costs: Fixture costs associated with starting Wired Bean are the following: 11 computers = $22,000, two printers = $1,000, one scanner = $500, one espresso machine = $10,700, one automatic espresso grinder = $795, two coffee/food preparation counters = $1,000, one information display counter = $1,000, one drinking/eating counter = $500, sixteen stools = $1,600, six computer desks w/chairs = $2,400, stationary goods = $500, two telephones = $200, decoration expense = $14,110 for a total fixture cost of $50,000.

Salaries Expense: The founder of Wired Bean, Peter Jones, will receive a salary of $24,000 in year 1, $36,000 in year 2 and $48,000 in year 3.

Payroll Expense: Wired Bean intends to hire six part-time employees at $5.75/hour and a full-time technician at $10.00/hour. The total cost of employing seven people at these rates for the first year is $7,240/month.

Rent Expense: Wired Bean is leasing a 1700 square foot facility at $.85/sq. foot. The lease agreement Wired Bean signed specifies that we pay $1445/month for a total of 36 months. At the end of the third year, the lease is open for negotiations and Wired Bean may or may not re-sign the lease depending on the demands of the leasor.

Utilities Expense: As stated in the contract, the lessor is responsible for the payment of utilities including: gas, and garbage disposal and real estate taxes. The only utilities expense that Wired Bean must pay is the phone bill generated by fifteen phone lines; thirteen will be dedicated to modems and two for business purposes. The basic monthly service charge for each line provided by US West is $17.29. The 13 lines used to connect the modems will make local calls to the network provided by Capitol resulting in a monthly charge of $224.77. The two additional lines used for business communication will cost $34.58/month plus long distance fees. Wired Bean assumes that it will not make more than $40.00/month in long distance calls. Therefore, the total cost associated with the two business lines is estimated at $74.58/month and the total phone expense at $299.35/month. In addition, there will be an additional utility expense of $800 for estimated EWEB bills.

Marketing Expense: Wired Bean will allocate $5,000 for promotional expenses at the time of start-up. These dollars will be used for advertising in local newspapers in order to build consumer awareness. For additional information please refer to section 5.0 of the business plan.

Insurance Expense: Wired Bean has allocated $1,440 for insurance for the first year. As revenue increases in the second and third year of business, Wired Bean intends to invest more money for additional insurance coverage.

Legal and Consulting Fees: The cost of obtaining legal consultation in order to draw up the paper work necessary for an LLC is $1,000.

Depreciation: In depreciating our capital equipment, Wired Bean used the Modified Accelerated Cost Recovery Method. We depreciated our computers over a five year time period and our fixtures over seven years.

Taxes: Wired Bean is an LLC and as an entity it is not taxed. However, there is a 26% payroll burden.

Accounts Payable: Wired Bean acquired a $24,000 loan from a bank at a 10% interest rate. The loan will be paid back at $750/month over the next three years. The $9,290 short term loan will be paid back at a rate of 8%.

**Appendix:
Personnel Plan**

Personnel Plan

Job title	Jan-96	Feb-96	Mar-96	Apr-96	May-96	Jun-96
Owner	$2,000	$2,000	$2,000	$2,000	$2,000	$2,000
Part Time 1	$660	$660	$660	$660	$660	$660
Part Time 2	$660	$660	$660	$660	$660	$660
Part Time 3	$660	$660	$660	$660	$660	$660
Part Time 4	$660	$660	$660	$660	$660	$660
Part Time 5	$660	$660	$660	$660	$660	$660
Part Time 6	$660	$660	$660	$660	$660	$660
Technician	$1,280	$1,280	$1,280	$1,280	$1,280	$1,280
Other	$0	$0	$0	$0	$0	$0
Subtotal	$7,240	$7,240	$7,240	$7,240	$7,240	$7,240

Jul-96	Aug-96	Sep-96	Oct-96	Nov-96	Dec-96	1996	1997	1998
$2,000	$2,000	$2,000	$2,000	$2,000	$2,000	$24,000	$36,000	$48,000
$660	$660	$660	$660	$660	$660	$7,920	$8,158	$8,402
$660	$660	$660	$660	$660	$660	$7,920	$8,158	$8,402
$660	$660	$660	$660	$660	$660	$7,920	$8,158	$8,402
$660	$660	$660	$660	$660	$660	$7,920	$8,158	$8,402
$660	$660	$660	$660	$660	$660	$7,920	$8,158	$8,402
$660	$660	$660	$660	$660	$660	$7,920	$8,158	$8,402
$1,280	$1,280	$1,280	$1,280	$1,280	$1,280	$15,360	$15,821	$16,295
$0	$0	$0	$0	$0	$0	$0	$0	$0
$7,240	$7,240	$7,240	$7,240	$7,240	$7,240	$86,880	$100,766	$114,709

Marketing Consultancy

BUSINESS PLAN

MERIDIAN CONSULTING

3439 San Jose Blvd.
Santa Monica CA 60677

This plan describes an effort to launch a business on an international scale. Because of the nature of the business, the plan considers the business's positioning in the world marketplace and the heavy competition already in the arena. This plan was compiled using Business Plan Pro, by Palo Alto Software ©.

- EXECUTIVE SUMMARY

- COMPANY SUMMARY

- COMPANY SERVICES

- MARKET ANALYSIS SUMMARY

- STRATEGY SUMMARY

- MANAGEMENT SUMMARY

- FINANCIAL PLAN

MARKETING CONSULTANCY
BUSINESS PLAN

**EXECUTIVE
SUMMARY**

Meridian Consulting will be formed as a consulting complany specializing in marketing of high-technology products in international markets. Its founders are former marketers of consulting services, personal computers, and market research, all in international markets. They are founding Meridian to formalize the consulting services they offer.

Objectives

1. Sales of $350 thousand in 1995 and $1 million by 1997..

2. Gross margin higher than 80%.

3. Net income more than 10% of sales by the third year.

Mission

Meridian Consulting offers high-tech manufacturers a reliable, high-quality alternative to in-house resources for business development, market development, and channel development on an international scale. A true alternative to in-house resources offers a very high level of practical experience, know-how, contacts, and confidentiality. Clients must know that working with Meridian is a more professional, less risky way to develop new areas even than working completely in-house with their own people. Meridian must also be able to maintain financial balance, charging a high value for its services, and delivering an even higher value to its clients. Initial focus will be development in the European and Latin American markets, or for European clients in the United States market.

Keys to Success

1. Excellence in fulfilling the promise — completely confidential, reliable, trustworthy expertise and information.

2. Developing visibility to generate new business leads.

3. Leveraging from a single pool of expertise into multiple revenue generation opportunities: retainer consulting, project consulting, market research, and market research published reports.

**COMPANY
SUMMARY**

Meridian Consulting is a new company providing high-level expertise in international high-tech business development, channel development, distribution strategies, and marketing of high-tech products. It will focus initially on providing two kinds of international triangles:

•Providing United States clients with development for European and Latin American markets.

•Providing European clients with development for the United States and Latin American markets.

As it grows it will take on people and consulting work in related markets, such as the rest of Latin America, and the Far East, and similar markets. As it grows it will look for additional leverage by taking brokerage positions and representation positions to create percentage holdings in product results.

**Company
Ownership**

Meridian Consulting will be created as a California C corporation based in Santa Marita County, owned by its principal investors and principal operators. As of this writing it has not been chartered yet and is still considering alternatives of legal formation.

Total start-up expense (including legal costs, logo design, stationery and related expenses) come to $73,000. Start-up assets required include $3,000 in short-term assets (office furniture, etc.) and $1,000,000 in initial cash to handle the first few months of consulting operations as sales and accounts receivable play through the cash flow. The details are included in Table 1.

Start-up Summary

Start-up Plan

Start-up Expenses
Legal $1,000
Stationery etc. $3,000
Brochures $5,000
Consultants $5,000
Insurance $350
Expensed equipment $3,000
Other $1,000
Total Start-up Expense $18,350

Start-up Assets Needed
Cash requirements $25,000
Start-up inventory $50,000
Other Short-term Assets $7,000
Total Short-term Assets $32,000
Long-term Assets
Capital Assets $0
Total Assets $32,000

Total Start-up Requirements: $50,350
Left to finance: $0

Start-up Funding Plan

Investment
Investor 1 $20,000
Investor 2 $20,000
Other $10,000
Total investment $50,000

Short-term borrowing
Unpaid expenses $5,000
Short-term loans $0
Interest-free short-term loans $0
Subtotal Short-term Borrowing $5,000
Long-term Borrowing $0
Total Borrowing $5,000

Loss at start-up	($23,000)
Total Equity	$27,000
Total Debt and Equity	$32,000
Checkline	$0

COMPANY SERVICES

Meridian offers expertise in channel distribution, channel development, and market development, sold and packaged in various ways that allow clients to choose their preferred relationship: these include retainer consulting relationships, project-based consulting, relationship and alliance brokering, sales representation and market representation, project-based market research, published market research, and information forum events.

Services

Meridian offers the expertise a high-technology company needs to develop new product distribution and new market segments in new markets. This can be taken as high-level retainerconsulting, market research reports, or project-based consulting.

Service Description

1. Retainer consulting: we represent a client company as an extension of its business development and market development functions. This begins with complete understanding of the client company's situation, objectives, and constraints. We then represent the client company quietly and confidentially, sifting through new market developments and new opportunities as is appropriate to the client, representing the client in initial talks with possible allies, vendors, and channels.

2. Project consulting: Proposed and billed on a per-project and per-milestone basis, project consulting offers a client company a way to harness our specific qualities and use our expertise to solve specific problems, develop and/or implement plans, develop specific information.

3. Market research: group studies available to selected clients at $5,000 per unit. A group study is packaged and published, a complete study of a specific market, channel, or topic. Examples might be studies of developing consumer channels in Japan or Mexico, or implications of changing margins in software.

Competitive Comparison

The competition comes in several forms

1. The most significant competition is no consulting at all, companies choosing to do business development and channel development and market research in-house. Their own managers do this on their own, as part of their regular business functions. Our key advantage in competition with in-house development is that managers are already overloaded with responsibilities, they don't have time for additional responsibilities in new market development or new channel development. Also, Meridian can approach alliances, vendors, and channels on a confidential basis, gathering information and making initial contacts in ways that the corporate managers can't.

2. The high-level prestige management consulting: McKinsey, Bain, Arthur Anderson, Boston Consulting Group, etc. These are essentially generalists who take their name-brand management consulting into specialty areas. Their other very important weakness is the management structure that has the partners selling new jobs, and inexperienced associates delivering the work. We compete against them as experts in our specific fields, and with the guarantee that our clients will have the top-level people doing the actual work.

3. The third general kind of competitor is the international market research company: International Data Corporation (IDC), Dataquest, Stanford Research Institute, etc. These companies are formidable competitors for published market research and market forums, but cannot provide the kind of high-level consulting that Meridian will provide.

4. The fourth kind of competition is the market-specific smaller house. For example: NomuraResearch in Japan, Select S.A. de C.V. in Mexico (now affiliated with IDC).

5. Sales representation, brokering, and deal catalysts are an ad-hoc business form that will be defined in detail by the specific nature of each individual case.

The business will begin with a general corporate brochure establishing the positioning. This brochure will be developed as part of the start-up expenses.   **Sales Literature**

Literature and mailings for the initial market forums will be very important, with the need to establish a high-quality look and feel for

1. The key fulfillment and delivery will be provided by the principals of the business. The real core value is professional expertise, provided by a combination of experience, hard work. and education (in that order).   **Sourcing**

2. We will turn to qualified professionals for free-lance back-up in market research and presentation and report development, which are areas that we can afford to contract out without risking the core values provided to the clients.

Meridian Consulting will maintain latest Windows and Macintosh capabilities including: **Technology**

1. Complete Email facilities in Internet, Compuserve, America-Online, and Applelink, for working with clients directly through email delivery of drafts and information.

2. Complete presentation facilities for preparation and delivery of multimedia presentations on Macintosh or Windows machines, in formats including on-disk presentation, live presentation, or video presentation.

3. Complete desktop publishing facilities for delivery of regular retainer reports, project output reports, marketing materials, market research reports.

In the future, Meridian will broaden the coverage by expanding into coverage of additional markets (e.g. all of Latin America, Far East, Western Europe) and additional product areas (e.g. telecommunications and technology integration).   **Future Services**

We are also studying the possibility of newsletter or electronic newsletter services, or perhaps special on-topic reports.

Meridian will be focusing on high-technology manufacturers of computer hardware and software, services, and networking, who want to sell into markets in the United States, Europe, and Latin America. These are mostly larger companies, and occasionally medium-sized companies.   **MARKET ANALYSIS SUMMARY**

Our most important group of potential customers are executives in larger corporations. These are marketing managers, general managers, and sales managers, sometimes charged with international focus and sometimes charged with market or even specific channel focus. They do not want to waste their time or risk their money looking for bargain information or questionnable expertise. As they go into markets looking at new opportunities, they are very sensitive to risking their company's name and reputation. Professional experience

Market Segmentation

1. Large manufacturer corporations: our most important market segment is the large manufacturer of high-technology products, such as Apple, Hewlett-Packard, IBM, Microsoft, Siemens, or Olivetti. These companies will be calling on Meridian for development functions that are better spun off than managed in-house, and for market research, and for market forums.

2. Medium-sized growth companies: particularly in software, multimedia, and some related high-growth fields, Meridian will be able to offer an attractive development alternative to the company that is management constrained and unable to address opportunities in new markets and new market segments.

Industry Analysis

Connsulting "industry" is pulverized and disorganized, thousands of smaller consulting organizations and individual consultants for every one of the few dozen well-known companies.

Consulting is a disorganized industry, with participants ranging from major international name-brand consultants to tens of thousands of individuals. One of Meridian's challenges will be establishing itself as a "real" consulting company, positioned as a relatively risk-free corporate purchase.

Industry Participants

Consulting "industry" is pulverized and disorganized, thousands of smaller consulting organizations and individual consultants for every one of the few dozen well-known companies.

At the highest level are the few well-established major names in management consulting. Most of these are organized as partnerships established in major markets around the world, linked together by interconnecting directors and sharing the name and corporate wisdom. Some evolved from accounting companies (e.g. Arthur Anderson, Touche Ross) and some from managementconsulting (McKinsey, Bain). These companies charge very high rates for consulting, and maintain relatively high overhead structures and fulfillment structures based on partners selling and junior associates fulfilling.

At the intermediate level are some function-specific or market specific consultants, such as the market research firms (IDC, Dataquest) or channel development firms (ChannelCorp, Channel Strategies, ChannelMark).

Some kinds of consulting is little more than contract expertise provided by somebody looking for a job and offering consulting services as a stop-gap measure while looking.

Distribution Patterns

Consulting is sold and purchased mainly on a word-of-mouth basis, with relationships and previous experience being by far the most important factor.

The major name-brand houses have locations in major cities and major markets, and executive-level managers or partners develop new business through industry associations, business associations, and chambers of commerce and industry, etc., even in some cases social associations such as country clubs.

The medium-level houses are generally area-specific or function specific, and are not easily able to leverage their business through distribution.

The key element in purchase decisions made at the Meridian client level is trust in the professional reputation and reliability of the consulting firm.

Competition and Buying Patterns

Main Competitors

1. High-level prestige management consulting.

Strengths: international locations managed by owner-partners with a high level of presentation and understanding of general business. Enviable reputations which make purchase of consulting an easy decision for a manager, despite the very high prices.

Weaknesses: General business knowledge doesn't substitute for the specific market, channel, and distribution expertise of Meridian, focusing on high-technology markets and products only. Also, fees are extremely expensive, and work is generally done by very junior-level consultants, even though sold by high-level partners.

2. The international market research company

Strengths: International offices, specific market knowledge, permanent staff developing marketresearch information on permanent basis, good relationships with potential client companies.

Weaknesses: market numbers are not marketing, not channel development or market development. Although these companies compete for some of the business Meridian is after, they cannot really offer the same level of business understanding at a high level.

3. Market specific or function-specific experts

Strengths: expertise in market or functional areas. Meridian should not try to compete with Normura or Select in their markets with market research, or with ChannelCorp in channel management.

Weaknesses: the inability to spread beyond a specific focus, or to rise above a specific focus, to provide actual management expertise, experience, and wisdom beyond the specifics.

The most significant competition is no consulting at all, companies choosing to do business development and channel development and market research in-house.

Strengths: no incremental cost except travel; also, the general work is done by the people who are entirely responsible, the planning done by those who will implement.

Weaknesses: most managers are terribly overburdened already, unable to find incremental resources in time and people to apply to incremental opportunities. Also, there is a lot of additional risk in market development and channel development done in house from the ground up. Finally, retainer-based antenna consultants can greatly enhance a company's reach and extend its position into conversations that might otherwise never hanve taken place.

Market Analysis

As indicated by Table 2, we must focus on a few thousand well-chosen potential customers in the United States, Europe, and Latin America. These few thousand high-tech manufacturing companies are the key customers for Meridian.

Market Analysis

Potential Customers	Customers	Growth rate
U.S. High Tech	5,000	10%
European High Tech	1,000	15%
Latin America	250	35%
Other	10,000	2%
Total	16,250	6.27%

STRATEGY SUMMARY

Meridian will focus on three geographical markets, the United States, Europe, and Latin America, and in limited product segments: personal computers, software, networks, telecommunications, personal organizers, and technology integration products.

The target customer is usually a manager in a larger corporation, and occasionally an owner or president of a medium-sized corporation in a high-growth period.

Pricing Strategy

Meridian Consulting will be priced at the upper edge of what the market will bear, competing with the name brand consultants. The pricing fits with the general positioning of Meridian as high-level expertise.

Consulting should be based on $5,000 per day for project consulting, $2,000 per day for market research, and $10,000 per month and up for retainer consulting. Market research reports should be priced at $5,000 per report, which will of course require that reports be very well planned and focused on very important topics that are very well presented.

Sales Forecast

The sales forecast monthly summary is included in the appendix. The annual sales projections are included here in Table 3.

Sales Forecast

Sales	1996	1997	1998
Retainer Consulting	$200,000	$350,000	$425,000
Project Consulting	$270,000	$325,000	$350,000
Market Research	$122,000	$150,000	$200,000
Strategic Reports	$0	$50,000	$125,000
Other	$0	$0	$0
Total Sales	$592,000	$875,000	$1,100,000

Direct Costs	1996	1997	1998
Retainer Consulting	$30,000	$38,000	$48,000
Project Consulting	$45,000	$56,000	$70,000
Market Research	$84,000	$105,000	$131,000
Strategic Reports	$0	$20,000	$40,000
Other	$0	$0	$0
Subtotal Direct Cost of Sales	$159,000	$219,000	$289,000

At this writing strategic alliances with Morgan and Daley are possibilities, given the content of existing discussions. Given the background of prospective partners, we might also be talking to European companies including Siemens and Olivetti and others, and to United States companies related to Apple Computer. In Latin America we would be looking at the key localhigh-technology vendors, beginning with Printaform.

Strategic Alliances

The initial management team depends on the founders themselves, with little back-up. As we grow we will take on additional consulting help, plus graphic/editorial, sales, and marketing.

MANAGEMENT SUMMARY

Meridian should be managed by working partners, in a structure taken mainly from Morgan Partners. In the beginning we assume 3-5 partners:

•Richard Wiley

•At least one, probably two partners from Morgan and Daley

•One strong European partner, based in Paris.

•The organization has to be very flat in the beginning, with each of the founders reponsible for his or her own work and management.

•One other strong partner

Organizational Structure

The Meridian business requires a very high level of international experience and expertise, which means that it will not be easily leveragable in the common consulting company mode - in which partners run the business and make sales, while associates fulfill. Partners will necessarily be involved in the fulfillment of the core business proposition, providing the expertise to the clients.

The initial personnel plan is still tentative. It should involve 3-5 partners, 1-3 consultants, 1 strong editorial/graphic person with good staff support, 1 strong marketing person, an office manager, and a secretary. Later we add more partners, consultants and sales staff.

Management Team

The detailed monthly personnel plan for the first year is included in the appendices. The annual personal estimates are included here as Table 5.

Personnel Plan

Personnel Plan

		1996	1997	1998
Partners	1.4	$144,000	$175,000	$200,000
Consultants	1.25	$0	$50,000	$63,000
Editorial/graphic	1.2	$18,000	$22,000	$26,000
VP Marketing	1.1	$20,000	$50,000	$55,000
Sales people	1.1	$0	$30,000	$33,000
Office Manager	1.1	$7,500	$30,000	$33,000
Secretarial	1.1	$5,250	$20,000	$22,000
Other	1.1	$0	$0	$0
Subtotal		$194,750	$377,000	$432,000

**FINANCI AL
PLAN**

**Important
Assumptions**

Table 6 summarizes key financial assumptions, including 45-day average collection days, sales entirely on invoice basis, expenses mainly on net 30 basis, 35 days on average for payment of invoices, and present-day interest rates.

General Assumptions

	1996	1997	1998
Short Term Interest Rate	8.00%	8.00%	8.00%
Long Term Interest Rate	10.00%	10.00%	10.00%
Payment days	35	35	35
Collection days	45	60	60
Tax Rate Percent	25.00%	25.00%	25.00%
Expenses in cash%	25.00%	25.00%	25.00%
Sales on credit	100.00%	100.00%	100.00%
Personnel Burden %	14.00%	14.00%	14.00%

Note: Ratios in assumptions are used as estimators and may therefore have different values than ratios calculated in the ratios section.

**Key Financial
Indicators**

The following benchmark chart indicates our key financial indicators for the first three years. We foresee major growth in sales and operating expenses, and a bump in our collection days as we spread the business during expansion.

**Break-even
Analysis**

Table 7 summarizes key financial assumptions, including 45-day average collection days, sales entirely on invoice basis, expenses mainly on net 30 basis, 35 days on average for payment of invoices, and present-day interest rates.

Break Even Analysis
Monthly Units Break-even $12,500
Monthly Sales Break-even $12,500

Assumptions
Average Unit Sale $1.00
Average Per-Unit Cost $0.20
Fixed Cost $10,000

The detailed monthly pro-forma income statement for the first year is included in the appendices. The annual estimates are included here.

Pro-forma Income Statement

	1996	1997	1998
Sales	$592,000	$875,000	$1,100,000
Cost of Sales	$159,000	$219,000	$289,000
Other	$0	$0	$0
Total Cost of Sales	$159,000	$219,000	$289,000
Gross margin	$433,000	$656,000	$811,000
Gross margin percent	73.14%	74.97%	73.73%
Operating expenses:			
Advertising/Promotion			
10.00%	$36,000	$40,000	$44,000
Public Relations			
10.00%	$30,000	$30,000	$33,000
Travel			
10.00%	$90,000	$60,000	$110,000
Miscellaneous			
10.00%	$6,000	$7,000	$8,000
Payroll expense	$194,750	$377,000	$432,000
Leased Equipment	$6,000	$7,000	$7,000
Utilities	$12,000	$12,000	$12,000
Insurance	$3,600	$2,000	$2,000
Rent	$18,000	$0	$0
Depreciation	$200	$450	$600
Payroll Burden	$27,265	$52,780	$60,480
Contract/Consultants	$0	$0	$0
Other	$0	$0	$0
Total Operating Expenses			
	$423,815	$588,230	$709,080
Profit Before Interest			
and Taxes	$9,185	$67,770	$101,920
Interest Expense ST	$3,600	$12,800	$12,800
Interest Expense LT	$5,000	$5,000	$5,000
Taxes Incurred	$146	$12,493	$21,030
Net Profit	$439	$37,478	$63,090
Net Profit/Sales	0.07%	4.28%	5.74%

Projected Cash Flow

Cash flow projections are critical to our success. The annual cash flow figures are included here as Table 8. Detailed monthly numbers are included in the appendices.

Pro-Forma Cash Flow

	1996	1997	1998
Net Profit:	$439	$37,478	$63,090
Plus:			
Depreciation	$18,000	$0	$0
Change in Accounts Payable	$26,068	$1,434	$11,035
Current Borrowing (repayment)	$60,000	$100,000	$0
Increase (decrease) Other Liabilities	$0	$0	$0
Long-term Borrowing (repayment)	$50,000	$0	$0
Capital Input	$0	$0	$0
Subtotal	$154,507	$138,911	$74,125
Less:	1905	1905	1905
Change in Accounts Receivable	$100,000	$97,072	$50,676
Change in Inventory	$0	$0	$0
Change in Other ST Assets	$0	$0	$0
Capital Expenditure	$0	$0	$0
Dividends	$0	$0	$0
Subtotal	$100,000	$97,072	$50,676
Net Cash Flow	$54,507	$41,839	$23,449
Cash balance	$79,507	$121,346	$144,796

Projected Balance Sheet

The balance sheet shows healthy growth of net worth, and strong financial position. The monthly estimates are included in the appendices.

Pro-forma Balance Sheet

	1996	1997	1998
Short-term Assets Starting Balances			
Cash	$25,000	$79,507	$121,346	$144,796
Accounts receivable	$0	$100,000	$197,072	$247,748
Inventory	$0	$0	$0	$0
Other Short-term Assets	$7,000	$7,000	$7,000	$7,000
Total Short-term Assets	$32,000	$186,507	$325,418	$399,543
Long-term Assets				
Capital Assets	$0	$0	$0	$0
Accumulated Depreciation	$0	$18,000	$18,000	$18,000
Total Long-term Assets	$0	($18,000)	($18,000)	($18,000)
Total Assets	$32,000	$168,507	$307,418	$381,543
Debt and Equity				
Accounts Payable	$5,000	$31,068	$32,502	$43,537
Short-term Notes	$0	$60,000	$160,000	$160,000
Other ST Liabilities	$0	$0	$0	$0
Subtotal Short-term Liabilities	$5,000	$91,068	$192,502	$203,537
Long-term Liabilities	$0	$50,000	$50,000	$50,000
Total Liabilities	$5,000	$141,068	$242,502	$253,537
Paid in Capital	$50,000	$50,000	$50,000	$50,000
Retained Earnings	($23,000)	($23,000)	($22,561)	$14,916
Earnings	$0	$439	$37,478	$63,090
Total Equity	$27,000	$27,439	$64,916	$128,006
Total Debt and Equity	$32,000	$168,507	$307,418	$381,543
Net Worth	$27,000	$27,439	$64,916	$128,006

The following table shows the projected businesses ratios. We expect to maintain healthy ratios for profitability, risk, and return.

Ratio Analysis

Profitability Ratios:	1996	1997	1998	RMA
Gross margin	73.14%	74.97%	73.73%	0
Net profit margin	0.07%	4.28%	5.74%	0
Return on Assets	0.26%	12.19%	16.54%	0
Return on Equity	1.60%	57.73%	49.29%	0
Activity Ratios				
AR Turnover	5.92	4.44	4.44	0
Collection days	31	62	74	0
Inventory Turnover	0.00	0.00	0.00	0
Accts payable turnover	8.71	8.71	8.71	0
Total asset turnover	3.51	2.85	2.88	0

Debt Ratios:	1996	1997	1998	RMA
Debt to net Worth	5.14	3.74	1.98	0
Short-term Debt to Liab.	0.65	0.79	0.80	0

Liquidity ratios

	1996	1997	1998	RMA
Current Ratio	2.05	1.69	1.96	0
Quick Ratio	2.05	1.69	1.96	0
Net Working Capital	$95,439	$132,916	$196,006	0
Interest Coverage	1.07	3.81	5.73	0

Additional ratios	1996	1997	1998	RMA
Assets to sales	0.28	0.35	0.35	0
Debt/Assets	84%	79%	66%	0
Current debt/Total Assets	54%	63%	53%	0
Acid Test	0.95	0.67	0.75	0
Asset Turnover	3.51	2.85	2.88	0
Sales/Net Worth	21.58	13.48	8.59	0

Appendix: Pro-forma Balance Sheet
**Projected Balance
Sheet**

	Jan-96	Feb-96	Mar-96	Apr-96	May-96	Jun-96	Jul-96
Short-term Assets Starting Balances							
Cash	$25,000	$58,428	$39,767	$36,494	$43,163	$48,312	$44,086
Accounts receivable	$0	$10,000	$14,795	$29,589	$44,000	$75,000	$104,000
Inventory	$0	$0	$0	$0	$0	$0	$0
Other Short-term Assets	$7,000	$7,000	$7,000	$7,000	$7,000	$7,000	$7,000
Total Short-term Assets	$32,000	$75,428	$61,561	$73,083	$94,163	$130,312	$155,086
Long-term Assets							
Capital Assets	$0	$0	$0	$0	$0	$0	$0
Accumulated Depreciation	$0	$1,500	$3,000	$4,500	$6,000	$7,500	$9,000
Total Long-term Assets	$0	($1,500)	($3,000)	($4,500)	($6,000)	($7,500)	($9,000)
Total Assets	$32,000	$73,928	$58,561	$68,583	$88,163	$122,812	$146,086

Debt and Equity

	Jan-96	Feb-96	Mar-96	Apr-96	May-96	Jun-96	Jul-96
Accounts Payable	$5,000	$14,475	$16,656	$17,951	$21,403	$26,149	$30,896
Short-term Notes	$0	$0	$0	$20,000	$40,000	$60,000	$60,000
Other ST Liabilities	$0	$0	$0	$0	$0	$0	$0
Subtotal Short-term Liabilities	$5,000	$14,475	$16,656	$37,951	$61,403	$86,149	$90,896
Long-term Liabilities	$0	$50,000	$50,000	$50,000	$50,000	$50,000	$50,000
Total Liabilities	$5,000	$64,475	$66,656	$87,951	$111,403	$136,149	$140,896
Paid in Capital	$50,000	$50,000	$50,000	$50,000	$50,000	$50,000	$50,000
Retained Earnings	($23,000)	($23,000)	($23,000)	($23,000)	($23,000)	($23,000)	($23,000)
Earnings	$0	($17,548)	($35,095)	($46,368)	($50,240)	($40,338)	($21,810)
Total Equity	$27,000	$9,453	($8,095)	($19,368)	($23,240)	($13,338)	$5,190
Total Debt and Equity	$32,000	$73,928	$58,561	$68,583	$88,163	$122,812	$146,086
Net Worth	$27,000	$9,453	($8,095)	($19,368)	($23,240)	($13,337)	$5,190

Aug-96	Sep-96	Oct-96	Nov-96	Dec-96	1996	1997	1998
$61,072	$83,398	$77,676	$58,072	$60,174	$79,507	$79,507	$121,346
$87,500	$60,000	$87,500	$120,000	$132,500	$100,000	$100,000	$197,072
$0	$0	$0	$0	$0	$0	$0	$0
$7,000	$7,000	$7,000	$7,000	$7,000	$7,000	$7,000	$7,000
$155,572	$150,398	$172,176	$185,0 72	$199,674	$186,507	$186,507	$325,418
$0	$0	$0	$0	$0	$0	$0	$0
$10,500	$12,000	$13,500	$15,000	$16,500	$18,000	$18,000	$18,000
($10,500)	($12,000)	($13,500)	($15,000)	($16,500)	($18,000)	($18,000)	($18,000)
$145,072	$138,398	$158,676	$170,072	$183,174	$168,507	$168,507	$307,418

Aug-96	Sep-96	Oct-96	Nov-96	Dec-96	1996	1997	1998
$24,855	$21,403	$33,053	$35,211	$36,074	$31,068	$31,068	$32,502
$60,000	$60,000	$60,000	$60,000	$60,000	$60,000	$160,000	$160,000
$0	$0	$0	$0	$0	$0	$0	$0
$84,855	$81,403	$93,053	$95,211	$96,074	$91,068	$91,068	$192,502
$50,000	$50,000	$50,000	$50,000	$50,000	$50,000	$50,000	$50,000
$134,855	$131,403	$143,053	$145,211	$146,074	$141,068	$141,068	$242,502
$50,000	$50,000	$50,000	$50,000	$50,000	$50,000	$50,000	$50,000
($23,000)	($23,000)	($23,000)	($23,000)	($23,000)	($23,000)	($23,000)	($22,561)
($16,783)	($20,005)	($11,378)	($2,139)	$10,100	$439	$439	$37,478
$10,218	$6,995	$15,623	$24,861	$37,100	$27,439	$27,439	$64,916
$145,072	$138,398	$158,676	$170,072	$183,174	$168,507	$168,507	$307,418
$10,218	$6,995	$15,623	$24,861	$37,100	$27,439	$27,439	$64,916

Appendix: Projected Cash Flow

Pro-Forma Cash Flow

	Jan-96	Feb-96	Mar-96	Apr-96	May-96	Jun-96
Net Profit:	($17,548)	($17,548)	($11,273)	($3,873)	$9,903	$18,528
Plus:						
Depreciation	$1,500	$1,500	$1,500	$1,500	$1,500	$1,500
Change in Accounts Payable	$9,475	$2,181	$1,295	$3,452	$4,747	$4,747
Current Borrowing (repayment)	$0	$0	$20,000	$20,000	$20,000	$0
Increase (decrease) Other Liabilities	$0	$0	$0	$0	$0	$0
Long-term Borrowing (repayment)	$50,000	$0	$0	$0	$0	$0
Capital Input	$0	$0	$0	$0	$0	$0
Subtotal	$43,428	($13,866)	$11,522	$21,080	$36,149	$24,774
Less:	Jan	Feb	Mar	Apr	May	Jun
Change in Accounts Receivable	$10,000	$4,795	$14,795	$14,411	$31,000	$29,000
Change in Inventory	$0	$0	$0	$0	$0	$0
Change in Other ST Assets	$0	$0	$0	$0	$0	$0
Capital Expenditure	$0	$0	$0	$0	$0	$0
Dividends	$0	$0	$0	$0	$0	$0
Subtotal	$10,000	$4,795	$14,795	$14,411	$31,000	$29,000
Net Cash Flow	$33,428	($18,661)	($3,273)	$6,669	$5,149	($4,226)
Cash balance	$58,428	$39,767	$36,494	$43,163	$48,312	$44,086

Appendix: Important Assumptions

General Assumptions

	Jan-96	Feb-96	Mar-96	Apr-96	May-96	Jun-96
Short Term Interest Rate	8.00%	8.00%	8.00%	8.00%	8.00%	8.00%
Long Term Interest Rate	10.00%	10.00%	10.00%	10.00%	10.00%	10.00%
Payment days	35	35	35	35	35	35
Collection days	45	45	45	45	45	45
Tax Rate Percent	25.00%	25.00%	25.00%	25.00%	25.00%	25.00%
Expenses in cash%	25.00%	25.00%	25.00%	25.00%	25.00%	25.00%
Sales on credit	100.00%	100.00%	100.00%	100.00%	100.00%	100.00%
Personnel Burden %	14.00%	14.00%	14.00%	14.00%	14.00%	14.00%

Jul-96	Aug-96	Sep-96	Oct-96	Nov-96	Dec-96	1	1997	1998
$5,028	($3,223)	$8,628	$9,239	$12,239	($9,661)	$	$37,478	$63,090
$1,500	$1,500	$1,500	$1,500	$1,500	$1,500	$18.	$0	$0
($6,041)	($3,452)	$11,651	$2,158	$863	($5,005)	$26.	$1,434	
$0	$0	$0	$0	$0	$0	$60.	$100,000	
$0	$0	$0	$0	$0	$0		$0	
$0	$0	$0	$0	$0	$0	$50.	$0	
$0	$0	$0	$0	$0	$0		$0	$0
$486	($5,175)	$21,778	$12,896	$14,602	($13,167)	$154.	$138,911	$74,125
Jul	Aug	Sep	Oct	Nov	Dec	1	1905	1905
($16,500)	($27,500)	$27,500	$32,500	$12,500	($32,500)	$100.	$97,072	
$0	$0	$0	$0	$0	$0		$0	$0
$0	$0	$0	$0	$0	$0		$0	
$0	$0	$0	$0	$0	$0		$0	$0
$0	$0	$0	$0	$0	$0		$0	$0
($16,500)	($27,500)	$27,500	$32,500	$12,500	($32,500)	$100.	$97,072	$50,676
$16,986	$22,325	($5,722)	($19,604)	$2,102	$19,333	$54.	$41,839	$23,449
$61,072	$83,398	$77,676	$58,072	$60,174	$79,507	$79.	$121,346	$144,796

Note: Ratios in assumptions are used as estimators and may therefore have different values than ratios calculated in the ratios section.

Jul-96	Aug-96	Sep-96	Oct-96	Nov-96	Dec-96	1996	1997	1998
8.00%	0%	8.00%	8.00%	8.00%	8.00%	8.00%	8.00%	8.00%
10.00%	10.00%	10.00%	10.00%	10.00%	10.00%	10.00%	10.00%	10.00%
35	35	35	35	35	35	35	35	35
45	45	45	45	45	45	45	60	60
25.00%	25.00%	25.00%	25.00%	25.00%	25.00%	25.00%	25.00%	25.00%
25.00%	25.00%	25.00%	25.00%	25.00%	25.00%	25.00%	25.00%	25.00%
100.00%	100.00%	100.00%	100.00%	100.00%	100.00%	100.00%	100.00%	100.00%
14.00%	14.00%	14.00%	14.00%	14.00%	14.00%	14.00%	14.00%	14.00%

Appendix:
Personnel Plan

Personnel Plan

		Jan-96	Feb-96	Mar-96	Apr-96	May-96	Jun-96
Partners	1.4	$12,000	$12,000	$12,000	$12,000	$12,000	$12,000
Consultants	1.25	$0	$0	$0	$0	$0	$0
Editorial/graphic	1.2	$0	$0	$0	$0	$0	$0
VP Marketing	1.1	$0	$0	$0	$0	$0	$0
Sales people	1.1	$0	$0	$0	$0	$0	$0
Office Manager	1.1	$0	$0	$0	$0	$0	$0
Secretarial	1.1	$0	$0	$0	$0	$0	$0
Other	1.1	$0	$0	$0	$0	$0	$0
Subtotal		$12,000	$12,000	$12,000	$12,000	$12,000	$12,000

Appendix:
Projected Profit
and Loss

Pro-forma Income Statement

		Jan-96	Feb-96	Mar-96	Apr-96	May-96	Jun-96
Sales		$10,000	$10,000	$20,000	$34,000	$58,000	$75,000
Cost of Sales		$2,500	$2,500	$4,000	$8,000	$13,500	$19,000
Total Cost of Sales		$2,500	$2,500	$4,000	$8,000	$13,500	$19,000
Gross margin		$7,500	$7,500	$16,000	$26,000	$44,500	$56,000
Gross margin percent		75.00%	75.00%	80.00%	76.47%	76.72%	74.67%
Operating expenses:							
Advertising/Promotion	10.00%	$3,000	$3,000	$3,000	$3,000	$3,000	$3,000
Public Relations	10.00%	$2,500	$2,500	$2,500	$2,500	$2,500	$2,500
Travel	10.00%	$7,500	$7,500	$7,500	$7,500	$7,500	$7,500
Miscellaneous	10.00%	$500	$500	$500	$500	$500	$500
Payroll expense		$12,000	$12,000	$12,000	$12,000	$12,000	$12,000
Leased Equipment		$500	$500	$500	$500	$500	$500
Utilities		$1,000	$1,000	$1,000	$1,000	$1,000	$1,000
Insurance		$300	$300	$300	$300	$300	$300
Rent		$1,500	$1,500	$1,500	$1,500	$1,500	$1,500
Depreciation		$0	$0	$0	$0	$0	$0
Payroll Burden		$1,680	$1,680	$1,680	$1,680	$1,680	$1,680
Total Operating Expenses		$30,480	$30,480	$30,480	$30,480	$30,480	$30,480
Profit Before Interest and Taxes		($22,980)	($22,980)	($14,480)	($4,480)	$14,020	$25,520
Interest Expense ST		$0	$0	$133	$267	$400	$400
Interest Expense LT		$417	$417	$417	$417	$417	$417
Taxes Incurred	($5,849)	($5,849)	($3,758)	($1,291)	$3,301	$6,176	$1,676
Net Profit	($17,548)	($17,548)	($11,273)	($3,873)	$9,903	$18,528	$5,028
Net Profit/Sales		-175.48%	-175.48%	-56.36%	-11.39%	17.07%	24.70%

Jul-96	Aug-96	Sep-96	Oct-96	Nov-96	Dec-96	1996	1997	1998
$12,000	$12,000	$12,000	$12,000	$12,000	$12,000	$144,000	$175,000	$200,000
$0	$0	$0	$0	$0	$0	$0	$50,000	$63,000
$0	$0	$0	$6,000	$6,000	$6,000	$18,000	$22,000	$26,000
$0	$0	$5,000	$5,000	$5,000	$5,000	$20,000	$50,000	$55,000
$0	$0	$0	$0	$0	$0	$0	$30,000	$33,000
$0	$0	$0	$2,500	$2,500	$2,500	$7,500	$30,000	$33,000
$0	$0	$0	$1,750	$1,750	$1,750	$5,250	$20,000	$22,000
$0	$0	$0	$0	$0	$0	$0	$0	$0
$12,000	$12,000	$17,000	$27,250	$27,250	$27,250	$194,750	$377,000	$432,000

Jul-96	Aug-96	Sep-96	Oct-96	Nov-96	Dec-96	1996	1997	1998
$50,000	$35,000	$70,000	$85,000	$90,000	$55,000	$592,000	$875,000	$1,100,000
$12,000	$8,000	$21,500	$24,000	$25,000	$19,000	$159,000	$219,000	$289,000
$12,000	$8,000	$21,500	$24,000	$25,000	$19,000	$159,000	$219,000	$289,000
$38,000	$27,000	$48,500	$61,000	$65,000	$36,000	$433,000	$656,000	$811,000
76.00%	77.14%	69.29%	71.76%	72.22%	65.45%	73.14%	74.97%	73.73%
$3,000	$3,000	$3,000	$3,000	$3,000	$3,000	$36,000	$40,000	$44,000
$2,500	$2,500	$2,500	$2,500	$2,500	$2,500	$30,000	$30,000	$33,000
$7,500	$7,500	$7,500	$7,500	$7,500	$7,500	$90,000	$60,000	$110,000
$500	$500	$500	$500	$500	$500	$6,000	$7,000	$8,000
$12,000	$12,000	$17,000	$27,250	$27,250	$27,250	$194,750	$377,000	$432,000
$500	$500	$500	$500	$500	$500	$6,000	$7,000	$7,000
$1,000	$1,000	$1,000	$1,000	$1,000	$1,000	$12,000	$12,000	$12,000
$300	$300	$300	$300	$300	$300	$3,600	$2,000	$2,000
$1,500	$1,500	$1,500	$1,500	$1,500	$1,500	$18,000	$0	$0
$0	$0	$0	$0	$0	$200	$200	$450	$600
$1,680	$1,680	$2,380	$3,815	$3,815	$3,815	$27,265	$52,780	$60,480
$30,480	$30,480	$36,180	$47,865	$47,865	$48,065	$423,815	$588,230	$709,080
$7,520	($3,480)	$12,320	$13,135	$17,135	($12,065)	$9,185	$67,770	$101,920
$400	$400	$400	$400	$400	$400	$3,600	$12,800	$12,800
$417	$417	$417	$417	$417	$417	$5,000	$5,000	$5,000
($1,074)	$2,876	$3,080	$4,080	($3,220)	$146	$12,493	$21,030	
($3,223)	$8,628	$9,239	$12,239	($9,661)	$439	$37,478	$63,090	
10.06%	-9.21%	12.33%	10.87%	13.60%	-17.57%	0.07%	4.28%	5.74%

Appendix: Sales
Forecast

Sales Forecast

Sales	Jan-96	Feb-96	Mar-96	Apr-96	May-96	Jun-96
Retainer Consulting	$10,000	$10,000	$10,000	$10,000	$20,000	$20,000
Project Consulting	$0	$0	$10,000	$20,000	$30,000	$40,000
Market Research	$0	$0	$0	$4,000	$8,000	$15,000
Strategic Reports	$0	$0	$0	$0	$0	$0
Other	$0	$0	$0	$0	$0	$0
Total Sales	$10,000	$10,000	$20,000	$34,000	$58,000	$75,000

Direct Costs	Jan-96	Feb-96	Mar-96	Apr-96	May-96	Jun-96
Retainer Consulting	$2,500	$2,500	$2,500	$2,500	$2,500	$2,500
Project Consulting	$0	$0	$1,500	$3,500	$5,000	$6,500
Market Research	$0	$0	$0	$2,000	$6,000	$10,000
Strategic Reports	$0	$0	$0	$0	$0	$0
Other	$0	$0	$0	$0	$0	$0
Subtotal Direct Cost of Sales	$2,500	$2,500	$4,000	$8,000	$13,500	$19,000

	Jul-96	Aug-96	Sep-96	Oct 96	Nov-96	Dec-96	1996	1997	1998
	$20,000	$20,000	$20,000	$20,000	$20,000	$20,000	$200,000	$350,000	$425,000
	$20,000	$10,000	$30,000	$45,000	$50,000	$15,000	$270,000	$325,000	$350,000
	$10,000	$5,000	$20,000	$20,000	$20,000	$20,000	$122,000	$150,000	$200,000
	$0	$0	$0	$0	$0	$0	$0	$50,000	$125,000
	$0	$0	$0	$0	$0	$0	$0	$0	$0
	$50,000	$35,000	$70,000	$85,000	$90,000	$55,000	$592,000	$875,000	$1,100,000

	Jul-96	Aug-96	Sep-96	Oct-96	Nov-96	Dec-96	1996	1997	1998
	$2,500	$2,500	$2,500	$2,500	$2,500	$2,500	$30,000	$38,000	$48,000
	$3,500	$1,500	$5,000	$7,500	$8,500	$2,500	$45,000	$56,000	$70,000
	$6,000	$4,000	$14,000	$14,000	$14,000	$14,000	$84,000	$105,000	$131,000
	$0	$0	$0	$0	$0	$0	$0	$20,000	$40,000
	$0	$0	$0	$0	$0	$0	$0	$0	$0
	$12,000	$8,000	$21,500	$24,000	$25,000	$19,000	$159,000	$219,000	$289,000

Metal Shop

BUSINESS PLAN

KROSNOW METAL WORKS

6500 East River Street
Cincinnati, OH 44612

This business plan will be of particular interest to entrepreneurs wishing to take advantage of the changing climate of international trade. It examines a business venture begun by American citizens in Poland and covers, among other things, banking procedures relevant to this country. Also note the estimates for projected revenues and costs; although doing business overseas may seem risky and unfamiliar, given the correct preparation, it is as likely to succeed as any business in North America.

- INTRODUCTION

- EXECUTIVE SUMMARY

- OBJECTIVES

- MISSION

- KEYS TO SUCCESS

- COMPANY SUMMARY

- PRODUCTS

- STRATEGY AND IMPLEMENTATION SUMMARY

- MANAGEMENT SUMMARY

- FINANCIAL PLANNING

METAL SHOP
BUSINESS PLAN

INTRODUCTION

In the decade of the 90s Poland has been the scene of an enormous and successful experiment. A nationwide transition from a centrally planned economy to a free market was initiated and implemented here for the first time in world history.

Commencing in January 1990, a comprehensive program of economic reforms Poland freed-up prices, introduced convertibility of its currency, stabilized the exchange rate and, as a rule, demonopolized business and opened the economy. These measures resulted in a notable development of a private sector, increase of competition and general revival of the economic dynamism. Poland was the first country in Central and Eastern Europe to show signs of economic recovery already in 1992. Once begun, the positive trends in the Polish economy grew stronger in the subsequent years, finally making Poland the fastest growing major economy in all of Europe.

From the very beginning of its profound transformation, Poland has been continuously attracting the attention of the international business community. In the fall of 1993, the influential New York City investment bank, Morgan Stanley, was the first to use the expression "European tiger" in referring to the Polish economy. In 1994, US Department of Commerce officially named Poland one of the world's ten Big Emerging Markets. The next year, the renowned British business newspaper Financial Times in its March special edition summarized the Polish economy's 5-year achievements by the phrase "Shock therapy works a miracle". And at the end of 1995, Busines Week magazine in its feature article on Poland presented the Polish economy as the "hottest" in Europe.

Today's Poland offers enormous business opportunities. Various investments made so far by American and Western European firms have already proven to be successful and profitable. No doubt, these successes have been largely possible due to the unique business advantages offered by Poland's marketplace, its size, geographical location, economic potential and international ties.

Leaders of experienced US and European companies urge the international business community to look closely at Poland. "We at P&G are betting heavily on the future of Poland... We are doing so with a lot of confidence. I would counsel other globally oriented businesses to do the same" stated J.E. Pepper, CEO of Procter and Gamble, Midwest-based consumer products manufacturer.

The message is simple: If you are looking for new significant business opportunities in the world marketplace, consider Poland - the most dynamic economy in Europe.

EXECUTIVE SUMMARY

Poland is a significant untapped business opportunity. Most Polish businesses were government-owned and inefficient with old sub-standard equipment. By utilizing existing order commit-ments, key contacts within the Polish Government and with the principals' dual cultural background, Krosnow Metal Works will set up a high technology metal working facility within Poland.

OBJECTIVES

1. Start up manufacturing production in Poland within 6 months of obtaining financing.
2. Have first year revenues of $90,000,000.
3. Show a profit in the first year of operation of the business of over $900,000.
4. Double sales revenue in 2nd year of operation.

Krosnow Metal Works will be a startup high technology manufacturing company in Poland that aims to provide high quality, low cost machined metal parts to Polish industry. Also, Europe presents itself as an excellent market to whom to export this superior technology and machined metal parts.

We intend to generate a fair return to our investors and to finance continued growth.
We also intend to create a work environment that facilitates training of employees in the use of high technology machine tools.

MISSION

The keys to success in this business are:
1. Follow thru on the existing letter of intent to buy machined metal parts from us to ensure that they materialize into orders.
2. Cordial relationships with Polish government's economic development authorities.
3. Employees well trained in the use of high technology metal-working machinery.

KEYS TO SUCCESS

Krosnow Metal Works is a startup metal-working manufacturer to be located in Poland. The principals' extensive machining skills, their excellent relations with the Polish government and their existing order commitments will ensure the success of this startup venture.

COMPANY SUMMARY

Krosnow Metal Works is a privately held Ohio corporation. The company is equally owned by Vaclav Wysocki and Piotr Puzdrowski.

Company Ownership

Our start-up costs come to $2,000,000 which will be primarily used to purchase new production equipment. The start-up costs are to be financed 15% by individual investors and 85% by a bank loan from a national bank in Poland.

Startup Summary

Start-up Expenses

Legal	$5,000
Salaries	$28,800
Brochures	$5,000
Travel	$5,000
Insurance $0	
Rent	$6,000
Office expenses	$5,000
Expensed equipment	$10,000
Other	$0
Total Start-up Expense	$64,800
Start-up Assets Needed	
Cash requirements	$100,000
Start-up inventory	$100,000
Other Short-term Assets	$100,000
Total Short-term Assets	$300,000
Long-term Assets	$1,700,000

Total Assets	$2,000,000
Total Start-up Requirements	$2,064,800
Left to finance	$64,800

Start-up Funding Plan

Investment	
Investor 1	$100,000
Investor 2	$100,000
Other	$100,000
Total investment	$300,000
Short-term borrowing	
Unpaid expenses	$0
Short-term loans	$0
Interest-free short-term loans	$0
Subtotal Short-term Borrowing	$0
Long-term Borrowing	$1,700,000
Total Borrowing	$1,700,000
Loss at start-up	$0
Total Equity	$300,000
Total Debt and Equity	$2,000,000
Checkline	$0

COMPANY PRODUCTS

Krosnow Metal Works will machine metal parts as subcontracted by major manufacturers in Poland. These orders may be from automobile plants, machine tool manufactures or others.

By offering new and better technology Krosnow Metal Works can produce high quality, low cost parts and win business from these manufacturers that they may have done in house or subcontracted with other Polish companies with lower quality equipment.

COMPANY LOCATIONS AND FACILITIES

The manufacturing plant will be located in Krosnow Poland which is 90 kilometers (65 miles) north of Gdansk. The plant will have 12,000-sq. ft. of manufacturing space and 1,000 sq. ft of office space.

PRODUCTS

Krosnow Metal Works will machine metal parts for large manufacturing customers. The raw material for most of these parts will also be provided by these customers.

Competitive Comparison

As Poland moves to a modern market-based economy, its manufacturers will generate an enormous demand for specialized machined metal parts from subcontracting job shops.

Existing metal-working job shops in Poland use old style machine tools that are very labor intensive and unreliable, in their product quality. Consequently, their products are low quality and high cost.

Krosnow Metal Works, equipped with new computer controlled machine tools, will be able to produce high volume, high quality and low cost machined metal parts. Poland's existing job shops cannot match our technological advances.

Krosnow Metal Works machines metal parts that in most cases have been supplied by their customer. Our machining process adds value to the part. As a consequence, this production has real no raw material cost but a material cost of 10% of sales is assumed to cover other circumstances.

Sourcing

Metal-working has been a part of the manufacturing process for years. Machine tools such as lathes and milling machines were developed in the 1930s and 1940s to improve quality and productivity of the metal-working process.

Technology

In the 1970s computers were connected to machine tools to further streamline the machining processes. These machines are termed CNC for Computer Numerical Control.
While CNC machines have been vastly deployed in the West, a poor economy and limited investment capital have kept this technology out of Poland.

As product demand progresses, Krosnow Metal Works will diversify its manufacturing processes and equipment to match its customer/partners needs. In addition, its success in training its machinists in the new computer controlled equipment will be used to sell training services to other companies within Poland.

Future Products

Our strategy is based upon bringing high technology manufacturing into a market currently serviced by old and obsolete technology.

STRATEGY AND IMPLEMENTATION SUMMARY

Initially, we are focusing on servicing the Polish machine tool industry. But this will be extended beyond Poland and to service other industries besides machine tools.

Marketing Strategy

Krosnow Metal Works intends to price its metal-working services about the same $50/hour as its competitors. However, with its high technology equipment Krosnow Metal Works will be able to produce better quality products and have a 75% greater production rate.

Pricing Strategy

Krosnow Metal Works will use the support of the Polish Government's economic development organization and Krosnow Metal Works's business partners to find new customers and spread the word about the company's high technology resources.

Promotion Strategy

We expect sales to grow rapidly once word gets out about Krosnow Metal Works's high quality, low cost production capability.

Sales Strategy

The following table and related charts show our present sales forecast.

Sales Forecast

Sales Forecast

Type	1997	1998	1999
Sales	$9,000,000	$25,600,000.00	$68,000,000.00
Direct Cost of Sales	$900,000	$2,560,000.00	$6,800,000.00

Strategic Alliances

We have opportunities to build strategic alliances with the Polish machine tool manufacturers and with the Polish Government's economic development offices in their efforts to bring high technology to Poland.

MANAGEMENT SUMMARY

Growth in Krosnow Metal Works's business over the 3 year plan period will result in minimal additional hiring.

Management Team

Vaclav Wysocki is a highly experienced precision CNC programmer and has dual citizenship with the USA and Poland. He is also fluent in Polish and English. Piotr Puzdrowski is also a highly experienced precision CNC programmer.

Management Team Gaps

The management team is strong on metal-working machining and cross cultural contacts. The present team will be supplemented with an American CPA and American attorney.

Personnel Plan

Immediate personnel plans call for increases from 18 people at start up to 24 in three year's time.

Production	1997	1998	1999
Machinists and Inspectors	$900,000	$2,560,000	$6,800,000
Other	$0	$0	$0
Subtotal	$900,000	$2,560,000	$6,800,000
Sales and Marketing			
Salesman	$3,600	$3,900	$4,200
Commissions	$5,400	$5,000	$5,000
Other	$0	$0	$0
Subtotal	$9,000	$8,900	$9,200
Administration			
Owners	$172,500	$100,000	$110,000
Office personnel	$23,000	$13,000	$14,000
Other	$0	$0	$0
Subtotal	$195,500	$113,000	$124,000
Other			
Name or title	$0	$0	$0
Other	$0	$0	$0
Subtotal	$0	$0	$0
Total Headcount	18	21	24
Total Payroll	$1,104,500	$2,681,900	$6,933,200
Payroll Burden	$0	$0	$0
Total Payroll Expenditures	$1,104,500	$2,681,900	$6,933,200

The financial plan depends on the following assumptions.

The break-even analysis shows that Krosnow Metal Works break-even production would be 25,000 units a month while the sales forecast for the first year calls for the production of 50,000 units per month on average.

Monthly Units Break-even	25,000
Monthly Sales Break-even	$375,000

Assumptions:

Average Unit Sale	$15.00
Average Per-Unit Cost	$3.00
Fixed Cost	$3,000,000

We expect income to hit over 4 million for the first year and it should increase too more than 38 million by the third year of the plan.

	1997	1998	1999
Sales	$9,000,000	$25,600,000	$68,000,000
Direct Cost of Sales	$900,000	$2,560,000	$6,800,000
Production payroll	$900,000	$2,560,000	$6,800,000
35% Workers tax	$360,000	$896,000	$2,380,000
Tools	$9,996	$12,000	$14,000
Repairs	$5,040	$6,000	$7,000
Plant Supervision	$12,000	$13,000	$14,000
Utilities	$90,000	$90,000	$90,000
Total Cost of Sales	$2,277,036	$6,137,000	$16,105,000
Gross margin	$6,722,964	$19,463,000	$51,895,000
Gross margin percent	74.70%	76.03%	76.32%
Operating expenses:			
Sales and marketing expenses			
Sales/Marketing Salaries	$9,000	$8,900	$9,200
Advertising/Promotion	$2,400	$2,000	$2,000
Travel	$0	$0	$0
Miscellaneous	$4,800	$5,000	$5,000
Other	$0	$0	$0
Total Sales and Marketing Expense	$16,200	$15,900	$16,200
Sales and Marketing Percent	0.18%	0.06%	0.02%
General & Administrative Expenses			
G&A Salaries	$195,500	$113,000	$124,000
Office Expenses	$39,800	$10,000	$10,000
Legal and Accounting	$10,200	$5,000	$5,000
Travel	$8,004	$7,000	$8,000
Rent	$2,256	$2,000	$2,000
Telephone	$0		
Depreciation	$240,000	$240,000	$240,000

Payroll Burden	$0	$0	$0
Payroll Taxes	$39,000	$45,000	$50,000
Total General and Administrative Expense	$534,760	$422,000	$439,000
General and Administrative Percent	5.94%	1.65%	0.65%
Other Operating Expenses			
Other Salaries	$0	$0	$0
Contract/Consultants	$0	$0	$0
Other	$0	$0	$0
Total Other Operating Expenses	$0	$0	$0
Percent of Sales	0.00%	0.00%	0.00%
Total Operating Expenses	$550,960	$437,900	$455,200
Profit Before Interest and Taxes	$6,172,004	$19,025,100	$51,439,800
Interest Expense ST	$25,000	$0	$0
Interest Expense LT	$320,000	$100,000	$100,000
Taxes Incurred	$1,456,751	$4,731,275	$12,834,950
Net Profit	$4,370,253	$14,193,825	$38,504,850
Net Profit/Sales	48.56%	55.44%	56.62%

Projected Cash Flow

We expect to manage cash flow over the next 3 years with an initial $300,000 of equity investment, a bank loan from a national bank in Poland for $1,700,000 and working capital generated by the retained earnings of the business.

	1997	1998	1999
Net Profit:	$4,370,253	$14,193,825	$38,504,850
Plus:			
Depreciation	$240,000	$240,000	$240,000
Change in Accounts Payable	$140,647	$177,044	$467,928
Current Borrowing (repayment)	$0	$0	$0
Increase (decrease) Other Liabilities	$0	$0	$0
Long-term Borrowing (repayment)	$(1,200,000)	$0	$0
Capital Input	$0	$0	$0
Subtotal	$3,550,900	$14,610,869	$39,212,778
Less:	1997	1998	1999
Change in Accounts Receivable	$750,000	$1,383,333	$3,533,333
Change in Inventory	$279,506	$643,327	$1,661,333
Change in Other ST Assets	$0	$0	$0
Capital Expenditure	$0	$0	$0
Dividends	$0	$0	$0
Subtotal	$1,029,506	$2,026,661	$5,194,667
Net Cash Flow	$2,521,394	$12,584,209	$34,018,111
Cash balance	$2,621,394	$15,205,603	$49,223,715

Projected Balance Sheet

As shown in the balance sheet in the table, we expect a healthy growth in net worth, from $300,000 are start up to $58 million at the end of the three year period.

	1997	1998	1999
Short-term Assets			
Cash	$2,621,394	$15,205,603	$49,223,715
Accounts receivable	$750,000	$2,133,333	$5,666,667
Inventory	$379,506	$1,022,833	$2,684,167
Other Short-term Assets	$100,000	$100,000	$100,000
Total Short-term Assets	$3,850,900	$18,461,770	$57,674,548
Long-term Assets			
Capital Assets	$1,700,000	$1,700,000	$1,700,000
Accumulated Depreciation	$240,000	$480,000	$720,000
Total Long-term Assets	$1,460,000	$1,220,000	$980,000
Total Assets	$5,310,900	$19,681,770	$58,654,548

Debt and Equity			
	1997	1998	1999
Accounts Payable	$140,647	$317,692	$785,620
Short-term Notes	$0	$0	$0
Other ST Liabilities	$0	$0	$0
Subtotal Short-term Liabilities	$140,647	$317,692	$785,620
Long-term Liabilities	$500,000	$500,000	$500,000
Total Liabilities	$640,647	$817,692	$1,285,620
Paid in Capital	$300,000	$300,000	$300,000
Retained Earnings	$0	$4,370,253	$18,564,078
Earnings	$4,370,253	$14,193,825	$38,504,850
Total Equity	$4,670,253	$18,864,078	$57,368,928
Total Debt and Equity	$5,310,900	$19,681,770	$58,654,548
Net Worth	$4,670,253	$18,864,078	$57,368,928

Standard business ratios are included in the table that follows.

Business Ratios

Profitability Ratios:	1997	1998	1999
Gross margin	74.70%	76.03%	76.32%
Net profit margin	48.56%	55.44%	56.62%
Return on Assets	82.29%	72.12%	65.65%
Return on Equity	93.58%	75.24%	67.12%
Activity Ratios			
AR Turnover	12.00	12.00	12.00
Collection days	15	21	21
Inventory Turnover	9.50	8.75	8.69
Accts payable turnover	11.03	11.03	11.03
Total asset turnover	1.69	1.3	1.16
Debt Ratios:	1997	1998	1999
Debt to net Worth	0.14	0.04	0.02
Short-term Debt to Liab.	0.22	0.39	0.61
Liquidity ratios			
Current Ratio	27.38	58.11	73.41

Quick Ratio	24.68	54.89	70.00
Net Working Capital	$3,710,253	$18,144,078	$56,888,928
Interest Coverage	17.89	190.25	514.40
Additional ratios	1997	1998	1999
Assets to sales	0.59	0.77	0.86
Debt/Assets	12%	4%	2%
Current debt/Total Assets	3%	2%	1%
Acid Test	19.35	48.18	62.78
Asset Turnover	1.69	1.30	1.16
Sales/Net Worth	1.93	1.36	1.19

Business Biography of Vaclav Wysocki

Vaclav Wysocki was born in a small town in Poland on August 20, 1961. He moved to Olsztyn so he could study at the Technical School of Metallurgy. He specialized in the field planer operations. Vaclav worked at the "Byson" getting an education in the manufacturing of both tools and machines. He honed his skills there for 5 years until he was called into the Polish army. He married in 1986 and moved to the United States. His dual Polish-American citizenship gives him many advantages in Poland. He can buy land and businesses in Poland and get tax advantages for his company. Vaclav further sharpened his skills at the K.S. Machine shop and General Machine Products. Because of his knowledge he was promoted to shift supervisor. Meanwhile, he attended Hamilton Community College where he studied computer programming on CNC machines. He is currently working at Encore Mfg. Co. as an executive CNC programmer. Vaclav will move back to Poland where his skills, education and experience will be a tremendous asset in starting Krosnow Metal Works on the road to becoming a successful and profitable company.

Business Biography of Piotr Puzdrowski

Piotr Puzdrowski started his metalworking training back when he was in high school. He started his machining training right out of high school by working at a variety of jobs in machineshops. During this training period he was trained in all aspects of the machining industry. During the last six years of his fourteen year career he has spent working on Computer Numerically Controlled (CNC) machines. He has been awarded two Certificates of Training. One has been for proficiency in CNC and the other for completion of training in Statistical Process Control (SPC). During his working and training periods he developed the skills and knowledge to use various types of inspection equipment and high-tolerance technology that insure precision products at low cost. Piotr has the training, knowledge and experience to make Krosnow Metal Works a leader in the manufacturing industry. Piotr is married and lives in Cincinnati with his wife and young child.

Letter of Intent I

(Translation from Polish to English Language)

NUMERI-TECH
(Address in Poland)
6500 East River Street
Cincinnati, Ohio 44612

Krosnow Milling Machine Factory is offering a lease of a portion of production space area of 1200 m2 for $2.50 per m2 monthly. The cost does not include electricity, water, compressed air or heating.

Electricity, water and compressed air can be provided according to meter readings (necessary to install).

The cost of heating is $1.00 per m2 in the heating season, which is November through April. On our side we guarantee combined total value of orders worth about 1500 work hours per month on conventional machines under the condition that prices offered by you will be lower than the cost of production.

In addition, I see a chance of putting into motion a large scale production (additional 200 thousand/year) details according to the enclosed drawings and even increasing the assortment of other details if offered prices are attractive.

For your information, the actual cost of 1 KWh is $0.10, the cost of m3 of water is $0.55 and the cost of m3 of compressed air is $0.03.

Kindly waiting for your response.

Respectfully,

Temporary Director CFO

I, K. Toroska, translator, certify that the above statement is a true and exact translation of the attached document

Translator
Sate of Ohio
County of Hamilton

Sworn and subscribed to before me, a notary public, this 16th day of July 1996 at Cincinnati, Ohio.

FABRYKA OBRABIAREK PRECYZYJNYCH "AVIA"
ul. Siedluska 32, 42-997 Gdansk

Letter of Intent II

Mr. Vaclav Wysocki
President Krosnow Metal Works
6500 East River Street
Cincinnati, Ohio 44612

In reference to our meeting in Gdansk and conducted conversations, I am presenting an outline of future collaboration between our factory in Gdansk and the firm Krosnow Metal Works in Cincinnati. The Factory of Precision Milling Machines Avia in Gdansk is a producer of conventional milling machines and CNC centro milling equipment and feed shafts. A high technical level of production allows for continual increase of sales. For this reason the factory must free up new areas of installation, increasing continuously the boundary of cooperation. Proposals presented by the Krosnow Metal Works firm, based on the purchase of CNC milling machines production centers and numerical controlled inspection equipment are very interesting to our factory.

After establishing production in Poland by the firm Krosnow Metal Works, AVIA will establish permanent working cooperation with that firm and will supply appropriate details necessary for production and equipment storage-park. The quality of work and the price will decide the level of involvement. Also, I wish to underline that in Poland there are very few firms that have modern machine parks and at the same time specialize in cooperation in the machine industry.

This is why many other factories are in a situation similar to Avia.

At this point we are waiting to hear from Krosnow Metal Works about their future plans in Poland.

J. Krol,
General Director

I.K. Toroska, translator, certify that the above statement is a true and exact translation of theattached document.

Translator

State of Ohio
County of Hamilton

Sworn and subscribed to before me, a notary public, this 16th day of July 1996 at Cincinnati, Ohio.
Notary Public

Letter of Intent III

From:
Panakowski Kasa Oszczednosci
Ul. Mitria 5
88-665 Gdansk

To:
Krosnow Metal Works
6500 East River St.
Cincinnati, Ohio 44612

In reference to your letter we wish to present credit offers which are available in our bank. Financing is available for investment, and as operational credit. We provide loans in polish currency (PLN), and in western currency (USD), and (DEM). We provide investment credit in the form of a credit account and may be used for the purchase of new equipment which is necessary in the production start-up process, also this form of credit may be used for purchasing machines to replace existing equipment. This type of credit must be repaid in five years, or longer in cases of long term investments. The amount of credit must be verified as the actual cost of investment and not to exceed 80% of entire investment (20% of own resources). Interest rates for credit in polish currency is at 26% for short term loans (no longer than 12 months) and 27% for long term loans (over 12 months). Interest rates are set by the board of directors PKO BP. These rates are expected to change (in our predictions they will be lower in the near future).

Operational credit is available in the form of ongoing accounts, no longer than 12 months. Interest rates for this form of credit are at 21.3% and are expected to lower. Interest rates for this form of credit depend on risk of investment and may be 1 and 8 points. Interest rates for loans in western currency (USDand DEM0 depend on interest rates offered on international financing markets, bank charges, and may be between 2 and 7 points for investment credit, and 0.5 to points for operational credit.

Terms of payment are a matter of negotiation and may be monthly or quarterly for client convenience. In cases of investment credit, payments may start after reaching full production ability. Interest charges in this case must be paid monthly or quarterly.

Bank charges are:

    1. application fee of 0.5 to 2% of entire amount.
    2. unused fee of 0.25% to 0.5% of interest charges for unused amount (does not apply to operational credit).

When applying for investment credit our bank requires the following documents:

    1. credit application filed by client
    2. IRS confirmation (tax being paid)
    3. articles of incorporation
    4. bank account statements
    5. letters of intent and other signed contracts
    6. ownership title of properties or lease agreement
    7. business plan analyzed by independent expert
    8. local government investment approval
    9. other in some cases

Loan will be approved automatically when:

    1. ownership title is used for collateral
    2. equipment titles are used for collateral
    3. authorization to freeze accounts is given by client
    4. additional bank cosigns
    5. all shares held by client are used for collateral
    6. client agrees to reassign all accounts receivable to bank
    7. equitable cosigner

At this time PKO BP can finance single subjects up to 58 mil. USD. In some cases we will finance up to 78 mil. USD, but only with special permission of central offices. Besides credit, we may also cosign on loans from other banks. Bank charges then are from 2 to 2.5% of entire amount.

Additionally our bank provides service in international transactions in several ways. All of these offers are of a basic concept and is a matter of individual negotiations.

For more information please contact:

Regional Office PKO BP Gdansk
ul. Selewska 10/09
00-955 Gdansk

Sales Forecast

Type	Jan-97	Feb-97	Mar-97	Apr-97	May-97
Sales	$750,000.00	$750,000.00	$750,000.00	$750,000.00	$750,000.00
Direct Cost of Sales	$75,000.00	$75,000.00	$75,000.00	$75,000.00	$75,000.00

Personnel Plan

Production	Jan-97	Feb-97	Mar-97	Apr-97	May-97
Machinists and Inspectors	$75,000	$75,000	$75,000	$75,000	$75,000
Other	$0	$0	$0	$0	$0
Subtotal	$75,000	$75,000	$75,000	$75,000	$75,000
Sales and Marketing					
Salesman	$300	$300	$300	$300	$300
Commissions	$450	$450	$450	$450	$450
Other	$0	$0	$0	$0	$0
Subtotal	$750	$750	$750	$750	$750
Administration					
Owners	$7,500	$7,500	$7,500	$7,500	$7,500
Office personnel	$1,000	$1,000	$1,000	$1,000	$1,000
Other	$0	$0	$0	$0	$0
Subtotal	$8,500	$8,500	$8,500	$8,500	$8,500
Other					
Name or title	$0	$0	$0	$0	$0
Other	$0	$0	$0	$0	$0
Subtotal	$0	$0	$0	$0	$0
Total Headcount	18	18	18	18	18
Total Payroll	$84,250	$84,250	$84,250	$84,250	$84,250
Payroll Burden	$0	$0	$0	$0	$0
Total Payroll Expenditures	$84,250	$84,250	$84,250	$84,250	$84,250

General Assumptions

	Jan-97	Feb-97	Mar-97	Apr-97	May-97
Short Term Interest Rate	20.00%	20.00%	20.00%	20.00%	20.00%
Long Term Interest Rate	20.00%	20.00%	20.00%	20.00%	20.00%
Payment days	30	30	30	30	30
Collection days	30	30	30	30	30
Inventory Turnover	6.00	6.00	6.00	6.00	6.00
Tax Rate Percent	25.00%	25.00%	25.00%	25.00%	25.00%
Expenses in cash %	10.00%	10.00%	10.00%	10.00%	10.00%
Sales on credit	100.00%	100.00%	100.00%	100.00%	100.00%
Personnel Burden %	0.00%	0.00%	0.00%	0.00%	0.00%

Note: Ratios in assumptions are used as estimators and may therefore have different values than ratios calculated in the ratios section.

	Jun-97	Jul-97	Aug-97	Sep-97	Oct-97	Nov-97	Dec-97
	$750,000.00	$750,000.00	$750,000.00	$750,000.00	$750,000.00	$750,000.00	$750,000.00
	$75,000.00	$75,000.00	$75,000.00	$75,000.00	$75,000.00	$75,000.00	$75,000.00

	Jun-97	Jul-97	Aug-97	Sep-97	Oct-97	Nov-97	Dec-97
	$75,000	$75,000	$75,000	$75,000	$75,000	$75,000	$75,000
	$0	$0	$0	$0	$0	$0	$0
	$75,000	$75,000	$75,000	$75,000	$75,000	$75,000	$75,000
	$300	$300	$300	$300	$300	$300	$300
	$450	$450	$450	$450	$450	$450	$450
	$0	$0	$0	$0	$0	$0	$0
	$750	$750	$750	$750	$750	$750	$750
	$7,500	$7,500	$7,500	$7,500	$7,500	$7,500	$90,000
	$1,000	$1,000	$1,000	$1,000	$1,000	$1,000	$12,000
	$0	$0	$0	$0	$0	$0	$0
	$8,500	$8,500	$8,500	$8,500	$8,500	$8,500	$102,000
	$0	$0	$0	$0	$0	$0	$0
	$0	$0	$0	$0	$0	$0	$0
	$0	$0	$0	$0	$0	$0	$0
	18	18	18	18	18	18	18
	$84,250	$84,250	$84,250	$84,250	$84,250	$84,250	$177,750
	$0	$0	$0	$0	$0	$0	$0
	$84,250	$84,250	$84,250	$84,250	$84,250	$84,250	$177,750

	Jun-97	Jul-97	Aug-97	Sep-97	Oct-97	Nov-97	Dec-97
	20.00%	20.00%	20.00%	20.00%	20.00%	20.00%	20.00%
	20.00%	20.00%	20.00%	20.00%	20.00%	20.00%	20.00%
	30	30	30	30	30	30	30
	30	30	30	30	30	30	30
	6.00	6.00	6.00	6.00	6.00	6.00	6.00
	25.00%	25.00%	25.00%	25.00%	25.00%	25.00%	25.00%
	10.00%	10.00%	10.00%	10.00%	10.00%	10.00%	10.00%
	100.00%	100.00%	100.00%	100.00%	100.00%	100.00%	100.00%
	0.00%	0.00%	0.00%	0.00%	0.00%	0.00%	0.00%

Projected Profit and Loss

	Jan-97	Feb-97	Mar-97	Apr-97	May-97
Sales	$750,000	$750,000	$750,000	$750,000	$750,000
Direct Cost of Sales	$75,000	$75,000	$75,000	$75,000	$75,000
Production payroll	$75,000	$75,000	$75,000	$75,000	$75,000
35% Workers tax	$30,000	$30,000	$30,000	$30,000	$30,000
Tools	$833	$833	$833	$833	$833
Repairs	$420	$420	$420	$420	$420
Plant Supervision	$1,000	$1,000	$1,000	$1,000	$1,000
Utilities	$7,500	$7,500	$7,500	$7,500	$7,500
Total Cost of Sales	$189,753	$189,753	$189,753	$189,753	$189,753
Gross margin	$560,247	$560,247	$560,247	$560,247	$560,247
Gross margin percent	74.70%	74.70%	74.70%	74.70%	74.70%
Operating expenses:					
Sales and marketing expenses					
Sales/Marketing Salaries	$750	$750	$750	$750	$750
Advertising/Promotion	$200	$200	$200	$200	$200
Travel	$0	$0	$0	$0	$0
Miscellaneous	$400	$400	$400	$400	$400
Other	$0	$0	$0	$0	$0
Total Sales and Marketing Expense	$1,350	$1,350	$1,350	$1,350	$1,350
Sales and Marketing Percent	0.18%	0.18%	0.18%	0.18%	0.18%
General & Administrative Expenses					
G&A Salaries	$8,500	$8,500	$8,500	$8,500	$8,500
Office Expenses	$1,800	$1,800	$1,800	$1,800	$1,800
Legal and Accounting	$850	$850	$850	$850	$850
Travel	$667	$667	$667	$667	$667
Rent	$188	$188	$188	$188	$188
Telephone					
Depreciation	$20,000	$20,000	$20,000	$20,000	$20,000
Payroll Burden	$0	$0	$0	$0	$0

Jun-97	Jul-97	Aug-97	Sep-97	Oct-97	Nov-97	Dec-97
$750,000	$750,000	$750,000	$750,000	$750,000	$750,000	$750,000
$75,000	$75,000	$75,000	$75,000	$75,000	$75,000	$75,000
$75,000	$75,000	$75,000	$75,000	$75,000	$75,000	$75,000
$30,000	$30,000	$30,000	$30,000	$30,000	$30,000	$30,000
$833	$833	$833	$833	$833	$833	$833
$420	$420	$420	$420	$420	$420	$420
$1,000	$1,000	$1,000	$1,000	$1,000	$1,000	$1,000
$7,500	$7,500	$7,500	$7,500	$7,500	$7,500	$7,500
$189,753	$189,753	$189,753	$189,753	$189,753	$189,753	$189,753
$560,247	$560,247	$560,247	$560,247	$560,247	$560,247	$560,247
74.70%	74.70%	74.70%	74.70%	74.70%	74.70%	74.70%
$750	$750	$750	$750	$750	$750	$750
$200	$200	$200	$200	$200	$200	$200
$0	$0	$0	$0	$0	$0	$0
$400	$400	$400	$400	$400	$400	$400
$0	$0	$0	$0	$0	$0	$0
$1,350	$1,350	$1,350	$1,350	$1,350	$1,350	$1,350
0.18%	0.18%	0.18%	0.18%	0.18%	0.18%	0.18%
$8,500	$8,500	$8,500	$8,500	$8,500	$8,500	$102,000
$1,800	$1,800	$1,800	$1,800	$1,800	$1,800	$20,000
$850	$850	$850	$850	$850	$850	$850
$667	$667	$667	$667	$667	$667	$667
$188	$188	$188	$188	$188	$188	$188
$20,000	$20,000	$20,000	$20,000	$20,000	$20,000	$20,000
$0	$0	$0	$0	$0	$0	$0

Projected Cash Flow

	Jan-97	Feb-97	Mar-97	Apr-97	May-97
Net Profit:	$365,044	$365,044	$365,044	$371,294	$373,544
Plus:					
Depreciation	$20,000	$20,000	$20,000	$20,000	$20,000
Change in Accounts Payable	$124,704	$0	$0	$0	($2,628)
Current Borrowing (repayment)	$500,000.00	$0	$0	($500,000)	$0
Increase (decrease) Other Liabilities	$0	$0	$0	$0	$0
Long-term Borrowing (repayment)	$0	$0	$0	$0	$0
Capital Input	$0	$0	$0	$0	$0
Subtotal	$1,009,748	$385,044	$385,044	($108,706)	$390,916
Less:	Jan	Feb	Mar	Apr	May
Change in Accounts Receivable	$739,726	$0	$0	$10,274	$0
Change in Inventory	$279,506	$0	$0	$0	$0
Change in Other ST Assets	$0	$0	$0	$0	$0
Capital Expenditure	$0	$0	$0	$0	$0
Dividends	$0	$0	$0	$0	$0
Subtotal	$1,019,232	$0	$0	$10,274	$0
Net Cash Flow	($9,484)	$385,044	$385,044	($118,980)	$390,916
Cash balance	$90,516	$475,560	$860,604	$741,624	$1,132,540

Jun-97	Jul-97	Aug-97	Sep-97	Oct-97	Nov-97	Dec-97
$371,294	$371,294	$371,294	$371,294	$371,294	$371,294	$302,519
$20,000	$20,000	$20,000	$20,000	$20,000	$20,000	$20,000
$2,628	$0	$0	$0	$0	$0	$15,943
$0	$0	$0	$0	$0	$0	$0
$0	$0	$0	$0	$0	$0	$0
$0	$0	$0	$0	$0	$0	($1,200,000)
$0	$0	$0	$0	$0	$0	$0
$393,922	$391,294	$391,294	$391,294	$391,294	$391,294	($861,538)

Jun	Jul	Aug	Sep	Oct	Nov	Dec
$0	$0	$0	$0	$0	$0	$0
$0	$0	$0	$0	$0	$0	$0
$0	$0	$0	$0	$0	$0	$0
$0	$0	$0	$0	$0	$0	$0
$0	$0	$0	$0	$0	$0	$0
$0	$0	$0	$0	$0	$0	$0
$393,922	$391,294	$391,294	$391,294	$391,294	$391,294	($861,538)
$1,526,462	$1,917,756	$2,309,050	$2,700,344	$3,091,638	$3,482,932	$2,621,394

Projected Balance Sheet

	Jan-97	Feb-97	Mar-97	Apr-97	May-97
Short-term Assets					
Cash	$90,516	$475,560	$860,604	$741,624	$1,132,540
Accounts receivable	$739,726	$739,726	$739,726	$750,000	$750,000
Inventory	$379,506	$379,506	$379,506	$379,506	$379,506
Other Short-term Assets	$100,000	$100,000	$100,000	$100,000	$100,000
Total Short-term Assets	$1,309,748	$1,694,792	$2,079,836	$1,971,130	$2,362,046
Long-term Assets					
Capital Assets	$1,700,000	$1,700,000	$1,700,000	$1,700,000	$1,700,000
Accumulated Depreciation	$20,000	$40,000	$60,000	$80,000	$100,000
Total Long-term Assets	$1,680,000	$1,660,000	$1,640,000	$1,620,000	$1,600,000
Total Assets	$2,989,748	$3,354,792	$3,719,836	$3,591,130	$3,962,046

Debt and Equilty	Jan-97	Feb-97	Mar-97	Apr-97	May-97
Accounts Payable	$124,704	$124,704	$124,704	$124,704	$122,076
Short-term Notes	$500,000	$500,000	$500,000	$0	$0
Other ST Liabilities	$0	$0	$0	$0	$0
Subtotal Short-term Liabilities	$624,704	$624,704	$624,704	$124,704	$122,076
Long-term Liabilities	$1,700,000	$1,700,000	$1,700,000	$1,700,000	$1,700,000
Total Liabilities	$2,324,704	$2,324,704	$2,324,704	$1,824,704	$1,822,076
Paid in Capital	$300,000	$300,000	$300,000	$300,000	$300,000
Retained Earnings	$0	$0	$0	$0	$0
Earnings	$365,044	$730,088	$1,095,132	$1,466,426	$1,839,970
Total Equilty	$665,044	$1,030,088	$1,395,132	$1,766,426	$2,139,970
Total Debt and Equilty	$2,989,748	$3,354,792	$3,719,836	$3,591,130	$3,962,046
Net Worth	$665,044	$1,030,088	$1,395,132	$1,766,426	$2,139,970
Payroll Taxes	$3,500	$3,500	$3,500	$3,500	$500
Total General and Admin. Expense	$35,505	$35,505	$35,505	$35,505	$32,505
General and Administrative Percent	4.73%	4.73%	4.73%	4.73%	4.33%
Other Operating Expenses					
Other Salaries	$0	$0	$0	$0	$0
Contract/Consultants	$0	$0	$0	$0	$0
Other	$0	$0	$0	$0	$0
Total Other Operating Expenses	$0	$0	$0	$0	$0
Percent of Sales	0.00%	0.00%	0.00%	0.00%	0.00%
Total Operating Expenses	$36,855	$36,855	$36,855	$36,855	$33,855
Profit Before Interest and Taxes	$523,392	$523,392	$523,392	$523,392	$526,392
Interest Expense ST	$8,333	$8,333	$8,333	$0	$0
Interest Expense LT	$28,333	$28,333	$28,333	$28,333	$28,333
Taxes Incurred	$121,681	$121,681	$121,681	$123,765	$124,515
Net Profit	$365,044	$365,044	$365,044	$371,294	$373,544
Net Profit/Sales	48.67%	48.67%	48.67%	49.51%	49.81%

	Jun-97	Jul-97	Aug-97	Sep-97	Oct-97	Nov-97	Dec-97
	$1,526,462	$1,917,756	$2,309,050	$2,700,344	$3,091,638	$3,482,932	$2,621,394
	$750,000	$750,000	$750,000	$750,000	$750,000	$750,000	$750,000
	$379,506	$379,506	$379,506	$379,506	$379,506	$379,506	$379,506
	$100,000	$100,000	$100,000	$100,000	$100,000	$100,000	$100,000
	$2,755,968	$3,147,262	$3,538,556	$3,929,850	$4,321,144	$4,712,438	$3,850,900
	$1,700,000	$1,700,000	$1,700,000	$1,700,000	$1,700,000	$1,700,000	$1,700,000
	$120,000	$140,000	$160,000	$180,000	$200,000	$220,000	$240,000
	$1,580,000	$1,560,000	$1,540,000	$1,520,000	$1,500,000	$1,480,000	$1,460,000
	$4,335,968	$4,707,262	$5,078,556	$5,449,850	$5,821,144	$6,192,438	$5,310,900

	Jun-97	Jul-97	Aug-97	Sep-97	Oct-97	Nov-97	Dec-97
	$124,704	$124,704	$124,704	$124,704	$124,704	$124,704	$140,647
	$0	$0	$0	$0	$0	$0	$0
	$0	$0	$0	$0	$0	$0	$0
	$124,704	$124,704	$124,704	$124,704	$124,704	$124,704	$140,647
	$1,700,000	$1,700,000	$1,700,000	$1,700,000	$1,700,000	$1,700,000	$500,000
	$1,824,704	$1,824,704	$1,824,704	$1,824,704	$1,824,704	$1,824,704	$640,647
	$300,000	$300,000	$300,000	$300,000	$300,000	$300,000	$300,000
	$0	$0	$0	$0	$0	$0	$0
	$2,211,264	$2,582,558	$2,953,852	$3,325,146	$3,696,440	$4,067,734	$4,370,253
	$2,511,264	$2,882,558	$3,253,852	$3,625,146	$3,996,440	$4,367,734	$4,670,253
	$4,335,968	$4,707,262	$5,078,556	$5,449,850	$5,821,144	$6,192,438	$5,310,900
	$2,511,264	$2,882,558	$3,253,852	$3,625,146	$3,996,440	$4,367,734	$4,670,253
	$3,500	$3,500	$3,500	$3,500	$3,500	$3,500	$3,500
	$35,505	$35,505	$35,505	$35,505	$35,505	$35,505	$147,205
	4.73%	4.73%	4.73%	4.73%	4.73%	4.73%	19.63%
	$0	$0	$0	$0	$0	$0	$0
	$0	$0	$0	$0	$0	$0	$0
	$0	$0	$0	$0	$0	$0	$0
	$0	$0	$0	$0	$0	$0	$0
	0.00%	0.00%	0.00%	0.00%	0.00%	0.00%	0.00%
	$36,855	$36,855	$36,855	$36,855	$36,855	$36,855	$148,555
	$523,392	$523,392	$523,392	$523,392	$523,392	$523,392	$411,692
	$0	$0	$0	$0	$0	$0	$0
	$28,333	$28,333	$28,333	$28,333	$28,333	$28,333	$8,333
	$123,765	$123,765	$123,765	$123,765	$123,765	$123,765	$100,840
	$371,294	$371,294	$371,294	$371,294	$371,294	$371,294	$302,519
	49.51%	49.51%	49.51%	49.51%	49.51%	49.51%	40.34%

Novelty Shop

BUSINESS PLAN

THE GREAT PRETENDER

555 Main St.
Ten Rivers, MI 49887

This plan is an example of a business capitalizing on a venture with a proven track record, but in a market with no existing compeition. A previous gag and novelty store stopped doing business in the area, but not because of lack of customers, so this owner will start a similar business in its place. In this case, interest has already been established, so this experienced entrepreneur will be in a good position for success in her market.

- EXECUTIVE SUMMARY
- THE COMPANY
- PRODUCTS/SERVICES
- PRODUCTION
- MARKETS
- COMPETITION
- MARKETING
- RISKS
- FINANCES
- MILESTONES

NOVELTY SHOP
BUSINESS PLAN

EXECUTIVE SUMMARY

Everyone is familiar with the summer tourism season in Ten Rivers. The Great Pretender, a unique novelty, gag, costume, and collectible retail store, plans to exploit this market by opening an 1100 sq. ft. store in the heart of the Downtown Shopping District on E. Mitchell Street. Its market segment includes the estimated 27,000 people in Emerald County and the surrounding communities, not to mention the influx of summer residents and tourists.

A former store of its kind did phenomenal business, so the need has already been established. The location is close to anchor businesses that draw year round traffic, such as JCPenney, Bentley's and Record World, which make it, without question, the best possible location. The idea is something I planned to do in December of 1998, but this location is prime-- my best opportunity is now.

Competition for The Great Pretender is scarce. The closest store of its kind is in downtown Traverse City. The store will carry things that can't be found at other stores... things found in your imagination. The fact that there is no immediate competition, coupled with the great location, will make this a profitable business.

The Great Pretender will be a sole proprietorship founded by Marianna Peters, sole owner. The idea began from a past management position of a successful, similar store. I will bring four years of accumulated customers and knowledge to The Great Pretender. I feel this gives the business a sales and marketing edge by using this existing customer base.

To date, I have applied for Michigan State Tax License, Assumed Name and Wholesale Suppliers. I have invested $1,000 to hold the building at 555 Main St., Ten Rivers, I am seeking an additional $25,000 in loans to start the sole proprietorship. Major costs include

- Shop rent
- Inventory
- Remodeling
- Equipment
- Salaries

This totals approximately $24,000 allowing for last minute items.

Projected sales during the first three months. based on market and past experience. should average close to $4,000 per month. The main piece of profit per year is the month of October, when sales should be over $24,000 for the month: With proper budgeting the large profit from that month, approximately $14,000, with pay rent/utilities for the quieter months we all experience here in Northern/Michigan. Although, the established anchor stores on either ends of the block will help generate winter business tremendously

Opening day is planned for Saturday June 20, 1998, at the very beginning of our summer season. Loan payoff can be achieved by December 1998, at which time I receive my trust fund of $47,000. Along with the trust fund for collateral, I am also willing to put up clear titles to both my 1989 Ford Ranger and 1987 Manistique Mobile Home (see financial chapter). I also have a cosigner, if necessary.

While The Great Pretender has the potential for high growth in the current market, it's first two to three years will be largely dedicated to achieving company financial stability.

THE COMPANY

The Great Pretender has been an idea of mine for three to four years. It is something I've been planning to do in December 1998 when, on my 30th birthday, I will receive my trust fund totaling $47,000.00. I believe there is need for a novelty, collectible, gag, and costume retail business in this area. My previous management of a similar store will bring not only experience but a lengthy customer following as well. Many of the customers from the previous store have expressed interest to me about such a place. I feel this gives me an inside look about what people want and are willing to pay for.

The company's immediate goals are to achieve opening by June 20, 1998, in time to reap the rewards of a lucrative summer tourism season. I will employ parttime help in the months of October, otherwise I will be the sole employee .

The Great Pretender is in the process of securing $25,000 in start up financing, which will be paid in full in eight months. I wish to have enough financing to cover inventory, beginning advertising, salary and utilities.

PRODUCTS AND SERVICES

The Great Pretender is a retail store that will sell a wide variety of specialty items.

- Practical jokes and gags
- Magic tricks and cards cards
- Juggling and clowning supplies
- Costumes
- Collectibles

Literally something for everyone, by no means your ordinary gift shop. During specific seasons, the largest being Halloween, The Great Pretender will sell large quantities of both adult and childrens costumes, wigs, makeup and other accessories.

Having been a former manager of this type of store, I have experienced the need first hand. Since that store is no longer operating (not due to financial reasons), many former customers have expressed to me a need for such products. There is no such speciality shop in the immediate area, the closest being Traverse City. It will appeal to many different people through its enormous selection of products.

Though The Great Pretender will only employ myself in the beginning, next summer I hope to have staff for both clowning and magic shows for various events, such as birthday parties. Again, this is a need already expressed to me.

Rental costumes and mascots are also something I am investigating for the future. Not only would they be profitable in the Halloween season, but throughout the year for use at such events as grand openings and parades. I feel they would be a great investment.

The building I have rented at 555 Main St., Ten Rivers has 1100 sq. ft. in the main level. It also has a finished basement with an additional 1500 sq. ft., which for now will be utilized as the needarises.

PRODUCTION

The Great Pretender will obtain products at wholesale prices from multiple suppliers. Because items are purchased by the dozen or gross, cost is kept to a minimum, which allows for a markup of 200%-250% . Shipping and delivery time varies from one to two weeks making products easily accessible when needed.

The Great Pretender will have a storage unit in the basement. Because the products come prepackaged, ready for sale, production is almost eliminated. Each, carton will be inspected forquantity and damage as it arrives. Items will be priced and put on the shelf or in storage.

Currently, inventory will be handled on paper, but in the future a computerized inventory system will be implemented. By having inventory kept on computer, I can have an accurate daily count and never run out of a much-needed item.

MARKET

The Great Pretender will encompass: extremely wide market. Its unique products will appeal to both young and old, male and female. It will be stocked with something for all economic backgrounds: items for children, teens, working people, homemakers, retirees, collectors. retirees, collectors....literally something for everyone.

Recent demographics compiled by the Ten Rivers Chamber of Commerce show over 27,000 residents in Emerald County and nearly three time/ that number in the busy summer months. Tourism continues to be a major economic force and has now grown include to winter attractions as well.

The Great Pretender will be centrally located at 555 Main St. in the heart of the Downtown Shopping District. It will also neighbor well-established businesses that attract year round traffic. Pedestrian traffic is heavy along Mitchell Street, which is used year round by students, the working class for lunch, evening stroll, and shopping.

COMPETITION

Generally speaking, there is not another store of its kind the immediate area, so competition is very limited. The closest store to purchase novelties, magic tricks, etc. would be in Traverse City, over a one hour drive.

Seasonal items such as the costumes and accessories can be found at department stores, such as WalMart and KMart.

The main weakness common to competitors is the fact that they have a limited stock of styles and variety. Much of their space and capital is used for other products. Human physiques and tastes vary considerably in a county of 27,000 and our wide selection will draw customers who can't find what they're looking for elsewhere.

During the month of October, which by far is the busiest month for The Great Pretender, I will counter the threat of department stores with extra advertising, including print and radio. Also, the great display window in the downtown area lends itself to excellent advertising at no additional cost.

MARKETING

The main advertising of The Great Pretender will be its store display window. Sincesignificant numbers of pedestrians pass the shop window each day, I will use a variety of displays changed at two-week intervals. I will also have an advertisement in the local phone guide yellow pages listed under Costumes and Novelties.

For the StartUp advertising and Grand Opening, will be placed in the Ten Rivers News Review, The Guardian-Review, and The Image publication, which is read by thousands of tourists weekly.

During seasonal events, The Great Pretender will have 30-second radio spots and flyers in the newspapers. We will also participate in downtown events such as July 4th and Christmas parades.

The most serious risk to The Great Pretender is a very tight budget. If we fail to draw customers the first few months, we may default on our loan payments. To counter this, I plan to open at the busiest time of the year and limit overhead, such as payroll by only employing myself. For the first four months, due to summer heat and longer daylight hours, utility is reduced.

Another risk is the winter months, which are considerably slower for the downtown retailers. This is anticipated and planned for with proper budgeting from the profitable month of October. We will also counter that slow time by capitalizing on the increasing popularity of such holidays as New Year's and St. Patrick's Day. having surrounding anchor stores close by will also increase winter traffic.

The products are quickly accessible, eliminating the need for high dollars tied up in backstock. The Great Pretender will use caution when ordering and only order the necessary quantities.

RISKS

FINANCES

Personal Financial Statement

Income	
Salary/Wages	$14,560
Dividend/Interest	
Capital Gains from Trust	$2,030
TOTAL ANNUAL INCOME	$16,590
Debits	
Dept. Loans	
Visa ($50/mo)	$600
Real Estate	
Lot Rent ($165/mo)	$1,980
(mobile home)	
Taxes	
Delinquent State Tax Owed ($80/mo)	$720
Insurance Premiums	
Auto	$900
Living Expenses	
Utilities	$3,060
Home/Personal	$2,640
Other Expenses	
Medical Bills	$1,200
Auto Repairs	$800
TOTAL ANNUAL DEBITS	$11,900
Personal Financial Statement	
Income After Expenses	
Total Annual Income	$16,590
Total Annual Debits	$11,900
TOTAL INCOME AFTER EXPENSES	$4,690

Personal Financial Statement

Assets
Automobiles
Car $3,500
Stocks/Bonds etc.
Trust Fund Due December 1998 $46,400
Other Assets
Mobile Home $5,000

TOTAL ASSETS $54,900

Personal Financial Statement Liabilities
Credit Cards
Visa $400
Other Liabilities
Delinquent Taxes Owed $720

Business Financial Statement

Cost of Sales

	Expected Sales	Cost/Sale	Total Cost of Sales
Costumes	$30,000	45%	$13,500
Gags/Novelties	$22,000	35%	$7,700
Magic	$15,000	40%	$6,000
Total (per year)	$67,000		$27,200
Total (per month)	$5,583		$2,267

Operating Expenses
Wages $1,100
Rent $1,100
Insurance $100
Utilities $150
Bookkeeping $50
Advertising $50
Loan Payment $600

TOTAL MONTHLY OPERATING EXPENSES $3,150

Profit and Loss
Total Sales Revenue $5,583
Total Cost of Sales   -$2,267
Total Operating Expense   -$3,150

PROFIT $166

Start Up Costs
Beginning Inventory $13,000
Equipment $5,000
Marketing $500
Loan Payment $5,700

TOTAL START UP $24,200

Bank Loan* $25,000

1994-1998	Idea in the making
April 8, 1998	Saw building for rent
April 15	Started business plan
April 20	Applied for tax # and assumed name
April 21	Secured building 442 E. Mitchell Street for $1,000
May 1	Present loan application
May 15	Loan secured
May 18	Ordered inventory
May 19	Construction, painting, shelving begin
May 26	Secure cash register
May 27	Obtain sign
June 1	Construction, painting, shelving complete
June 1	Lease begins
June 3	Inventory begins arriving
June 12	Ads begin running
June 17	Signs hung
June 20	Opening Day
July 4	Grand Opening Celebration
October 1998	Peak season - longer hours
	Hire 2-3 part-time employees
December 1998	Loan pay off
June 1999	Expand to basement

Office Furniture Retailer

BUSINESS PLAN   POWERLINE OF NORTHERN MINNESOTA

982 Delaney Circle
Johnsonville MN 77821

This business plan garnered it's owner the loan it requests. Should a business owner compile a business plan in advance of requesting a loan, it can help the loan process go more smoothly. This plan, in addition to its succinctness, has a very comprehensive consideration of the marketplace.

- STATEMENT OF PURPOSE

- EXECUTIVE SUMMARY

- MARKET ANALYSIS

- MANAGEMENT

STATEMENT OF PURPOSE

PowerLine of Northern Minnesota, dba of Habitat, Inc., is a PowerLine studio providing design services and a selection of PowerLine furniture and cabinetry in a showroom environment. Studio products and services focus on general business and health care markets in a territory north of Garnet including most of Minnesota's northern regions, based in Petoskey.

The company requires start up capital in the amount of $60,000, to be used for leasehold improvements, displays and accessories, inventory, office equipment, tools, forms, signage, opening costs and operating capital. Funding is needed for a projected opening of April 1995. Two months are necessary for ordering and set up of displays.

The operation of PowerLine of Northern Minnesota will result in a net profit sufficient to repay the loan and interest within five years. The loan can be secured with home equity funds in the amount of $30,000 and retirement.and stock funds of the pricipals.

EXECUTIVE SUMMARY

PowerLine of Northern Minnesota is a PowerLine Studio. The studio concept was developed in 1966 by Mitchell Camden and Associates, the manufacturers of PowerLine furniture and cabinetry. PowerLine studios are the distribution system for their product to the general business and health care markets. PowerLine of Northern Minnesota joins a network of 50 independently owned Studios located throughout the United States. .

The PowerLine of Northern Minnesota Studio provides design assistance and sales of Tachline components for furniture, cabinetry, office systems, seating and closet systems. The success of PowerLine of Northern Minnesota is in providing high quality, adaptable, moderately pricedproducts paired with design expertise to customize each client's storage needs.

The PowerLine Studio's mix of products targets two market niches within the general business and health care markets. In the general business market, the focus is professional home offices and small businesses. PowerLine' provides attractive and functional office organization in a variety of sized components for maximum space utilization at a lower cost than traditional steel office furniture.

In the health care market, the niche is medical office buildings and outpatient facilities. PowerLine fills this market's need for specialty, modular, medical cabinetry that is code approved and can be installed and rearranged as required in this rapidly growing industry.

Additionally, PowerLine of Northern Minnesota provides multipurpose storage components for residential home entertainment systems, home office and closets.

PowerLine products are purchased factory direct and are shipped RTA (ready to assemble) or preassembled. The Studio maintains a protected sales territory and is assisted by extensive factory supported training, product updates, dealer networking and factory representative visits.

To complete the office design, PowerLine of Northern Minnesota sells seating products, decorative accessories, lighting and desk storage accessories.

MARKET ANALYSIS

Northern Minnesota communities are peopled with small business owners and professionals. The greater Petoskey area, drawing from Landry, Caledonia and Holiday counties, is experiencing population growth and is becoming a destination point for consumers of goods and services.

These two facts define the market focus for one product group of PowerLine of Northern Minnesota, Small office/Home office. This potential market numbers over 1200 in the surrounding area; physicians, dentists, accountants, attorneys, building contractors, insurance and real estate agents, allied medical professionals, college and local government officials, and home business owners are PowerLine customers.

These business people require an uncomplicated system for organization of the reception area; work stations with computer equipment, phone, fax and filing; conference areas; manager's office; employee lounges. Priorities for the small business are adaptability for changing needs, reasonable cost and enduring style and colors. PowerLine fulfills each of these requirements.

Another concern of the small business person is limited time to plan or make changes in an inadequate office or workspace. Doing the daily business takes precedence over how an office functions or what it looks like. Providing the service of analysis of storage needs, formulation of a workable plan, and the implementation of the design into the workplace, PowerLine of Northern Minnesota takes the time to personalize a business' storage needs. Assistance with installation, decorating and accessorizing completes the project.

The PowerLine of Northern Minnesota professional will coordinate with the business' vendors of phone and business equipment to minimize disruption in the workplace and assure a smooth transition into the new office environment.

Because of the uniformity of sizes and consistency of colors of the PowerLine products, as the business grows or relocates, their office fixtures can be moved, rearranged and added to. Repeat business becomes a reliable barometer for success.

The most effective way to interact with the small business market is a face to face meeting. An introductory mailing to the 1200 professionals of a PowerLine color postcard targeted to the individual's type of business, will be followed up with a visit to the workplace by way of introduction. This personal expression is more welcome than a ringing telephone. At that time, a future appointment is made at the business person's convenience.

PowerLine of Northern Minnesota has the territory to service small business from north of Garnet to the Minnesota border, and will market regionally to raise market awareness and market specifically to the greater Petoskey area.

Business owners surveyed feel there is a void of product between the traditional, costly, steel office furniture and inexpensive, poor quality and selection, discount brand furniture. Local sources for the former, office supply stores, include Caledonia Office Supply, Franklin Office Supply, and Minnesota Officeways. They present themselves as purveyors of high end office furnishings-such as Steelcase, Herman Miller, Kimball, Haworth, and Knoll. While brand awareness is important, product suitability for the small business needs is overlooked.

Some of the above mentioned sources do offer some lower priced alternatives, as do some furniture stores and mail order companies. A computer stand, a desk or a file cabinet purchased

by itself is a start. The frustration occurs as a business needs an adjoining printer stand, another desk, or expansion of filing and storage systems. Are other pieces available to match that initial purchase? Was the original piece suggested with future needs in mind? Was help offered in planning for eventual storage and growth needs? The total office concept is addressed and provided for with PowerLine of Northern Minnesota's products and services.

PowerLine is a highly versatile, quality casework system. No other manufacturer can meet PowerLine's range of products at an affordable cost. PowerLine of Northern Minnesota's

MARKET ANALYSIS
...continued

MARKET ANALYSIS
...continued

competitive advantage is its expertise to assist the client in the design of the cabinetry and then deliver and install a quality product in a short time frame, approximately four weeks.

PowerLine of Northern Minnesota's other market focus is health care. Petoskey, with its' Northern Minnesota Hospital, Benson Clinic, and TotalHealth Group subsidiaries, is a natural hub for health care services in this region. By the year 2000, health care is predicted to be 20% of the country's GNP. The trend toward ambulatory centers and outpatient services necessitates new building and remodeling of older ambulatory centers, physician's clinics, and group practice clinics. The Benson Clinic is expecting to expand its' physician staff to 140 in the coming year.

In the health care market, PowerLine is a well-known name. Mitchell Camden and Associates, the manufacturers of PowerLine, is an architectural firm specializing in the design and con

struction of medical facilities. PowerLine furniture and cabinetry is designed and manufactured to the exacting specifications of the health care industry and is used in all Mitchell Camden buildings. In the northern Minnesota area, Camden facilities in 21 locations. These facilities serve as a base of customers for additional PowerLine purchases.

There is tremendous pressure to hold down costs in the health care market. This fast growing industry is constantly adapting to convert existing spaces to better uses and to construct satellite facilities to make health care more accessible, especially in the rural areas of northern Minnesota. PowerLine medical cabinetry utilizes a modular design that permits the product to be mass produced at a lower cost. This also allows for health care users to reconfigure and reuse cabinets as needs change. Over the long term, the cost of cabinets is lower because the life of the product is much longer.

The decision makers in the health care market list cost and quality as important factors. Past experiences with local cabinet shops have produced lover quality and guarantees that outlived the cabinet business. Cabinetry manufacturers typically produce for residential udes that do not address the demands of the health care user. The only local cabinet maker that is capable of providing an acceptable quality and cost is Jordan Design. They are a business that has grown with the area and has reached the deciding point; further growth and a compromise of quality and service, or maintain its, market along with its' service to satisfy existing customers. Their focus is divided between kitchen design and commercial applications.

The health care market is reached by direct contact to architects, administrators, purchasing' agents, general contractors, developers, and designers. The showroom is used as a tool to visually show and explain the product. PowerLine of Northern Minnesota's competitive advantage in this market is the expertise to assist the client in the design of the cabinetry and then deliver and install a quality product in a short time frame.

Letters of introduction as this area's distributor of PowerLine cabinetry will go to existing facilities that are using PowerLine and color postcards to potential customers will be a visual introduction to the product. Follow up phone calls will determine if the information has gotten to the appropriate decision maker and appointments will be made.

Marketing of the PowerLine of Northern Minnesota Studio is crucial in establishing brand recognition and community visibility. Target marketing to the two market niches, general business and health care, will focus on direct mailing of specialized color post cards featuring the aspect of PowerLine most suitable to the targeted customer's needs. Visits to these businesses will position PowerLine of Northern Minnesota as being there for the customer, when they are ready to purchase.

Being an active participant in the community is key to a successful marketing plan. PowerLine of Northern Minnesota will be a member of the Chamber of Commerce and involved in community functions. Business after Hours, Business Expo and Studio Open Houses will acquaint potential customers with products and services.

Local newspaper publications will feature a press release upon opening and subsequent Studio seminars or newsworthy media events will be covered. Newspaper advertising will supplement direct mailings and announce special events or sales. Special interest publications put out by the newspaper, such as business or health related tabs, would be appropriate for advertising as well as features written by Colleen Jackson, an often quoted source for cabinetry and design articles.

Cross merchandising with other related business merchants will produce additional exposure for both. PowerLine computer furniture can be displayed at a business selling computer hardware or office equipment. Electronics can be shown in a home entertainment setting.

A data base of all PowerLine of Northern Minnesota customers will be maintained for mailings of product updates, special events and a newsletter of storage related information and trends. Mailings to new residents via Welcome Wagon lists will reach prospects for business or home office PowerLine users. A complementary letter opener with PowerLine of Northern Minnesota logo, can be distributed in the Welcome Wagon packet provided to newcomers.

Yellow Pages advertising under headings of cabinetry and office furniture will provide an introduction to PowerLine of Northern Minnesota's products and services. Public radio underwriting will reach a discerning population likely to appreciate the style, value and service of PowerLine of Northern Minnesota.

Business cards, stationery, presentation folders, signage and advertising will all feature the PowerLine style of printing and layout that signifies genuine PowerLine product. The mobility of the population means that more people coming into the area will have heard of or own PowerLine products. Familiarity with the product and satisfaction with both product and service will help to establish and grow PowerLine of Northern Minnesota. Studios report that after their second year, one-half of all sales are from previous customers.

PowerLine of Northern Minnesota is incorporated as Habitat, Inc., and is headed by Colleen Jackson, president; Bill Jackson, vice president; Judy Farmer, secretary/treasurer.

MANAGEMENT

PowerLine of Northern Minnesota is a PowerLine Studio providing traditional design services along with a selection of PowerLine furniture and cabinetry in a showroom environment. The Studio is approved by Mitchell Camden and Associates to market and sell PowerLine products in an exclusive territory north of Garnet to the northern border. PowerLine furniture is sold on a non-exclusive basis.

The Studio's market niches are general business and health care markets, providing exceptional quality furniture and cabinetry and design expertise to answer the organization and storage needs of its clients. Qualified to head the PowerLine of Northern Minnesota Studio is Colleen Jackson.

Colleen has, for the last ten years, managed Greenwich Kitchen & Bath in Petoskey. Beginning the Design Department inside Kelly Danforth Building Center, she establihed the design standards, product lines, displays and staffing requirements. Through her direction, Greenwich has evolved from a 600 square foot, sub-department with $35,000 in sales, to a 3000 square foot, freestanding showroom with sales of $1.8 million. From a single designer operation, Colleen now designs and oversees a staff of four designers, two assistants, an office manager and delivery person.

MANAGEMENT
...continued

Design and sales of cabinetry for residential and business applications has provided Colleen with the expertise to successfully market the PowerLine products. She is well known in the Petoskey area with business people, designers, builders, trades people and health care professionals. The local newspaper has interviewd her on several occasions as an expert on design trends.

Further, Colleen's degree and background is in Interior Design, having been on the design staff Johnson Interiors in Petoskey, Kerry's in East Lansing, and Randall's Furniture in Lansing.

Customer service was the focus of Colleen's career as a service representative for American Power and Light. Listening skills and organizational habits were emphasized during these four years.

Colleen has continually expanded her knowlege and skills through courses including Dale Carnegie Leadership and Sales Training, Health Focus Facilities Design Seminar, Inc. World7 Business Conference, Chicago Merchandise Mart Design-Conferences, computer training classes, CAD (computer aided design) training, and stays informed of market trends and product developments through numerous trade publications.

Colleen Jackson will provide the design, marketing and management. for PowerLine of Northern Minnesota. She will oversee the day to day functioning of the business and make sales calls to clients.

Assisting in the Studio showroom will be Judy Farmer. She is responsible for greeting customers in the showroom, answering phone inquiries, setting up appointments, management of the database, correspondence, scheduling shipments and deliveries, and providing customer service to clients. Judy's background is in department management of Sanderling's Bakery where she was resonsible for the daily production and staff management. She also has training in clerical and customer relations procedures.

Bill Jackson will provide warehouse, assembly and installation services on a part time basis. He is skilled in all facets of PowerLine construction and is experienced in cabinet installation and construction. Bill has worked with customers for twenty years as an installation and service technician for American Power and Light. He is very competent in customer service and will provide clients with a positive last impression upon completion of the installation.

As business needs require, additional warehouse, installation and sales people will be added. Subcontractors will be used on a temporary basis to supplement larger installations.

Custom countertop fabrications will be done by an independent top shop. Appropriate specialists will be called upon as client needs or installations warrant. Moving and delivery personnel may be hired as needed.

Accounting will be handled by a CPA. Daily bookkeeping functions will be done in the Studio by Judy Farmer.

Parts Manufacturer

BUSINESS PLAN

ZEMENS METAL CORPORATION

177 Hill St.
Rochester, MN 87882

This business plan is a good example of an established business re-visiting goals and objectives to achieve continuous improvment. Note that all phases of operation, from production and safety to cash flow and employee relations, are examined for opportunities for growth. This an exemplary plan for a business in any industry to use as a starting point for measuring their own business' health and well-being.

- COMPANY VISION

- COMPANY MISSION STATEMENT

- DEPARTMENTAL GOALS AND MEASURES

- MARKET STRATEGY AND FUTURE PLANS

- FINANCIAL PROJECTIONS

COMPANY VISION

To set the standard for industries we serve and to be the organization against which others are measured.

To continually strive for excellence in all that we do.

To provide the highest quality deep drawn components and assemblies to our customers.

To provide the highest level of customer service in the industry.

To maintain the highest standards of honesty and integrity in all our relationships.

COMPANY MISSION STATEMENT

It is the goal of Zemens Metal Corporation to set the standard for the industries we serve and to be the organization against which others are measured.

The following principles will dictate our actions as we continue our quest for excellence in all we do:

1. Strive to achieve a company-wide commitment to continuous improvement in all areas of our business.
2. Maintain the highest standards of honesty and integrity in all relationships with our employees, customers, suppliers, service groups and community.
3. Utilize the best technologies in mechanical, statistical and management techniques to effectively bring high quality products to the marketplace and to ensure employee and customer satisfaction.
4. Embrace change as a vehicle to the future.
5. Dedicate ourselves to the principle of craftsmanship and the notion that the customers, suppliers and the work force, being brought together with mutual respect for each one's contribution, has created today what is Zemens Metal Corporation.

DEPARTMENTAL GOALS AND MEASURES

The following section contains the goals which have been identified for each individual department within the company. The method of measuring each goal is also identified. It is assumed that attainment of these goals supports our efforts towards continuous improvement andmaintains our status as the premier manufacturer of deep drawn metal components. Implied in all of these goals is our commitment to the highest level of service to our customers.

The goals established should not be viewed as static; rather they should be seen as a living expression of our attempts to identify opportunities for ongoing improvement and growth of the company.

These goals will be assessed on a regular basis (i.e. quarterly) and modified, deleted, or new goals established as current situations dictate.

Engineering Department

I. TO INTEGRATE ENGINEERING FUNCTION IN All ASPECTS OF A JOB-QUOTING, DESIGN, TOOLING, GAUGING, PRODUCTION, AND CLEANING/SHIPPING.

Goal
Increase engineering's technical knowledge of their total function in the manufacturing of deep drawn metal components and assemblies.

Current
We currently have a total quality systems manual which details the comprehensive function of the Engineering Department.

Measures

1. Adhere to the advanced quality principles detailed in the Quality Manual.
2. Maintain engineering turnaround time of 24 hours on quotes.
3. Establish a thru production feedback loop/team consisting of an engineer, quality represen
   tative, toolmaker and setup technician. This team will meet during the engineering,
   toolmaking and first setup of the job and document these meetings. The goal is 100%
   compliance by June 1, 1995. This will be monitored by the quality systems manager as part
   of the yearly audit of the TQS Plan.
4. Assess setup time and running efficiency between actuals and quote estimate. This data will
   be gathered starting 1/1/96 after proper education of production personnel.

1. ANALYSIS OF INTERNAL vs. EXTERNAL TOOLING USE AND EFFICIENCY OF BOTH | **Tooling Department**

Goal

Assure the healthy and proper mix of internal and external tooling to provide for the company's
long term profitability.

Current

ABD is our first outside source for new tooling based on their ability to meet our budget and
time frame.

Measures

A. Actual cost of tooling versus budgeted tooling.
B. Delivery date versus stated need time specified on sales order.

Goal | **Apprenticeship Program**

To have an established training program, approved by the Department of Labor, which meets
our needs for quality tool & die makers.

Current

We currently have three people enrolled in our training program.

Measures

A. To have one person at each of the 4 levels of the program.
B. Apprentices are adhering to the established time lines.
C. Regular (semiannual) evaluation of an apprentice's performance within the program.
D. Yearly assessment of the effectiveness of the program with any necessary modifications
   reviewed.

SAFETY | **Production Department**
Goal
Zero accidents (injury-free work environment).

Current

3 year (1992-1994) average of 26 accidents per year.

**Production
Department**
...continued

Measures

A. Reduction of 5 accidents per year to goal.

      1995 - 21 meets, 19 exceeds, 17 excellent
      1996 - 16 meets, 14 exceeds, 12 excellent
      1997 - 11 meets, 9 exceeds, 7 excellent

B. Measure quarterly during course of year and publicize.

HOUSEKEEPING
Goal

On a scale of 1 (low) to 10 (high) we strive for perfection, but establish a minimum standard of 8 on this scale.

Current

No current measure.

Measure

A housekeeping committee will be established and will rate each department on a monthly basis. A deduction of .5 points will be taken for each housekeeping deficiency. Department performance, and the company as a whole performance, will be publicized monthly.

PRESS UPTIME
Goal

A goal of 75% uptime of gross press capacity (# of presses x 20 hours = total press time per day x 5 = gross capacity).

Current

We currently average 60% uptime of available hours worked based on # of presses x 17 hours

Measure

We will measure uptime for each of our 3 production units. This measure will be the uptime hours as a percentage of gross press capacity.

COMMUNICATION
Goal

A board visible within the plant and office areas to show performance in the areas of safety, housekeeping, and press uptime on a monthly basis. Discussion at State-of-the-Business Meeting three times yearly.

Measure

Board kept current.

IDENTIFY NEEDS FOR IMPROVEMENT
Goal

Develop an effective plan to identify individual strengths and weaknesses as they relate to standards established for the department.

Measure

A matrix of essential and desired skills for each job will be established and each team member will be assessed in these areas during their semiannual performance review.

RECOGNITION OF POSITIVE PERFORMANCE
Goal
Consistent and regular recognition (feedback) of positive performance. This recognition can be tangible rewards or intangible rewards.

Measure
Written feedback for outstanding performance will be placed in each team members personnel file.

PROMOTE QUALITY THROUGHOUT THE ORGANIZATION   **Quality Department**
Goal
Increased awareness of quality issues for all Zemens Metal personnel.

Current
We currently compile monthly scrap reports.

Measures
1. Attain QS-9000 certification in 1995. Need a milestone record and list of achievements towards milestones.
2. Pursue Malcolm-Baldridge Award. Need a milestone record and list of achievements towards milestones.
3. Item related to quality improvements in each newsletter.
4. Monthly internal quality newsletter.

Integration results - examples include:
1. Production - scrap report, production uptime.
2. Shipping - periodic audit once a quarter.
5. Reduce total scrap (rejects, sorting & rework costs, machine scrap)

    1995 - 2.05% (of sales)
    1996 - 1.90% (of sales)
    1997 - 1.80% (of sales)

6. Audit the execution of the quality systems as detailed in the existing Quality Manual on an annual basis. This process will be segmented for quarterly review. The results of the audit will be provided to senior management who, in turn, will review with department managers. The quality systems manager will monitor adherence to any follow-up actions identified through the audit. The total quality goal will be:

    85% compliance - 1995
    90% compliance - 1996
    95% compliance - 1997

TO IDENTIFY PHYSICAL AND PERFORMANCE BARRIERS WHICH IMPEDE ON-TIME SHIPMENT   **Shipping Department**
Goal
To have 100% on-time shipment.

Current

We estimate that we are near 95-96% on-time at this time.

Measures

1. Assess daily shipments versus shipping schedule.
2. Any product received by Shipping (including outside services) will be packaged and ready to ship within 24 hours.

> 24 hours - meets
> 20 hours - exceeds
> 16 hours - excellent

Sales Department

IMPROVE OUR RESPONSE TO CUSTOMERS

Goals

1. To improve customer service through:
   - Accurate lead times.
   - Streamlined communications
2. To improve our quote and no quote ratio.
3. Monitor customer potential.
4. To increase sales.

Measures

1. Quotes will be completed within 3 days. Quote log maintained by Sales.
2. Production job new order completed within 4-6 weeks. This will be measured by customer order and initial M.F.C. ship date.
3. Improve the ratio of accepted quotes by 15% over 1993 and 1994 levels without reducing the number of new tooling jobs.
4. Sales to have regular contact with new and existing customers regarding availability of other work possible within that company. Sales will provide monthly feedback to senior management regarding their assessment of long term potential for selected customers. Log kept available at all times updated by Sales at all times.
5. Sales will increase to the following levels:

> 1995 - $21.0MM
> 1996 - $24.0MM
> 1997 - $28.0MM

6. Customer surveys will be completed on a yearly basis.

Purchasing Department

TO ESTABLISH STANDARDS FOR INVENTORY TURN RATIOS. TO IMPROVE LEVEL OF COORDINATION WITH SUPPLIERS TO MANAGE COSTS AND ASSIST WITH TURN RATIO GOAL.

Goal

To have a 7-10 day period for material on-site to production. 10 days (fully effective), 8 days (exceeds), 7 days (exceptional). Zero stock outs.

Current

We are currently at 20 days. We currently have stock outs and need to establish baseline incidence figures.

Measures

1. The Purchasing Department will gather cumulative data related to date material received and date used in production. This information will be reported weekly.
2. Measure stock outs - zero stock outs. Reported weekly.

TO MAINTAIN A FINANCIAL REPORTING SYSTEM TO SERVE AS A BASIS FOR CONTINUOUS IMPROVEMENT

Accounting Department

Goals

1. Accurate and timely reports.
2. Develop a costing system with senior management.

Measures

1. End of month report available within 10 working days from last day of the month. This report will include trends against goals and action items to address trends.
2. Preliminary report on a costing system by 7/1/95.

MAINTAIN AN EFFECTIVE WORK FORCE
MAINTAIN EFFECTIVE AND TIMELY COMMUNICATIONS

Human Resources Department

Goals

1. To have a well trained and sufficient work force.
2. To have a well informed work force.

Measures

1. Newsletter - 4 times a year
   (January, April, July and October).
2. State-of-the-Business Meetings - 3 times a year
   (January, May and September).
3. Develop and monitor apprenticeship programs in tool & die and setup specialist.
4. Provide feedback to senior management on cost of benefits, benefit enhancements, and comparison of M.F.C. wage and benefits with local companies and PMA companies. This will be done at least once a year.
5. Assist all members of the Zemens Metal team in remaining cognizant of our responsibility to provide timely and appropriate motivational enhancements to all Zemens Metal personnel.

Zemens Metal Corporation is keenly aware of the continued and increasing trend of globalization within the automotive industry. Competitive pricing, cost containment and continuous improvement are on-going initiatives; the successful supplier now has to satisfy the industry's demands for shorter lead times coupled with more frequent, on-time deliveries.

MARKET STRATEGY AND FUTURE PLANS

Zemens Metal will blend its' sales, scheduling, purchasing and shipping departments towards the goal of providing on-time parts within 4-6 weeks of order placement. To accomplish this goal, the following changes will be made:

- Sales will get more involved with customer releasing departments to obtain realistic part usage rates and build schedules.
- Scheduling will encompass three separate, but interactive areas: order entry, production and shipping scheduling, and customer service.
- Purchasing will assume responsibility for all outside services including, but not limited to, expediting and receiving functions.
- Shipping will focus on cleaning parts, packaging and shipping.

While our dependency on the highly cyclical automotive market continues, it has not been a detriment to us. In fact, it has fueled our rapid growth in the past few years. Nevertheless, we continue to diversify our product base outside the automotive industry and have set a goal of 12% non-automotive business by 1997. To accomplish this, we will seek out sales agencies associated with diverse industries in various geographic areas with a goal of adding at least one new agency per year. We will attend at least two domestic trade shows per year, one of which will be in an area new to us, to continue our exposure in new markets and industries.

Zemens Metal realizes that, as it moves into new markets and expands its' customer base, competition with other metal forming companies will intensify. Our efforts towards continuous improvement in the areas of pricing, quality and delivery are constants. We will focus future efforts on developing new processes and capabilities which allow us to expand our product Offerings. Along these lines, securing work for our new, larger presses and expanding our value-added assembly capabilities will allow us to offer a wide range of complete products to our customers. With all projects, our emphasis will be on high volume and emerging product lines while minimizing our reliance on maturing product lines.

Integral to all future plans is maintaining the highest level of customer service. We will intensify our efforts to cultivate long-term relationships with existing and new customers by involving personnel at all levels of our organization in assuring customer satisfaction with our products and service. We will continue to monitor our performance and customer satisfaction with an annual survey sent to all customers in the fall of each year. Our goal will be to improve our ratings by 1/4 of 1 point (5 point scale) in each of the next 3 years.

Our sales dollar objectives, along with targeted automotive to non-automotive sales mix, is shown below. We will monitor our margins closely and, if it becomes apparent that shifting away from automotive work tends to decrease these margins, a restructuring of our strategy will be needed.

Year	Sales	Increase	Automotive	Non-Automotive
1994	17.2MM	26.5	91%	9%
1995	21.0MM	22.1	90%	0%
1996	24.0MM	14.3	89%	1%
1997	28.0MM	16.7	88%	2%

Given the projected annual growth from 1995 through 1997 and our desire to expand our customer and product base, additional personnel and equipment will be needed. We anticipate that our current facility will adequately accommodate our growth. However, changes in the existing facility, due for completion in 1995, include the addition of a health center and air-conditioning for the manufacturing area. These changes are seen as enhancements to our facility which benefit all of our personnel and helps them achieve the goals established in this business plan. Anticipated equipment and personnel needs are detailed below.

Production

- 3-4 experienced die-setters each year at a cost of approximately $37,000 per person.
- 2 production apprentices per year at a cost of approximately $21,000 per person.

Toolroom

- 3 machinists by late 1995 at an approximate cost of $30,000 per person.
- 2 toolroom apprentices per year at an approximate cost of $21,000 per person.

Engineering

- 1 tooling engineer by June 1996 at an approximate cost of $33,000.

Purchasing

- 1 "Buyer" by mid-1996 at an approximate cost of $36,000.

Quality Assurance

- 1 final auditor by late 1995 at an approximate cost of $27,000.
- 2 floor inspectors by mid-1996 at an approximate cost of $27,000 each.

Shipping/Cleaning

- none anticipated with equipment purchases.

Personnel

FINANCIAL PROJECTIONS

Forecast of Major Balance Sheet Categories

	1995	1996	1997
Assets			
Cash/Investments	$1,944.3	$3,190.5	$4,628.1
Accts. Receivable	$3,540.6	$4,500.6	$5,620.6
Inventory	$1,119.6	$1,287.6	$1,545.1
Other Assets/Prepaids	$240.5	$245.3	$250.2
Net Plant & Equipt	$624.5	$664.5	$774.5
Total Assets	$7,469.5	$9,888.5	$12,818.5
Liabilities			
Line of Credit	$300.0	$300.0	$300.0
Trade Payables	$1,500.0	$1,600.0	$1,700.0
Accrued Expenses	$600.0	$700.0	$800.0
Officers Notes Pay	$0.0	$0.0	$0.0
Bank Debt	$815.9	$1,090.9	$1,440.9
Total Liabilities	$3,215.9	$3,690.9	$4,240.9
Equity	$4,253.6	$6,197.6	$8,577.6
Total Liabilities and Equity	$7,469.5	$9,888.5	$12,818.5
Debt to Equity Ratio From Operations	0.76	0.6	0.49

**Forecast of
Cash Flows**

	1995	1996	1997
Cash Flows From Operations			
Net income (loss)-per tax before discretionary adj.			
Adjustments to reconcile net income (loss) to			
net cash provided by operating activities			
Depreciation (non-cash exp.)	$330.0	$360.0	$390.0
(Increase)/Decrease in accts. rec.	($840.0)	($960.0)	($1,120.0)
Increase/(Decrease) in trade accts.pay.	$277.7	$100.0	$100.0
(Increase)/Decrease in inventories	($223.9)	($167.9)	($257.5)
(Increase)/Decrease in Other/P.P. Assets	($4.7)	($4.8)	($4.9)
Increase/(Decrease) in accrued expenses	$227.0	$100.0	$100.0
Income Taxes	($1,648.5)	($1,944.0)	($2,380.0)
Net Cash Flow Provided by Operating Activities	$1,414.6	$1,371.2	$1,587.6
Cash Flows From Plant and Equipment			
(Purchase)/disposition of property, plant & equip.	($300.0)	($400.0)	($500.0)
Net Cash Flow Provided by Capital Asset Activity	($300.0)	($400.0)	($500.0)
Cash Flows From Financing Activities			
Line of Credit Increase/(Decrease)	$176.0	$0.0	$0.0
Net Bank Debt Increase/(Decrease)	$200.0	$275.0	$350.0
Officers Debt Increase/(Decrease)	($500.0)	$0.0	$0.0
Net Cash Flow Provided By Financing Activities	($124.0)	$275.0	$350.0
Net Increase (Decrease) In Cash	$990.6	$1,246.2	$1,437.6
Cash - Beginning of Period	$953.7	$1,944.3	$3,190.5
Cash - End of Period			
(Before Year-End Discretionary Adj.)	$1,944.3	$3,190.5	$4,628.1

Department	1993	1994	1995	1996	1997	**Forecast of Personnel Needs**
Hourly	Act	Act	Est	Est	Est	
Production	23	29	35	40	45	
Quality Assurance	11	14	16	18	18	
Maintenance	7	7	7	8	8	
Toolroom/Toolcrib	11	13	19	21	23	
Shipping/Receiving	5	8	10	10	10	
Engineering	4	3	4	5	5	
Office	5	5	5	5	6	
Total - Hourly	66	79	96	107	115	
% Inc.		19.7%	21.5%	11.5%	7.5%	
Salaried						
Management	2	2	3	3	3	
Production	4	4	6	6	6	
Quality Assurance	1	1	2	2	2	
Engineering	4	5	4	5	5	
Sales	1	2	2	2	3	
Human Resources	0	0	1	1	1	
Finance	1	1	2	2	2	
Total - Saleried	13	15	20	21	22	
% Inc.		15.4%	33.3%	5.0%	4.8%	
Total - Company	79	94	116	128	137	
% Inc.		19.0%	23.4%	10.3%	7.0%	

Forecast of Capital Asset Needs

Department	Item	1995 Est	1996 Est	1997 Est
Production	250T. Komatsu		$750.0	
	2012 Presses (2)		$200.0	$200.0
	1512 Presses (2)		$150.0	$150.0
	1212 Press		$80.0	
	Speed Lathes (2)		$20.0	
	Turning Lathe		$15.0	
	Auto. Stock Reels (30)	$50.0	$50.0	$65.0
	Air Cond. Plant	$250.0		
	Surface Grinder		$9.0	
	Total	$300.0	$1,274.0	$415.0
Toolroom	ID/OD Grinder	$100.0		
	Lathe	$40.0		
	Milling Machine	$25.0		
	C.N.C. Turning Ctrs (2)		$100.0	$100.0
	Total	$165.0	$100.0	$100.0
Engineering	Cad Stations(2)	$20.0	$20.0	
	Quote Computer	$4.0		
	Printer	$3.0		
	Cad Stations-Prod(6)		$18.0	
	Total	$27.0	$38.0	$0.0
Quality Assurance	Comparator		$10.0	
	Vision System		$40.0	
	Total	$0.0	$50.0	$0.0
Shipping/Rec.	Boxing System		$15.0	
	Cleaning Machine			$125.0
	H2O Treatment System			$15.0
	Total	$0.0	$15.0	$140.0
Miscellaneous		$50.0	$50.0	$50.0
Grand Total		$542.0	$1,527.0	$705.0

Production

Item	Year	Cost
1 250-Ton Komatsu	1996	750K
2 2012	1996, 1997	175-200K Each
2 1512	1996, 1997	125-150K Each
1 1212	1996	80K
2 Speed Lathes	1996	10K Each
1 Turning Lathe	1996	15K
30 Automatic Stock Realers	2/mo.	5500 Each
1 Surface Grinder	1996	9K

Toolroom

Item	Year	Cost
1 I.D./O.D. Grinder	1995	85-95K
1 Lathe	1995	30-40K
1 Milling Machine	1995	18-25K
2 C.N.C. Turning Centers	1996, 1997	80-100K Each

Engineering

Item	Year	Cost
2 CAD Stations	1995, 1996	20K Each
Update Quoting Computer	1995	4K
1 Printer (Color)	1995	3K
6 Computer Stations For Production	1996	3K Each

Quality Assurance

Item	Year	Cost
1 Comparator	1996	8-10K
1 Vision System	1996	30-40K

Shipping/Cleaning

Item	Year	Cost
1 Packaging System	1996	10-15K
1 Cleaning Machine	1997	125K
1 Water Treatment System	1997	15K

Equipment

Income Statement
Recap From
Operations

Year			Sales			COS		
Month		Parts	Other	Total	Parts	Other	Total
Total 1993	A	$11,913.4	$1,656.5	$13,569.9	$4,084.2	$2,768.2	$6,852.4
Total 1994	A	$15,510.5	$1,718.2	$17,228.7	$5,143.8	$3,315.4	$8,459.2
Total 1995	E	$19,000.0	$2,000.0	$21,000.0	$6,301.0	$4,094.0	$10,395.0
Total 1996	E	$22,000.0	$2,000.0	$24,000.0	$7,295.9	$4,584.1	$11,880.0
Total 1997	E	$26,000.0	$2,000.0	$28,000.0	$8,622.5	$5,237.5	$13,860.0

A=Actual E=Estimate
(Pre-Tax and Prior to Discretionary Y-E- Adjustments)

% To Sales	MGF. Exp.	% To Sales	Admin. Exp.	% To Sales	Net Inc'l	% To Sales
50.5%	$3,498.3	25.8%	$1,252.8	9.2%	$1,966.4	14.5%
49.1%	$4,825.1	28.0%	$1,417.6	8.2%	$2,526.8	14.7%
49.5%	$5,628.0	26.8%	$1,680.0	8.0%	$3,297.0	15.7%
49.5%	$6,360.0	26.5%	$1,872.0	7.8%	$3,888.0	16.2%
49.5%	$7,280.0	26.0%	$2,100.0	7.5%	$4,760.0	17.0%

Party Supply Store

BUSINESS PLAN

CELEBRATIONS

1100 Sutton Ave.
Kokomo, IN 55872

This business plan for a party supply retailer is a nearly exhaustive consideration of the party planning industry's potential in this owner's market. This entrepreneur has considered not only his initial startup, but related businesses that can be developed as adjuncts. Note the use of available data to get a commanding picture of the business' possibility for success.

- CASH FLOW ASSUMPTIONS AND CONSIDERATIONS

- EXECUTIVE SUMMARY

- COMPANY DESCRIPTION

- INDUSTRY ANALYSIS

- MARKET ANALYSIS

- MARKETING PLAN

- FACILITIES AND EQUIPMENT

- MANAGEMENT

- SALES VOLUME PROJECTIONS

- USE OF FUNDS STATEMENT

- START-UP COSTS

- CAPITAL REQUIREMENTS, RESOURCES, AND PROPOSED LOAN

- COLLATERAL PROPERTY DESCRIPTIONS

- OPENING BALANCE STATEMENT

- PROFIT AND LOSS STATEMENT YEAR 1

- CASH FLOW PROJECTIONS YEAR 1

CASH FLOW ASSUMPTIONS AND CONSIDERATIONS

The market research data is based on a limited geographical sales area, the central counties of the state of Indiana. Actual market area includes parts of nine counties from the central Indiana, about 7% of the state.

All costs and expenses are taken from the high side of any estimates or ranges. The sales figures are deliberately figured from the low side of any projections. This was done to present the project in the most conservative manner.

Targeted market share projections are very conservative considering that we will be the only store of this type in the market area. The nearest full line competitors are 70 miles away.

The cash flow chart does not account for four weeks in the year. For ease of accounting all months are assumed to have exactly four weeks. This action allows for some buffer effect in cash flow assumptions.

The size of the store's inventory and projected sales figures have prompted some sizable discounts on the costs of inventory. Manufacturers are offering an additional 20% to 40% off the costs of selected lines of paper goods. These savings are not reflected in the cash flow estimates, as they are not locked in until the actual purchases are made and are based on the size and the timing of the order.

The landlord, recognizing that the store will be a magnet store that will draw customers, offered an excellent lease at about half the going rate for the area that we are located in. We will generate shopping traffic for the other businesses in the building.

The purchases figures in the cash flow projections are calculated to include a 2% return and allowances amount.

The depreciation expense account in the cash flow projections is based on MACR schedules for assets in the 7 year category.

The cash flow projections sheet, at the beginning of the second year, shows an expenses for $10,000 for the purchase of etching and engraving machinery. This follows the business plan for growth of the business and is expected to generate $20,000 to $25,000 in direct sales.

EXECUTIVE SUMMARY

This plan covers three distinct stages. The first is to open Celebrations of Kokomo. This will be a retail store selling three lines of merchandise.

- 1st. Paper products such as plates, napkins, tablecloths, balloons, decorations, and banners.
- 2nd. A full line of wedding accessories such as bridal pillows, cake tops, server sets, and so forth.
- 3rd. Etched glassware such as wine glasses and wedding and anniversary gift sets of glass and crystal and a careful selection of items suitable for gifts for weddings, anniversaries, and special occasions.

The first stage of this plan is projected to cost $90,300. Of this amount we need to finance about $75,000. The break even point of sales vs. expenses occurs in the 5th month of operation. Debt service is paid from the first month of operation. Total accumulated profits compared to all accumulated expenses become positive in the 10th month of the first year.

In stage two we hope to expand the business to include event planning and coordination of peripheral services such as hall, rentals, limos, and caterers. This stage does not require financing and will be implemented, as it becomes viable.

The retail market in the tri-county are of Jackson, Green, and Yardley counties is estimated at 3.2 Billion Dollars. The wedding and party accessories is about $1,070,000. After three years of operation, we project a market share of 30%, giving us gross sales of about $421,000 per year at that point.

Competitive advantages are:
   Location: our nearest full line competitor is 70 miles away.
   Selection: a complete line of merchandise to be offered in depth.
   Price: Volume and selection will allow moderate pricing strategies.

Management skills of the owners:
Greg Rivers: B.S. in Business Management from Lake Superior State University, office experience with Randolph Construction, Selling experience in both wholesale and retail sales.

June Rivers: 28 years experience in billing, collection, scheduling, and office operations.

COMPANY DESCRIPTION

Name of Company: Celebrations of Kokomo.

Name of Owners: June J. and Greg M. Rivers

Legal structure of the company: "S" Corporation

Type of Business: Retail sales of decorations, paper goods and accessories for weddings, birthdays, anniversaries and all types of parties and occasions.

Reasons for formation of the company:
The main reasons for starting this company are to provide a useful and needed service to the community, to fulfil lifelong ambitions of being in charge of our destines, to work for our own economic welfare, and to function at our potential.

Goals

The short term goals for this business are to establish a thriving and competitive presence in the accessories niche of the wedding and party business, and provide a local alternative to what is now a major trip to the nearest competitor. We also want to provide glassware engraving, a unique and specialized service that will be recognized for high quality and considered to be an appropriate gift for very special occasions.

The long term goals start with cementing the position of the business as a reasonably priced, full line, service center for the paper products and of the wedding and party accessories business. We plan to expand this service to include printing services, consulting and organizing for weddings and other events, and some rentals for these types of events.

The etching and engraving part of the business is planned to expand to provide products and services to a wider area. We would like to be a supplier of personalized, etched to order, stemware and glassware in the Indiana, Ohio, and Michigan area.

Product/Service Analysis

Description

The business intends to compete in three areas. The first area is paperware. This includes all the plates, napkins, balloon, tablecloths, banners, decorations, and so forth, that are needed to have a party or reception. This will be the largest portion of the inventory and will require the most display space.

The second area is centered around the wedding accessory market. These type of products include items such as unity candles, ring pillows, toasting glasses, garters, guest books, gift books, pompoms, and wedding albums. It is planned to expand this area to include a wedding and event co-ordinating service to provide one stop planning of all peripheral services such as the limo, hall, flowers, organist, soloist, horse and carriage, photographer or any other service that would enhance the event.

The third area is engraving and etching of stem ware and glasses. The ability to engrave names, dates, and patterns on champagne and wine toasting glasses will enhance the bridal part of the business. For other events such as birthdays, gag gifts, souvenirs and anniversaries the ability to engrave or etch names, dates, and patterns on the spot will create its own traffic. There is also a large market to be exploited in supplying other stores, businesses, and service clubs with both previously engraved glassware and glassware engraved per order.

Advantages

In the local market place there is limited direct competition in the paper products area, there are no engraving places that cater to the glassware market, and the wedding accessories market does not have business that offers a full line, in depth selection.

None of these products are necessities, but they compete in a selected market that has several advantages. Despite the ups and downs of the market place, weddings will continue to consume these products and services. People will still continue to celebrate events and occasions and they tend to view the purchase of these types of products and services as being of importance to the occasion. We believe that the business will compete very favorable in terms of price, location, and selection

INDUSTRY ANALYSIS

Growth and Competition

As a whole, the wedding and party paperware industry has shown remarkable resilience in the market place. In the last few years there has been an upswing in the purchase of these types of products. The number of suppliers has also increased significantly. Locally, there has been little attempt at serving this market.

The wedding accessory industry has been a solid part of the economy for a number of years. There is no expectation in this industry of relinquishing market share or slowing its steady growth.

As far as I can determine the glassware etching and engraving business per order is so scattered and fragmented that there is no practical industry to relate to. I have found one business in Florida that engraves glassware and one company in Plymouth, Michigan that actually does what I envision the market requires. They are in such diverse markets that trying to use their data for market size and share is impractical. There is some competition in peripheral areas from other businesses such as stained glass companies that etch or frost glass. They typically do not do stemware or glassware, however.

I anticipate slow to steady growth in the paperware and wedding accessory parts of the business. The growth of the etching and engraving business will be a little more explosive. There is no direct competition and the primary markets, tourism and giftware, are experiencing great growth.

The wedding industry has two major focuses in the year. Spring and fall weddings account for the majority of weddings. There is however, a long lead time in the planning and purchasing of the products in this area. This tends to flatten the purchasing cycle. The purchase of paper products for special events such as parties, anniversaries, and holiday celebrations are spread out pretty well and help keep the business in a good cash flow position. The glassware end of the business will follow the wedding and paperware cycles, but will also be influenced by the flux of the tourist seasons.

Seasonality and Cycles of Business

There are no licensing requirements, no franchising fees, or obligatory memberships in trade associations. The biggest impediments will be inventory costs, advertising budgets, and the cost of either renting or purchasing a location. The only social or economic factors that would influence the business would be a major re-adjustment in how people perceive the importance of their wedding, anniversary, birthday or holiday parties.

Barriers and Incentives to Entry

MARKET ANALYSIS

Customers

This will be a retail operation on the wedding and paperware side and both wholesale and retail on the engraving side of the business. In general the demographics of the retail customers, reflect the broad spectrum of income and lifestyles of the surrounding community. Sales in the areas I have selected are not limited to any specific segment of society or level of income. However, the level of spending per event rises with the level of income of the particular customer. The products will, in general, appeal more to women than men. Hobbies, education, profession, or age will not impact the buying decisions. Customers tend to purchase on the basis of price, quality, location, and service.

Competition

The competition in the paperware part of the business is mainly from one paperware retailer 70 miles away. Local competition is provided by two stationary stores, several drugstores, and a large, broad spectrum marketer. In the wedding accessory part of the business, the competition flower shops offer some accessories and the two bridal shops in the marketing area do not offer a broad spectrum, full line selection of bridal accessories. The etching and engraving part of the business shave no direct competition. There are business have no direct competition. That are businesses in the area that do stain or etch plate glass, but none that focus on stemware or barware.

The greatest competition my business will face will be Indiana Paper Products Company of Indianapolis, Indiana. They are a full line, well positioned company. They are at present, the best option available for the purchase of paperware products and for wedding accessories. Their price structure reflects their dominant position in the market. Their greatest attraction is the full spectrum of choices available to their customers.

Another strong competitor is Kokomo Bridal Salon. The area of competition is in wedding accessories. Quality and service are excellent, but the selection and price are limited. They are the dominant business in the wedding dress and tuxedo business in Kokomo.

Suppliers

In the wedding accessory market the main suppliers re the Hortense B. Hewitt co. of Rexburg, Idaho, Jamie Lynn Co. of Chicago, and Treasure Masters of Derry, NM.

The main paperware products supplier is Creative Expressions, a division of the James River Corporation. Alternative suppliers are Amscan, Inc., of Harrison, N.Y., Francis Mayer Inc. of Savannah, Ga., Prestige Balloons from Gardena Ca, and Oddity Inc. of Pottsville, PA.

Anchor Hocking and the Lumar co. are just two of many glassware suppliers that can provide plain stemware and glasses suitable for engraving and etching.

MARKETING PLAN

Market Positioning

Price: The strategy is to offer competitive prices that are lower that the market leader, yet set to indicate value and worth. Initial customer surveys indicate that a 50% mark-up is acceptable in the paperproducts part of the sales mix. The engraving and etching prices will try to reflect the idea that these are great gifts in the intermediate price rage. Priced high enough to make them quality gifts, yet low enough to attract a wide section of customers. The price range will be from $10 to $20 per set in general, with high-
end sets available.

Quality: The product quality will have to be very good as the products will be showcased in highly visible situations. This attitude will be prevalent in all three areas of the business.

Service: Highly individual service is the key to success in these types of businesses. Personal attention to the customers will result in higher sales and word of mouth advertising. Everyone's wedding or special event is very important to them and deserve attentive service.

Advantages

The business has some good advantages in this market place. The first is location. The nearest large competitor is 70 miles away. The second is range and depth of selection. The local competing companies are not in the paperware market. At best they have some products and some selection. Another advantage will be synergistic. We will offer all these products in one place and they tend to complement one another. Customers will save a three hour tip and enjoy great prices.

Entry Strategy

I will be the only company in this area to offer this combination of products. This fact combined with a good advertising strategy, aimed at brides and party givers, will make our presence known. Word of mouth will also play a large part in the introduction of this company. Physical location and a good sign will also help. Sales promotions are not viewed as good marketing strategy for entry to this market. I would much rather rely on the advantages indicated above.

Another important part of the entry strategy is our presence in the various bridal shows, and local bridal magazines. Television and radio are too expensive for inclusion in this market entry strategy at this time. Direct marketing aimed at specific customers such as graduating students is possible by market research, direct mail, and inserts in the local papers.

Sales

Presentation and selection will catch the customers attention as well as how the merchandise is displayed and how easy it is to find the items wanted. Signs marking the product sections should be attractive and bright. Displays are planned in four feet sections and will be kept in areas that are related. For example, all tablecloths, paper, plastic, and cloth should be located in the same area for comparison and customer convenience.

Sales strategy also includes a knowledgeable, courteous sales staff. Knowledge about the products and the right attitude toward the customers are part of the image the store will try to project and foster. This strategy is aimed at establishing a large volume of repeat sales.

The suggested retail prices in the catalogs seem to be very competitive and attractive to the potential customers I have surveyed. The mark up seems to average about 100%. [See attachment]. I planto offer no discounts or promotional sales at this time. Credit sales will be limited to the sale of engraved or etched glassware to other stores. The policies will be net 30 and an appropriate % rate to be determined. Engraved or etched to order will require up-front payment. Warranties will be offered that reflect the manufacturers warranties. Refunds will require the sales slip and the item purchased. All refunds will require the initials of the manager or owner.

Pricing Policies

Advertising in the local newspaper seems to offer the best mix of market penetration and price advantage. Creativity is easy to achieve and fast response times are attractive also. The advertising budget will determine the frequency of advertising budget will determine the frequency of ad runs, and the number of new ads to be created. Inserts in the newspaper are also a good buy and offer excellent market presentation.

Advertising and Promotion

There is a wedding apparel fashion show in the area that can present the business to a lot of new customers. The show takes place two to three times a year and reaches 200 to 500 brides-to-be. It is excellent for presenting this business on a one to one basis. There is also a local bridal magazine that covers the market area.

Selected mailings to those who register at county offices for marriage licenses and word of mouth are also strategies that are under consideration.

Donating products and services to schools and churches also is a part of the advertising plan. Advertising in school papers target a prime segment of potential customers, and sponsorship of school functions reinforces our presence.

Advertising in the yellow pages listing can also be an important factor in drawing new business and the major cost of advertising is borne by the phone company. Recognition by new customers of the effectiveness of the yellow pages will draw a large volume of new business.

Visibility of the business location by means of a sign and the building itself are a primary party of the advertising package and are cost effective.

At this time, advertising in radio or television are not within the means of the budget.

The industry average for turnaround on orders is about three days in house and another two to five days on the road. Minimum orders rage from $50 to $350, depending on the supplier. In certain cases when the order totals $350, the freight costs are paid by the shipper. Initial inventory is projected to be $45,000. Replenishment orders will made weekly or as needed.

Inventory and Ordering

FACILITIES & EQUIPMENT

Facilities

The business will be located in the downtown area of the city of Kokomo, Indiana. the requirements are adequate parking, easy access, visibility, affordability, and at least 1500 to 2000 sq. ft. of floor space.

The usual rental agreement for this area is in the rage of $700 to $1500 per month, depending on location and condition of the building. Renovation and repair costs will depend on the condition of the building and the amount of re-arranging necessary.

Equipment and display shelving

Shelving and racks will be built or assembled by myself. Used racks and display units are available from a business in Muncie, Indiana. Other office equipment is already on hand, and includes adding machines, desk, file cabinets, and a computer.

MANAGEMENT

Owners

The owners of the business are June & Greg Rivers. Mr. Rivers is a graduate of Lake State University with a degree in Business Administration. He has experience in accounting and sales. He has taught accounting in the school system and been a tax accountant. He has held positions in both retail and wholesales sales, and has always been involved in customer relations.

Mrs. Rivers has experience in account collections, telephone work, retail sales, billing procedures, and insurance forms. She has worked in these areas for over 25 years. Another family member, who is an accountant of over fifty years experience, will help in the office.

Compensation

The compensation plan includes a salary base and bonus package. Medical and retirement plans are options that will be implemented as the business grows. Compensation will be limited in scale until profits warrant and increase.

Management Skills

The primary skills needed by a business of this type are concentrated in the personal skills area. The ability to interact with people determines the success or failure of the business. Not only customers must be handled with care, but management of any employees and relationships with suppliers are critical to success.

Prior knowledge of this type of business is not critical. The skill and experience of the sales representatives of many of the supplier companies can fill this gap. The personal skills listed above complement the reps input. Necessary skills in the advertising, insurance, tax, accounting, and other technical areas are hired as necessary.

FINANCIAL DOCUMENTS

Sales Volume Projections

Prepared with assistance from manufacturers representatives. Data from the Kokomo Regional Chamber of Commerce, the Central Indiana Council of Governments, the Extension Office of Jackson County, the Edward Lowe Foundation, and Ameritech.

This report was based on data representing a 40 mile area centered on Kokomo, Indiana. This area includes all of Jackson, Green, and Yardley counties. The extended sales area actually served by this business also includes parts of five other counties. These extended sales areas are not include in the projections listed below.

General Market Data

Population	121,283
Number of Households	46,717
Median Household Income	$27,118
Spendable Income after Taxes for the sales area	$950,153,000

Wedding Accessories

Number of Weddings per year	700
Estimated amounts spent on accessories	$200
Potential Market – Wedding Accessories	$140,000

Party goods, paper goods, decorations, and accessories

Number of Households	46,717
Amount spent per Household	$20
Potential market – Paper goods	$934,240

Total Potential Sales for this market area $1,074,340

Targeted Market Share

Year 1	17%	$180,000
Year 2	25%	$265,800
Year 3	30%	$320,400

Capital Requirements

Equipment	$1,753.00
Start up Costs and Deposits	$3,213.00
Renovation Costs	$10,650.00
Furnishings	$7,000.00
Insurance, legal, and permit fees	$2,384.00
Beginning inventory	$45,000.00
Working Capital	$8,000.00
Automobiles	$7,300.00
Advertising	$2,500.00
Travel Expenses	$2,500.00
Total	$90,300.00

Financial Resources
Personal Investment

Cash	$8,000.00
Automobiles	$7,300.00
Total	$15,300.00

Proposed Loan

Amount:	$75,000.00

Length: 7 years
Terms: 11% for 7 years, Mthly paym'ts.of $1284.18

Total	$90,300.00

**Use of Funds
Statement**

Amount of Loan	$75,000.00
Personal Funds Invested	$8,000.00
Company Vehicles & Equipment invested as Capital	$7,300.00

Expenditures:

Deposits, Licenses, Permits, Gas, Electric, Phone &Tra	$612.00
Rental Deposits (Security and 1st month)	$2,600.00
Legal Fees	$750.00
Incorporation Fees	$327.00
Insurance Premiums (Building, Contents, & Liability)	$1,307.00
Office Equipment (See Start-Up Costs)	$1,753.00
Display Racks and Shelving	$7,000.00
Material and Construction Costs	$8,150.00
Contractor's fees for inspections and upgrades	$2,500.00
Electrical &Structural	
Plumbing and Gas	
Inventory (2160 Sq. Ft. of display & Shelving Area)	$45,000.00
Advertising:	$2,500.00
Local News Inserts	
Media Consultant Fee	
Telephone & Travel Expenses	$2,500.00
Total Expenditures	$75,000.00
Cash On Hand	$8,000.00
Vehicles	$7,300.00
Totals	$90,300.00

Miscellaneous:

Gas	$300.00
Electric	$-
Phone	$84.00
Trash	$29.00
Licenses and Permits	$200.00
Legal Fees	$750.00

Insurance Premiums:

Building	$300.00	Ann. Premium
Contents	$628.00	Ann. Premium
Liability	$379.00	Ann. Premium
Total	$2,670.00	

Office Equipment:

Cash Register	$300.00	ER-240 Samsung
Desk	$200.00	Used
Office Chair	$200.00	Used
Staplers and desk equip.	$150.00	
Fire Extinguishers	$120.00	6 ea. 1A-10B Dry
Smoke Alarms	$40.00	4ea. Life Saver Co.
Cards, Paper, and labels	$200.00	Letterhead
Business Checks	$60.00	
Telephone	$80.00	SW Bell 2 line phone
Adding Machine	$60.00	
Balloon gas & machine	$165.00	Lease Cost
Helium	$58.00	Contents
Nozzels for balloons	$50.00	
Saftey chart for tank	$70.00	
Interior Furnishings	$7,000.00	Display Racks, Slotwall system with hooks & baskets

Subtotal	$8,753.00
Total	$11,423.00

**Opening
Balance Sheet**

Assets			
Cash	$8,000.00		
Inventory	$45,000.00		
Prepaid Startup Costs	$21,247.00		
Current Assets		$74,247.00	
Office Equipment	$1,753.00		
Shelving	$7,000.00		
Vehicles	$7,300.00		
Accumulated Depreciation	$-		
Net Fixed Assets		$16,053.00	
Total Assets			$90,300.00
Liabilities			
Payables	$0		
Current portion of Long Term Debt	$597.00		
Current Liabilities		$597.00	
Bank Loan	$74,403.00		
Long Term Liabilities	$74,403.00		
Owners Equity			
Paid In Capital	$15,300.00		
Total Net Worth		$15,300.00	
Total Liabilitiers and Net Worth			$90,300.00

**Profit & Loss
Statement For the
End of Year 1**

Sales		$180,000.00
Less Returns & Allowances		$0
Net Sales		$180,000.00
Expenses:		
Purchases	$93,600.00	
Wages	$15,600.00	
Outside Services	$1,200.00	
Supplies	$2,400.00	
Repairs & Maintenance	$2,400.00	
Advertising	$6,000.00	
Automobile & Travel	$2,400.00	
Rent	$15,600.00	
Telephone	$2,400.00	
Utilities	$2,400.00	
Insurance	$2,400.00	
Shipping	$2,400.00	
Depreciation	$1,248.00	
Loan	$7,877.00	
Miscellaneous	$2,400.00	
Total Expenses		$160,325.00
Net Profit		$19,675.00

Sales	$265,800.00	**Profit & Loss**
Less Returns & Allowances	$0	**Statement For the**
Net Sales	$265,800.00	**End of Year 2**

Expenses:

Purchases	$138,216.00
Wages	$36,000.00
Outside Services	$2,400.00
Supplies	$3,600.00
Repairs & Maintenance	$2,400.00
Advertising	$9,000.00
Automobile & Travel	$3,600.00
Rent	$16,800.00
Telephone	$3,600.00
Utilities	$3,600.00
Insurance	$3,000.00
Shipping	$3,600.00
Depreciation	$1,248.00
Loan Interest	$7,006.00
Miscellaneous	$4,800.00

Total Expenses	$238,870.00
Net Profit	$26,930.00

Sales	$380,400.00	**Profit & Loss**
Less Returns & Allowances	$0	**Statement For the**
Net Sales	$380,400.00	**End of Year 3**

Expenses:

Purchases	$166,608.00
Wages	$48,000.00
Outside Services	$3,600.00
Supplies	$3,600.00
Repairs & Maintenance	$2,400.00
Advertising	$12,000.00
Automobile & Travel	$3,600.00
Rent	$18,000.00
Telephone	$4,800.00
Utilities	$3,600.00
Insurance	$3,600.00
Shipping	$4,800.00
Depreciation	$1,248.00
Loan Interest	$6,032.00
Miscellaneous	$4,800.00

Total Expenses	$287,888
Net Profit	$32,512

**First Year
Cash Flow**

	January	February	March	April	May	June
Cash on Hand-B.O.M.	$15,000.00	$10,986.00	$7,743.00	$4,881.00	$2,019.00	$309.00
Cash Receipts						
Cash Sales	$4,800.00	$6,000.00	$7,200.00	$7,200.00	$9,600.00	$10,800.00
Collections	$0	$0	$0	$0	$0	$0
Loans	$0	$0	$0	$0	$0	$0
Capital	$0	$0	$0	$0	$0	$0
Total Cash Receipts	$4,800.00	$6,000.00	$7,200.00	$7,200.00	$9,600.00	$10,800.00
Total Cash	$19,800.00	$16,986.00	$14,943.00	$12,081.00	$11,619.00	$11,109.00
Expenses						
Purchases	$2,496.00	$3,120.00	$3,744.00	$3,744.00	$4,992.00	$5,616.00
Wages	$2,000.00	$2,000.00	$2,000.00	$2,000.00	$2,000.00	$2,000.00
Payroll Exp.	$100.00	$100.00	$100.00	$100.00	$100.00	$100.00
Supplies	$200.00	$200.00	$200.00	$200.00	$200.00	$200.00
Repairs & Maint.	$200.00	$200.00	$200.00	$200.00	$200.00	$200.00
Advertising	$500.00	$500.00	$500.00	$500.00	$500.00	$500.00
Auto Exp.	$200.00	$200.00	$200.00	$200.00	$200.00	$200.00
Shipping	$200.00	$200.00	$200.00	$200.00	$200.00	$200.00
Acct. & Legal	$0	$0	$0	$0	$0	$0
Rent	$0	$0	$0	$0	$0	$0
Telephone	$200.00	$5.00	$200.00	$200.00	$200.00	$200.00
Utilities	$200.00	$200.00	$200.00	$200.00	$200.00	$200.00
Insurance	$200.00	$200.00	$200.00	$200.00	$200.00	$200.00
Taxes (Real Est.)	$100.00	$100.00	$100.00	$100.00	$100.00	$100.00
Interest	$100.00	$100.00	$100.00	$100.00	$100.00	$100.00
Other Exp.	$100.00	$100.00	$100.00	$100.00	$100.00	$100.00
Depr. Equip. Exp.	$0	$0	$0	$0	$0	$0
Depr. Bld. Exp.	$100.00	$100.00	$100.00	$100.00	$100.00	$100.00
Misc. Exp.	$50.00	$50.00	$50.00	$50.00	$50.00	$50.00
Subtotal Expenses	$6,946.00	$7,375.00	$8,194.00	$8,194.00	$9,442.00	$10,066.00
Loan Paymt.	$1,868.00	$1,868.00	$1,868.00	$1,868.00	$1,868.00	$1,868.00
Total Cash Paid Out	$8,814.00	$9,243.00	$10,062.00	$10,062.00	$11,310.00	$11,934.00
Cash Position-E.O.D.	$10,986.00	$7,743.00	$4,881.00	$2,019.00	$309.00	$(825.00)
Gross Profit	$(4,014.00)	$(3,243.00)	$(2,862.00)	$(2,862.00)	$(1,710.00)	$(1,134.00)
Operating Data						
Sales Volume	$200.00	$250.00	$300.00	$300.00	$400.00	$450.00
Bad Debts						
Inventory on Hand	$41,000.00					
Accts. Payable						
Depreciation Accumulated	$100.00	$200.00	$300.00	$400.00	$500.00	$600.00

July	August	September	October	November	December	Yearly Total
$(825.00)	$(1,383.00)	$(1,365.00)	$(771.00)	$399.00	$1,569.00	$3,315.00
$12,000.00	$13,200.00	$14,400.00	$15,600.00	$15,600.00	$16,800.00	$133,200.00
$0	$0	$0	$0	$0	$0	$0
$0	$0	$0	$0	$0	$0	$0
$0	$0	$0	$0	$0	$0	$0
$12,000.00	$13,200.00	$14,400.00	$15,600.00	$15,600.00	$16,800.00	$133,200.00
$11,175.00	$11,817.00	$13,035.00	$14,829.00	$15,999.00	$18,369.00	$136,515.00
$6,240.00	$6,864.00	$7,488.00	$8,112.00	$8,112.00	$8,736.00	$69,264.00
$2,000.00	$2,000.00	$2,000.00	$2,000.00	$2,000.00	$2,000.00	$24,000.00
$100.00	$100.00	$100.00	$100.00	$100.00	$100.00	$1,200.00
$200.00	$200.00	$200.00	$200.00	$200.00	$200.00	$2,400.00
$200.00	$200.00	$200.00	$200.00	$200.00	$200.00	$2,400.00
$500.00	$500.00	$500.00	$500.00	$500.00	$500.00	$6,000.00
$200.00	$200.00	$200.00	$200.00	$200.00	$200.00	$2,400.00
$200.00	$200.00	$200.00	$200.00	$200.00	$200.00	$2,400.00
$0	$0	$0	$0	$0	$0	$0
$0	$0	$0	$0	$0	$0	$0
$200.00	$200.00	$200.00	$200.00	$200.00	$200.00	$2,205.00
$200.00	$200.00	$200.00	$200.00	$200.00	$200.00	$2,400.00
$200.00	$200.00	$200.00	$200.00	$200.00	$200.00	$2,400.00
$100.00	$100.00	$100.00	$100.00	$100.00	$100.00	$1,200.00
$100.00	$100.00	$100.00	$100.00	$100.00	$100.00	$1,200.00
$100.00	$100.00	$100.00	$100.00	$100.00	$100.00	$1,200.00
$0	$0	$0	$0	$0	$0	$0
$100.00	$100.00	$100.00	$100.00	$100.00	$100.00	$1,200.00
$50.00	$50.00	$50.00	$50.00	$50.00	$50.00	$600.00
$10,690.00	$11,314.00	$11,938.00	$12,562.00	$12,562.00	$13,186.00	$122,469.00
$1,868.00	$1,868.00	$1,868.00	$1,868.00	$1,868.00	$1,868.00	$22,416.00
$12,558.00	$13,182.00	$13,806.00	$14,430.00	$14,430.00	$15,054.00	$144,885.00
$(1,383.00)	$(1,365.00)	$(771.00)	$399.00	$1,569.00	$3,315.00	$(8,370.00)
$(558.00)	$18.00	$594.00	$1,170.00	$1,170.00	$1,746.00	$(11,685.00)
$500.00	$550.00	$600.00	$650.00	$650.00	$700.00	
						$41,000.00
$700.00	$800.00	$900.00	$1,000.00	$1,100.00	$1,200.00	$1,200.00

Pasta Franchise

BUSINESS PLAN

PASTA EXPRESS

117 High St.
Jordan, MI 49775

This business plan examines a take-out pasta franchise with a careful consideration of the marketplace, a crucial step, considering the highly competitive marekt in which the store will operate. This new concept in food service has a good location, but so do its competitors, all of which are located in a highly trafficked upscale shopping area. Note that promotional adverstising is a high percentage of sales.

- EXECUTIVE SUMMARY

- DESCRIPTION OF BUSINESS

- MARKET ANALYSIS

- COMPETITIVE ANALYSIS

- DESIGN AND DEVELOPMENT PLANS

- OPERATIONS AND MANAGEMENT PLANS

- FINANCIAL COMPONENTS

PASTA FRANCHISE
BUSINESS PLAN

EXECUTIVE SUMMARY

The market demand has never been greater for food that is healthy, economically priced, and great tasting. This is the last market with wide open potential for growth to the American consumer. Traditionally, pasta has been consumed in fine restaurants, usually in a more formal or sit down atmosphere at medium to high prices. As pasta has moved to the center stage as a product that both tastes good, and is good for you, Pasta Express has positioned itself to provide the services in demand by the American consumer; a variety of healthy pastas, moderate price and very good taste. The basic focus is to provide the consumer with a healthy, quality meal which is economically priced. This is a concept that will never grow old.

Pasta Express is a franchise system of fast food pasta restaurants with dine in, take out and delivery service, with ongoing support from the national franchiser. National assistance includes; site selection, restaurant design, comprehensive training, support of ongoing operations through marketing assistance, quality control programs, research and development.

Pasta Express of Jordan, MI will require a total financial commitment of $110,000. The franchise fee for the Jordan restaurant will be $10,000. Additional rights to two (2) more stores (located within the protected territory of Jordan, Jordan Hills, Landview Township and Whistler Heights) has been purchased for $10,000 each, with $5,000 payable up front and $5,000 payable when each additional store is opened. Any (all) store openings after initial three will not have any franchise fees. The initial equity contribution of $110,000 will be provided by Pirko, Inc., owners and operators of the Jordan store.

DESCRIPTION OF BUSINESS

History

Pasta Express of Jordan, MI is being structured to operate franchises of the national chain Pasta Express. Pasta Express is owned by Frank Taylor of FT Pasta, Inc. and headquarted in Freemont, MI.

The national Pasta Express chain was established in 1987 with the opening of the original Pasta Express in Freemont, Mi. The company has been franchising since 1991. Recent growth has been in the Detroit area where there are currently 12 stores in operation. Pasta Express has signed master franchise agreements in Wisconsin, Texas, and Indiana to open stores within the next ten years. There are currently restaurants opened and operating in each of the areas.

Ownership Structure

Ownership of the business is in the form of an S Corporation with 50% of the stock owned by Thomas McAffee and the remaining 50% of the stock owned by Carol McAffee.

Business/ Professional qualifications

Thomas McAffee has worked in Computer Systems management for the last fifteeen years. He is a graduate of Michigan State University with a Liberal Arts degree. He also holds an Associates degree in Business from Washtenaw Community College. He does not have any restaurant ownership experience.

Carol McAffee has worked in a retail environment for over three years and in a doctor's office for the last year. She has attended Wayne County Community College. She does not have any restaurant ownership experience.

The objectives for the first five years of the business are as follows:
> Obtain training from the Franchiser
> Open and establish the first restaurant within the community
> Make the restaurant profitable
> Expand into a minimum of three restaurants within ten years

Pasta Express is a fast food pasta chain that focuses on the drawing power of an Italian restaurant that meets the needs of people on the go who still want a healthy product at reasonable prices.

For many years, the only place you could get a variety of quality pasta was a sit down Italian restaurant that was much more expensive and did not meet the needs of the customer who is in a hurry.

The Pasta Express menu is centered around pasta dishes, with a variety of sauces. The majority of the sauces are cooked on site from Pasta Express recipes. For diversity, Pasta Express also offers individual pizza's (in some stores), a line of hot Italian sandwiches, and a good selection of salads. The Pasta Express menu items are available for dine in, carry out, and delivery. Pasta Express also carries a large party, or catering, menu.

The service is exceptional. The #1 goal of each employee will be customer service and satisfaction. Pasta Express believes in the old fashion motto "the customer is always right". In today's society where customer service is often lacking, Pasta Express will structure the business to provide the best service possible in a friendly, helpful atmosphere.

Geographical Area

Pasta Express will draw customers primarily from the Jordan, Jordan Hills, and Landview Township communities.

Pasta Express will draw on the Jordan communities reputation as growing upper middle class community with a thriving old fashion downtown area. The Pasta Express franchises are structured to operate in areas with populations of a minimum of 25,000 people.

There are no physical limitations to the market area since the Jordan area is well served by several major roads, and interstate 75 and M-59.

Pasta Express relies on customer volume with no specific major customer groups. However, the customers can be categorized as:

> 1) baby boomers with families
> 2) Office/retail employees
> 3) young adults (teens to early 20's)
> 4) Adults over 50

Pasta Express is structured to operate in strip mall type locations. The corporate headquarters provides detailed site selection assistance, including lease negotiations.

Pasta Express is designed to function in a 1,500 square foot store. A drive up window can be utilized if a suitable site for such is located.

The final site has been identified for the first store:

117 High St. in downtown Jordan

The equipment necessary for the operation of Pasta Express is part of the purchase agreement with the Pasta Express Franchiser (FT Pasta, Inc.) and will supplied before store opening.

Organization

Pasta Express's staff will be divided into three functional areas, Operations, Administration and Marketing. Each division will be headed by one of the principals:

> Operations: Carol McAffee
> Administration: Thomas McAffee
> Marketing: Thomas McAffee

MARKET ANALYSIS

Geography/ Demographics

The national trend for eating out has increased over the last five years and will continue into the future. In 1993, the amount of money spent on eating out was equal to what was spent for consumption inside the home. The is the first time that consumers spent as much for "eat out" food as they did for "at home" food. According to the American Demographics magazine, in year 1996, spending on restaurants and take out food overtook the nation's grocery bill. The market demand has never been greater for food that is healthy, economically priced, and great tasting. The recent health oriented menu options added to national chains like Taco Bell, Subway, and even McDonald's, point to the nations desire for healthy food.

In an analysis of casual dining Restaurant Business magazine noted that baby boomers, and others, are coming face to face with the realization that youth is ephemeral. With that realization has come the emphasis on healthy dining alternatives like pasta.

The Jordan area has a very good mix of retail and industrial businesses along with a combination of single family homes and apartments. There are also two high schools, one university, and one community college in the area.

There are many competing, well established food outlet in the area, however, few of them are currently providing a similar product all the same price point.

Customers

The customers for restaurants in the geographical area served by Pasta Express,Jordan, can be categorized as follows:

> 1) baby boomers with families
> 2) Office/retail employees
> 3) young adults (teens to early 20's)
> 4) Adults over 50

There are several identifiable characteristics of the market area that determine the segment as listed. Since this area is rapidly growing, as opposed to mature, there are new home buyers who tend to have families and dine out often. According to American Demographics Magazine baby boomers and their families eat out an average of four times a week.

Within the Jordan and Jordan areas, there is a good mix of retail, office, and industrial trade. This should provide Pasta Express with an opportunity for a good luncheon business.

There are two high schools within the Jordan Hills boundaries, along with one university. In a neighboring community, there is a large community college. This should give the Pasta Express an opportunity at capturing some of the young adult market.

The final group, adults over 50, dine out an average of 2.4 times per week. Recent trends indicate that adults age 50+ are dining out less often, but they are more attracted to restaurants that offer food to be eaten at home. Pasta Express can satisfy their needs.

The strategic goals and plans for Pasta Express are based on the following assumptions:

Assumptions

1. The National and local trends toward consumption of healthy food will continue. All indications from national publications consulted agree that healthy food which is reasonably priced will continue it's popularity well into the next century.

2. The trend towards dining out will remain steady. Indications are that dining out will actually increase over the next five to seven years.

The restaurant industry in the United States has been characterized by rapid change. During the 50's and 60's, dining out was quite a new experience to a country feeling the affects of post-war affluence. Also, the various wars have increased the awareness many Americans have with foods from different cultures. This has spawned a trend toward restaurants featuring food from Europe and Asia.

Supply and Demand

An American original, the diner, spread across the country and soon evolved into chain restaurants operated by local, regional, and national corporations. During this period, a newrestaurant concept grew up from the local hamburger stand. The fast food restaurant was started from such humble beginnings and quickly multiplied. Over the next two decades fast food matured and changed at the same time to meet the changing tastes of the public.

While fast food chains experienced significant growth, restaurants evolved also. During the late 60's and 70's, "natural" food restaurants became popular only to give way to nouvelle cuisine in the 80s. The trend in the 90s is to healthy food, low in fat, cholesterol, and sugar.

The national restaurant industry includes approximately 125,000 restaurants plus 235,000 fast food restaurants according to the National Restaurant Owners Association (NROA). NROA estimates that combined restaurant sales reached 4.5 billion dollars in 1994.

The local market reflects the national trends. As pasta has moved to the center stage as a product that both tastes good and is good for you, Pasta Express has positioned itself to provide the services in demand by the American consumer; a variety of healthy pastas, moderate price, and very good taste.

The number of restaurants will grow at an annual rate of 7.3% for the next five years according to a report from the U.S. Department of Agriculture.

Growth Factors

The growth can be attributed to many factors such as a continued trend toward two worker families, thus eating out more for lunches and having little time to prepare a meal after work. The biggest potential for growth involves food prepared for consumption, or take-out food. As the name, Pasta Express, implies, we are positioned to take advantage of either market segment.

The local Jordan area will experience a growth rate above the national average due to the rapid growth of the population throughout Langston county. Numerous subdivisions are being developed along with major construction of retail and multi family housing in the downtown Jordan area.

Product Lifestyle

The restaurant industry is in a rapidly growing phase. Although this growth trend means opportunities for increased sales volume and higher profit margins, overhead must be closely monitored. The importance of quality control, purchasing, low overhead, advertising and marketing cannot be overstated.

At all of the Pasta Express franchise locations, customer loyalty has been developed through its excellent service and popular menu. Attention must be paid to trends, however, and changes should be made early in both the menu and decor before customers become bored and move on to another experience.

Price Structure

Pasta Express is structured to present excellent tasting food at reasonable prices. As such, Pasta Express operates with food costs at 34% of gross. This figure is somewhat higher than industry standards for the same type of menu, however, Pasta Express strives to maintain affordable prices. Pasta Express will keep menu prices at reasonable levels to attract the largest share possible from its demographic base.

Marketing Process

Pasta Express will market food and service of its restaurant using a custom designed campaign by the Franchiser. Franchise fees of 2% of gross sales will be applied for corporate advertising in addition to a minimum of 2% of gross sales to be applied to advertising for individual stores.

Advertising campaigns will utilize newspaper and direct coupon marketing. Pasta Express will also market its catering (or Pasta trays) through the same advertising means.

Some of the advertising means used will be:

Life and Style News: Advertisements and flyers will be distributed through the newspaper on a regular basis.
Mini Market Share: Advertisements will be place periodically by the Franchisor in this mailer package.
Bounce back Flyer's and coupons: will be put in every customers food order to help create return business.
Downtown Jordan Promotions: Advertising campaigns will be done on these special yearly events:

    1) May: Pioneer Days
    2) July: Sidewalk Sale
    3) August: Music Festival
    4) September: Arts and Crafts Festival

Tom-A-To Man costume: Costume will be rented for special occasions.

Pasta Express will have intense direct and indirect competition in the Jordan market for the food dollar. City records show that there are a number of businesses listed in the broadcategory of restaurants. Of these, many feature some form of pasta as a menu item. Additionally, a few Italian restaurants are listed each with several pasta items.

The main competition for the fast food dollar will come from the pizza chains and the national fast food chains such as McDonald's, Kentucky Fried Chicken, Arby's, etc.

Downtown Area:

The Dairy Bar, 304 High St.: Mainly fast food, hamburger dishes with an old fashioned dairy bar. Mostly dine in with some take out.

BigTime Pizza Cafe, 401 High St.: Full service medium priced Italian restaurant featuring pizza, pasta and drinks.

Gringo House, 124 W. 4th: Full service medium priced Mexican food restaurant with drinks.

Hungry Howies, 606 High St.: Take out pizza, subs, with delivery.

Krazy Kathy's, 111 University: Fast food Coney Island hot dogs. Dine in restaurant

Jordan Pub, 327 High St.: Full service moderate to expensive dine in restaurant with some carry out. Competition is in the pasta dishes.

Tony Coney, 621 High St.: Fast food Coney Island hot dogs. Dine in restaurant.

Fritz's, 423 High St.: Medium priced full service restaurant and bar. Competition is in some pasta dishes.

Grant's Steakhouse, 543 High St.: Moderate to expensive bar and dine in restaurant.

Lunch to go, 606 High St.: Take out sandwich shop geared to the luncheon crowd.

Jordan Chop House, 306 High St.: Expensive full service restaurant with vale parking.

Lebanon Kitchen, 543 High St.: Lebanese and Italian food. Moderate to expensive, dine in restaurant.

Subway, 408 High St.: Dine in and take out sandwich (sub) shop.

Polish Inn, 121 High St.: Dine in and take out inexpensive Polish style restaurant.

Renaissance Tea Room, 11 W. 3rd: Moderate priced dine in food.

Mario's Pizza, 140 High St.: Take out pizza, subs, calzones with delivery.

Brothers Pizza, 107 E. Second: Take out pizza, subs, calzones with delivery. Competition is in Lasagna.

Competition
...continued

Domino's Pizza, 121 E. University: Take out pizza with delivery.

Jet's Pizza, 816 High St.: Take out pizza and subs with delivery.

Petey's Pizza, 334 High St.: Mainly a dine in full service pizzeria.

Roberto's, High St.: Full service medium priced Italian restaurant. Competition is in pasta dishes.

Jordan Hills:

Little Caesar's, Kmart Plaza: Dine in and take out pizza.

Papa Romano's, 1322 Canner: Take out pizza, subs with delivery. Competion is in a small number of pasta dishes and catering.

Sir Pizza, 290 Willton: Take out pizza with delivery.

Smoky's Pizza and Subs, Jordan Rd.: Take out pizza, subs with delivery. Competion is in Lasagna and a small number of pasta dishes and catering.

McDonald's, Jordan Rd.: Mainly fast food, hamburger and chicken dishes. Dine in and take out.

Kentucky Fried Chicken: Mainly fast food, chicken dishes.

Arby's, 744 Jordan Rd.: Mainly fast food, roast beef, turkey and chicken dishes. Dine in and take out.

Burger King, 1106 Jordan Rd.: Mainly fast food, hamburger and chicken dishes. Dine in and take out.

Family Place, 870 Jordan Rd.: Full service, low priced family restaurant. Competition with some pasta dishes.

Ocean Side, 650 Jordan Rd.: Full service, low priced family restaurant. Competition with some pasta dishes.

Lao Tzu Palace, 173 Livernois: Chinese food, moderate price, dine in and carry out.

Advantages

1. *Healthy food*

The current fast food market does not provide for fast healthy food. Pasta Express fills some of the void by allowing customers to obtain fast food which is healthy for them, and their family.

2 *Price*

Pasta Express offers Italian food at lower prices then typical sit down full service Italian restaurants.

3. Service

Pasta Express operates with the motto "the customer is always right". In today's busy world, the customer aspect of the restaurant business is often overlooked.

4. Delivery

Pasta Express will have free delivery to everyone in the downtown area and only a $1.00 charge for delivery outside of the downtown area. This is below the customary $2.00 charge from the pizza chains.

5. Untapped market

Pasta Express will offer an alternative not readily available in the Jordan marketplace.

1. Name recognition

Disadvantages

As a fast food outlet, Pasta Express, does not have the name recognition of other local, regional and national chains.

2. New Food Concept

Italian food, in general, and more specifically, pasta, are new concepts in fast food.

3. Rental Costs

Prime rental locations are extremely costly.

4. Location

The current location rented presents some problems in regards to visibility from the street. Parking is located on the side of the building. Automobiles making northbound left turns intothe complex will find it difficult.

**DESIGN AND
DEVELOPMENT
PLANS**

GOAL#1
Opening of the first Pasta Express restaurant in June of 1996.

Goals

GOAL#2
Achieve $180,000 in gross sales in the first year.

GOAL#3
Achieve a 10% increase in gross sales in the second and third year of operation.

Risk Analysis

- Operational stability and support from the Franchiser
- High failure rate of restaurants (although failure rates for franchises are much less).
- Location of the operation
- Intense competition
- Scarcity of available workers

Evaluation Methods

Pasta Express will evaluate the achievement of its stated goals by measuring financial factors.

Pasta Express will monitor monthly sales volume as compared to monthly operating costs. Monthly increases (seasonal) will be expected in the gross sales category, along with year to date increases.

Opening of additional franchise locations will be determined based on gross sales and net profit levels of the first restaurant.

Strategic Actions

Strategy 1

The goal is to open the Jordan Pasta Express restaurant by June 1996. The location has beensecured and most of the interior of the building has been completed.

Start up housewares, and beginning inventory needs to be ordered, along with detailing the grand opening advertising package.

Strategy 2

The goal is to achieve $180,000 in gross sales the first year of operation. This will be accomplished through a marketing plan which is constructed by the corporate office of Pasta Express.

The corporate office plan is to include direct mailing and newspaper advertising along with in store promotions.

Strategy 3

The goal is to increase sales 10% in the second and third year of operation. This will be accomplished by:

Working with the Landview County Small Business Association and the Franchiser to build a complete marketing plan

Reviewing operations (budgets/costs) monthly with the franchiser and accountant

Providing superior products and services, exceeding customer expectations

Schedule For Goal 1

Develop/complete a business plan by May 1996.

Complete grand opening marketing plan by May 1st, 1996.

Hire an Accountant by May 1st, 1996.

Complete the physical construction of the restaurant by June 1st,1996.

Order all startup equipment and stock by June 1st, 1996.

Print menus by June 15th, 1996

Hire and train employees by June 15th, 1996.

Open the restaurant by June 20th, 1996.

Schedule For Goal 2

Evaluate monthly sales to provide for increases on a monthly basis (seasonally adjusted).

Meet with the president (franchiser) of Pasta Express to review the entire operation and make recommendations for improving sales.

Review menu for items which are popular and unpopular, make adjustments accordingly.

Complete and implement an aggressive marketing plan.

Schedule For Goal 3

Evaluate effectiveness of the marketing plan. Make necessary adjustments.

Meet with Landview County Small Business Association and review the business plan.

Receive marketing assistance from the Franchiser.

Review and adjust cost of goods sold and pricing as necessary.

Reviews all costs on an ongoing basis to ensure money is expended wisely.

...continued

FINANCIAL COMPONENTS

Cash Flow Chart (6 months)

Description	Year 1	% to sales	Year 2	% to sales	Year 3	% to sales
Sales	90,000		189,000		198,000	
Cost of Sales						
Beverages	1,900	2.11%	4,000	2.12%	4,500	2.27%
Deliveries	400	0.44%	900	0.48%	1,000	0.51%
Food Products	27,000	30.00%	50,000	26.46%	52,000	26.26%
Linen and Laundry	300	0.33%	400	0.21%	450	0.23%
Paper products, containers	3,000	3.33%	5,000	2.65%	5,200	2.63%
Payroll	12,000	13.33%	17,000	8.99	17,000	8.59%
Produce	2,000	2.22%	4,100	2.17%	4,300	2.17%
Supplies	500	0.56%	500	0.26%	500	0.25%
Taxes-Payroll	1,500	1.67%	2,000	1.06%	2,000	1.01%
Operating Expenses						
Advertising	5,500	6.11%	6,700	3.54%	7,000	3.54%
Amortization	1,750	1.94%	3,000	1.59%	3,000	1.52%
Bank Charges	1,000	1.11%	1,000	0.53%	1,000	0.51%
Contributions	100	0.11%	500	0.26%	500	0.25%
Depreciation	6,000	6.67%	6,000	3.17%	6,000	3.03%
Insurance	800	0.89%	800	0.42%	800	0.40%
Legal and Accounting	1,000	1.11%	2,000	1.06%	2,200	1.11%
Maintenance	400	0.44%	700	0.37%	700	0.35%
Payroll-Officer	8,000	8.89%	10,000	5.29%	10,000	5.05%
Rent	12,000	13.33%	20,500	10.85%	20,500	10.35%
Royalties	3,600	4.00%	7,560	4.00%	7,920	4.00%
Sales Tax	5,400	6.00%	11,340	6.00%	11,880	6.00%
Tax - personal property	300	0.33%	600	0.32%	600	0.30%
Telephone	700	0.78%	1,300	0.69%	1,300	0.66%
Trash Removal	200	0.22%	400	0.21%	400	0.20%
Utilities	3,000	3.33%	6,200	3.28%	6,500	3.28%
TOTAL	(8,350)	109.28%	26,500	85.98%	30,750	84.47%

ASSETS

Current Assets:				
Cash in Bank	21,000	21,000		
Fixed Assets:				
Equipment	22,000			
Leasehold Improvements	38,000	60,000		
Other Assets:				
Franchise Fees	20,000			
Startup Costs	7,000			
Rent Escrow	2,000	29,000		
Total Assets			110,000	

LIABILITIES

Current Liabilities				
Long Term Liabilities				
Loan - Shareholder	105,000	105,000		
Equity				
Common Stock	5,000	5,000		
Total Liabilities			110,000	

STATEMENT OF ASSETS AND LIABILITIES

Restaurant

BUSINESS PLAN

KELLY HOUSE INN

337 Delaney St.
Kimble, MI 48667

A second effort for these entrepreneurs, their experience is evident in this plan. This restaurant will be one of the area's full-service dining establishments. Located in a burgeoning area of the country, the timing is evidently correct. Note the careful surveying of relevant data to support their business goals.

- EXECUTIVE SUMM
- MISSION STATEM
- PURPOSE
- DESCRIPTION OF BUSINESS
- MARKETING
- COMPETITION
- OWNERSHIP AND MANAGEMENT STRUCTURE
- PROFILES

RESTAURANT
BUSINESS PLAN

EXECUTIVE SUMMARY

The concept for Kelly House Inn revolves around several key words: Quality, innovation, Value, Freshness and Service.

Kelly House Inn will be a superior, fullservice restaurant, located in the heart of downtown Kimble, serving lunch and dinner, and featuring responsible alcohol service. This new restaurant will give downtown Kimble the opportunity to offer residents, visitors and businesspeople a unique and welcome alternative in casual dining.

The need for such a quality establishment is well documented in a recent extensive study commissioned by the Downtown Kimble Area Economic Enhancement Strategy Task Force. The "Kingston-Howard Downtown Kimble Economic Enhancement Strategy 1996" report projects population growth as well as retail sales growth, along with a demand for additional downtown office space and downtown housing. Such growth will increase demand for other services and products. The study makes at least 50 references to the need for additional restaurants in downtown Kimble, with emphasis on excellent food, outdoor seating and dining alternatives (variety).

In addition, when residents were asked by Kingston-Howard what specific types of businesses would attract them to downtown more often, more restaurants and food establishments were at the top of their list.

There is little competition in the same category as Kelly House Inn. Most existing establishments that serve alcohol are pubtype places. The Inn would further distinguish itself with a menu of food items that are innovative, topquality, fresh and "housemade."

It will operate seven days a week under experienced management, headed by Vincent Freemont, coowner with Anna Freemont of the Inn's sister restaurant, The Coffee Grinder Cafe. Kelly House Inn would draw on the strengths and capitalize on the excellent reputation of The Coffee Grinder, yet have its own personality, featuring unique selections of hot and grilled foods.

Vincent and Anna Freemont are active members of this community and experienced restaurateurs. Vincent Freemont has a 20 year history of extensive restaurant management in privately owned and corporate chain restaurants. He has a B.A. degree in restaurant and hotel management from Michigan State University. Anna Freemont is a registered dietitian and worked for Bellevue Corporation in the food service management division.

Anticipated sales during the first year of operation is $600,000, with projected 20% increases during the following two years. This is based on the history of sales increases at The Coffee Grinder Cafe.

One of the primary goals of this new restaurant is to provide Value to the customer. Menu pricing will be set based on the objective to have an average dinner check be $15.00 and an average lunch check to be $7.00.

Emphasis will be placed on friendly service that will not only meet, but exceed guests' expectations. And while excellence is hard to define, oftentimes others will define it for you. An excellent track record at the awardwinning The Coffee Grinder Cafe will help sell this new venture, as will value combined with imagination.

Kelly House Inn will be the area's full service restaurant of choice, providing the best value for fresh and wholesome food, innovative menu selections and memorable service.

MISSION STATEMENT

This plan is designed to establish the feasibility of a successful outcome for this new restaurant business venture, and to provide all necessary information and supporting materials to:

PURPOSE

- Set business strategies based on experience and existing research data
- Obtain adequate financing

This document will demonstrate the need for a restaurant of this caliber in downtown Kimble and its chances for success. It will serve as a road map that will set the course for further planning and for the implementation process.

Anticipated financing is 75% of $260,000 for the use of total startup costs and $30,000 of reserveto use for operating funds in the first months. This financing will help ensure a timely start to the project in order to take advantage of the upcoming tourist season. Opening the Kelly House Inn by the summer of 1997 will keep the financial projections on track and increase the likelihood of success.

Repayment will be through cash flow of the restaurant, on a scheduled basis.

DESCRIPTION OF BUSINESS

This new business will be a superior, fullservice restaurant, serving lunch and dinner, and featuring responsible alcohol service. The hallmark of Kelly House Inn will be Excellence in all aspects:

Overview

- menu selections and complementing wines
- variety of foods and beverages
- friendly and competent service

Business hours:

Sunday-Thursday 11 a.m. to 9 p.m.
Friday & Saturday 11 a.m. to 11 p.m.

Square footage: 2,800

Kelly House Inn's casual ambience will contribute to the comfort diners will feel in a relaxed tmosphere, whether starting out with a beer or lingering over a final cup of coffee or glass of wine after dinner.

Atmosphere

The menu and pricing is designed for outstanding perceived value, with a generous selection of innovative and appealing menu items that emphasize freshness and quality. The menu entrees will enhance the numerous selections of beer and wines bytheglass.

Menu & Pricing

Location

Kelly House Inn will be located in the heart of downtown Kimble, taking advantage of downtown's bustling tourist industry, and offering an attractive alternative for seasonal and yearround residents, as well as business owners and employees.

MARKETING

Research. A recent intensive study, commissioned by the Downtown Kimble Area Economic Enhancement Strategy Task Force, supports the need for additional restaurants, based on existing consumer demands and projected population/use growth.

The "Kingston-Howard Downtown Kimble Economic Enhancement Strategy 1996" makes 50 references to the need for additional restaurants in downtown Kimble, with the focus on excellent food, as well as outdoor seating and dining alternatives (variety). The study outlines:

Retail sales growth potential from its "current level of approximately 29% to between 32% and 34% by the year 2002."

A demand for additional office space "between 10% and 15% during the next 6 years, based on...further enhancement of the area and anticipated increase in area households...."

A recommendation to develop upper floors of commercial building for additional downtown housing.

These statistics suggest and Kingston-Howard recommends that businesses be developed now to accommodate the projected growth patterns that are anticipated in a relatively short period of time. Additional shoppers, business owners, employees and residents mean additional opportunities for dining establishments to serve this new influx of clientele.

The study also recommends, as a course of action, that "current Downtown business owners should consider opening multiple operations to provide variety and a range of price points to the market."

Demand for more restaurants topped the list for residents who were asked what specific type of business would attract them to downtown more often. And visitors named food as the top item purchased when in downtown.

In order to accommodate existing customers and to draw more people into downtown, Kingston-Howard says that two retail clusters should be formed: the first consisting of prepared food establishments, including fine dining and moderate priced restaurants, as well as other food and specialty retail businesses. The second cluster should also contain restaurants. The study recommends additional "anchors" to be created in downtown and suggests that these should include unique, nonchain food establishments...."

Target Markets

The demographics for proposed target markets are wide in range, which bodes well for the success of this venture:

- Men and women
- Primarily 25 years old and older
- Families
- Residents of Emmet and nearby counties
- Visitors to the area from outofcouty and outofstate
- Current clientele of sister restaurant, The Coffee Grinder Cafe
- People "using" downtown as outlined in Kingston-Howard (for shopping, banking, dining,personal business, service businesses and post office, in addition to downtown workers)

Specific target markets by serving time:

Target market for lunch: Downtown business owners, employees, shoppers, tourists, seasonal and yearround residents.

Target market for dinner: Tourists, seasonal and yearround residents. Kelly House Inn would be a eatery "destination location," and would draw on clientele attending theater and other downtown promotions.

To create and maintain awareness by the public of Kelly House Inn, several methods of publicity will be utilized:

Promotions & Publicity

Advertising primarily in the Kimble News Guardian and Hamilton Magazine. Hamilton Magazine reaches out-of-county and out-of-state visitors, and has been an effective source of new business at The Coffee Grinder Cafe.

Crosspromotions with Kimble's Gaslight Cinema and McCune Arts Center productions, and with Kelly House Inn's sister restaurant, The Coffee Grinder Café. Other tie-ins with community events as appropriate.

Key messages in advertising:

- •Quality
- •Freshness
- •Affordable
- •Variety
- •Value
- •Service
- •Connection with The Coffee Grinder (an established, successful sister restaurant)

Anticipated Sales* & Expenses

First year (June 15, 1997 to June 14, 1998)	$600,000
Second year (20% increase)	$720,000
Third year (20% increase)	$864,000

Based on the history of sales increases over the previous year at The Coffee Grinder Cafe:

- • 66% first year
- • 41% second year
- • 22% third year

Anticipated food and liquor sales mix is 88% and 12% respectively.

- • Food cost goal is 33%.
- • Beverage cost goal is 30%.
- • Total Labor is 25%.
- • Operating supplies is 4.5%.
- • Rent is 4.2%.

Menu Pricing

- Average dinner check $15.00
- Average lunch check $7.00

Menu pricing will be determined considering the following:

- Goal of less than $15.00 for an average dinner check
- Goal of less than $7.00 for an average lunch check
- Achieving desired food cost through total menu mix
- Guests' perceptions of value for the quantity, quality and uniqueness of the product

COMPETITION

The Kingston-Howard study concluded that there is a demand for more dining diversity in downtown Kimble. Currently, there are four downtown eating establishments that serve alcohol: Main Street Pub, Larry's Pub & Grub, The Kimble Hotel (Dining Room) and Knockin' Around Room, and the Green Door Cafe. The remaining downtown restaurants do not provide the combination of full table service and alcoholic beverages.

Main Street Pub and Larry's Pub & Grub are perceived as bars that serve "pubtype" food and have a lower check average than anticipated at Kelly House Inn. They do little advertising. The Dining Dining Room at the Kimble Hotel is more of a fine dining experience, with a higher check average than anticipated at Kelly House Inn. The Knockin' Around Room is geared more to a "pub of dining and food, with lower pricing than anticipated at the Inn. The Green Door Cafe is probably the most similar competitor in terms of menu pricing and casual dining atmosphere.

Kelly House Inn would differentiate itself from its competition with a menu of food items that are innovative, top quality, fresh, and "housemade," which is always a marketing plus.

Another unique concept at Kelly House Inn will be found in its method of ordering. A la carte selections will allow diners to select the amount and kinds of food they wish and not be locked into a preselected array of side dishes.

The Inn would draw on the strengths and capitalize on the excellent reputation of its sister restaurant, The Coffee Grinder Cafe, by offering topnotch quality food at affordable prices, but with a unique fare and flare. Kelly House Inn would complement The Coffee Grinder by giving diners the option of hot and grilled foods.

OWNERSHIP AND MANAGEMENT STRUCTURE

Kelly House Inn is a limited liability company. The members are Paul and Marie Hanson, attorneys; and Vincent and Anna Freemont, owners of The Coffee Grinder Cafe.

Paul and Marie Hanson contribute legal expertise as well as broad knowledge of food and wine.

Vincent Freemont has a 20 year history of extensive restaurant management experience in a privatelyowned restaurant as well as corporate chain restaurants. His education includes a B.A. in restaurant and hotel management from Michigan State University. Besides opening his own successful restaurant, The Coffee Grinder Cafe, he has been responsible for the openings of approximately 20 new restaurants with the Hanover Food Service Company.

Anna Freemont is a registered dietitian and had worked for Bellevue Corporation, food service management division, for 10 years. She also opened and manages The Coffee Grinder Cafe.

Day-to-day operations will be handled by a general manager and a chef, and by trained key personnel operating as shift leaders.

Organizational structure:

- General Manager Vincent Freemont
- Assistant Manager
- Kitchen Manager
- Dining Room Supervisor
- (2) Kitchen Shift Leaders

PROFILES

Vincent and Anna Freemont are dedicated businesspeople who are committed to giving their customers at The Coffee Grinder Cafe the best product at an affordable price. Their efforts at providing quality and innovative food items has earned them several awards, including the Kimble Regional Chamber of Commerce Service Excellence Award in 1996 and Hamilton Magazine's Readers' Choice for Soups, Lunches and Coffee for the past three consecutive years.

Familyoriented and conscientious members of the community, Vincent and Anna participate in local events and their children's school activities.

Anna has chaired the Kimble Thanksgiving Parade for the last two years, each year enhancing this event with more zeal than the year before. This year, she secured major donations to purchase and fill a giant 45-foot nutcracker balloon. Anna also teaches a soupcooking class through the Kimble Adult Education Program.

Vincent teaches a coffee appreciation class through the Adult Ed Program. He is a member of the Breakfast for Champions Committee and the Promotions Committee of the Kimble Gaslight Downtown Association.

Menu

Appetizers

Spring Rolls
Skewered Shrimp
Chicken Nachos
Bean Nachos
Calamari
Shrimp & Rice Fritters
Wild Mushroom Ravioli
Black Bean Soup
Cheese Onion Soup
Fontina, Corn, and
Jalapeno Quesadilla
Mussels

...continued

**Sandwiches, Salads,
& Light Courses**

Tuna Melt
Shrimp Melt
Grilled Hamburger with Bleu Cheese
Grilled Marinated Tuna Steak Sandwich
Pork Sandwich with Chipolte BBQ Sauce
Mustard Chicken with Mixed Greens
Black Bean and Vegetable Burritos
Caesar Salad with Grilled Shrimp
Spinach Salad with Prosciutto Dressing
Open-Faced Roasted Pepper and Mozzarella Sandwich
North City Salad
Caesar Salad

Entrees

Grilled Beef Tenderloin with red wine, shallot and mushroom sauce
Grilled Tuna Steak with Soy Ginger Sauce
Grilled Herbed Salmon with Red Wine Sauce
Northern Catch of the Day
Ratatouille
Grilled Flank Steak with Soy-rosemary Marinade
Pork Medallions with Balsamic Vinegar and Sage
Penne with Sundried Tomatoes, Mushrooms and Artichoke Hearts
Pasta Shells with Feta and Herbs
Linguine with Summer Peppers and Sausage
Chicken with Port Mushroom Sauce
Jamaican Jerk Chicken with Black Beans
Citrus-Grilled Chicken with Mesquite Honey

Funding Total

Equipment Total	45,556.00
HVAC Improvements	7,000.00
Hood vent with return air	15,000.00
Register system	6,000.00
Smallwares	15,000.00
Chairs	4,000.00
Tables	12,000.00
Remaining construction allowance	75,000.00

     *Tile
     *Artifact
     *Painting
     *Exterior
     *Sectioning
     *Ceiling
     *Signature
     *Neon
     *Lighting

*Bathrooms	179,556.00
Training & opening food	7,500.00
Pre-opening	187,056.00

60" Sandwich station reach-in refrigerator - 3	1,395.00	4,185.00	
54" Two door reach-in refrigerator	1,855.00	1,855.00	
30" Ice cream cabinet	675.00	675.00	
92" Keg dispenser	2,075.00	2,075.00	
80" Black bottle cooler	1,260.00	1,260.00	
Ice cream dipwell	105.00	105.00	
30" Ice maker cubers - 459 lbs	1,630.00	1,630.00	
Ice bin 270-340 capacity	545.00	545.00	
Draft box tapping kit	115.00	115.00	
Walk-in refrigerator box	3,415.00	3,415.00	
Refrigerator for walk-in - 1 1/2 H.P.	2,270.00	2,270.00	
Freezer - 2 door - 54"	2,375.00	2,375.00	
Boiler - 42 1/4" - 3 burner	1,635.00	1,635.00	
6 Burner-Vulcan (2-oven w/convection, griddle & broiler)	3,685.00	3,685.00	
Casters	160.00	160.00	
Warming drawer - single	600.00	600.00	
750 Watt food warmer	160.00	160.00	
Microwave 1200 Watt	950.00	950.00	
Slicer Berkel - 10"	645.00	645.00	
Kitchen Aid - 5 qt.	380.00	380.00	
Food processor	435.00	435.00	
Dishwasher - Jackson	5,350.00	5,350.00	
Coffee brewer	535.00	535.00	
Water/service station	1,233.00	1,233.00	
Steam kettle - Cleveland - 6 gallon	2,246.00	2,246.00	
Dish tables	700.00	700.00	
Work table - 6	200.00	1,200.00	
3 Compartment dish sink - 2 drainboards - 127" x 27"	1,469.00	1,469.00	
Handsinks - 2	165.00	165.00	
Deep fat fryer	725.00	725.00	
Sub Total		42,778.00	
Tax		2,567.00	
TOTAL		45,556.00	

Projected Cash Flow

CASH	Year 1	Year 2
Beginning Balance		
Plus:	30,000.00	45,950.00
Cash receipts/sales	636,000.00	763,200.00
TOTAL CASH	666,000.00	809,150.00
DISBURSEMENTS		
Food cost	174,240.00	209,088.00
Beverage cost	21,600.00	25,920.00
Hourly payroll	150,000.00	172,800.00
Operating supplies	30,000.00	32,400.00
Repairs & maintenance	12,000.00	12,600.00
Utilities	14,000.00	14,700.00
Rent	25,200.00	25,875.00
Printing	2,000.00	2,000.00
Insurance	12,000.00	3,500.00
Advertising	9,000.00	10,800.00
Bank Charges	1,000.00	1,000.00
Dues	500.00	500.00
Personel Property	2,500.00	3,000.00
Use Tax	2,200.00	2,200.00
Single Business Tax	3,000.00	4,000.00
Licenses	2,500.00	2,500.00
Professional Fees	7,000.00	7,000.00
Miscellaneous	3,000.00	3,000.00
Management Labor with Taxes	50,000.00	60,000.00
Loan Repayment	30,960.00	30,960.00
Income Tax Payment	1,380.00	23,000.00
Sales Tax Payments	66,050.00	89,150.00
TOTAL **DISBURSEMENTS**	620,050.00	745,993.00
CASH FLOW	45,950.00	63,157.00

SALES	Year 1		Year 2		**Pro Forma Profit &**
Food	528,000.00	88	633,600.00	88	**Loss Statement**
Beverage	72,000.00	12	86,400.00	12	
TOTAL	600,000.00	100%	720,000.00	100%	
Cost Of Sales					
Food	174,240,00	33	209,088.00	33	
Beverage	21,600.00	30	25,920.00	30	
TOTAL	195,840.00	32.6	235,008.00	32.6	
Hourly Labor					
Total w/Payroll Tax	150,000.00	25	172,800.00	24	
Controllables					
Operating supplies	30,000.00	5	32,400.00	4.5	
Repairs & maintenance	12,000.00	2	12,600.00	1.8	
Total Controllables	42,000.00	7	45,000.00	6.3	
Profit After Controllables	212,160.00	35.4	267,192.00	37.1	

NON-CONTROLLABLES	Year 1		Year 2	
Utilities	14,000.00	2.3%	14,700.00	2.0%
Rent	25,200.00	4.2	25,875.00	3.6
Depreciation	30,000.00	5.0	30,000.00	4.2
Equipment write-off	16,400.00	2.7	10,000.00	1.4
Training labor	5,000.00	.8		
Training food	2,500.00	.4		
Printing	2,000.00	.3	2,000.00	.3
Insurance	12,000.00	2.0	13,500.00	1.9
Advertising	9,000.00	1.5	10,800.00	1.5
Bank charges	1,000.00	.2	1,000.00	.1
Dues	500.00	.1	500.00	.1
Personal property	2,500.00	.4	3,000.00	.4
Use tax	2,200.00	.4	2,200.00	.3
Single business tax	3,000.00	.5	4,000.00	.6
Licenses	2,500.00	.4	2,500.00	.3
Professional fees	7,000.00	1.2	7,000.00	1.0
Miscellaneous	3,000.00	.5	3,000.00	.4
Management labor	50,000.00	8.3	60,000.00	8.3
Interest expense	21,000.00	3.5	20,000.00	2.8
TOTAL NON-CONTROLLABLES	208,800.00	34.8	210,075.00	29.2
PROFIT	3,360.00	.6	57,117.00	7.9

Restaurant

BUSINESS PLAN

ROCK ISLAND TAVERN

30338 East Green Ave.
Williamston, PA 11898

This business plan shows a seasoned consideration of all aspects of assuming ownership of a business already in existence. Since the business simply changed hands, information that would normally be speculative, such as traffic, average check price, and income, is more reliable. Entrepreneurs considering purchasing a business rather than starting from the ground up will find this plan very useful.

- EXECUTIVE SUMMARY

- NATURE OF VENTURE

- MARKER DESCRIPTION AND ANALYSIS

- DESCRIPTION OF PRODUCTS AND SERVICES

- BUILDING AND EQUIPMENT

- MANAGEMENT TEAM AND OWNERSHIP

- BUSINESS STRATEGY

- FINANCIAL DATA

- EXHIBITS

EXECUTIVE SUMMARY

Andersen Enterprises, Inc. (AEI) was formed to own and operate the Rock Island Tavern. The tavern is located on East Green Avenue in Williamston, Oakland Township, Pellton County. Pellton County is one of the largest counties in the state and Oakland Township is one of the county's fastest growing townships.

Management will focus on maintaining the Tavern's loyal base of repeat customers and will attract new customers from surrounding communities by providing quality food and beverages at reasonable prices. In addition, AEI will feature good quality entertainment, attractive and comfortable surroundings and consistent, high quality service.

Management

Steven Gresboro, Owner

Steven Gresboro will be responsible for operational and financial management, sales, marketing and promotion. Mr. Gresboro has eight years of experience as a manager/bartender for Benedict Arnold's Pub in Jordan, PA and Junior's Joint in Kingstown, PA. His responsibilities included hiring, managing, and firing of staff personnel as well as food and beverage service, record keeping and inventory management. Mr. Gresboro has been a corporate lender for Penn Financial Corporation serving as Vice President in the middle market lending area for the past 11 years. He has extensive knowledge and experience in the field of banking, finance, sales and marketing. Mr. Gresboro graduated from Westminster University in 1983 with a B.S. in Business Administration Marketing. In May 1994, he received a Masters of Business Administration-Finance from St. Joseph's University.

Kevin Painter, Manager

Kevin Painter will be responsible for management of day to day operations. Mr. Painter's principal responsibilities will include staff management, purchasing, inventory management, marketing and promotions. Mr. Painter has seven years experience as a manager/bartender for Gridiron Sports Bar in Grimley, Pa. And Danny's in York River, Pa. His responsibilities included food and beverage service as well as staff management, purchasing, inventory management and recordkeeping.

Market

The company's target market will consist primarily of local residential customers ranging in age from 21 to 45 and local businesses. Research indicates that 90% of local tavern business comes from a three mile radius. The population of Oakland Township is approximately 7539 (estimated 1992) and has grown 7% since 1990 making it one of Pellton County's largest townships. The population demographics reveal a universe of people totaling 5448 in the age group 18 to 59. The local housing area consists of a mix of single family homes, townhouses, apartment dwellings and mobile home parks. The average household income is $43,221 (estimated 1989).

Products/Services

The tavern will feature a wide selection of alcoholic and non-alcoholic beverages including a variety of liquors, wines, and beers. The food menu will include a wide selection of appetizers along with grilled and cold sandwiches, steaks, hoagies, burgers and fries, dinner and dinner specials. AEI will feature live entertainment, a disc jockey, music, video games and amusements. Business hours will be Monday thru Sunday, 11:00 AM-2:00 AM.

AEI's competition within a three mile radius consists primarily of several local established taverns/pubs/fire halls. The Williamston Fire Hall is located on Rt. 73 one mile east of the Rock Island Tavern, and the Victorian Rose is approximately four miles west on Rt. 73 in Watertown. The Fire Hall is popular and features a good selection of food and beverages with occasional entertainment. However, it has limited hours of operation and is closed on Sundays. The Victorian Rose is established, but has limited food, entertainment and parking and attracts a transient customer base. The tavern is also closed on Sundays. Other local competition includes the Boston Inn located three miles north on Route 206 and the Hill Street Tavern located in Foley Pass.

Competition

The Rock Island Tavern has been in business for over 40 years and is considered a landmark in Williamston. The Tavern is known for its good food, comfortable surroundings, quality entertainment and amusement/games selection. Management will actively promote the tavern as the place to meet and socialize in Williamston. This message will be delivered through local advertisements, direct mail, promotional giveaways, special events (i.e. car shows), and through word-of-mouth.

Uniqueness

AEI Associates has offered $250M for the purchase of the assets of the Tavern excluding real estate. The assets to be purchased include equipment, machinery, fixtures, supplies, inventory and the liquor license. AEI will negotiate a ten year lease agreement with a ten year renewal option and the right of first refusal should the owner elect to sell the property.

Purchase Pric

AEI will provide an equity contribution of $125M in cash. The seller will take back a secured note for $125M over ten years at 9% fixed with no prepayment penalty. AEI will seek to obtain a $45M-$50M secured SBA guaranteed fixed rate term loan amortizing over five to seven years to finance certain initial costs and working capital requirements.

Financing

	1991	1992	1993	1994	1995
Sales	275657	418135	461075	444203	475198
Operating Expenses	65405	115429	122158	141348	146273
Pretax Profit	9570	30569	66278	36618	36487
Total Assets	57980	60212	62939	91676	93730
Total Liabilities	35274	33727	41478	65376	75562
Net Worth	22733	26485	21461	26300	18168

Summary of Historical Financial Results

	1997	1998	1999	2000	2001
Sales	49900	433930	581984	651822	749595
Operating Expenses	169685	177225	188425	205075	221325
Pretax Profit	14165	22622	32688	45979	70863
Total Assets	317664	308902	306168	309421	330103
Total Liabilities	292500	272500	254500	233500	215000
Net Worth	25164	35402	51688	75921	115103

Summary of Financial Projections

NATURE OF VENTURE

Background

The tavern/restaurant industry is mature and established, nevertheless, food and alcoholic beverage sales continue to rise nationally. Consumers spent roughly 215 billion at restaurants and taverns in 1995. This growth has been fueled by the long term rise in the portion of food and beverage dollars consumers spend on items prepared outside the home. In addition, changing work and leisure habits and increased advertising and promotion spearheaded by the alcoholic beverage industry have contributed to the industry's growth and have enhanced profitability.

Nature of Products/Services

AEI will offer a wide selection of alcoholic and non-alcoholic beverages, along with a full menu and complete selection of lunch, dinner and snack items. AEI will feature live entertainment on weekends including local and regional bands and music acts. On certain weekday and weekend nights, a disc jockey will complement and/or supplement the live music. For amusement, the Tavern will provide two pool tables, darts and a wide variety of popular video games. AEI will promote drink specials, promotional prizes, giveaways and special events such as (antique car shows) in the adjacent parking lot.

Location of Venture

The Rock Island Tavern is located along an active commercial section of East Green Avenue (Route 45) approximately ½ mile from Route 206 in Williamston, Pellton County, PA. The Tavern is approximately one-half mile east of Watertown and approximately ten miles north of Foley Pass. The surrounding businesses include several international fast food chains, retail shops, and service companies. The Tavern is located next to Gary's Farmer's Market, a very active retail established over 75 years ago.

According to Oakland Township authorities, the surrounding area is expected to continue to grow as a result of continued residential construction and commercial development. The site is locate within 1/4 mile of a new 50 lot single family housing development. The adjoining parcels have been zoned to accommodate additional townhouse development and further retail development to include a multi screen movie theater and strip center.

According to Pennsylvania Department of Transportation (PENNDOT), a 1996 traffic survey for Route 45 and Route 206 determined the average daily traffic counts to be as follows:

Route 45
• 17,960 vehicles
Route 206
• North Bound = 8,617 vehicles
• South Bound = 8,563 vehicles

MARKET DESCRIPTION AND ANALYSIS

AEI will target the local residents and businesses of Oakland Township and surrounding townships in order to develop a loyal base of repeat customers as well as draw new customers from the surrounding communities. In addition, the company will seek to attract the areas growing commuter traffic.

Market Trends

AEI's target market will consist of local residential customers, local businesses and commuter traffic. Research indicates that up to 90% of business comes from within a three mile radius. Consequently, the company will focus on attracting and developing a loyal customer base from the surrounding community. AEI expects to capture commuter traffic traveling to Dentworth, Foley Pass, and Watertown

Pellton County is an urban county of 689,996 persons (estimate 1992) situated in southeastern Pennsylvania. Three major employment centers are located within the county making Pellton County one of the leading industrial and trade complexes in the nation.

Pellton County experienced rapid growth in population, housing and employment following WWII. A residential construction boom occurred during the 1950's and 1960's and has remained strong ever since. Development is likely to remain strong particularly in the western part of the county due to the extensive road network, educated and skilled labor force and availability of land.

Demographic and Economic Trends

AEI's principal competition comes from local bars, and tavern/restaurants within a ten mile radius. The Williamston Fire Hall is locate within the town of Williamston approximately one mile east on Route 45 in an active commercial are. The Fire Hall is a popular location and features a good selection of alcoholic and non-alcoholic beverages, food and occasional live entertainment.
The Victorian Rose is an established tavern located approximately three miles west on Route 45 in Watertown on a busy residential/commercial area. The tavern attracts local residents but has a limited and average food selection and limited parking.

Current Competitors

DESCRIPTION OF PRODUCTS/ SERVICES

The Rock Island Tavern will differentiate itself from its many local competitors in a variety of ways. The tavern will continue to build upon its reputation as a favorite local spot for socializing, drinking, dining and entertainment. AEI will retain loyal customers and attract new customers by improving the selection of alcoholic beverages, upgrading promotional giveaways and prizes and featuring special events. Moreover, AEI will offer quality live entertainment, theme nights and a popular selection of video games and amusements.

Management will actively promote the tavern through local advertisements, cross couponing and advertising with local merchants, direct mail promotions and through promotional giveaways and special events.

Uniqueness of Products/Services

AEI's principal competitive advantages come from its ability to offer an attractive combination of beverages, food, music, and entertainment which will appeal to a large and growing target market. The principal competitors do not offer this combination and variety to their customers.

Advantages Over Competition

The property consists of a triangular shaped one-half acre lot situated on the east side of East Green Avenue. The building is zoned for general commercial use and consists of a two-story detached commercial dwelling of brick construction with aluminum siding and a shingle roof which is approximately 70 years old.

BUILDING AND EQUIPMENT

The first level consists of a horseshoe shaped bar with seating capacity for 22 customers along with a kitchen, adjoining dining/entertainment area and four separate rest rooms. The second floor contains a bedroom, bathroom, office area, conference room and attic. The basement area contains storage space and refrigeration and freezer units for beer and food storage.

The property will be leased to AEI Associates, Inc. under a ten-year lease agreement. However, the principals have the option to buy the property. An appraisal dated July 15, 1993 by Specht Realty, Inc. indicated a market value of $188,600. A purchase price has not yet been agreed upon. The principal equipment consists primarily of kitchen equipment such as a stove, refrigerators and freezers. Other assets include televisions, tables, chairs, air-conditioners, a cash register, desk bedroom and conference room furniture.

MANAGEMENT TEAM AND OWNERSHIP

AEI's management team will consist of Steven Gresboro and Kevin Painter. Steven and Kevin are highly focused, hard working, energetic and broadly experienced individuals whose combined talents provide a strong and qualified management team. Steven and Kevin provide the needed "hands on" experience in the tavern/restaurants business. In addition, Mr. Gresboro brings expertise in the areas of business administration, finance, sales and marketing. His extensive business background and academic credentials compliment the strengths and talents of Kevin Painter.

BUSINESS STRATEGIES

AEI will employ a differentiation strategy that will create value for the customer beyond that available from existing competition. The company will focus on providing a friendly, comfortable and entertaining environment that features a wide selection of quality spirits, beverages and food.

Marketing Plan and Supporting Strategies

AEI will support its differentiation strategy by effective execution of its marketing plan which contains sever integral supporting strategies, including product/service, promotional/sales and pricing.

AEI's product/service strategy will be to provide a wide selection of popular alcoholic and non-alcoholic beverages along with an extensive menu of popular snacks, lunch, and dinner selections. Management will strive to deliver the highest level of consistent, friendly, and courteous customer service to insure a pleasurable drinking and dining experience. In addition, the Tavern will feature a variety of popular live entertainment and music. AEI will also provide popular games and amusements including two pool tables, darts, and video games which will provide a strong source of additional income.

AEI will utilize multiple, constant, but limited advertising and promotional sources. These sources will be selected to maximize the return on allocated advertising/promotional dollars. The local community residents and businesses will be attracted through the yellow pages, local newspaper advertisements, flyers, coupons and periodic direct mail programs.

AEI will offer certain promotional giveaway items, such as T-shirts, key chains, calendars, coffee mugs, which will include the Rock Island Tavern's distinctive logo. In addition, the Tavern will sponsor special events such as a car show and golf outing which will include gifts and cash prizes. The company will also join certain industry associations, such as the Freestone Tavern and Restaurant Association and the local chamber of commerce. These associations provide valuable business tips, allow the business owner to develop industry contacts and build community relations.

AEI will utilize a combination of competitor based and prestige pricing. This will insure pricing is in line and local competitors for products and services where little value can be added such as in the case of games and amusements. However, prestige pricing will be employed such as premium micro-brews and liquors or dinner specials where AEI can offer higher quality. The company's strategy will be to position itself among the leading competitors and compete on quality, convenience and customer service, and lastly on price. By developing a high quality image and reputation AEI can maintain premium pricing and maintain its position as the preferred local tavern in the area.

The average customer is expected to spend between $5.00 and $20.00 per visit.

AEI will be owned and operated by Steven Gresboro who will own 100% of the company's capital stock.

Financial Strategy

AEI will seek to obtain a $45M-$50M secured SBA guaranteed term loan at a fixed rate amortizing over five to seven years to finance initial costs and working capital needs. The remaining balance of the required funding will be provided through a secured $125M seller note to be repaid over 10 years bearing interest at 9% fixed per annum. AEI's cash contribution will be $125M which will consist of an equity contribution and shareholder note.

AEI expects to realize strong consistent, sales and earnings growth in year one that will increase steadily by year five. This growth will be principally attributable to the increase in local population as a result of continued expansion of residential housing developments and from the establishments of new local businesses within immediate area. A new 50 lot single family home development is under construction within one-quarter mile of the Tavern. AEI expects the other surrounding land parcels will be sold for commercial development to include a large townhouse development, multi-screen movie theater and a retail strip center. The company expects to develop additional loyal customers through execution of this advertising/promotional programs, and will focus on attracting the areas growing commuter traffic. Through the five year period, management will effectively control purchases and overhead to maximize operating efficiency and profitability. In addition, operating expenditures will be carefully managed to insure incremental revenue growth results in increased bottom-line profitability.

Overall Growth Strategy

FINANCIAL DATA

For the purposes of this projection it is assumed AEI took over operations on January 1, 1997. A brief analysis of the 1995 financial statements is as follows:

Historical Financial Statement Analysis

1995 Income Statement

Sales

Sales increased by 6.9% in 1995 and have increased by an average (16.2% over the past four years). Management attributes this growth to increased advertising and promotion efforts in conjunction with an upgraded food, beverage, games/amusement selection.

Operating Expenses

Management has demonstrated effective control of expenses over the past four years in relation to sales growth. Operating expenses increased by $5M in 1995 but declined in a percentage of sales by 1% to 30.8%. Major expense items include officer salaries, utilities, taxes, rent and insurance costs.

<u>1995 Balance Sheet</u>

Inventory

Inventory levels have been very stable year after year and are comprised primarily of liquor, food and beer. Minimum inventory levels are maintained due to the perishable nature of the aforementioned items. Management purchases liquor and food on a weekly basis. Beer is purchased twice a week.

Fixed Assets

Equipment includes principally kitchen appliances and accessories, refrigerators, beer coolers, compressors, freezers, furniture and fixtures.

Long Term Debt

This represents the remaining balance of a bank term loan to finance equipment purchases and building improvements. In addition, the principal has provided periodic loans to the company to support working capital requirements and for renovations and improvements.

Estimated Initial Costs

Desired Minimum Cash Balance		$20,000
Initial Expenditures		
License/Permit Fees	1,500	
Wages/Payroll Taxes	5,000	
Prepaid Insurance	8,400	
Inventory	5,000	
Deposits	1,400	
Bank Fees	2,000	
Advertising and Promotion	2,000	
Legal and Accounting	2,000	
Total Initial Expenditures		$47,300
Assets Purchased		
Equipment	150,000	
Liquor License	50,000	
Goodwill	50,000	
Total Assets Purchased		250,000
Total Initial Costs		297,300
Financing Requirements		
Seller Note	125,000	
Bank Financing	47,000	
Equity Investment	125,000	
Total Financing Requirements $297,300		

These Financial Projections are based on estimates and assumptions set forth therein, and have been delivered for the information and convenience of persons who wish to evaluate the feasibility of the company's strategy and goals. Each such person who has received them realizes that financial projections are inherently speculative. The Financial Projections are based upon the company's Assumptions reflecting conditions it expects to exist or the course of action it expects to take. Because events and circumstance do not occur as anticipated, there will be difference between the Financial Projections and actual results, and those differences may be material. The Financial Projections are based upon detailed underlying assumptions.

Income Statement

Sales

Sales are projected to reach $499,000 in 1997 and increase by 7% in 1998, 9% in 1999, 12% in 2000 and 15% in 2001. Sales through the projection period will be fueled by the increase in local population as a result of continued expansion of residential housing developments and from the establishment of new local businesses within the immediate area. AEI will attract and develop new customers through execution of its advertising/promotional programs.

AEI's principal sources of revenue will be generated through the sale of beer and liquor. Beer sales are expected to represent approximately 50% of total revenue. Draft and bottle beer sales will comprise the bulk of total beer revenue. Liquor sales are projected to represent approximately 15% of total revenue which is in line with historical percentage. This percentage is projected to remain relatively stable year to year as beer continues to be the dominant beverage. Food sales will comprise the remaining 35% of sales. Sales of food are expected to grow moderately year to year due to management's focus on beverage sales. The gross margin is expected to remain relatively stable at 40% of sales through the projection period. This assumption is based onhistorical figures and industry averages.

Operating Expenses

Due to significant sales growth through the projection period, expenses are forecasted to increase although decline as percentage of sales, but remaining within industry averages. Operating expenses are projected to decline as a percentage of sales from 34.0% in 1997 to 29.5% by 2001 as a result of effective management and control of expenses.

Taxes

The effective tax rate is projected to be 40%.

Balance Sheet

Fixed Assets

Fixed assets are stated at cost. Depreciation is provided over the estimated useful lines of the assets under the straight-line method for financial reporting purpose and accelerated methods for income tax purposes. Fixed assets include principally machinery and equipment to be depreciated over seven years.

Goodwill

The excess of the purchase price over the fair market value of the assets acquired is being amortized using the straight-line method over a 15 year period.

**Five Year
Financial Projects
and Assumptions**

...continued

Liquor License

The liquor license will be amortized using the straight line method over a 15 year period.

Accounts Payable

The majority of suppliers are expected to extend 30-day terms and AEI will pay within those terms.

Long Term Debt

Long term debt will consist of the remaining principal balance of a bank term loan amortizing over five to seven years. Also included, will be the remaining principal balance of the seller note amortizing over ten years at a fixed rate of 9% per annum. In addition, a shareholder note will pay the minimum interest allowable with no specific repayment schedule.

Net Worth

AEI expects to achieve profitability in 1997 and thereafter. The company plans to financegrowth through cash flow from operations. No additional equity will be required after 1997. Net worth is expected to improve from 1997 and thereafter comprising a greater percentage of total capitalization.

Annual Projections
Cash Flow Analysis

	12/31/97	12/31/98	12/31/99	12/31/00	12/31/01
Cash flow from operating activities:					
Net income (loss)	$5,164	$10,238	$16,266	$24,252	39183
Depreciation & amortization	28,120	25,260	25,260	25,260	25,260
(Increase) decrease in inventory	(9000)	(500)	(500)		
Incr. (decr.) in payables & accruals	12,500	3,500	3,500	1,500	4,000
(Increase) decrease in intagibles	(100000)				
(Increase) decrease in other/deposits	(3000)				
Net case from operating activities	$(66,216)	$38,498	$44,526	$51,012	$68,443
Cash flows from investment activities:					
(Purchase) Sale of equipment/RE	$(150,000)	$20,000			
Net cash from investment activities	$(150,000)	$20,000			
Cash flow from financing activities:					
Increase (decrease) in CPLTD	$22,500				
Increase (decrease) in long term debt	257,500	(22,500)	(22,500)	(22,500)	(22,500)
Increase in additional paid in capital	20,000				
Net cash from financing activities	$300,000	$(22,500)	$(22,500)	$(22,500)	$(22,500)
Net change in cash:					
Increase (decrease) in cash	83,784	35,998	22,026	28,512	45,943
Cash-Beginning of year	83,784	119,782	141,808	170,321	
Cash-End of year	$83,784	$119,782	$141,808	$170,321	$216,263
Core cash required	$19,192	$20,536	$22,384	$25,070	$28,831
Cumulative excess cash flow	$64,592	$99,246	$119,424	$145,250	$187,433

**Historical
Financial
Statements:
Balance Sheet**

	FYE 12/31/91		FYE 12/31/92	
ASSETS				
Current assets:				
Cash & equivalents	$1,034	1.8%	$401	0.7%
Accounts receivable	400	0.7%	400	0.7%
Inventories	9,899	17.1%	9,473	15.7%
Total current assets	$11,333	19.5%	$10,274	17.1%
Gross fixed assets	$25,506	44.0%	$32,056	53.2%
Less: accumulated depreciation	1,612	2.8%	5,171	8.6%
Net fixed assets	$23,894	41.2%	$26,885	44.7%
Other assets:				
Shareholder loans	$2,753	4.7%	$2,753	4.6%
Other assets-Liquor license	20,000	34.5%	20,000	33.2%
Prepaids	0.0%	300	0.5%	840
Loan origination fees	0.0%	0.0%	10,036	15.9%
TOTAL ASSETS	$57,980	100.0%	$60,212	100.0%
LIABILITIES				
Accounts payable	$3,668	6.3%	$5,013	8.3%
Current long term debt-bank	812	1.4%	3,462	5.7%
Current long term debt-seller	5,975	10.3%	3,922	6.5%
Accruals	0.0%	0.0%	0.0%	0.0%
Total current liabilities	$10,455	18.0%	$12,397	20.6%
Long term debt-bank	$24,792	42.8%	$21,330	35.4%
Long term debt-shareholder	0.0%	0.0%	6,355	10.1%
TOTAL LIABILITIES	$35,247	60.8%	$33,727	56.0%
NET WORTH				
Common stock	$100	0.2%	$100	0.2%
Additional paid in capital	12,999	22.4%	12,999	21.6%
Retained earnings (deficit)	9,634	16.6%	13,386	22.2%
Total net worth	$22,733	39.2%	$26,485	44.0%
TOTAL LIABILITIES & NET WORTH	$57,980	100.0%	$60,212	100.0%

	FYE 12/31/93		FYE 12/31/94		FYE 12/31/95	
$210	0.3%	$843	0.9%	$202	0.2%
400	0.6%	400	0.4%	400	0.4%
8,494	13.5%	8,919	9.7%	8,473	9.0%
$9,104	14.5%	$10,162	11.1%	$9,075	9.7%
$32,809	52.1%	$67,059	73.1%	$83,075	88.6%
9858	15.7%	15,418	16.8%	26,279	28.0%
$22,951	36.5%	$51,641	56.3%	$56,796	60.6%
0.0%	0.0%	0.0%			
20,000	31.8%	20,000	21.8%	20,000	21.3%
1.3%	1,850	2.0%	1,850	2.0%	
8,023	8.8%	6,010	6.4%		
$62,931	100.0%	$91,676	100.0%	$93,731	100.0%
$5,555	8.8%	$3,060	3.3%	$7,072	7.5%
3,462	5.5%	825	0.9%	2,375	2.5%
5,382	8.6%	4,498	4.9%	4,794	5.1%
0.0%					
$14,399	22.9%	$8,383	9.1%	$14,241	15.2%
$20,724	32.9%	$22,566	24.6%	$21,644	23.1%
34,427	37.6%	39,677	42.3%		
$41,478	65.9%	$65,376	71.3%	$75,562	80.6%
$100	0.2%	$100	0.1%	$100	0.1%
12,999	20.7%	12,999	14.2%	12,999	13.9%
8,362	13.3%	13,201	14.4%	5,068	5.4%
$21,461	34.1%	$26,300	28.7%	$18,167	19.4%
$62,939	100.0%	$91,676	100.0%	$93,729	100.0%

**Annual
Projections:
Balance Sheet**

	PROJ 12/31/97		PROJ 12/31/98	
ASSETS				
Current assets:				
Cash & equivalents	$83,784	26.4%	$119,782	38.8%
Inventories	9,000	2.8%	9,500	3.1%
Total Current assets	$92,784	29.2%	$129,282	41.9%
Gross fixed assets	$150,000	47.2%	$130,000	42.1%
Less: accumulated depreciation	21,450	6.8%	40,040	13.0%
Net fixed assets	$128,550	40.5%	$89,960	29.1%
Other assets:				
Prepaids	$2,000	0.6%	$2,000	0.6%
Deposits	1,000	0.3%	1,000	0.3%
Other assets-Liquor license	46,665	14.7%	43,330	14.0%
Goodwill	46,665	14.7%	43,330	14.0%
TOTAL ASSETS	$317,664	100.0%	$308,902	100.0%
LIABILITIES				
Notes payable@P+1%	$	0.0%	$	0.0%
Accounts payable	7,500	2.4%	8,500	2.8%
Current long term debt-bank	10,000	3.1%	10,000	3.2%
Current long term debt-seller	12,500	3.9%	12,500	4.0%
Accruals	5,000	1.6%	7,500	2.4%
Total current liabilities	$35,000	11.0%	$38,500	12.5%
Long term debt-bank@9%	$40,000	12.6%	$30,000	9.7%
Long term debt-seller@9%	112,500	35.4%	100,000	32.4%
Long term debt-shareholder	105,000	33.1%	105,000	34.0%
TOTAL LIABILITIES	$292,500	92.1%	$273,500	88.5%
NET WORTH				
Common stock	$100	0.0%	$100	0.0%
Additional paid in capital	19,900	6.3%	19,900	6.4%
Retained earnings (deficit)	5,164	1.6%	15,402	5.0%
Total net worth	$25,164	7.9%	$35,402	11.5%
TOTAL LIABILITIES & NET WORTH	$317,664	100.0%	$308,902	100.0%

	PROJ 12/31/99		PROJ 12/31/100		PROJ 12/31/101
$141,808	46.3%	$170,321	55.0%	$216,263	65.5%
10,000	3.3%	10,000	3.2%	10,000	3.0%
$151,808	49.6%	$180,321	58.3%	$226,263	68.5%
$130,000	42.5%	$130,000	42.0%	$130,000	39.4%
58,630	19.1%	77,220	25.0%	95,810	29.0%
$71,370	23.3%	$52,780	17.1%	$34,190	10.4%
$2,000	0.7%	$2,000	0.6%	$2,000	0.6%
1,000	0.3%	1,000	0.3%	1,000	0.3%
39,995	13.1%	36,660	11.8%	33,325	10.1%
39,995	13.1%	36,660	11.8%	33,325	10.1%
$306,168	100.0%	$309,421	100.0%	$309,421	100.0%
$	0.0%	$	0.0%	$	0.0%
10,000	3.3%	10,000	3.2%	12,000	3.6%
10,000	3.3%	10,000	3.2%	10,000	3.0%
12,500	4.1%	12,500	4.0%	12,500	3.8%
9,500	3.1%	11,000	3.6%	13,000	3.9%
$42,000	13.7%	$43,500	14.1%	$47,500	14.4%
$20,000	6.5%	$10,000	3.2%	$	0.0%
87,500	28.6%	75,000	24.2%	62,500	18.9%
105,000	34.3%	105,000	33.9%	105,000	31.8%
$254,500	83.1%	$233,500	75.5%	$215,000	65.1%
$100	0.0%	$100	0.0%	$100	0.0%
19,900	6.5%	19,900	6.4%	19,900	6.0%
31,668	10.3%	55,921	18.1%	95,103	28.8%
$51,668	16.9%	$75,921	24.5%	$115,103	34.9%
$306,168	100.0%	$309,421	100.0%	$330,103	100.0%

**Historical
Financial
Statements:
Income Statement**

	FYE 12/31/91		FYE 12/31/92	
Net sales	$275,657	100.0%	$418,135	100.0%
Cost of sales	199,205	72.3%	269,589	64.5%
Gross profit	$76,452	27.7%	$148,546	35.5%
Operating expenses:				
Officers salaries	$	0.0%	$2,250	0.5%
Utilities	13,430	4.9%	20,424	4.9%
Supplies	266	0.1%	556	0.1%
License & permits	3,284	1.2%	2,930	0.7%
Telephone	979	0.4%	1,725	0.4%
Trash removal	1,293	0.5%	2,343	0.6%
Insurance	1,892	0.7%	14,886	3.6%
Payroll taxes	11,513	4.2%	14,044	3.4%
Accounting & legal	1,759	0.6%	5,010	1.2%
Repairs & maintenance	4,630	1.7%	8,988	2.1%
Rent	19,596	7.1%	28,540	6.8%
Depreciation & amortization	1,613	0.6%	3,558	0.9%
Bank charges	670	0.2%	886	0.2%
Office expense	1,187	0.4%	0.0%	419
Advertising & promotion	1,750	0.6%	6.333	1.5%
Cleaning & exterminating	517	0.2%	983	0.2%
Coil cleaning & water testing	68	0.0%	149	0.0%
Dues & subscriptions	173	0.1%	182	0.0%
Linen & laundry	587	0.2%	1,642	0.4%
Theft & loss	0.0%	0.0%	0.0%	0.0%
Miscellaneous	118	0.0%	0.0%	225
Total operating expenses:	$65,325	23.7%	$115,429	27.6%
Operating profit (loss)	$11,127	4.0%	$33,117	7.9%
Interest expense	$1,812	0.7%	$2,650	0.6%
Other income (expense)	355	0.1%	102	0.0%
Pretax income (loss)	$9,670	3.5%	$30,569	7.3%
Taxes	$	0.0%	$	0.0%
Net income (loss)	$9,670	3.5%	$30,569	7.3%

	FYE 12/31/93		FYE 12/31/94		FYE 12/31/95
$461,075	100.0%	$444,203	100.0%	$475,198	100.0%
270,210	58.6%	264,168	59.5%	290,382	61.1%
$190,865	41.4%	$180,035	40.5%	$184,816	38.9%
$11,225	2.4%	$17,300	3.9%	$20,800	4.4%
21,245	4.6%	23,681	5.3%	19,633	4.1%
	0.0%	9,860	2.2%	13,025	2.7%
1,370	0.3%	642	0.1%	550	0.1%
1,595	0.2%	1,722	0.4%	1,634	0.3%
2,400	0.5%	2,340	0.5%	2,184	0.5%
8,999	2.0%	11,444	2.6%	11.334	2.4%
12,677	2.7%	15,213	3.4%	15,727	3.3%
3,593	0.8%	3,960	0.9%	2,440	0.5%
8,938	1.9%	5,005	1.1%	6,037	1.3%
31,100	6.7%	31,200	7.0%	31,375	6.6%
3,954	0.9%	6,398	1.4%	7,129	1.5%
1,010	0.2%	1,155	0.3%	1,037	0.2%
	0.1%	511	0.1%	527	0.1%
8,311	1.8%	6,726	1.5%	5,084	1.1%
814	0.2%	248	0.1%	562	0.1%
191	0.0%	659	0.1%	1,021	0.2%
225	0.0%		0.0%	200	0.0%
3,867	0.8%	2,059	0.5%	24	0.0%
4,700	1.0%				
	0.0%	1,225	0.3%	1,250	0.3%
$122,158	27.6%	$141,348	31.8%	$146,273	30.8%
$68,707	14.9%	$38,687	8.7%	$38,543	8.1%
$2,506	0.5%	$2,174	0.5%	$2,199	0.5%
77	0.0%	105	0.0%	143	0.0%
$66,278	14.4%	$36,618	8.2%	$36,487	7.7%
$	0.0%	$	0.0%	$	0.0%
$66,278	14.4%	$36,618	8.2%	$36,487	7.7%

**Annual
Projections:
Income Statement**

	PROJ 12/31/97		PROJ 12/31/98	
Net sales	$499,000	100.0%	$533,930	100.0%
Cost of sales	299,400	60.0%	320,358	60.0%
Gross profit	$199,600	40.0%	$213,572	40.0%
Operating expenses:				
Officers salaries	$50,000	10.0%	$53,000	9.9%
Utilities	24,900	5.0%	26,200	4.9%
Supplies	1,000	0.2%	1,000	0.2%
License & permits	1,500	0.3%	1,500	0.3%
Telephone	1,800	0.4%	1,800	0.3%
Trash removal	2,500	0.5%	2,600	0.5%
Insurance	12,000	2.4%	12,500	2.3%
Payroll taxes	16,000	3.2%	17,000	3.2%
Accounting & legal	2,000	0.4%	1,500	0.3%
Repairs & maintenance	3,000	0.6%	3,500	0.7%
Rent	16,800	3.4%	16,800	3.1%
Depreciation-Fixed assets	21,450	4.3%	18,590	3.5%
Amortization-Liquor license	3,335	0.7%	3,335	0.6%
Bank charges	1,000	0.2%	1,000	0.2%
Office expense	500	0.1%	600	0.1%
Advertising & promotion	5,000	1.0%	7,000	1.3%
Cleaning & exterminating	500	0.1%	500	0.1%
Coil cleaning & water testing	1,000	0.2%	1,100	0.2%
Dues & subscriptions	200	0.0%	200	0.0%
Linen & laundry	3,000	0.6%	3,200	0.6%
Theft & loss	2,000	0.4%	4,000	0.7%
Miscellaneous	200	0.0%	300	0.1%
Total operating expenses:	$169,685	34.0%	$177,225	33.2%
Operating profit (loss)	$29,915	6.0%	$36,347	6.8%
Interest expense	$15,750	3.2%	$13,725	2.6%
Other income (expense)	0.0%	0.0%	0.0%	0.0%
Pretax income (loss)	$14,165	2.8%	$22,622	4.2%
Taxes	$5,666	1.1%	$9,049	1.7%
Amortization-Goodwill	$3,335	0.7%	$3,335	0.6%
Net income (loss)	$5,164	1.0%	$10,238	1.9%

	PROJ 12/31/99		PROJ 12/31/100		PROJ 12/31/101
$581,984	100.0%	$651,822	100.0%	$749,595	100.0%
349,190	60.0%	391,093	60.0%	449,757	60.0%
$232,793	40.0%	$260,729	40.0%	$299,838	40.0%
$56,000	9.6%	$59,000	9.1%	$62,000	8.3%
28,000	4.8%	32,600	5.0%	37,500	5.0%
1,200	0.2%	1,400	0.2%	1,600	0.2%
1,700	0.3%	1,900	0.3%	2,100	0.3%
1,900	0.3%	1,900	0.3%	2,100	0.3%
2,700	0.5%	2,800	0.4%	3,000	0.4%
13,000	2.2%	14,000	2.1%	15,000	2.0%
18,100	3.1%	20,000	3.1%	22,500	3.0%
1,700	0.3%	1,900	0.3%	2,100	0.3%
4,500	0.8%	5,000	0.8%	5,000	0.7%
16,800	2.9%	16,800	2.6%	16,800	2.2%
18,590	3.2%	18,590	2.9%	18,590	2.5%
3,335	0.6%	3,335	0.5%	3,335	0.4%
1,200	0.2%	1,400	0.2%	1,500	0.2%
700	0.1%	800	0.1%	1,000	0.1%
9,000	1.5%	12,000	1.8%	15,000	2.0%
600	0.1%	700	0.1%	800	0.1%
1,300	0.2%	1,500	0.2%	1,600	0.2%
350	0.1%	350	0.1%	300	0.0%
3,400	0.6%	3,600	0.6%	3,900	0.5%
4,000	0.7%	5,000	0.8%	5,000	0.7%
350	0.1%	500	0.1%	600	0.1%
$188,425	32.4%	$205,075	31.5%	$221,325	29.5%
$44,368	7.6%	$55,654	8.5%	$78,513	10.5%
$11,700	2.0%	$9,675	1.5%	$7,650	1.0%
0.0%					
$32,668	5.6%	$45,979	7.1%	$70,863	9.5%
$13,067	2.2%	$18,391	2.8%	$28,345	3.8%
$3,335	0.6%	$3,335	0.5%	$3,335	0.4%
$16,266	2.8%	$24,252	3.7%	$39,183	5.2%

Restaurant/Microbrewery

BUSINESS PLAN

HOMESTEADERS' PUB & GRUB

5297 Kingswood
Marble River, WA 98922

This business plan is exemplary in it's thoroughness and consideration of every detail. It's clear vision and enthusiasm underscore the owners' qualifications for the undertaking. Note the complementary nature of the business and it's environment. Their suitedness for each other lends uniqueness to the venture and ambience to the establishment.

- CONFIDENTIALITY STATEMENT

- EXECUTIVE SUMMARY

- CURRENT POSITION AND FUTURE OUTLOOK

- MANAGEMENT AND OWNERSHIP

- UNIQUENESS OF THE ESTABLISHMENT

- FUNDS SOUGHT AND USAGE

- BUSINESS DESCRIPTION

- SITUATION ANALYSIS

- VISION AND MISSION STATEMENT

- OBJECTIVES

- STRATEGIES

- MANAGEMENT/OWNERSHIP

- THE UNFILLED NEED/UNIQUENESS OF THE ESTABLISHMENT

- PRICING AND VALUE

- MARKET RESEARCH AND ASSUMPTIONS/ MARKET OVERVIEW

- MARKET SEGMENTS/COMPETITION

- CUSTOMER PROFILE/MARKET SHARE

- GEOGRAPHIC MARKET FACTORS

- MARKET STRATEGIES

- SALES FORECASTS

- THEME, MENU, SERVICE AND DELIVERY

- ADVERTISING AND PROMOTIONS

- CUSTOMER CONTACT/EMPLOYMENT AND PERSONNEL PLANS

- BUYING AND STOCKING PLANS

- FACILITY PLANS

- RISK ANALYSIS

- BUSINESS PROJECTED FINANCIAL STATEMENTS

- PERSONAL PROJECTED FINANCIAL STATEMENTS

RESTAURANT/MICROBREWERY
BUSINESS PLAN

CONFIDENTIALITY STATEMENT

The information, data, and drawings embodied in this business plan are strictlyconfidential and are supplied on the understanding that they will be held confidentially and not disclosed to third parties without the prior written consent of the authors of this document.

EXECUTIVE SUMMARY

Homesteaders' Pub & Grub will be a people friendly restaurant and tavern. It will provide comfortable surroundings for people to bring family and friends to enjoy a reasonably priced meal and a wide variety of American microbrewed beers and American wines. The business will be established at the current site of Howie's, located on the riverfront in Marble River, Washington. With some remodeling, and the use of most of the existing equipment, we will turn what was once a drive-in, into a gathering spot for people who have an appreciation for the natural environment. It will not matter whether our guests are local people or visitors to our town. All will be made to feel comfortable. Customers will find a love of the outdoors portrayed, friendliness, warmth and a special appreciation for the mountains and all the activities relating to this area.

CURRENT POSITION AND FUTURE OUTLOOK

The strength of our business will be in the quality of the products we serve; the food, beer, wine, the environment and most of all the service we provide our guests. Within 2-3 years we plan to add a microbrewery onsite. This addition will give us even a more unique draw for customers. National statistics show micro/restaurant openings increasing markedly and the failure rate in the US is a low 1 out of 7.

Marble River Washington is one of the gateways to North Cascades National Park. The northeast entrance (at the top of the "Sawtooth Highway" above Marble River) logged over 190,000 visitors last year. With the current 10 year, 21 million dollar development plan for the ski area, and the fine 18 hole championship golf course, the community and it's present leadership are demonstrating their commitment to the future growth of the area. Marble River is on its' way to becoming a competitor with Big Sky, Montana, Jackson Hole, Wyoming and Sun Valley, Idaho as a destination year round recreation center in the west.

MANAGEMENT AND OWNERSHIP

Gary and Diane Danforth are husband and wife and will be joint owners. Gary Danforth (41) has been an educator/coach for 20 years in both Michigan and Wyoming. He has received awards as both a teacher and a coach. Gary has also served an internship in a microbrewery/restaurant in northern Michigan. He has recently received extensive training to become a brew master at a The Siebel Institute this summer.

Diane Danforth (34) has spent her career in the business sector. Diane started in public accounting after college then moved to the private sector. She currently works for three separate corporations (all the same owners) and holds the positions of General Manager/CFO/Controller.

UNIQUENESS OF THE ESTABLISHMENT

Our company will differentiate itself from others in Marble River because of three factors. Foremost will be the "personal touch" provided by the owners. Gary and Diane have ample experience in serving and dealing with people. Gary brings people skills from education and Diane brings her skills from the public and private business sector. We will have a unique atmosphere. Presently there is no restaurant/pub that brings nature and the offerings of the North Cascades ecosystem inside. Finally, we will offer food and drink quality that will be hard to match. By serving fresh food, American beer and wine in wonderful atmosphere, people will come.

The business is seeking $350,000 in long term debt financing secured by a combination of business assets and personal assets. These funds combined with the $40,000 of our personal money will give us a total of $390,000. $265,000 will be used to purchase the property and building presently called Howie's in Marble River. $60,000 will be used in remodeling & additional furnishings. $25,000 will be used to purchase inventory for the restaurant. $40,000 will be used as working capital. All of the funds to purchase the property, building, fixtures, etc. will be loaned to Gary & Diane personally, with the reasoning to follow.

Homesteaders' Pub & Grub will operate as a corporation with Diane owning 51% of the stock and Gary owning 49%. This ratio is used so that the corporation may receive some future benefits of a woman owner (in some instances classified as a minority). The building will be owned by Gary & Diane personally, and rented to the corporation. This will be done for tax purposes.

Homesteaders' Pub & Grub will be a restaurant/pub, specializing in good food, and American beer and wines. We feel that the rebirth of the brewing industry in this country and the many fine wineries throughout the United States will allow us to serve top quality American fare without the need to import beer and wine. Eventually we will open a microbrewery on premise to complete the total package. The microbrewing industry is expanding throughout this country. There are over 300 such places in this country. We will begin however, as a restaurant/pub specializing in specialty American brews and wines.

The current facilities will be remodeled to accommodate an actual sit down bar area and a sit down dining room with table service. We would like to open the room up so the appearance will be more appealing and more practical from a serving stand point. Our projected seating capacity will be over 60 dining seats and 10 bar seats

FUNDS SOUGHT AND USAGE

The restaurant/pub market is described as a risky venture. It will take much time and work. Presently the building we are seeking serves the community as a seasonal drive-in type restaurant. We will remodel the facility and make it into an attractive sit down restaurant/pub. Diane and Gary bring a wealth of people, management and motivational skills to the business. Gary also brings a knowledge of the brewing industry and Diane brings hands on management, business and accounting knowledge. We are both recognized as outstanding cooks and are gifted in the art of entertaining people. We will make this work. Our ideas, energy and people skills willmake this happen. When the brewing operation comes online there will be added benefits of local and regional distribution of the products.

SITUATION ANALYSIS

The microbrewery/pub experience is expanding all over the United States. The failure rate is 1 in 7 start ups. That is quite good. Basically that means if you won't work, you won't make it. The Danforths will work.

We envision a thriving restaurant/pub operation for the first two to three years. We intend to then begin a microbrewing operation. At that point, we will have the ability to market our beer product locally and regionally. The advantage of an on site brewery attached to the restaurant will only make our position in the dining market of Marble River stronger. The uniqueness of having an operating brewing operation in full view of dining customers will add even more ambience to our friendly establishment. The ability to enjoy fresh, high quality beer with a top notch meal will be hard to beat.

The company's mission is to provide the people of Marble River, Washington and the visitors to the area, the highest quality service, food and drink at a reasonable cost. We further plan

VISION AND MISSION STATEMENT

to provide an environment that brings a touch of the natural wonders of the North Cascades ecosystem inside to the patrons. We will target all residents of Miner County as well as all visitors to the area.

OBJECTIVES

- To be "the" premier restaurant/pub in Marble River
- To expand our business with the addition of a microbrewery on site within two to three years.
- To realize a 10% increase in sales over the next three years and a 15% increase when the microbrewery is open.
- To become an integral part of the city of Marble River and it's future.

STRATEGIES

- To secure financing for the purchase of the established building, remodeling costs, inventory, and operating capital.
- To provide service to the customer that is second to none.
- To provide an atmosphere for dining and drinking that truly reflects the greater North Cascades ecosystem and it's history.
- To provide a stimulating menu that crosses a variety of food styles.
- The food served will be of the highest quality and best value for the money spent.
- Seek out and find the highest quality American microbrewed beers to serve to our customers.
- Seek out and find the highest quality American wines to serve to our customers.

MANAGEMENT/ OWNERSHIP

The management team will be Gary and Diane Danforth. Gary & Diane decided to go into business for themselves seven years ago. They evaluated their life styles and decided they were ready for a change. They began to focus on long term planning to make this plan a reality. They knew they wanted to return to the west and most of all to the mountains. They became familiar with the microbrewery industry when they helped a friend open one in northern Michigan. Their dream then became to have a restaurant microbrewery in the west. In the spring of 1996 they put their lakefront home up for sale and began to expedite their plan. They focussed their planned move to the city of Marble River. They were familiar with this town because both used to live in Freemont, Washington before moving east. Marble River had always been a favorite spot. Their house sold in December of 1996. They liquidated their other debts with their profits and put the rest in the bank . They began a serious search for a piece of property to fit their needs. In February of 1997 they came across the Howie's site. With some imagination they decided this would be the place to recognize their dreams.

Both Gary and Diane have a lot of experience in the people and service business. The intention is to run the business with the owners as primary employees, adding staff as the need arises. The Danforths will manage all operations and employees will report to them.

The Homesteaders' Pub & Grub will be operated as a corporation. Diane Danforth will own 51% of the corporation and Gary Danforth will own 49%. The land, building and fixtures will be owned by Gary and Diane personally and leased to the corporation. This ownership structure may have to change once the brewery is brought on line. The corporation will register it's trade name to ensure that promotional activities, articles, and decor are protected. Management believes that the unique combination of marketing and products can only be protected in this manner.

Marble River needs a restaurant and pub that highlights the North Cascades environment and Miner County's history. The town needs a place where people can meet over a cold brew, good food, and enjoy the special ambience of the establishment. There needs to be a spot in town that stimulates the urge in all of us to get out and enjoy the natural surroundings (the Sawtooth Wilderness and the Cascade Range). We also need a spot where those of us that are interested in these out of door activities can meet to plan future adventures.

The restaurant will cater to the largely unfilled need for a spot to view North Cascades and thesurrounding wilderness areas through pictures, photographs, and detailed maps. The mineral history of Miner County, mainly coal, will also be highlighted. The history of the area's famous mountain men will be on display. The image of the restaurant will be designed to provoke a desire to explore the area by car, walking the trails, or backpacking in the high country. The owners want their customers to see and explore the amazing country that surrounds them.

We will target both tourists and local residents to frequent the establishment. The restaurant will be located near many of the local motels. Parking will be "outside the door" and ample.

The beer and wine selections will attract a variety of customers from the outdoor enthusiast, to the professional, to families, to older established connoisseurs of these beverages. Pricing on the menu will be moderate. The menu will be a cross section of food styles. Portions will be generous and of top quality The service will be friendly and prompt.

THE UNFILLED NEED/ UNIQUENESS OF THE ESTABLISHMENT

The menu pricing structure was established based on competition locally and throughout the industry for similar menus. With our competitors in mind we also looked at labor and ingredient costs to arrive at a pricing scheme. We used what is known in the industry as "combination pricing" to arrive at our final figures. Combination pricing is a combination of the factor method, gross margin pricing, prime cost method and competition pricing.

In designing our menu we looked at the customers we are trying to attract. We tried to design a menu that would appeal to this audience. Our menu has a wide range of prices and selections.

PRICING AND VALUE

The restaurant and pub industry are well established in the Miner County area. In fact Marble River boasts itself as having "more restaurants per capita than any other community in Washington." The careful reader can understand this statement when you examine Marble River's major industry: tourism. To support the large visiting population (190,000 used the north entrance to North Cascades last year) the current food service industry in this area doesn't seem so large.

Marble River currently offers a variety of food choices. We feel our establishment will fit nicely into this market. We will be unique in our menu, service and decor. We will also provide easy parking and access to the main road. Visitors to our establishment will enjoy a great view of the city, the mountains, and the creek.

Being one of many good restaurants in the area can only help this community. With so many people coming through this area every year, a good meal in several locations will make them speak fondly of the area, return to the area, and encourage others to visit.

MARKET RESEARCH AND ASSUMPTIONS/ MARKET OVERVIEW AND SIZE

MARKET SEGMENTS/ COMPETITION

One of every 3 meals eaten in this country is eaten away from the home. This equates to 42% of the consumers food budget being spent at restaurants. We will capture our share of these national statistics. More importantly though, our restaurant's growth potential is tied directly to the growth of the community of Marble River. While census data shows Miner County realizing about a 5% annual growth rate, Marble River has been seeing close to 15% growth during the same recent intervals. Our food menu, beer and wine selections will be able to keep up with this growth. The owners feel that this establishment will exceed the areas projected growth rate because it will become known for it's quality of food, selection of beer and wines, superior service, location, and atmosphere.

We expect with the addition of a microbrewery we will see a growth in sales by as much as 20% due to the uniqueness and the addition of off site sales and distribution.

The restaurant and pub competition in Marble River is varied and intense. Each existing establishments holds a unique place in the market. Because Marble River has this variety though, people from the surrounding areas come and enjoy! Our addition to this market will attract even more people.

We look at competition as a positive. Competition can only make us better. The owner both strive to be the best in all they do. That intrinsic motivation both owners have will not go away. It will only grow with competition.

CUSTOMER PROFILE/ MARKET SHARE

Our customer base will be large and varied. We intend to attract local people, vacationers to the North Cascades area, skiers who come for the skiing, "car campers" who are on road tours, golfers, and backcountry enthusiasts who enjoy the area and all it has to offer. We do not intend to forget the weekenders who come from surrounding communities just to enjoy this special town at all times of year.

We will welcome all ages, from infants to senior citizens. We will provide an environment that makes them all feel welcome.

It is hard to determine what share we will have of the market because we are combining two areas. Combining quality food with a pub atmosphere and potential microbrewery is new to this area. The previous owner operated this piece of property as a drive-in, which is very different from our perception of how we'll operate it.

GEOGRAPHIC MARKET FACTORS

This piece of property is usually the last place you see (convenient for take out sales) when leaving Marble River towards the mountains or the first place you see when entering town from the mountains. It has 200' of creek frontage and it has it's own parking lot making it convenient for motorhomes, travel trailers and snow mobile trailers. The outside of the building will attract interest as people pass by, making them say "Lets go back to that first place we saw" or "Lets stop here, this looks perfect." Being first and last does have its advantages.

We believe in the growth of the area. This town is one of the best kept secrets in the United States. It is sixty miles from Bellingham, Washington and all that city has to offer. It is the gateway to some of the most spectacular wilderness left in the world. The majority of the community seems to want slow, planned, well-thought-out growth and we very much agree in this approach.

Marble River has location, recreation (golf, skiing, camping, fishing, hunting, back packing, etc.), and most importantly, great people from many cultural backgrounds.

This is a great place to be and a great time to be here. We will work hard to be a positive part of the community and it's future.

The restaurant and pub will attract locals with monthly promotional events; like an English pint club, daily food specials, a changing variety of microbrewed beers and American wines. We will cater to local businesses by providing a fax order system far lunches. We will advertise in the local and regional newspapers and hotel fliers to attract out of town guests. We will make the building appealing and intriguing both inside and out so people will want to stop.

The owners will pride themselves in being present (one or the other or both) during most working hours. We will let the customer know we are here and that we value their business and we are always there for them. We hope to meet most all the customers and help them enjoy themselves. We will provide that extra service that everyone appreciates.

The restaurant & pubs' strategy for service will include a well-trained staff that will offer any type of service to the customer when asked (i.e. special orders, special seating, special dietary needs, information about the area and directions). Thus our unconditional guarantee: If you are not satisfied, we will make it right.

MARKET STRATEGIES

The receipts for Homesteaders' Pub & Grub are forecasted to remain steady in 1998 and increase by 10% in 1999, to $277,860 in 1999. We assume the average ticket will be $15.00 in 1997 and 1998. A combination of increased customers as well as an increase in the average ticket will account for this growth. This will be achieved by targeting our local customer base and visitors to Marble River

The projected sales breakdown by customer in 1998 is as follows:

SALES FORECASTS

	% of Sales
Under 30 Young adults	10
Over 50 couples	20
Other families	30
Others	10

Homesteaders' Pub & Grub will serve a variety of dishes. This variety is based on the fact that we are attempting to attract a variety of customers for both lunch and dinner. We will offer vegetarian items, traditional restaurant and pub fare, and a children's menu. Salads and fresh bread will compliment the service. The addition of the microbrewery in a few years will add a unique image and aroma to the facilities relaxing, natural, and subdued ambience. The pricing on the menu is moderate and compares favorably to other menus in town. Dinner service is forecast to be our highest revenue generator with more than 60% of the sales. The hours from 3:00 p.m. to 10:00 p.m. will be key for our establishment as this is the time that travelers and recreationalists are settling in for the evening and looking for a great spot to eat and enjoy a beverage.

THEME, MENU SERVICE AND DELIVERY

Once a patron walks in the door, customer service begins. Customers will be shown to a seat or allowed to choose a seat if that is their preference. A member of the staff will then offer a menu and ask if they have a drink preference. Once the meal is ordered, the ticket will be taken to the kitchen and the order prepared in an expedient manner. Food will be delivered in a timely manner. Wait staff will be available and pleasant at all times during a customer's meal. Once the meal is completed, busing will be done as unobtrusively as possible. The wait staff will ask if anything else is desired. If the patron requires something else it will be provided, if not, the customer will receive his/her ticket (bill). We will accept cash and major credit cards as a method of payment.

ADVERTISING AND PROMOTIONS

Promotional activities for Homesteaders' Pub & Grub will focus on the unique theme and image Of the establishment. The primary advertising will be in the local newspapers and local radio. We will also advertise in promotional publications and flyers that are directed to the local tourist industry. The establishment's logo will be prominent in all advertising. This logo will also be displayed on several types of apparel that will be worn by the staff and for sale in the restaurant. We also intend to help sponsor local events in the community that will allow our name or logo to be displayed.

The owners plan to be active in the community. This may be the single biggest promotional tool for the business. By building goodwill we feel we will be building a strong community base that will support our business.

More advertising may be explored as the business is established and funds permit.

CUSTOMER CONTACT/ EMPLOYMENT AND PERSONNEL PLANS

The Homesteaders' Pub & Grub will look for outgoing, intelligent, and fun-loving employees. Eating out is fun if we are entertained and coddled. Going to a restaurant is similar to going to the theater. The "action" around you is for your benefit, to satisfy your wants and needs. Our staff will be trained to unconditionally guarantee satisfaction to all patrons. Once our customers arrive they will be made to feel at all times as if, individually and collectively, they are at center stage. The decor, menu and the wait staff will help to make this a reality.

In addition to the two owners, the plan is to hire two part time employees to keep throughout the year. These employees will be utilized in the kitchen and compensated at $8.00 per hour. In July and August the forecast is to employ two additional part time people to serve as wait staff for $4.00 per hour plus tips.

The owners will share the cooking and management duties unless a competent cook can be found. the shortage of motivated personnel and higher than average employee turnover is predicted. That seems to be a fact of life in the restaurant business. The owners will employ a motivational plan, as well as various incentives to keep employees committed to "their" pub and restaurant. Training and performance evaluations will be an integral part of employee motivation. Moving employees towards "taking ownership" of their job, their responsibilities, and the business operation will be the primary goal.

BUYING AND STOCKING PLANS

Bellingham, Washington which is 60 miles west of Marble River has a number of restaurant equipment and supply companies. Items such as detergents, kitchen supplies, specialty food equipment, fresh produce, and food can be purchased there. Whenever possible we will purchase items locally. A large food service company called Sysco Food Services of Washington will be a primary supplier. They will come "right to the room." That company will be hard to beat price wise. They offer most everything that we will need. Repair items and specialty goods will be available in Bellingham.

We will search out local sources for our meats. Beef especially, is raised right in our area and we can't imagine the need to look elsewhere.

Our beer and wine products will be purchased from distributors in Bellingham. Franklin Beverage, Digby Distributing, Greely Brewing, Inc., and Mountainside Distributing Co. each will be evaluated as to price, selection, and quality.

Because we will be starting as a small operation we see our stocking inventory as easily manageable. We will inventory our goods at least twice monthly. This will help to discipline us, so that we can monitor our purchases carefully. This will reveal which items are used most frequently and which are slow moving. This info will also tell us about our customers tastes, seasonal changes, and other fluctuations that may lead to menu selection improvement or change. Accurate inventory control will also help us monitor our cost of sales.

Finally keeping a close accounting of our stock will allow us to order proper quantities at the most opportune times. This we feel will cut down on spoilage as well as tying up funds in excess inventory that is not needed.

The internal structure of the restaurant will be gutted when the building if first purchased. The remodeling will emphasize a personal relaxed atmosphere, rather than the current dining hall/drive-in effect. A bar will be installed that seats up to 12 people. The interior design coordination will be handled by the owners. Kitchen facilities will be substantially improved by changing the preparation, cooking and storage areas. Replacement of older and broken equipment, within cost constraints, will be undertaken. The remodeling will improve security and reduce maintenance. The process will be completed within six weeks. Parking will be evaluated once the restaurant is up and running. To keep costs manageable the owners will start out using the present parking facilities.

FACILITY PLANS

The two major issues to be dealt with the first year or two in the life of Homesteaders' Pub & Grub are seasonal slowdowns and making ourselves known. Marketing, advertising, getting involved in the community, and time in the market will be the keys to both. The first problem will be the most difficult. Time in our location will be the key we feel. If we become very profitable during the busy season, we feel we'll be able to weather the slower times. If we can maintain a minimum level of profitability during the first two years as we build relationships with local clients, we will become a very successful year around operation. We will do very well during the busy season and well during the slower times. The experiences the owners have had with people during their lives have truly been, "build it, they will come." If you provide a "total package" that people want and enjoy you will be successful! We intend to be successful!

RISK ANALYSIS

Projected Balance Sheet for Homesteaders' as of 9/30/97

Assets:		Liabilities:	
Cash	$40,100.00	Note Payable Officer	$90,000.00
Inventory	25,000.00	Total Liabilities	90,000.00
Beer & Wine License	25,000.00		
Total Assets	$90,100.00	Stockholders Equity:	
		Common Stock	100.00
		Retained Earnings	
		Total Stockholders Equity	100.00
		Liabilities & Stockholders Equity	$90,100.00

Projected Balance Sheet for Homesteaders' as of 12/31/97

Assets:		Liabilities:	
Cash	$37,796.47	Note Payable Officer	$90,000.00
Inventory	25,000.00	Total Liabilities	90,000.00
Beer & Wine License	25,000.00		
Less Amortization	-125.00		
Total Assets	$87,671.47	Stockholders Equity:	
		Common Stock	100.00
		Retained Earnings	-2428.53
		Total Stockholders Equity	-2328.53
		Liabilities & Stockholders Equity	$87,671.47

Projected Balance Sheet for Homesteaders' as of 12/31/98

Assets:		Liabilities:	
Cash	$56.006.96	Note Payable Officer	$90,000.00
Inventory	25,000.00	Total Liabilities	90,000.00
Beer & Wine License	25,000.00		
Less Amortization	-1,875.00		
Total Assets	$104,131.96	Stockholders Equity:	
		Common Stock	100.00
		Retained Earnings	14,031.96
		Total Stockholders Equity	14,131.96
		Liabilities & Stockholders Equity	$104,131.96

Assets:		Liabilities:	
Cash	$79,025.57	Note Payable Officer	$90,000.00
Inventory	25,000.00	Total Liabilities	90,000.00
Beer & Wine License	25,000.00		
Less Amortization	-3,125.00		
Total Assets	$125,900.57	Stockholders Equity:	
		Common Stock	100.00
		Retained Earnings	35,800.57
		Total Stockholders Equity	35,900.57
		Liabilities &	
		Stockholders Equity	$125,900.57

Projected Balance Sheet for Homesteaders' as of 12/31/99

Assets:		Liabilities:	
Cash	$107,695.37	Note Payable Officer	$90,000.00
Inventory	$25,000.00	Total Liabilities	$90,000.00
Beer & Wine License	$25,000.00		
Less Amortization	$(4,375.00)		
Total Assets	$153,320.37	Stockholders Equity:	
		Common Stock	$100.00
		Retained Earnings	$63,220.37
		Total Stockholders Equity	$63,320.37
		Liabilities &	
		Stockholders Equity	$153,320.37

Projected Balance Sheet for Homesteaders' as of 12/31/2000

Assets:		Liabilities:	
Cash	$142,668.79	Note Payable Officer	$90,000.00
Inventory	28,000.00	Total Liabilities	90,000.00
Beer & Wine License	28,000.00		
Less Amortization	-5,625.00		
Total Assets	$190,063.79	Stockholders Equity:	
		Common Stock	100.00
		Retained Earnings	99,963.79
		Total Stockholders Equity	100,063.79
		Liabilities &	
		Stockholders Equity	$190,063.79

Projected Balance Sheet for Homesteaders' as of 12/31/2000

Projected Balance Sheet for Homesteaders' as of 12/31/2002

Assets:		Liabilities:	
Cash	$189,403.69	Note Payable Officer	$90,000.00
Inventory	30,000.00	Total Liabilities	90,000.00
Beer & Wine License	25,000.00		
Less Amortization	-6,875.00		
Total Assets	$237,528.69	Stockholders Equity:	
		Common Stock	100.00
		Retained Earnings	147,428.69
		Total Stockholders Equity	147,528.69
		Liabilities &	
		Stockholders Equity	$237,528.69

Personal Balance Sheet as of 8/31/97

Assets:		Liabilities:	
Cash	$40,000.00	Notes Payable:	
Vehicles	13,000.00	Insurance	$16,543.45
Life Insurance	12,951.00	Vehicles	10,461.88
TSA'S	100,386.00	Other	3,000.00
Total Assets	$166,337.00	Total Liabilities	$30,005.33
		Net Worth	136331.67
		Total Liabilities & Net Worth	$166,337.00

Projected Personal Balance Sheet as of 9/30/97

Assets:		Liabilities:	
Cash	$4,900.00	Notes Payable:	
Note Receivable Corp.	90,000.00	Building	$350,000.00
Land	100,000.00		
Building	100,000.00	Insurance	16,543.45
Building Improvements	60,000.00	Vehicles	10,461.88
Equipment	40,000.00		
Vehicles	13,000.00	Other	3,000.00
Life Insurance	12,951.00	Total Liabilities	$380,005.33
TSA'S	100,386.00		
Stock Corporation	100.00	Net Worth	$141,331.67
Total Assets	$521,337.00		
		Total Liabilities & Net Worth	$521,337.00

Assets:

Cash	$9,765.03
Note Receivable Corp.	90,000.00
Land	100,000.00
Building	100,000.00
Building Improvements	60,000.00
Equipment	40,000.00
Less Depreciation	(1,142.93)
Vehicles	13,000.00
Life Insurance	12,951.00
TSA'S	109,755.36
Stock Corporation	100.00
Investment in Corporation	-2,428.53
Total Assets	$531,999.93

Liabilities:

Notes Payable:	
Building	$349,475.96
Insurance	10,097.99
Vehicles	9,513.16
Other	4,000.00
Total Liabilities	$373,087.11
Net Worth	$158,912.82
Total Liabilities & Net Worth	$531,999.93

Projected Personal Balance Sheet as of 12/31/97

Income:

Wages Corporation	7,714.00
Rent Income	3,414.67
Interest Payment	666.67
Total Income	11,795.34

Expenses:

Interest Expense	
Building Loan	2,625.00
Insurance Loan	0.00
Vehicle	948.71
Depreciation	1,142.83
Total Expenses Before Taxes	4,716.54
Income (Loss) Before Taxes	7,078.80
Taxes	2123.64
Income (Loss) After Taxes	$4,955.16

Projected Personal Income Statement as of 12/31/97

Cash Sources:

Wages Corporation	6,650.00
Rent Income	3,414.67
Interest Income	666.67
Total Sources	10,731.34

Cash Uses:

Interest Expense	3,127.94
Loan Payoff	1,472.75
Taxes	0.00
Living Expenses	1,000.00
Total Uses	5,600.69
Cash Increase/(Decrease)	5,130.65
Beginning Cash	4,900.00
Ending Cash	$10,030.65

Projected Personal Cash Flow Statement 12/31/97

Projected Personal Balance Sheet as of 12/31/98

Assets:		Liabilities:	
Cash	$9,742.27	Notes Payable:	
Note Receivable C.	90,000.00	Building	$342,872.31
Land	100,000.00	Insurance	10,097.98
Building	100,000.00	Vehicles	5,517.15
Building Improvements	60,000.00	Other	4,000.00
Equipment	40,000.00	Total Liabilities	$362,487.44
Less Depreciation	(14,856.93)		
Vehicles	12,000.00		
Life Insurance	12,951.00		
TSA'S	122,926.00	Net Worth	$184,406.86
Stock Corporation	100.00		
Investment in Corporation	14,031.96		
Total Assets	$546,894.30	Total Liabilities & Net Worth	$546,894.30

Projected Personal Income Statement as of 12/31/98

Wages Corporation	$18,280.00
Rent Income	40,976.00
Interest Payment	8,000.00
Total Income	67,256.00

Expenses:

Interest Expense	
Building Loan	31,184.85
Insurance Loan	635.99
Vehicle	949.79
Depreciation	13,714.00
Total Expenses Before Taxes	46,484.63
Income (Loss) Before Taxes	20,771.37
Taxes	6707.15
Income (Loss) After Taxes	$14,064.23

Projected Personal Cash Flow Statement as of 12/31/99

Cash Sources:

Wages Corporation	$18,280.00
Rent Income	40,976.00
Interest Income	8,000.00
Total Sources	67,256.00

Cash Uses:

Interest Expense	32,770.63
Loan Payoff	15,800.99
Taxes	6707.15
Living Expenses	12,000.00
Total Uses	67,278.77
Cash Increase/(Decrease)	(22.76)
Beginning Cash	9,765.03
Ending Cash	$9,742.27

Assets:

Cash	$6,314.86	
Note Receivable Corporation	90,000.00	
Land	100,000.00	
Building	100,000.00	
Building Improvements	60,000.00	
Equipment	40,000.00	
Less Depreciation	(28,570.93)	
Vehicles	10,000.00	
Life Insurance	12,951.00	
TSA'S	135,218.60	
Stock Corporation	100.00	
Investment in Corporation	35,800.57	
Total Assets	$561,814.10	

Liabilities:

Notes Payable:	
Building	$335,649.20
Insurance	4,517.42
Vehicles	1,178.69
Other	0.00
Total Liabilities	$341,345.31
Net Worth	$220,468.79
Total Liabilities & Net Worth	$561,814.10

Projected Personal Balance Sheet as of 12/31/99

Income:

Wages Corporation	$18,280.00
Rent Income	40,976.00
Interest Payment	8,000.00
Total Income	67,256.00

Expenses:

Interest Expense	
Building Loan	30,565.37
Insurance Loan	293.55
Vehicle	570.56
Depreciation	13,714.00
Total Expenses Before Taxes	45,143.48
Income (Loss) Before Taxes	22,112.52
Taxes	6892.99
Income (Loss) After Taxes	$15,219.53

Projected Personal Income Statement as of 12/31/99

Cash Sources:

Wages Corporation	$18,280.00
Rent Income	40,976.00
Interest Income	8,000.00
Total Sources	67,256.00

Cash Uses:

Interest Expense	31,429.48
Loan Payoff	17,142.12
Taxes	6892.99
Living Expenses	15,000.00
Total Uses	70,464.59
Cash Increase/(Decrease)	(3,208.59)
Beginning Cash	9,523.45
Ending Cash	$6,314.86

Projected Personal Cash Flow Statement as of 12/31/99

Personal Balance Sheet as of 12/31/2000

Assets:		Liabilities:	
Cash	$19,593.60	Notes Payable:	$327,748.51
Note Receivable Corp.	$90,000.00	Building	$0
Land	$100,000.00	Insurance	$0
Building	$100,000.00	Vehicles	$0
Building Improvements	$60,000.00	Other	$0
Equipment	$40,000.00	Total Liabilities	$327,748.51
Less Depreciation	$42,284.93		
Vehicles	$10,000.00		
Life Insurance	$12,951.00		
TSA's	$148,740.46	Net Worth	$274,571.99
Stock Corporation	$100.00		
Investment in Corporation	$63,220.37		
Total Assets	$602,320.50	Total Liabilities & Net Worth	$602,320.50

Projected Personal Income Statement as of 12/31/2000

Income:	
Wages Corporation	$42,257.15
Rent Income	$40,976.00
Interest Payment	$8,000.00
Total Income	$91,233.15

Expenses:	
Interest Expense:	
Building Loan	$29,887.80
Insurance Loan	$163.65
Vehicle	$16.76
Depreciation	$13,714.00
Total Expenses Before Taxes	$43,714.00
Income (Loss) Before Taxes	$47,450.94
Taxes	$14,289.41
Income (Loss) After Taxes	$33,161.54

Projected Personal Cash Flow Statement as of 12/31/2000

Cash Sources:	
Wages Corporation	$42,257.15
Rent Income	$40,976.00
Interest Income	$8,000.00
Total Sources	$91,233.15
Cash Uses:	
Interest Expense	$30,068.21
Loan Payoff	$13,596.80
Taxes	$14,289.41
Living Expenses	$20,000.00
Total Uses	$77,954.42
Cash Increase/(Decrease)	$13,278.74
Beginning Cash	$6,314.86
Ending Cash	$19,593.60

Assets:

		Liabilities:	
Cash	$30,787.86	Notes Payable:	
Note Receivable Corp.	90,000.00	Building	$319,106.68
Land	100,000.00	Insurance	0.00
Building	100,000.00	Vehicles	0.00
Building Improvements	60,000.00	Other	0.00
Equipment	40,000.00	Total Liabilities	$319,106.68
Less Depreciation	(55,998.93)		
Vehicles	5,000.00		
Life Insurance	12,951.00		
TSA'S	163,614.51	Net Worth	$327,311.55
Stock Corporation	100.00		
Investment in Corporation	99,963.79		
Total Assets	$646,418.23	Total Liabilities & Net Worth	$646,418.23

Projected Personal Balance Sheet as of 12/31/2001

Income:

Wages Corporation	$48,535.72
Rent Income	40,976.00
Interest Payment	8,000.00
Total Income	97,571.72

Expenses:

Interest Expense	
Building Loan	29,146.64
Depreciation	13,714.00
Total Expenses Before Taxes	42,860.66
Income (Loss) Before Taxes	54,711.06
Taxes	16,413.32
Income (Loss) After Taxes	$38,297.74

Projected Personal Income Statement as of 12/31/2001

Cash Sources:	
Wages Corporation	$48,595.72
Rent Income	40,976.00
Interest Income	8,000.00
Total Sources	97,571.72
Cash Uses:	
Interest Expense	29,146.66
Loan Payoff	8,641.83
Taxes	16,413.32
Living Expenses	28,000.00
Total Uses	82,201.81
Cash Increase/(Decrease)	15,369.91
Beginning Cash	15,417.95

Projected Personal Cash Flow Statement as of 12/31/2001

Projected Personal Balance Sheet as of 12/31/2002

Assets:		Liabilities:	
Cash	$37,004.55	Notes Payable:	
Note Receivable Corp.	90,000.00	Building	$309,654.19
Land	100,000.00	Insurance	0.00
Building	100,000.00	Vehicles	0.00
Building Improvements	60,000.00	Other	0.00
Equipment	40,000.00	Total Liabilities	$309,654.19
Less Depreciation	(69,712.93)		
Vehicles	5,000.00		
Life Insurance	12,951.00		
TSA'S	179,975.96	Net Worth	$393,093.08
Stock Corporation	100.00		
Investment in Corporation	147,428.69		
Total Assets	$702,747.27	Total Liabilities & Net Worth	$702,747.27

Projected Personal Income Statement as of 12/31/2000

Income:	
Wages Corporation	$55,885.08
Rent Income	40,976.00
Interest Payment	8,000.00
Total Income	104,861.08

Expenses:	
Interest Expense	
Building Loan	28,336.00
Depreciation	13,714.00
Total Expenses Before Taxes	42,050.00
Income (Loss) Before Taxes	62,811.08
Taxes	18,843.32
Income (Loss) After Taxes	$43,967.75

Projected Personal Cash Flow Statement as of 12/31/2002

Cash Sources:	
Wages Corporation	$55,885.08
Rent Income	40,976.00
Interest Income	8,000.00
Total Sources	104,861.08

Cash Uses:	
Interest Expense	28,336.00
Loan Payoff	19,339.11
Taxes	18,843.32
Living Expenses	30,000.00
Total Uses	96,518.43
Cash Increase/(Decrease)	8,342.64
Beginning Cash	28,661.91
Ending Cash	$37,004.55

	12/31/97
Sales	$15,750.00
Cost of Goods Sold:	
Supplies	8,138.00
Labor	4,650.00
Total Cost of Goods Sold	12,788.00
Gross Profit	2,962.00
Expenses:	
Payroll Taxes	360.68
Rent/Utilities/Telephone	3,776.91
Insurance/Legal/Accounting	315.00
Office & Supplies	63.00
Equipment Expense	157.50
Maintenance	173.25
Auto Expense	94.50
Advertising	630.00
Travel & Entertainment	78.75
Interest	667.00
Amortization	125.00
Other	200.00
Total Expenses	6,641.59
Profit (Loss) Before Taxes	-3,679.59
Taxes	-1,251.06
Net Income (Loss)	($2,428.53)

Projected Monthly Income Statement as of 12/31/97

	12/31/99	12/31/100	12/31/101	12/31/102
Sales	$277,860.00	$305.651.00	$351,502.00	404227.30
Cost of Goods Sold:				
Supplies	97,251.00	106,977.85	123,025.70	141,479.56
Labor	55,572.00	61,130.20	700,300.40	80,845.46
Total COGS	152,823.00	168,108.05	193,326.10	222,325.02
Gross Profit	125,037.00	137,542.95	158,175.90	181,902.29
Expenses:				
Payroll Taxes	6,362.99	6,999.41	8,049.40	9,256.81
Rent/Utils/Phone	477,366.70	48,005.89	49,060.47	50,273.15
Insurance/Legal/Acct	5,557.20	6,113.02	7,030.04	8,084.55
Office & Supplies	1,111.44	1,222.60	1,406.01	1,616.91
Equipment Expense	2,778.60	3,056.51	3,515.02	4,042.27
Maintenance	3,056.46	3,362.16	3,866.52	4,446.50
Auto Expense	1,167.16	1,833.91	2,109.01	2,425.36
Advertising	11,114.40	12,226.04	14,060.08	16,169.09
Travel & Entertainment	1,389.30	1,528.26	1,757.51	2,021.14
Interest	8,000.00	8,000.00	8,000.00	8,000.00
Amortization	1,250.00	1,250.00	1,250.00	1,250.00
Other	2,400.00	2,400.00	2,400.00	2,400.00
Total Expenses	92,054.25	95,997.80	102,504.05	109,985.77
Profit (loss) Before Taxes	32,982.75	41,545.15	55,671.85	71,916.51
Taxes	11214.13	14125.35	18928.43	24451.61
Net Income (Loss)	$21,768.61	$27,419.80	$36,743.42	$47,464.90

Projected Income Statements for Homesteaders' for Years' Ending...

**Projected Monthly
Income Statements
for Homesteaders'
for Twelve Months
Ending 12/31/98**

	1/31/98	2/28/98	3/31/98	4/30/98	5/31/98	6/30/98
Sales	$23,250.00	$23,250.00	$15,750.00	$15,750.00	$15,750.00	$23,250.00
Cost of Goods Sold:						
Supplies	8,138.00	8,138.00	5,513.00	5,513.00	5,513.00	8,138.00
Labor	4,650.00	4,650.00	3,150.00	3,150.00	3,150.00	4,650.00
Total Cost of Goods Sold	12,788.00	12,788.00	8,663.00	8,663.00	8,663.00	12,788.00
Gross Profit	10,462.00	10,462.00	7,087.00	7,087.00	7,087.00	10,462.00
Expenses:						
Payroll Taxes	532.43	532.43	360.68	360.68	360.68	532.43
Rent/Utilities/Telephone	3,949.41	3,949.41	3,776.91	3,776.91	3,776.91	3,949.41
Insurance/Legal/Accounting	465.00	465.00	315.00	315.00	315.00	465.00
Office & Supplies	93.00	93.00	63.00	63.00	63.00	93.00
Equipment Expense	232.50	232.50	157.50	157.5	157.50	232.50
Maintenance	255.75	255.75	173.25	173.25	173.25	255.75
Auto Expense	139.50	139.50	94.50	94.50	94.50	139.50
Advertising	930.00	930.00	630.00	630.00	630.00	930.00
Travel & Entertainment	116.25	116.25	78.75	78.75	78.75	116.25
Interest	667.00	667.00	667.00	667.00	667.00	667.00
Amortization	125.00	125.00	125.00	125.00	125.00	125.00
Other	200.00	200.00	200.00	200.00	200.00	200.00
Total Expenses	7,705.84	7,705.84	6,641.59	6,641.59	6,641.59	7,705.84
Profit (Loss) Before Taxes	2,756.17	2,756.17	445.42	445.42	445.42	2,756.17
Taxes	937.10	937.10	151.44	151.44	151.44	937.10
Net Income (Loss)	$1,819.07	$1,819.07	$293.97	$293.97	$293.97	$1,819.07

7/31/98	8/31/98	9/30/98	10/31/98	11/30/98	12/31/98	TOTAL
$32,550.00	$32,550.00	$15,750.00	$15,750.00	$15,750.00	$23,250.00	$252,600.00
11,393.00	11,393.00	5,513.00	5,513.00	5,513.00	8,138.00	88,416.00
6,510.00	6,510.00	3,150.00	3,150.00	3,150.00	4,650.00	50,520.00
17,903.00	17,903.00	8663	8,663.00	8,663.00	12,788.00	138,936.00
14,647.00	14,647.00	7,087.00	7,087.00	7,087.00	10,462.00	113,664.00
745.40	745.40	360.68	360.68	360.68	532.43	5,784.54
4,163.31	4,163.31	3,776.91	3,776.91	3,776.91	3,949.41	46,785.72
651.00	651.00	315.00	315.00	315.00	465.00	5,052.00
130.20	130.20	63.00	63.00	63.00	93.00	1,010.40
325.50	325.50	157.50	157.50	157.50	232.50	2,526.00
358.05	358.05	173.25	173.25	173.25	255.75	2,778.60
195.30	195.30	94.50	94.50	94.50	139.50	1,515.60
1,302.00	1,302.00	630.00	630.00	630.00	930.00	10,104.00
162.75	162.75	78.75	78.75	78.75	116.25	1,263.00
667.00	667.00	667.00	667.00	667.00	667.00	8,004.00
125.00	125.00	125.00	125.00	125.00	125.00	1,500.00
200.00	200.00	200.00	200.00	200.00	200.00	2,400.00
9,025.51	9,025.51	6,641.59	6,641.59	6,641.59	7,705.84	88,723.86
5,621.50	5,621.50	445.42	445.42	445.42	8,156.17	24,940.14
1,911.31	1,911.31	151.44	151.44	151.44	937.10	8,479.65
$3,710.19	$293.97	$293.97	$293.97	$293.97	$1,819.07	$16,460.49

Taxi Service

BUSINESS PLAN

LAKEVIEW TAXI

27000 Kingsborough Ave.
Toledo, OH 32311

This businsess plan presents a persuasive and innovative system for organizing and running an alternative taxi service. An entrepreneur with a new improvement on a traditional business will find this plan's clear logic instructive. Note the comprehensive overview of industry practices and their shortcomings.

TAXI SERVICE
BUSINESS PLAN

MISSION STATEMENT

The mission of Lakeview Taxi is twofold. The first mission is to serve the general public in a fair and honest way. The second is to do this from a Christian perspective. While performing these tasks, it is hoped for and expected that a decent profit will be gathered from our efforts. There are many problems with the current taxi organizations in existence and it is hoped that by adding an alterantive to the services out there, the public will really appreciate our efforts.

BUSINESS ORIENTATION

The business of Lakeview Taxi will be transportation. Not just taxi service, but package delivery and other types of transportation such as Go Bus (a federally sponsored program) and even Ambucab (transportation on for the elderly) type services. The taxi service will be located in Toledo, Ohio in an office located on South Williams avenue.

MARKETING PLAN

Demographics

The amount of taxi business in the Toledo area is strong and growing. The population in the greater metropolitan area exceeds 500,000 people and the community is dynamic and getting more vibrant with each passing day. The entire area has a low unemployment rate, a diversified economy, and wonderful year round events which attract tourist dollars and people to the region.

Customer Profile

A taxi comapny attracts two main types of business. The first type is a commercial charge account business, and the second is direct consumer business. The commercial accounts usually have either package delivery or pay for passengers as their main function and are usually charge accounts. The direct consumer accounts are people from throughout the city who need taxi service for various reasons, to run errands, get to work etc. Consumer accounts are usually cub accounts and payable immediately. The customer never comes to the place of business of the taxi service, all taxis are dispatched to the customers place of business and the sole representative view that the customer has of the taxi service is through the cleanliness of the vehicle and the driver, and the promptness of their response. Any value added services just enhance these basic considerations of the customer.

Need for Services

There is a pressing need for reliable public transportation in the Toledo area, Bus service is not a viable option for many people due to the limited scope of operation of bus service in the area. The buses here do not run very long during the day and they are very restricted as to routes and times during the weekend and off-peak times. As a result, public transportation is always needed for those whom the bus cannot serve.

Economic Factors

Not only is there a strong and growing industrial base in the region, the city has been quietly developing the downtown area for quite some time. New projects are being planned and built daily and the entire downtown property is expanding at a very fist rate. In the last ten years, there has been an explosion of new venues which have attracted people to the downtown area. The city has recently seen the implementation of several sports franchises, an auto race, expanded concert venues, hotel construction, and are planning a downtown convention center which should pull in business from the surrounding cities in Ohio and throughout the United States. A state-of-the-art cancer research center is also being developed in addition to the world's first mall for children. Toledo is a city of opportunity and that expansion and growth fuels the need for more reliable transportation.

There are currently three other taxicab companies in the area. Each company is severely flawed and yet still manages to generate incredible amounts of revenue. Only one company, Maumee Taxi, the largest one, could be considered serious competition. This firm is prosperous and quite skillful at handling large numbers of clients. They currently have 56 taxis in their fleet and have most of the prestigious accounts in town. The other two companies still manage to thrive in spite of the fact that they have much smaller income bases and essentially are driving outdated equipment in poor condition. During busy times, none of the companies can keep up with demand and customers have been known to wait for up to four hours. During normal operating scenarios, wait times still range from approximately twenty to thirty minutes. This wait time is unnecessary and quite destructive to customer support. Taxi companies typically do not fail in this area. Other cities have a higher turnover of taxi companies, but they usually have a much larger presence. Metro Columbus has a population base of one million and 14,000 cabs. Toledo has a population base of 500,000 and 150 cabs. That is quite a difference. The reason for such a large spread is that Toledo is an affluent area and taxi service is not as pressing as in the impoverished areas surrounding Columbus. Another reason is that only recently has Toledo developed a significant downtown business. As the downtown continues to develop, taxi service will be required to increase exponentially.

ATTRACTING CUSTOMERS

Image

The current image of a taxi driver in Toledo is not a pleasant one. Drivers are looked at as unprofessional and discourteous. One reason that this is true is the nature of the business. Most taxi companies operate in the best and the worst areas of town and drivers have to deal with a wide variety of people. The drivers that are hired are not professional and are given virtually no training before they are sent out to deal with the public. Lakeview Taxi can change that. Training costs can be reduced through an apprenticeship program. Drivers can ride with several drivers and learn all of the necessary skills without incurring a large cost. In addition, training materials can be written down and provided at the start of training and a simple test can be administered to gauge the skills obtained by the driver. Knowledge of the city, command of the English language, and knowledge of charge account operations would go a long way towards improving the basic professionalism of the driver. Uniforms which are both comfortable and easy to maintain would also strive to complete the look that the public deserves and should expect. Of course, cleanliness of the cars is a must. A monthly inspection of vehicles would eliminate a large number of problems associated with operating a fleet and would ensure that the licensing authority would not bother with inspections of their own. We can control the image of Lakeview Taxi and it is possible to do so with a minimum of intrusiveness.

Pricing

Pricing is fixed by the city using regulated meters. Prices can fluctuate when the city council votes for a meter rate increase. Increases are usually annual and as a result, meter errata are high in the Toledo area and need minimal adjustment. The only meter problem would actually be the problem associated with metered waiting time. A factor that could be adjusted quite easily. Flag drop is currently 1.65 and the rate is then .17 per click every 1/9th of a mile. This rate is quite reasonable and is a good value to the customer as well.

Credit

Most taxi companies currently do not offer to take major credit cards. This is a huge mistake and there are a wide range of people who would use taxis more if this simple problem could be eradicated.

Customer Service

Customer service is a priority at Lakeview Taxi. The customer cares most about the promptness of the taxi that he or she is riding in. One way to ensure that customers would be served in a much better fashion would be to implement a zoned taxi dispatch system. A zoned system is essentially a first come/first served system of dispatching that eliminates much of the delay that occurs during ordinary dispatching. There are no real drawbacks to the system except that it would take a short while for drivers to get used to such a system. It is the quickest and easiest way to operate a taxi company. The current system, which relies on the closest cab to an order bidding on the order, means that orders are constantly being held up while the bidding takes place. It also means that orders are much more selective. Selecting a specific order is fine for the the driver, but it is a slow process that inconveniences the customer. If the drivers were switched over to a different system, in the long run, they would actually make more money and the entire system would speed up immensely.

Advertising

Advertising is minimal in the taxi service business, but could be maximized with the use of a little creativity. Currently a yellow page ad listing is the only necessary requirement to generate business. Many customers will immediately try the new taxi company in town to see if it has a faster response time than the other services in the area. Other people will try the new service if favorable word-of-mouth advertising is received. A large pool of customers is always available for a new company to have. In fact, most services that start up actually have a problem keeping up with the large volume of orders that come with just opening the doors to business. That pattern has repeated itself with each new taxi business that has developed within the last ten years.

Customer Incentives

Customers could be lured to try a new company by the use of incentives. It is illegal to charge more than the regulated price on taxi fares. It is not illegal to give a discount for first time riders of the service and it would strongly enhance repeat business to do so. Also, customers could be lured by giving away an occasional free ride or by using coupons distributed in the Advance Newspaper or the Toledo Press. These coupons could also be distributed in the taxis themselves as any driver who had a passenger could pass one out and any driver who did not have a fare could stop at local businesses and pass them out. That technique has been tried before with amazing success. However, as soon as the taxi company gets a steady base, all sales activity seems to stop. The company starts to generate sales so high they cannot handle the volume. In fact, most new companies lose business because they are too successful.

Customer Incentives

A satisfied customer in the taxi business will stay with that company for a long period of time. Sometimes as long as twenty years. Once a customer is satisfied, it is hard to get them to switch companies. Any measure of reasonable success recognizes that the repeat or "regular" customer is the one we all strive to get and maintain. There are a lot of ideas that have not been implemented simply because the business is so strong in this area. Hotels are constantly asking that cabs service them and hotels need shuttles for their overnight guests. A taxi company that catered to this market would do extremely well.

Additional Sources of Revenue

Even though taxi companies are by and large successful, they could be made even more so by adding additional revenue streams. Taxis can be painted with advertisements and turned into independent marketing venues of their own. Drivers could pass out flyers and could direct customers to certain establishments that had a reciprocal relationship with the company. Value added services could include food deliveries and other types of deliveries that other companies make on a routine basis. The horizon is truly unlimited when it comes to the taxi business. A little creativity would go a long way in furthering that horizon.

Taxi brokering is a unique concept. It allows drivers to own their own vehicles and operate them in a manner consistent with the company's policies and procedures. The standard practice for most taxi companies is to have each driver be an independent contractor and not an employee. The IRS has upheld this practice as standard in the industry. Many times, however, a taxi company and other companies treat their independent contractors as employees and they expose themselves and their company to massive tax liability if a tax ruling should happen to go against them. This is not wise policy, but it certainly exists in most taxi companies in the United States. There is a way to avoid liability and yet still maintain reasonable control over the drivers through applying the principles of taxi brokering. When a driver owns his or her own vehicle, there is an enormous savings to be had at all levels in the company. The advantages are spelled out below.

Overhead is reduced enormously when the company does not have to own and operate a fleet of vehicles. The savings on maintenance costs alone justifies using this tactic. In addition to direct cost savings, there is an operation personnel cost savings as well. There is no need for mechanics, no need for a scheduler, in fact, office staff can be reduced to a point where it is almost not necessary.

Overhead

The high turnover rate that plagues the industry is entirely avoided. Brokers are responsible for procuring their own drivers and even if it becomes difficult for them to locate drivers, the broker simply works more time during his shift to make up the difference. Almost all personnel problems are avoided when utilizing brokers.

Controlling Turnover

Brokers take care of their own vehicles. There is no hassle associated with keeping vehicles on the road and no responsibility for ensuring cleanliness. That burden is borne entirely by the broker and most brokers in the past have shown that they have a high regard for their vehicles and they have every reason to keep them running and in good condition. In fact, inspecting the fleet becomes much easier for management when they do not have to attend to the myriad of other details that goes into running a company-owned fleet.

Shifting Ownership Burden

Brokers tend to be careful drivers. It is their equipment, so they tend to treat it more carefully and have a better understanding of any drivers that they hire to work under them. As such, insurance rates will eventually go to show that careful drivers translates into lower costs for everyone involved. Further, insurance costs can also be minimized by reducing the collision coverage for vehicles. Part of the operational costs paid for by the brokers could be used to maintain a collision fund to help pay for repairs when needed while greatly reducing insurance costs, which shall be discussed in further detail shortly.

Better Drivers Result

Because brokers help so much to reduce costs across-the board, operational fees (the cost charged to the broker on a daily or weekly basis) can be reduced to an absolute minimum. This ensures that most brokers will succeed in their investment and will have an added incentive to add taxis at their earliest opportunity.

Fees Minimized

With brokers acting as owner-operators, another unique opportunity presents itself for use, that of eliminating a paid dispatch system. Since brokers are experienced drivers and have an investment in the company, they can be utilized as dispatchers for the company. Once again, the cost savings are substantial and using brokers as dispatchers is a good way to promote a

Rotating Dispatch System

solid working relationship among the members of the company. Teamwork is a foreign concept to many drivers now working under exploitive conditions. Having brokers dispatch taxis while using a zone system is not only workable, but more equitable to the drivers because it reduces the possibility of corruption and gives them an opportunity to be continuously trained in all facets of the business.

COMPANY ORGANIZATION

The company shall be organized with the president of the company overseeing total operations and the vice-president or operations director handling administrative duties. There may or may not be office personnel to contend with, but that will all be handled administratively by the vice-president or operations director. There is no need for mechanics, dispatchers (if using rotating dispatch set-up), or schedulers. All of those duties would be eliminated by the change in company structure resulting from using a brokered system..

PROPOSED METHOD OF FINANCING

Conventional bank financing seems likely due to the collateral that can be presented as security for the loan. This loan security should be enough to get the financing necessary to fund the start-up. In the unlikely event that it does not, a private stock distribution could provide for optional financing.

REVENUE AND CASH FLOW PROJECTIONS

Operational Fees and Their Impact

The revenue from taxi operations is relatively easy to project. All revenue is based on one factor, the operational fee charged to the brokers. The initial figure given for start-up purposes is $250.00 per week per vehicle to be paid on a daily $50.00 basis for five days. This is $90.00 a week less than all of the other companies in town and is highly competitive. Not only that, but since the fleet would be comprised entirely of brokers, this fee could be adjusted downwards from the first day of operation. When brokers in other companies see lower fees at Lakeview, they will be inclined to bring their cars over. Any time fees were further lowered, a ripple effect would be likely to occur and make bringing over brokers from other companies highly likely. Because the competition could not compete with these lower fees due to their much higher cost structure, they would be placed under tremendous pressure just to continue operations. Bringing over brokers would also mean automatically attracting more customers as some drivers bring with them a certain volume of customers. There is no telling how low operational fees could go with enough volume.

Revenue Formula

The revenue formula for Lakeview Taxi is as follows:

$250.00 x number of vehicles x per week = total revenue per week

The competition (one company) is currently running 56 taxis in the Toledo area. Using the above formula, we arrive at a revenue of $14,000.00 per week, or $56,000 per month, or $728,000.00 per year. Even though the start-up number of taxis would be closer to 10 vehicles, there is still a weekly gross profit potential of $2500.00 or $10,000 per month. Given Toledo size and potential development, it could easily support a taxi fleet of 300 or more within five years. The potential is there and growing every day.

Cash flow in a taxi company is good. The revenue is dependable and stable and is affected by only a couple of problems. One is that some cars have to be given downtime to help with time spent off of the road. Usually only a token amount is collected. This is a minor factor, but worth mentioning from a cash flow standpoint. This factor is mitigated somewhat by the way fees are charged. Because they are due on Friday for the previous five days, weekends are always free for drivers and many would see that time as an ideal opportunity to effect repairs on their vehicle. Of greater concern is the charge account problem. Drivers and brokers alike are used to receiving their money or credit for charges right away while the charge accounts sometimes have a thirty or sixty day turnaround. This problem could be solved or lessened in one of several ways. Those ways are examined below:

Cash Flow

Charge customers could be assessed a fee for the extension of credit by the taxi company. Extending credit is not as necessary as in the taxi business as in some industries; however, a significant portion of package revenue does come in the form of charge accounts, so it is useful to a degree. The fee could be nominal, in the 5% to 10% range for most customers. This money would be placed in a pool to fund payout to brokers and drivers.

Customer Charged

Brokers could be assessed a fee ranging from 10% to 15% of the charge and that money could be used in the same pool as the one described previously, giving the charge pool a combined rate of 15% to 25%. This pool would be self-financing and would soon build up an incredible reserve of equity in the company. Not only that, but interest derived from the pool could be used as an additional revenue stream down the road. Charges would, out of necessity, have to be small at first and build volume as the fund pool grew of its own accord.

Broker Charged

Charges could be delayed pending payment by the customer. This would be the most unattractive option since the paperwork generated and the broker dissatisfaction would work against this option. A legitimate argument could be made for delaying payment, but this would likely become a contentious issue if presented.

Delayed Payment

Despite the problems just presented, for the most part, cash flow is easier to manage in this business than in many others, and cash flow at Lakeview Taxi would help get the business launched and running with almost instant revenue at start-up.

An additional source of revenue at start-up is the down payments brokers must make to place vehicles on the road. Brokers are currently paying $2000.00 per vehicle at the competition to put a car on the road. These down payments are supposed to cover insurance, cost of radios and meters, and miscellaneous expenses. The fact of the matter is that this is an additional source of revenue for the company at start-up because the costs associated with placing a vehicle on the road are often much less than what is charged to the broker.

Added Revenue

The start-up costs for running a taxi company is high for several reasons. These reasons are explained in detail below:

START-UP COSTS

Insurance: This is the highest cost factor involved in running the taxi company and the greatest hindrance in getting started. Taxis are usually insured at a rate high enough to account for a weekly charge. Taxi insurance is hard to obtain and is billed at between $60.00 and $100.00 per week to the company. This type of coverage is not even first class insurance, as the market for this type of insurance is so small. Other companies' careless use of taxi insurance has lead to the high rates. It is a challenge coming up with the premium down payment, which is usually set at around 20% (partially offset by broker down payments) of the total annual policy. Once insurance is obtained, however, the Lakeview Taxi system would eventually drive rates down in regards to our particular company due to the careful screening and other safe driving incentives mentioned earlier. Still, the obstacle is formidable, but not insurmountable.

Licensing: The cost of licensing is roughly $3000.00 per year and is not a problem if all of the taxis are painted and equipped for inspection.

Office Costs: Would be minimal. The customer never sees the office and therefore the primary consideration for space is simply a location with plenty of parking. The cost for space like the type that is being described here would be roughly $1000.00 per month.

Radios: This cost would also be borne by the broker at start-up, and would be minimal for the company.

Tower and Frequency Allocation: Would be minimal due to the fact that all tower operators wish to have their radio equipment purchased and will cut down the cost of tower space for exclusive purchasing of their equipment.

Meters: Are paid for by the brokers and installed by a servicing company. The meters are then set at a rate determined by the city.

Miscellaneous Costs: Will be estimated and broken down separately.

FINANCIAL DATA

The following financial data is presented as basic information and is not as complete as that following a financial audit by a certified professional. Please bear in mind that the data presented is only an estimate.

CONCLUSION

Lakeview Taxi is a viable service company that could provide great benefits to the city and generate large profits for the owners. It is completely possible to start this business with a small investment and produce large returns soon after its inception. The writers of this plan urge you to review the following information and if there is any that you feel is incomplete or inexplicable, please bring it to our attention. We can provide for transportation needs of the city not only now, but in years to come. Thank you for taking time to review this plan.

Assets (at market valuation)

Cash on hand	2400	
Stocks	1750	
Fixtures	3000	
Furnishings	6000	
Gun Collect.	4200	
Motorcycle	7000	
Car, Camry	18,000	
Residence	122,000	
Total Assets		164,350

Liabilities

First mortgage	76,000	
Auto loan	6,000	
Credit Cards	9,200	
Misc. Loans	6,700	
Misc. Debt	13,900	
Total Liabilities		111,800
Net Worth		52,550
Total Liabilities and Net		164,350

...continued

**Profit and
Loss By Month**

	January	February	March	April	May	June	July
Expenses							
Rent	1000	1000	1000	100	1000	1000	1000
Advertisi	150	150	150	150	150	150	150
Utilities	100	100	100	100	100	100	100
Wages	0	0	0	0	0	0	0
Insuranc	3000	3000	3000	3000	3000	3000	3000
Supplies	50	50	50	50	50	50	50
Licenses	250	250	250	250	250	250	250
Office	0	0	0	0	0	0	0
Radio	0	0	0	0	0	0	0
Tower	120	120	120	120	120	120	120
Misc.	300	300	300	300	300	300	300
	4970	4970	4970	4970	4970	4970	4970

August	Septemb	October	Novembe	Decembe	Total
1000	1000	1000	1000	1000	12,000
150	150	150	150	150	1,800
100	100	100	100	100	1,200
0	0	0	0	0	0
3000	3000	3000	3000	3000	36,000
50	50	50	50	50	600
250	250	250	250	250	3,000
0	0	0	0	0	0
0	0	0	0	0	0
120	120	120	120	120	1,440
300	300	300	300	300	3,600
4970	4970	4970	4970	4970	59,640

Profit before taxes   79,860

Appendix A - Business Plan Template

Business Plan Template

USING THIS TEMPLATE

A business plan carefully spells out a company's projected course of action over a period of time, usually the first two to three years after the start-up. In addition, banks, lenders, and other investors examine the information and financial documentation before deciding whether or not to finance a new business venture. Therefore, a business plan is an essential tool in obtaining financing and should describe the business itself in detail as well as all important factors influencing the company, including the market, industry, competition, operations and management policies, problem solving strategies, financial resources and needs, and other vital information. The plan enables the business owner to anticipate costs, plan for difficulties, and take advantage of opportunities, as well as design and implement strategies that keep the company running as smoothly as possible.

This template has been provided as a model to help you construct your own business plan. Please keep in mind that there is no single acceptable format for a business plan, and that this template is in no way comprehensive, but serves as an example.

The business plans provided in this section are fictional and have been used by small business agencies as models for clients to use in compiling their own business plans.

GENERIC BUSINESS PLAN

Main headings included below are topics that should be covered in a comprehensive business plan. They include:

Business Summary

Purpose
Provides a brief overview of your business, succinctly highlighting the main ideas of your plan.

Includes
- Name and Type of Business
- Description of Product/Service
- Business History and Development
- Location
- Market
- Competition
- Management
- Financial Information
- Business Strengths and Weaknesses
- Business Growth

Table of Contents

Purpose

Organized in an Outline Format, the Table of Contents illustrates the selection and arrangement of information contained in your plan.

Includes

○ Topic Headings and Subheadings
○ Page Number References

Business History and Industry Outlook

Purpose

Examines the conception and subsequent development of your business within an industry specific context.

Includes

○ Start-up Information
○ Owner/Key Personnel Experience
○ Location
○ Development Problems and Solutions
○ Investment/Funding Information
○ Future Plans and Goals
○ Market Trends and Statistics
○ Major Competitors
○ Product/Service Advantages
○ National, Regional, and Local Economic Impact

Product/Service

Purpose

Introduces, defines,and details the product and/or service that inspired the information of your business.

Includes

○ Unique Features
○ Niche Served
○ Market Comparison
○ Stage of Product/Service Development
○ Production
○ Facilities, Equipment, and Labor
○ Financial Requirements
○ Product/Service Life Cycle
○ Future Growth

Market Examination

Purpose
Assessment of product/service applications in relation to consumer buying cycles.

Includes
- Target Market
- Consumer Buying Habits
- Product/Service Applications
- Consumer Reactions
- Market Factors and Trends
- Penetration of the Market
- Market Share
- Research and Studies
- Cost
- Sales Volume and Goals

Competition

Purpose
Analysis of Competitors in the Marketplace.

Includes
- Competitor Information
- Product/Service Comparison
- Market Niche
- Product/Service Strengths and Weaknesses
- Future Product/Service Development

Marketing

Purpose
Identifies promotion and sales strategies for your product/service.

Includes
- Product/Service Sales Appeal
- Special and Unique Features
- Identification of Customers
- Sales and Marketing Staff
- Sales Cycles
- Type of Advertising/Promotion
- Pricing
- Competition
- Customer Services

Operations

Purpose

Traces product/service development from production/inception to the market environment.

Includes

- ◯Cost Effective Production Methods
- ◯Facility
- ◯Location
- ◯Equipment
- ◯Labor
- ◯Future Expansion

Administration and Management

Purpose

Offers a statement of your management philosophy with an in-depth focus on processes and procedures.

Includes

- ◯Management Philosophy
- ◯Structure of Organization
- ◯Reporting System
- ◯Methods of Communication
- ◯Employee Skills and Training
- ◯Employee Needs and Compensation
- ◯Work Environment
- ◯Management Policies and Procedures
- ◯Roles and Responsibilities

Key Personnel

Purpose

Describes the unique backgrounds of principle employees involved in business.

Includes

- ◯Owner(s)/Employee Education and Experience
- ◯Positions and Roles
- ◯Benefits and Salary
- ◯Duties and Responsibilities
- ◯Objectives and Goals

Potential Problems and Solutions

Purpose
Discussion of problem solving strategies that change issues into opportunities.

Includes
- Risks
- Litigation
- Future Competition
- Economic Impact
- Problem Solving Skills

Financial Information

Purpose
Secures needed funding and assistance through worksheets and projections detailing financial plans, methods of repayment, and future growth opportunities.

Includes
- Financial Statements
- Bank Loans
- Methods of Repayment
- Tax Returns
- Start-up Costs
- Projected Income (3 years)
- Projected Cash Flow (3 Years)
- Projected Balance Statements (3 years)

Appendices

Purpose
Supporting documents used to enhance your business proposal.

Includes
- Photographs of product, equipment, facilities, etc.
- Copyright/Trademark Documents
- Legal Agreements
- Marketing Materials
- Research and or Studies
- Operation Schedules
- Organizational Charts
- Job Descriptions
- Resumes
- Additional Financial Documentation

Food Distributor

FICTIONAL BUSINESS PLAN

COMMERCIAL FOODS, INC.

3003 Avondale Ave.
Knoxville, TN 37920

October 31, 1992

This plan demonstrates how a partnership can have a positive impact on a new business. It demonstrates how two individuals can carve a niche in the specialty foods market by offering gourmet foods to upscale restaurants and fine hotels. This plan is fictional and has not been used to gain funding from a bank or other lending institution.

- STATEMENT OF PURPOSE

- DESCRIPTION OF THE BUSINESS

- MANAGEMENT

- PERSONNEL

- LOCATION

- PRODUCTS AND SERVICES

- THE MARKET

- COMPETITION

- SUMMARY

- INCOME STATEMENT

- FINANCIAL STATEMENTS

FOOD DISTRIBUTOR
BUSINESS PLAN

STATEMENT OF PURPOSE

Commercial Food, Inc. seeks a loan of $75,000 to establish a new business. This sum together with $5,000 equity investment by the principals will be used as follows:

Merchandise inventory	$25,000
Office fixture/equipment	12,000
Warehouse equipment	14,000
One delivery truck	10,000
Working capital	39,000
Total	**$100,000**

DESCRIPTION OF THE BUSINESS

Commercial Foods, Inc. will be a distributor of specialty food service products to hotels and upscale restaurants in the geographical area in a 50 mile radius of Knoxville. Richard Roberts will direct the sales effort and John Williams will manage the warehouse operation and the office. One delivery truck will be used initially with a second truck added in the third year.

We expect to begin operation of the business within 30 days after securing the requested financing.

MANAGEMENT

A. Richard Roberts is a native of Memphis, Tennessee. He is a graduate of Memphis State University with a Bachelor's degree from the School of Business. After graduation, he worked for a major manufacturer of specialty food service products as a detail sales person for five years and for the past three years, he has served as a product sales manager for this firm.

B. John Williams is a native of Nashville, Tennessee. He holds a B.S. Degree in Food Technology from the University of Tennessee. His career includes five years as a product development chemist in gourmet food products and five years as operations manager for a food service distributor.

Both men are healthy and energetic. Their backgrounds complement each other which will ensure the success of Commercial Foods, Inc. They will set policies together and personnel decisions will be made jointly. Initial salaries for the owners will be $1,000 per month for the first few years. The spouses of both principals are successful in the business world and earn enough to support the families.

They have engaged the services of Foster Jones, CPA, and William Hale, Attorney to assist them in an advisory capacity.

PERSONNEL

The firm will employ one delivery truck driver at a wage of $8.00 per hour. One office worker will be employed at $7.50 per hour. One part-time employee will be used in the office at $5.00 per hour. The driver will load and unload his own trucks. Mr. Williams will assist in the warehouse operation as needed to assist one stock person at $7.00 per hour. An additional delivery truck and driver will be added the third year.

LOCATION

The firm will lease a 20,000 square foot building at 3003 Avondale Ave., in Knoxville, which contains warehouse and office areas equipped with two-door truck docks. The annual rental is $9,000. The building was previously used as a food service warehouse and very little modification to the building will be required.

The firm will offer specialty food service products such as soup bases, dessert mixes, sauce bases, pastry mixes, spices, and flavors, normally used by upscale restaurants and nice hotels. We are going after a niche in the market with high quality gourmet products. There is much less competition in this market than in standard run of the mill food service products. Through their work experiences, the principals have contacts with supply sources and with local chefs.

PRODUCTS AND SERVICES

We know from our market survey that there are over 200 hotels and upscale restaurants in the area we plan to serve. Customers will be attracted by a direct sales approach. We will offer samples of our products and product application data on use of our products in the finished prepared foods. We will cultivate the chefs in these establishments. The technical background of John Williams will be especially useful here.

THE MARKET

We find that we will be only distributor in the area offering a full line of gourmet food service products. Other foodservice distributors offer only a few such items in conjunction with their standard product line. Our survey shows that many of the chefs are ordering products from Atlanta and Memphis because of lack of adequate local supply.

COMPETITION

Commercial Foods, Inc. will be established as a foodservice distributor of specialty food in Knoxville. The principals, with excellent experience in the industry are seeking a $75,000 loan to establish the business. The principals are investing $25,000 as equity capital.

SUMMARY

The business will be set up as an "S" Corporation with each principal owning 50% of the common stock in the corporation.

Attached is a three year pro forma income statement we believe to be conservative. Also attached are personal financial statements of the principals and a projected cash flow statement for the first year.

	1st Year	2nd Year	3rd Year
Gross Sales	300,000	400,000	500,000
Less Allowances	1,000	1,000	2,000
Net Sales	299,000	399,000	498,000
Cost of Goods Sold	179,400	239,400	298,800
Gross Margin	119,600	159,600	199,200
Operating Expenses			
Utilities	1,200	1,500	1,700
Salaries	76,000	79,000	102,000
Payroll Taxes/Benefits	9,100	9,500	13,200
Advertising	3,000	4,500	5,000
Office Supplies	1,500	2,000	2,500
Insurance	1,200	1,500	1,800
Maintenance	1,000	1,500	2,000
Outside Services	3,000	3,000	3,000
Whse Supplies/Trucks	6,000	7,000	10,000
Telephone	900	1,000	1,200
Rent	9,000	9,500	9,900
Depreciation	2,500	2,000	3,000
Total Expenses	114,400	122,000	155,300
Other Expenses			
Bank Loan Payment	15,000	15,000	15,000
Bank Loan Interest	6,000	5,000	4,000
Total Expenses	**120,400**	**142,000**	**174,300**
Net Profit (Loss)	**(800)**	**17,600**	**24,900**

PRO FORMA INCOME STATEMENT

FINANCIAL STATEMENT I

Assets		Liabilities	
Cash	15,000		
1991 Olds	11,000	Unpaid Balance	8,000
Residence	140,000	Mortgage	105,000
Mutual Funds	12,000	Credit Cards	500
Furniture	5,000	Note Payable	4,000
Merck Stock	10,000		
	182,200		117,500
Net Worth		**64,700**	
	182,200		**182,200**

FINANCIAL STATEMENT II

Assets		Liabilities	
Cash	5,000		
1992 Buick Auto	15,000	Unpaid Balance	12,000
Residence	120,000	Mortgage	100,000
U.S. Treasury Bonds	5,000	Credit Cards	500
Home Furniture	4,000	Note Payable	2,500
AT&T Stock	3,000		
	147,000		115,000
Net Worth		**32,000**	
	147,000		**147,000**

Hardware Store

FICTIONAL BUSINESS PLAN

OSHKOSH HARDWARE, INC

123 Main St.
Oshkosh, WI 54901

June 1994

The following plan outlines how a small hardware store can survive competition from large discount chains by offering products and providing expert advice in the use of any product it sells. This plan is fictional and has not used to gain funding from a bank or other lending institution.

EXECUTIVE SUMMARY

Oshkosh Hardware, Inc. is a new corporation which is going to establish a retail hardware store in a strip mall in Oshkosh, Wisconsin. The store will sell hardware of all kinds, quality tools, paint and housewares. The business will make revenue and a profit by servicing its customers not only with needed hardware but also with expert advice in the use of any product it sells.

Oshkosh Hardware, Inc. will be operated by its sole shareholder, James Smith. The company will have a total of four employees. It will sell its products in the local market. Customers will buy our products because we will provide free advice on the use of all of our products and will also furnish a full refund warranty.

Oshkosh Hardware, Inc. will sell its products in the Oshkosh store staffed by three sales representatives. No additional employees will be needed to achieve its short and long range goals. The primary short range goal is to open the store by October 1, 1994. In order to achieve this goal a lease must be signed by July 1, 1994 and the complete inventory ordered by August 1, 1994.

Mr. James Smith will invest $30,000 in the business. In addition the company will have to borrow $150,000 during the first year to cover the investment in inventory, accounts receivable, and furniture and equipment. The company will be profitable after six months of operation and should be able to start repayment of the loan in the second year.

THE BUSINESS

The business will sell hardware of all kinds, quality tools, paint, and housewares. We will purchase our products from three large wholesale buying groups.

In general our customers are homeowners who do their own repair and maintenance, hobbyists, and housewives. Our business is unique in that we will have a complete line of all hardware items and will be able to get special orders by overnight delivery. The business makes revenue and profits by servicing our customers not only with needed hardware but also with expert advice in the use of any product we sell. Our major costs for bringing our products to market are cost of merchandise of 36%, salaries of $45,000, and occupancy costs of $60,000.

Oshkosh Hardware, Inc.'s retail outlet will be located at 1524 Frontage Road, which is in a newly developed retail center of Oshkosh. Our location helps facilitate accessibility from all parts of town and reduces our delivery costs. The store will occupy 7500 square feet of space. The major equipment involved in our business is counters and shelving, a computer, a paint mixing machine, and a truck.

THE MARKET

Oshkosh Hardware, Inc. will operate in the local market. There are 15,000 potential customers in this market area. We have three competitors who control approximately 98% of the market at present. We feel we can capture 25% of the market within the next four years. Our major reason for believing this is that our staff is technically competent to advise our customers in the correct use of all products we sell.

After a careful market analysis we have determined that approximately 60% of our customers are men and 40% are women. The percentage of customers that fall into the following age categories are:

Under 16:	0%
17-21:	5%
22-30:	30%
31-40:	30%

41-50:	20%
51-60:	10%
61-70:	5%
Over 70:	0%

The reasons our customers prefer our products is our complete knowledge of their use and our full refund warranty.

We get our information about what products our customers want by talking to existing customers. There seems to be an increasing demand for our product. The demand for our product is increasing in size based on the change in population characteristics.

At Oshkosh Hardware, Inc. we will employ 3 sales people and will not need any additional personnel to achieve our sales goals. These salespeople will need several years experience in home repair and power tool usage. We expect to attract 30% of our customers from newspaper ads, 5% of our customers from local directories, 5% of our customers from the yellow pages, 10% of our customers from family and friends and 50% of our customers from current customers. The most cost effect source will be current customers. In general our industry is growing.

SALES

We would evaluate the quality of our management staff as being excellent. Our manager is experienced and very motivated to achieve the various sales and quality assurance objectives we have set. We will use a management information system which produces key inventory, quality assurance and sales data on a weekly basis. All data is compared to previously established goals for that week and deviations are the primary focus of the management staff.

MANAGEMENT

The short term goals of our business are:

**GOALS
IMPLEMENTATION**

    1. Open the store by October 1, 1994
    2. Reach our breakeven point in two months
    3. Have sales of $100,000 in the first six months

In order to achieve our first short term goal we must:

    1. Sign the lease by July 1, 1994
    2. Order a complete inventory by August 1, 1994

In order to achieve our second short term goal we must:

    1. Advertise extensively in Sept. and Oct.
    2. Keep expenses to a minimum

In order to achieve our third short term goal we must:

    1. Promote power tool sales for the Christmas season
    2. Keep good customer traffic in Jan. and Feb.

The long term goals for our business are:

    1. Obtain sales volume of $600,000 in three years
    2. Become the largest hardware dealer in the city
    3. Open a second store in Fond du Lac

The most important thing we must do in order to achieve the long term goals for our business is to develop a highly profitable business with excellent cash flow.

FINANCE

Oshkosh Hardware, Inc. Faces some potential threats or risks to our business. They are discount house competition. We believe we can avoid or compensate for this by providing quality products complimented by quality advice on the use of every product we sell. The financial projections we have prepared are located at the end of this document.

JOB DESCRIPTION: GENERAL MANAGER

Sales

The General Manager of the business of the corporation will be the president of the corporation. He will be responsible for the complete operation of the retail hardware store which is owned by the corporation. A detailed description of his duties and responsibilities is as follows:

Train and supervise the three sales people. Develop programs to motivate and compensate these employees. Coordinate advertising and sales promotion effects to achieve sales totals as outlined in budget. Oversee purchasing function and inventory control procedures to insure adequate merchandise at all times at a reasonable cost.

Finance

Prepare monthly and annual budgets. Secure adequate line of credit from local banks. Supervise office personnel to insure timely preparation of records, statements, all government reports, control of receivables and payables and monthly financial statements.

Administration

Perform duties as required in the areas of personnel, building leasing and maintenance, licenses and permits and public relations.

QUARTERLY FORECASTED BALANCE SHEETS

	Beg Bal	1st Qtr	2nd Qtr	3rd Qtr	4th Qtr
Assets					
Cash	30,000	418	(463)	(3,574)	4,781
Accounts Receivable	0	20,000	13,333	33,333	33,333
Inventory	0	48,000	32,000	80,000	80,000
Other Current Assets	0	0	0	0	0
Total Current Assets	30,000	68,418	44,870	109,759	118,114
Land	0	0	0	0	0
Building & Improvements	0	0	0	0	0
Furniture & Equipment	0	75,000	75,000	75,000	75,000
Total Fixed Assets	0	75,000	75,000	75,000	75,000
Less Accum. Depreciation	0	1,875	3,750	5,625	7,500
Net Fixed Assets	0	73,125	71,250	69,375	67,500
Intangible Assets	0	0	0	0	0
Less Amortization	0	0	0	0	0
Net Intangible Assets	0	0	0	0	0
Other Assets	0	0	0	0	0
Total Assets	**30,000**	**141,543**	**116,120**	**179,134**	**185,614**

	Beg Bal	1st Qtr	2nd Qtr	3rd Qtr	4th Qtr
Liabilities and Shareholders' Equity					
Short-Term Debt	0	0	0	0	0
Accounts Payable	0	12,721	10,543	17,077	17,077
Dividends Payable	0	0	0	0	0
Income Taxes Payable	0	(1,031)	(2,867)	(2,355)	(1,843)
Accured Compensation	0	1,867	1,867	1,867	1,867
Other Current Liabilities	0	0	0	0	0
Total Current Liabilities	0	13,557	9,543	16,589	17,101
Long-Term Debt	0	110,000	110,000	160,000	160,000
Other Non-Current Liabilities	0	0	0	0	0
Total Liabilities	0	123,557	119,543	176,589	177,101
Common Stock	30,000	30,000	30,000	30,000	30,000
Retained Earnings	0	(12,014)	(33,423)	(27,455)	(21,487)
Shareholders' Equity	30,000	17,986	(3,423)	2,545	8,513
Total Liabilities & Shareholders' Equity	30,000	141,543	116,120	179,134	185,614

	Beg Actual	1st Qtr	2nd Qtr	3rd Qtr	4th Qtr	Total
Total Sales	0	60,000	40,000	100,000	100,000	300,000
Goods/Services	0	21,600	14,400	36,000	36,000	108,000
Gross Profit	0	38,400	25,600	64,000	64,000	192,000
Operating Expenses	0	47,645	45,045	52,845	52,845	198,380
Fixed Expenses						
Interest	0	1,925	1,925	2,800	2,800	9,450
Depreciation	0	1,875	1,875	1,875	1,875	7,500
Amortization	0	0	0	0	0	0
Total Fixed Expenses	0	3,800	3,800	4,675	4,675	16,950
Operating Profit (Loss)	0	(13,045)	(23,245)	6,480	6,480	(23,330)

QUARTERLY FORECASTED STATEMENTS OF EARNINGS AND RETAINED EARNINGS

BUSINESS PLAN TEMPLATE

	Beg Actual	1st Qtr	2nd Qtr	3rd Qtr	4th Qtr	Total
Other Income (Expense)	0	0	0	0	0	0
Interest Income	0	0	0	0	0	0
Earnings (Loss) Before Taxes	0	(13,045)	(23,245)	6,480	6,480	(23,330)
Income Taxes	0	(1,031)	(1,836)	512	512	(1,843)
Net Earnings	0	(12,014)	(21,409)	5,968	5,968	(21,487)
Retained Earnings, Beginning	0	0	(12,014)	(33,423)	(27,455)	0
Less Dividends	0	0	0	0	0	0
Retained Earnings, Ending	0	(12,014)	(33,423)	(27,455)	(21,487)	(21,487)

QUARTERLY FORECASTED STATEMENTS OF CHANGES IN FINANCIAL POSITION

	Beg Bal	1st Qtr	2nd Qtr	3rd Qtr	4th Qtr	Total
Sources (Uses) of Cash						
Net Earnings (Loss)	0	(12,014)	(21,409)	5,968	5,968	(21,487)
Depreciation & Amortization	0	1,875	1,875	1,875	1,875	7,500
Cash Provided by Operations	0	(10,139)	(19,534)	7,834	7,834	(13,987)
Dividends	0	0	0	0	0	0
Cash Provided by (Used For) Changes in						
Accounts Receivable	0	(20,000)	6,667	(20,000)	0	(33,333)
Inventory	0	(48,000)	16,000	(48,000)	0	(80,000)
Other Current Assets	0	0	0	0	0	0
Accounts Payable	0	12,	721	(2,178)	6,534 0	17,077
Income Taxes	0	(1,031)	(1,836)	512	512	(1,843)
Accrued Compensation	0	1,867	0	0	0	1,867
Dividends Payable	0	0	0	0	0	0
Other Current Liabilities	0	0	0	0	0	0

	Beg Bal	1st Qtr	2nd Qtr	3rd Qtr	4th Qtr	Total
Other Assests	0	0	0	0	0	0
Net Cash Provided by (Used For)						
Operating Activities	0	(54,443)	18,653	(60,954)	512	(96,233)
Investment Transactions						
Furniture & Equipment	0	(75,000)	0	0	0	(75,000)
Land	0	0	0	0	0	0
Building & Improvements	0	0	0	0	0	0
Intangible Assets	0	0	0	0	0	0
Net Cash From Investment Transactions	0	(75,000)	0	0	0	(75,000)
Financing Transactions						
Short-Term Debt	0	0	0	0	0	0
Long-Term Debt	0	110,000	0	50,000	0	160,000
Other Non-Current Liabilities	0	0	0	0	0	0
Sale of Common Stock	30,000	0	0	0	0	0
Net Cash from Financing Transactions	30,000	110,000	0	50,000	0	160,000
Net Increase (Decrease) in Cash	30,000	(29,582)	(881)	(3,111)	8,355	(25,219)
Cash, Beginning of Period	0	30,000	418	(463)	(3,574)	30,000
Cash, End of Period	30,000	418	(463)	(3,574)	4,781	4,781

**FINANCIAL
RATIO ANALYSIS**

	Beg Act	1st Qtr	2nd Qtr	3rd Qtr	4th Qtr
Overall Performance					
Return on Equity	0.00	(66.80)	625.45	234.50	70.10
Return on Total Assets	0.00	(8.49)	(18.44)	3.33	3.22
Operating Return	0.00	(9.22)	(20.02)	3.62	3.49
Profitability Measures					
Gross Profit Percent	0.00	64.00	64.00	64.00	64.00
Profit Margin (AIT)	0.00	(20.02)	(53.52)	5.97	5.97
Operating Income per Share	0.00	0.00	0.00	0.00	0.00
Earnings per Share	0.00	0.00	0.00	0.00	0.00
Test of Investment Utilization					
Asset Turnover	0.00	0.42	0.34	0.56	0.54
Equity Turnover	0.00	3.34	(11.69)	39.29	11.75
Fixed Asset Turnover	0.00	0.82	0.56	1.44	1.48
Average Collection Period	0.00	30.00	30.00	30.00	30.00
Days Inventory	0.00	200.00	200.00	200.00	200.00
Inventory Turnover	0.00	0.45	0.45	0.45	0.45
Working Capital Turns	0.00	1.09	1.13	1.07	0.99
Test of Financial Condition					
Current Ratio	0.00	5.05	4.70	6.62	6.91
Quick Ratio	0.00	1.51	1.35	1.79	2.23
Working Capital Ratio	1.00	0.43	0.33	0.57	0.60
Dividend Payout	0.00	0.00	0.00	0.00	0.00
Financial Leverage					
Total Assets	1.00	7.87	(33.92)	70.39	21.80

	Beg Act	1st Qtr	2nd Qtr	3rd Qtr	4th Qtr
Debt/Equity	0.00	6.87	(34.92)	69.39	20.80
Debt to Total Assets	0.00	0.87	1.03	0.99	0.95

Year-End Equity History

	Beg Act	1st Qtr	2nd Qtr	3rd Qtr	4th Qtr
Shares Outstanding	0	0	0	0	0
Market Price per Share (@20x's earnings)	0.00	0.00	0.00	0.00	0.00
Book Value per Share	0.00	0.00	0.00	0.00	0.00

Altman Analysis Ratio

	Beg Act	1st Qtr	2nd Qtr	3rd Qtr	4th Qtr
1.2x (1)	1.20	0.47	0.37	0.62	0.65
1.4x (2)	0.00	(0.12)	(0.40)	(0.21)	(0.16)
3.3x (3)	0.00	(0.35)	(0.72)	0.07	0.07
0.6x (4)	0.00	0.00	0.00	0.00	0.00
1.0x (5)	0.00	0.42	0.34	0.56	0.54
Z Value	1.20	.042	(.041)	1.04	1.10

DETAILS FOR QUARTERLY STATEMENTS OF EARNINGS

	Beg Act	1st Qtr	2nd Qtr	3rd Qtr	4th Qtr	Total	% Sales	Fixed
Sales								
Dollars Sales Forecasted								
Product 1	0	60,000	40,000	100,000	100,000	300,000		
Product 2	0	0	0	0	0	0		
Product 3	0	0	0	0	0	0		
Product 4	0	0	0	0	0	0		
Product 5	0	0	0	0	0	0		
Product 6	0	0	0	0	0	0		
Total Sales	0	60,000	40,000	100,000	100,000	300,000		

DETAILS FOR QUARTERLY STATEMENTS OF EARNINGS
...continued

	Beg Act	1st Qtr	2nd Qtr	3rd Qtr	4th Qtr	Total	%Sales	Fixed
Cost of Sales								
Dollar Cost Forecasted								
Product 1	0	21,600	14,400	36,000	36,000	108,000	36.00%	0
Product 2	0	0	0	0	0	0	0.00%	0
Product 3	0	0	0	0	0	0	0.00%	0
Product 4	0	0	0	0	0	0	0.00%	0
Product 5	0	0	0	0	0	0	0.00%	0
Product 6	0	0	0	0	0	0	0.00%	0
Total Cost of Sales	0	21,600	14,400	36,000	36,000	108,000		
Operating Expenses								
Payroll	0	12,000	12,000	12,000	12,000	48,000	0.00%	12,000
Paroll Taxes	0	950	950	950	950	3,800	0.00%	950
Advertising	0	4,800	3,200	8,000	8,000	24,000	8.00%	0
Automobile Expenses	0	0	0	0	0		0.00%	0
Bad Debts	0	0	0	0	0	0	0.00%	0
Commissions	0	3,000	2,000	5,000	5,000	15,000	5.00%	0
Computer Rental	0	1,200	1,200	1,200	1,200	4,800	0.00%	1,200
Computer Supplies	0	220	220	220	220	880	0.00%	220
Computer Maintenance	0	100	100	100	100	400	0.00%	100
Dealer Training	0	1,000	1,000	1,000	1,000	4,000	0.00%	1,000
Electricity	0	3,000	3,000	3,000	3,000	12,000	0.00%	3,000
Employment Ads and Fees	0	0	0	0	0	0	0.00%	0
Entertainment: Business	0	1,500	1,500	1,500	1,500	6,000	0.00%	1,500
General Insurance	0	800	800	800	800	32,000	0.00%	800
Health & W/C Insurance	0	0	0	0	0	0	.00%	0
Interest: LT Debt	0	2,500	2,500	2,500	2,500	10,000	0.00%	2,500
Legal & Accounting	0	1,500	1,500	1,500	1,500	6,000	0.00%	1,500
Maintenance & Repairs	0	460	460	460	460	1,840	0.00%	460

	Beg Act	1st Qtr	2nd Qtr	3rd Qtr	4th Qtr	Total	%Sales	Fixed
Office Supplies	0	270	270	270	270	1,080	0.00%	270
Postage	0	85	85	85	85	340	0.00%	85
Prof. Development	0	0	0	0	0	0	0.00%	0
Professional Fees	0	1,000	1,000	1,000	1,000	4,000	0.00%	1,000
Rent	0	8,000	8,000	8,000	8,000	32,000	0.00%	8,000
Shows & Conferences	0	0	0	0	0	0	0.00%	0
Subscriptions & Dues	0	285	285	285	285	1,140	0.00%	285
Telephone	0	1,225	1,225	1,225	1,225	4,900	0.00%	1,225
Temporary Employees	0	0	0	0	0	0	0.00%	0
Travel Expenses	0	750	750	750	750	3,000	0.00%	750
Utilities	0	3,000	3,000	3,000	3,000	12,000	0.00%	3,000
Research & Devlpmnt.	0	0	0	0	0	0	0.00%	0
Royalties	0	0	0	0	0	0	0.00%	0
Other 1	0	0	0	0	0	0	0.00%	0
Other 2	0	0	0	0	0	0	0.00%	0
Other 3	0	0	0	0	0	0	0.00%	0
Total Operating Expenses	0	47,645	45,045	52,845	52,845	198,380		
Percent of Sales	0.00	79.41	112.61	52.85	52.85	66.13		

DETAILS FOR QUARTERLY STATEMENT OF EARNINGS
...continued

Appendix - B
Organizations, Agencies and Consultants

Organizations, Agencies, & Consultants

A listing of Associations and Consultants of interest to entrepreneurs, followed by the 10 Small Business Administration Regional Offices, Small Business Development Centers, Service Corps of Retired Executives offices, and Venture Capital & Finance companies.

ASSOCIATIONS

This section contains a listing of associations and other agencies of interest to the small business owner. Entries are listed alphabetically by organization name.

American Association for Consumer
Benefits
PO Box 100279
Fort Worth, Texas 76185
Phone: (800)872-8896
Free: (800)872-8896
Fax: (817)377-5633
William Kirkman, Contact

American Federation of Small
Business
American Small Businesses
Association
1800 N. Kent St., Ste. 910
Arlington, Virginia 22209
Free: (800)235-3298
Vernon Castle, Exec. Dir.

American Society of Independent
Business
c/o Keith Wood
777 Main St., Ste. 1600
Fort Worth, Texas 76102
Phone: (817)870-1880
Keith Wood, Pres.

American Woman's Economic
Development Corporation
71 Vanderbilt Ave., 3rd Fl.
New York, New York 10169
Phone: (212)692-9100
Fax: (212)692-9296
Suzanne Tufts, Pres. & CEO

Association of Small Business
Development Centers
1300 Chain Bridge Rd., Ste. 201
Mc Lean, Virginia 22101-3967

Phone: (703)448-6124
Fax: (703)448-6125
E-mail: jjohns1012@aol.com
Max Summers, Pres.

BEST Employers Association
2515 McCabe Way
Irvine, California 92614
Phone: (714)756-1000
Free: (800)854-7417
Fax: (714)553-1232
E-mail: bestplans@bestplans.com
Donald R. Lawrenz, Exec. Sec.

Business Coalition for Fair
Competition
8421 Frost Way
Annandale, Virginia 22003
Phone: (703)280-4622
Fax: (703)280-0942
E-mail: kentonpi@aol.com
Kenton Pattie, Contact

Business Market Association
4131 N. Central Expy., Ste. 720
Dallas, Texas 75204
Phone: (214)559-3900
Fax: (214)559-4143
R. Mark King, Pres.

Coalition of Americans to Save the
Economy
1100 Connecticut Ave. NW, Ste.
1200
Washington, District of Columbia
20036-4101
Phone: (202)293-1414
Fax: (202)293-1702
Barry Maloney, Treas.

Family Firm Institute
12 Harris St.
Brookline, Massachusetts 02146
Phone: (617)738-1591
Fax: (617)738-4883
Judy L. Green, Ph.D., Exec.Dir.

International Association of Business
701 Highlander Blvd.
Arlington, Texas 76015
Phone: (817)465-2922
Fax: (817)467-5940
Paula Rainey, Pres.

International Association for Business
Organizations
PO Box 30149
Baltimore, Maryland 21270
Phone: (410)581-1373
Rudolph Lewis, Exec. Officer

International Council for Small
Business
c/o Jefferson Smurfit Center for
Entrepreneurial Studies
St. Louis University
3674 Lindell Blvd.
St. Louis, Missouri 63108
Phone: (314)977-3628
Fax: (314)977-3627
E-mail: icsb@sluvca.slu.edu
William I. Dennis, Jr., Pres.

ISBE Employers of America
520 S. Pierce, Ste. 224
Mason City, Iowa 50401
Phone: (515)424-3187
Free: (800)728-3187
Fax: (515)424-1673
Jim Collison, Pres.

National Alliance for Fair
Competition
3 Bethesda Metro Center, Ste. 1100
Bethesda, Maryland 20814
Phone: (410)235-7116
Fax: (410)235-7116
Tony Ponticelli, Exec. Dir.

National Association for Business
Organizations
PO Box 30149
Baltimore, Maryland 21270

Phone: (410)581-1373
Rudolph Lewis, Pres.

National Association of Private
Enterprise
PO Box 612147
Dallas, Texas 75261-2147
Free: (800)223-6273
Fax: (817)332-4525
Heidi Williams, Acct. Exec.

National Association for the Self-
Employed
PO Box 612067
Dallas, Texas 75261-2067
Free: (800)232-NASE
Fax: (800)551-4446
Bennie Thayer, Pres. & CEO

National Association of Small
Business Investment Companies
666 11th St. NW, No. 750
Washington, District of Columbia
20001
Phone: (202)628-5055
Fax: (202)628-5080
E-mail: nasbic@nasbic.org
Lee W. Mercer, Pres.

National Business Association
5151 Belt Line Rd., No. 1150
Dallas, Texas 75240-7545
Phone: (214)458-0900
Free: (800)456-0440
Fax: (214)960-9149
Robert G. Allen, Pres.

National Business Owners
Association
1033 N. Fairfax St., Ste. 402
Alexandria, Virginia 22314
Phone: (202)737-6501
Fax: (703)838-0149
J. Drew Hiatt, Exec. VP

National Council for Industrial
Innovation
National Federation of Independent
Business
53 Century Blvd., Ste. 300
Nashville, Tennessee 37214
Phone: (615)872-5800
Fax: (615)872-5899
Fred Holladay, VP & CFO

National Small Business Benefits
Association
2244 N. Grand Ave. E.
Springfield, Illinois 62702
Phone: (217)753-2558
Fax: (217)753-2558
Les Brewer, Exec. VP

National Small Business United
1155 15th St. NW, Ste. 710
Washington, District of Columbia
20005
Phone: (202)293-8830
Free: (800)345-6728
Fax: (202)872-8543
E-mail: nsbu@nsbu.org
John Paul Galles, Pres.

Network of Small Businesses
5420 Mayfield Rd., Ste. 205
Lyndhurst, Ohio 44124
Phone: (216)442-5600
Fax: (216)449-3227
Irwin Friedman, Chm.

The Score Association
Service Corps of Retired Executives
Association
409 3rd St. SW, 4th Fl.
Washington, District of Columbia
20024
Phone: (202)205-6762
Free: (800)634-0245
Fax: (202)205-7636
W. Kenneth Yancey, Jr., Exec. Dir.

Small Business Assistance Center
554 Main St.
PO Box 15014
Worcester, Massachusetts 01615-
0014
Phone: (508)756-3513
Fax: (508)791-4709
Francis R. Carroll, Pres.

Small Business Foundation of
America
1155 15th St.
Washington, District of Columbia
20005
Phone: (202)223-1103
Fax: (202)476-6534
Regina Tracy, Exec. Dir.

Small Business Legislative Council
1156 15th St. NW, Ste. 510
Washington, District of Columbia
20005
Phone: (202)639-8500
Fax: (202)296-5333
John Satagaj, Pres.

Small Business Network
PO Box 30149
Baltimore, Maryland 21270
Phone: (410)581-1373
E-mail: natibb@ix.netcom.com
Rudolph Lewis, CEO

Small Business Service Bureau
554 Main St.
PO Box 15014
Worcester, Massachusetts 01615-
0014
Phone: (508)756-3513
Fax: (508)791-4709
Francis R. Carroll, Pres.

Small Business Support Center
Association
c/o James S. Ryan
8811 Westheimer Rd., No. 210
Houston, Texas 77063-3617
James S. Ryan, Admin.

Support Services Alliance
PO Box 130
Schoharie, New York 12157-0130
Phone: (518)295-7966
Free: (800)322-3920
Fax: (518)295-8556
Robert M. Marquardt, Pres.

CONSULTANTS

*This section contains a listing of
consultants specializing in small business
development. It is arranged alphabetically
by country, then by state or province, then
by city, then by firm name.*

CANADA

Alberta

Varsity Consulting Group
2-45 Faculty of Business
University of Alberta

Edmonton, Alberta T6G 2R6
Phone: (403)492-2994
Fax: (403)492-5400
Web: http://www.ualberta.ca/
~mbaassoc/vcg

Viro Hospital Consulting
42 Commonwealth Bldg., 9912 - 106
St. NW
Edmonton, Alberta T5K 1C5
Phone: (403)425-3871
Fax: (403)425-3871
E-mail: rpb@freenet.edmonton.ab.ca

British Columbia

SRI Strategic Resources Inc.
4330 Kingsway, Ste. 1600
Burnaby, British Columbia V5H 4G7
Phone: (604)435-0627
Fax: (604)435-2782
E-mail: inquiry@sri.bc.ca
Web: http://www.sri.com

DeBoda & DeBoda
1523 Milford Ave.
Coquitlam, British Columbia
V3J 2V9
Phone: (604)936-4527
Fax: (604)936-4527

The Sage Group Ltd.
980 - 355 Burrard St.
744 W. Haistings, Ste. 410
Vancouver, British Columbia
V6C 1A5
Phone: (604)669-9269
Fax: (604)669-6622

Ontario

Cynton Co.
17 Massey St.
Brampton, Ontario L6S 2V6
Phone: (905)792-7769
Fax: (905)792-8116
E-mail: cynton@usa.net

Begley & Associates
RR 6
Cambridge, Ontario N1R 5S7
Phone: (519)740-3629
Fax: (519)740-3629
E-mail: begley@in.on.ca

Web: http://www.in.on.ca/~begley/
index.htm

Tikkanen-Bradley
RR No.1
Consecon, Ontario K0K 1T0
Phone: (604)669-0583
E-mail: consult@mortimer.com
Web: http://204.191.209/consult/

Task Enterprises
Box 69, RR 2 Hamilton
Flamborough, Ontario L8N 2Z7
Phone: (905)659-0153

HST Group Ltd.
430 Gilmour St.
Ottawa, Ontario K2P 0R8
Phone: (613)236-7303
Fax: (613)236-9893

Harrison Associates
BCE Place
181 Bay Street, Ste. 3740
PO Box 798
Toronto, Ontario M5J 2T3
Phone: (416)364-5441
Fax: (416)364-2875

Ken Wyman & Associates Inc.
64B Shuter St., Ste. 200
Toronto, Ontario M5B 1B1
Phone: (416)362-2926
Fax: (416)362-3039
E-mail: kenwyman@compuserve.com

JPL Business Consultants
82705 Metter Rd.
Wellandport, Ontario L0R 2J0
Phone: (905)386-7450
Fax: (905)386-7450
E-mail:
plamarch@freenet.npiec.on.ca

Quebec

The Zimmar Consulting Partnership
Inc.
Westmount
PO Box 98
Montreal, Quebec H3Z 2T1
Phone: (514)484-1459
Fax: (514)484-3063

UNITED STATES

Alabama

Business Planning Inc.
300 Office Park Dr.
Birmingham, Alabama 35223-2474
Phone: (205)870-7090
Fax: (205)870-7103

Tradebank of Eastern Alabama
546 Broad St., Ste. 3
Gadsden, Alabama 35901
Phone: (205)547-8700
Fax: (205)547-8718
E-mail: mansion@webex.com
Web: http://www.webex.com/~tea

Alaska

AK Business Development Center
3335 Arctic Blvd., Ste. 203
Anchorage, Alaska 99503
Phone: (907)562-0335
Fax: (907)562-6988

Business Matters
PO Box 287
Fairbanks, Alaska 99707
Phone: (907)452-5650

Arizona

Carefree Direct Marketing Corp.
8001 E. Serene St.
PO Box 3737
Carefree, Arizona 85377-3737
Phone: (602)488-4227
Fax: (602)488-2841

Trans Energy Corporation
1739 W. 7th Ave.
Mesa, Arizona 85202
Phone: (602)921-0433
Fax: (602)967-6601
E-mail: aha@getnet.com

CMAS
5125 N. 16th St.
Phoenix, Arizona 85016
Phone: (602)395-1001
Fax: (602)604-8180

Harvey C. Skoog
PO Box 26515
Prescott Valley, Arizona 86312

Phone: (520)772-1714
Fax: (520)772-2814

Louw's Management Corp.
8711 E. Pinnacle Peak Rd., No. 340
Scottsdale, Arizona 85255-3555
Phone: (602)585-7177
Fax: (602)585-5880
E-mail: louws@earthlink.com
Gary L. McLeod
PO Box 230
Sonoita, Arizona 85637
Fax: (602)455-5661

Van Cleve Associates
6932 E. 2nd St.
Tucson, Arizona 85710
Phone: (602)296-2587
Fax: (602)296-2587

California

Thomas E. Church & Associates, Inc.
PO Box 2439
Aptos, California 95001
Phone: (408)662-7950
Fax: (408)662-7955
E-mail: church@ix.netcom.com

Keck & Company Business
Consultants
410 Walsh Rd.
Atherton, California 94027
Phone: (650)854-9588
Fax: (650)854-7240
Web: http://www.keckco.com

Ben W. Laverty III, REA, CEI
4909 Stockdale Hwy., Ste. 132
Bakersfield, California 93309
Phone: (805)837-9933
Fax: (805)837-9936
E-mail: cstc@kern.com
Web: http://www.kern.com/cstc/

Lindquist Consultants-Venture
Planning
225 Arlington Ave.
Berkeley, California 94707
Phone: (510)524-6685
Fax: (510)527-6604

Larson Associates
PO Box 9005
Brea, California 92822

Phone: (714)529-4121
Fax: (714)572-3606

Kremer Management Consulting
PO Box 500
Carmel, California 93921
Phone: (408)626-8311
Fax: (408)624-2663
E-mail: ddkremer@aol.com

JB Associates
21118 Gardena Dr.
Cupertino, California 95014
Phone: (408)257-0214
Fax: (408)257-0216
E-mail: semarang@sirius.com

House Agricultural Consultants
PO Box 1615
Davis, California 95617-1615
Phone: (916)753-3361
Fax: (916)753-0464
E-mail: infoag@houseag.com
Web: http://www.houseag.com/

Technical Management Consultants
3624 Westfall Dr.
Encino, California 91436-4154
Phone: (818)784-0626
Fax: (818)501-5575
E-mail: tmcrs@aol.com

RAINWATER-GISH & Associates,
Business Finance & Development
317 Third St., Ste. 3
Eureka, California 95501
Phone: (707)443-0030
Fax: (707)443-5683

Strategic Business Group
800 Cienaga Dr.
Fullerton, California 92835
Phone: (714)449-1040
Fax: (714)525-1631

Burnes Consulting Group
20537 Wolf Creek Rd.
Grass Valley, California 95949
Phone: (916)346-8188
Fax: (916)346-7704
Free: (800)949-9021
E-mail: ktalk94@aol.com

Pioneer Business Consultants
9042 Garfield Ave., Ste. 312
Huntington Beach, California 92646

Phone: (714)964-7600

MCS Associates
18300 Von Karman, Ste. 1100
Irvine, California 92715
Phone: (714)263-8700
Fax: (714)553-0168
E-mail: mcs@earthlink.net

The Laresis Companies
PO Box 3284
La Jolla, California 92038
Phone: (619)452-2720
Fax: (619)452-8744

RCL & Co.
PO Box 1143
La Jolla, California 92038
Phone: (619)454-8883
Fax: (619)454-8880

General Business Services
3201 Lucas Cir.
Lafayette, California 94549
Phone: (510)283-8272

The Ribble Group
27601 Forbes Rd., Ste. 52
Laguna Niguel, California 92677
Phone: (714)582-1085
Fax: (714)582-6420
E-mail: ribble@deltanet.com

Norris Bernstein, CMC
9309 Marina Pacifica Dr. N
Long Beach, California 90803
Phone: (562)493-5458
Fax: (562)493-5459

Horizon Consulting Services
1315 Garthwick Dr.
Los Altos, California 94024
Phone: (415)967-0906
Fax: (415)967-0906

Brincko Associates, Inc.
1801 Ave. of the Stars, Ste. 1054
Los Angeles, California 90067
Phone: (310)553-4523
Fax: (310)553-6782

F.J. Schroeder & Associates
1926 Westholme Ave.
Los Angeles, California 90025
Phone: (310)470-2655
Fax: (310)470-6378

E-mail: fjsacons@aol.com
Web: http://www.mcninet.com/
GlobalLook/Fjschroe.html

Western Management Associates
8351 Vicksburg Ave.
Los Angeles, California 90045-3924
Phone: (310)645-1091
Fax: (310)645-1092
E-mail: CFOForRent@aol.com
Web: http://www.expert-market.com/
cfoforrent

Darrell Sell and Associates
Los Gatos, California 95030
Phone: (408)354-7794
E-mail: darrell@netcom.com

Leslie J. Zambo
3355 Michael Dr.
Marina, California 93933
Phone: (408)384-7086
Fax: (408)647-4199
E-mail:
104776.1552@compuserve.com

Marketing Services Management
PO Box 1377
Martinez, California 94553
Phone: (510)370-8527
Fax: (510)370-8527
E-mail: markserve@biotechnet.com

William M. Shine Consulting Service
PO Box 127
Moraga, California 94556-0127
Phone: (510)376-6516

W & J Partnership
3450 Bluegrass Court
PO Box 1108
Morgan Hill, California 95038-1108
Phone: (408)779-1714
Fax: (408)778-1305

Palo Alto Management Group, Inc.
2672 Bayshore Pkwy., Ste. 701
Mountain View, California 94043
Phone: (415)968-4374
Fax: (415)968-4245
E-mail: mburwen@pamg.com

The Market Connection
4020 Birch St., Ste. 203
Newport Beach, California 92660
Phone: (714)731-6273
Fax: (714)833-0253

Muller Associates
PO Box 7264
Newport Beach, California 92658
Phone: (714)646-1169
Fax: (714)646-1169

NEXUS - Consultants to Management
PO Box 1531
Novato, California 94948
Phone: (415)897-4400
Fax: (415)898-2252
E-mail: jimnexus@aol.com

Adelphi Communications
Incorporated
PO Box 28831
Oakland, California 94604-8831
Phone: (510)430-7444
Fax: (510)530-3411
Web: http://www.adelphi.com

Intelequest Corp.
722 Gailen Ave.
Palo Alto, California 94303
Phone: (415)968-3443
Fax: (415)493-6954
E-mail: frits@iqix.com

Business Research Consultants, Inc.
66 San Marino Cir.
Rancho Mirage, California 92270
Phone: (760)328-3700
Fax: (760)328-2474
E-mail: jackmcla@aol.com

Bay Area Tax Consultants and
Bayhill Financial Consultants
1150 Bayhill Dr., Ste. 1150
San Bruno, California 94066-3004
Phone: (415)952-8786
Fax: (415)588-4524
E-mail: baytax@compuserve.com
Web: http://www.baytax.com/

California Business Incubation
Network
101 W. Broadway, No. 480
San Diego, California 92101
Phone: (619)237-0559
Fax: (619)237-0521

G.R. Gordetsky Consultants Inc.
11414 Windy Summit Pl.
San Diego, California 92127
Phone: (619)487-4939
Fax: (619)487-5587

Freeman, Sullivan & Co.
131 Steuart St., Ste. 500
San Francisco, California 94105
Phone: (415)777-0707
Fax: (415)777-2420
Free: (800)777-0737
Web: http://www.fsc-research.com

Ideas Unlimited
2151 California St., Ste. 7
San Francisco, California 94115
Phone: (415)931-0641
Fax: (415)931-0880

Russell Miller Inc.
300 Montgomery St., Ste. 900
San Francisco, California 94104
Phone: (415)956-7474
Fax: (415)398-0620

PKF Consulting
425 California St., Ste. 1650
San Francisco, California 94104
Phone: (415)421-5378
Fax: (415)956-7708
E-mail: pkfcsf@aol.com
Web: http://www.cquest.com/
pkfb.html

Welling & Woodard, Inc.
1067 Broadway
San Francisco, California 94133
Phone: (415)776-4500
Fax: (415)776-5067

ORDIS, Inc.
6815 Trinidad Dr.
San Jose, California 95120-2056
Phone: (408)268-3321
Fax: (408)268-3582
Free: (800)446-7347
E-mail: ordis@aol.com
Web: http://www.ordis.com

Stanford Resources, Inc.
3150 Almaden Expy., Ste. 255
San Jose, California 95118
Phone: (408)448-4440
Fax: (408)448-4445
E-mail: stanres@ix.netcom.com
Web: http://
www.stanfordresources.com

Technology Properties Ltd., Inc.
4010 Moore Park, St. 215
San Jose, California 95117

Phone: (408)243-9898
Fax: (408)296-6637

Helfert Associates
1777 Borel Pl., Ste. 508
San Mateo, California 94402-3514
Phone: (415)377-0540
Fax: (415)377-0472

The Information Group, Inc.
PO Box Q
Santa Clara, California 95055-3756
Phone: (408)985-7877
Fax: (408)985-2945
E-mail: dvincent@tig.usa.com
Web: http://www.tig-usa.com

Cast Management Consultants
1620 26th St., Ste. 2040N
Santa Monica, California 90404
Phone: (310)828-7511
Fax: (310)453-6831

Cuma Consulting Management
Box 724
Santa Rosa, California 95402
Phone: (707)785-2477
Fax: (707)785-2478

The E-Myth Academy
131B Stony Circle, Ste. 2000
Santa Rosa, California 95401
Phone: (707)569-3600
Fax: (707)569-5700
Free: (800)221-0266
E-mail: emyth1@aol.com

Reilly, Connors & Ray
1743 Canyon Rd.
Spring Valley, California 91977
Phone: (619)698-4808
Fax: (619)460-3892
E-mail: davidray@adnc.com

Management Consultants
Sunnyvale, California 94087-4700
Phone: (408)773-0321

RJR Associates
1639 Lewiston Dr.
Sunnyvale, California 94087
Phone: (408)737-7720
Fax: (408)737-7720

Schwafel Associates
333 Cobalt Way, Ste. 107

Sunnyvale, California 94086
Phone: (408)720-0649
Fax: (408)720-1949
E-mail:
102065.234@compuserve.com
Web: http://www.patca.org/patca

Out of Your Mind. . .and Into the
Marketplace
13381 White Sand Dr.
Tustin, California 92780
Phone: (714)544-0248
Fax: (714)730-1414
Free: (800)419-1513
E-mail: lpinson@aol.com
Web: http://www.business-plan.com

Independent Research Services
PO Box 2426
Van Nuys, California 91404-2426
Phone: (818)993-3622

Ingman Company Inc.
7949 Woodley Ave., Ste. 120
Van Nuys, California 91406-1232
Phone: (818)375-5027
Fax: (818)894-5001

Innovative Technology Associates
3639 E. Harbor Blvd., Ste. 203E
Ventura, California 93001
Phone: (805)650-9353

Ridge Consultants, Inc.
100 Pringle Ave., Ste. 580
Walnut Creek, California 94596
Phone: (510)274-1990
Fax: (510)274-1956
E-mail: info@ridgecon.com
Web: http://www.ridgecon.com

Bell Springs Publishing
PO Box 1240
Willits, California 95490
Phone: (707)459-6372
E-mail: bellsprings@sabernet

Hutchinson Consulting and
Appraisals
23245 Sylvan St., Ste. 103
Woodland Hills, California 91367
Phone: (818)888-8175
Fax: (818)888-8220
Free: (800)977-7548
E-mail: hcac.@sprintmall.com

J.H. Robinson & Associates
20695 Deodar Dr., Ste. 100
PO Box 351
Yorba Linda, California 92686-0351
Phone: (714)970-1279

Colorado

Sam Boyer & Associates
4255 S. Buckley Rd., No. 136
Aurora, Colorado 80013
Free: (800)785-0485
E-mail: samboyer@samboyer.com
Web: http://www.samboyer.com/

GVNW, Inc./Management
2270 La Montana Way
PO Box 25969
Colorado Springs, Colorado 80936
Phone: (719)594-5800
Fax: (719)599-0968

M-Squared, Inc.
755 San Gabriel Pl.
Colorado Springs, Colorado 80906
Phone: (719)576-2554
Fax: (719)576-2554

Western Capital Holdings, Inc.
7500 E. Arapahoe Rd., Ste. 395
Englewood, Colorado 80112
Phone: (303)290-8482
Fax: (303)770-1945

Thornton Financial FNIC
1024 Centre Ave., Bldg. E
Fort Collins, Colorado 80526-1849
Phone: (970)221-2089
Fax: (970)484-5206

TenEyck Associates
1760 Cherryville Rd.
Greenwood Village, Colorado 80121-1503
Phone: (303)758-6129
Fax: (303)761-8286

Associated Enterprises Ltd.
13050 W. Ceder Dr., Unit 11
Lakewood, Colorado 80228
Phone: (303)988-6695
Fax: (303)988-6739
E-mail: ael1@classic.msn.com

Johnson & West Management
Consultants, Inc.
7612 S. Logan Dr.

Littleton, Colorado 80122
Phone: (303)730-2810
Fax: (303)730 3219

Connecticut

Stratman Group Inc.
40 Tower Ln.
Avon, Connecticut 06001-4222
Phone: (860)677-2898
Fax: (860)677-8210
Free: (800)551-0499

Cowherd Consulting Group, Inc.
106 Stephen Mather Rd.
Darien, Connecticut 06820
Phone: (203)655-2150
Fax: (203)655-6427

Greenwich Associates
8 Greenwich Office Park
Greenwich, Connecticut 06831-5149
Phone: (203)629-1200
Fax: (203)629-1229

Franchise Builders
185 Pine St., Ste. 818
Manchester, Connecticut 06040
Phone: (860)647-7542
Fax: (860)646-6544
E-mail: watchisle@.aol.com

JC Ventures, Inc.
4 Arnold St.
Old Greenwich, Connecticut 06870-1203
Phone: (203)698-1990
Fax: (203)698-2638
Free: (800)698-1997

Charles L. Hornung Associates
52 Ned's Mountain Rd.
Ridgefield, Connecticut 06877
Phone: (203)431-0297

Manus
100 Prospect St., S. Tower
Stamford, Connecticut 06901
Phone: (203)326-3880
Fax: (203)326-3890
Free: (800)445-0942
E-mail: manull@aol.com

Sternbach Associates International
16 Tamarac Rd.
Westport, Connecticut 06880

Phone: (203)227-2059
Fax: (203)454-7341

Delaware

Focus Marketing
51-7 Haver Dr.
Claymont, Delaware 19703
Phone: (302)793-3064

Daedalus Ventures, Ltd.
PO Box 1474
Hockessin, Delaware 19707
Phone: (302)239-6758
Fax: (302)239-9991
E-mail: daedalus@mail.del.net

The Formula Group
PO Box 866
Hockessin, Delaware 19707
Phone: (302)456-0952
Fax: (302)456-1354
E-mail: formula@netaxs.com

Selden Enterprises Inc.
2502 Silverside Rd., Ste. 1
Wilmington, Delaware 19810-3740
Phone: (302)529-7113
Fax: (302)529-7442
E-mail: seldenl@juno.com
Web: http://www.wld.com/id/w26209001750

District of Columbia

Enterprise Consulting, Inc.
2806 36th Pl. NW
Washington, District of Columbia 20007
Phone: (202)342-7640

Bruce W. McGee and Associates
7826 Eastern Ave. NW, Ste. 30
Washington, District of Columbia 20012
Phone: (202)726-7272
Fax: (202)726-2946

McManis Associates, Inc.
1900 K St. NW, Ste. 700
Washington, District of Columbia 20006
Phone: (202)466-7680
Fax: (202)872-1898

Florida

Whalen & Associates, Inc.
4255 Northwest 26 Ct.
Boca Raton, Florida 33434
Phone: (561)241-5950
Fax: (561)241-7414
E-mail: drwhalen@ix.netcom.com

Eric Sands Consulting Services
6193 Rock Island Rd., Ste. 412
Fort Lauderdale, Florida 33319
Phone: (954)721-4767
Fax: (954)720-2815

Host Media Corp.
3948 S. Third St., Ste. 191
Jacksonville Beach, Florida 32250
Phone: (904)285-3239
Fax: (904)285-5618
E-mail:
msconsulting@compuserve.com

William V. Hall
1925 Brickell, Ste. D-701
Miami, Florida 33129
Phone: (305)856-9622
Fax: (305)856-4113

Taxplan, Inc.
Mirasol International Center
2699 Collins Ave.
Miami Beach, Florida 33140
Phone: (305)538-3303

T.C. Brown & Associates
8415 Excalibur Cir., Apt. B1
Naples, Florida 34108
Phone: (941)594-1949
Fax: (941)594-0611

RLA International Consulting
713 Lagoon Dr.
North Palm Beach, Florida 33408
Phone: (407)626-4258
Fax: (407)626-5772

Comprehensive Franchising, Inc.
2465 Ridgecrest Ave.
Orange Park, Florida 32065
Phone: (904)272-6567
Fax: (904)272-6750
Free: (800)321-6567
E-mail: theimp@cris.com
Web: http://www.franchise411.com

Hunter G. Jackson Jr. - Consulting
Environmental Physicist
PO Box 618272
Orlando, Florida 32861-8272
Phone: (407)295-4188

F.A. McGee, Inc.
800 Claughton Island Dr., Ste. 401
Ormond Beach, Florida 32176
Phone: (305)377-9123

F. Newton Parks
210 El Brillo Way
Palm Beach, Florida 33480
Phone: (561)833-1727
Fax: (561)833-4541

Avery Business Development
Services
2506 St. Michel Ct.
Ponte Vedra Beach, Florida 32082
Phone: (904)285-6033
Fax: (904)285-6033

Strategic Business Planning Company
PO Box 821006
South Florida, Florida 33082-1006
Phone: (954)704-9100
Fax: (954)438-7333
E-mail: info@bizplan.com
Web: http://www.bizplan.com

Dufresne Consulting Group, Inc.
10014 N. Dale Mabry, Ste. 101
Tampa, Florida 33618-4426
Phone: (813)264-4775
Fax: (813)931-5845

Center for Simplified Strategic
Planning, Inc.
PO Box 3324
Vero Beach, Florida 32964-3324
Phone: (561)231-3636
Fax: (561)231-1099

Georgia

Marketing Spectrum Inc.
115 Perimeter Pl., Ste. 440
Atlanta, Georgia 30346
Phone: (770)395-7244
Fax: (770)393-4071

Business Ventures Corporation
6030 Dawson Blvd., Ste. E
Norcross, Georgia 30093

Phone: (770)729-8000
Fax: (770)729-8028

Informed Decisions Inc.
PO Box 219
Sautee Nacoochee, Georgia 30571
Fax: (706)878-1802
Free: (800)982-0676

Tom C. Davis & Associates, P.C.
3189 Perimeter Rd.
Valdosta, Georgia 31602
Phone: (912)247-9801
Fax: (912)244-7704
E-mail: mail@tcdcpa.com
Web: http://www.tcdcpa.com/

Illinois

TWD and Associates
431 S. Patton
Arlington Heights, Illinois 60005
Phone: (847)398-6410
Fax: (847)255-5095
E-mail: tdoo@aol.com

Management Planning Associates,
Inc.
2275 Half Day Rd., Ste. 350
Bannockburn, Illinois 60015-1277
Phone: (847)945-2421
Fax: (847)945-2425

Phil Faris Associates
86 Old Mill Ct.
Barrington, Illinois 60010
Phone: (847)382-4888

Seven Continents Technology
787 Stonebridge
Buffalo Grove, Illinois 60089
Phone: (708)577-9653
Fax: (708)870-1220

Grubb & Blue, Inc.
2404 Windsor Pl.
Champaign, Illinois 61820
Phone: (217)366-0052
Fax: (217)356-0117

ACE Accounting Service, Inc.
3128 N. Bernard St.
Chicago, Illinois 60618
Phone: (773)463-7854
Fax: (773)463-7854

AON Consulting
123 N. Wacker Dr.
Chicago, Illinois 60606
Phone: (312)701-4800
Fax: (312)701-4855
Free: (800)438-6487
Web: http://aonconsulting.com/

FMS Consultants
5801 N. Sheridan Rd., Ste. 3D
Chicago, Illinois 60660
Phone: (773)561-7362
Fax: (773)561-6274

Kingsbury International, Ltd.
1258 N. LaSalle St.
Chicago, Illinois 60610
Phone: (312)787-6756
Fax: (312)787-3136
E-mail: jetlag@mcs.com

MacDougall & Blake, Inc.
1414 N. Wells St., Ste. 311
Chicago, Illinois 60610-1306
Phone: (312)587-3330
Fax: (312)587-3699

James C. Osburn Ltd.
2701 W. Howard St.
Chicago, Illinois 60645
Phone: (773)262-4428
Fax: (773)262-6755

Tarifero & Tazewell Inc.
211 S. Clark
PO Box 2130
Chicago, Illinois 60690
Phone: (312)665-9714
Fax: (312)665-9716

William J. Igoe
3949 Earlston Rd.
Downers Grove, Illinois 60515
Phone: (630)960-1418

Human Energy Design Systems
620 Roosevelt Dr.
Edwardsville, Illinois 62025
Phone: (618)692-0258
Fax: (618)692-0819

BioLabs, Inc.
15 Sheffield Ct.
Lincolnshire, Illinois 60069
Phone: (847)945-2767

Clyde R. Goodheart
15 Sheffield Ct.
Lincolnshire, Illinois 60069
Phone: (847)945-2767

China Business Consultants Group
931 Dakota Cir.
Naperville, Illinois 60563
Phone: (630)778-7992
Fax: (630)778-7915
E-mail: cbcq@aol.com

Smith Associates
1320 White Mountain Dr.
Northbrook, Illinois 60062
Phone: (847)480-7200
Fax: (847)480-9828

Francorp, Inc.
20200 Governors Dr.
Olympia Fields, Illinois 60461
Phone: (708)481-2900
Fax: (708)481-5885
Free: (800)372-6244
E-mail: francorp@aol.com
Web: http://www.francorpinc.com

Camber Business Strategy
Consultants
PO Box 986
Palatine, Illinois 60078-0986
Phone: (847)705-0101
Fax: (847)705-0101

Partec Enterprise Group
5202 Keith Dr.
Richton Park, Illinois 60471
Phone: (708)503-4047
Fax: (708)503-9468

A.D. Star Consulting
320 Euclid
Winnetka, Illinois 60093
Phone: (847)446-7827
Fax: (847)446-7827
E-mail: adstar@ameritech.net

Indiana

Modular Consultants Inc.
3109 Crabtree Ln.
Elkhart, Indiana 46514
Phone: (219)264-5761
Fax: (219)264-5761

Midwest Marketing Research
PO Box 1077
Goshen, Indiana 46527
Phone: (219)533-0548
Fax: (219)533-0540
E-mail: 103365.654@compuserve

Ketchum Consulting Group
8021 Knue Rd., Ste. 112
Indianapolis, Indiana 46250
Phone: (317)845-5411
Fax: (317)842-9941

MDI Management Consulting
1519 Park Dr.
Munster, Indiana 46321
Phone: (219)838-7909
Fax: (219)838-7909

The Vincent Company Inc.
800 E. Jefferson, Ste. CD
South Bend, Indiana 46617
Phone: (219)287-9933
Fax: (219)288-6250
Free: (800)274-0733
E-mail: vincent@skyenet.net

Iowa

McCord Consulting Group, Inc.
4533 Pine View Dr. NE
PO Box 11024
Cedar Rapids, Iowa 52402
Phone: (319)378-0077
Fax: (319)378-1577
E-mail: sam_mtt@prodigy.com

McGladrey & Pullen, LLP
1699 E. Woodfield Rd., Ste. 300
Davenport, Iowa 52801-1822
Phone: (847)517-7070
Fax: (847)517-7067
Free: (800)365-8353
Web: http://www.mcgladrey.com

Management Solutions, L.C.
3815 Lincoln Place Dr.
Des Moines, Iowa 50312
Phone: (515)277-6408
Fax: (515)277-3506
E-mail:
102602.1561@compuserve.com

Grandview Marketing
15 Red Bridge Dr.

Sioux City, Iowa 51104
Phone: (712)239-3122
Fax: (712)258-7578
E-mail: eandrews@pionet.net

Maine

Edgemont Enterprises
PO Box 8354
Portland, Maine 04104
Phone: (207)871-8964
Fax: (207)871-8964

Pan Atlantic Consultants
148 Middle St.
Portland, Maine 04101
Phone: (207)871-8622
Fax: (207)772-4842
E-mail: panatl@worldnet.att.net

Maryland

Grant Thornton
2 Hopkins Plaza
Baltimore, Maryland 21201
Phone: (410)685-4000
Fax: (410)837-0587

Imperial Group, Limited
305 Washington Ave., Ste. 204
Baltimore, Maryland 21204-6009
Phone: (410)337-8500
Fax: (410)337-7641

Burdeshaw Associates, Ltd.
4701 Sangamore Rd.
Bethesda, Maryland 20816-2508
Phone: (301)229-5800
Fax: (301)229-5045
E-mail: bal@interramp.com

Michael E. Cohen
5225 Pooks Hill Rd., Ste. 1119 S
Bethesda, Maryland 20814
Phone: (301)530-5738
Fax: (301)493-9147

World Development Group, Inc.
4340 E. West Hwy., Ste. 105
Bethesda, Maryland 20814-4411
Phone: (301)652-1818
Fax: (301)652-1250
E-mail: wdg@has.com

Swartz Consulting
PO Box 4301

Crofton, Maryland 21114-4301
Phone: (301)262-6728

Software Solutions International Inc.
9633 Duffer Way
Gaithersburg, Maryland 20879
Phone: (301)330-4136

Strategies, Inc.
8 Park Center Ct., Ste. 200
Owings Mills, Maryland 21117
Phone: (410)363-6669
Fax: (410)363-1231

Hammer Marketing Resources
179 Inverness Rd.
Severna Park, Maryland 21146
Phone: (410)544-9191
Fax: (410)544-9189
Web: http://www.gohammer.com

Andrew Sussman & Associates
13731 Kretsinger
Smithsburg, Maryland 21783
Phone: (301)824-2943
Fax: (301)824-2943

Massachusetts

Geibel Marketing and Public
Relations
PO Box 611
Belmont, Massachusetts 02178-0005
Phone: (617)484-8285
Fax: (617)489-3567
E-mail: geibel@compuserve.com
Web: http://www.geibeler.com

Bain
2 Copley Pl.
Boston, Massachusetts 02117-0897
Phone: (617)572-2000
Fax: (617)572-2427
Web: http://www.rec.bain.com

Pendergast & Co.
4 Copley Place, Box 84
Boston, Massachusetts 02116
Phone: (617)720-0400
Fax: (617)266-8341

Mehr & Company
62 Kinnaird St.
Cambridge, Massachusetts 02139
Phone: (617)876-3311
Fax: (617)876-3023

Monitor Company, Inc.
25 First St.
Cambridge, Massachusetts 02141
Phone: (617)252-2000
Fax: (617)252-2100

Data and Strategies Group, Inc.
Three Speen St.
Framingham, Massachusetts 01701
Phone: (508)820-2500
Fax: (508)820-1626
Web: http://www.dsggroup.com

Information & Research Associates
PO Box 3121
Framingham, Massachusetts 01701
Phone: (508)788-0784

Easton Consultants Inc.
252 Pond St.
Hopkinton, Massachusetts 01748
Phone: (508)435-4882
Fax: (508)435-3971
Web: http://www.easton-consult.com

Jeffrey D. Marshall
102 Mitchell Rd.
Ipswich, Massachusetts 01938-1219
Phone: (508)356-1113
Fax: (508)356-2989

Consulting Resources Corporation
6 Northbrook Park
Lexington, Massachusetts 02173
Phone: (781)863-1222
Fax: (781)863-1441
E-mail: conres@world.std.com

The Planning Technologies Group,
Inc.
92 Hayden Ave.
Lexington, Massachusetts 02173
Phone: (781)861-0999
Fax: (781)861-1099
E-mail: ptg@plantcc.com

VMB Associates, Inc.
115 Ashland St.
Melrose, Massachusetts 02176
Phone: (617)665-0623

The Co. Doctor
14 Pudding Stone Ln.
Mendon, Massachusetts 01756
Phone: (508)478-1747
Fax: (508)478-0520

The Enterprise Group
73 Parker Rd.
Needham, Massachusetts 02194
Phone: (617)444-6631
Fax: (617)433-9991
E-mail: lsacco@world.std.com
Web: http://www.enterprise-
group.com

PSMJ Resources, Inc.
10 Midland Ave.
Newton, Massachusetts 02158
Phone: (617)965-0055
Fax: (617)965-5152
Free: (800)537-7765
E-mail: psmj@tiac.net
Web: http://www.psmj.com

IEEE Consultants' Network
255 Bear Hill Rd.
Waltham, Massachusetts 02154-1017
Phone: (617)890-5294
Fax: (617)890-5290

Kalba International, Inc.
1601 Trapelo Rd.
Waltham, Massachusetts 02154
Phone: (781)259-9589
Fax: (781)466-8440

Business Planning and Consulting
Services
20 Beechwood Terr.
Wellesley, Massachusetts 02181
Phone: (617)237-9151
Fax: (617)237-9151

Interim Management Associates
21 Avon Rd.
Wellesley, Massachusetts 02181
Phone: (617)237-0024

Michigan

Walter Frederick Consulting
1719 South Blvd.
Ann Arbor, Michigan 48104
Phone: (313)662-4336
Fax: (313)769-7505

G.G.W. and Associates
1213 Hampton
Jackson, Michigan 49203
Phone: (517)782-2255
Fax: (517)782-2255

Altamar Group Ltd.
6810 S. Cedar, Ste. 2-B
Lansing, Michigan 48911
Phone: (517)694-0910
Fax: (517)694-1377
Free: (800)443-2627

Sheffieck Consultants, Inc.
23610 Greening Dr.
Novi, Michigan 48375-3130
Phone: (248)347-3545
Fax: (248)347-3530

Rehmann, Robson PC
5800 Gratiot
PO Box 2025
Saginaw, Michigan 48605
Phone: (517)799-9580
Fax: (517)799-0227
Web: http://www.rrpc.com

Francis & Company
17200 W. Ten Mile Rd., Ste. 207
Southfield, Michigan 48075
Phone: (248)559-7600
Fax: (248)559-5249

Private Ventures, Inc.
16000 W. Nine Mile Rd., Ste. 504
Southfield, Michigan 48075
Phone: (248)569-1977
Fax: (248)569-1838
Free: (800)448-7614
E-mail: pventuresi@aol.com

JGK Associates
14464 Kerner Dr.
Sterling Heights, Michigan 48313
Phone: (810)247-9055

Minnesota

Consatech Inc.
PO Box 1047
Burnsville, Minnesota 55337
Phone: (612)953-1088
Fax: (612)435-2966

Robert F. Knotek
14960 Ironwood Ct.
Eden Prairie, Minnesota 55346
Phone: (612)949-2875

Kinnon Lilligren Associates
Incorporated
6211 Oakgreen Ave. S

Denmark Township
Hastings, Minnesota 55033-9153
Phone: (612)436-6530
Fax: (612)436-6530

Decker Business Consulting
6837 Booth Ave.
Inver Grove Heights, Minnesota
55076
Phone: (612)451-6600

Health Fitness Physical Therapy
3500 W. 80th St., Ste. 130
Minneapolis, Minnesota 55431
Phone: (612)831-6830
Fax: (612)831-7264

Minnesota Cooperation Office for
Small Business & Job Creation, Inc.
5001 W. 80th St., Ste. 825
Minneapolis, Minnesota 55437
Phone: (612)830-1230
Fax: (612)830-1232
E-mail: mncoop@msn.com

Power Systems Research
1301 Corporate Center Dr., Ste. 113
St. Paul, Minnesota 55121
Phone: (612)454-0144
Fax: (612)454-0760
Free: (800)433-7746
E-mail: Barb@Powersys.com
Web: http://www.powersys.com

Small Business Success
PO Box 21097
St. Paul, Minnesota 55121-0097
Phone: (612)454-2500
Fax: (612)456-9138

Missouri

Business Planning and Development
Inc.
4030 Charlotte St.
Kansas City, Missouri 64110
Phone: (816)753-0495
E-mail: humph@bpdev.demon.co.uk
Web: http://www.bpdev.demon.co.uk

Nebraska

International Management Consulting
Group, Inc.
1309 Harlan Dr., Ste. 205
Bellevue, Nebraska 68005

Phone: (402)291-4545
Fax: (402)291-4343
Free: (800)665-IMCG
E-mail: imcg@neonramp.com
Web: http://www.mgtconsulting.com

Heartland Management Consulting
Group
1904 Barrington Pkwy.
Papillion, Nebraska 68046
Phone: (402)339-1319
Fax: (402)339-1319

Nevada

The DuBois Group
800 Southwood Blvd., Ste. 206
Incline Village, Nevada 89451
Phone: (702)832-0550
Fax: (702)832-0556
Free: (800)375-2935

New Hampshire

Wolff Consultants
10 Buck Rd.
PO Box 1003
Hanover, New Hampshire 03755
Phone: (603)643-6015

New Jersey

ConMar International, Ltd.
283 Dayton-Jamesburg Rd.
PO Box 437
Dayton, New Jersey 08810
Phone: (908)274-1100
Fax: (908)274-1199

Kumar Associates, Inc.
260 Columbia Ave.
Fort Lee, New Jersey 07024
Phone: (201)224-9480
Fax: (201)585-2343

John Hall & Company, Inc.
PO Box 187
Glen Ridge, New Jersey 07028
Phone: (201)680-4449
Fax: (201)680-4581
E-mail: jhcompany@aol.com

Strategic Management Group
PO Box 402
Maplewood, New Jersey 07040
Phone: (201)378-2470

Vanguard Communications Corp.
100 American Rd.
Morris Plains, New Jersey 07950
Phone: (201)605-8000
Fax: (201)605-8329
Web: http://www.vanguard.net/

KLW New Products
156 Cedar Dr.
Old Tappan, New Jersey 07675
Phone: (201)358-1300
Fax: (201)664-2594
E-mail: /rlarsenunited states of america.net

PA Consulting Group
315 A Enterprise Dr.
Plainsboro, New Jersey 08536
Phone: (609)936-8300
Fax: (609)936-8811
Web: http://www.pa-consulting.com

Aurora Marketing Management, Inc.
212 Carnegie Ctr., Ste. 206
Princeton, New Jersey 08540-6233
Phone: (609)520-8863

Smart Business Supersite
88 Orchard Rd., CN-5219
Princeton, New Jersey 08543
Phone: (908)321-1924
Fax: (908)321-5156
E-mail: irv@smartbiz.com
Web: http://www.smartbiz.com

Tracelin Associates
1171 Main St., Ste. 6K
Rahway, New Jersey 07065
Phone: (908)381-3288

Schkeeper Inc.
130-6 Bodman Pl.
Red Bank, New Jersey 07701
Phone: (908)219-1965

Henry Branch Associates
2502 Harmon Cove Tower
Secaucus, New Jersey 07094
Phone: (201)866-2008
Fax: (201)601-0101
E-mail: HDPW18A@prodigy.com
Web: http://www.mcninet.com/
globallook/hbranch.html

Robert Gibbons & Co., Inc.
46 Knoll Rd.

Tenafly, New Jersey 07670-1050
Phone: (201)871-3933
Fax: (201)871-2173
E-mail: crisisbob@aol.com

PMC Management Consultants, Inc.
11 Thistle Ln.
PO Box 332
Three Bridges, New Jersey 08887-0332
Phone: (908)788-1014
Fax: (908)806-7287

R.W. Bankart & Associates
20 Valley Ave., Ste. D-2
Westwood, New Jersey 07675-3607
Phone: (201)664-7672

New Mexico

Vondle & Associates, Inc.
4926 Calle de Tierra, NE
Albuquerque, New Mexico 87111
Phone: (505)292-8961
Fax: (505)296-2790

InfoNewMexico
2207 Black Hills Road, NE
Rio Rancho, New Mexico 87124
Phone: (505)891-2462
Fax: (505)896-8971

New York

Powers Research and Training Institute
PO Box 78
Bayville, New York 11709
Phone: (516)628-2250
Fax: (516)628-2252
E-mail: 73313.1315@compuserve.com
Web: http://www.coachfederation.org/crs/67.nancy.powers.htm

Consortium House
139 Wittenberg Rd.
Bearsville, New York 12409
Phone: (914)679-8867
Fax: (914)679-9248
E-mail: eugenegs@aol.com
Web: http://www.chpub.com

Progressive Finance Corporation (PFC)
3549 Tiemann Ave.
Bronx, New York 10469
Phone: (718)405-9029
Fax: (718)405-1170
Free: (800)225-8381

Wave Hill Associates
2621 Palisade Ave., Ste. 15-C
Riverdale
Bronx, New York 10463
Phone: (718)549-7368
Fax: (718)601-9670

Overton Financial
7 Allen Rd.
Cortlandt Manor, New York 10566
Phone: (914)737-4649
Fax: (914)737-4696

Samani International Enterprises,
Marions Panyaught Consultancy
2028 Parsons
Flushing, New York 11357-3436
Phone: (917)287-8087
Fax: (800)873-8939
E-mail: vjp2@compuserve.com
Web: http://www.dorsai.org/~vjp2

Marketing Resources Group
71-58 Austin St.
Forest Hills, New York 11375
Phone: (718)261-8882

Group I Financial Services
PO Box 922
Highland, New York 12528
Phone: (914)451-7625
E-mail: 103107.227@compuserve.com

North Star Enterprises
670 N. Terrace Ave.
Mount Vernon, New York 10552
Phone: (914)668-9433

E.N. Rysso & Associates
21 Jordan Rd.
New Hartford, New York 13413-2311
Phone: (315)732-2206
Fax: (315)732-2206

Boice Dunham Group
437 Madison Ave.
New York, New York 10022

Phone: (212)752-5550
Fax: (212)752-7055

Elizabeth Capen
27 E. 95th St.
New York, New York 10128
Phone: (212)427-7654

Dunham & Marcus Inc.
575 Madison Ave., 10th Fl.
New York, New York 10022-1304
Phone: (212)605-0571
Fax: (212)605-0589

Haver Analytics
60 E. 42nd St., Ste. 2424
New York, New York 10017
Phone: (212)986-9300
Fax: (212)986-5857
E-mail: data@haver.com
Web: http://www.haver.com

The Jordan, Edmiston Group, Inc.
150 E 52nd Ave., 18th Fl.
New York, New York 10022
Phone: (212)754-0710
Fax: (212)754-0337

KPMG Peat Marwick - Management
Consultants
345 Park Ave.
New York, New York 10154
Phone: (212)909-5000
Fax: (212)738-9819
Web: http://www.kpmg.com

Mahoney Cohen Consulting Corp.
111 W. 40th St., 12th Fl.
New York, New York 10018
Phone: (212)490-8000
Fax: (212)790-5913

Management Practice, Inc.
342 Madison Ave.
Ste. 1230
New York, New York 10173-1230
Phone: (212)867-7948
Fax: (212)972-5188
Web: http://www.mpiweb.com

Moseley Associates, Inc.
342 Madison Ave., Ste. 1414
New York, New York 10016
Phone: (212)213-6673
Fax: (212)687-1520

Practice Development Counsel
60 Sutton Pl. S
New York, New York 10022
Phone: (212)593-1549
Fax: (212)980-7940
E-mail: phaserot@counsel.com

The Van Tulleken Company Limited
126 E. 56th St.
New York, New York 10022
Phone: (212)355-1390
Fax: (212)755-3061
E-mail: newyork@vantelleken.com

Vencon Management, Incorporated
301 W. 53rd St.
New York, New York 10019
Phone: (212)581-8787
Fax: (212)397-4126

R.A. Walsh Consultants
429 E. 52nd St.
New York, New York 10022
Phone: (212)688-6047
Fax: (212)535-4075

Werner International Inc.
55 East 52nd, 29th floor
New York, New York 10055
Phone: (212)909-1260
Fax: (212)909-1273

Zimmerman Business Consulting,
Inc.
44 E. 92nd St., Ste. 5-B
New York, New York 10128
Phone: (212)860-3107
Fax: (212)860-7730
E-mail: lj22bci@aol.com

Stromberg Consulting
2500 Westchester Ave.
Purchase, New York 10577
Phone: (914)251-1515
Fax: (914)251-1562

ComputerEase Co.
9 Hachaliah Brown Dr.
Somers, New York 10589
Phone: (914)277-5317
Fax: (914)277-5317
E-mail: crawfordc@juno.com

Innovation Management Consulting,
Inc.
209 Dewitt Rd.

Syracuse, New York 13214-2006
Phone: (315)425-5144
Fax: (315)445-8989
E-mail: missonneb@axess.net

M. Clifford Agrcss
891 Fulton St.
Valley Stream, New York 11580
Phone: (516)825-8955
Fax: (516)825-8955

Destiny Kinal Marketing Consultancy
105 Chemung St.
Waverly, New York 14892
Phone: (607)565-8317
Fax: (607)565-4083

Management Insight
96 Arlington Rd.
Williamsville, New York 14221
Phone: (716)631-3319
Fax: (716)631-0203
Free: (800)643-3319

North Carolina

Norelli & Company
Nations Bank Corporation Center
100 N. Tyron St., Ste. 3220
Charlotte, North Carolina 28202-4000
Phone: (704)376-5484
Fax: (704)376-5485

North Dakota

Center for Innovation
4300 Dartmouth Dr.
Grand Forks, North Dakota 58202
Phone: (701)777-3132
Fax: (701)777-2339
Web: http://www.und.nodak.edu/dept/
cibd/welcome.htm

Ohio

Transportation Technology Services
208 Harmon Rd.
Aurora, Ohio 44202
Phone: (330)562-3596

Delta Planning, Inc.
PO Box 22618
Beachwood, Ohio 44122
Phone: (216)831-2521
Fax: (216)831-7616

Free: (800)672-0762
E-mail: delta@planet.net

Empro Systems, Inc.
4777 Red Bank Expy., Ste. 1
Cincinnati, Ohio 45227-1542
Phone: (513)271-2042
Fax: (513)271-2042

Poppe Tyson
1301 E. 9th St., Ste. 3400
Cleveland, Ohio 44114
Phone: (216)623-1511
Fax: (216)623-1501

Cory Dillon Associates
111 Schreyer Pl. E
Columbus, Ohio 43214
Phone: (614)262-8211
Fax: (614)262-3806

Holcomb Gallagher Adams
300 Marconi, Ste. 303
Columbus, Ohio 43215
Phone: (614)221-3343
Fax: (614)221-3367
E-mail: riadams@acme.freenet.oh.us

Ransom & Associates -
COMPETITIVEdge Group
106 E. Pacemont Rd.
Columbus, Ohio 43202-1225
Phone: (614)267-7100
Fax: (614)267-7199
E-mail: wjrnetworkWalk.com

Herman Associates Inc.
PO Box 5351
Fairlawn, Ohio 44333
Phone: (330)836-5656
Fax: (330)836-3311
Free: (800)227-3566
E-mail:
75473.2217@compuserve.com

Young & Associates
PO Box 711
Kent, Ohio 44240
Phone: (330)678-0524
Fax: (330)678-6219
Free: (800)525-9775
Web: http://www.younginc.com

Robert A. Westman & Associates
8981 Inversary Dr. SE
Warren, Ohio 44484-2551

Phone: (330)856-4149
Fax: (330)856-2564

Oklahoma

Innovative Resources Inc.
4900 Richmond Sq., Ste. 100
Oklahoma City, Oklahoma 73118
Phone: (405)840-0033
Fax: (405)843-8359
E-mail: ipartners@juno.com

Oregon

INTERCON - The International
Converting Institute
5200 Badger Rd.
Crooked River Ranch, Oregon 97760
Phone: (541)548-1447
Fax: (541)548-1618
E-mail: intercon@transport.com

Talbott ARM
HC 60, Box 5620
Lakeview, Oregon 97630
Phone: (541)635-8587
Fax: (503)947-3482

Management Technology Associates,
Ltd.
1618 SW 1st Ave., Ste. 315
Portland, Oregon 97201
Phone: (503)224-5220
Fax: (503)224-6704

Pennsylvania

Problem Solvers for Industry
345 Park Ave.
Chalfont, Pennsylvania 18914
Phone: (215)822-9695
Fax: (215)822-8086

Elayne Howard & Associates, Inc.
3501 Masons Mill Rd., Ste. 501
Huntingdon Valley, Pennsylvania
19006-3509
Phone: (215)657-9550

GRA, Incorporated
115 West Ave., Ste. 201
Jenkintown, Pennsylvania 19046
Phone: (215)884-7500
Fax: (215)884-1385
E-mail: dkfinn@hslc.org

Mifflin County Industrial
Development Corporation
Mifflin County Industrial Plaza
6395 SR 103 N
Bldg. 50
Lewistown, Pennsylvania 17044
Phone: (717)242-0393
Fax: (717)242-1842
E-mail: mcide@acsworld.net

Autech Products
1289 Revere Rd.
Morrisville, Pennsylvania 19067
Phone: (215)493-3759
Fax: (215)493-3759

Advantage Associates
434 Avon Dr.
Pittsburgh, Pennsylvania 15228
Phone: (412)343-1558
Fax: (412)362-1684
E-mail: ecocba1@aol.com

Regis J. Sheehan & Associates
291 Foxcroft Rd.
Pittsburgh, Pennsylvania 15220
Phone: (412)279-1207

James W. Davidson Co., Inc.
23 Forest View Rd.
Wallingford, Pennsylvania 19086
Phone: (610)566-1462

Puerto Rico

Diego Chevere & Co.
Ste. 301, Metro Parque 7
Metro Office Park
Caparra Heights, Puerto Rico 00920
Phone: (787)782-9595
Fax: (787)782-9532

Manuel L. Porrata and Associates
898 Munoz Rivera Ave., Ste. 201
Rio Piedras, Puerto Rico 00927
Phone: (809)765-2140
Fax: (809)754-3285

South Carolina

Aquafood Business Associates
PO Box 16190
Charleston, South Carolina 29412
Phone: (803)795-9506
Fax: (803)795-9477

Strategic Innovations International
12 Executive Court
Lake Wylie, South Carolina 29710
Phone: (803)831-1225
Fax: (803)831-1177
E-mail: strat@aol.com

Minus Stage
Box 4436
Rock Hill, South Carolina 29731
Phone: (803)328-0705
Fax: (803)329-9948

Tennessee

Daniel Petchers & Associates
8820 Fernwood CV
Germantown, Tennessee 38138
Phone: (901)755-9896

CFP Business Choices
1114 Forest Harbor, Ste. 300
Hendersonville, Tennessee 37075-9694
Phone: (615)822-8692
Fax: (615)822-8692
Free: (800)737-8382
E-mail: bz-ch@juno.com

RCFA Healthcare Management
Services
9648 Kingston Pike, Ste. 8
Knoxville, Tennessee 37922
Phone: (423)531-0176
Fax: (423)531-0722
Web: http://www.rcfa.com

Growth Consultants of America
3917 Trimble Rd.
PO Box 158382
Nashville, Tennessee 37215
Phone: (615)383-0550
Fax: (615)269-8940
E-mail: 70244.451@compuserve.com

Texas

Lori Williams
1000 Leslie Ct.
Arlington, Texas 76012
Phone: (817)459-3934
Fax: (817)459-3934

Erisa Adminstrative Services Inc.
12325 Haymeadow Dr., Bldg. 4

Austin, Texas 78750-1847
Phone: (512)250-9020
Fax: (512)250-9487
Web: http://www.cserisa.com

R. Miller Hicks & Company
1011 W. 11th St.
Austin, Texas 78703
Phone: (512)477-7000
Fax: (512)477-9697
E-mail: millerhicks@rmhicks.com

Pragmatic Tactics, Inc.
3303 Westchester Ave.
College Station, Texas 77845
Phone: (409)696-5294
Fax: (409)696-4994
Free: (800)570-5294
E-mail: ptactics@aol.com
Web: http://www.ptatics.com

Perot Systems
12377 Merit Dr., Ste. 1100
Dallas, Texas 75251
Phone: (972)383-5600
Free: (800)688-4333
E-mail: corp.comm@ps.net
Web: http://www.ps.net

High Technology Associates -
Division of Global Technologies, Inc.
1775 St. James Pl., Ste. 105
Houston, Texas 77056
Phone: (713)963-9300
Fax: (713)963-8341
E-mail: wta@infohwy.com

PROTEC
4607 Linden Pl.
Pearland, Texas 77584
Phone: (281)997-9872
Fax: (281)997-9895
E-mail: p.oman@ix.netcom.com

Business Strategy Development
Consultants
PO Box 690365
San Antonio, Texas 78269
Phone: (210)696-8000
Fax: (210)696-8000
Free: (800)927-BSDC

Tom Welch, CPC
6900 San Pedro Ave., Ste. 147
San Antonio, Texas 78216-6207

Phone: (210)737-7022
Fax: (210)737-7022
E-mail: bplan@iamerica.nct
Web: http://www.moneywords.com

Utah

CAPCON, Ltd.
8746 S. Rustler Rd.
Sandy, Utah 84093
Phone: (801)943-6339
Fax: (801)942-2864

Virginia

Elliott B. Jaffa
2530-B S. Walter Reed Dr.
Arlington, Virginia 22206
Phone: (703)931-0040

Koach Enterprises - USA
5529 N. 18th St.
Arlington, Virginia 22205
Phone: (703)241-8361
Fax: (703)241-8623

Federal Market Development
5650 Chapel Run Ct.
Centreville, Virginia 22020-3601
Phone: (703)502-8930
Fax: (703)502-8929
Free: (800)821-5003

Barringer, Huff & Stuart
2107 Graves Mills Rd., Ste. C
Forest, Virginia 24551
Phone: (804)316-9356
Fax: (804)316-9357

Performance Support Systems
11835 Canon Blvd., Ste. C-101
Newport News, Virginia 23606
Phone: (757)873-3700
Fax: (757)873-3288
Free: (800)488-6463
E-mail: pss2@aol.com
Web: http://www.2020insight.net

Charles Scott Pugh (Investor)
4101 Pittaway Dr.
Richmond, Virginia 23235-1022
Phone: (804)560-0979
Fax: (804)560-4670

John C. Randall and Associates, Inc.
PO Box 15127

Richmond, Virginia 23227
Phone: (804)746-4450
Fax: (804)747-7426

McLeod & Co.
410 1st St.
Roanoke, Virginia 24011
Phone: (540)342-6911
Fax: (540)344-6367
Web: http://www.mcleodco.com/

The Small Business Counselor
12423 Hedges Run Dr., Ste. 153
Woodbridge, Virginia 22192
Phone: (703)490-6755
Fax: (703)490-1356

Washington

Perry L. Smith Consulting
800 Bellevue Way NE, Ste. 400
Bellevue, Washington 98004-4208
Phone: (425)462-2072
Fax: (425)462-5638

ECG Management Consultants, Inc.
1111 3rd Ave., Ste. 2700
Seattle, Washington 98101-3201
Phone: (206)689-2200
Fax: (206)689-2209
E-mail: ecg@ecgmc.com
Web: http://www.ecgmc.com

Northwest Trade Adjustment
Assistance Center
900 4th Ave., Ste. 2430
Seattle, Washington 98164-1003
Phone: (206)622-2730
Fax: (206)622-1105
E-mail: nwtaac@sprynet.com

Business Planning Consultants
S. 3510 Ridgeview Dr.
Spokane, Washington 99206
Phone: (509)928-0332
Fax: (509)921-0842
E-mail: bpci@nextdim.com

Wisconsin

White & Associates, Inc.
5349 Somerset Ln. S
Greenfield, Wisconsin 53221
Phone: (414)281-7373
Fax: (414)281-7006
E-mail: wna@eworld.com

SMALL BUSINESS ADMINISTRATION REGIONAL OFFICES

This section contains a listing of Small Business Administration offices arranged numerically by region. Service areas are provided. Contact the appropriate office for a referral to the nearest field office.

Region 1

U.S. Small Business Administration
10 Causeway St., Rm. 812
Boston, Massachusetts 02222
Phone: (617)565-8415
Fax: (617)565-8420
Serves Connecticut, Maine, Massachusetts, New Hampshire, Rhode Island, and Vermont.

Region 2

U.S. Small Business Administration
26 Federal Plz., Rm. 3108
New York, New York 10278
Phone: (212)264-1450
Fax: (212)264-0038
Serves New Jersey, New York, Puerto Rico, and the Virgin Islands.

Region 3

U.S. Small Business Administration
475 Allendale Rd., Ste. 201
King of Prussia, Pennsylvania 19406
Phone: (610)962-3710
Fax: (610)962-3743
Serves Delaware, the District of Columbia, Maryland, Pennsylvania, Virginia, and West Virginia.

Region 4

U.S. Small Business Administration
1375 Peachtree St. NE, Rm. 500
Atlanta, Georgia 30367-8102
Phone: (404)347-4999
Fax: (404)347-2355
Serves Alabama, Florida, Georgia, Kentucky, Mississippi, North Carolina, South Carolina, and Tennessee.

Region 5

U.S. Small Business Administration
Gateway IV Bldg., Ste. 1975 South
300 S. Riverside Plz.
Chicago, Illinois 60606-6611
Phone: (312)353-8089
Fax: (312)353-3426
Serves Illinois, Indiana, Michigan, Minnesota, Ohio, and Wisconsin.

Region 6

U.S. Small Business Administration
8625 King George Dr., Bldg. C
Dallas, Texas 75235-3391
Phone: (214)767-7611
Fax: (214)767-7870
Serves Arkansas, Louisiana, New Mexico, Oklahoma, and Texas.

Region 7

U.S. Small Business Administration
Lucas Place, Ste. 307
323 W. 8th St.
Kansas City, Missouri 64105
Phone: (816)374-6380
Fax: (816)374-6339
Serves Iowa, Kansas, Missouri, and Nebraska.

Region 8

U.S. Small Business Administration
633 17th St., 7th Fl.
Denver, Colorado 80202
Phone: (303)294-7186
Fax: (303)294-7153
Serves Colorado, Montana, North Dakota, South Dakota, Utah, and Wyoming.

Region 9

U.S. Small Business Administration
71 Stevenson St., 20th Fl.
San Francisco, California 94105
Phone: (415)744-6404
Serves American Samoa, Arizona, California, Guam, Hawaii, Nevada, and the Trust Territory of the Pacific Islands.

Region 10

U.S. Small Business Administration
1200 6th Ave., Ste. 1805
Seattle, Washington 98101-1128
Phone: (206)553-5676
Fax: (206)553-4155
Serves Alaska, Idaho, Oregon, and
Washington.

SMALL BUSINESS DEVELOPMENT CENTERS

This section contains a listing of all Small Business Development Centers organized alphabetically by state/U.S. territory name, then by city, then by agency name.

Alabama

Auburn University
SBDC
E-mail:
ghannem@business.auburn.edu
108 College of Business
Auburn, Alabama 36849-5243
Phone: (334)844-4220
Fax: (334)844-4268
Garry Hannem, Dir.

Auburn University
Small Business Development Center
108 College of Business
Auburn, Alabama 36849-5243
Phone: (334)844-4220
Fax: (334)844-4268
Gary Hannem, Dir.
E-mail:
ghannem@business.auburn.edu

Alabama Small Business
Development Center
University of Alabama at
Birmingham
SBDC
E-mail:
asbd003@uabdpo.dpo.uab.edu
Medical Towers Bldg.
1717 11th Ave. S., Ste. 419
Birmingham, Alabama 35294-4410
Phone: (205)934-7260
Fax: (205)934-7645
John Sandefur, State Dir.

Alabama Small Business Procurement
System
University of Alabama at
Birmingham
SBDC
Small Business Development Center
1717 11th Ave. S., Ste. 419
Birmingham, Alabama 35294-4410
Phone: (205)934-7260
Fax: (205)934-7645
Charles Hobson, Procurement Dir.

Alabama Technology Assistance
Program
University of Alabama at
Birmingham
SBDC
E-mail:
asbd009@uabdpo.dpo.uab.edu
1717 11th Ave. S., Ste. 419
Birmingham, Alabama 35294-4410
Phone: (205)934-7260
Fax: (205)934-7645
Susan Armour, Associate State Dir.

University of Alabama at
Birmingham
SBDC
1601 11th Ave. S.
Birmingham, Alabama 35294-2180
Phone: (205)934-6760
Fax: (205)934-0538

University of Alabama at
Birmingham
Small Business Development Center
1717 11th Ave. S., Ste. 419
Birmingham, Alabama 35294-4410
Phone: (205)934-7260
Fax: (205)934-7645
Charles Hobson, Dir.

University of North Alabama
Small Business Development Center
Box 5248, Keller Hall
Florence, Alabama 35632-0001
Phone: (205)760-4629
Fax: (205)760-4813
Kerry Gatlin, Dir.

University of North Alabama
SBDC
PO Box 5248, Keller Hall
Florence, Alabama 35632-0001
Phone: (205)760-4629

Fax: (205)760-4813
Kerry Gatlin, Dir.

Alabama A&M University
University of Alabama (Huntsville)
North East Alabama Regional Small
Business Development Center
225 Church St. NW
PO Box 168
Huntsville, Alabama 35804-0168
Phone: (205)535-2061
Fax: (205)535-2050
Jeff Thompson, Dir.
E-mail: thompsonj@email.uah.edu

N. E. Alabama Regional
Alabama A&M University
University of Alabama at Huntsville
SBDC
E-mail: thompsonj@email.uah.edu
P.O. Box 168
225 Church St., N.W.
Huntsville, Alabama 35804-0168
Phone: (205)535-2061
Fax: (205)535-2050
Jeff Thompson, Dir.

Jacksonville State University
SBDC
114 Merrill Hall
700 Pelham Rd. N.
Jacksonville, Alabama 36265
Phone: (205)782-5271
Fax: (205)782-5179
Pat Shaddix, Dir.

Jacksonville State University
Small Business Development Center
700 Pelham Rd. N
114 Merrill Hall
Jacksonville, Alabama 36265
Phone: (205)782-5271
Fax: (205)782-5179
Pat Shaddix, Dir.

Livingston University
Small Business Development Center
Station 35
Livingston, Alabama 35470
Phone: (205)652-9661
Fax: (205)652-9318
Paul Garner, Dir.

Livingston University
SBDC
Station 35

Livingston, Alabama 35470
Phone: (205)652-9661
Fax: (205)652-9318
Paul Garner, Dir.

University of South Alabama
SBDC
College of Business Rm. 8
Mobile, Alabama 36688
Phone: (334)460-6004
Fax: (334)460-6246

University of South Alabama
Small Business Development Center
College of Business, Rm. 8
Mobile, Alabama 36688
Phone: (334)460-6004
Fax: (334)460-6246

Alabama State University
Small Business Development Center
915 S. Jackson St.
Montgomery, Alabama 36195
Phone: (334)229-4138
Fax: (334)269-1102
Lorenza G. Patrick, Dir.

Alabama State University
SBDC
915 S. Jackson St.
Montgomery, Alabama 36195
Phone: (334)229-4138
Fax: (334)269-1102
Lorenza G. Patrick, Dir.

Troy State University
SBDC
E-mail: jkerv@asntsu.asn.net
Bibb Graves, Rm. 102
Troy, Alabama 36082-0001
Phone: (205)670-3771
Fax: (205)670-3636

Troy State University
Small Business Development Center
Bibb Graves, Rm. 102
Troy, Alabama 36082-0001
Phone: (205)670-3771
Fax: (205)670-3636
Janet W. Kervin, Dir.
E-mail: jkerv@asntsu.asn.net

Alabama International Trade Center
University of Alabama
SBDC
Bidgood Hall, Rm. 201

PO Box 870396
Tuscaloosa, Alabama 35487-0396
Phone: (205)348-7621
Fax: (205)348-6974
Brian Davis, Dir.
E-mail: aitc@aitc.cba.ua.edu

University of Alabama
SBDC
E-mail: phaninen@ua1vm.ua.edu
P.O. Box 870397
Bidgood Hall, Rm. 250
Tuscaloosa, Alabama 35487-0397
Phone: (205)348-7011
Fax: (205)348-9644
Paavo Hanninen, Dir.

University of Alabama
Alabama International Trade Center
Small Business Devlopment Center
Bidgood Hall, Rm. 201
Box 870396
Tuscaloosa, Alabama 35487-0396
Phone: (205)348-7621
Fax: (205)348-6974
Brian Davis, Dir.
E-mail: aitc@aitc.cba.ua.edu

Alaska

University of Alaska (Fairbanks)
Small Business Development Center
510 Second Ave., Ste. 101
Fairbanks, Alaska 99701
Phone: (907)456-1701
Free: (800)478-1701
Fax: (907)456-1873
Theresa Proenza, Contact

University of Alaska (Juneau)
Small Business Development Center
400 Willoughby St., Ste. 211
Juneau, Alaska 99801
Phone: (907)463-3789
Free: (800)478-6655
Fax: (907)463-3929
Charles Northrip, Dir.

Kenai Peninsula Small Business
Development Center
110 S. Willow St., Ste. 106
Kenai, Alaska 99611-7744
Phone: (907)283-3335
Fax: (907)283-3913
William L. Root, Dir.

University of Alaska (Matanuska-
Susitna)
Small Business Development Center
1801 Parks Hwy., Ste. C-18
Wasilla, Alaska 99654
Phone: (907)373-7232
Fax: (907)373-2560
Marian Romano, Dir.

Arizona

Central Arizona College
Small Business Development Center
8470 N. Overfield Rd.
Coolidge, Arizona 85228
Phone: (520)426-4341
Fax: (520)426-4284
Donald Biggerstaff, Dir.

Coconino County Community
College
Small Business Development Center
3000 N. 4th St., Ste. 25
Flagstaff, Arizona 86004
Phone: (520)526-5072
Fax: (520)526-8693
Stephen West, Dir.

Northland Pioneer College
Small Business Development Center
PO Box 610
Holbrook, Arizona 86025
Phone: (520)537-2976
Fax: (520)524-2227
Joel Eittreim, Dir.

Mohave Community College
Small Business Development Center
1971 Jagerson Ave.
Kingman, Arizona 86401
Phone: (520)757-0894
Fax: (520)757-0836
Jennee Miles, Dir.

Yavapai College
Small Business Development Center
117 E. Gurley St., Ste. 206
Prescott, Arizona 86301
Phone: (520)778-3088
Fax: (520)778-3109
Richard Senopole, Contact

Cochise College
Small Business Development Center
901 N. Colombo, Rm. 411

Sierra Vista, Arizona 85635
Phone: (520)515-5443
Fax: (520)515-5478
Debbie Elver, Dir.

Arizona Small Business Development
Center Network
E-mail: york@maricopa.bitnet
2411 W. 14th St., Ste. 132
Tempe, Arizona 85281
Phone: (602)731-8720
Fax: (602)731-8729
Michael York, State Dir.

Maricopa Community Colleges
SBDC
1414 W. Broadway, Ste. 165
Tempe, Arizona 85281
Phone: (602)966-7786
Fax: (602)966-8541
Christina Gonzalez, Dir.
Sonny Quinonez, Dir.

Eastern Arizona College
SBDC
622 College Ave.
Thatcher, Arizona 85552-0769
Phone: (520)428-8590
Fax: (520)428-8462
Greg Roers, Dir.

Eastern Arizona College
Small Business Development Center
622 College Ave.
Thatcher, Arizona 85552-0769
Phone: (520)428-8590
Fax: (520)428-8462
Greg Roers, Dir.

Pima Community College
Small Business Development Center
4905-A E. Broadway Blvd., Ste. 101
Tucson, Arizona 85709-1260
Phone: (520)748-4906
Fax: (520)748-4585
Linda Andrews, Dir.

Arizona Western College
Small Business Development Center
Century Plz., No. 152
281 W. 24th St.
Yuma, Arizona 85364
Phone: (520)341-1650
Fax: (520)726-2636
Hank Pinto, Dir.

Arkansas

Henderson State University
Small Business Development Center
1100 Henderson St.
PO Box 7624
Arkadelphia, Arkansas 71923
Phone: (501)230-5224
Fax: (501)230 5236
Bill Akin, Dir.

University of Central Arkansas
Small Business Development Center
College of Business Administration
Burdick Business Administration
Bldg., Rm. 212
201 Donaghey Ave.
Conway, Arkansas 72035-0001
Phone: (501)450-3190
Fax: (501)450-5302

Genesis Technology Incubator
SBDC Satellite Office
University of Arkansas Engineering
Research Center
Fayetteville, Arkansas 72701-1201
Phone: (501)575-7473
Fax: (501)575-7446
Bob Penquite, Business Consultant

University of Arkansas at Fayetteville
Small Business Development Center
College of Business
BADM 1172, Ste. 106
Fayetteville, Arkansas 72701
Phone: (501)575-5148
Fax: (501)575-4013
Ms. Jimmie Wilkins, Dir.

SBDC
1109 S. 16th St.
P.O. Box 2067
Fort Smith, Arkansas 72901
Phone: (501)785-1376
Fax: (501)785-1964
Byron "Twig" Branch, Business
Consultant

University of Arkansas at Little Rock,
Regional Office (Fort Smith)
Small Business Development Center
1109 S. 16th St.
PO Box 2067
Fort Smith, Arkansas 72901
Phone: (501)785-1376

Fax: (501)785-1964
Byron Branch, Business Specialist

University of Arkansas at Little Rock,
Regional Office (Harrison)
Small Business Development Center
818 Hwy. 62-65-412 N
PO Box 190
Harrison, Arkansas 72601
Phone: (501)741-8009
Fax: (501)741-1905
Bob Penquite, Business Consultant

University of Arkansas at Little Rock,
Regional Office (Hot Springs)
Small Business Development Center
835 Central Ave., Box 402D
Hot Springs, Arkansas 71901
Phone: (501)624-5448
Fax: (501)624-6632
Richard Evans, Business Consultant

Arkansas State University
Small Business Development Center
PO Drawer 2605
Jonesboro, Arkansas 72402-2605
Phone: (501)932-3517
Fax: (501)972-3868
Herb Lawrence, Dir.

University of Arkansas At Little Rock
Arkansas SBDC
Little Rock Techonology Center
Bldg.
100 S. Main St., Ste. 401
Little Rock, Arkansas 72201
Phone: (501)324-9043
Fax: (501)324-9049
Janet Nye, State Dir.

University of Arkansas Little Rock
SBDC
100 S. Main, Ste. 401
Little Rock, Arkansas 72201
Phone: (501)324-9043
Fax: (501)324-9049
John Harrison, Business Consultant

University of Arkansas at Little Rock,
Regional Office (Magnolia)
Small Business Development Center
600 Bessie
PO Box 767
Magnolia, Arkansas 71753
Phone: (501)234-4030

Fax: (501)234-0135
Mr. Lairie Kincaid, Business
Consultant

University of Arkansas at Little Rock,
Regional Office (Pine Bluff)
Small Business Development Center
The Enterprise Center III
400 Main, Ste. 117
Pine Bluff, Arkansas 71601
Phone: (501)536-0654
Fax: (501)536-7713
Vonelle Vanzant, Business Consultant

University of Arkansas at Little Rock,
Regional Office (Stuttgart)
Small Business Development Center
301 S. Grand, Ste. 101
PO Box 289
Stuttgart, Arkansas 72160
Phone: (501)673-8707
Larry LeFler, Business Consultant

Mid-South Community College
SBDC
2000 W. Broadway
P.O. Box 2067
West Memphis, Arkansas 72303-2067
Phone: (501)733-6767

California

Central Coast Small Business
Development Center
6500 Soquel Dr.
Aptos, California 95003
Phone: (408)479-6136
Fax: (408)479-6166
Teresa Thomae, Dir.

Sierra College Small Business
Development Center
560 Wall St., Ste. J
Auburn, California 95603
Phone: (916)885-5488
Fax: (916)823-2831
Mary Wollesen, Dir.

Weill Institute Small Business
Development Center
1706 Chester Ave., Ste. 200
Bakersfield, California 93301
Phone: (805)322-5881
Fax: (805)322-5663
Jeffrey Johnson, Dir.

Butte College
Small Business Development Center
260 Cohasset Rd., Ste. A
Chico, California 95926
Phone: (916)895-9017
Fax: (916)895-9099
Kay Zimmerlee, Dir.

Southwestern College Small Business
Development and International Trade
Center
900 Otay Lakes Rd., Bldg. 1600
Chula Vista, California 91910
Phone: (619)482-6393
Fax: (619)482-6402
Mary Wylie, Dir.

Yuba College SBDC
15145 Lakeshore Dr.
PO Box 4550
Clearlake, California 95422-4550
Phone: (707)995-3440
Fax: (707)995-3605
George McQueen, Dir.

Contra Costa SBDC
2425 Bisso Ln., Ste. 200
Concord, California 94520
Phone: (510)646-5377
Fax: (510)646-5299
Debra Longwood, Dir.

North Coast Small Business
Development Center
207 Price Mall, Ste. 500
Crescent City, California 95531
Phone: (707)464-2168
Fax: (707)465-6008
Fran Clark, Dir.

Imperial Valley Satellite SBDC
Town & Country Shopping Center
301 N. Imperial Ave., Ste. B
El Centro, California 92243
Phone: (619)312-9800
Fax: (619)312-9838
Debbie Trujillo, Satellite Mgr.

Export SBDC/E1 Monte Outreach
Center
10501 Valley Blvd., Ste. 106
El Monte, California 91731
Phone: (818)459-4111
Fax: (818)443-0463
Charles Blythe, Manager

North Coast/Satellite Center
520 E. St.
Eureka, California 95501
Phone: (707)445-9720
Fax: (707)445-9652
Duff Heuttner, Bus. Counselor

Central California
Small Business Development Center
3419 W. Shaw Ave., Ste. 102
Fresno, California 93711
Phone: (209)275-1223
Fax: (209)275-1499
Dennis Winans, Dir.

Gavilan College Small Business
Development Center
7436 Monterey St.
Gilroy, California 95020
Phone: (408)847-0373
Fax: (408)847-0393
Peter Graff, Dir.

Accelerate Technology Assistance
Small Business Development Center
4199 Campus Dr.
University Towers, Ste. 240
Irvine, California 92715
Phone: (714)509-2990
Fax: (714)509-2997
Tiffany Haugen, Dir.

Amador SBDC
P.O. Box 1077
222 N. Hwy. 49
Jackson, California 95642
Phone: (209)223-0351
Fax: (209)223-5237

Greater San Diego Chamber of
Commerce Small Business
Development Center
4275 Executive Sq., Ste. 920
La Jolla, California 92037
Phone: (619)453-9388
Fax: (619)450-1997
Hal Lefkowitz, Dir.

East Los Angeles SBDC
5161 East Pomona Blvd., Ste. 212
Los Angeles, California 90022
Phone: (213)262-9797
Fax: (213)262-2704

Export Small Business Development
Center of Southern California

110 E. 9th, Ste. A669
Los Angeles, California 90079
Phone: (213)892-1111
Fax: (213)892-8232
Gladys Moreau, Dir.

South Central LA/Satellite
SBDC
4060 S. Figueroa St.
Los Angeles, California 90037
Phone: (213)846-1710
Fax: (213)535-1686
Cope Norcross, Satellite Mgr.

Alpine SBDC
P.O. Box 265
3 Webster St.
Markleeville, California 96120
Phone: (916)694-2475
Fax: (916)694-2478

Yuba/Sutter Satellite
SBDC
429 10th St.
Marysville, California 95901
Phone: (916)749-0153
Fax: (916)749-0152

Valley Sierra SBDC
Merced Satellite
1632 N St.
Merced, California 95340
Phone: (209)725-3800
Fax: (209)383-4959
Nick Starianoudakis, Satellite Mgr.

Valley Sierra Small Business
Development Center
1012 11th St., Ste. 300
Modesto, California 95354
Phone: (209)521-6177
Fax: (209)521-9373
Kelly Bearden, Dir.

Napa Valley College Small Business
Development Center
1556 First St., Ste. 103
Napa, California 94559
Phone: (707)253-3210
Fax: (707)253-3068
Michael Kauffman, Dir.

Inland Empire Business Incubator
SBDC
Building 409
Norton Air Force Base, California

92509
Phone: (909)382-0065
Fax: (909)382-8543
Chuck Eason, Inubator Mgr.

East Bay Small Business
Development Center
519 17th. St., Ste. 210
Oakland, California 94612
Phone: (510)893-4114
Fax: (510)893-5532
Napoleon Britt, Dir.

International Trade Office
SBDC
3282 E. Guasti Rd., Ste. 100
Ontario, California 91761
Phone: (909)390-8071
Fax: (909)390-8077
John Hernandez, Trade Manager

Coachella Valley SBDC
Palm Springs Satellite Center
501 S. Indian Canyon Dr., Ste. 222
Palm Springs, California 92264
Phone: (619)864-1311
Fax: (619)864-1319
Brad Mix, Satellite Mgr.

Pasadena Satellite
SBDC
2061 N. Los Robles, Ste. 106
Pasadena, California 91104
Phone: (818)398-9031
Fax: (818)398-3059
David Ryal, Satellite Mgr.

Pico Rivera SBDC
9058 E. Washington Blvd.
Pico Rivera, California 90660
Phone: (310)942-9965
Fax: (310)942-9745
Beverly Taylor, Satellite Mgr.

Eastern Los Angeles County Small
Business Development Center
375 S. Main St., Ste. 101
Pomona, California 91766
Phone: (909)629-2247
Fax: (909)629-8310
Toni Valdez, Dir.

Pomona SBDC
375 S. Main St., Ste. 101
Pomona, California 91766
Phone: (909)629-2247

Fax: (909)629-8310
Paul Hischar, Satellite Manager

Cascade Small Business Development
Center
737 Auditorium Dr., Ste. A
Redding, California 96001
Phone: (916)247-8100
Fax: (916)241-1712
Carole Enmark, Dir.

Inland Empire Small Business
Development Center
2002 Iowa Ave., Bldg. D, Ste. D-110
Riverside, California 92507
Phone: (909)781-2345
Free: (800)750-2353
Fax: (909)781-2353
Terri Corrazini Ooms, Dir.

California Trade and Commerce
Agency
California SBDC
801 K St. Ste. 1700
Sacramento, California 95814
Phone: (916)324-5068
Fax: (916)322-5084
Kim Neri, State Dir.

Greater Sacramento SBDC
1410 Ethan Way
Sacramento, California 95825
Phone: (916)563-3210
Fax: (916)563-3264
Cynthia Steimle, Director

Calaveras SBDC
P.O. Box 431
3 N. Main St.
San Andreas, California 95249
Phone: (209)754-1834
Fax: (209)754-4107

San Francisco SBDC
711 Van Ness, Ste. 305
San Francisco, California 94102
Phone: (415)561-1890
Fax: (415)561-1894
Tim Sprinkles, Director

Orange County Small Business
Development Center
901 E. Santa Ana Blvd., Ste. 101
Santa Ana, California 92701
Phone: (714)647-1172
Fax: (714)835-9008
Gregory Kishel, Dir.

Southwest Los Angeles County
Westside Satellite
SBDC
3233 Donald Douglas Loop S., Ste. C
Santa Monica, California 90405
Phone: (310)398-8883
Fax: (310)398-3024
Ken Davis, Admin. Asst.

Redwood Empire Small Business
Development Center
520 Mendocino Ave., Ste. 210
Santa Rosa, California 95401
Phone: (707)524-1770
Fax: (707)524-1772
Charles Robbins, Dir.

San Joaquin Delta College Small
Business Development Center
814 N. Hunter St.
Stockton, California 95202
Phone: (209)474-5089
Fax: (209)474-5605
Gillian Murphy, Dir.

Silicon Valley SBDC
298 S. Sunnyvale Ave., Ste. 204
Sunnyvale, California 94086
Phone: (408)736-0680
Fax: (408)736-0679
Eliza Minor, Director

Southwest Los Angeles County Small
Business Development Center
21221 Western Ave., Ste. 110
Torrance, California 90501
Phone: (310)787-6466
Fax: (310)782-8607
Susan Hunter, Dir.

West Company SBDC
367 N. State St., Ste. 208
Ukiah, California 95482
Phone: (707)468-3553
Fax: (707)462-8945
Sheilah Rogers, Director

North Los Angeles Small Business
Development Center
14540 Victory Blvd., Ste. 206
Van Nuys, California 91411
Phone: (818)373-7092
Fax: (818)373-7740
Wilma Berglund, Dir.

Export SBDC Satellite Center
5700 Ralston St., Ste. 310
Ventura, California 93003
Phone: (805)644-6191
Fax: (805)658-2252
Heather Wicka, Manager

Gold Coast SBDC
5700 Ralston St., Ste. 310
Ventura, California 93003
Phone: (805)644-6191
Fax: (805)658-2252
Heather Wicka, Manager

High Desert SBDC
Victorville Satellite Center
15490 Civic Dr., Ste. 102
Victorville, California 92392
Phone: (619)951-1592
Fax: (619)951-8929
Megan Partington, Business
Consultant

Central California /Visalia Satellite
SBDC
430 W. Caldwell Ave., Ste. D
Visalia, California 93277
Phone: (209)625-3051
Fax: (209)625-3053
Randy Mason, Satellite Mgr.

Colorado

Adams State College
Small Business Development Center
Business Bldg., No. 105
Alamosa, Colorado 81102
Phone: (719)587-7372
Fax: (719)587-7603
Peggy Micklich, Dir.

Community College of Aurora
Small Business Development Center
9905 E. Colfax
Aurora, Colorado 80010-2119
Phone: (303)341-4849
Fax: (303)361-2953
Randy Johnson, Dir.

Front Range Community College
(Boulder)
Small Business Development Center
Boulder Chamber of Commerce
2440 Pearl St.
Boulder, Colorado 80302

Phone: (303)442-1475
Fax: (303)938-8837
Joe Bell, Dir.

Pueblo Community College (Canon
City)
Small Business Development Center
402 Valley Rd.
Canon City, Colorado 81212
Phone: (719)275-5335
Fax: (719)275-4400
Elwin Boody, Dir.

Pikes Peak Community College
Small Business Development Center
Colorado Springs Chamber of
Commerce
PO Drawer B
Colorado Springs, Colorado 80901-
3002
Phone: (303)471-4836
Fax: (303)635-1571

Colorado Northwestern Community
College
Small Business Development Center
50 College Dr.
Craig, Colorado 81625
Phone: (970)824-7078
Fax: (970)824-3527
Ken Farmer, Dir.

Delta Small Business Development
Center
Delta Montrose Vocational School
1765 US Hwy. 50
Delta, Colorado 81416
Phone: (970)874-8772
Fax: (970)874-8796
Steve Schrock, Dir.

Community College of Denver
Small Business Development Center
Greater Denver Chamber of
Commerce
1445 Market St.
Denver, Colorado 80202
Phone: (303)620-8076
Fax: (303)534-3200
Tamela Lee, Dir.

Office of Business Development
Colorado SBDC
1625 Broadway, Ste. 1710
Denver, Colorado 80202

Phone: (303)892-3809
Fax: (303)892-3848
Joe Bell, Dir.

Fort Lewis College
Small Business Development Center
1000 Rim Dr.
Durango, Colorado 81301
Phone: (970)247-7009
Fax: (970)247-7623
Jim Reser, Dir.
E-mail: reser-j@fortlewis.edu

Front Range Community College
(Fort Collins)
Small Business Development Center
2627 Redwing Rd., Ste. 105
Fort Collins, Colorado 80526
Phone: (970)226-0881
Fax: (970)204-0385
Frank Pryor, Dir.

Morgan Community College (Fort
Morgan)
Small Business Development Center
300 Main St.
Fort Morgan, Colorado 80701
Phone: (970)867-3351
Fax: (970)867-3352
Lori Slinn, Dir.

Colorado Mountain College
(Glenwood Springs)
Small Business Development Center
215 9th St.
Glenwood Springs, Colorado 81601
Phone: (970)928-0120
Free: (800)621-1647
Fax: (970)945-1531
Susan Glenn-James, Dir.

SBDC
1726 Cole Blvd., Ste. 310
Golden, Colorado 80401
Phone: (303)277-1840
Fax: (303)277-1899

Mesa State College
Small Business Development Center
304 W. Main St.
Grand Junction, Colorado 81505-
1606
Phone: (970)243-5242
Fax: (970)241-0771

Greeley/Weld Chamber of Commerce
Small Business Development Center
Aims Community College
902 7th Ave.
Greeley, Colorado 80631
Phone: (970)352-3661
Fax: (970)352-3572

Red Rocks Community College Small
Business Development Center
777 S. Wadsworth Blvd., Ste. 254
Bldg. 4
Lakewood, Colorado 80226
Phone: (303)987-0710
Fax: (303)987-1331
Jayne Reiter, Acting Dir.

Lamar Community College
Small Business Development Center
2400 S. Main
Lamar, Colorado 81052
Phone: (719)336-8141
Fax: (719)336-2448
Elwood Gillis, Dir.

Small Business Development Center
Arapahoe Community College
South Metro Chamber of Commerce
7901 S. Park Plz., Ste. 110
Littleton, Colorado 80120
Phone: (303)795-5855
Fax: (303)795-7520
Selma Kristel, Dir.

Pueblo Community College Small
Business Development Center
900 W. Orman Ave.
Pueblo, Colorado 81004
Phone: (719)549-3224
Fax: (719)546-2413
Rita Friberg, Dir.

Morgan Community College
(Stratton)
Small Business Development Center
PO Box 28
Stratton, Colorado 80836
Phone: (719)348-5596
Fax: (719)348-5887
Roni Carr, Dir.

Trinidad State Junior College
Small Business Development Center
136 W. Main St.
Davis Bldg.

Trinidad, Colorado 81082
Phone: (719)846-5645
Fax: (719)846-4550
Dennis O'Connor, Dir.

Front Range Community College
(Westminster)
Small Business and International
Development Center
3645 W. 112th Ave.
Westminster, Colorado 80030
Phone: (303)460-1032
Fax: (303)469-7143
Michael Lenzini, Dir.

Connecticut

Bridgeport Regional Business
Council
Small Business Development Center
10 Middle St., 14th Fl.
Bridgeport, Connecticut 06604-4229
Phone: (203)330-4813
Fax: (203)366-0105
Juan Scott, Dir.

Quinebaug Valley Community
Technical College
Small Business Development Center
742 Upper Maple St.
Danielson, Connecticut 06239-1440
Phone: (203)774-1133
Fax: (203)774-7768
Roger Doty, Dir.

University of Connecticut (Groton)
Small Business Development Center
Administration Bldg., Rm. 300
1084 Shennecossett Rd.
Groton, Connecticut 06340-6097
Phone: (860)449-1188
Fax: (860)445-3415
William Lockwood, Dir.

Middlesex Country Chamber of
Commerce
SBDC
393 Main St.
Middletown, Connecticut 06457
Phone: (860)344-2158
Fax: (860)346-1043
John Serignese

Greater New Haven Chamber of
Commerce
Small Business Development Center
195 Church St.
New Haven, Connecticut 06510-2009
Phone: (203)782-4390
Fax: (203)787-6730
Pete Rivera, Dir.

Southwestern Area Commerce and
Industry Association
Small Business Development Center
1 Landmark Sq., Ste. 230
Stamford, Connecticut 06901
Phone: (203)359-3220
Fax: (203)967-8294
George Ahl, Dir.

University of Connecticut
School of Business Administration
Connecticut SBDC
E-mail: oconnor@ct.sbdc.uconn.edu
2 Bourn Place, U-94
Storrs Mansfield, Connecticut 06269
Phone: (860)486-4135
Fax: (860)486-1576
John O'Connor, State Dir.

Connecticut SBDC
101 S. Main St.
Waterbury, Connecticut 06706-1042
Phone: (203)757-8937
Fax: (203)756-9077
Ilene Oppenheim

University of Connecticut (Greater
Hartford Campus)
Small Business Development Center
1800 Asylum Ave.
West Hartford, Connecticut 06117
Phone: (860)241-4986
Fax: (860)241-4907
Zaiga Antonetti, Assoc. State Dir.

Eastern Connecticut State University
Small Business Development Center
83 Windham St.
Williamantic, Connecticut 06226-
2211
Phone: (860)465-5349
Fax: (860)465-5143
Henry Reed, Dir.

Delaware

Delaware State University
School of Business Economics
SBDC
1200 N. Dupont Hwy.
Dover, Delaware 19901
Phone: (302)678-1555
Fax: (302)739-2333
Jim Crisfield, Director

Delaware Technical and Community
College
SBDC
Industrial Training Bldg.
PO Box 610
Georgetown, Delaware 19947
Phone: (302)856-1555
Fax: (302)856-5779
William F. Pfaff, Dir.

University of Delaware
Delaware SBDC
Purnell Hall-Ste. 005
Newark, Delaware 19716-2711
Phone: (302)831-1555
Fax: (302)831-1423
Clinton Tymes, State Dir.

Small Business Resource &
Information Center
SBDC
1318 N. Market St.
Wilmington, Delaware 19801
Phone: (302)571-1555
Barbara Necarsulmer, Mgr.

District of Columbia

George Washington University
East of the River Community
Development Corp.
SBDC
3101 MLK Jr., Ave., SE, 3rd Fl.
Washington, District of Columbia
20010
Phone: (202)561-4975
Howard Johnson, Counselor

George Washington University
National Law Center
Small Business Clinic
720 20th St. NW
Washington, District of Columbia
20052

Phone: (202)994-7463
Fax: (202)994-4946
Susan Jones, Dir.

Howard University
SBDC
2000 14th St., NW, 2nd Fl.
Washington, District of Columbia
20009
Phone: (202)396-1200
Jose Hernandez, Counselor

Marshall Heights Community
Development Organization
SBDC
3917 Minnesota Ave., NE
Washington, District of Columbia
20019
Phone: (202)396-1200
Terry Strong, Counselor

Metropolitan Washington
SBDC
6th & Fairmont Sts., N.W., Rm. 128
Washington, District of Columbia
20059
Phone: (202)806-1550
Fax: (202)806-1777
Woodrow "Woody" McCutchen,
Regional Dir.

Ward Five Community Development
Corp.
SBDC
Satellite Location
901 Newton St., NE, Ste. 103
Washington, District of Columbia
20017
Phone: (202)396-1200
Fax: (202)396-4106
Terry Strong

Washington District Office
Business Information Center
SBDC
1110 Vermont Ave., NW, 9th Fl.
Washington, District of Columbia
20005
Phone: (202)606-4000
Carmen Long, Counselor

Florida

SBDC (Bartow)
600 N. Broadway, Ste. 300

Bartow, Florida 33830
Phone: (941)534-4370
Fax: (941)533-1247
Marcela Stanislaus, Vice President

Florida Atlantic University (Boca Raton)
Small Business Development Center
PO Box 3091
Bldg. T9
Boca Raton, Florida 33431
Phone: (407)362-5620
Fax: (407)362-5623
Nancy Young, Dir.

UCF Brevard Campus
Small Business Development Center
1519 Clearlake Rd.
Cocoa, Florida 32922
Phone: (407)951-1060

Dania Small Business Development Center
46 SW 1st Ave.
Dania, Florida 33304-3607
Phone: (954)987-0100
William Healy, Regional Mgr.

Florida Regional SBDC
Daytona Beach Community College
1200 W. International Speedway Blvd.
Daytona Beach, Florida 32114
Phone: (904)947-3141
Fax: (904)254-4465

Florida Atlantic University
Commercial Campus
Small Business Development Center
1515 W. Commercial Blvd., Rm. 11
Fort Lauderdale, Florida 33309
Phone: (954)771-6520
Fax: (954)776-6645
John Hudson, Regional Mgr.

Minority Business Development Center
SBDC
5950 West Oakland Park Blvd., Ste. 307
Fort Lauderdale, Florida 33313
Phone: (954)485-5333
Fax: (954)485-2514

Edison Community College
Small Business Development Center

8099 College Pky. SW
Fort Myers, Florida 33919
Phone: (941)489-9200
Fax: (941)489-9051
Dan Regelski, Management Consultant

Florida Gulf Coast University
The Midway Center
Small Business Development Center
17595 S. Tamiami Trail, Ste. 200
Midway Ctr.
Ft. Myers, Florida 33908-4500
Phone: (941)590-1053

Indian River Community College
Small Business Development Center
3209 Virginia Ave., Rm. 114
Fort Pierce, Florida 34981-5599
Phone: (407)462-4756
Fax: (407)462-4796
Richard Carreno, Dir.

Okaloosa-Walton Community College
SBDC
1170 Martin Luther King, Jr. Blvd.
Fort Walton Beach, Florida 32547
Phone: (904)863-6543
Fax: (904)863-6564
Walter Craft, Mgr.

University of North Florida (Gainesville)
Small Business Development Center
505 NW 2nd Ave., Ste. D
PO Box 2518
Gainesville, Florida 32601-2518
Phone: (352)377-5621
Fax: (352)372-4132
Bill Stensgaard, Regional Mgr.

University of North Florida (Jacksonville)
Small Business Development Center
College of Business
4567 St. John's Bluff Rd. S
Bldg. 11, Rm. 2163
Jacksonville, Florida 32216
Phone: (904)646-2476
Fax: (904)646-2594
Lowell Salter, Dir.

Gulf Coast Community College
SBDC
2500 Minnesota Ave.

Lynn Haven, Florida 32444
Phone: (904)271-1108
Fax: (904)271-1109
Doug Davis, Dir.

Brevard Community College (Melbourne)
Small Business Development Center
3865 N. Wickham Rd., CM 207
Melbourne, Florida 32935
Phone: (407)632-1111
Fax: (407)232-1111
Victoria Peak, Mgr.

Florida International University
Small Business Development Center
University Park
EAS-2620
Miami, Florida 33199
Phone: (305)348-2272
Marvin Nesbit, Regional Dir.

Florida International University (North Miami Campus)
Small Business Development Center
Academic Bldg. No. 1, Rm. 350
NE 151 and Biscayne Blvd.
Miami, Florida 33181
Phone: (305)940-5790
Fax: (305)348-2965
Royland Jarrett, Regional Mgr.

Miami Dade Community College
Small Business Development Center
6300 NW 7th Ave.
Miami, Florida 33150
Phone: (305)237-1906
Fax: (305)237-1908
Frederick Bonneau, Dir.

Ocala Small Business Development Center
110 E. Silver Springs Blvd.
PO Box 1210
Ocala, Florida 34470-6613
Phone: (352)629-8051
Philip Geist, Regional Mgr.

University of Central Florida
Small Business Development Center
College of Business Administration, 309
PO Box 161530
Orlando, Florida 32816-1530
Phone: (407)823-5554

Fax: (407)823-3073
Al Polfer, Dir.

Palm Beach Gardens
Florida Atlantic University
SBDC
Northrop Center
3970 RCA Blvd., Ste. 7323
Palm Beach Gardens, Florida 33410
Phone: (407)691-8550
Fax: (407)692-8502
Steve Windhaus, Regional Mgr.

Procurement Technical Assistance
Program
University of West Florida
Small Business Development Center
11000 University Pky., Bldg. 8
Pensacola, Florida 32514
Phone: (904)474-2908
Fax: (904)474-2126
Martha Cobb, Dir.

University of West Florida
Downtown Center
Florida SBDC
19 West Garden St. Ste. 300
Pensacola, Florida 32501
Phone: (904)444-2066
Fax: (904)444-2070
Jerry Cartwright, State Dir.

Seminole Community College
SBDC
100 Weldon Blvd., Bldg. R
Sanford, Florida 32773-6199
Phone: (407)328-4722
Fax: (407)330-4489

Florida Agricultural and Mechanical
University
Small Business Development Center
1157 E. Tennessee St.
Tallahassee, Florida 32308
Phone: (904)599-3407
Fax: (904)561-2395
Patricia McGowan, Dir.

SBDC Training Center
Skipper Palms Shopping Center
1111 N. Westshore Dr., Annex B
Tampa, Florida 33607
Phone: (813)554-2341
Fax: (813)554-2356
Charles Attardo, Mgr.

E-mail:
SBDC@smtc_fla.enterprise.state.fl.us

University of South Florida (Tampa)
Small Business Development Center
College of Business Adminstration
4202 E. Fowler Ave., BSN 3403
Tampa, Florida 33620
Phone: (813)974-4371
Free: (800)733-7232
Fax: (813)974-5020
Dick Hardesty, Mgr.

Georgia

Darton College
Southwest Georgia District Small
Business Development Center
E-mail: sbdcalb@uga.cc.uga.edu
Business and Technology Center
230 S. Jackson St., Ste. 333
Albany, Georgia 31701-2885
Phone: (912)430-4303
Fax: (912)430-3933
Sue Ford, District Dir.

Georgia SBDC
Chicopee Complex
University of Georgia
1180 E. Broad St.
Athens, Georgia 30602-5412
Phone: (706)542-6762
Fax: (706)542-6776
Hank Logan, State Dir.
E-mail: sbdcath@uga.cc.uga.edu

NE Georgia District
SBDC
University of Georgia
1180 E. Broad St.
Athens, Georgia 30602-5412
Phone: (706)542-7436
Fax: (706)542-6823
Gayle Rosenthal, Mgr.

NW Georgia District
University of Georgia
SBDC
1180 E. Broad St.
Athens, Georgia 30602-5412
Phone: (706)542-6756
Fax: (706)542-6776

Georgia State University
Small Business Development Center

E-mail: sbdcatl@uga.cc.uga.edu
Box 874
University Plz.
Atlanta, Georgia 30303-3083
Phone: (404)651-3550
Fax: (404)651-1035
Lee Quarterman, Center Mgr.

Morris Brown College
Small Business Development Center
643 Martin Luther King, Jr., Dr. NW
Atlanta, Georgia 30314
Phone: (404)220-0205
Fax: (404)688-5985
Ray Johnson, Center Mgr.

Augusta College
Small Business Development Center
1061 Katherine St.
Augusta, Georgia 30904-6105
Phone: (706)737-1790
Fax: (706)731-7937
Jeff Sanford, Center Mgr.
E-mail: sbdcaug@uga.cc.uga.edu

University of Georgia (Brunswick)
Small Business Development Center
1107 Fountain Lake Dr.
Brunswick, Georgia 31525-3039
Phone: (912)264-7343
Fax: (912)262-3095
George Eckerd, Center Mgr.
E-mail: sbdcrun@uga.cc.uga.edu

Columbus College
Small Business Development Center
E-mail: sbdccolu@uga.cc.uga.edu
928 45th St.
North Bdlg., Rm. 523
Columbus, Georgia 31904-6572
Phone: (708)649-7433
Fax: (708)649-1928
Tom Snyder, Center Mgr.

DeKalb Small Business Development
Center
DeKalb Chamber of Commerce
750 Commerce Dr., Ste. 201
Decatur, Georgia 30030-2622
Phone: (404)378-8000
Fax: (404)378-3397
Eric Bonaparte, Center Mgr.

Gainesville Small Business
Development Center
E-mail: sbdcgain@uga.cc.uga.edu

500 Jesse Jewel Pky., Ste. 304
Gainesville, Georgia 30501-4203
Phone: (706)531-5681
Fax: (706)531-5684
Ron Simmons, Center Mgr.

Kennesaw State College
Small Business Development Center
1000 Chastain Rd.
Kennesaw, Georgia 30144-5591
Phone: (770)423-6450
Fax: (770)423-6564
Carlotta Roberts, Center Mgr.
E-mail:
carobert@kscmail.kennesaw.edu

Southeast Georgia District (Macon)
Small Business Development Center
E-mail: sbdcmac@uga.cc.uga.edu
PO Box 13212
401 Cherry St., Ste. 701
Macon, Georgia 31208-3212
Phone: (912)751-6592
Fax: (912)751-6607
David Mills, District Mgr.

Clayton State College
Small Business Development Center
E-mail: sbdcmorr@uga.cc.uga.edu
PO Box 285
Morrow, Georgia 30260
Phone: (404)961-3440
Fax: (404)961-3428
Alex Ferdinand, Center Mgr.

UGA SBDC
1770 Indian Trail Rd., Ste. 410
Norcross, Georgia 30093
Phone: (770)806-2124
Robert Dixon, District Dir.
Robert Andoh, Center Mgr.

Floyd Junior College
Small Business Development Center
E-mail: sbdcrome@uga.cc.uga.edu
PO Box 1864
Rome, Georgia 30162-1864
Phone: (404)295-6326
Fax: (404)295-6732
Drew Tonsmeire, Center Mgr.

Southeast Georgia District
(Savannah)
Small Business Development Center
450 Mall Blvd., Ste. H

Savannah, Georgia 31406-4824
Phone: (912)356-2755
Fax: (912)353-3033
Harry O'Brien, Center Mgr.
E-mail: sbdcsav@uga.u.uga.edu

University of Georgia (Statesboro)
Small Business Development Center
325 S. Main St.
Statesboro, Georgia 30460
Phone: (912)681-5194
Fax: (912)681-0648
David Lewis, Center Mgr.
E-mail: sbdcstat@uga.cc.uga.edu

Valdosta Small Business
Development Center
Baytree W. Professional Offices
1205 Baytree Rd., Ste. 9
Valdosta, Georgia 31602-2782
Phone: (912)245-3738
Fax: (912)245-3741
Suzanne Barnett, Center Mgr.
E-mail: sbdcval@uga.cc.uga.edu

Warner Robins Small Business
Development Center
151 Osigian Blvd.
Warner Robins, Georgia 31088
Phone: (912)953-9356
Fax: (912)953-9376
Ronald Reaves, Center Mgr.

Guam

Guam SBDC
University of Guam
PO Box 5061
UOG Station
Mangilao, Guam 96923
Phone: (671)735-2590
Fax: (671)735-2002
Dr. Sephen L Marder, Executive

Hawaii

Kona Circuit Rider
SBDC
200 West Kawili St.
Hilo, Hawaii 96720-4091
Phone: (808)933-3515
Fax: (808)933-3683
Jean Geer, Business Consultant

University of Hawaii at Hilo
Hawaii SBDC
200 W. Kawili St.
Hilo, Hawaii 96720-4091
Phone: (808)933-3515
Fax: (808)933-3683
Darryl Mleynek, State Dir.

University of Hawaii, West Oahu
SBDC
130 Merchant St., Ste. 1030
Honolulu, Hawaii 96813
Phone: (808)522-8131
Fax: (808)522-8135
Laura Noda, Center Dir.

Business Research Library
University of HI-Hilo
SBDC
590 Lipoa Pkwy. #128
Kihei, Hawaii 96753
Phone: (808)875-2400
Fax: (808)875-2452

Maui Community College
Small Business Development Center
Maui Research and Technology
Center
590 Lipoa Pky., No. 130
Kihei, Hawaii 96753-6900
Phone: (808)875-2402
Fax: (808)875-2452
David B. Fisher, Dir.

Kauai Community College
Small Business Development Center
3-1901 Kaumualii Hwy.
Lihue, Hawaii 96766-9591
Phone: (808)246-1748
Fax: (808)246-5102
Randy Gringas, Center Dir.

Idaho

Boise State University
Small Business Development Center
1910 University Dr.
Boise, Idaho 83725
Phone: (208)385-3875
Free: (800)225-3815
Fax: (208)385-3877
Robert Shepard, Regional Dir.

Boise State University
College of Business

Idaho SBDC
1910 University Dr.
Boise, Idaho 83725
Phone: (208)385-1640
Free: (800)225-3815
Fax: (208)385-3877
James Hogge, State Dir.

Idaho State University (Idaho Falls)
Small Business Development Center
2300 N. Yellowstone
Idaho Falls, Idaho 83401
Phone: (208)523-1087
Free: (800)658-3829
Fax: (208)523-1049
Betty Capps, Regional Dir.

Lewis-Clark State College
Small Business Development Center
500 8th Ave.
Lewiston, Idaho 83501
Phone: (208)799-2465
Fax: (208)799-2878
Helen LeBoeuf-Binninger, Regional
Dir.

Idaho Small Business Development
Center
305 E. Park St. Ste. 405
McCall, Idaho 83638
Phone: (208)634-2883
Larry Smith, Associate Editor
Consultant

Idaho State University (Pocatello)
Small Business Development Center
1651 Alvin Ricken Dr.
Pocatello, Idaho 83201
Phone: (208)232-4921
Free: (800)232-4921
Fax: (208)233-0268
Paul Cox, Regional Dir.

North Idaho College
SBDC
525 W. Clearwater Loop
Post Falls, Idaho 83854
Phone: (208)769-3296
Fax: (208)769-3223
John Lynn, Regional Dir.

College of Southern Idaho
Small Business Development Center
315 Falls Ave.
PO Box 1238

Twin Falls, Idaho 83303-1238
Phone: (208)733-9554
Fax: (208)733-9316
Cindy Bond, Regional Dir.

Illinois

Waubonsee Community College
(Aurora Campus)
Small Business Development Center
5 E. Galena Blvd.
Aurora, Illinois 60506
Phone: (630)892-3334
Fax: (630)892-3374
Mike O'Kelley, Dir.

Southern Illinois University at
Carbondale
Small Business Development Center
College of Business Administration
Carbondale, Illinois 62901-6702
Phone: (618)536-2424
Fax: (618)453-5040
Dennis Cody, Dir.

John A. Logan College
Small Business Development Center
RR 2
Carterville, Illinois 62918
Phone: (618)985-3741
Fax: (618)985-2248
Richard Fyke, Dir.

Kaskaskia College
Small Business Development Center
27210 College Rd.
Centralia, Illinois 62801
Phone: (618)532-2049
Fax: (618)532-4983
Richard McCullum, Dir.

University of Illinois at Urbana-
Champaign
Small Business Development Center
428 Commerce W.
1206 S. 6th St.
Champaign, Illinois 61820
Phone: (217)244-1585
Fax: (217)333-7410
Helen Lesieur, Dir.

Asian American Alliance
SBDC
6246 N. Pulaski Rd., Ste. 101
Chicago, Illinois 60646

Phone: (312)202-0600
Fax: (312)202-1007
Joon H. Lee, Dir.

Back of the Yards Neighborhood
Council
Small Business Development Center
1751 W. 47th St.
Chicago, Illinois 60609
Phone: (312)523-4419
Fax: (312)254-3525
Paul Ladniak, Dir.

Chicago Small Business Development
Center
DCCA James R. Thompson Center
100 W. Randolph, Ste. 3-400
Chicago, Illinois 60601
Phone: (312)814-6111
Fax: (312)814-2807
Carson Gallagher, Dir.

Eighteenth Street Development Corp.
Small Business Development Center
1839 S. Carpenter
Chicago, Illinois 60608
Phone: (312)733-2287
Fax: (312)733-7315
Maria Munoz, Dir.

Greater North Pulaski Development
Corp.
Small Business Development Center
4054 W. North Ave.
Chicago, Illinois 60639
Phone: (312)384-2262
Fax: (312)384-3850
Paul Peterson, Dir.

Industrial Council of Northwest
Chicago
Small Business Development Center
2023 W. Carroll
Chicago, Illinois 60612
Phone: (312)421-3941
Fax: (312)421-1871
Melvin Eisland, Dir.

Latin American Chamber of
Commerce
Small Business Development Center
2539 N. Kedzie, Ste. 11
Chicago, Illinois 60647
Phone: (312)252-5211
Fax: (312)252-7065
Arturo Venecia, Dir.

North Business and Industrial Council
(NORBIC)
SBDC
2500 W. Bradley Pl.
Chicago, Illinois 60618
Phone: (312)588-5855
Fax: (312)588-0734
Tom Kamykowski, Dir.

Richard J. Daley College
Small Business Development Center
7500 S. Pulaski Rd., Bldg. 200
Chicago, Illinois 60652
Phone: (312)838-0319
Fax: (312)838-0303
Jim Charney, Dir.

Women's Business Development
Center
Small Business Development Center
8 S. Michigan, Ste. 400
Chicago, Illinois 60603
Phone: (312)853-3477
Fax: (312)853-0145
Paul Carlin, Dir.

McHenry County College
Small Business Development Center
8900 U.S. Hwy. 14
Crystal Lake, Illinois 60012-2761
Phone: (815)455-6098
Fax: (815)455-9319
Susan Whitfield, Dir.

Danville Area Community College
Small Business Development Center
28 W. North St.
Danville, Illinois 61832
Phone: (217)442-7232
Fax: (217)442-6228
Ed Adrain, Dir.

Cooperative Extension Service
SBDC
985 W. Pershing Rd., Ste. F-4
Decatur, Illinois 62526
Phone: (217)875-8284
Fax: (217)875-8288
Rick Russell, Dir.

Sauk Valley Community College
Small Business Development Center
173 Illinois, Rte. 2
Dixon, Illinois 61021-9110
Phone: (815)288-5111

Fax: (815)288-5958
John Nelson, Dir.

Black Hawk College
Small Business Development Center
301 42nd Ave.
East Moline, Illinois 61244
Phone: (309)755-2200
Fax: (309)755-9847
Donna Scalf, Dir.

East St. Louis Small Business
Development Center
DCCA, State Office Bldg.
650 Missouri Ave., Ste. G32
East St. Louis, Illinois 62201
Phone: (618)482-3833
Fax: (618)482-3832
Robert Ahart, Dir.

Southern Illinois University at
Edwardsville
Small Business Development Center
Center for Advanced Manufacturing
and Production
Campus Box 1107
Edwardsville, Illinois 62026
Phone: (618)692-2929
Fax: (618)692-2647
Alan Hauff, Dir.

Elgin Community College
Small Business Development Center
1700 Spartan Dr., Office B-15
Elgin, Illinois 60123
Phone: (847)888-7675
Fax: (847)888-7995
Craig Fowler, Dir.

Evanston Business and Technology
Center
Small Business Development Center
1840 Oak Ave.
Evanston, Illinois 60201
Phone: (847)866-1817
Fax: (847)866-1808
Rick Holbrook, Dir.

College of DuPage
Small Business Development Center
22nd St. & Lambert Rd.
Glen Ellyn, Illinois 60137
Phone: (630)942-2600
Fax: (630)942-3789
David Gay, Dir.

Lewis and Clark Community College
SBDC
5800 Godfrey Rd.
Godfrey, Illinois 62035
Phone: (618)466-3411
Fax: (618)466-0810
Bob Duane, Dir.

College of Lake County
Small Business Development Center
19351 W. Washington St.
Grayslake, Illinois 60030
Phone: (847)223-3633
Fax: (847)223-9371
Linda Jorn, Dir.

Southeastern Illinois College
Small Business Development Center
303 S. Commercial
Harrisburg, Illinois 62946-2125
Phone: (618)252-5001
Fax: (618)252-0210
Becky Williams, Dir.

Rend Lake College
Small Business Development Center
Rte. 1
Ina, Illinois 62846
Phone: (618)437-5321
Fax: (618)437-5677
Lisa Payne, Dir.

Joliet Junior College
Small Business Development Center
Renaissance Center, Rm. 312
214 N. Ottawa St.
Joliet, Illinois 60431
Phone: (815)727-6544
Fax: (815)722-1895
Denise Mikulski, Dir.

Kankakee Community College
Small Business Development Center
101 S. Schuyler Ave.
Kankakee, Illinois 60901
Phone: (815)933-0376
Fax: (815)933-0380
JoAnn Seggebruch, Dir.

Western Illinois University
Small Business Development Center
114 Seal Hall
Macomb, Illinois 61455
Phone: (309)298-2211
Fax: (309)298-2520
Dan Voorhis, Dir.

Maple City Business and Technology
Center
Small Business Development Center
620 S. Main St.
Monmouth, Illinois 61462
Phone: (309)734-4664
Fax: (309)734-8579
Carol Cook, Dir.

Illinois Valley Community College
Small Business Development Center
815 N. Orlando Smith Ave., Bldg. 11
Oglesby, Illinois 61348
Phone: (815)223-1740
Fax: (815)224-3033
Boyd Palmer, Dir.

Illinois Eastern Community College
Small Business Development Center
401 E. Main St.
Olney, Illinois 62450
Phone: (618)395-3011
Fax: (618)395-1922
John Spitz, Dir.

Moraine Valley College
Small Business Development Center
10900 S. 88th Ave.
Palos Hills, Illinois 60465
Phone: (708)974-5468
Fax: (708)974-0078
Hilary Gereg, Dir.

Bradley University
Small Business Development Center
141 N. Jobst Hall, 1st Fl.
Peoria, Illinois 61625
Phone: (309)677-2992
Fax: (309)677-3386
Roger Luman, Dir.

Illinois Central College
Small Business Development Center
124 SW Adams St., Ste. 300
Peoria, Illinois 61602
Phone: (309)676-7500
Fax: (309)676-7534
Susan Gorman, Dir.

Quincy Procurement Technical
Assistance Center
Small Business Development Center
301 Oak St.
Quincy, Illinois 62301
Phone: (217)228-5511
Edward Van Leer, Dir.

Rock Valley College
Small Business Development Center
1220 Rock St., Ste. 180
Rockford, Illinois 61101-1437
Phone: (815)968-4087
Fax: (815)968-4157
Beverly Kingsley, Dir.

Department of Commerce &
Community Affairs
Illinois SBDC
620 East Adams St., Third Fl.
Springfield, Illinois 62701
Phone: (217)524-5856
Fax: (217)785-6328
Jeff Mitchell, State Dir.

Lincoln Land Community College
Small Business Development Center
100 N. 11th St.
Springfield, Illinois 62703
Phone: (217)789-1017
Fax: (217)789-0958

Shawnee Community College
Small Business Development Center
Shawnee College Rd.
Ullin, Illinois 62992
Phone: (618)634-9618
Fax: (618)634-9028
Donald Denny, Dir.

Governors State University
Small Business Development Center
University Park, Illinois 60466
Phone: (708)534-4929
Fax: (708)534-8457
Christine Cochrane, Dir.

Indiana

Batesville Office of Economic
Development
SBDC
132 S. Main
Batesville, Indiana 47006
Phone: (812)933-6110

Bedford Chamber of Commerce
SBDC
1116 W. 16th St.
Bedford, Indiana 47421
Phone: (812)275-4493

Bloomfield Chamber of Commerce
SBDC

c/o Harrah Realty Co.
23 S. Washfington St.
Bloomfield, Indiana 47424
Phone: (812)275-4493

Bloomington Area Small Business
Development Center
116 W. 6th St., No. 100
Bloomington, Indiana 47404
Phone: (812)339-8937
Fax: (812)336-0651
David Miller. Dir.

Clay Count Chamber of Commerce
SBDC
12 N. Walnut St.
Brazil, Indiana 47834
Phone: (812)448-8457

Brookville Chamber of Commerce
SBDC
PO Box 211
Brookville, Indiana 47012
Phone: (317)647-3177

Clinton Chamber of Commerce
SBDC
292 N. 9th St.
Clinton, Indiana 47842
Phone: (812)832-3844

Columbia City Chamber of
Commerce
SBDC
112 N. Main St.
Columbia City, Indiana 46725
Phone: (219)248-8131

Columbus Regional Small Business
Development Center
4920 N. Warren Dr.
Columbus, Indiana 47203
Phone: (812)372-6480
Free: (800)282-7232
Fax: (812)372-0228
Glenn Dunlap, Dir.

Connerville SBDC
504 Central
Connersville, Indiana 47331
Phone: (317)825-8328

Chamber of Commerce of Harrison
County
310 N. Elm St.
Corydon, Indiana 47112

Phone: (812)738-2137
Fax: (812)738-2137

Montgomery County Chamber of
Commerce
SBDC
211 S. Washington St.
Crawfordsville, Indiana 47933
Phone: (317)654-5507

Decatur Chamber of Commerce
SBDC
125 E. Monroe St.
Decatur, Indiana 46733
Phone: (219)724-2604

City of Delphi Community
Development
SBDC
201 S. Union
Delphi, Indiana 46923
Phone: (317)564-6692

Southwestern Indiana Small Business
Development Center
100 NW 2nd St., Ste. 200
Evansville, Indiana 47708
Phone: (812)425-7232
Fax: (812)421-5883
Jeff Lake, Dir.

Northeast Indiana Small Business
Development Center
1830 Wayne Trace
Fort Wayne, Indiana 46803
Phone: (219)426-0040
Fax: (219)424-0024
A. V. Fleming, Dir.

Clinton County Chamber of
Commerce
SBDC
207 S. Main St.
Frankfort, Indiana 46041
Phone: (317)654-5507

Northlake Small Business
Development Center
487 Broadway, Ste. 201
Gary, Indiana 46402
Phone: (219)882-2000

Greencastle Partnership Center
SBDC
2 S. Jackson St.
Greencastle, Indiana 46135
Phone: (317)653-4517

Greensburg Area Chamber of
Commerce
SBDC
125 W. Main St.
Greensburg, Indiana 47240
Phone: (812)663-2832

Hammond Development Corp.
SBDC
649 Conkey St.
Hammond, Indiana 46324
Phone: (219)853-6399

Blackford County Economic
Development
SBDC
PO Box 43
Hartford, Indiana 47001-0043
Phone: (317)348-4944

Indiana SBDC Network
E-mail: sthrash@in.net
One North Capitol, Ste. 420
Indianapolis, Indiana 46204
Phone: (317)264-6871
Fax: (317)264-3102

Indianapolis Regional Small Business
Development Center
342 N. Senate Ave.
Indianapolis, Indiana 46204-1708
Phone: (317)261-3030
Fax: (317)261-3053
Tim Tichenar, Dir.

Southern Indiana Small Business
Development Center
4100 Charlestown Road
New Albany, Indiana 47150
Phone: (812)945-0054
Fax: (812)948-4664
Gretchen Mahaffey, Dir.

Kendallville Chamber of Commerce
SBDC
228 S. Main St.
Kendallville, Indiana 46755
Phone: (219)347-1554

Kokomo-Howard County Small
Business Development Center
106 N. Washington
Kokomo, Indiana 46901
Phone: (317)457-5301
Fax: (317)452-4564
Todd Moser, Dir.

LaPorte Small Business Development
Center
414 Lincolnway
La Porte, Indiana 46350
Phone: (219)326-7232

Greater Lafayette Area Small
Business Development Center
122 N. 3rd
Lafayette, Indiana 47901
Phone: (317)742-2394
Fax: (317)742-6276
Susan Davis, Dir.

Union County Chamber of Commerce
SBDC
102 N. Main St., No. 6
Liberty, Indiana 47353-1039
Phone: (317)458-5976

Linton/Stockton Chamber of
Commerce
SBDC
PO Box 208
Linton, Indiana 47441
Phone: (812)847-4846

Southeastern Indiana Small Business
Development Center
301 E. Main St.
Madison, Indiana 47250
Phone: (812)265-3127
Fax: (812)265-2923
Rose Marie Roberts, Dir.

Greater Martinsville Chamber of
Commerce
SBDC
210 N. Marion St.
Martinsville, Indiana 46151
Phone: (317)342-8110

Lake County Public Library
Small Business Development Center
1919 W. 81st. Ave.
Merrillville, Indiana 46410-5382
Phone: (219)756-7232

First Citizens Bank
SBDC
515 N. Franklin Sq.
Michigan City, Indiana 46360
Phone: (219)874-9245

Mitchell Chamber of Commerce
SBDC
1st National Bank

Main Street
Mitchell, Indiana 47446
Phone: (812)849-4441

Mount Vernon Chamber of
Commerce
SBDC
405 E. 4th St.
Mt. Vernon, Indiana 47620
Phone: (812)838-3639

East Central Indiana Small Business
Development Center
401 S. High St.
PO Box 842
Muncie, Indiana 47308
Phone: (317)284-8144
Fax: (317)741-5489
Barbara Armstrong, Dir.

Brown County Chamber of
Commerce
SBDC
PO Box 164
Nashville, Indiana 47448
Phone: (812)988-6647

Henry County Economic
Development Corp.
SBDC
1325 Broad St., Ste. B
New Castle, Indiana 47362
Phone: (317)529-4635

Jennings County Chamber of
Commerce
SBDC
PO Box 340
North Vernon, Indiana 47265
Phone: (812)346-2339

Paoli Chamber of Commerce
210 S. W. Court St.
P.O. Box 22
Paoli, Indiana 47454
Phone: (812)723-4769
Fax: (812)723-4769

Northwest Indiana (Portage)
Small Business Development Center
6100 Southport Rd.
Portage, Indiana 46368
Phone: (219)762-1696
Fax: (219)942-5806

Jay County Development Corp.
SBDC

121 W. Main St., Ste. A
Portland, Indiana 47371
Phone: (219)726-9311

Richmond-Wayne County Small
Business Development Center
33 S. 7th St.
Richmond, Indiana 47374
Phone: (317)962-2887
Fax: (317)966-0882
Doug Peters, Dir.

Rochester and Lake Manitou
Chamber of Commerce
Fulton Economic Development
Center
SBDC
617 Main St.
Rochester, Indiana 46975
Phone: (219)223-6773

Rushville Chamber of Commerce
SBDC
PO Box 156
Rushville, Indiana 46173
Phone: (317)932-2222

Washington County Chamber of
Commerce
210 N. Main St.
Salem, Indiana 47167-2031
Phone: (812)883-4303
Fax: (812)883-6008

St. Mary of the Woods College
SBDC
St. Mary-of-the-Woods, Indiana
47876
Phone: (812)535-5151

Greater Scott County Chamber of
Commerce
90 N. Main St., #B
Scottsburg, Indiana 47170
Phone: (812)752-4080
Fax: (812)752-7272

Seymour Chamber of Commerce
SBDC
PO Box 43
Seymour, Indiana 47274
Phone: (812)522-3681

Minority Business Development
Project Future
SBDC
401 Col

South Bend, Indiana 46634
Phone: (219)234-0051

South Bend Area Small Business
Development Center
300 N. Michigan
South Bend, Indiana 46601
Phone: (219)282-4350
Fax: (219)282-4344
Carolyn Anderson, Dir.

Economic Development Office
SBDC
46 E. Market St.
Spencer, Indiana 47460
Phone: (812)829-3245

Sullivan Chamber of Commerce
SBDC
10 S. Crt. St.
Sullivan, Indiana 47882
Phone: (812)268-4836

Tell City Chamber of Commerce
SBDC
Regional Federal Bldg.
645 Main St.
Tell City, Indiana 47586
Phone: (812)547-2385
Fax: (812)547-8378

Terre Haute Area Small Business
Development Center
Indiana State University
School of Business, Rm. 510
Terre Haute, Indiana 47809
Phone: (812)237-7676
Fax: (812)237-7675
William Minnis, Dir.

Tipton County Economic
Development Corp.
SBDC
136 E. Jefferson
Tipton, Indiana 46072
Phone: (317)675-7300

Porter County
SBDC
911 Wall St.
Valparaiso, Indiana 46383
Phone: (219)477-5256

Vevay/Switzerland Country
Foundation
SBDC
PO Box 193

Vevay, Indiana 47043
Phone: (812)427-2533

Vincennes University
SBDC
PO Box 887
Vincennes, Indiana 47591
Phone: (812)885-5749

Wabash Area Chamber of Commerce
Wabash Economic Development
Corp.
SBDC
67 S. Wabash
Wabash, Indiana 46992
Phone: (219)563-1168

Washington Daviess County
SBDC
1 Train Depot St.
Washington, Indiana 47501
Phone: (812)254-5262
Fax: (812)254-2550
Mark Brochin, Dir.

Purdue University
SBDC
Business & Industrial Development
Center
1220 Potter Dr.
West Lafayette, Indiana 47906
Phone: (317)494-5858

Randolph County Economic
Development Foundation
SBDC
111 S. Main St.
Winchester, Indiana 47394
Phone: (317)584-3266

Iowa

Iowa State University
Iowa SBDC
College of Business Administration
137 Lynn Ave.
Ames, Iowa 50014
Phone: (515)292-6351
Free: (800)373-7232
Fax: (515)292-0020
Ronald Manning, State Dir.

Iowa State University
Small Business Development Center
ISU Branch Office

2501 N. Loop Dr.
Bldg. 1, Ste. 608
Ames, Iowa 50010-8283
Phone: (515)296-7828
Free: (800)373-7232
Fax: (515)296-9910
Steve Carter, Dir.

DMACC Small Business
Development Center
Circle West Incubator
PO Box 204
Audubon, Iowa 50025
Phone: (712)563-2623
Fax: (712)563-2301
Lori Harmening-Webb, Dir.

University of Northern Iowa
Small Business Development Center
Business Bldg., Ste. 5
Cedar Falls, Iowa 50614-0120
Phone: (319)273-2696
Fax: (319)273-6830
Lyle Bowlin, Dir.

Iowa Western Community College
Small Business Development Center
2700 College Rd., Box 4C
Council Bluffs, Iowa 51502
Phone: (712)325-3260
Fax: (712)325-3408
Ronald Helms, Dir.

Southwestern Community College
Small Business Development Center
1501 W. Townline Rd.
Creston, Iowa 50801
Phone: (515)782-4161
Fax: (515)782-4164
Paul Havick, Dir.

Eastern Iowa Community College
District
Eastern Iowa Small Business
Development Center
304 W. 2nd St.
Davenport, Iowa 52801
Phone: (319)322-4499
Fax: (319)322-8241
Jon Ryan, Dir.

Drake University
Small Business Development Center
Drake Business Center
2429 University Ave.

Des Moines, Iowa 50311-4505
Phone: (515)271-2655
Fax: (515)271-4540
Benjamin Swartz, Dir.

Northeast Iowa Small Business
Development Center
770 Town Clock Plz.
Dubuque, Iowa 52001
Phone: (319)588-3350
Fax: (319)557-1591
Charles Tonn, Contact

Iowa Central Community College
SBDC
900 Central Ave., Ste. 4
Fort Dodge, Iowa 50501
Phone: (515)576-0099
Fax: (515)576-0826
Todd Madson, Dir.

University of Iowa
Small Business Development Center
108 Papajohn Business
Administration Bldg., Ste. S-160
Iowa City, Iowa 52242-1000
Phone: (319)335-3742
Free: (800)253-7232
Fax: (319)353-2445
Paul Heath, Dir.
E-mail: paul-heath@uiowa.edu

Kirkwood Community College
Small Business Development Center
2901 10th Ave.
Marion,Iowa 52302
Phone: (319)377-8256
Fax: (319)377-5667
Jim Anderson, Dir.

North Iowa Area Community College
Small Business Development Center
500 College Dr.
Mason City, Iowa 50401
Phone: (515)421-4342
Fax: (515)423-0931
Richard Petersen, Dir.

Indian Hills Community College
Small Business Development Center
525 Grandview Ave.
Ottumwa, Iowa 52501
Phone: (515)683-5127
Fax: (515)683-5263
Bryan Ziegler, Dir.

Western Iowa Tech Community
College
Small Business Development Center
4647 Stone Ave., Bldg. B
Box 265
Sioux City, Iowa 51102-0265
Phone: (712)274-6418
Free: (800)352-4649
Fax: (712)274-6429
Dennis Bogenrief, Dir.

Iowa Lakes Community College
(Spencer)
Small Business Development Center
Gateway Center
Hwy. 71 N
Spencer, Iowa 51301
Phone: (712)262-4213
Fax: (712)262-4047
John Beneke, Dir.

Southeastern Community College
Small Business Development Center
Drawer F
West Burlington, Iowa 52655
Phone: (319)752-2731
Fax: (319)752-3407

Kansas

Bendictine College
SBDC
1020 N. 2nd St.
Atchison, Kansas 66002
Phone: (913)367-5340
Fax: (913)367-6102
Don Laney, Dir.

Butler County Community College
Small Business Development Center
600 Walnut
Augusta, Kansas 67010
Phone: (316)775-1124
Fax: (316)775-1370
Dorinda Rolle, Dir.

Neosho County Community College
SBDC
1000 S. Allen
Chanute, Kansas 66720
Phone: (316)431-2820
Fax: (316)431-0082
Duane Clum, Dir.

Coffeyville Community College
SBDC

11th and Willow Sts.
Coffeyville, Kansas 67337-5064
Phone: (316)251-7700
Fax: (316)252-7098
Charles Shaver, Dir.

Colby Community College
Small Business Development Center
1255 S. Range
Colby, Kansas 67701
Phone: (913)462-3984
Fax: (913)462-8315
Robert Selby, Dir.

Cloud County Community College
SBDC
2221 Campus Dr.
PO Box 1002
Concordia, Kansas 66901
Phone: (913)243-1435
Fax: (913)243-1459
Tony Foster, Dir.

Dodge City Community College
Small Business Development Center
2501 N. 14th Ave.
Dodge City, Kansas 67801
Phone: (316)227-9247
Fax: (316)227-9200
Wayne E. Shiplet, Dir.

Emporia State University
Small Business Development Center
207 Cremer Hall
Emporia, Kansas 66801
Phone: (316)342-7162
Fax: (316)341-5418
Lisa Brumbaugh, Dir.

Fort Scott Community College
SBDC
2108 S. Horton
Fort Scott, Kansas 66701
Phone: (316)223-2700
Fax: (316)223-6530
Steve Pammenter, Dir.

Garden City Community College
SBDC
801 Campus Dr.
Garden City, Kansas 67846
Phone: (316)276-9632
Fax: (316)276-9630
Vern Kinderknecht, Regional Dir.

Fort Hays State University
Small Business Development Center
109 W. 10th St.
Hays, Kansas 67601
Phone: (913)628-5340
Fax: (913)628-1471
Clare Gustin, Dir.

Hutchinson Community College
Small Business Development Center
815 N. Walnut, Ste. 225
Hutchinson, Kansas 67501
Phone: (316)665-4950
Free: (800)289-3501
Fax: (316)665-8354
Clark Jacobs, Dir.

Independence Community College
SBDC
College Ave. & Brookside
PO Box 708
Independence, Kansas 67301
Phone: (316)331-4100
Fax: (316)331-5344
Preston Haddan, Dir.

Allen County Community College
SBDC
1801 N. Cottonwood
Iola, Kansas 66749
Phone: (316)365-5116
Fax: (316)365-3284

University of Kansas
Small Business Development Center
734 Vermont St., Ste. 104
Lawrence, Kansas 66044
Phone: (913)843-8844
Fax: (913)865-4400
Mike O'Donnell, Dir.

Seward County Community College
Small Business Development Center
1801 N. Kansas
PO Box 1137
Liberal, Kansas 67901
Phone: (316)624-1951
Fax: (316)624-0637
Tom Cornelius, Dir.

Kansas State University (Manhattan)
Small Business Development Center
College of Business Administration
2323 Anderson Ave., Ste. 100
Manhattan, Kansas 66502-2947

Phone: (913)532-5529
Fax: (913)532-5827
Fred Rice, Regional Dir.

Ottawa University
SBDC
College Ave., Box 70
Ottawa, Kansas 66067
Phone: (913)242-5200
Fax: (913)242-7429
Lori Kravets, Dir.

Johnson County Community College
Small Business Development Center
CEC Bldg., Rm. 223
Overland Park, Kansas 66210-1299
Phone: (913)469-3878
Fax: (913)469-4415
Glenda Sapp, Dir.

Labette Community College
SBDC
200 S. 14th
Parsons, Kansas 67357
Phone: (316)421-6700
Fax: (316)421-0921
Mark Turnbull, Dir.

Pittsburg State University
Small Business Development Center
Shirk Hall
Pittsburg, Kansas 66762
Phone: (316)235-4920
Fax: (316)232-6440
Kathryn Richard, Dir.

Pratt Community College
Small Business Development Center
Hwy. 61
Pratt, Kansas 67124
Phone: (316)672-5641
Fax: (316)672-5288
Pat Gordon, Dir.

Kansas State University (Salina)
Small Business Development Center
2409 Scanlan Ave.
Salina, Kansas 67401
Phone: (913)826-2622
Fax: (913)826-2936
Pat Mills, Dir.

Kansas SBDC
214 SW 6th St., Ste. 205
Topeka, Kansas 66603-3261
Phone: (913)296-6514

Fax: (913)296-3490
Debbie Bishop, Dir.

Washburn University of Topeka
SBDC
School of Business
101 Henderson Learning Center
Topeka, Kansas 66621
Phone: (913)231-1010
Fax: (913)231-1063
Wayne Glass, Regional Dir.
E-mail: zzglas@acc.wuacc.edu

Wichita State University
SBDC
1845 Fairmont
Wichita, Kansas 67208-0148
Phone: (316)689-3193
Fax: (316)689-3647
Joann Ard, Dir.

Kentucky

Ashland Small Business Development
Center
Morehead State University College of
Business
PO Box 830
207 15th St.
Ashland, Kentucky 41105-0830
Phone: (606)329-8011
Fax: (606)325-4607
Kimberly A. Jenkins, Dir.

Western Kentucky University
Bowling Green Small Business
Development Center
245 Grise Hall
Bowling Green, Kentucky 42101
Phone: (502)745-2901
Fax: (502)745-2902
Rick Horn, Dir.

Elizabethtown Small Business
Development Center
238 W. Dixie Ave.
Elizabethtown, Kentucky 42701
Phone: (502)765-6737
Fax: (502)769-5095
Lou Ann Allen, Dir.

Northern Kentucky University
SBDC
BEP Center 468
Highland Heights, Kentucky 41076

Phone: (606)572-6524
Fax: (606)572-5566
Sutton Landry, Dir.

Hopkinsville Small Business
Development Center
Murray State University
300 Hammond Dr.
Hopkinsville, Kentucky 42240
Phone: (502)886-8666
Fax: (502)886-3211
Mike Cartner, Dir.

SBDC
Lexington Public Library, 4th Fl.
140 Main St.
Lexington, Kentucky 40507-1376
Phone: (606)257-7666
Fax: (606)257-1751
Barbara Biroschik, Program
Coordinator

University of Kentucky
Center for Business Development
Kentucky SBDC
225 Business and Economics Bldg.
Lexington, Kentucky 40506-0034
Phone: (606)257-7668
Fax: (606)323-1907

Bellarmine College
Small Business Development Center
School of Business
600 W. Main St., Ste. 219
Louisville, Kentucky 40202
Phone: (502)574-4770
Fax: (502)574-4771
Thomas G. Daley, Dir.

University of Louisville
Small Business Development Centers
Center for Entrepreneurship and
Technology
Burhans Hall, Shelby Campus, Rm.
122
Louisville, Kentucky 40292
Phone: (502)588-7854
Fax: (502)588-8573
Lou Dickie, Dir.

Southeast Community College
SBDC
1300 Chichester Ave.
Middlesboro, Kentucky 40965-2265
Phone: (606)242-4514

Fax: (606)242-4514
Kathleen Moats, Dir.

Morehead State University
Small Business Development Center
207 Downing Hall
Morehead, Kentucky 40351
Phone: (606)783-2895
Fax: (606)783-5020
Wilson Grier, Dir.

Murray State University
West Kentucky Small Business
Development Center
College of Business and Public
Affairs
Business Bldg., Rm 253
Murray, Kentucky 42071
Phone: (502)762-2856
Fax: (502)762-3049
Rosemary Miller, Dir.

Owensboro Small Business
Development Center
Murray State University
3860 U.S. Hwy. 60 W
Owensboro, Kentucky 42301
Phone: (502)926-8085
Fax: (502)684-0714
Mickey Johnson, Dir.

Pikeville Small Business
Development Center
Moorehead State University
Rte. 7
110 Village St.
Pikeville, Kentucky 41501
Phone: (606)432-5848
Fax: (606)432-8924
Mike Morley, Dir.

Eastern Kentucky University
South Central Small Business
Development Center
107 W. Mt. Vernon St.
Somerset, Kentucky 42501
Phone: (606)678-5520
Fax: (606)678-8349
Donald R. Snyder, Dir.

Louisiana

Alexandria SBDC
Hibernia National Bank Bldg., Ste.
510
934 3rd St.

Alexandria, Louisiana 71301
Phone: (318)484-2123
Fax: (318)484-2126
Kathey Hunter, Consultant

Capital Small Business Development
Center
Southern University
1933 Wooddale Blvd., Ste. E
Baton Rouge, Louisiana 70806
Phone: (504)922-0998
Fax: (504)922-0999
Greg Spann, Dir.

Southeastern Louisiana University
Small Business Development Center
College of Business Administration
Box 522, SLU Sta.
Hammond, Louisiana 70402
Phone: (504)549-3831
Fax: (504)549-2127
William Joubert, Dir.

University of Southwestern Louisiana
Acadiana Small Business
Development Center
Box 43732
College of Business Administration
Lafayette, Louisiana 70504
Phone: (318)262-5344
Fax: (318)262-5296
Dan Lavergne, Dir.

McNeese State University
Small Business Development Center
College of Business Administration
Lake Charles, Louisiana 70609
Phone: (318)475-5529
Fax: (318)475-5012
Paul Arnold, Dir.

College of Business Administration
Northeast Louisiana University
Louisiana SBDC
700 University Ave.
Room 2-57
Monroe, Louisiana 71209
Phone: (318)342-5506
Fax: (318)342-5510
Dr. John Baker, State Dir.
Dr. Lesa Lawrence, Associate State
Dir.

Louisiana Electronic Assistance
Program
SBDC

NE Louisiana, College of Business
Administration
Monroe, Louisiana 71209
Phone: (318)342-1215
Fax: (318)342-1209
Dr. Jerry Wall, Dir.

Northeast Louisiana University
Small Business Development Center
College of Business Administration,
Rm. 2-57
Monroe, Louisiana 71209
Phone: (318)342-1224
Fax: (318)342-1209
Paul Dunn, Dir.

Northwestern State University
Small Business Development Center
College of Business Administration
Natchitoches, Louisiana 71497
Phone: (318)357-5611
Fax: (318)357-6810
Mary Lynn Wilkerson, Dir.

Louisiana International Trade Center
SBDC
World Trade Center, Ste. 2926
2 Canal St.
New Orleans, Louisiana 70130
Phone: (504)568-8222
Fax: (504)568-8228
Ruperto Chavarri, Dir.

Loyola University
Small Business Development Center
College of Business Administration
Box 134
New Orleans, Louisiana 70118
Phone: (504)865-3474
Fax: (504)865-3496
Ronald Schroeder, Dir.

Southern University—New Orleans
Small Business Development Center
College of Business Administration
New Orleans, Louisiana 70126
Phone: (504)286-5308
Fax: (504)286-3131
Jon Johnson, Dir.

University of New Orleans
Small Business Development Center
1600 Canal St., Ste. 620
New Orleans, Louisiana 70112
Phone: (504)539-9292
Fax: (504)539-9205
Norma Grace, Dir.

Louisiana Tech University
Small Business Development Center
College of Business Administration
Box 10318, Tech Sta.
Ruston, Louisiana 71271-0046
Phone: (318)257-3537
Fax: (318)257-4253

Louisiana State University at
Shreveport
Small Business Development Center
College of Business Administration
1 University Dr.
Shreveport, Louisiana 71115
Phone: (318)797-5144
Fax: (318)797-5208
James O. Hicks, Dir.

Nicholls State University
Small Business Development Center
College of Business Administration
PO Box 2015
Thibodaux, Louisiana 70310
Phone: (504)448-4242
Fax: (504)448-4922
Weston Hull, Dir.

Maine

Androscoggin Valley Council of
Governments
Small Business Development Center
125 Manley Rd.
Auburn, Maine 04210
Phone: (207)783-9186
Fax: (207)783-5211

SBDC
Weston Bldg.
7 N. Chestnut St.
Augusta, Maine 04330
Phone: (207)621-0245
Fax: (207)622-9739

Eastern Maine Development Corp.
Small Business Development Center
1 Cumberland Pl., Ste. 300
PO Box 2579
Bangor, Maine 04402-2579
Phone: (207)942-6389
Free: (800)339-6389
Fax: (207)942-3548
Ron Loyd, Dir.

Belfast Satellite
Waldo County Development Corp.

SBDC
67 Church St.
Belfast, Maine 04915
Phone: (207)942-6389
Fax: (800)339-6389

Brunswick Satellite
Midcoast Council for Business
Development
SBDC
8 Lincoln St.
Brunswick, Maine 04011
Phone: (207)882-4340

Northern Maine Development
Commission
Small Business Development Center
2 S. Main St.
PO Box 779
Caribou, Maine 04736
Phone: (207)498-8736
Free: (800)427-8736
Fax: (207)498-3108
Rodney Thompson, Dir.

East Millinocket Satellite
Katahdin Regional Development
Corp.
SBDC
58 Main St.
East Millinocket, Maine 04430
Phone: (207)746-5338
Fax: (207)746-9535

East Wilton Satellite
Robinhood Plaza
Rte. 2 & 4
East Wilton, Maine 04234
Phone: (207)783-9186

Fort Kent Satellite
SBDC
Aroostook County Registry of Deeds
Corner of Elm and Hall Streets
Fort Kent, Maine 04743
Phone: (207)498-8736
Free: (800)427-8736

Houlton Satellite
SBDC
Superior Ct. House
Ct. St.
Houlton, Maine 04730
Phone: (207)498-8736
Free: (800)427-8736

Lewiston Satellite
Business Information Center (BIC)
SBDC
Bates Mill Complex
35 Canal St.
Lewiston, Maine 04240
Phone: (207)783-9186

Machias Satellite
Sunrise County Economic Council
(Calais Area)
SBDC
Washington County Economic
Planning Commission
63 Main St., PO Box 679
Machias, Maine 04654
Phone: (207)454-2430
Fax: (207)255-0983

University of Southern Maine
Maine SBDC
96 Falmouth St.
P.O. Box 9300
Portland, Maine 04104-9300
Phone: (207)780-4420
Fax: (207)780-4810
Charles Davis, Dir.

Rockland Satellite
SBDC
Key Bank of Maine
331 Main St
Rockland, Maine 04841
Phone: (207)882-4340

Rumford Satellite
River Valley Growth Council
Hotel Harris Bldg.
23 Hartford St.
Rumford, Maine 04276
Phone: (207)783-9186

Biddeford Satellite
Biddeford-Saco Chamber of
Commerce and Industry
110 Main St.
Saco, Maine 04072
Phone: (207)282-1567
Fax: (207)282-3149

Southern Maine Regional Planning
Commission
Small Business Development Center
255 Main St.
PO Box Q

Sanford, Maine 04073
Phone: (207)324-0316
Fax: (207)324-2958
Joseph Vitko, Dir.

Skowhegan Satellite
SBDC
Norridgewock Ave.
Skowhegan, Maine 04976
Phone: (207)621-0245

South Paris Satellite
SBDC
166 Main St.
South Paris, Maine 04281
Phone: (207)783-9186

Waterville Satellite
Thomas College
SBDC
Administrative Bldg. - Library
180 W. River Rd.
Waterville, Maine 04901
Phone: (207)621-0245

Coastal Enterprises, Inc. (Wiscasset)
Small Business Development Center
Water St.
PO Box 268
Wiscasset, Maine 04578
Phone: (207)882-4340
Fax: (207)882-4456
James Burbank, Dir.

York Chamber of Commerce
SBDC
449 Rte. 1
York, Maine 03909
Phone: (207)363-4422

Maryland

Anne Arundel, Office of Economic
Development
SBDC
2666 Riva Rd., Ste. 200
Annapolis, Maryland 21401
Phone: (410)224-4205
Fax: (410)222-7415
Mike Fish, Consultant

Central Maryland
SBDC
University of Baltimore
1420 N. Charles St., Rm 142
Baltimore, Maryland 21201-5779

Phone: (410)837-4141
Fax: (410)837-4151
Barney Wilson, Executive Dir.

Hartford County Economic
Development Office
SBDC
220 S. Main St.
Bel Air, Maryland 21014
Phone: (410)893-3837
Fax: (410)879-8043
Maurice Brown, Consultant

Maryland Small Business
Development Center
7100 Baltimore Ave., Ste. 401
College Park, Maryland 20740
Phone: (301)403-8300
Fax: (301)403-8303
James N. Graham, State Dir.

University of Maryland
SBDC
Dingman Center for Entrepreneurship
College of Business and Management
College Park, Maryland 20742-1815
Phone: (301)405-2144
Fax: (301)314-9152

Howard County Economic
Development Office
SBDC
6751 Gateway Dr., Ste. 500
Columbia, Maryland 21044
Phone: (410)313-6552
Fax: (410)313-6556
Ellin Dize, Consultant

Western Region
SBDC
3 Commerce Dr.
Cumberland, Maryland 21502
Phone: (301)724-6716
Free: (800)457-7232
Fax: (301)777-7504
Rubert Douglas, Exec.Dir.

Cecil County Chamber of Commerce
SBDC
135 E. Main St.
Elkton, Maryland 21921
Phone: (410)392-0597
Fax: (410)392-6225
Maurice Brown, Consultant

Frederick Community College
SBDC
7932 Opossumtown Pike
Frederick, Maryland 21702
Phone: (301)846-2683
Fax: (301)846-2689
Mary Ann Garst, Program Dir.

Arundel Center N.
SBDC
101 Crain Hwy., NW, Rm. 110B
Glen Burnie, Maryland 21061
Phone: (410)766-1910
Fax: (410)766-1911
Mike Fish, Consultant

Community College at Saint Mary's
County
SBDC
PO Box 98, Great Mills Rd.
Great Mills, Maryland 20634
Phone: (301)868-6679
Fax: (301)868-7392
James Shepherd, E-mail: Business
Analyst

Hagerstown Junior College
SBDC
Technology Innovation Center
11404 Robinwood Dr.
Hagerstown, Maryland 21740
Phone: (301)797-0327
Fax: (301)777-7504
Tonya Fleming Brockett, Dir.

Suburban Washington Region Small
Business Development Center
1400 McCormick Dr., Ste. 282
Landover, Maryland 20785
Phone: (301)883-6491
Fax: (301)883-6479
Monika Wilkerson, Executive Dir.

Landover SBDC
7950 New Hampshire Ave., 2nd Fl.
Langley Park, Maryland 20783
Phone: (301)445-7324
Fax: (301)883-6479
Avon Evans, Consultant

Southern Maryland
Charles County Community College
SBDC
P.O. Box 910
Mitchell Rd.
LaPlata, Maryland 20646

Phone: (301)934-7580
Fax: (301)934-7681
Betsy Cooksey, Dir.

Garrett Community College
SBDC
Mosser Rd.
McHenry, Maryland 21541
Phone: (301)387-6666
Fax: (301)387-3096
Sandy Major, Business Analyst

Salisbury State University
Eastern Shore Region Small Business
Development Center
Power Professional Bldg., Ste. 400
Salisbury, Maryland 21801
Phone: (410)546-4325
Free: (800)999SBDC
Fax: (410)548-5389
John Dillard, Exec.Dir.

Baltimore County Chamber of
Commerce
SBDC
102 W. Pennsylvania Ave., Ste. 402
Towson, Maryland 21204
Phone: (410)832-5866
Fax: (410)821-9901
John Casper, Consultant

Carrol County Economic
Development Office
SBDC
125 N. Court St., Rm. 101
Westminster, Maryland 21157
Phone: (410)857-8166
Fax: (410)848-0003
Michael Fish, Consultant

Eastern Region - Upper Shore SBDC
Chesapeake College
PO Box 8
Wye Mills, Maryland 21679
Phone: (410)822-5400
Free: (800)762SBDC
Fax: (410)827-5286
Patricia Ann Marie Schaller,
Consultant

Massachusetts

International Trade Center
University of Massachusetts Amherst
SBDC

205 School of Management
Amherst, Massachusetts 01003-4935
Phone: (413)545-6301
Fax: (413)545-1273

University of Massachusetts
Massachusetts SBDC
205 School of Management
Amherst, Massachusetts 01003-4935
Phone: (413)545-6301
Fax: (413)545-1273
John Ciccarelli, State Dir.

Massachusetts Export Center
World Trade Center, Ste. 315
Boston, Massachusetts 02210
Phone: (617)478-4133
Fax: (617)478-4135
Paula Murphy, Dir.

Minority Business Assistance Center
SBDC
University of Massachusetts Boston
Boston College of Management, 5th
Fl.
Boston, Massachusetts 02125-3393
Phone: (617)287-7750
Fax: (617)287-7767
Hank Turner, Dir.

Capital Formation Service
Boston College
SBDC
96 College Rd.-Rahner House
Chestnut Hill, Massachusetts 02167
Phone: (617)552-4091
Fax: (617)552-2730
Don Reilley, Dir.

Metropolitan Boston Small Business
Development Center Regional Office
Boston College
96 College Rd., Rahner House
Chestnut Hill, Massachusetts 02167
Phone: (617)552-4091
Fax: (617)552-2730
Dr. Jack McKiernan, Regional Dir.

Southeastern Massachusetts Small
Business Development Center
Regional Office
University of Massachusetts-
Dartmouth
200 Pocasset St.
PO Box 2785

Fall River, Massachusetts 02722
Phone: (508)673-9783
Fax: (508)674-1929
Clyde Mitchell, Regional Dir.

North Shore Massachusetts Small
Business Development Center
Regional Office
Salem State College
197 Essex St.
Salem, Massachusetts 01970
Phone: (508)741-6343
Fax: (508)741-6345
Frederick Young, Dir.

Western Massachusetts Small
Business Development Center
Regional Office
University of Massachusetts-Amherst
101 State St., Ste. 424
Springfield, Massachusetts 01103
Phone: (413)737-6712
Fax: (413)737-2312
Dianne Fuller Doherty, Dir.

Clark University
Central Massachusetts Small Business
Development Center Regional Office
950 Main St.
Dana Commons
Worcester, Massachusetts 01610
Phone: (617)793-7615
Fax: (617)793-8890
Laurence March, Dir.

Michigan

Lenawee County Chamber of
Commerce
SBDC
202 N. Main St., Ste. A
Adrian, Michigan 49221-2713
Phone: (517)266-1465
Fax: (517)263-6065
David B. Munson, Dir.

Allegan County Economic Alliance
SBDC
Allegan Intermediate School Bldg.
2891 M-277
P.O. Box 277
Allegan, Michigan 49010-8042
Phone: (616)673-8442
Fax: (616)650-8042
Chuck Birr, Dir.

Ottawa County Economic
Development Office, Inc.
Small Business Development Center
6676 Lake Michigan Dr.
PO Box 539
Allendale, Michigan 49401-0539
Phone: (616)892-4120
Fax: (616)895-6670
Ken Rizzio, Dir.

Gratiot Area Chamber of Commerce
SBDC
110 W. Superior St.
P.O. Box 516
Alma, Michigan 48801-0516
Phone: (517)463-5525

Alpena Community College
SBDC
666 Johnson St.
Alpena, Michigan 49707
Phone: (517)356-9021
Fax: (517)356-7507
Bob Munroe, Dir.

MMTC SBDC
2901 Hubbard Rd.
PO Box 1485
Ann Arbor, Michigan 48106-1485
Phone: (313)769-4110
Fax: (313)769-4064
Bill Loomis, Dir.

Huron County Economic
Development Corp.
Small Business Development Center
Huron County Bldg., Rm. 303
250 E. Huron
Bad Axe, Michigan 48413
Phone: (517)269-6431
Fax: (517)269-7221
Carl Osentoski, Dir.

Battle Creek Area Chamber of
Commerce
SBDC
4 Riverwalk Centre
34 W. Jackson, Ste. A
Battle Creek, Michigan 49017
Phone: (616)962-4076
Fax: (616)962-4076
Kathy Perrett, Dir.

Bay Area Chamber of Commerce
SBDC
901 Saginaw

Bay City, Michigan 48708
Phone: (517)893-4567
Fax: (517)893-7016
Cheryl Hiner, Dir.

Lake Michigan College Corporation
and Community Development
Small Business Development Center
2755 E. Napier
Benton Harbor, Michigan 49022-1899
Phone: (616)927-8179
Fax: (616)927-8103
Milt Richter, Dir.

Ferris State University
Small Business Development Center
330 Oak St.
West 115
Big Rapids, Michigan 49307
Phone: (616)592-3553
Fax: (616)592-3539
Lora Swenson, Dir.
E-mail: yc26@ferris.bitnet

Northern Lakes Economic Alliance
SBDC
1048 East Main St.
P.O. Box 8
Boyne City, Michigan 49712-0008
Phone: (616)582-6482
Fax: (616)582-3213
Thomas Johnson, Dir.

Livingston County Small Business
Development Center (Brighton)
131 S. Hyne
Brighton, Michigan 48116
Phone: (810)227-3556
Fax: (810)227-3080
Dennis Whitney, Dir.

Buchanan Chamber of Commerce
SBDC
119 Main St.
Buchanan, Michigan 49107
Phone: (616)695-3291
Fax: (616)695-4250
Marlene Gauer, Dir.

Tuscola County Economic
Development Corp.
Small Business Development Center
194 N. State St., Ste. 200
Caro, Michigan 48723
Phone: (517)673-2849

Fax: (517)673-2517
James McLoskey, Dir.

Branch County Economic Growth
Alliance
SBDC
20 Division St.
Coldwater, Michigan 49036
Phone: (517)278-4146
Fax: (517)278-8369
Joyce Elferdink, Dir.

University of Detroit Mercy
NILAC Small Business Development
Center
4001 W. McNichols, Rm. 105
Commerce and Finance Bldg.
PO Box 19900
Detroit, Michigan 48219-0900
Phone: (313)993-1115
Fax: (313)993-1115
Ram Kesavan, Dir.

Wayne State University
Michigan SBDC
E-mail:
stateoffice@misbdc.wayne.edu
2727 Second Ave.
Detroit, Michigan 48201
Phone: (313)964-1798
Fax: (313)964-3648
Ronald R. Hall, State Dir.

Wayne State University
2727 2nd Ave., Rm. 107
Detroit, Michigan 48201
Phone: (313)577-4850
Fax: (313)577-8933
Kevin Lauderdale, Dir.

First Step, Inc.
Small Business Development Center
2415 14th Ave., S.
Escanaba, Michigan 49829
Phone: (906)786-9234
Fax: (906)786-4422
David Gillis, Dir.

Community Capital Development
Corp.
SBDC
711 N. Saginaw, Ste. 123
Walter Ruether Center
Flint, Michigan 48503
Phone: (810)239-5847

Fax: (810)239-5575
Bobby Wells, Dir.

Center For Continuing Education-
Macomb Community College
SBDC
32101 Caroline
Fraser, Michigan 48026
Phone: (810)296-3516
Fax: (810)293-0427

North Central Michigan College
SBDC
800 Livingston Blvd.
Gaylord, Michigan 49735
Phone: (517)731-0071

Association of Commerce and
Industry
SBDC
1 S. Harbor Ave.
PO Box 509
Grand Haven, Michigan 49417
Phone: (616)846-3153
Fax: (616)842-0379
Karen K. Benson, Dir.

Grand Valley State University
SBDC
301 W. Fulton St., Ste. 718S
Grand Rapids, Michigan 49504
Phone: (616)771-6693
Fax: (616)771-6805
Carol R. Lopucki, Dir.

The Right Place Program
SBDC
820 Monroe NW, Ste. 350
Grand Rapids, Michigan 49503-1423
Phone: (616)771-0571
Fax: (616)458-3768
Raymond P. DeWinkle, Dir.

Oceana County Economic
Development Corp.
100 State St.
PO Box 168
Hart, Michigan 49420-0168
Phone: (616)873-7141
Fax: (616)873-5914
Charles Persenaire, Dir.

Hastings Industrial Incubator
SBDC
1035 E. State St.
Hastings, Michigan 49058

Phone: (616)948-2305
Fax: (616)948-2947
Joe Rahn, Dir.

Greater Gratiot Development, Inc.
Small Business Center
136 S. Main
Ithaca, Michigan 48847
Phone: (517)875-2083
Fax: (517)875-2990
Don Schurr, Dir.

Jackson Business Development
Center
414 N. Jackson St.
Jackson, Michigan 49201
Phone: (517)787-0442
Fax: (517)787-3960
Dwayne K. Miller, Dir.

Kalamazoo College
Small Business Development Center
Stryker Center for Management
Studies
1327 Academy St.
Kalamazoo, Michigan 49006-3200
Phone: (616)337-7350
Fax: (616)337-7415
Carl R. Shook, Dir.

Lansing Community College
Small Business Development Center
PO Box 40010
Lansing, Michigan 48901-7210
Phone: (517)483-1921
Fax: (517)483-1675
Deleski Smith, Dir.

Lapeer Development Corp.
Small Business Development Center
449 McCormick Dr.
Lapeer, Michigan 48446
Phone: (810)667-0080
Fax: (810)667-3541
Patricia Crawford Lucas, Dir.

Midland Chamber of Commerce
SBDC
300 Rodd St.
Midland, Michigan 48640
Phone: (517)839-9901
Fax: (517)835-3701
Sam Boeke, Dir.

Genesis Center for Entrepreneurial
Development
SBDC

111 Conant Ave.
Monroe, Michigan 48161
Phone: (313)243-5947
Fax: (313)242-0009
Dani Topolski, Dir.

Macomb County Business Assistance
Network
Small Business Development Center
115 S. Groesbeck Hwy.
Mount Clemens, Michigan 48043
Phone: (810)469-5118
Fax: (810)469-6787
Donald Morandini, Dir.

Central Michigan University
Small Business Development Center
256 Applied Business Studies
Complex
Mount Pleasant, Michigan 48859
Phone: (517)774-3270
Fax: (517)774-7992
Charles Fitzpatrick, Dir.

Muskegon Economic Growth
Alliance
Small Business Development Center
230 Terrace Plz.
PO Box 1087
Muskegon, Michigan 49443-1087
Phone: (616)722-3751
Fax: (616)728-7251
Mert Johnson, Dir.

Harbor County Chamber of
Commerce
SBDC
3 W. Buffalo
New Buffalo, Michigan 49117
Phone: (616)469-5409
Fax: (616)469-2257

Greater Niles Economic Development
Fund
SBDC
1105 N. Front St.
Niles, Michigan 49120
Phone: (616)683-1833
Fax: (616)683-7515
Chris Brynes, Dir.

Huron Shores Campus
SBDC
5800 Skeel Ave.
Oscoda, Michigan 48750

Phone: (517)739-1445
Fax: (517)739-1161
Dave Wentworth, Dir.

St. Clair County Community Small
Business Development Center
800 Military St., Ste. 320
Port Huron, Michigan 48060-5015
Phone: (810)982-9511
Fax: (810)982-9531
Todd Brian, Dir.

Kirtland Community College
SBDC
10775 N. St. Helen Rd.
Roscommon, Michigan 48653
Phone: (517)275-5121
Fax: (517)275-8510

Saginaw County Chamber of
Commerce
SBDC
901 S. Washington Ave.
Saginaw, Michigan 48601
Phone: (517)752-7161
Fax: (517)752-9055
James Bockelman, Dir.

Saginaw Future, Inc.
Small Business Development Center
301 E. Genesee, 3rd Fl.
Saginaw, Michigan 48607
Phone: (517)754-8222
Fax: (517)754-1715
Matthew Hufnagel, Dir.

Washtenaw Community College
SBDC
740 Woodland
Saline, Michigan 48176
Phone: (313)944-1016
Fax: (313)944-0165
Daniel Stotz, Dir.

West Shore Community College
Small Business Development Center
Business and Industrial Development
Institute
3000 N. Stiles Rd.
PO Box 277
Scottville, Michigan 49454-0277
Phone: (616)845-6211
Fax: (616)845-0207
Mark Bergstrom, Dir.

South Haven Chamber of Commerce
SBDC
300 Broadway
South Haven, Michigan 49090
Phone: (616)637-5171
Fax: (616)639-1570
Larry King, Dir.

Downriver Small Business
Development Center
15100 Northline Rd.
Southgate, Michigan 48195
Phone: (313)281-0700
Fax: (313)281-3418
Paula Boase, Dir.

Arenac County Extension Service
SBDC
County Bldg.
P.O. Box 745
Standish, Michigan 48658
Phone: (517)846-4111

Sterling Heights Area Chamber of
Commerce
Small Business Development Center
12900 Hall Rd., Ste. 110
Sterling Heights, Michigan 48313
Phone: (810)731-5400
Fax: (810)731-3521

Greater Northwest Regional Small
Business Development Center
2200 Dendrinos Dr.
PO Box 506
Traverse City, Michigan 49685-0506
Phone: (616)929-5000
Fax: (616)929-5012
Richard Beldin, Dir.

Northwestern Michigan College
Small Business Development Center
Center for Business and Industry
1701 E. Front St.
Traverse City, Michigan 49686-3061
Phone: (616)922-1720
Fax: (616)922-1722
Cheryl Troop, Dir.

Traverse Bay Economic Development
Corp.
Small Business Development Center
202 E. Grandview Pky.
PO Box 387
Traverse City, Michigan 49684

Phone: (616)946-1596
Fax: (616)946-2565
Charles Blankenship, Pres.

Traverse City Area Chamber of
Commerce
Small Business Development Center
202 E. Grandview Pky.
PO Box 387
Traverse City, Michigan 49684
Phone: (616)947-5075
Fax: (616)946-2565
Matthew Meadors, Dir.

Business Enterprise Development
Center
Walsh College/OCC
1301 W. Long Lake Rd., Ste. 150
Troy, Michigan 48098
Phone: (810)952-5800
Fax: (810)952-1875
Daniel V. Belknap, Dir.

Saginaw Valley State University
Small Business Development Center
Business and Industrial Development
Institute
7400 Bay Rd.
University Center, Michigan 48710-
0001
Phone: (517)790-4388
Fax: (517)790-4983
Christine Greue, Dir.

Macomb Community College
SBDC
14500 12 Mile Rd.
Warren, Michigan 48093
Phone: (810)445-7348
Fax: (810)445-7316
Geary Maiurini, Dir.

Warren-Center Line Sterling Heights
Chamber of Commerce
SBDC
30500 Van Dyke, #118
Warren, Michigan 48093
Phone: (313)751-3939
Fax: (313)751-3995
Janet E. Masi, Dir.

Warren Chamber of Commerce
Small Business Development Center
30500 Van Dyke, Ste. 118
Warren, Michigan 48093

Phone: (313)751-3939
Fax: (313)751-3995
Janet Masi, Dir.

Minnesota

Northwest Technical College
SBDC
905 Grant Ave., SE
Bemidji, Minnesota 56601
Phone: (218)755-4286
Fax: (218)755-4289
Susan Kozojed, Dir.

Normandale Community College
(Bloomington)
Small Business Development Center
9700 France Ave. S
Bloomington, Minnesota 55431
Phone: (612)832-6560
Fax: (612)832-6352
Betty Walton, Dir.

Brainerd Technical College
Small Business Development Center
300 Quince St.
Brainerd, Minnesota 56401
Phone: (218)828-5302
Fax: (218)828-5321
Pamela Thomsen, Dir.

University of Minnesota at Duluth
Small Business Development Center
10 University Dr., 157 SBE
Duluth, Minnesota 55812-2496
Phone: (218)726-8758
Fax: (218)726-6338

Itasca Development Corp.
Grand Rapids Small Business
Development Center
19 NE 3rd St.
Grand Rapids, Minnesota 55744
Phone: (218)327-2241
Fax: (218)327-2242
John Damjanovich, Dir.

Hibbing Community College
Small Business Development Center
1515 E. 25th St.
Hibbing, Minnesota 55746
Phone: (218)262-6703
Fax: (218)262-6717
Allen Jackson, Dir.

Rainy River Community College
Small Business Development Center
1501 Hwy. 71
International Falls, Minnesota 56649
Phone: (218)285-2255
Fax: (218)285-2239

Region Nine Development
Commission
SBDC
410 Jackson St.
PO Box 3367
Mankato, Minnesota 56002-3367
Phone: (507)387-5643
Fax: (507)387-7105
Alison McKenzie, Dir.

Southwest State University
Small Business Development Center
Science and Technical Resource
Center, Ste. 105
Marshall, Minnesota 56258
Phone: (507)537-7386
Fax: (507)537-6094
Jack Hawk, Dir.

Minnesota Project Innovation
Small Business Development Center
The Mill Pl., Ste. 400
111 3rd Ave. S., Ste. 100
Minneapolis, Minnesota 55401
Phone: (612)338-3280
Fax: (612)338-3483
Randall Olson, Dir.

University of St. Thomas
SBDC
1000 La Salle Ave.
Ste. MPL 100
Minneapolis, Minnesota 55403
Phone: (612)962-4500
Fax: (612)962-4410
Gregg Schneider, Dir.

Moorhead State University
Small Business Development Center
1104 7th Ave. S.
SU Box 303
Moorhead, Minnesota 56563
Phone: (218)236-2289
Fax: (218)236-2280
Len Sliwoski, Dir.

Owatonna Incubator, Inc. SBDC
560 Dunnell Dr., Ste. 203

PO Box 505
Owatonna, Minnesota 55060
Phone: (507)451-0517
Fax: (507)455-2788
Lisa McGinnis, Dir.

Pine Technical College
Small Business Development Center
1100 4th St.
Pine City, Minnesota 55063
Phone: (612)629-7340
Fax: (612)629-7603
John Sparling, Dir.

Hennepin Technical College
SBDC
1820 N. Xenium Lane
Plymouth, Minnesota 55441
Phone: (612)550-7218
Fax: (612)550-7272
Danelle Wolf, Dir.

Pottery Business and Tech. Center
Small Business Development Center
2000 Pottery Pl. Dr., Ste. 339
Red Wing, Minnesota 55066
Phone: (612)388-4079
Fax: (612)385-2251
Marv Bollum, Dir.

Rochester Community College
Small Business Development Center
Hwy. 14 E.
851 30th Ave. SE
Rochester, Minnesota 55904
Phone: (507)285-7536
Fax: (507)280-5502
Ellen Nelson, Dir.

Dakota County Technical College
SBDC
1300 145th St. E.
Rosemount, Minnesota 55068
Phone: (612)423-8262
Fax: (612)322-5156
Tom Trutna, Dir.

Dakota County Technical College
Small Business Development Center
1300 E. 145th St.
Rosemount, Minnesota 55068
Phone: (612)423-8262
Fax: (612)322-5156
Tom Trutna, Dir.

Southeast Minnesota Development
Corp.
SBDC
111 W. Jessie St.
Rushford, Minnesota 55971
Phone: (507)864-7557
Fax: (507)864-2091
Terry Erickson, Dir.

St. Cloud State University
Small Business Development Center
4191 2nd St. S.
St. Cloud, Minnesota 56301-3761
Phone: (612)255-4842
Fax: (612)255-4957
Dawn Jensen-Ragnier, Dir.

Department of Trade and Economic
Development
Minnesota SBDC
500 Metro Sq.
121 7th Pl. E.
St. Paul, Minnesota 55101-2146
Phone: (612)297-5770
Fax: (612)296-1290

Mesabi Community College
Small Business Development Center
820-N. 9th St., Olcott Plaza, Ste. 140
Virginia, Minnesota 55792
Phone: (218)741-4251
Fax: (218)741-4249
John Freeland, Dir.

Wadena Chamber of Commerce
SBDC
222 2nd St., SE
Wadena, Minnesota 56482
Phone: (218)631-1502
Fax: (218)631-2396
Paul Kinn, Dir.

Northeast Metro Technical College
SBDC
3300 Century Ave., N., Ste. 200-D
White Bear Lake, Minnesota 55110-
1894
Phone: (612)779-5764
Fax: (612)779-5802
Bob Rodine, Dir.

Mississippi

Northeast Mississippi Community
College
SBDC

Holiday Hall, 2nd Fl.
Booneville, Mississippi 38829
Phone: (601)728-7751
Fax: (601)728-1165
Kenny Holt, Dir.

Delta State University
Small Business Development Center
PO Box 3235 DSU
Cleveland, Mississippi 38733
Phone: (601)846-4236
Fax: (601)846-4235
John Brandon, Dir.

East Central Community College
SBDC
PO Box 129
Decatur, Mississippi 39327
Phone: (601)635-2111
Fax: (601)635-2150
Ronald Westbrook, Dir.

Jones County Junior College
SBDC
900 Court St.
Ellisville, Mississippi 39437
Phone: (601)477-4165
Fax: (601)477-4152
Ken Dupre, Dir.

Gulf Coast Community College
SBDC
Jackson County Campus
PO Box 100
Gautier, Mississippi 39553
Phone: (601)497-9595
Fax: (601)497-9604
Dean Brown, Dir.

Mississippi Delta Community College
Small Business Development Center
PO Box 5607
Greenville, Mississippi 38704-5607
Phone: (601)378-8183
Fax: (601)378-5349
Chuck Herring, Dir.

MS Delta Community College
SBDC
P.O. Box 5607
Greenville, Mississippi 38704-5607
Phone: (601)378-8183
Fax: (601)378-5349
Chuch Herring, Dir.

Mississippi Contract Procurement
Center
SBDC
3015 12th St.
PO Box 610
Gulfport, Mississippi 39502-0610
Phone: (601)864-2961
Fax: (601)864-2969
C. W. "Skip" Ryland, Exec. Dir.

Pearl River Community College
Small Business Development Center
5448 U.S. Hwy. 49 S.
Hattiesburg, Mississippi 39401
Phone: (601)544-0030
Fax: (601)544-0032
Heidi McDuffie, Dir.

Mississippi Valley State University
Affiliate SBDC
Itta Bena, Mississippi 38941
Phone: (601)254-3601
Fax: (601)254-6704
Dr. Cliff Williams, Dir.

Jackson State University
Small Business Development Center
Jackson Enterprise Center, Ste. A-1
931 Hwy. 80 W
Box 43
Jackson, Mississippi 39204
Phone: (601)968-2795
Fax: (601)968-2796
Henry Thomas, Dir.

University of Southern Mississippi
Small Business Development Center
136 Beach Park Pl.
Long Beach, Mississippi 39560
Phone: (601)865-4578
Fax: (601)865-4581
Lucy Betcher, Dir.

Alcorn State University
SBDC
PO Box 90
Lorman, Mississippi 39096-9402
Phone: (601)877-6684
Fax: (601)877-6266
Sharon Witty, Dir.

Meridian Community College
Small Business Development Center
910 Hwy. 19 N
Meridian, Mississippi 39307

Phone: (601)482-7445
Fax: (601)482-5803
Kathy Braddock, Dir.

Mississippi State University
Small Business Development Center
PO Drawer 5288
Mississippi State, Mississippi 39762
Phone: (601)325-8684
Fax: (601)325-4016
Sonny Fisher, Dir.

Copiah-Lincoln Community College
Small Business Development Center
823 Hwy. 61 N.
Natchez, Mississippi 39120
Phone: (601)445-5254
Fax: (601)445-5254
Bob D. Russ, Dir.

Hinds Community College
Small Business Development Center/
International Trade Center
PO Box 1170
Raymond, Mississippi 39154
Phone: (601)857-3537
Fax: (601)857-3535
Marguerita Wall, Dir.

Holmes Community College
SBDC
412 W. Ridgeland Ave.
Ridgeland, Mississippi 39157
Phone: (601)853-0827
Fax: (601)853-0844
John Deddens, Dir.

Northwest Mississippi Community
College
SBDC
8700 Northwest Dr.
DeSoto Ctr.
Southaven, Mississippi 38671
Phone: (601)342-7648
Fax: (601)342-7648
Jody Dunning, Dir.

Southwest Mississippi Community
College
SBDC
College Dr.
Summit, Mississippi 39666
Phone: (601)276-3890
Fax: (601)276-3867
Kathryn Durham, Dir.

Itawamba Community College
Small Business Development Center
653 Eason Blvd.
Tupelo, Mississippi 38801
Phone: (601)680-8515
Fax: (601)842-6885
Rex Hollingsworth, Dir.

University of Mississippi
SBDC
Old Chemistry Bldg., Ste. 216
University, Mississippi 38677
Phone: (601)234-2120
Fax: (601)232-5650
Michael Vanderlip, Dir.

University of Mississippi
Mississippi SBDC
Old Chemistry Bldg., Ste. 216
University, Mississippi 38677
Phone: (601)232-5001
Fax: (601)232-5650
Raleigh Byars, State Dir.

Missouri

Camden County
SBDC Extension Center
113 Kansas
PO Box 1405
Camdenton, Missouri 65020
Phone: (573)346-2644
Fax: (573)346-2694
Jackie Rasmussen, B&I Spec.

Missouri PAC - Southeastern
Missouri State University
SBDC
222 N. Pacific
Cape Girardeau, Missouri 63701
Phone: (573)290-5965
Fax: (573)651-5005
George Williams, Dir.

Southeast Missouri State University
Small Business Development Center
222 N. Pacific
Cape Girardeau, Missouri 63701
Phone: (573)290-5965
Fax: (573)651-5005
Frank "Buz" Sutherland, Dir.
E-mail: SBDC-
CG@EXT.MISSOURI.EDU

Chillicothe City Hall
SBDC

715 Washington
Chillicothe, Missouri 64601
Phone: (816)646-6920
Fax: (816)646-6811
Nanette Anderjaska, Dir.

East Central Missouri/St. Louis
County
Extension Center
121 S. Meramac, Ste. 501
Clayton, Missouri 63105
Phone: (314)889-2911
Fax: (314)854-6147
Carole Leriche-Price, B&I Specialist

Boone County Extension Center
SBDC
1012 N. Hwy UU
Columbia, Missouri 65203
Phone: (573)445-9792
Fax: (573)445-9807
Mr. Casey Venters, B&I Specialist

MO PAC-Central Region
University of Missouri-Columbia
SBDC
E-mail: mopcik@ext.missouri.edu
1800 University Pl.
Columbia, Missouri 65211
Phone: (573)882-3597
Fax: (573)884-4297
Morris Hudson, Dir.

University of Missouri
Missouri SBDC
300 University Pl.
Columbia, Missouri 65211
Phone: (573)882-0344
Fax: (573)884-4297
Max E. Summers, State Dir.

University of Missouri—Columbia
Small Business Development Center
1800 University Pl.
Columbia, Missouri 65211
Phone: (573)882-7096
Fax: (573)882-6156
Frank Siebert, Dir.
E-mail: SBDC-
C@EXT.MISSOURI.EDU

Hannibal Satellite Center
Hannibal, Missouri 63401
Phone: (816)385-6550
Fax: (816)385-6568

Jefferson County
Courthouse, Annex No. 203
Extension Center
Courthouse, Annex 203
725 Maple St.
PO Box 497
Hillsboro, Missouri 63050
Phone: (573)789-5391
Fax: (573)789-5059

Cape Girardeau County
SBDC Extension Center
815 Hwy. 25S
PO Box 408
Jackson, Missouri 63755
Phone: (314)243-3581
Fax: (314)243-1606
Richard Sparks, Specialist

Cole County Extension Center
SBDC
2436 Tanner Bridge Rd.
Jefferson City, Missouri 65101
Phone: (573)634-2824
Fax: (573)634-5463
Mr. Chris Bouchard

Missouri Southern State College
Small Business Development Center
3950 Newman Rd.
107 Matthews Hall
Joplin, Missouri 64801-1595
Phone: 417625-9313
Fax: 417926-4588
Jim Krudwig, Dir.

Rockhurst College
Small Business Development Center
1100 Rockhurst Rd.
VanAckeren Hall, Rm. 205
Kansas City, Missouri 64110-2599
Phone: (816)926-4572
Fax: (816)926-4588
Judith Burngen, Dir.

Northeast Missouri State University
Small Business Development Center
207 E. Patterson
Kirksville, Missouri 63501-4419
Phone: (816)785-4307
Fax: (816)785-4181
Glen Giboney, Dir.
E-mail: SBDC-
K@EXT.MISSOURI.EDU

Thomas Hill Enterprise Center
SBDC
PO Box 246
Macon, Missouri 63552
Phone: (816)385-6550
Jane Vanderham, Dir.

Northwest Missouri State University
Small Business Development Center
127 S. Buchanan
Maryville, Missouri 64468
Phone: (816)562-1701
Fax: (816)562-1900
Brad Anderson

Audrain County
Extension Center
101 Jefferson
4th Fl. Courthouse
Mexico, Missouri 65265
Phone: (573)581-3231
Fax: (573)581-3232
Judy Moss, B&I Specialist

Randolph County
Extension Center
417 E. Urbandale
Moberly, Missouri 65270
Phone: (816)263-3534
Fax: (816)263-1874
Ray Marshall, B&I Specialist

Mineral Area College
SBDC
PO Box 1000
Park Hills, Missouri 63653
Phone: (573)431-4593
Fax: (573)431-2144
Bruce Epps, Dir.
E-mail: SBDC-
FR@EXT.MISSOURI.EDU

Three Rivers Community College
Small Business Development Center
Business Incubator Bldg.
3019 Fair St.
Poplar Bluff, Missouri 63901
Phone: (314)686-3499
Fax: (314)686-5467
John Bonifield, Dir.
E-mail: SBDC-
PB@EXT.MISSOURI.EDU

Washington County SBDC
102 N. Missouri
Potosi, Missouri 63664

Phone: (573)438-2671
LaDonna McCuan, B&I Specialist

Center for Technology Transfer and
Economic Development
University of Missouri—Rolla
Nagogami Ter., Bldg. 1, Rm. 104
Rolla, Missouri 65401-0249
Phone: (573)341-4559
Fax: (573)346-2694
Fred Goss, Dir.
E-mail: SBDC-
RT@EXT.MISSOURI.EDU

Missouri Enterprise Business
Assistance Center
SBDC
800 W 14th St., Ste. 111
Rolla, Missouri 65401
Phone: (573)364-8570
Fax: (573)341-6495
Rick Pugh, Dir.
E-mail:
MOPROLLA@EXE.MISSOURI.EDU

Phelps County
SBDC Extension Center
Courthouse, 200 N. Main
PO Box 725
Rolla, Missouri 65401
Phone: (573)364-3147
Fax: (573)364-0436
Paul Cretin, B&I Spec.

Missouri PAC - Eastern Region
SBDC
975 Hornet Dr., Bldg. 279- Wing B
St. Louis, Missouri 63101
Phone: (314)731-3533
Ken Konchel, Dir.
E-mail:
MOPSTL@EXT.MISSOURI.EDU

St. Louis County
Extension Center
207 Marillac, UMSL
8001 Natural Bridge Rd.
St. Louis, Missouri 63121
Phone: (314)553-5944
John Henschke, Specialist

St. Louis University
Small Business State University
SBDC
E-mail: sbdc-stl@ext.missouri.edu
3750 Lindell Blvd.

Saint Louis, Missouri 63108-3412
Phone: (314)977-7232
Fax: (314)977-7241
Viginia Campbell, Dir.

St. Louis County Economic Council
St. Charles County
SBDC Extension Center
260 Brown Rd.
St. Peters, Missouri 63376
Phone: (314)970-3000
Fax: (314)970-3000
Tim Wathen, B&I Specialist

Pettis County
Extension Center
1012A Thompson Blvd.
Sedalia, Missouri 65301
Phone: (816)827-0591
Fax: (816)826-8599
Betty Lorton, B&I Specialist

Southwest Missouri State University
Small Business Development Center
Center for Business Research
901 S. National
Box 88
Springfield, Missouri 65804-0089
Phone: (417)836-5685
Fax: (417)836-6337
Jane Peterson, Dir.

Franklin County
SBDC Extension Center
414 E. Main
PO Box 71
Union, Missouri 63084
Phone: (573)583-5141
Fax: (573)583-5145
Rebecca How, B&I Specialist

Central Missouri State University
SBDC
Grinstead 75
Warrensburg, Missouri 64093-5037
Phone: (816)543-4402
Fax: (816)747-1653
Bernie Sarbaugh, Coordinator

Central Missouri State University
Center for Technology
Grinstead, No. 75
Warrensburg, Missouri 64093-5037
Phone: (816)543-4402
Fax: (816)747-1653
Cindy Tanck, Coordinator

Howell County
SBDC Extension Center
217 S. Aid Ave.
West Plains, Missouri 65775
Phone: (417)256-2391
Fax: (417)256-8569
Mick Gilliam, B&I Spec.

Montana

Billings Area Business Incubator
Small Business Development Center
Montana Tradepost Authority
115 N. Broadway, 2nd Fl.
Billings, Montana 59101
Phone: (406)256-6875
Fax: (406)256-6877
Jerry Thomas, Contact

Bozeman Small Business
Development Center
Gallatin Development Corp.
222 E. Main, Ste. 102
Bozeman, Montana 59715
Phone: (406)587-3113
Fax: (406)587-9565
Darrell Berger, Contact

Butte Small Business Development
Center
Rural Economic Development
Incubator
305 W. Mercury, Ste. 211
Butte, Montana 59701
Phone: (406)782-7333
Fax: (406)782-9675
Ralph Kloser, Contact

High Plains Development Authority
SBDC
710 1st. Ave. N.
P.O. Box 2568
Great Falls, Montana 59401
Phone: (406)454-1934
Fax: (406)454-2995
Suzie David

Havre Small Business Development
Center
Bear Paw Development Corp.
PO Box 1549
Havre, Montana 59501
Phone: (406)265-9226
Fax: (406)265-3777
Randy Hanson, Contact

Montana Department of Commerce
Montana SBDC
1424 9th Ave.
Helena, Montana 59620
Phone: (406)444-4780
Fax: (406)444-1872
David Elenbaas, Acting State Dir.

Kalispell Small Business
Development Center
Flathead Valley Community College
777 Grandview Dr.
Kalispell, Montana 59901
Phone: (406)756-8333
Fax: (406)756-3815
Dan Manning, Contact

Missoula Small Business
Development Center
Missoula Business Incubator
127 N. Higgins, 3rd Fl.
Missoula, Montana 59802
Phone: (406)728-9234
Fax: (406)721-4584
Leslie Jensen, Contact

Sidney Small Business Development
Center
Eastern Plains RC&D
123 W. Main
Sidney, Montana 59270
Phone: (406)482-5024
Fax: (406)482-5306
Dwayne Heintz, Contact

Nebraska

Chadron State College
NBDC-Chadron
Administration Bldg.
Chadron, Nebraska 69337
Phone: (308)432-6282
Fax: (308)432-6430
Cliff Hanson, Dir.
E-mail: chanson@cscl.csc.edu

University of Nebraska at Kearney
NBDC-Kearney
Welch Hall
19th St. and College Dr.
Kearney, Nebraska 68849-3035
Phone: (308)865-8344
Fax: (308)865-8153
Kay Payne, Dir.

University of Nebraska at Lincoln
NBDC-Lincoln
Cornhusker Bank Bldg., Ste. 302
11th and Cornhusker Hwy.
Lincoln, Nebraska 68521
Phone: (402)472-3358
Fax: (402)472-0328
Irene Cherhoniak, Dir.

Mid-Plains Community College
NBDC-North Platte
416 N. Jeffers, Rm. 26
North Platte, Nebraska 69101
Phone: (308)534-5115
Fax: (308)534-5117
Dean Kurth, Dir.

Nebraska SBDC
University of Nebraska at Omaha
60th & Dodge Sts.
CBA Rm. 407
Omaha, Nebraska 68182
Phone: (402)554-2521
Fax: (402)554-3747
Robert Bernier, State Dir.

Nebraska Small Business
Development Center
Omaha Business and Technology
Center
2505 N. 24 St., Ste. 101
Omaha, Nebraska 68110
Phone: (402)595-3511
Fax: (402)595-3524
Tom McCabe, Dir.

Peter Kiewit Conference Center
SBDC
1313 Farnam-on-the-Mall, Ste. 132
Omaha, Nebraska 68182-0248
Phone: (402)595-2381
Fax: (402)595-2385
Jeanne Eibes, Dir.

Peru State College
NBDC-Peru
T.J. Majors Hall, Rm. 248
Peru, Nebraska 68421
Phone: (402)872-2274
Fax: (402)872-2422
David Ruenholl, Dir.

Western Nebraska Community
College
NBDC-Scottsbluff

Nebraska Public Power Bldg.
1721 Broadway, Rm. 408
Scottsbluff, Nebraska 69361
Phone: (308)635-7513
Fax: (308)635-6596
Ingrid Battershell, Dir.

Wayne State College
NBDC-Wayne
Gardner Hall
1111 Main St.
Wayne, Nebraska 68787
Phone: (402)375-7575
Fax: (402)375-7574
Loren Kucera, Dir.

Carson City Chamber of Commerce
Small Business Development Center
1900 S. Carson St., Ste. 100
Carson City, Nevada 89701
Phone: (702)882-1565
Fax: (702)882-4179
Larry Osborne, Dir.

Great Basin College
Small Business Development Center
1500 College Pkwy.
Elko, Nevada 89801
Phone: (702)753-2245
Fax: (702)753-2242
John Pryor, Dir.

Incline Village Chamber of
Commerce
SBDC
969 Tahoe Blvd.
Incline Village, Nevada 89451
Phone: (702)831-4440
Fax: (702)832-1605
Sheri Woods, Exec. Dir.

Foreign Trade Zone Office
SBDC
1111 Grier Dr.
Las Vegas, Nevada 89119
Phone: (702)896-4496
Fax: (702)896-8351
Robert Holland, Bus. Dev. Specialist

University of Nevada at Las Vegas
Small Business Development Center
Box 456011
Las Vegas, Nevada 89154-6011
Phone: (702)895-0852
Fax: (702)895-4095

Sharolyn Craft, Dir.

North Las Vegas Small Business
Development Center
19 W. 4th St.
North Las Vegas, Nevada 89030
Phone: (702)399-6300
Fax: (702)399-6301
Janis Stevenson, Consultant

University of Nevada at Reno
Small Business Development Center
College of Business Administration
Business Bdlg., Rm. 411
Reno, Nevada 89557-0100
Phone: (702)784-1717
Fax: (702)784-4337
Sam Males, Dir.

Tri-County Development Authority
Small Business Development Center
50 W. 4th St.
PO Box 820
Winnemucca, Nevada 89446
Phone: (702)623-5777
Fax: (702)623-5999
Terri Williams, Dir.

New Hampshire

University of New Hampshire
Small Business Development Center
108 McConnell Hall
Durham, New Hampshire 03824-3593
Phone: (603)862-2200
Fax: (603)862-4876
Elizabeth Lamoureaux, Dir.
E-mail: 1m1@christa.unh.edu

Keene State College
Small Business Development Center
Blake House
Keene, New Hampshire 03435-2101
Phone: (603)358-2602
Fax: (603)358-2612
Gary Cloutier, Regional Mgr.
E-mail: gc@cchrista.unh.edu

Littleton Small Business
Development Center
120 Main St.
Littleton, New Hampshire 03561
Phone: (603)444-1053
Fax: (603)444-5463
Liz Ward, Regional Mgr.

E-mail: eaward@christa.unh.edu

Office of Economic Initiatives
SBDC
E-mail: ahj@hopper.unh.edu
1000 Elm St.. 14th Fl.
Manchester, New Hampshire 03101
Phone: (603)634-2796
Amy Jennings, Dir.

Small Business Development Center
(Manchester, NH)
1000 Elm St., 14th Fl.
Manchester, New Hampshire 03101
Phone: (603)624-2000
Fax: (603)647-4410
Bob Ebberson, Regional Mgr.
E-mail: rte@christa.unh.edu

New Hampshire Small Business
Development Center
c/o Center for Economic
Development
1 Indian Head Plz., Ste. 510
Nashua, New Hampshire 03060
Phone: (603)886-1233
Fax: (603)598-1164
Bob Wilburn, Regional Mgr.
E-mail: sbdc~bw@mv.mv.com

Plymouth State College
Small Business Development Center
Hyde Hall
Plymouth, New Hampshire 03264-
1595
Phone: (603)535-2523
Fax: (603)535-2850
Janice Kitchen, Regional Mgr.
E-mail: janice.kitchen@plymouth.edu

SBDC
18 S. Main St., Ste. 3A
Rochester, New Hampshire 03867
Phone: (603)330-1929
Fax: (603)330-1948

New Jersey

Greater Atlantic City Chamber of
Commerce
Small Business Development Center
1301 Atlantic Ave.
Atlantic City, New Jersey 08401
Phone: (609)345-5600
Fax: (609)345-4524

William R. McGinley, Dir.

Rutgers University Schools of
Business
Small Business Development Center
Business and Science Bldg., 2nd Fl.
Camden, New Jersey 08102
Phone: (609)757-6221
Fax: (609)225-6231
Patricia Peacock, Dir.

Brookdale Community College
Small Business Development Center
Newman Springs Rd.
Lincroft, New Jersey 07738
Phone: (908)842-1900
Fax: (908)842-0203
Bill Nunnally, Dir.

Rutgers University
New Jersey SBDC
180 University Ave.
3rd. Fl. Ackerson Hall
Newark, New Jersey 07102
Phone: (201)648-5950
Fax: (201)648-1110
Brenda B. Hopper, State Dir.

Bergen Community College
SBDC
400 Paramus Rd.
Paramus, New Jersey 07652-1595
Phone: (201)447-7841
Fax: (201)447-7495
Melody Irvin, Dir.

Mercer County Community College
Small Business Development Center
1200 Old Trenton Rd.
PO Box B
Trenton, New Jersey 08690
Phone: (609)586-4800
Fax: (609)890-6338
Herb Spiegel, Dir.

Kean College
Small Business Development Center
East Campus, Rm. 242
Union, New Jersey 07083
Phone: (908)527-2946
Fax: (908)527-2960

Warren County Community College
Small Business Development Center
Rte. 57 W.
Washington, New Jersey 07882

Phone: (908)689-9620
Fax: (908)689-7488
Robert Cerutti, Dir.

New Mexico

New Mexico State University at
Alamogordo
Small Business Development Center
2230 Lawrence Blvd.
Alamogordo, New Mexico 88310
Phone: (505)434-5272
Fax: (505)434-5272
Dwight Harp, Dir.

Albuquerque Technical-Vocational
Institute
Small Business Development Center
525 Buena Vista SE
Albuquerque, New Mexico 87106
Phone: (505)224-4246
Fax: (505)224-4251
Roslyn Block, Dir.

South Valley
SBDC
933 Sunset SW
Albuquerque, New Mexico 87105
Phone: (505)248-0132
Fax: (505)248-0127
Steven Becerra, Dir.

New Mexico State University at
Carlsbad
Small Business Development Center
PO Box 1090
Carlsbad, New Mexico 88220
Phone: (505)887-6562
Fax: (505)885-0818
Larry Coalson, Dir.

Clovis Community College
Small Business Development Center
417 Schepps Blvd.
Clovis, New Mexico 88101
Phone: (505)769-4136
Fax: (505)769-4190

Northern New Mexico Community
College
Small Business Development Center
1002 N. Onate St.
Espanola, New Mexico 87532
Phone: (505)747-2236
Fax: (505)747-2180
Darien Cabral, Dir.

San Juan College
Small Business Development Center
4601 College Blvd.
Farmington, New Mexico 87402
Phone: (505)599-0528
Cal Tingey, Dir.

University of New Mexico at Gallup
Small Business Development Center
PO Box 1395
Gallup, New Mexico 87305
Phone: (505)722-2220
Fax: (505)863-6006
Elsie Sanchez, Dir.

New Mexico State University at
Grants
Small Business Development Center
709 E. Roosevelt Ave.
Grants, New Mexico 87020
Phone: (505)287-8221
Fax: (505)287-2125
Clemente Sanchez, Dir.

New Mexico Junior College
Small Business Development Center
5317 Lovington Hwy.
Hobbs, New Mexico 88240
Phone: (505)392-4510
Fax: (505)392-2526
Don Leach, Dir.

New Mexico State University—Dona
Ana Branch
Small Business Development Center
3400 S. Espina St.
Dept. 3DA, Box 30001
Las Cruces, New Mexico 88003-0001
Phone: (505)527-7601
Fax: (505)527-7515
Terry Sullivan, Dir.

Luna Vocational-Technical Institute
Small Business Development Center
Luna Campus
PO Drawer K
Las Vegas, New Mexico 88701
Phone: (505)454-2595
Fax: (505)454-2518
Michael Rivera, Dir.

University of New Mexico at Los
Alamos
Small Business Development Center
901 18th St., No. 18

PO Box 715
Los Alamos, New Mexico 87544
Phone: (505)662-0001
Fax: (505)662-0099
Jim Greenwood, Dir.

University of New Mexico at
Valencia
Small Business Development Center
280 La Entrada
Los Lunas, New Mexico 87031
Phone: (505)866-5348
Fax: (505)865-3095
Ray Garcia, Dir.

Eastern New Mexico University at
Roswell
Small Business Development Center
57 Univ. Ave.
PO Box 6000
Roswell, New Mexico 88201-6000
Phone: (505)624-7133
Fax: (505)624-7132
Eugene Simmons, Dir.

Santa Fe Community College
New Mexico SBDC
P.O. Box 4187
Santa Fe, New Mexico 87502-4187
Phone: (505)438-1362
Free: (800)281-SBDC
Fax: (505)438-1237
Roy Miller, Dir.

Western New Mexico University
Small Business Development Center
PO Box 2672
Silver City, New Mexico 88062
Phone: (505)538-6320
Fax: (505)538-6341
Linda K. Jones, Dir.

Mesa Technical College
Small Business Development Center
PO Box 1143
Tucumcari, New Mexico 88401
Phone: (505)461-4413
Fax: (505)461-1901
Richard Spooner, Dir.

New York

State University of New York at
Albany
Small Business Development Center

Draper Hall, Rm. 107
135 Western Ave.
Albany, New York 12222
Phone: (518)442-5577
Fax: (518)442-5582
Peter George III, Dir.

State University of New York (Suny)
New York SBDCS
E-mail: kingjl@cc.sunycentral.edu
Suny Plaza, S-523
Albany, New York 12246
Phone: (518)443-5398
Free: (800)732-SBDC
Fax: (518)465-4992
James L. King, State Dir.

Binghamton University
Small Business Development Center
PO Box 6000
Binghamton, New York 13902-6000
Phone: (607)777-4024
Fax: (607)777-4029
Joanne Bauman, Dir.
E-mail: sbdcbu@spectra.net

State University of New York
Small Business Development Center
74 N. Main St.
Brockport, New York 14420
Phone: (716)637-6660
Fax: (716)637-2102
Wilfred Bordeau, Dir.

Bronx Community College
Small Business Development Center
McCracken Hall, Rm.14
W. 181st & University Ave.
Bronx, New York 10453
Phone: (718)563-3570
Fax: (718)563-3572
Eugene Williams, Dir.

Bronx Outreach Center
Con Edison
SBDC
560 Cortlandt Ave.
Bronx, New York 10451
Phone: (718)563-9204

Downtown Brooklyn Outreach Center
Kingsborough Community College
SBDC
395 Flatbush Ave. Extension Rm. 413
Brooklyn, New York 11201

Phone: (718)260-9783
Fax: (718)260-9797

Kingsboro Community College
Small Business Development Center
2001 Oriental Blvd. Rm. 4204
Manhattan Beach
Brooklyn, New York 11235
Phone: (718)368-4619
Fax: (718)368-4629
Edward O'Brien, Dir.

State University of New York at
Buffalo
Small Business Development Center
1300 Elmwood Ave.
Bacon Hall 117
Buffalo, New York 14222
Phone: (716)878-4030
Fax: (716)878-4067
Susan McCartney, Dir.

Canton Outreach Center
Jefferson Community College
SBDC
SUNY Canton
Canton, New York 13617
Phone: (315)386-7312
Fax: (315)386-7945

Cobleskill Outreach Center
SBDC
SUNY Cobleskill
State University of New York
Warner Hall, Rm. 218
Cobleskill, New York 12043
Phone: (518)234-5528
Fax: (518)234-5272

Corning Community College
Small Business Development Center
24 Denison Pky. W
Corning, New York 14830
Phone: (607)962-9461
Free: (800)358-7171
Fax: (607)936-6642
Bonnie Gestwicki, Dir.

Mercy College/Westchester Outreach
Center
SBDC
555 Broadway
Dobbs Ferry, New York 10522-1189
Phone: (914)674-7485
Fax: (914)693-4996
Tom Milton, Coordinator

State University of New York at
Farmingdale
Small Business Development Center
Campus Commons Bldg.
2350 Route 110
Farmingdale, New York 11735
Phone: (516)420-2765
Fax: (516)293-5343
Joseph Schwartz, Dir.

Marist College Outreach Center
SBDC
Fishkill Extension Center
2600 Rte. 9, Unit 90
Fishkill, New York 12524-2001
Phone: (914)897-2607
Fax: (914)897-4653

Niagara Community College
Geneseo Outreach Center
1 College Circle
South Hall, No. 111
Geneseo, New York 14454
Phone: (716)245-5429
Fax: (716)245-5430
Charles VanArsdale, Dir.

Geneva Outreach Center
SBDC
122 N. Genesee St.
Geneva, New York 14456
Phone: (315)781-1253
Sandy Bordeau, Administrative Dir.

Hempstead Outreach Center
SBDC
269 Fulton Ave.
Hempstead, New York 11550
Phone: (516)564-8672
Fax: (516)481-4938

York College/City University of New
York
Small Business Development Center
94-50 159th St.
Science Bldg. Rm. 107
Jamaica, New York 11451
Phone: (718)262-2880
Fax: (718)262-2881
James A. Heyliger

Jamestown Community College
Small Business Development Center
PO Box 20
Jamestown, New York 14702-0020
Phone: (716)665-5754

Free: (800)522-7232
Fax: (716)665-6733
Irene Dobies, Dir.

Kingston Small Business
Development Center
1 Development Ct.
Kingston, New York 12401
Phone: (914)339-0025
Fax: (914)339-1631
Patricia La Susa, Dir.

Baruch College
Mid-Town Outreach Center
SBDC
360 Park Ave. S., Rm. 1101
New York, New York 10010
Phone: (212)802-6620
Fax: (212)802-6613
Barrie Phillip, Coordinator

East Harlem Outreach Center
SBDC
145 E. 116th St., 3rd Fl.
New York, New York 10029
Phone: (212)346-1900
Fax: (212)534-4576
Anthony Sanchez, Coordinator

Harlem Outreach Center
SBDC
163 W. 125th St., Rm. 1307
New York, New York 10027
Phone: (212)346-1900
Fax: (212)534-4576
Anthony Sanchez, Coordinator

Mid-Town Outreach Ctr.
Baruch College
SBDC
360 Park Ave. S. Rm. 1101
New York, New York 10010
Phone: (212)802-6620
Fax: (212)802-6613
Barrie Phillip, Coordinator

Pace University
Small Business Development Center
1 Pace Plz., Rm. W483
New York, New York 10038
Phone: (212)346-1900
Fax: (212)346-1613
Ira Davidson, Dir.

Niagara Falls Satellite Office
Niagara Community College

SBDC
Carborundum Center
345 3rd St.
Niagara Falls, New York 14303-1117
Phone: (716)285-4793
Fax: (716)285-4797

Onondaga Community College/
Oswego Outreach Center
SBDC
44 W. Bridge St.
Oswego, New York 13126
Phone: (315)343-1545
Fax: (315)343-1546

Clinton Community College
SBDC
136 Clinton Pointe Dr.
Lake Shore Rd., Rte. 9
Plattsburgh, New York 12901
Phone: (518)562-4260
Fax: (518)563-9759
Merry Gwynn, Coordinator

Suffolk County Community College
Riverhead Outreach Center
SBDC
Riverhead, New York 11901
Phone: (516)369-1409
Fax: (516)369-3255

SUNY at Brockport
State University at Brockport
SBDC
Temple Bldg.
14 Franklin St., Ste. 200
Rochester, New York 14604
Phone: (716)232-7310
Fax: (716)637-2182

Niagara County Community College
Small Business Development Center
3111 Saunders Settlement Rd.
Sanborn, New York 14132
Phone: (716)693-1910
Fax: (716)731-3595
Richard Gorko, Dir.

Long Island University at
Southhampton/Southampton Outreach
Center
Suny StonyBrook
Abney Peak, Montauk Hwy.
Southampton, New York 11968
Phone: (516)287-0059
Fax: (516)287-8287

College of Staten Island
SBDC
2800 Victory Blvd.
Bldg 1A, Rm. 211
Staten Island, New York 10314-9806
Phone: (718)982-2560
Fax: (718)982-2323
Dr. Ronald Sheppard, Dir.

SUNY at Stony Brook
SBDC
Harriman Hall, Rm. 103
Stony Brook, New York 11794-3775
Phone: (516)632-9070
Fax: (516)632-7176
Judith McEvoy, Dir.

Rockland Community College
Small Business Development Center
145 College Rd.
Suffern, New York 10901-3620
Phone: (914)356-0370
Fax: (914)356-0381
Thomas J. Morley, Dir.

Onondaga Community College
Small Business Development Center
4969 Onondaga Rd.
Excell Bldg., Rm. 108
Syracuse, New York 13215-1944
Phone: (315)492-3029
Fax: (315)492-3704
Robert Varney, Dir.

Manufacturing Field Office
SBDC
Rensselaer Technology Park
385 Jordan Rd.
Troy, New York 12180-7602
Phone: (518)286-1014
Fax: (518)286-1006
Thomas Reynolds, Dir.

State University Institute of
Technology
Small Business Development Center
PO Box 3050
Utica, New York 13504-3050
Phone: (315)792-7546
Fax: (315)792-7554
David Mallen, Dir.

SUNY Institute of Technology at
Utica/Rome
SBDC
P.O. Box 3050

Utica, New York 13504-3050
Phone: (315)792-7546
Fax: (315)792-7554
David Mallen, Dir.

Jefferson Community College
Small Business Development Center
Coffeen St.
Watertown, New York 13601
Phone: (315)782-9262
Fax: (315)782-0901
John F. Tanner, Dir.

SBDC Outreach Small Business
Resource Center
222 Bloomingdale Rd., 3rd Fl.
White Plains, New York 10605-1500
Phone: (914)644-4116
Fax: (914)644-2184
Maria Circosta, Coordinator

North Carolina

Asheville SBTDC
34 Wall St., Ste. 707
Asheville, North Carolina 28805
Phone: (704)251-6025

Appalachian State University
Small Business and Technology
Development Center (Northwestern
Region)
Walker College of Business
2123 Raley Hall
Boone, North Carolina 28608
Phone: (704)262-2492
Fax: (704)262-2027
Bill Parrish, Regional Dir.

University of North Carolina at
Chapel Hill
Central Carolina Regional Small
Business Development Center
608 Airport Rd., Ste. B
Chapel Hill, North Carolina 27514
Phone: (919)962-0389
Fax: (919)962-3291
Dan Parks, Dir.

University of North Carolina at
Charlotte
Small Business and Technology
Development Center (Southern
Piedmont Region)
8701 Mallard Creek Rd.
Charlotte, North Carolina 28262

Phone: (704)548-1090
Fax: (704)548-9050
George McAllister, Dir.

Western Carolina University
Small Business and Technology
Development Center (Western
Region)
Center for Improving Mountain
Living
Bird Bldg.
Cullowhee, North Carolina 28723
Phone: (704)227-7494
Fax: (704)227-7422
Allan Steinburg, Dir.

Elizabeth City State University
Small Business and Technology
Development Center (Northeastern
Region)
1704 Weeksville Rd.
PO Box 874
Elizabeth City, North Carolina 27909
Phone: (919)335-3247
Fax: (919)355-3648
Wauna Dooms, Dir.

Fayetteville State University
Cape Fear Small Business and
Technology Development Center
PO Box 1334
Fayetteville, North Carolina 28302
Phone: (910)486-1727
Fax: (910)486-1949
Sid Gautam, Dir.

North Carolina A&T State University
Northern Piedmont Small Business
and Technology Development Center
(Eastern Region)
C. H. Moore Agricultural Research
Center
1601 E. Market St.
PO Box D-22
Greensboro, North Carolina 27411
Phone: (910)334-7005
Fax: (910)334-7073
Cynthia Clemons, Dir.

East Carolina University
Small Business and Technology
Development Center (Eastern Region)
Willis Bldg.
300 East 1st St.
Greenville, North Carolina 27858-
4353

Phone: (919)328-6157
Fax: (919)328-6992
Walter Fitts, Dir.

Catawba Valley Region
SBTDC
514 Hwy. 321 NW, Ste. A
Hickory, North Carolina 28601
Phone: (704)345-1110
Fax: (704)326-9117
Rand Riedrich, Dir.

Pembroke State University
Office of Economic Development and
SBTDC
SBDC
Pembroke, North Carolina 28372
Phone: (910)521-6603
Fax: (910)521-6550

North Carolina SBTDC
SBDC
333 Fayette St. Mall, Ste. 1150
Raleigh, North Carolina 27601
Phone: (919)715-7272
Fax: (919)715-7777
Scott R. Daugherty, Executive Dir.

North Carolina State University
Capital Region
SBTDC
MCI Small Business Resource Center
800 1/2 S. Salisbury St.
Raleigh, North Carolina 27601
Phone: (919)715-0520
Fax: (919)715-0518
Gary Palin, Dir.

North Carolina Wesleyan College
SBTDC
3400 N. Wesleyan Blvd.
Rocky Mount, North Carolina 27804
Phone: (919)985-5130
Fax: (919)977-3701

University of North Carolina at
Wilmington
Southeastern Region
SBTDC
601 S. College Rd.
Wilmington, North Carolina 28403
Phone: (910)395-3744
Fax: (910)350-3990
Mike Bradley, Acting Dir.

University of North Carolina at
Wilmington
Small Business and Technology
Development Center (Southeast
Region)
601 S. College Rd.
Cameron Hall, Rm. 131
Wilmington, North Carolina 28403
Phone: (910)395-3744
Fax: (910)350-3990
Mike Bradley, Dir.

Winston-Salem State University
Northern Piedmont Small Business
and Technology Center
PO Box 13025
Winston Salem, North Carolina
27110
Phone: (910)750-2030
Fax: (910)750-2031
Bill Dowa, Dir.

North Dakota

Bismarck Regional Small Business
Development Center
400 E. Broadway, Ste. 416
Bismarck, North Dakota 58501
Phone: (701)223-8583
Fax: (701)222-3843
Jan M. Peterson, Regional Dir.

Devils Lake Outreach Center
SBDC
417 5th St.
Devils Lake, North Dakota 58301
Free: (800)445-7232
Gordon Synder, Regional Dir.

Dickinson Regional Center
Small Business Development Center
314 3rd Ave. W
Drawer L
Dickinson, North Dakota 58602
Phone: (701)227-2096
Fax: (701)225-5116
Bryan Vendsel, Regional Dir.

Fargo Regional Small Business
Development Center
417 Main Ave., Ste. 402
Fargo, North Dakota 58103
Phone: (701)237-0986
Fax: (701)237-9734
Jon Grinager, Regional Mgr.

Procurement Assistance Center
SBDC
417 Main St.
Fargo, North Dakota 58103
Phone: (701)237-9678
Free: (800)698-5726
Fax: (701)237-9734

Red River Regional Planning Council
SBDC
Grafton Outreach Center
SBDC
PO Box 633
Grafton, North Dakota 58237
Free: (800)445-7232
Gordon Snyder, Regional Dir.

Grand Forks Regional Small Business
Development Center
202 N. 3rd St., Ste. 200
The Hemmp Center
Grand Forks, North Dakota 58203
Phone: (701)772-8502
Fax: (701)772-2772
Gordon Snyder, Regional Dir.

University of North Dakota
North Dakota SBDC
118 Gamble Hall
University Station Box 7308
Grand Forks, North Dakota 58202-7308
Phone: (701)777-3700
Fax: (701)777-3225
Walter "Wally" Kearns, State Dir.

Jamestown Outreach Ctr.
SBDC
210 10th St.
S.E.P.O Box 1530
Jamestown, North Dakota 58402
Phone: (701)252-9243
Fax: (701)251-2488
Jon Grinager, Regional Dir.

North Dakota Small Business
Development Center
210 10th St.
SE PO Box 1530
Jamestown, North Dakota 58402
Phone: (701)252-9243
Fax: (701)251-2488
Jon Grinager, Regional Dir.

Minot Regional
SBDC

900 N. Broadway, Ste. 300
Minot, North Dakota 58703
Phone: (701)852-8861
Fax: (701)858-3831
Brian Argabright, Regional

Williston Outreach Center
SBDC
PO Box 2047
Williston, North Dakota 58801
Free: (800)445-7232
Bryan Vendsel, Regional Dir.

Ohio

Akron Regional Development Board
Small Business Development Center
1 Cascade Plz., 8th Fl.
Akron, Ohio 44308-1192
Phone: (330)379-3170
Fax: (330)379-3164
Charles Smith, Dir.

Women's Entrepreneurial Growth
Organization
Small Business Development Center
The University of Akron
Buckingham Bldg., Rm. 55
PO Box 544
Akron, Ohio 44309
Phone: (330)972-5179
Fax: (330)972-5513
Dr. Penny Marquette, Dir.

Women's Network
SBDC
1540 West Market St., Ste. 100
Akron, Ohio 44313
Phone: (330)864-5636
Fax: (330)884-6526
Marlene Miller, Dir.

Enterprise Development Corp.
SBDC
900 E. State St.
Athens, Ohio 45701
Phone: (614)592-1188
Fax: (614)593-8283
Karen Paton, Dir.

Ohio University Innovation Center
Small Business Development Center
Technical & Enterprise Bldg.
20 East Circle Dr., Ste. 153
Athens, Ohio 45701
Phone: (614)593-1797

Fax: (614)593-1795
Marianne Vermeer, Dir.
E-mail:
vermeer@ouvata.cats.ohiou.edu

WSOS Community Action
Commision, Inc.
Wood County SBDC
WSOS Community Action
Commission, Inc.
121 E. Wooster St.
PO Box 539
Bowling Green, Ohio 43402
Phone: (419)352-7469
Fax: (419)353-3291
Tom Blaha, Dir.

Kent State University/Stark Campus
SBDC
6000 Frank Ave., NW
Canton, Ohio 44720
Phone: (330)499-9600
Fax: (330)494-6121

Women's Business Development
Center
SBDC
2400 Cleveland Ae., NW
Canton, Ohio 44709
Phone: (330)453-3867
Fax: (330)773-2992

Wright State University—Lake
Campus
Small Business Development Center
7600 State Rte. 703
Celina, Ohio 45822
Phone: (419)586-0355
Free: (800)237-1477
Fax: (419)586-0358
Tom Knapke, Dir.

Clermont County Area
SBDC
Clermont County Chamber of
Commerce
4440 Glen Este-Withamsville Rd.
Cincinnati, Ohio 45245
Phone: (513)753-7141
Fax: (513)753-7146
Dennis Begue, Dir.

University of Cincinnati
SBDC
IAMS Research Pk., MC189
1111 Edison Ave.

Cincinnati, Ohio 45216-2265
Phone: (513)948-2082
Fax: (513)948-2007
Bill Floretti, Dir.

Greater Cleveland Growth
Association
Small Business Development Center
200 Tower City Center
50 Public Sq.
Cleveland, Ohio 44113-2291
Phone: (216)621-3300
Fax: (216)621-4617
Janet Haar, Dir.

Northern Ohio Manufacturing
SBDC
Prospect Park Bldg.
4600 Prospect Ave.
Cleveland, Ohio 44103-4314
Phone: (216)432-5364
Fax: (216)361-2900
Gretchen Faro, Dir.

Centrqal Ohio Manufacturing
SBDC
1250 Arthur E. Adams Dr.
Columbus, Ohio 43221
Phone: (614)688-5176
Fax: (614)688-5001

Department of Development
Ohio SBDC
77 S. High St., 28th Fl.
Columbus, Ohio 43216-1001
Phone: (614)466-2711
Fax: (614)466-0829
Holly I. Schick, State Dir.

Greater Columbus Area Chamber of
Commerce
SBDC
37 N. High St.
Columbus, Ohio 43215-3065
Phone: (614)225-6082
Fax: (614)469-8250
Linda Steward, Dir.

Dayton Area Chamber of Commerce
Small Business Development Center
Chamber Plz.
5th & Main Sts.
Dayton, Ohio 45402-2400
Phone: (513)226-8239
Fax: (513)226-8254

Harry Bumgarner, Dir.

Wright State University/Dayton
SBDC
Center for Small Business Assistance,
College of Business 31
College of Business
310 Rike Hall
Dayton, Ohio 45435
Phone: (513)873-3503
Dr. Jeanette Davy, Dir.

Northwest Private Industry Council
SBDC
1935 E. 2nd St., Ste. D
Defiance, Ohio 43512
Phone: (419)784-3777
Fax: (419)782-4649
Don Wright, Dir.

Northwest Technical College
Small Business Development Center
1935 E. 2nd St., Ste. D
Defiance, Ohio 43512
Phone: (419)784-3777
Fax: (419)782-4649
Don Wright, Dir.

Terra Community College
Small Business Development Center
1220 Cedar St.
Fremont, Ohio 43420
Phone: (419)332-1002
Fax: (419)314-2300
Joe Wilson, Dir.

Enterprise Center
Small Business Development Center
129 E. Main St.
PO Box 756
Hillsboro, Ohio 45133
Phone: (513)393-9599
Fax: (513)393-8159
Bill Grunkemeyer, Dir.

Ashtabula County Economic
Development Council, Inc.
Small Business Development Center
36 W. Walnut St.
Jefferson, Ohio 44047
Phone: (216)576-9134
Fax: (216)576-5003
Sarah Bogardus, Dir.

Kent State University Partnership
SBDC

Kent State University
College of Business Administration
Rm. 300A
Kent, Ohio 44242
Phone: (330)672-2772
Fax: (330)672-2448
Linda Yost, Dir.

EMTEC/Southern Area
Manufacturing
SBDC
3171 Research Park
Kettering, Ohio 45420
Phone: (513)259-1361
Fax: (513)259-1303
James Ackley, Dir.

Lima Technical College
Small Business Development Center
545 W. Market St., Ste. 305
Lima, Ohio 45801-4717
Phone: (419)229-5320
Fax: (419)229-5424
Gerald J. Biedenharn, Dir.

Lorain County Chamber of
Commerce
SBDC
6100 S. Boadway
Lorain, Ohio 44053
Phone: (216)233-6500
Dennis Jones, Dir.

Mid-Ohio Small Business
Development Center
246 E. 4th St.
PO Box 1208
Mansfield, Ohio 44901
Free: (800)366-7232
Fax: (419)522-6811
Tim Bowersock, Dir.

Marietta College
SBDC
213 Fourth St.
Marietta, Ohio 45750
Phone: (614)376-4901
Fax: (614)376-4832
Emerson Shimp, Dir.

Marion Area Chamber of Commerce
SBDC
206 S. Prospect St.
Marion, Ohio 43302
Phone: (614)387-0188

Fax: (614)387-7722
Lynn Lovell, Dir.

Lake County Economic Development
Center
SBDC
Lakeland Community College
750 Clocktower Dr.
Mentor, Ohio 44060
Phone: (216)951-1290
Fax: (216)951-7336
Jerry Loth, Dir.

Tuscarawas SBDC
Tuscarawas SBDC
Kent State University
300 University Dr., NE
New Philadelphia, Ohio 44663-9447
Phone: (330)339-3391
Fax: (330)339-2637
Tom Farbizo, Dir.

Miami University
Small Business Development Center
336 Upham Hall
Oxford, Ohio 45056
Phone: (513)529-4841
Fax: (513)529-1469
Dr. Michael Broida, Dir.

Upper Valley Joint Vocational School
Small Business Development Center
8811 Career Dr.
N. Country Rd., 25A
Piqua, Ohio 45356
Phone: (513)778-8419
Free: (800)589-6963
Fax: (513)778-9237
Carol Baumhauer, Dir.

Ohio Valley Minority Business
Association
SBDC
1208 Waller St.
P.O. Box 1757
Portsmouth, Ohio 45662
Phone: (614)353-8395
Fax: (614)353-2695
Clemmy Womack, Dir.

Department of Development of the
CIC of Belmont County
Small Business Development Center
100 E. Main St.
St. Clairsville, Ohio 43950

Phone: (614)695-9678
Fax: (614)695-1536
Mike Campbell, Dir.

Kent State University/Salem Campus
SBDC
2491 State, Rte. 45 S.
Salem, Ohio 44460
Phone: (330)332-0361
Fax: (330)332-9256
Deanne Taylor, Dir.

Lawrence County Chamber of
Commerce
Small Business Development Center
U.S. Rte. 52 & Solida Rd.
PO Box 488
South Point, Ohio 45680
Phone: (614)894-3838
Fax: (614)894-3836
Lou-Ann Walden, Dir.

Springfield Small Business
Development Center
300 E. Auburn Ave.
Springfield, Ohio 45505
Phone: (513)322-7821
Fax: (513)322-7824
Rafeal Underwood, Exec.

Jefferson County Small Business
Development Center
Greater Steubenville Chamber of
Commerce
630 Market St.
PO Box 278
Steubenville, Ohio 43952
Phone: (614)282-6226
Fax: (614)282-6285
Jeff Castner, Dir.

Toledo Small Business Development
Center
300 Madison Ave., Ste. 200
Toledo, Ohio 43604-1575
Phone: (419)252-2700
Fax: (419)252-2724
Linda Fayerweather, Dir.

Youngstown/Warren SBDC
Region Chamber of Commerce
180 E. Market St.
Warren, Ohio 44482
Phone: (330)393-2565
Patricia Veisz, Mgr.

Youngstown State University
SBDC
Cushwa Center for Industrial
Development
241 Federal Plaza W.
Youngstown, Ohio 44503
Phone: (330)746-3350
Fax: (330)746-3324
Patricia Veisz, Mgr.

Zanesville Area Chamber of
Commerce
Small Business Development Center
217 N. 5th St.
Zanesville, Ohio 43701
Phone: (614)452-4868
Fax: (614)454-2963
Bonnie J. Winnett, Dir.

Oklahoma

East Central University
Small Business Development Center
1036 E. 10th St.
Ada, Oklahoma 74820
Phone: (405)436-3190
Fax: (405)436-3190
Frank Vater
E-mail: osbdcecu@chickasaw.com

Northwestern Oklahoma State
University
Small Business Development Center
709 Oklahoma Blvd.
Alva, Oklahoma 73717
Phone: (405)327-8608
Fax: (405)327-0560
Connie Murrell, Dir.

Southeastern Oklahoma State
University
Oklahoma SBDC
517 University
Station A, Box 2584
Durant, Oklahoma 74701
Phone: (800)522-6154
Fax: (405)920-7471
Dr. Grady Pennington, State Dir.

Phillips University
Small Business Development Center
100 S. University Ave.
Enid, Oklahoma 73701
Phone: (405)242-7989
Fax: (405)237-1607
Bill Gregory, Coordinator

Langston University Center
Small Business Development Center
Hwy. 33 E.
Langston, Oklahoma 73050
Phone: (405)466-3256
Fax: (405)466-2909
Robert Allen, Dir.

Lawton Satellite
Small Business Development Center
American National Bank Bldg.
601 SW "D" Ave., Ste. 209
Lawton, Oklahoma 73501
Phone: (405)248-4946
Fax: (405)355-3560
Linda Strelecki

NE Oklahoma A&M
Miami Satellite
SBDC
Dyer Hall, Rm. 307
200 I St. NE
Miami, Oklahoma 74354
Phone: (918)540-0575
Fax: (918)540-0575
Hugh Simon, Specialist

Rose State College
SBDC
Procurement Speciality Center
6420 Southeast 15th St.
Midwest City, Oklahoma 73110
Phone: (405)733-7348
Fax: (405)733-7495
Judy Robbins, Dir.
Michael Cure, Bus. Dev. Specialist

Carl Albert College
Small Business Development Center
1507 S. McKenna
Poteau, Oklahoma 74953
Phone: (918)647-4019
Fax: (918)647-1218
Dean Qualls, Dir.

Northeastern Oklahoma State
University
Small Business Development Center
Oklahoma Small Business
Development Center
Tahlequah, Oklahoma 74464
Phone: (918)458-0802
Fax: (918)458-2105
Danielle Coursey

Tulsa Satellite
Small Business Development Center
State Office Bldg.
440 S. Houston, Ste. 507
Tulsa, Oklahoma 74127
Phone: (918)581-2502
Fax: (918)581-2745
Jeff Horvath, Dir.

Southwestern Oklahoma State
University
Small Business Development Center
100 Campus Dr.
Weatherford, Oklahoma 73096
Phone: (405)774-1040
Fax: (405)774-7091
Chuck Felz, Dir.

Oregon

Linn-Benton Community College
Small Business Development Center
6500 SW. Pacific Blvd.
Albany, Oregon 97321
Phone: (541)917-4923
Fax: (541)917-4445
Dennis Sargent, Dir.

Southern Oregon State College/
Ashland
Small Business Development Center
Regional Services Institute
Ashland, Oregon 97520
Phone: (541)482-5838
Fax: (541)482-1115
Liz Shelby, Dir.

Central Oregon Community College
Small Business Development Center
2600 NW College Way
Bend, Oregon 97701
Phone: (541)383-7290
Fax: (541)383-7503
Bob Newhart, Dir.

Southwestern Oregon Community
College
Small Business Development Center
2110 Newmark Ave.
Coos Bay, Oregon 97420
Phone: (541)888-7100
Fax: (541)888-7113
Jon Richards, Dir.

Columbia Gorge Community College
SBDC

212 Washington
The Dalles, Oregon 97058
Phone: (541)298-3118
Fax: (541)298-3119
Mr. Bob Cole, Dir.

Lane Community College
Oregon SBDC
44 W. Broadway, Ste. 501
Eugene, Oregon 97401-3021
Phone: (541)726-2250
Fax: (541)345-6006
Dr. Edward Cutler, State Dir.

Rogue Community College
Small Business Development Center
214 SW 4th St.
Grants Pass, Oregon 97526
Phone: (541)471-3515
Fax: (541)471-3589
Lee Merritt, Dir.

Mount Hood Community College
Small Business Development Center
323 NE Roberts St.
Gresham, Oregon 97030
Phone: (503)667-7658
Fax: (503)666-1140
Don King, Dir.

Oregon Institute of Technology
Small Business Development Center
3201 Campus Dr. S. 314
Klamath Falls, Oregon 97601
Phone: (541)885-1760
Fax: (541)885-1855
Jamie Albert, Dir.

Eastern Oregon State College
Small Business Development Center
Regional Services Institute
1410 L Ave.
La Grande, Oregon 97850
Phone: (541)962-3391
Free: (800)452-8639
Fax: (541)962-3668
Joni Woodwell, Dir.

Oregon Coast Community College
Small Business Development Center
4157 NW Hwy. 101, Ste. 123
PO Box 419
Lincoln City, Oregon 97367
Phone: (541)994-4166
Fax: (541)996-4958
Rose Seminary, Contact

Southern Oregon State College/
Medford
Small Business Development Center
Regional Service Institute
229 N. Bartlett
Medford, Oregon 97501
Phone: (541)772-3478
Fax: (541)776-2224
Liz Shelby, Dir.

Clackamas Community College
Small Business Development Center
7616 SE Harmony Rd.
Milwaukie, Oregon 97222
Phone: (503)656-4447
Fax: (503)652-0389
Jan Stennick, Dir.

Treasure Valley Community College
Small Business Development Center
88 SW 3rd Ave.
Ontario, Oregon 97914
Phone: (541)889-2617
Fax: (541)889-8331
Kathy Simko, Dir.

Blue Mountain Community College
Small Business Development Center
37 SE Dorion
Pendleton, Oregon 97801
Phone: (541)276-6233
Fax: (541)276-6819
Betty Udy, Contact

Portland Community College
Small Business International Trade
Program
121 SW Salmon St., Ste. 210
Portland, Oregon 97204
Phone: (503)274-7482
Fax: (503)228-6350
Tom Niland, Dir.

Portland Community College
Small Business Development Center
123 NW 2nd Ave., Ste. 321
Portland, Oregon 97209
Phone: (503)414-2828
Fax: (503)294-0725
Robert Keyser, Dir.

Umpqua Community College
Small Business Development Center
744 SE Rose
Roseburg, Oregon 97470
Phone: (541)672-2535

Fax: (541)672-3679
Terry Swagerty, Dir.

Chemeketa Community College
Small Business Development Center
365 Ferry St. SE
Salem, Oregon 97301
Phone: (503)399-5181
Fax: (503)581-6017
Bobbie Clyde, Dir.

Clatsop Community College
Small Business Development Center
1240 S. Holladay
Seaside, Oregon 97138
Phone: (503)738-3347
Fax: (503)738-7843
Kennetyh McCune, Dir.

Tillamook Bay Community College
Small Business Development Center
401 B Main St.
Tillamook, Oregon 97141
Phone: (503)842-2551
Fax: (503)842-2555
Mike Harris, Dir.

Pennsylvania

Lehigh University
Small Business Development Center
Ranch Business Ctr., No. 37
Bethlehem, Pennsylvania 18015
Phone: (610)758-3980
Fax: (610)758-5205
Dr. Larry A. Strain, Dir.

Clarion University of Pennsylvania
Small Business Development Center
Dana Still Bldg., Rm. 102
Clarion, Pennsylvania 16214
Phone: (814)226-2060
Fax: (814)226-2636
Dr. Woodrow Yeaney, Dir.

Bucks County SBDC Outreach Center
2 E. Court St.
Doylestown, Pennsylvania 18901
Phone: (215)230-7150
Bruce Love, Dir.

Gannon University
Small Business Development Center
120 W. 9th St.
Erie, Pennsylvania 16501
Phone: (814)871-7569

Fax: (814)871-7383
Ernie Post, Dir.

Kutztown University
Small Business Development Center
2986 N. 2nd St.
Harrisburg, Pennsylvania 17110
Phone: (717)720-4230
Fax: (717)233-3181
Katherine Wilson, Dir.

Duquesne University
SBDC
Robert Shaw Bldg.
Indiana, Pennsylvania 15705
Phone: (412)357-7915
Fax: (412)357-4514
Dr. Mary T. McKinney, Dir.

St. Vincent College
Small Business Development Center
300 Fraser Purchase Rd.
Latrobe, Pennsylvania 15650
Phone: (412)537-4572
Fax: (412)537-0919
Jack Fabean, Dir.

Bucknell University
Small Business Development Center
126 Dana Engineering Bldg., 1st Fl.
Lewisburg, Pennsylvania 17837
Phone: (717)524-1249
Fax: (717)524-1768
Charles Coder, Dir.

St. Francis College
Small Business Development Center
Business Resource Center
Loretto, Pennsylvania 15940
Phone: (814)472-3200
Fax: (814)472-3202
John A. Palko, Dir.

LaSalle University
Small Business Development Center
1900 W. Olney Ave.
Box 365
Philadelphia, Pennsylvania 19141
Phone: (215)951-1416
Fax: (215)951-1597
Andrew Lamas, Dir.

Temple University
Small Business Development Center
Rm. 6, Speakman Hall, 006-00
Philadelphia, Pennsylvania 19122

Phone: (215)204-7282
Fax: (215)204-4554
Geraldine Perkins, Dir.

University Of Pennsylvania
Pennsylvania SBDC
E-mail:
ghiggins@sec1.wharton.upenn.edu
The Wharton School
423 Vance Hall
3733 Spruce St.
Philadelphia, Pennsylvania 19104-6374
Phone: (215)898-1219
Fax: (215)573-2135
Gregory L. Higgins, Jr., State Dir.

Duquesne University
Small Business Development Center
Rockwell Hall, Rm. 10, Concourse
600 Forbes Ave.
Pittsburgh, Pennsylvania 15282
Phone: (412)396-6233
Fax: (412)396-5884
Mary T. McKinney, Dir.

University of Pittsburgh
Small Business Development Center
The Joseph M. Katz Graduate School
of Business
208 Bellefield
315 S. Bellefield Ave.
Pittsburgh, Pennsylvania 15213
Phone: (412)648-1544
Fax: (412)648-1636
Ann Dugan, Dir.

University of Scranton
Small Business Development Center
St. Thomas Hall, Rm. 588
Scranton, Pennsylvania 18510
Phone: (717)941-7588
Fax: (717)941-4053
Elaine M. Tweedy, Dir.

West Chester University
SBDC
319 Anderson Hall
West Chester, Pennsylvania 19383
Phone: (610)436-2162
Fax: (610)436-3170

Wilkes University
Small Business Development Center
Hollenback Hall

192 S. Franklin St.
Wilkes Barre, Pennsylvania 18766-0001
Phone: (717)831-4340
Fax: (717)824-2245
Jeffrey Alves, Dir.

Puerto Rico

SBDC
Edificio Union Plaza, Ste. 701
416 Ponce de Leon Ave.
Hato Rey, Puerto Rico 00918
Phone: (787)763-5108
Fax: (787)763-4629
Carmen Marti, State Dir.

Rhode Island

Northern Rhode Island Chamber of
Commerce
SBDC
640 George Washington Hwy.
Lincoln, Rhode Island 02865
Phone: (401)334-1000
Fax: (401)334-1009
Robert D. Hamlin, Case Mgr.

Newport County Chamber of
Commerce
E. Bay Small Business Development
Center
45 Valley Rd.
Middletown, Rhode Island 02842-6306
Phone: (401)849-6900
Fax: (401)849-5848
Sam Carr, Case Mgr.

Fishing Community Program Office
SBDC
PO Box 178
Narragansett, Rhode Island 02882
Phone: (401)783-2466
Angela Caporelli, Program Mgr.

South County SBDC
QP/D Industrial Park
35 Belver Ave., Rm. 212
North Kingstown, Rhode Island
02852-7556
Phone: (401)294-1227
Fax: (401)294-6897
Sue Barker, Asst. Dir.

Enterprise Community SBDC
550 Broad St.
Providence, Rhode Island 02905
Phone: (940)1 0272-1083
Evette McCray, Mgr.

Rhode Island/DOT
SBDC Supportive Services Program
2 Capitol Hill, Rm. 106
Providence, Rhode Island 02903
Phone: (401)277-4576
Fax: (401)277-6168
O.J. Silas, Program Mgr.

Bryant College
Export Assistance Center
SBDC
1150 Douglas Pike
Smithfield, Rhode Island 02917
Phone: (401)232-6407
Fax: (401)232-6416
Raymond Fogarty, Dir.

Bryant College
Rhode Island SBDC
1150 Douglas Pike
Smithfield, Rhode Island 02917
Phone: (401)232-6111
Fax: (401)232-6933
Douglas Jobling, State Dir.

Bryant College Koffler Technology
Center
Bryant College
1150 Douglas Pke.
Smithfield, Rhode Island 02917
Phone: (401)232-0220
Fax: (401)232-0242
Christopher Langton, Dir.

Entrepreneurship Training Program
Bryant College
SBDC
1150 Douglas Pike
Smithfield, Rhode Island 02917
Cheryl Faria, Program Mgr.

Bristol County Chamber of
Commerce
SBDC
P.O. Box 250
Warren, Rhode Island 02885
Phone: (401)245-0750
Fax: (401)245-0110

Central RI Chamber of Commerce
SBDC
P.O. Box 7243
Warwick, Rhode Island 02887
Phone: (401)732-1100
Fax: (401)732-1107
Mr. William Nash, Case Mgr.

South Carolina

Aiken Small Business Development
Center
171 University Pky., Ste. 100
Aiken, South Carolina 29801
Phone: (803)641-3646
Fax: (803)641-3647
Jackie Moore, Area Mgr.

University of South Carolina at
Beaufort
Small Business Development Center
800 Carteret St.
Beaufort, South Carolina 29902
Phone: (803)521-4143
Fax: (803)521-4142
Martin Goodman, Area Mgr.

Clemson University
Small Business Development Center
College of Commerce and Industry
425 Sirrine Hall
Box 341392
Clemson, South Carolina 29634-1392
Phone: (803)656-3227
Fax: (803)656-4869
Becky Hobart, Regional Dir.

University of South Carolina
College of Business Administration
South Carolina SBDC
1710 College St.
Columbia, South Carolina 29208
Phone: (803)777-4907
Fax: (803)777-4403
John Lenti, State Director

USC Regional Small Business
Development Center
University of South Carolina
College of Business Administration
Columbia, South Carolina 29208
Phone: (803)777-5118
Fax: (803)777-4403
James Brazell, Dir.
E-mail:
brazell@univscvm.csd.scarolina.edu

Coastal Carolina College
Small Business Development Center
School of Business Administration
PO Box 1954
Conway, South Carolina 29526
Phone: (803)349-2170
Fax: (803)349-2455
Tim Lowery, Area Mgr.

Florence-Darlington Technical
College
Small Business Development Center
PO Box 100548
Florence, South Carolina 29501-0548
Phone: (803)661-8256
Fax: (803)661-8041
David Raines, Area Mgr.

Greenville Chamber of Commerce
Small Business Development Center
24 Cleveland St.
Greenville, South Carolina 29601
Phone: (803)271-4259
Fax: (803)282-8549

SBDC Manufacturing Field Office
53 E. Antrim Dr.
Greenville, South Carolina 29607
Phone: (803)271-3005

Upper Savannah Council of
Government
Small Business Development Center
Exchange Building
222 Phoenix St., Ste. 200
SBDC Exchange Bldg.
PO Box 1366
Greenwood, South Carolina 29648
Phone: (803)941-8071
Fax: (803)941-8090
George Long, Area Mgr.

University of South Carolina at Hilton
Head
Small Business Development Center
Kiawah Bldg., Ste. 300
10 Office Park Rd.
Hilton Head, South Carolina 29928-
7535
Phone: (803)785-3995
Fax: (803)777-0333
Jim DeMartin, Consultant

Charleston SBDC
5900 Core Dr., Ste. 104
North Charleston, South Carolina
29406

Phone: (803)740-6160
Fax: (803)740-1607
Merry Boone, Area Mrg.

South Carolina State College
Small Business Development Center
School of Business Administration
300 College Ave.
Orangeburg, South Carolina 29117
Phone: (803)536-8445
Fax: (803)536-8066
John Gadson, Regional Dir.

Winthrop College
Winthrop Regional Small Business
Development Center
School of Business Administration
119 Thurman Bldg.
Rock Hill, South Carolina 29733
Phone: (803)323-2283
Fax: (803)323-4281
Nate Barber, Regional Dir.

Spartanburg Chamber of Commerce
Small Business Development Center
105 Pine St.
PO Box 1636
Spartanburg, South Carolina 29304
Phone: (803)594-5080
Fax: (803)594-5055
John Keagle, Area Mgr.

South Dakota

Aberdeen Small Business
Development Center
226 Citizens Bldg.
Aberdeen, South Dakota 57401
Phone: (605)626-2252
Fax: (605)626-2667
Bryce Anderson, Dir.

Pierre Small Business Development
Center
105 S. Euclid, Ste. C
Pierre, South Dakota 57501
Phone: (605)773-5941
Fax: (605)773-5942
Greg Sund, Dir.

Rapid City Small Business
Development Center
444 N. Mount Rushmore Rd., Rm.
208
Rapid City, South Dakota 57701
Phone: (605)394-5311

Fax: (605)394-6140
Matthew Johnson, Dir.

Sioux Falls Region
SBDC
405 S. 3rd Ave., Ste. 101
Sioux Falls, South Dakota 57104
Phone: (605)367-5757
Fax: (605)367-5755
Duane Fladland, Regional Dir.

University of South Dakota
School of Business
South Dakota SBDC
414 E. Clark
Vermillion, South Dakota 57069
Phone: (605)677-5498
Fax: (605)677-5272
Robert E. Ashley, Jr., State Dir.

Watertown Small Business
Development Center
124 1st. Ave., N.W.
Watertown, South Dakota 57201
Phone: (605)886-7224
Fax: (605)882-5049

Tennessee

Chattanooga State Technical
Community College
SBDC
4501 Amnicola Hwy.
Chattanooga, Tennessee 37406-1097
Phone: (423)697-4410
Fax: (423)698-5653
Alan Artress, Specialist

Southeast Tennessee Development
District
Small Business Development Center
PO Box 4757
Chattanooga, Tennessee 37405
Phone: (423)266-5781
Fax: (423)267-7705
Vann Cunningham, Dir.

Austin Peay State University
Small Business Development Center
College of Business
Clarksville, Tennessee 37044
Phone: (615)648-7764
Fax: (615)648-5985
John Volker, Dir.

Cleveland State Community College
Small Business Development Center
Adkisson Dr.
PO Box 3570
Cleveland, Tennessee 37320
Phone: (423)478-6247
Fax: (423)478-6251
Don Green, Dir.

SBDC (Columbia)
Memorial Bldg., Rm. 205
308 W. 7th St.
Columbia, Tennessee 38401
Phone: (615)388-5674
Fax: (615)388-5474
Richard Prince, Senior Specialist

Tennessee Technological University
SBDC
College of Business Administration
PO Box 5023
Cookeville, Tennessee 38505
Phone: (615)372-6634
Fax: (615)372-6249

Dyersburg State Community College
Small Business Development Center
1510 Lake Rd.
Dyersburg, Tennessee 38024
Phone: (901)286-3201
Fax: (901)286-3271
Bob Wylie

Four Lakes Regional Industrial
Development Authority
SBDC
PO Box 63
Hartsville, Tennessee 37074-0063
Phone: (615)374-9521
Fax: (615)374-4608
Dorothy Vaden, SB Specialist

Jackson State Community College
Small Business Development Center
2046 N. Parkway St.
Jackson, Tennessee 38305
Phone: (901)424-5389
Fax: (901)425-2647
David L. Brown, Lambuth University
SBDC
705 Lambuth Blvd.
Jackson, Tennessee 38301
Phone: (901)425-3326
Fax: (901)425-3327
Phillip Ramsey, SB Specialist

East Tennessee State University
College of Business
SBDC
P.O. Box 70698
Johnson City, Tennessee 37614
Phone: (423)929-5630
Fax: (423)461-7080
Bob Justice, Dir.

International Trade Center
SBDC
301 E. Church Ave.
Knoxville, Tennessee 37915
Phone: (423)637-4283
Fax: (423)523-2071
Richard Vogler, IT Specialist

Pellissippi State Technical
Community College
Small Business Development Center
301 East Church Ave.
Knoxville, Tennessee 37915
Phone: (423)525-0277
Fax: (423)971-4439

University of Memphis
International Trade Center
SBDC
Memphis, Tennessee 38152
Phone: (901)678-4174
Fax: (901)678-4072
Philip Johnson, Dir.

University of Memphis
Tennessee SBDC
S. Campus (Getwell Road)
Building #1
Memphis, Tennessee 38152
Phone: (901)678-2500
Fax: (901)678-4072
Dr. Kenneth J. Burns, State Dir.

Walters State Community College
Tennessee Small Business
Development Center
500 S. Davy Crockett Pky.
Morristown, Tennessee 37813
Phone: (423)585-2675
Fax: (423)585-2679
Jack Tucker, Dir.
E-mail: jtucker@wscc.cc.tn.us

Middle Tennessee State University
Small Business Development Center
College of Business

1417 E. Main St.
PO Box 487
Murfreesboro, Tennessee 37132
Phone: (615)898-2745
Fax: (615)898-2681
Patrick Geho, Dir.

Tennessee State University
Small Business Development Center
College of Business
330 10th Ave. N.
Nashville, Tennessee 37203-3401
Phone: (615)963-7179
Fax: (615)963-7160
Billy E. Lowe, Dir.

Texas

Abilene Christian University
Small Business Development Center
College of Business Administration
648 E. Hwy. 80
Abilene, Texas 79601
Phone: (915)670-0300
Fax: (915)670-0311
Judy Wilhelm, Dir.

Sul Ross State University
Big Bend SBDC Satellite
PO Box C-47, Rm. 319
Alpine, Texas 79832
Phone: (915)837-8694
Fax: (915)837-8104
Michael Levine, Dir.

Alvin Community College
Small Business Development Center
3110 Mustang Rd.
Alvin, Texas 77511-4898
Phone: (713)388-4686
Fax: (713)388-4903
Gina Mattei, Dir.

West Texas A&M University
Small Business Development Center
T. Boone Pickens School of Business
1800 S. Washington, Ste. 209
Amarillo, Texas 79102
Phone: (806)372-5151
Fax: (806)372-5261
Don Taylor, Dir.

Trinity Valley Community College
Small Business Development Center
500 S. Prairieville

Athens, Texas 75751
Phone: (903)675-7403
Free: (800)335-7232
Fax: (903)675-5199
Judy Loden, Dir.

Lower Colorado River Authority
Small Business Development Center
3700 Lake Austin Blvd.
PO Box 220
Austin, Texas 78767
Phone: (512)473-3510
Fax: (512)473-3285
Larry Lucero, Dir.

Lee College
Small Business Development Center
PO Box 818
Rundell Hall
Baytown, Texas 77522-0818
Phone: (713)425-6307
Fax: (713)425-6309
Kenneth Voytek, Contact

Lamar University
Small Business Development Center
855 Florida Ave.
Beaumont, Texas 77705
Phone: (409)880-2367
Fax: (409)880-2201
Gene Arnold, Dir.

Bonham Satellite
Chamber of Commerce
SBDC
110 W. 1st
Bonham, Texas 75418
Phone: (903)583-4811
Fax: (903)583-6706
Darroll Martin, Coordinator

Blinn College
Small Business Development Center
902 College Ave.
Brenham, Texas 77833
Phone: (409)830-4137
Fax: (409)830-4135
Phillis Nelson, Dir.

Bryan/College Station Chamber of
Commerce
Small Business Development Center
PO Box 3695
Bryan, Texas 77805-3695
Phone: (409)260-5222

Fax: (409)260-5208
Sam Harwell, Contact

Greater Corpus Christi Business
Alliance
Small Business Development Center
1201 N. Shoreline
Corpus Christi, Texas 78403
Phone: (512)881-1847
Fax: (512)882-4256
Oscar Martinez, Dir.

Corsicana Small Business
Development Center
120 N. 12th St.
Corsicana, Texas 75110
Phone: (903)874-0658
Free: (800)320-7232
Fax: (903)874-4187
Leon Allard, Dir.

Dallas County Community College
North Texas SBDC
1402 Corinth St.
Dallas, Texas 75215
Phone: (800)350-7232
Fax: (214)860-5813
Elizabeth (Liz) Klimback, Regional
Dir.

International Trade Center
SBDC
World Trade Center, Ste. 150
2050 Stemmons Fwy.
PO Box 58299
Dallas, Texas 75258
Phone: (214)747-1300
Free: (800)337-7232
Fax: (214)748-5774
Beth Huddleston, Dir.

Bill J. #Priest Institute for Economic
Development
North Texas-Dallas Small Business
Development Center
1402 Corinth St.
Dallas, Texas 75215
Phone: (214)860-5842
Free: (800)348-7232
Fax: (214)860-5881
Pamela Speraw, Dir.

Technology Assistance Center
SBDC
1402 Corinth St.

Dallas, Texas 75215
Phone: (800)355-7232
Fax: (214)860-5881
Pamela Speraw, Dir.

Texas Center for Government
Contracting
Small Business Development Center
1402 Corinth
Dallas, Texas 75215
Phone: (214)860-5850
Fax: (214)860-5857
Al Salgado, Dir.

Grayson County College
Small Business Development Center
6101 Grayson Dr.
Denison, Texas 75020
Phone: (903)786-3551
Free: (800)316-7232
Fax: (903)786-6284
Cynthia Flowers-Whitfield, Dir.

Denton Small Business Development
Center
PO Drawer P
Denton, Texas 76202
Phone: (817)380-1849
Fax: (817)382-0040
Carolyn Birkhead, Coordinator

Best Southwest
SBDC
214 S, Main, Ste. 102A
Duncanville, Texas 75116
Phone: (214)709-5878
Free: (800)317-7232
Fax: (214)709-6089
Herb Kamm, Dir.

DeSoto Small Business Development
Center
214 S. Main, Ste. 102A
Duncanville, Texas 75116
Phone: (214)709-5878
Free: (800)317-7232
Fax: (214)709-6089

University of Texas—Pan American
Small Business Development Center
1201 W. University Dr.
Center for Entrepreneurship &
Economic Development
Edinburg, Texas 78539-2999
Phone: (210)316-2610

Fax: (210)316-2612
Juan Garcia, Dir.

El Paso Community College
Small Business Development Center
103 Montana Ave., Ste. 202
El Paso, Texas 79902-3929
Phone: (915)534-3410
Fax: (915)534-4625
Roque Segura, Dir.

Automation and Robotics Research
Institute
SBDC
7300 Jack Newell Blvd., S.
Fort Worth, Texas 76118
Phone: (817)794-5900
Fax: (817)794-5952
Don Liles, Dir.

Tarrant County Junior College
Small Business Development Center
Mary Owen Center
1500 Houston St., Rm. 163
Fort Worth, Texas 76102
Phone: (817)244-7158
Fax: (817)244-0627
Truitt Leake, Dir.

Cooke County Community College
Small Business Development Center
1525 W. California
Gainesville, Texas 76240
Phone: (817)668-4220
Free: (800)351-7232
Fax: (817)668-6049
Cathy Keeler, Dir.

Galveston College
Small Business Development Center
4015 Avenue Q
Galveston, Texas 77550
Phone: (409)740-7380
Fax: (409)740-7381
Joe Harper, Contact/Dir.

Western Bank and Trust Satellite
SBDC
PO Box 461545
Garland, Texas 75046
Phone: (214)860-5850
Fax: (214)860-5857
Al Salgado, Dir.

Grand Prairie Satellite
SBDC

Chamber of Commerce
900 Conover Dr.
Grand Prairie, Texas 75053
Phone: (214)860-5850
Fax: (214)860-5857
Al Salgado, Dir.

Houston International Trade Center
Small Business Development Center
1100 Louisiana, Ste. 500
Houston, Texas 77002
Phone: (713)752-8404
Fax: (713)756-1500
Mr. Carlos Lopez, Dir.

North Harris Montgomery
Community College District
Small Business Development Center
250 N. Sam Houston Pky.
Houston, Texas 77060
Phone: (713)591-9320
Fax: (713)591-3513
Ray Laughter, Contact

Texas Product Development Center
Small Business Development Center
1100 Louisiana, Ste. 500
Houston, Texas 77002
Phone: (713)752-8477
Fax: (713)756-1515
Jacqueline Taylor, Dir.

University of Houston
Texas Product Development Center
1100 Louisiana, Ste. 500
Houston, Texas 77002
Susan Macy, Dir.

University of Houston
Small Business Development Center
1100 Louisiana, Ste. 500
Houston, Texas 77002
Phone: (713)752-8400
Fax: (713)756-1500
Mike Young, Dir.

University of Houston
Southeastern Texas SBDC
1100 Louisiana, Ste. 500
Houston, Texas 77002
Phone: (713)752-8444
Fax: (713)756-1500
J.E."Ted" Cadou, Reg. Dir.

Sam Houston State University
Small Business Development Center

College of Business Administration
PO Box 2058
Huntsville, Texas 77341-2058
Phone: (409)294-3737
Fax: (409)294-3738
Bob Barragan, Dir.

Kingsville Chamber of Commerce
Small Business Development Center
635 E. King
Kingsville, Texas 78363
Phone: (512)595-5088
Fax: (512)592-0866
Elizabeth Soliz, Contact

Brazosport College
Small Business Development Center
500 College Dr.
Lake Jackson, Texas 77566
Phone: (409)266-3380
Fax: (409)265-7208
Patricia Leyendecker, Dir.

Laredo Development Foundation
Small Business Development Center
Division of Business Administration
616 Leal St.
Laredo, Texas 78041
Phone: (210)722-0563
Fax: (210)722-6247
David Puig, Contact

Kilgore College
Triple Creek Shopping Plaza
SBDC
110 Triple Creek Dr., Ste. 70
Longview, Texas 75601
Phone: (903)757-5857
Free: (800)338-7232
Fax: (903)753-7920
Brad Bunt, Dir.

Texas Tech University
Northwestern Texas SBDC
Spectrum Plaza
2579 S. Loop 289, Ste. 114
Lubbock,. Texas 79423
Phone: (806)745-3973
Fax: (806)745-6207
Craig Bean, Regional Dir.

Angelina Community College
Small Business Development Center
PO Box 1768
Lufkin, Texas 75902
Phone: (409)639-1887

Fax: (409)639-1887
Chuck Stemple, Dir.

Midlothian SBDC
330 N. 8th St., Ste. 203
Midlothian, Texas 76065-0609
Phone: (214)775-4336
Fax: (214)775-4337

Northeast Texarkana
Small Business Development Center
PO Box 1307
Mount Pleasant, Texas 75455
Phone: (903)572-1911
Free: (800)357-7232
Fax: (903)572-0598
Bob Wall, Dir.

University of Texas—Permian Basin
Small Business Development Center
College of Management
4901 E. University
Odessa, Texas 79762
Phone: (915)552-2455
Fax: (915)552-2433
Karl Painter, Dir.

Paris Junior College
Small Business Development Center
2400 Clarksville St.
Paris, Texas 75460
Phone: (903)784-1802
Fax: (903)784-1801
Pat Bell, Dir.

Courtyard Center for Professional and
Economic Development
Collin Small Business Development
Center
Piano Market Sq.
4800 Preston Park Blvd., Ste. A126,
Box 15
Plano, Texas 75093
Phone: (214)985-3770
Fax: (214)985-3775
Chris Jones, Dir.

Angelo State University
Small Business Development Center
2610 West Ave. N.
Campus Box 10910
San Angelo, Texas 76909
Phone: (915)942-2098
Fax: (915)942-2096
Patty Warrington, Dir.

University of Texas at San Antonio
Technology Center
University of Texas, San Antonio
1222 N. Main St., Ste. 450
San Antonio, Texas 78212
Phone: (210)458-2458
Fax: (210)458-2464
Judith Ingalls, Dir.

University of Texas at San Antonio
International Trade Center
SBDC
1222 N. Main, Ste. 450
San Antonio, Texas 78212
Phone: (210)458-2470
Fax: (210)458-2464
Sara Jackson, Dir.

University of Texas at San Antonio
Downtown
South Texas Border SBDC
E-mail: rmckinle@utsadt.utsa.edu
1222 N. Main, Ste. 450
San Antonio, Texas 78212
Phone: (210)458-2450
Fax: (210)458-2464
Robert McKinley, Regional Dir.

Houston Community College System
Small Business Development Center
13600 Murphy Rd.
Stafford, Texas 77477
Phone: (713)499-4870
Fax: (713)499-8194
Ted Charlesworth, Acting Dir.

Tarleton State University
Small Business Development Center
School of Business Administration
Box T-0650
Stephenville, Texas 76402
Phone: (817)968-9330
Fax: (817)968-9329
Rusty Freed, Dir.

College of the Mainland
Small Business Development Center
1200 Amburn Rd.
Texas City, Texas 77591
Phone: (409)938-7578
Free: (800)246-7232
Fax: (409)935-5186
Elizabeth Boudreau, Dir.

Tyler Junior College
Small Business Development Center

1530 South SW Loop 323, Ste. 100
Tyler, Texas 75701
Phone: (903)510-2975
Fax: (903)510-2978
Frank Viso, Dir.

Middle Rio Grande Development
Council
Small Business Development Center
209 N. Getty St.
Uvalde, Texas 78801
Phone: (210)278-2527
Fax: (210)278-2929
Patrick Gibbons, Dir.

University of Houston—Victoria
Small Business Development Center
700 Main Center, Ste. 102
Victoria, Texas 77901
Phone: (512)575-8944
Fax: (512)575-8852
Carole Parks, Dir.
E-mail: parks@jade.vic.uh.edu

McLennan Community College
Small Business Development Center
4601 N. 19th, Ste. A-15
Waco, Texas 76708
Phone: (817)750-3600
Free: (800)349-7232
Fax: (817)750-3620
Lu Billings, Dir.

LCRA Coastal Plains
SBDC
301 W. Milam
Wharton, Texas 77488
Phone: (409)532-1007
Lynn Polson, Dir.

Midwestern State University
Small Business Development Center
Division of Business Administration
3410 Taft Blvd.
Wichita Falls, Texas 76308
Phone: (817)689-4373
Fax: (817)689-4374
Tim Thomas, Dir.

Utah

Southern Utah University
Small Business Development Center
351 W. Center
Cedar City, Utah 84720

Phone: (801)586-5400
Fax: (801)586-5493
Greg Powell, Dir.

Snow College
Small Business Development Center
345 W. 100 N.
Ephraim, Utah 84627
Phone: (801)283-4021
Fax: (801)283-6913
Russell Johnson, Dir.

Utah State University
Small Business Development Center
E. Campus Bldg., Rm. 24
Logan, Utah 84322-8330
Phone: (801)797-2277
Fax: (801)797-3317
Franklin C. Prante, Dir.

Weber State University
Small Business Development Center
College of Business and Economics
Ogden, Utah 84401
Phone: (801)626-6070
Fax: (801)626-7423
Bruce Davis, Dir.

Utah Valley State College
Utah Small Business Development
Center
800 West 1200 South
Orem, Utah 84058
Phone: (801)222-8230
Fax: (801)225-1229
Michael Finnerty, Contact

College of Eastern Utah
Small Business Development Center
451 East 400 North
Price, Utah 84501
Phone: (801)637-1995
Fax: (801)637-4102
Patrick Glenn, Dir.

Utah State University Extension
Office
SBDC
987 Lagoon St.
Roosevelt, Utah 84066
Phone: (801)722-2294
Matt Redd, Dir.

Dixie College
Small Business Development Center
225 South 700 East

St. George, Utah 84770-3876
Phone: (801)652-7751
Fax: (801)652-7870
Jill Ellis, Dir.

Salt Lake Community College
SBDC
1623 State St.
Salt Lake City, Utah 84115
Phone: (801)957-3480
Fax: (801)957-3489
Pamela Hunt, Dir.

Utah SBDC
1623 S. State St.
Salt Lake City, Utah 84115
Phone: (801)957-3480
Fax: (801)957-3489
Mike Finnerty, State Dir.

Salt Lake Community College
Sandy SBDC
8811 S. 700 E.
Sandy, Utah 84070
Phone: (801)255-5878
Fax: (801)255-6393
Barry Bartlett, Dir.

Vermont

Brattleboro Development Credit
Corp.
SBDC
PO Box 1177
Brattleboro, Vermont 05301-1177
Phone: (802)257-7731
Fax: (802)258-3886
William McGrath, Executive V. P.

Northwestern Vermont Small
Business Development Center
Greater Burlington Industrial Corp
PO Box 786
Burlington, Vermont 05402-0786
Phone: (802)658-9228
Fax: (802)860-1899
Thomas D. Schroeder, Specialist

Addison County Economic
Development Corp.
SBDC
2 Court St.
Middlebury, Vermont 05753
Phone: (802)388-7953
Fax: (802)388-8066
William Kenerson, Exec. Dir.

Central Vermont Economic
Development Center
SBDC
PO Box 1439
Montpelier, Vermont 05601-1439
Phone: (802)223-4654
Fax: (802)223-4655
Donald Rowan, Exec. Dir.

Lamoille Economic Development
Corp.
SBDC
P.O. Box 455
Morrisville, Vermont 05661-0455
Phone: (802)888-4923
Chris D'Elia, Executive Dir.

Bennington County Industrial Corp.
SBDC
PO Box 357
North Bennington, Vermont 05257-
0357
Phone: (802)442-8975
Fax: (802)442-1101
Chris Hunsinger, Executive Dir.

Lake Champlain Island Chamber of
Commerce
SBDC
PO Box 213
North Hero, Vermont 05474-0213
Phone: (802)372-5683
Fax: (802)372-6104
Barbara Mooney, Exec. Dir.

Vermont Technical College
Small Business Development Center
PO Box 422
Randolph Center, Vermont 05061
Phone: (802)728-9101
Fax: (802)728-3026
Donald L. Kelpinski, State Dir.

Southwestern Vermont Small
Business Development Center
Rutland Economic Development
Corp.
256 N. Main St.
Rutland, Vermont 05701-0039
Phone: (802)773-9147
Fax: (802)773-2772
James B. Stewart, SBDC Specialist

Franklin County Industrial
Development Corp.
SBDC

PO Box 1099
St. Albans, Vermont 05478-1099
Phone: (802)524-2194
Fax: (802)527-5258
Timothy J. Soule, Executive Dir.

Northeastern Vermont Small Business
Development Center
PO Box 630
St. Johnsbury, Vermont 05819-0630
Phone: (802)748-1014
Fax: (802)748-1223
Charles E. Carter, Exec. Dir.

Southeastern Vermont Small Business
Development Center
Springfield Development Corp.
PO Box 58
Springfield, Vermont 05156-0058
Phone: (802)885-2071
Fax: (802)885-3027
Al Moulton, Executive Dir.

Green Mountain Economic
Development Corporation
SBDC
PO Box 246
White River Jct., Vermont 05001-
0246
Phone: (802)295-3710
Fax: (802)295-3779
Lenne Quillen-Blume, SBDC
Specialist
Peter Markou, Executive Dir.

Virgin Islands

University of the Virgin Islands
(Charlotte Amalie)
Small Business Development Center
8000 Nisky Center, Ste. 202
Charlotte Amalie, Virgin Islands
00802-5804
Phone: (809)776-3206
Fax: (809)775-3756
Ian Hodge

University of the Virgin Islands
Small Business Development Center
Sunshine Mall
No.1 Estate Cane, Ste. 104
Frederiksted, Virgin Islands 00840
Phone: (809)692-5270
Fax: (809)692-5629
Chester Williams, State Dir.

Virginia

Virginia Highlands SBDC
PO Box 828
Abingdon, Virginia 24212
Phone: (703)676-5615
Fax: (703)628-7576
Jim Tilley, Dir.

Arlington Small Business
Development Center
George Mason University, Arlington
Campus
3401 N. Fair Dr.
Arlington, Virginia 22201
Phone: (703)993-8128
Fax: (703)993-8130
Paul Hall, Dir.

Virginia Eastern Shore Corp.
SBDC
36076 Lankford Hwy.
PO Box 395
Belle Haven, Virginia 23306
Phone: (757)442-7179
Fax: (757)442-7181

Mount Empire Community College
Southwest Small Business
Development Center
Drawer 700, Rte. 23, S.
Big Stone Gap, Virginia 24219
Phone: (703)523-6529
Fax: (703)523-8139
Tim Blankenbecler, Dir.

Central Virginia Small Business
Development Center
918 Emmet St., N. Ste. 200
Charlottesville, Virginia 22903-4878
Phone: (804)295-8198
Fax: (804)295-7066
Charles Kulp, Dir.

Hampton Roads Chamber of
Commerce
SBDC
400 Volvo Pkwy.
P.O. Box 1776
Chesapeake, Virginia 23320
Phone: (757)664-2590
Fax: (757)548-1835
William J. Holoran, Jr., Dir.

Northern Virginia Small Business
Development Center
George Mason University

4031 University Dr., Ste. 200
Fairfax, Virginia 22030
Phone: (703)993-2131
Fax: (703)993-2126
Michael Kehoe, Dir.

Longwood College (Farmville)
Small Business Development Center
515 Main St.
Farmville, Virginia 23901
Phone: (804)395-2086
Fax: (804)395-2359
Gerald L. Hughes, Jr., Dir.

Rappahannock Region Small
Business Development Center
1301 College Ave.
Seacobeck Hall
Fredericksburg, Virginia 22401
Phone: (540)654-1060
Fax: (540)654-1070
Jeffrey R. Sneddon, Dir.

Thomas Nelson Community College
525 Butler Farm Rd., Ste. 102
Hampton, Virginia 23666
Phone: (757)825-2957
Fax: (757)825-2960

James Madison University
Small Business Development Center
JMU College of Business
Zane Showker Hall, Rm. 523
Harrisonburg, Virginia 22807
Phone: (703)568-3227
Fax: (703)568-3299
Karen Wigginton, Dir.

Lynchburg Regional Small Business
Development Center
147 Mill Ridge Rd.
Lynchburg, Virginia 24502-4341
Phone: (804)582-6170
Free: (800)876-7232
Barry Lyons, Contact

Flory Small Business Development
Center
10311 Sudley Manor Dr.
Manassas, Virginia 22110
Phone: (703)335-2500
Linda Decker, Dir.

SBDC Satellite Office
P.O. Box 709
115 Broad St.

Martinsville, Virginia 24114
Phone: (540)632-4462
Fax: (540)632-5059
Ken Copeland, Dir.

Lord Fairfax Community College
SBDC
PO Box 47
Skirmisher Ln.
Middletown, Virginia 22645
Phone: (703)869-6649
Fax: (703)868-7002
Robert Crosen, Dir.

Small Business Development Center
of Hampton Roads, Inc. (Norfolk)
420 Bank St.
PO Box 327
Norfolk, Virginia 23501
Phone: (757)664-2528
Fax: (757)622-5563
Warren Snyder, Dir.

New River Valley
SBDC
600-H Norwood St.
PO Box 3726
Radford, Virginia 24141
Phone: (540)831-6056
David Shanks

Southwest Virginia Community
College
Southwest Small Business
Development Center
PO Box SVCC, Rte. 19
Richlands, Virginia 24641
Phone: (703)964-7345
Fax: (703)964-5788
Jim Boyd, Dir.

Capital Area Small Business
Development Center
1 N. 5th St., Ste. 510
Richmond, Virginia 23219
Free: (800)646-SBDC
Fax: (804)648-7849
Taylor Cousins, Dir.

Commonwealth of Virginia
Department of Economic
Development
Virginia SBDC
901 E. Byrd St., Ste. 1800
Richmond, Virginia 23219

Phone: (804)371-8253
Fax: (804)225-3384
Bob Wilburn, State Dir.

Blue Ridge Small Business
Development Center
Western Virginia SBDC Consortium
310 1st St., SW Mezzanine
Roanoke, Virginia 24011
Phone: (703)983-0717
Fax: (703)983-0723
John Jennings, Dir.

Longwood
Small Business Development Center
South Boston Branch
515 Broad St.
PO Box 1116
South Boston, Virginia 24592
Phone: (804)575-0444
Fax: (804)572-4087
Vincent Decker, Bus. Analyst

Loudoun County Small Business
Development Center
21515 Ridge Top Cir., Ste. 200
Sterling, Virginia 22170
Phone: (703)430-7222
Fax: (703)430-9562
Joseph Messina, Dir.

Warsaw Small Business Development
Center
106 W. Richmond Rd.
PO Box 490
Warsaw, Virginia 22572
Phone: (804)333-0286
Fax: (804)333-0187
John Clickener, Dir.

Wytheville Small Business
Development Center
Wytheville Community College
1000 E. Main St.
Wytheville, Virginia 24382
Phone: (703)223-4798
Free: (800)468-1195
Fax: (703)223-4850
Rob Edwards, Dir.

Washington

Bellevue Small Business
Development Center
Bellevue Community College

3000 Landerholm Circle SE
Bellevue, Washington 98007-6484
Phone: (206)643-2888
Fax: (206)649-3113
Bill Huenefeld, Contact

Western Washington University
Small Business Development Center
308 Parks Hall
Bellingham, Washington 98225-9073
Phone: (360)650-3899
Fax: (360)650-4844
Lynn Trzynka, Contact

Centralia Community College
Small Business Development Center
600 W. Locust St.
Centralia, Washington 98531
Phone: (360)736-9391
Fax: (360)753-3404
Don Hays, Contact

Columbia Basin College—TRIDEC
Small Business Development Center
901 N. Colorado
Kennewick, Washington 99336
Phone: (509)735-6222
Fax: (509)735-6609
Glynn Lamberson, Contact

Edmonds Community College
Small Business Development Center
20000 68th Ave. W.
Lynnwood, Washington 98036
Phone: (206)640-1435
Fax: (206)640-1532
Jack Wicks, Contact

Big Bend Community College
Small Business Development Center
7662 Chanute St., Bldg. 1500
Moses Lake, Washington 98837-3299
Phone: (509)762-6289
Fax: (509)762-6329
Ed Baroch, Contact

Skagit Valley College
Small Business Development Center
2405 College Way
Mount Vernon, Washington 98273
Phone: (360)428-1282
Fax: (360)336-6116
Peter Stroosma, Contact

Wenatchee Valley College
SBDC
Box 741

Okanogan, Washington 98840
Phone: (509)826-5107
Fax: (509)826-1812
Ron Neilsen, Specialist

Washington State University
(Olympia)
Small Business Development Center
721 Columbia St. SW
Olympia, Washington 98501
Phone: (360)753-5616
Fax: (360)586-5493
Douglas Hammel, Contact

Washington State University
(Pullman)
Small Business Development Center
501 Johnson Tower
PO Box 644851
Pullman, Washington 99164-4727
Phone: (509)335-1576
Fax: (509)335-0949
Carol Riesenberg, Dir.

Duwamish Industrial Education
Center
Small Business Development Center
6770 E. Marginal Way S
Seattle, Washington 98108-3405
Phone: (206)768-6855
Ruth Ann Halford, Contact

International Trade Institute
North Seattle Community College
Small Business Development Center
2001 6th Ave., Ste. 650
Seattle, Washington 98121
Phone: (206)553-0052
Ann Tamura, Contact
Washington Small Business
Development Center (Seattle)
180 Nickerson, Ste. 207
Seattle, Washington 98109
Phone: (206)464-5450
Fax: (206)464-6357
Bill Jacobs, Contact

Washington State University
(Spokane)
Small Business Development Center
665 North Riverpoint Blvd.
Spokane, Washington 99204-0399
Phone: (509)358-2051
Fax: (509)358-2059
Terry Chambers, Contact

Washington Small Business
Development Center (Tacoma)
950 Pacific Ave., Ste. 300
PO Box 1933
Tacoma, Washington 98401-1933
Phone: (206)272-7232
Fax: (206)597-7305
Neil Delisanti, Contact

Columbia River Economic
Development Council
Small Business Development Center
100 E. Columbia Way
Vancouver, Washington 98660-3156
Phone: (360)693-2555
Fax: (360)694-9927
Janet Harte, Contact

Port of Walla Walla SBDC
500 Tausick Way
Walla Walla, Washington 99362
Phone: (509)527-4681
Fax: (509)525-3101
Rich Monacelli, Specialist

Wenatchee Small Business
Development Center
327 East Penny Rd.
Industrial Bldg. 2, Ste. D.
Wenatchee, Washington 98801
Phone: (509)662-8016
Fax: (509)663-0455
Jeff Martin, Contact

Yakima Valley College
Small Business Development Center
PO Box 1647
Yakima, Washington 98907
Phone: (509)454-3608
Fax: (509)454-4155
Corey Hansen, Contact

West Virginia

College of West Virginia
SBDC
PO Box AG
Beckley, West Virginia 25802
Phone: (304)255-4022
Fax: (304)255-4022
Ken Peters, Program Mgr.

Governor's Office of Community and
Industrial Development
SBDC
950 Kanawha Blvd. E.

Charleston, West Virginia 25301
Phone: (304)558-2960
Fax: (304)348-0127

Elkins Satellite
SBDC
10 Eleventh St., Ste. 1
Elkins, West Virginia 26241
Phone: (304)637-7205
Fax: (304)637-4902
James Martin, Business Analyst

Fairmont State College
Small Business Development Center
Locust Ave.
Fairmont, West Virginia 26554
Phone: (304)367-4125
Fax: (304)366-4870
Dale Bradley, Program Mgr.

Marshall University
Small Business Development Center
1050 4th Ave.
Huntington, West Virginia 25755-2126
Phone: (304)696-6789
Fax: (304)696-6277
Edna McClain, Program Mgr.

West Virginia Institute of Technology
Small Business Development Center
Engineering Bldg., Rm. 102
Montgomery, West Virginia 25136
Phone: (304)442-5501
Fax: (304)442-3307
James Epling, Program Mgr.

West Virginia University
Small Business Development Center
PO Box 6025
Morgantown, West Virginia 26506-6025
Phone: (304)293-5839
Fax: (304)293-7061
Stan Kloc, Program Mgr.

West Virginia University
(Parkersburg)
Small Business Development Center
Rte. 5, Box 167-A
Parkersburg, West Virginia 26101-9577
Phone: (304)424-8277
Fax: (304)424-8315
Greg Hill, Program Mgr.

Shepherd College
Small Business Development Center
120 N. Princess St.
Shepherdstown, West Virginia 25443
Phone: (304)876-5261
Fax: (304)876-5117
Fred Baer, Program Mgr.

West Virginia Northern Community College
Small Business Development Center
1701 Market St.
College Sq.
Wheeling, West Virginia 26003
Phone: (304)233-5900
Fax: (304)232-9065
Ed Huttenhower, Program Mgr.

Wisconsin

University of Wisconsin—Eau Claire
Small Business Development Center
PO Box 4004
Eau Claire, Wisconsin 54702-4004
Phone: (715)836-5811
Fax: (715)836-5263
Fred Waedt, Dir.

University of Wisconsin—Green Bay
Small Business Development Center
Wood Hall, Ste. 460
Green Bay, Wisconsin 54301
Phone: (414)465-2089
Fax: (414)465-2660
James Holly, Dir.
E-mail: hollyj@uwgb.edu

University of Wisconsin—Parkside
Small Business Development Center
284, Tallent Hall
Kenosha, Wisconsin 53141-2000
Phone: (414)595-2189
Fax: (414)595-2513
Patricia Deutsch, Dir.
E-mail: pduetsch@vm.uwp.edu

University of Wisconsin—La Crosse
Small Business Development Center
120 N. Hall
La Crosse, Wisconsin 54601
Phone: (608)785-8782
Fax: (608)785-6919
Jan Gallagher, Dir.
E-mail: jgallagh@uwlax.edu

University of Wisconsin
Wisconsin SBDC
432 N. Lake St., Rm. 423
Madison, Wisconsin 53706
Phone: (608)263-7794
Fax: (608)262-3878

University of Wisconsin—Madison
Small Business Development Center
975 University Ave., Rm. 3260
Grainger Hall
Madison, Wisconsin 53706
Phone: (608)263-2221
Fax: (608)263-0818
Joan Gillman, Dir.
E-mail: jtg@mi.bus.wisc.edu

University of Wisconsin—Milwaukee
Small Business Development Center
161 W. Wisconsin Ave., Ste. 600
Milwaukee, Wisconsin 53203
Phone: (414)227-3240
Fax: (414)227-3142
Sara Murray, Dir.

University of Wisconsin—Oshkosh
Small Business Development Center
157 Clow Faculty Bldg., 800 Algoma Blvd.
Oshkosh, Wisconsin 54901
Phone: (414)424-1453
Fax: (414)424-7413
Rita Janaky, Dir.
E-mail:
mozingo@vaxa.cis.uwash.edu

University of Wisconsin—Stevens Point
Small Business Development Center
Lower Level Main Bldg.
Stevens Point, Wisconsin 54481
Phone: (715)346-2004
Fax: (715)346-4045
Mark Stover, Dir.
E-mail: mstover@uwspmail.uwsp.edu

University of Wisconsin—Superior
Small Business Development Center
29 Sundquist Hall
Superior, Wisconsin 54880
Phone: (715)394-8352
Fax: (715)394-8454
Neil Hensrud, Dir.
E-mail: nhensrud@wpo.uwsuper.edu

University of Wisconsin—
Whitewater
Small Business Development Center
Carlson Bldg., No. 2000
Whitewater, Wisconsin 53190
Phone: (414)472-3217
Fax: (414)472-4863
Carla Lenk, Dir.
E-mail: lenkc@uwwvax.uww.edu

Wisconsin Innovation Service Center
SBDC
University of Wisconsin at
Whitewater
402 McCutchan Hall
Whitewater, Wisconsin 53190
Phone: (414)472-1365
Fax: (414)472-1600
Debra Malewicki, Dir.

Wisconsin Technology Access Center
SBDC
E-mail: malewicd@uwwvax.uww.edu
University of Wisconsin at
Whitewater
416 McCutchen Hall
Whitewater, Wisconsin 53190
Phone: (414)472-1365
Fax: (414)472-1600
Debra Malewicki, Dir.

Wyoming

Casper Small Business Development
Center
Region III
111 W. 2nd St., Ste. 502
Casper, Wyoming 82601
Phone: (307)234-6683
Free: (800)348-5207
Fax: (307)577-7014
Leonard Holler, Dir.

Laramie County Enterprise Center
1400 E. College Dr.
Cheyenne, Wyoming 82007-5208
Phone: (307)632-6141
Free: (800)348-5208
Fax: (307)632-6061
Arlene Soto, Regional Dir.

Wyoming Small Business
Development Center
State Office
University of Wyoming

PO Box 3622
Laramie, Wyoming 82071-3622
Phone: (307)766-3505
Free: (800)348-5194
Fax: (307)766-3406
Diane Wolverton, State Dir.

Northwest Community College
Small Business Development Center
Northwest College
John Dewitt Student Center
Powell, Wyoming 82435
Phone: (307)754-6067
Free: (800)348-5203
Fax: (307)754-6069
Dwane Heintz, Dir.

Rock Springs Small Business
Development Center
Region I
PO Box 1168
Rock Springs, Wyoming 82902
Phone: (307)352-6894
Free: (800)348-5205

SERVICE CORPS OF RETIRED EXECUTIVES (SCORE) OFFICES

This section contains a listing of all SCORE offices organized alphabetically by state/U.S. territory name, then by city, then by agency name.

Alabama

SCORE Office (Columbus)
SCORE Office (Anniston)
c/o Calhoun County Chamber of
Commerce
PO Box 1087
Anniston, Alabama 36202
Phone: (205)237-3536

SCORE Office (North Alabama)
1601 11th Ave. S
Birmingham, Alabama 35294-4552
Phone: (205)934-6868

SCORE Office (Fairhope)
c/o Fairhope Chamber of Commerce
327 Fairhope Ave.
Fairhope, Alabama 36532
Phone: (334)928-8799

SCORE Office (Florence)
104 S. Pine St.
Florence, Alabama 35630
Phone: (205)764-4661
Fax: (205)766-9017

SCORE Office (Foley)
c/o Foley Chamber of Commerce
PO Box 1117
Foley, Alabama 36536
Phone: (334)943-3291
Fax: (334)943-6810

SCORE Office (Mobile)
c/o Mobile Area Chamber of
Commerce
PO Box 2187
Mobile, Alabama 36652
Phone: (334)433-6951

SCORE Office (Alabama Capitol
City)
c/o Montgomery Area Chamber of
Commerce
41 Commerce St.
PO Box 79
Montgomery, Alabama 36101-1114
Phone: (334)240-9295

SCORE Office (Tuscaloosa)
2200 University Blvd.
PO Box 020410
Tuscaloosa, Alabama 35402
Phone: (205)758-7588

Alaska

SCORE Office (Anchorage)
c/o U.S. Small Business
Administration
222 W. 8th Ave., No. 67
Anchorage, Alaska 99513-7559
Phone: (907)271-4022

Arizona

SCORE Office (Casa Grande)
Chamber of Commerce
575 N. Marshall
Casa Grande, Arizona 85222
Phone: (520)836-2125
Fax: (520)836-3623

SCORE Office (Cottonwood)
1010 S. Main St.
Cottonwood, Arizona 86326

Phone: (520)634-7593
Fax: (520)634-7594

SCORE Office (Flagstaff)
1 E. Rte. 66
Flagstaff, Arizona 86001
Phone: (520)556-7333

SCORE Office (Glendale)
7105 N. 59th Ave.
Glendale, Arizona 85311
Phone: (602)937-4754
Fax: (602)937-3333

SCORE Office (Green Valley)
W. Continental Rd.
PO Box 270
Green Valley, Arizona 85614
Phone: (602)625-7575
Fax: (602)648-6154

SCORE Office (Holbrook)
100 E. Arizona St.
Holbrook, Arizona 86025
Phone: (520)524-6558
Fax: (602)524-1719

SCORE Office (Kingman)
c/o Bill Murie
1070 Palo Verde
Kingman, Arizona 86401
Phone: (520)753-6106

SCORE Office (Lake Havasu)
Mohave Community College
1977 W. Acoma Blvd.
Lake Havasu City, Arizona 86403
Phone: (520)855-7812

SCORE Office (Pinetop)
592 W. White Mountain Blvd.
Lakeside, Arizona 85929
Phone: (602)367-4290

SCORE Office (East Valley)
Federal Bldg., Rm. 104
26 N. MacDonald St.
Mesa, Arizona 85201
Phone: (602)379-3100

SCORE Office (Payson)
PO Box 1380
Payson, Arizona 85547
Phone: (520)474-4515
Fax: (520)474-8812

SCORE Office (Phoenix)
2828 N. Central Ave., Ste. 800

Phoenix, Arizona 85004
Phone: (602)640-2329

SCORE Office (Northern Arizona)
Post Office Bldg., Ste. 307
101 W. Goodwin St.
Prescott, Arizona 86303
Phone: (520)778-7438

SCORE Office (St. Johns)
PO Box 178
St. Johns, Arizona 85936
Phone: (520)337-2000

SCORE Office (Sedona)
Forest & 89th Ave.
PO Box 478
Sedona, Arizona 86339
Phone: (520)282-7722

SCORE Office (Show Low)
PO Box 1083
Show Low, Arizona 85901
Phone: (520)537-2326
Fax: (520)537-2326

SCORE Office (Snowflake)
PO Box 776
Snowflake, Arizona 85937
Phone: (520)536-4331

SCORE Office (Springerville)
PO Box 31
Springerville, Arizona 85938
Phone: (520)333-2123
Fax: (520)333-5690

SCORE Office (Tucson)
c/o Tucson Art Council
240 N. Stone
Tucson, Arizona 85701
Phone: (520)884-9602

Arkansas

SCORE Office (South Central)
PO Box 1271
El Dorado, Arkansas 71731
Phone: (501)863-6113

SCORE Office (Ozark)
c/o Margaret B. Parrish
1141 Eastwood Dr.
Fayetteville, Arkansas 72701
Phone: (501)442-7619

SCORE Office (Northwest Arkansas)
Glenn Haven Dr., No. 4

Fort Smith, Arkansas 72901
Phone: (501)783-3556

SCORE Office (Garland County)
330 Kleinshore, No. 32
Hot Springs Village, Arkansas 71913
Phone: (501)922-0020

SCORE Office (Little Rock)
U.S. Small Business Administration
2120 Riverfront Dr., Rm. 100
Little Rock, Arkansas 72202-1747
Phone: (501)324-5893

SCORE Office (Southeast Arkansas)
PO Box 6866
Pine Bluff, Arkansas 71611
Phone: (501)535-7189

California

SCORE Office (Agoura)
5935 Kanan Rd.
Agoura Hills, California 91301
Phone: (818)889-3150
Fax: (818)889-3366

SCORE Office (Angels Camp)
1211 S. Main St.
Box 637
Angels Camp, California 95222
Phone: (209)736-0049
Fax: (209)736-9124

SCORE Office (Arroyo Grande)
800 W. Branch, Ste. A
Arroyo Grande, California 93420
Phone: (805)489-1488
Fax: (805)489-2239

SCORE Office (Atascadero)
6550 El Camino Real
Atascadero, California 93422
Phone: (805)466-2044
Fax: (805)466-9218

SCORE Office (Golden Empire)
1033 Truxton Ave.
PO Box 1947
Bakersfield, California 93301
Phone: (805)327-4421

SCORE Office (Kernville)
c/o Kernville Chamber of Commerce
1330 22nd St., Ste. B
Bakersfield, California 93301

SCORE Office (Bellflower)
9729 E. Flower St.
Bellflower, California 90706
Phone: (310)867-1744
Fax: (310)866-7545

SCORE Office (Brawley)
204 S. Empirial
Brawley, California 92227
Phone: (619)344-3160
Fax: (619)344-7611

SCORE Office (Burbank)
200 W. Magnolia Blvd.
Burbank, California 91502
Phone: (818)846-3111
Fax: (818)846-0109

SCORE Office (Calexico)
PO Box 948
Calexico, California 92231
Phone: (619)357-1166
Fax: (619)357-9043

SCORE Office (California City)
c/o California City Chamber of
Commerce
8048 California City Blvd.
PO Box 8001
California City, California 93504
Phone: (619)373-8676

SCORE Office (Camarillo)
c/o Camarillo Chamber of Commerce
632 Las Posas Rd.
Camarillo, California 93010
Phone: (805)484-4383

SCORE Office (Cambria)
c/o Cambria Chamber of Commerce
767 Main St.
Cambria, California 93428
Phone: (805)927-3624
Fax: (805)927-9426

SCORE Office (Canoga Park)
7248 Owensmouth Ave.
Canoga Park, California 91303
Phone: (818)884-4222

SCORE Office (Capitola)
621B Capitola Ave.
Capitola, California 95010
Phone: (408)475-6522
Free: (800)474-6522
Fax: (408)475-6530

SCORE Office (Carlsbad)
PO Box 10605
Carlsbad, California 92018
Phone: (619)931-8400
Fax: (619)931-9153

SCORE Office (Carpinteria)
PO Box 956
Carpinteria, California 93014
Phone: (805)684-5479
Fax: (805)684-3477

SCORE Office (Greater Chico Area)
1324 Mangrove St., Ste. 114
Chico, California 95926
Phone: (916)342-8932

SCORE Office (Chino)
13134 Central Ave.
Chino, California 91710
Phone: (909)627-6177
Fax: (909)627-4180

SCORE Office (Chula Vista)
233 4th Ave.
Chula Vista, California 91910
Phone: (619)420-6602
Fax: (619)420-1269

SCORE Office (Claremont)
205 Yale Ave.
Claremont, California 91711
Phone: (909)624-1681
Fax: (909)624-6629

SCORE Office (Clearlake)
PO Box 629
Clearlake, California 95422
Phone: (707)994-3600
Fax: (707)994-6410

SCORE Office (Colton)
620 N. Lacadena Dr.
Colton, California 92324
Phone: (909)825-2222
Fax: (909)824-1630

SCORE Office (Concord)
2151-A Salvio St., Ste. B
Concord, California 94520
Phone: (510)685-1181
Fax: (510)685-5623

SCORE Office (Covina)
935 W. Badillo St.
Covina, California 91723

Phone: (818)967-4191
Fax: (818)966-9660

SCORE Office (Rancho Cucamonga)
8280 Utica, Ste. 160
Cucamonga, California 91730
Phone: (909)987-1012
Fax: (909)987-5917

SCORE Office (Culver City)
PO Box 707
Culver City, California 90232-0707
Phone: (310)287-3850
Fax: (310)287-1350

SCORE Office (Danville)
380 Diablo Rd., Ste. 103
Danville, California 94526
Phone: (510)837-4400

SCORE Office (Downey)
11131 Brookshire Ave.
Downey, California 90241
Phone: (310)923-2191
Fax: (310)864-0461

SCORE Office (El Cajon)
109 Rea Ave.
El Cajon, California 92020
Phone: (619)444-1327
Fax: (619)440-6164

SCORE Office (El Centro)
1100 Main St.
El Centro, California 92243
Phone: (619)352-3681
Fax: (619)352-3246

SCORE Office (Escondido)
720 N. Broadway
Escondido, California 92025
Phone: (619)745-2125
Fax: (619)745-1183

SCORE Office (Fairfield)
1111 Webster St.
Fairfield, California 94533
Phone: (707)425-4625
Fax: (707)425-0826

SCORE Office (Fontana)
17009 Valley Blvd., Ste. B
Fontana, California 92335
Phone: (909)822-4433
Fax: (909)822-6238

SCORE Office (Foster City)
1125 E. Hillsdale Blvd.
Foster City, California 94404
Phone: (415)573-7600
Fax: (415)573-5201

SCORE Office (Fremont)
2201 Walnut Ave., Ste. 110
Fremont, California 94538
Phone: (510)795-2244
Fax: (510)795-2240

SCORE Office (Central California)
2719 N. Air Fresno Dr., Ste. 107
Fresno, California 93727-1547
Phone: (209)487-5605

SCORE Office (Gardena)
1204 W. Gardena Blvd.
Gardena, California 90247
Phone: (310)532-9905
Fax: (310)515-4893

SCORE Office (Glendale)
330 N. Brand Blvd., Rm. 190
Glendale, California 91203
Phone: (818)552-3206

SCORE Office (Lompoc)
c/o Lompoc Chamber of Commerce
330 N. Brand Blvd., Ste. 190
Glendale, California 91203-2304
Phone: (818)552-3206
Fax: (818)552-3260

SCORE Office (Glendora)
131 E. Foothill Blvd.
Glendora, California 91741
Phone: (818)963-4128
Fax: (818)914-4822

SCORE Office (Grover Beach)
177 S. 8th St.
Grover Beach, California 93433
Phone: (805)489-9091
Fax: (805)489-9091

SCORE Office (Hawthorne)
12477 Hawthorne Blvd.
Hawthorne, California 90250
Phone: (310)676-1163
Fax: (310)676-7661

SCORE Office (Hayward)
22300 Foothill Blvd., Ste. 303
Hayward, California 94541
Phone: (510)537-2424

SCORE Office (Hemet)
1700 E. Florida Ave.
Hemet, California 92544
Phone: (909)652-4390

SCORE Office (Hesperia)
16367 Main St.
PO Box 403656
Hesperia, California 92340
Phone: (619)244-2135

SCORE Office (Holloster)
c/o Holloster Small Business
Development Center
321 San Felipe Rd., No. 11
Hollister, California 95023

SCORE Office (Hollywood)
7018 Hollywood Blvd.
Hollywood, California 90028
Phone: (213)469-8311
Fax: (213)469-2805

SCORE Office (Indio)
82503 Hwy. 111
PO Drawer TTT
Indio, California 92202
Phone: (619)347-0676

SCORE Office (Inglewood)
330 Queen St.
Inglewood, California 90301
Phone: (818)552-3206

SCORE Office (La Puente)
218 N. Grendanda St. D.
La Puente, California 91744
Phone: (818)330-3216
Fax: (818)330-9524

SCORE Office (La Verne)
2078 Bonita Ave.
La Verne, California 91570
Phone: (909)593-5265
Fax: (714)929-8475

SCORE Office (Lake Elsinore)
132 W. Graham Ave.
Lake Elsinore, California 92530
Phone: (909)674-2577

SCORE Office (Lakeport)
PO Box 295
Lakeport, California 95453
Phone: (707)263-5092

SCORE Office (Lakewood)
5445 E. Del Amo Blvd., Ste. 2

Lakewood, California 90714
Phone: (213)920-7737

SCORE Office (Antelope Valley)
c/o Bruce Finlayson, Chair
747 E. Ave. K-7
Lancaster, California 93535
Phone: (805)948-4518

SCORE Office (Long Beach)
1 World Trade Center
Long Beach, California 90831

SCORE Office (Los Alamitos)
901 W. Civic Center Dr., Ste. 160
Los Alamitos, California 90720

SCORE Office (Los Altos)
c/o Los Altos Chamber of Commerce
321 University Ave.
Los Altos, California 94022
Phone: (415)948-1455

SCORE Office (Los Angeles)
404 S. Bixel
Los Angeles, California 90071

SCORE Office (Manhattan Beach)
PO Box 3007
Manhattan Beach, California 90266
Phone: (310)545-5313
Fax: (310)545-7203

SCORE Office (Merced)
1632 N. St.
Merced, California 95340
Phone: (209)725-3800
Fax: (209)383-4959

SCORE Office (Milpitas)
75 S. Milpitas Blvd., Ste. 205
Milpitas, California 95035
Phone: (408)262-2613
Fax: (408)262-2823

SCORE Office (Yosemite)
c/o Stanislaus County Economic
Development Corp.
1012 11th St., Ste. 300
Modesto, California 95354
Phone: (209)521-9333

SCORE Office (Montclair)
5220 Benito Ave.
Montclair, California 91763

SCORE Office (Monterey)
Montery Penninsula Chamber of

Commerce
380 Alvarado St.
Monterey, California 93940-1770
Phone: (408)649-1770

SCORE Office (Moreno Valley)
25480 Alessandro
Moreno Valley, California 92553

SCORE Office (Morgan Hill)
Morgan Hill Chamber of Commerce
25 W. 1st St.
PO Box 786
Morgan Hill, California 95038
Phone: (408)779-9444
Fax: (408)778-1786

SCORE Office (Morro Bay)
Morro Bay Chamber of Commerce
880 Main St.
Morro Bay, California 93442
Phone: (805)772-4467

SCORE Office (Mountain View)
580 Castro St.
Mountain View, California 94041
Phone: (415)968-8378
Fax: (415)968-5668

SCORE Office (Napa)
1556 1st St.
Napa, California 94559
Phone: (707)226-7455
Fax: (707)226-1171

SCORE Office (North Hollywood)
5019 Lankershim Blvd.
North Hollywood, California 91601
Phone: (818)552-3206

SCORE Office (Northridge)
8801 Reseda Blvd.
Northridge, California 91324
Phone: (818)349-5676

SCORE Office (Novato)
807 De Long Ave.
Novato, California 94945
Phone: (415)897-1164
Fax: (415)898-9097

SCORE Office (East Bay)
2201 Broadway, Ste. 701
Oakland, California 94612
Phone: (510)273-6611

SCORE Office (Oceanside)
928 N. Coast Hwy.
Oceanside, California 92054
Phone: (619)722-1534

SCORE Office (Ontario)
121 West B. St.
Ontario, California 91762
Fax: (714)984-6439

SCORE Office (Oxnard)
c/o Oxnard Chamber of Commerce
PO Box 867
Oxnard, California 93032
Phone: (805)385-8860
Fax: (805)487-1763

SCORE Office (Pacifica)
450 Dundee Way, Ste. 2
Pacifica, California 94044
Phone: (415)355-4122

SCORE Office (Palm Desert)
72990 Hwy. 111
Palm Desert, California 92260
Phone: (619)346-6111
Fax: (619)346-3463

SCORE Office (Palm Springs)
555 S. Palm Canyon, Rm. A206
Palm Springs, California 92264
Phone: (619)320-6682

SCORE Office (Lakeside)
c/o Paul Heindel
2150 Low Tree
Palmdale, California 93551
Phone: (805)948-4518
Fax: (805)949-1212

SCORE Office (Palo Alto)
Thoits/Love, Hershaberger, Inc.
325 Forest Ave.
Palo Alto, California 94301
Phone: (415)324-3121
Fax: (415)324-1215

SCORE Office (Pasadena)
117 E. Colorado Blvd., Ste. 100
Pasadena, California 91105
Phone: (818)795-3355
Fax: (818)795-5663

SCORE Office (Paso Robles)
c/o Paso Robles Chamber of
Commerce

1225 Park St.
Paso Robles, California 93446-2234
Phone: (805)238-0506
Fax: (805)238-0527

SCORE Office (Petaluma)
799 Baywood Dr., Ste. 3
Petaluma, California 94954
Phone: (707)762-2785
Fax: (707)762-4721

SCORE Office (Pico Rivera)
9122 E. Washington Blvd.
Pico Rivera, California 90660

SCORE Office (Pittsburg)
2700 E. Leland Rd.
Pittsburg, California 94565
Phone: (510)439-2181
Fax: (510)427-1599

SCORE Office (Pleasanton)
777 Peters Ave.
Pleasanton, California 94566
Phone: (510)846-9697

SCORE Office (Monterey Park)
485 N. Garey
Pomona, California 91769

SCORE Office (Pomona)
c/o Pomona Chamber of Commerce
485 N. Garey Ave.
PO Box 1457
Pomona, California 91769-1457
Phone: (909)622-1256

SCORE Office (Shasta)
c/o Shasta Chamber of Commerce
747 Auditorium Dr.
Redding, California 96099
Phone: (916)225-4433

SCORE Office (Redwood City)
1675 Broadway
Redwood City, California 94063
Phone: (415)364-1722
Fax: (415)364-1729

SCORE Office (Richmond)
3925 MacDonald Ave.
Richmond, California 94805

SCORE Office (Ridgecrest)
c/o Ridgecrest Chamber of Commerce
PO Box 771
Ridgecrest, California 93555

Phone: (619)375-8331
Fax: (619)375-0365

SCORE Office (Riverside)
3685 Main St., Ste. 350
Riverside, California 92501
Phone: (909)683-7100

SCORE Office (Sacramento)
660 J St., Ste. 215
Sacramento, California 95814-2413
Phone: (916)498-6420

SCORE Office (Salinas)
c/o Salinas Chamber of Commerce
PO Box 1170
Salinas, California 93902
Phone: (408)424-7611
Fax: (408)424-8639

SCORE Office (Inland Empire)
777 E. Rialto Ave.
Purchasing
San Bernardino, California 92415-0760
Phone: (909)386-8278

SCORE Office (Inland Empire)
San Bernardino Chamber of Commerce
PO Box 658
San Bernardino, California 92402
Phone: (909)885-7515

SCORE Office (San Carlos)
San Carlos Chamber of Commerce
PO Box 1086
San Carlos, California 94070
Phone: (415)593-1068
Fax: (415)593-9108

SCORE Office (Encinitas)
550 W. C St., Ste. 550
San Diego, California 92101-3540
Phone: (619)557-7272
Fax: (619)557-5894

SCORE Office (San Diego)
c/o U.S. Small Business Administration
550 West C. St., Ste. 550
San Diego, California 92101-3540
Phone: (619)557-7272

SCORE Office (Menlo Park)
1100 Merrill St.
San Francisco, California 94105

Phone: (415)325-2818
Fax: (415)325-0920

SCORE Office (San Francisco)
U.S. Small Business Administration
211 Main St., 4th Fl.
San Francisco, California 94105
Phone: (415)744-6827

SCORE Office (San Gabriel)
401 W. Las Tunas Dr.
San Gabriel, California 91776
Phone: (818)576-2525
Fax: (818)289-2901

SCORE Office (San Jose)
Small Business Institute
Deanza College
201 S. 1st. St., Ste. 137
San Jose, California 95113
Phone: (408)288-8479

SCORE Office (Santa Clara County)
280 S. 1st St., Rm. 137
San Jose, California 95113
Phone: (408)288-8479

SCORE Office (San Luis Obispo)
3566 S. Hiquera
San Luis Obispo, California 93401
Phone: (805)547-0779

SCORE Office (San Mateo)
1021 S. El Camino, 2nd Fl.
San Mateo, California 94402
Phone: (415)341-5679

SCORE Office (San Pedro)
390 W. 7th St.
San Pedro, California 90731
Phone: (310)832-7272

SCORE Office (Orange County)
200 W. Santa Anna Blvd., Ste. 700
Santa Ana, California 92701
Phone: (714)550-7369

SCORE Office (Santa Barbara)
PO Box 30291
Santa Barbara, California 93130
Phone: (805)563-0084

SCORE Office (Central Coast)
1650 E. Clark Ave., No. 252
Santa Maria, California 93455
Phone: (805)934-2620

SCORE Office (Santa Maria)
Santa Maria Chamber of Commerce
614 S. Broadway
Santa Maria, California 93454-5111
Phone: (805)925-2403
Fax: (805)928-7559

SCORE Office (Santa Monica)
501 Colorado, Ste. 150
Santa Monica, California 90401
Phone: (310)393-9825
Fax: (310)394-1868

SCORE Office (Santa Rosa)
777 Sonoma Ave., Rm. 115E
Santa Rosa, California 95404
Phone: (707)571-8342

SCORE Office (Scotts Valley)
c/o Scotts Valley Chamber of Commerce
4 Camp Evers Ln.
Scotts Valley, California 95066
Phone: (408)438-1010
Fax: (408)438-6544

SCORE Office (Simi Valley)
c/o Simi Valley Chamber of Commerce
40 W. Cochran St., Ste. 100
Simi Valley, California 93065
Phone: (805)526-3900
Fax: (805)526-6234

SCORE Office (Sonoma)
453 1st St. E
Sonoma, California 95476
Phone: (707)996-1033

SCORE Office (Los Banos)
222 S. Shepard St.
Sonora, California 95370
Phone: (209)532-4212

SCORE Office (Tuolumne County)
c/o Tuolumne County Chamber of Commerce
222 S. Shepherd St.
Sonora, California 95370
Phone: (209)532-4212

SCORE Office (South San Francisco)
c/o South San Francisco Chamber of Commerce
PO Box 469
South San Francisco, California 94080

Phone: (415)588-1911
Fax: (415)588-1529

SCORE Office (Stockton)
401 N. San Joaquin St., Rm. 215
Stockton, California 95202
Phone: (209)946-6293

SCORE Office (Taft)
314 4th St.
Taft, California 93268
Phone: (805)765-2165
Fax: (805)765-6639

SCORE Office (Conejo Valley)
c/o Conejo Valley Chamber of
Commerce
625 W. Hillcrest Dr.
Thousand Oaks, California 91360
Phone: (805)499-1993
Fax: (805)498-7264

SCORE Office (Torrance)
Torrance Chamber of Commerce
3400 Torrance Blvd., Ste. 100
Torrance, California 90503
Phone: (310)540-5858
Fax: (310)540-7662

SCORE Office (Truckee)
PO Box 2757
Truckee, California 96160
Phone: (916)587-2757
Fax: (916)587-2439

SCORE Office (Visalia)
c/o Tulare County E.D.C.
113 S. M St,
Tulare, California 93274
Phone: (209)627-0766
Fax: (209)627-8149

SCORE Office (Upland)
c/o Upland Chamber of Commerce
433 N. 2nd Ave.
Upland, California 91786
Phone: (909)931-4108

SCORE Office (Vallejo)
2 Florida St.
Vallejo, California 94590
Phone: (707)644-5551
Fax: (707)644-5590

SCORE Office (Van Nuys)
14540 Victory Blvd.

Van Nuys, California 91411
Phone: (818)989-0300
Fax: (818)989-3836

SCORE Office (Ventura)
Gold Coast Small Business
Development Center
5700 Ralston St., Ste. 310
Ventura, California 93003
Phone: (818)552-3210

SCORE Office (Vista)
201 E. Washington St.
Vista, California 92084
Phone: (619)726-1122
Fax: (619)226-8654

SCORE Office (Watsonville)
PO Box 1748
Watsonville, California 95077
Phone: (408)724-3849
Fax: (408)728-5300

SCORE Office (West Covina)
c/o West Covina Chamber of
Commerce
811 S. Sunset Ave.
West Covina, California 91790
Phone: (818)338-8496
Fax: (818)960-0511

SCORE Office (Westlake)
c/o Westlake Chamber of Commerce
30893 Thousand Oaks Blvd.
Westlake Village, California 91362
Phone: (805)496-5630
Fax: (818)991-1754

Colorado

SCORE Office (Colorado Springs)
2 N. Cascade Ave., Ste. 110
Colorado Springs, Colorado 80903
Phone: (719)636-3074

SCORE Office (Denver)
US Custom's House, 4th Fl.
721 19th St.
Denver, Colorado 80201-0660
Phone: (303)844-3985

SCORE Office (Tri-River)
1102 Grand Ave.
Glenwood Springs, Colorado 81601
Phone: (970)945-6589

SCORE Office (Grand Junction)
c/o Grand Junction Chamber of
Commerce
360 Grand Ave.
Grand Junction, Colorado 81501
Phone: (303)242-3214

SCORE Office (Gunnison)
c/o Russ Gregg
608 N. 11th
Gunnison, Colorado 81230
Phone: (303)641-4422

SCORE Office (Montrose)
1214 Peppertree Dr.
Montrose, Colorado 81401
Phone: (970)249-6080

SCORE Office (Pagosa Springs)
c/o Will Cotton
PO Box 4381
Pagosa Springs, Colorado 81157
Phone: (970)731-4890

SCORE Office (Rifle)
0854 W. Battlement Pky., Apt. C106
Parachute, Colorado 81635
Phone: (970)285-9390

SCORE Office (Pueblo)
302 N. Santa Fe
Pueblo, Colorado 81003
Phone: (719)542-1704

SCORE Office (Ridgway)
c/o Ken Hanson
143 Poplar Pl.
Ridgway, Colorado 81432

SCORE Office (Silverton)
c/o EF Homann
PO Box 480
Silverton, Colorado 81433
Phone: (303)387-5430

SCORE Office (Minturn)
PO Box 2066
Vail, Colorado 81658
Phone: (970)476-1224

Connecticut

SCORE Office (Greater Bridgeport)
10 Middle St., 14th Fl.
PO Box 999
Bridgeport, Connecticut 06601-0999
Phone: (203)335-3800

SCORE Office (Bristol)
10 Main St. 1st. Fl.
Bristol, Connecticut 06010
Phone: (203)584-4718
Fax: (203)584-4722

SCORE Office (Greater Danbury)
100 Mill Plain Rd.
Danbury, Connecticut 06811
Phone: (203)791-3804

SCORE Office (Eastern Connecticut)
University of Connecticut
Administration Bldg., Rm. 313
PO 625
61 Main St. (Chapter 579)
Groton, Connecticut 06475
Phone: (203)388-9508

SCORE Office (Greater Hartford
County)
330 Main St.
Hartford, Connecticut 06106
Phone: (203)240-4640

SCORE Office (Manchester)
c/o Manchester Chamber of
Commerce
20 Hartford Rd.
Manchester, Connecticut 06040
Phone: (203)646-2223
Fax: (203)646-5871

SCORE Office (New Britain)
185 Main St.,Ste. 431
New Britain, Connecticut 06051
Phone: (203)827-4492
Fax: (203)827-4480

SCORE Office (New Haven)
25 Science Pk., Bldg. 25, Rm. 366
New Haven, Connecticut 06511
Phone: (203)865-7645

SCORE Office (Fairfield County)
24 Beldon Ave., 5th Fl.
Norwalk, Connecticut 06850
Phone: (203)847-7348

SCORE Office (Old Saybrook)
c/o Old Saybrook Chamber of
Commerce
146 Main St.
PO Box 625
Old Saybrook, Connecticut 06475
Phone: (203)388-9508

SCORE Office (Simsbury)
Simsbury Chamber of Commerce
Box 244
Simsbury, Connecticut 06070
Phone: (203)651-7307
Fax: (203)651-1933

SCORE Office (Torrington)
Northwest Chamber of Commerce
23 North Rd.
Torrington, Connecticut 06791
Phone: (203)482-6586

Delaware

SCORE Office (Dover)
Dover Chamber of Commerce
Treadway Towers
P.O. Box 576
Dover, Delaware 19903
Phone: (302)678-0892
Fax: (302)678-0189

SCORE Office (Lewes)
PO Box 1
Lewes, Delaware 19958
Phone: (302)645-8073
Fax: (302)645-8412

SCORE Office (Milford)
Milford Chamber of Commerce
204 NE Front St.
Milford, Delaware 19963
Phone: (302)422-3301

SCORE Office (Wilmington)
824 Market St., Ste. 610
Wilmington, Delaware 19801
Phone: (302)573-6552
Fax: (302)573-6060

District of Columbia

SCORE Office (George Mason
University)
409 3rd St. SW, 4th Fl.
Washington, District of Columbia
20024
Free: (800)634-0245

SCORE Office (Washington DC)
1110 Vermont Ave. NW, 9th Fl.
PO Box 34346
Washington, District of Columbia
20043
Phone: (202)606-4000

Florida

SCORE Office (Desota County
Chamber of Commerce)
16 South Velucia Ave.
Arcadia, Florida 34266
Phone: (941)494-4033

SCORE Office (Suncoast/Pinellas)
Airport Business Ctr.
4707 - 140th Ave. N, No. 311
Clearwater, Florida 34622
Phone: (813)532-6800

SCORE Office (Dade)
1320 S. Dixie Hwy., Ste. 501
Coral Gables, Florida 33146
Phone: (305)536-5521

SCORE Office (Daytona Beach)
First Union Bldg., Ste. 365
444 Seabreeze Blvd.
Daytona Beach, Florida 32118
Phone: (904)255-6889

SCORE Office (DeLand)
DeLand Chamber of Commerce
336 N. Woodland Blvd.
DeLand, Florida 32720
Phone: (904)734-4331
Fax: (904)734-4333

SCORE Office (South Palm Beach)
1050 S. Federal Hwy., Ste. 132
Delray Beach, Florida 33483
Phone: (407)278-7752

SCORE Office (Ft. Lauderdale)
Federal Bldg., Ste. 123
299 E. Broward Blvd.
Ft. Lauderdale, Florida 33301
Phone: (305)356-7263

SCORE Office (Southwest Florida)
The Renaissance
8695 College Pky., Ste. 345 & 346
Fort Myers, Florida 33919
Phone: (813)489-2935

SCORE Office (Indian River)
Treasure Coast Professional Center,
Ste. 2
3229 S. US No. 1
Fort Pierce, Florida 34982
Phone: (407)489-0548

SCORE Office (Gainesville)
101 SE 2nd Pl., Ste. 104
Gainesville, Florida 32601
Phone: (904)375-8278

SCORE Office (Hialeah Dade
Chamber)
c/o Serry Stein
59 W. 5th St.
Hialeah, Florida 33010
Phone: (305)887-1515
Fax: (305)887-2453

SCORE Office (South Broward)
3475 Sheridian St., Ste. 203
Hollywood, Florida 33021
Phone: (305)966-8415

SCORE Office (Jacksonville)
7825 Baymeadows Way, Ste. 100-B
Jacksonville, Florida 32256-7504
Phone: (904)443-1911

SCORE Office (Jacksonville
Satellite)
c/o Jacksonville Chamber of
Commerce
3 Independent Dr.
Jacksonville, Florida 32202
Phone: (904)366-6600
Fax: (904)632-0617

SCORE Office (Central Florida)
404 N. Ingraham Ave.
Lakeland, Florida 33801
Phone: (813)688-4060

SCORE Office (Lakeland)
Lakeland Public Library
100 Lake Morton Dr.
Lakeland, Florida 33801
Phone: (941)686-2168

SCORE Office (St. Petersburg)
800 W. Bay Dr., Ste. 505
Largo, Florida 33712
Phone: (813)585-4571

SCORE Office (Leesburg)
Lake Sumter Community College
9501 US Hwy. 441
Leesburg, Florida 34788-8751
Phone: (352)365-3556
Fax: (352)365-3501

SCORE Office (BCC/Space Coast)
Space Coast

Melbourn Professional Complex
1600 Sarno, Ste. 205
Melbourne, Florida 32935
Phone: (407)254-2288

SCORE Office (Cocoa)
1600 Farno Rd., Unit 205
Melbourne, Florida 32935
Phone: (407)254-2288

SCORE Office (Melbourne)
Space Coast
Melbourne Professional Complex
1600 Samo, Ste. 205
Melbourne, Florida 32935
Phone: (407)254-2288

SCORE Office (Merritt Island)
1600 Farno Rd., Unit 205
Melbourne, Florida 32935
Phone: (407)254-2288

SCORE Office (Naples of Collier)
Sun Bank Naples
3301 Danis Blvd.
PO Box 413002
Naples, Florida 33941-3002
Phone: (941)643-0333

SCORE Office (Pasco County)
6014 US Hwy. 19, Ste. 302
New Port Richey, Florida 34652
Phone: (813)842-4638

SCORE Office (Southeast Volusia)
Chamber of Commerce
115 Canal St.
New Smyrna Beach, Florida 32168
Phone: (904)428-2449
Fax: (904)423-3512

SCORE Office (Ocala)
Ocala-Marion Chamber of Commerce
110 E. Silver Springs Blvd.
Ocala, Florida 34470-6613
Phone: (904)629-5959

Clay County SCORE Office
Clay County Chamber of Commerce
1734 Kingsdey Ave.
PO Box 1441
Orange Park, Florida 32073
Phone: (904)264-2651
Fax: (904)269-0363

SCORE Office (Orlando)
Federal Bldg., Rm. 455

80 N. Hughey Ave.
Orlando, Florida 32801
Phone: (407)648-6476

SCORE Office (Emerald Coast)
19 W. Garden St., No. 325
Pensacola, Florida 32501
Phone: (904)444-2060
Fax: (904)444-2070

SCORE Office (Charlotte County)
Punta Gorda Professional Center
201 W. Marion Ave., Ste. 211
Punta Gorda, Florida 33950
Phone: (813)575-1818

SCORE Office (St. Augustine)
c/o St. Augustine Chamber of
Commerce
1 Riberia St.
St. Augustine, Florida 32084
Phone: (904)829-5681
Fax: (904)829-6477

SCORE Office (Bradenton)
2801 Fruitville, Ste. 280
Sarasota, Florida 34237
Phone: (813)955-1029

SCORE Office (Manasota)
2801 Fruitville Rd., Ste. 280
Sarasota, Florida 34237
Phone: (813)955-1029

SCORE Office (Tallahassee)
c/o Leon County Library
200 W. Park Ave.
Tallahassee, Florida 32302
Phone: (904)487-2665

SCORE Office (Hillsborough)
4732 Dale Mabry Hwy. N, Ste. 400
Tampa, Florida 33614-6509
Phone: (813)870-0125

SCORE Office (Lake Sumter)
First Union National Bank
122 E. Main St.
Tavares, Florida 32778
Phone: (904)365-3556

SCORE Office (Titusville)
2000 S. Washington Ave.
Titusville, Florida 32780
Phone: (407)267-3036
Fax: (407)264-0127

SCORE Office (Venice)
257 N. Tamiami Trl.
Venice, Florida 34285
Phone: (941)488-2236
Fax: (941)484-5903

SCORE Office (Palm Beach)
500 Australian Ave. S, Ste. 100
West Palm Beach, Florida 33401
Phone: (407)833-1672

SCORE Office (Wildwood)
Sumter County Small Business
Services
103 N. Webster St.
Wildwood, Florida 34785

Georgia

SCORE Office (Atlanta)
1720 Peachtree Rd. NW, 6th Fl.
Atlanta, Georgia 30309
Phone: (404)347-2442

SCORE Office (Augusta)
3126 Oxford Rd.
Augusta, Georgia 30909
Phone: (706)869-9100

SCORE Office (Columbus)
School Bldg.
P.O. Box 40
Columbus, Georgia 31901
Phone: (706)327-3654

SCORE Office (Dalton-Whitfield)
PO Box 1941
Dalton, Georgia 30722-1941
Phone: (706)279-3383

SCORE Office (Gainesville)
Chamber of Commerce
PO Box 374
Gainesville, Georgia 30503
Phone: (770)532-6206
Fax: (770)535-8419

SCORE Office (Macon)
711 Grand Bdlg.
Macon, Georgia 31201
Phone: (912)751-6160

SCORE Office (Brunswick)
4 Glen Ave.
St. Simons Island, Georgia 31520
Phone: (912)265-0620
Fax: (912)265-0629

SCORE Office (Savannah)
33 Bull St., Ste. 580
Savannah, Georgia 31401
Phone: (912)652-4335

Guam

SCORE Office (Guam)
Pacific News Bldg., Rm. 103
238 Archbishop Flores St.
Agana, Guam 96910-5100
Phone: (671)472-7308

Hawaii

SCORE Office (Honolulu)
SCORE of Hawaii, Inc.
300 Ala Moana Blvd., No. 2213
PO Box 50207
Honolulu, Hawaii 96850-3212
Phone: (808)541-2977

SCORE Office (Kahului)
SCORE of Maine Inc.
c/o Chamber of Commerce
250 Alamaha, Unit N16A
Kahului, Hawaii 96732
Phone: (808)871-7711

Idaho

SCORE Office (Treasure Valley)
1020 Main St., No. 290
Boise, Idaho 83702
Phone: (208)334-1780

SCORE Office (Eastern Idaho)
2300 N. Yellowstone, Ste. 119
Idaho Falls, Idaho 83401
Phone: (208)523-1022

Illinois

SCORE Office (Fox Valley)
Greater Aurora Chamber of
Commerce
40 W. Downer Pl.
PO Box 277
Aurora, Illinois 60507
Phone: (708)897-9214

SCORE Office (Greater Belvidere)
Greater Belvidere Chamber of
Commerce
419 S. State St.
Belvidere, Illinois 61008

Phone: (815)544-4357
Fax: (815)547-7654

SCORE Office (Bensenville)
Greater O'Hare Association
1050 Busse Hwy. Suite 100
Bensenville, Illinois 60106
Phone: (708)350-2944
Fax: (708)350-2979

SCORE Office (Southern Illinois)
150 E. Pleasant Hill Rd.
Box 1
Carbondale, Illinois 62901
Phone: (618)453-6654

SCORE Office (Chicago)
Northwest Atrium Center
500 W. Madison St., No. 1250
Chicago, Illinois 60661
Phone: (312)353-7724

SCORE Office (Chicago—Oliver
Harvey College)
Oliver Harvey College
Small Business Development Center
Pullman Bldg.
1000 E. 11th St., 7th Fl.
Chicago, Illinois 60628
Fax: (312)468-8086

SCORE Office (Danville)
Danville Area Chamber of Commerce
28 W. N. Street
Danville, Illinois 61832
Phone: (217)442-7232
Fax: (217)442-6228

SCORE Office (Decatur)
Millikin University
1184 W. Main St.
Decatur, Illinois 62522
Phone: (217)424-6297

SCORE Office (Downers Grove)
Downers Grove Chamber of
Commerce
925 Curtis
Downers Grove, Illinois 60515
Phone: (708)968-4050
Fax: (708)968-8368

SCORE Office (Elgin)
Elgin Area Chamber of Commerce
24 E. Chicago, 3rd Fl.
PO Box 648
Elgin, Illinois 60120

Phone: (847)741-5660
Fax: (847)741-5677

SCORE Office (Freeport Area)
Freeport Area Chamber of Commerce
26 S. Galena Ave.
Freeport, Illinois 61032
Phone: (815)233-1350
Fax: (815)235-4038

SCORE Office (Galesburg)
Galesburg Area Chamber of
Commerce
292 E. Simmons St.
PO Box 749
Galesburg, Illinois 61401
Phone: (309)343-1194
Fax: (309)343-1195

SCORE Office (Glen Ellyn)
Glen Ellyn Chamber of Commerce
500 Pennsylvania
Glen Ellyn, Illinois 60137
Phone: (708)469-0907
Fax: (708)469-0426

SCORE Office (Alton)
Lewis & Clark Community College
Alden Hall
5800 Godfrey Rd.
Godfrey, Illinois 62035-2466
Phone: (618)467-2280

SCORE Office (Grayslake)
College of Lake County
19351 W. Washington St.
Grayslake, Illinois 60030
Phone: (708)223-3633
Fax: (708)223-9371

SCORE Office (Harrisburg)
Ec. Devel. Services Center
303 S. Commercial
Harrisburg, Illinois 62946-1528
Phone: (618)252-8528
Fax: (618)252-0210

SCORE Office (Joliet)
Joliet Region Chamber of Commerce
100 N. Chicago
Joliet, Illinois 60432
Phone: (815)727-5371
Fax: (815)727-5374

SCORE Office (Kankakee)
Kankakee Small Business

Development Center
101 S. Schuyler Ave.
Kankakee, Illinois 60901
Phone: (815)933-0376
Fax: (815)933-0380

SCORE Office (Macomb)
Western Illinois University
216 Seal Hall, Rm. 214
Macomb, Illinois 61455
Phone: (309)298-1128
Fax: (309)298-2520

SCORE Office (Matteson)
Prairie State College
210 Lincoln Mall
Matteson, Illinois 60443
Phone: (708)709-3750
Fax: (708)503-9322

SCORE Office (Mattoon)
Mattoon Association of Commerce
1701 Wabash Ave.
Mattoon, Illinois 61938
Phone: (217)235-5661
Fax: (217)234-6544

SCORE Office (Quad City)
Quad City Chamber of Commerce
622 19th St.
Moline, Illinois 61265
Phone: (309)797-0082

SCORE Office (Naperville)
Naperville Area Chamber of
Commerce
131 W. Jefferson Ave.
Naperville, Illinois 60540
Phone: (708)355-4141
Fax: (708)355-8355

SCORE Office (Northbrook)
Northbrook Chamber of Commerce
2002 Walters Ave.
Northbrook, Illinois 60062
Phone: (847)498-5555
Fax: (847)498-5510

SCORE Office (Palos Hills)
Moraine Valley Community College
Small Business Development Center
10900 S. 88th Ave.
Palos Hills, Illinois 60465
Phone: (847)974-5468
Fax: (847)974-0078

SCORE Office (Peoria)
c/o Peoria Chamber of Commerce
124 SW Adams, Ste. 300
Peoria, Illinois 61602
Phone: (309)676-0755

SCORE Office (Prospect Heights)
Harper College, Northeast Center
1375 Wolf Rd.
Prospect Heights, Illinois 60070
Phone: (847)537-8660
Fax: (847)537-7138

SCORE Office (Quincy Tri-State)
Quincy Chamber of Commerce
300 Civic Center Plz., Ste. 245
Quincy, Illinois 62301
Phone: (217)222-8093

SCORE Office (River Grove)
Triton College
2000 5th Ave.
River Grove, Illinois 60171
Phone: (708)456-0300
Fax: (708)583-3121

SCORE Office (Northern Illinois)
Rockford Illinois Chamber of
Commerce
515 N. Court St.
Rockford, Illinois 61103
Phone: (815)962-0122

SCORE Office (St. Charles)
St. Charles Chamber of Commerce
103 N. 1st Ave.
St. Charles, Illinois 60174-1982
Phone: (847)584-8384
Fax: (847)584-6065

SCORE Office (Springfield)
U.S. Small Business Administration
511 W. Capitol Ave., Ste. 302
Springfield, Illinois 62704
Phone: (217)492-4416
Fax: (217)492-4867

SCORE Office (Sycamore)
Greater Sycamore Chamber of
Commerce
112 Somunak St.
Sycamore, Illinois 60178
Phone: (815)895-3456
Fax: (815)895-0125

SCORE Office (University)
Governors State University

Hwy. 50 & Stuenkel Rd. Ste. C3305
University Park, Illinois 60466
Phone: (708)534-5000
Fax: (708)534-8457

Indiana

SCORE Office (Anderson)
c/o Anderson Chamber of Commerce
205 W. 11th St.
PO Box 469
Anderson, Indiana 46015
Phone: (317)642-0264

SCORE Office (Bloomington)
c/o Bloomington Chamber of
Commerce
400 W. 7th St., Ste. 102
Bloomington, Indiana 47404
Phone: (812)336-6381

SCORE Office (Southeast)
c/o Columbus Chamber of Commerce
500 Franklin St.
Box 29
Columbus, Indiana 47201
Phone: (812)379-4457

SCORE Office (Corydon)
310 N. Elm St.
Corydon, Indiana 47112
Phone: (812)738-2137
Fax: (812)738-6438

SCORE Office (Crown Point)
Old Courthouse Sq. Ste. 206
P.O. Box 43
Crown Point, Indiana 46307
Phone: (219)663-1800

SCORE Office (Elkhart)
418 S. Main St.
P.O. Box 428
Elkhart, Indiana 46515
Phone: (219)293-1531

SCORE Office (Evansville)
Old Post Office Pl.
100 NW 2nd St., No. 300
Evansville, Indiana 47708
Phone: (812)421-5879

SCORE Office (Fort Wayne)
1300 S. Harrison St.
Fort Wayne, Indiana 46802
Phone: (219)422-2601

SCORE Office (Gary)
973 W. 6th Ave., Rm. 326
Gary, Indiana 46402
Phone: (219)882-3918

SCORE Office (Hammond)
7034 Indianapolis Blvd.
Hammond, Indiana 46324
Phone: (219)931-1000
Fax: (219)845-9548

SCORE Office (Indianapolis)
429 N. Pennsylvania St., Ste. 100
Indianapolis, Indiana 46204-1873
Phone: (317)226-7264

SCORE Office (Jasper)
PO Box 307
Jasper, Indiana 47547-0307
Phone: (812)482-6866

SCORE Office (Kokomo/Howard
Counties)
106 N. Washington
PO Box 731
Kokomo, Indiana 46903-0731
Phone: (317)457-5301
Fax: (317)452-4564

SCORE Office (Logansport)
Logansport County Chamber of
Commerce
300 E. Broadway, Ste. 103
Logansport, Indiana 46947
Phone: (219)753-6388

SCORE Office (Madison)
301 E. Main St.
Madison, Indiana 47250
Phone: (812)265-3135
Fax: (812)265-2923

SCORE Office (Marengo)
c/o Marengo Chamber of Commerce
Rt. 1 Box 224D
Marengo, Indiana 47140
Fax: (812)365-2793

SCORE Office (Marion/Grant
Counties)
215 S. Adams
Marion, Indiana 46952
Phone: (317)664-5107

SCORE Office (Merrillville)
255 W. 80th Pl.

Merrillville, Indiana 46410
Phone: (219)769-8180
Fax: (219)736-6223

SCORE Office (Michigan City)
200 E. Michigan Blvd.
Michigan City, Indiana 46360
Phone: (219)874-6221
Fax: (219)873-1204

SCORE Office (South Central
Indiana)
1702 E. Spring St.
PO Box 653
New Albany, Indiana 47150
Phone: (812)945-0054

SCORE Office (Rensselaer)
104 W. Washington
Rensselaer, Indiana 47978

SCORE Office (Salem)
c/o Salem Chamber of Commerce
210 N. Main St.
Salem, Indiana 47167
Phone: (812)883-4303
Fax: (812)883-1467

SCORE Office (South Bend)
300 N. Michigan St.
South Bend, Indiana 46601
Phone: (219)282-4350

SCORE Office (Valparaiso)
150 Lincolnway
Valparaiso, Indiana 46383
Phone: (219)462-1105
Fax: (219)469-5710

SCORE Office (Vincennes)
Vincennes Chamber of Commerce
27 N. 3rd
P.O. Box 553
Vincennes, Indiana 47591
Phone: (812)882-6440
Fax: (812)882-6441

SCORE Office (Wabash)
PO Box 371
Wabash, Indiana 46992
Phone: (219)563-1168
Fax: (219)563-6920

Iowa

SCORE Office (Burlington)
Federal Bldg.

300 N. Main St.
Burlington, Iowa 52601
Phone: (319)752-2967

SCORE Office (Cedar Rapids)
Lattner Building, Ste. 200
215-4th Avenue, SE
Cedar Rapids, Iowa 52401-1806
Phone: (319)362-6405
Fax: (319)362-7861

SCORE Office (Southwest Iowa)
700 W. Clark
Clarinda, Iowa 51632
Phone: (712)542-2906

SCORE Office (Illowa)
River City Chamber of Commerce
333 4th Ave. S
Clinton, Iowa 52732
Phone: (319)242-5702

SCORE Office (Council Bluffs)
Council Bluffs Chamber of
Commerce
P.O. Box 1565
Council Bluffs, Iowa 51502-1565
Phone: (712)325-1000

SCORE Office (Northeast Iowa)
3404 285th St.
Cresco, Iowa 52136
Phone: (319)547-3377

SCORE Office (Des Moines)
Federal Bldg., Rm. 749
210 Walnut St.
Des Moines, Iowa 50309-2186
Phone: (515)284-4760

SCORE Office (Fort Dodge)
Federal Bdlg., Rm. 436
205 S. 8th St.
Fort Dodge, Iowa 50501
Phone: (515)955-2622

SCORE Office (Independence)
Independence Area Chamber of
Commerce
110 1st. St. east
Independence, Iowa 50644
Phone: (319)334-7178
Fax: (319)334-7179

SCORE Office (Iowa City)
210 Federal Bdlg.
PO Box 1853

Iowa City, Iowa 52240-1853
Phone: (319)338-1662

SCORE Office (Keokuk)
Keokuk Area Chamber of Commerce
Pierce Bldg., No. 1
401 Main St.
Keokuk, Iowa 52632
Phone: (319)524-5055

SCORE Office (Central Iowa)
Fisher Community Center
709 S. Center
Marshalltown, Iowa 50158
Phone: (515)753-6645

SCORE Office (River City)
15 West State St.
P.O. Box 1128
Mason City, Iowa 50401
Phone: (515)423-5724

SCORE Office (South Central)
c/o Indian Hills Community College
525 Grandview Ave.
Ottumwa, Iowa 52501
Phone: (515)683-5127
Fax: (515)683-5263

SCORE Office (Dubuque)
Northeast Iowa Community College
10250 Sundown Road
Peosta, Iowa 52068
Phone: (319)556-5110

SCORE Office (Shenandoah)
Chamber of Commerce
403 W. Sheridan
Shenandoah, Iowa 51601
Phone: (712)542-2906

SCORE Office (Sioux City)
c/o Sioux City Federal Bldg.
320 6th St.
Sioux City, Iowa 51101
Phone: (712)277-2325

SCORE Office (Iowa Lakes)
21 W. 5th St., Rm. 5
PO Box 7026
Spencer, Iowa 51301-3059
Phone: (712)262-3059

SCORE Office (Vista)
Storm Lake Chamber of Commerce
119 W. 6th St.

Storm Lake, Iowa 50588
Phone: (712)732-3780

SCORE Office (Waterloo)
Waterloo Chamber of Commerce
215 E. 4th
Waterloo, Iowa 50703
Phone: (319)233-8431

Kansas

SCORE Office (Southwest Kansas)
Dodge City Area Chamber of
Commerce
PO Box 939
Dodge City, Kansas 67801
Phone: (316)227-3119

SCORE Office (Emporia)
Emporia Chamber of Commerce
427 Commercial
Emporia, Kansas 66801
Phone: (316)342-1600

SCORE Office (Golden Belt)
Chamber of Commerce
1307 Williams
Great Bend, Kansas 67530
Phone: (316)792-2401

SCORE Office (Hays)
c/o Empire Bank
PO Box 400
Hays, Kansas 67601
Phone: (913)625-6595

SCORE Office (Hutchinson)
One E. 9th St.
Hutchinson, Kansas 67501
Phone: (316)665-8468

SCORE Office (Southeast Kansas)
404 Westminster Pl.
PO Box 886
Independence, Kansas 67301-0886
Phone: (316)331-4741

SCORE Office (McPherson)
McPherson Chamber of Commerce
306 N. Main
McPherson, Kansas 67460
Phone: (316)241-3303

SCORE Office (Salina)
PO Box 586
Salina, Kansas 67401
Phone: (913)827-9301

SCORE Office (Topeka)
1700 College
Topeka, Kansas 66621
Phone: (913)231-1010

SCORE Office (Wichita)
U.S. Small Business Administration
100 E. English, Ste. 510
Wichita, Kansas 67202
Phone: (316)269-6273

SCORE Office (Ark Valley)
Box 314
Winfield, Kansas 67156
Phone: (316)221-1617

Kentucky

SCORE Office (Ashland)
PO Box 830
Ashland, Kentucky 41105
Phone: (606)329-8011
Fax: (606)325-4607

SCORE Office (Bowling Green)
Bowling Green-Warren Chamber of
Commerce
812 State St.
P.O. Box 51
Bowling Green, Kentucky 42101
Phone: (502)781-3200
Fax: (502)843-0458

SCORE Office (Tri-Lakes)
508 Barbee Way
Danville, Kentucky 40422-1548
Phone: (606)231-9902

SCORE Office (Glasgow)
301 W. Main St.
Glasgow, Kentucky 42141
Phone: (502)651-3161
Fax: (502)651-3122

SCORE Office (Hazard)
B & I Technical Center
100 Airport Gardens Rd.
Hazard, Kentucky 41701
Phone: (606)439-5856
Fax: (606)439-1808

SCORE Office (Lexington)
1460 Newton Pke., Ste. A
Lexington, Kentucky 40511
Phone: (606)231-9902

SCORE Office (Louisville)
188 Federal Office Bldg.
600 Dr. Martin L. King Jr. Pl.
Louisville, Kentucky 40202
Phone: (502)582-5976

SCORE Office (Madisonville)
257 N. Main
Madisonville, Kentucky 42431
Phone: (502)825-1399
Fax: (502)825-1396

SCORE Office (Paducah)
Federal Office Bldg.
501 Broadway, Rm. B-36
Paducah, Kentucky 42001
Phone: (502)442-5685

Louisiana

SCORE Office (Central Louisiana)
802 3rd St.
PO Box 992
Alexandria, Louisiana 71309
Phone: (318)442-6671

SCORE Office (Baton Rouge)
564 Laurel St.
PO Box 3217
Baton Rouge, Louisiana 70801
Phone: (504)381-7125

SCORE Office (NorthShore)
PO Box 1458
Hammond, Louisiana 70404
Phone: (504)345-4457

SCORE Office (Lafayette)
Lafayette Chamber of Commerce
804 St. Mary Blvd.
PO Drawer 51307
Lafayette, Louisiana 70505-1307
Phone: (318)233-2705

SCORE Office (Lake Charles)
120 W. Pujo
Lake Charles, Louisiana 70601
Phone: (318)433-3632

SCORE Office (New Orleans)
365 Canal St., Ste. 2250
New Orleans, Louisiana 70130
Phone: (504)589-2356

SCORE Office (Shreveport)
400 Edwards St.

Shreveport, Louisiana 71101
Phone: (318)677-2509

Maine

SCORE Office (Augusta)
40 Western Ave.
Augusta, Maine 04330
Phone: (207)622-8509

SCORE Office (Bangor)
Husson College
Peabody Hall, Rm. 229
One College Cir.
Bangor, Maine 04401
Phone: (207)941-9707

SCORE Office (Central & Northern
Arrostock)
111 High St.
PO Box 357
Caribou, Maine 04736
Phone: (207)498-6156

SCORE Office (Penquis)
Chamber of Commerce
South St.
Dover Foxcroft, Maine 04426
Phone: (207)564-7021

SCORE Office (Maine Coastal)
Federal Bldg.
Main & Water St.
Box 1105
Ellsworth, Maine 04605
Phone: (207)667-5800

SCORE Office (Lewiston-Auburn)
c/o Chamber of Commerce
179 Lisbon St.
Lewiston, Maine 04240
Phone: (207)782-3708

SCORE Office (Portland)
66 Pearl St., Rm. 210
Portland, Maine 04101
Phone: (207)772-1147

SCORE Office (Western Mountains)
c/o Fleet Bank
108 Congress St.
PO Box 400
Rumford, Maine 04276
Phone: (207)364-3733

SCORE Office (Oxford Hills)
166 Main St.
South Paris, Maine 04281
Phone: (207)743-0499
Fax: (207)743-5917

Maryland

SCORE Office (Southern Maryland)
2525 Riva Rd., Ste. 110
Annapolis, Maryland 21401
Phone: (410)267-6206

SCORE Office (Baltimore)
The City Crescent Bldg., 6th Fl.
10 S. Howard St.
Baltimore, Maryland 21201
Phone: (410)962-2233
Fax: (410)962-1805

SCORE Office (Dundalk)
Eastern Baltimore Chamber of
Commerce
2200 Broening Hwy. Ste. 102
Baltimore, Maryland 21224
Phone: (410)282-9100
Fax: (410)631-9099

SCORE Office (Bel Air)
Bel Air Chamber of Commerce
108 S. Bond St.
Bel Air, Maryland 21014
Phone: (410)838-2020
Fax: (410)893-4715

SCORE Office (Bethesda)
7910 Woodmont Ave., Ste. 1204
Bethesda, Maryland 20814
Phone: (301)652-4900
Fax: (301)657-1973

SCORE Office (Bowie)
6670 Race Track Rd.
Bowie, Maryland 20715
Phone: (301)262-0920
Fax: (301)262-0921

SCORE Office (Dorchester County)
c/o Chamber of Commerce
203 Sunburst Hwy.
Cambridge, Maryland 21613
Phone: (410)228-3575

SCORE Office (Upper Shore)
c/o Talbout County Chamber of
Commerce

PO Box 1366
Easton, Maryland 21601
Phone: (410)822-4606
Fax: (410)822-7922

SCORE Office (Frederick County)
43A S. Market St.
Frederick, Maryland 21701
Phone: (301)662-4164

SCORE Office (Gaithersburg)
9 Park Ave.
Gaithersburg, Maryland 20877
Phone: (301)840-1400
Fax: (301)963-3918

SCORE Office (Glen Burnie)
Glen Burnie Chamber of Commerce
103 Crain Hwy. SE
Glen Burnie, Maryland 21061
Phone: (410)766-8282
Fax: (410)766-9722

SCORE Office (Hagerstown)
111 W. Washington St.
Hagerstown, Maryland 21740
Phone: (301)739-2015

SCORE Office (Laurel)
7901 Sandy Spring Rd. Ste. 501
Laurel, Maryland 20707
Phone: (301)725-4000
Fax: (301)725-0776

SCORE Office (Salisbury)
c/o Salisbury Chamber of Commerce
300 E. Main St.
Salisbury, Maryland 21801
Phone: (410)749-0185

Massachusetts

SCORE Office (Boston)
10 Causeway St., Rm. 265
Boston, Massachusetts 02222
Phone: (617)565-5591
Fax: (617)565-5598

SCORE Office (Southeastern
Massachusetts)
60 School St.
Brockton, Massachusetts 02401
Phone: (508)587-2673

SCORE Office (North Adams)
Northern Berkshire Development
Corp.

820 N. State Rd.
Cheshire, Massachusetts 01225
Phone: (413)743-5100

SCORE Office (Clinton Satellite)
c/o Clinton Chamber of Commerce
1 Green St.
Clinton, Massachusetts 01510
Fax: (508)368-7689

SCORE Office (Northeastern
Massachusetts)
Danvers Savings Bank
1 Conant St.
Danvers, Massachusetts 01923
Phone: (508)777-2200

SCORE Office (Bristol/Plymouth
Counties)
Fall River Area Chamber of
Commerce and Industry
PO Box 1871
Fall River, Massachusetts 02722-1871
Phone: (508)676-8226

SCORE Office (Greenfield)
PO Box 898
Greenfield, Massachusetts 01302
Phone: (413)773-5463
Fax: (413)773-7008

SCORE Office (Haverhill)
Haverhill Chamber
87 Winter St.
Haverhill, Massachusetts 01830
Phone: (508)373-5663
Fax: (508)373-8060

SCORE Office (Hudson Satellite)
c/o Hudson Chamber of Commerce
PO Box 578
Hudson, Massachusetts 01749
Phone: (508)568-0360
Fax: (508)568-0360

SCORE Office (Hyannis)
Independence Pk., Ste. 5B
270 Communications Way
Hyannis, Massachusetts 02601
Phone: (508)775-4884

SCORE Office (Lawrence)
264 Essex St.
Lawrence, Massachusetts 01840
Phone: (508)686-0900
Fax: (508)794-9953

SCORE Office (Leominster Satellite)
c/o Leominster Chamber of
Commerce
110 Erdman Way
Leominster, Massachusetts 01453
Phone: (508)840-4300
Fax: (508)840-4896

SCORE Office (Newburyport)
29 State St.
Newburyport, Massachusetts 01950
Phone: (617)462-6680

SCORE Office (Pittsfield)
Central Berkshire Chamber
66 West St.
Pittsfield, Massachusetts 01201
Phone: (413)499-2485

SCORE Office (Haverhill-Salem)
32 Derby Sq.
Salem, Massachusetts 01970
Phone: (508)745-0330
Fax: (508)745-3855

SCORE Office (Springfield)
1550 Main St., Ste. 212
Springfield, Massachusetts 01103
Phone: (413)785-0314

SCORE Office (Carver)
12 Taunton Green, Ste. 201
Taunton, Massachusetts 02780
Phone: (508)824-4068
Fax: (508)824-4069

SCORE Office (Cape Cod)
c/o Martha's Vineyard Chamber of
Commerce
Beach Rd.
PO Box 1698
Vineyard Haven, Massachusetts
02568
Phone: (508)693-0085

SCORE Office (Worcester)
33 Waldo St.
Worcester, Massachusetts 01608
Phone: (508)753-2924

Michigan

SCORE Office (Allegan)
c/o Allegan Chamber of Commerce
PO Box 338
Allegan, Michigan 49010
Phone: (616)673-2479

SCORE Office (Ann Arbor)
425 S. Main St., Ste. 103
Ann Arbor, Michigan 48104
Phone: (313)665-4433

SCORE Office (Battle Creek)
c/o Battle Creek Chamber of
Commerce
34 W. Jackson Ste. 4A
Battle Creek, Michigan 49017-3505
Phone: (616)962-4076
Fax: (616)962-6309

SCORE Office (Cadillac)
c/o Cadillac Chamber of Commerce
222 Lake St.
Cadillac, Michigan 49601
Phone: (616)775-9776
Fax: (616)775-1440

SCORE Office (Detroit)
477 Michigan Ave., Rm. 515
Detroit, Michigan 48226
Phone: (313)226-7947

SCORE Office (Flint)
Mott Community College
708 Root Rd., Rm. 308
Flint, Michigan 48503
Phone: (810)233-6846

SCORE Office (Grand Rapids)
110 Michigan Ave.
Grand Rapids, Michigan 49503
Phone: (616)771-0305

SCORE Office (Holland)
c/o Holland Chamber of Commerce
480 State St.
Holland, Michigan 49423
Phone: (616)396-9472

SCORE Office (Jackson)
Jackson Chamber of Commerce
209 East Washington
PO Box 80
Jackson, Michigan 49204
Phone: (517)782-8221
Fax: (517)782-0061

SCORE Office (Kalamazoo)
128 N. Kalamazoo Mall
Kalamazoo, Michigan 49007
Phone: (616)381-5382

SCORE Office (Lansing)
117 E. Allegan

PO Box 14030
Lansing, Michigan 48901
Phone: (517)487-6340
Fax: (517)484-6910

SCORE Office (Livonia)
Livonia Chamber of Commerce
15401 Farmington Rd.
Livonia, Michigan 48154
Phone: (313)427-2122
Fax: (313)427-6055

SCORE Office (Madison Heights)
26345 John R
Madison Heights, Michigan 48071
Phone: (810)542-5010
Fax: (810)542-6821

SCORE Office (Monroe)
Monroe Chamber of Commerce
111 E. 1st
Monroe, Michigan 48161
Phone: (313)242-3366
Fax: (313)242-7253

SCORE Office (Mount Clemens)
Macomb County Chamber of
Commerce
58 S/B Gratiot
Mount Clemens, Michigan 48043
Phone: (810)463-1528
Fax: (810)463-6541

SCORE Office (Muskegon)
c/o Muskegon Chamber of Commerce
PO Box 1087
230 Terrace Plz.
Muskegon, Michigan 49443
Phone: (616)722-3751
Fax: (616)728-7251

SCORE Office (Petoskey)
c/o Petoskey Chamber of Commerce
401 E. Mitchell St.
Petoskey, Michigan 49770-9961
Phone: (616)347-4150

SCORE Office (Pontiac)
Pontiac Chamber of Commerce
PO Box 430025
Pontiac, Michigan 48343
Phone: (810)335-9600

SCORE Office (Pontiac)
Oakland County Economic
Development Group
Executive Office Bldg.

1200 N. Telegraph Rd.
Pontiac, Michigan 48341
Phone: (810)975-9555

SCORE Office (Port Huron)
920 Pinegrove Ave.
Port Huron, Michigan 48060
Phone: (810)985-7101

SCORE Office (Rochester)
Rochester Chamber of Commerce
71 Walnut Ste. 110
Rochester, Michigan 48307
Phone: (810)651-6700
Fax: (810)651-5270

SCORE Office (Saginaw)
901 S. Washington Ave.
Saginaw, Michigan 48601
Phone: (517)752-7161
Fax: (517)752-9055

SCORE Office (Upper Peninsula)
c/o Chamber of Commerce
2581 I-75 Business Spur
Sault Sainte Marie, Michigan 49783
Phone: (906)632-3301

SCORE Office (Southfield)
21000 W. 10 Mile Rd.
Southfield, Michigan 48075
Phone: (810)204-3050
Fax: (810)204-3099

SCORE Office (Traverse City)
202 E. Grandview Pkwy.
PO Box 387
Traverse City, Michigan 49685
Phone: (616)947-5075

SCORE Office (Warren)
Warren Chamber of Commerce
30500 Van Dyke, Ste. 118
Warren, Michigan 48093
Phone: (810)751-3939

Minnesota

SCORE Office (Aitkin)
c/o Donald F. Gode
Aitkin, Minnesota 56431
Phone: (218)741-3906

SCORE Office (Albert Lea)
Albert Lea Chamber of Commerce
202 N. Broadway Ave.

Albert Lea, Minnesota 56007
Phone: (507)373-7487

SCORE Office (Austin)
PO Box 864
Austin, Minnesota 55912
Phone: (507)437-4561
Fax: (507)437-4869

SCORE Office (South Metro)
Burnsville Chamber of Commerce
101 W. Burnsville Pkwy., No. 150
Burnsville, Minnesota 55337
Phone: (612)435-6000

SCORE Office (Fairmont)
c/o Fairmont Chamber of Commerce
PO Box 826
Fairmont, Minnesota 56031
Phone: (507)235-5547
Fax: (507)235-8411

SCORE Office (Southwest
Minnesota)
112 Riverfront St.
Box 999
Mankato, Minnesota 56001
Phone: (507)345-4519

SCORE Office (Minneapolis)
North Plaza Bldg., Ste. 51
5217 Wayzata Blvd.
Minneapolis, Minnesota 55416
Phone: (612)591-0539

SCORE Office (Owatonna)
PO Box 331
Owatonna, Minnesota 55060
Phone: (507)451-7970
Fax: (507)451-7972

SCORE Office (Red Wing)
2000 W. Main St., Ste. 324
Red Wing, Minnesota 55066
Phone: (612)388-4079

SCORE Office (Southeastern
Minnesota)
Mashall Chamber of Commerce
220 S. Broadway, Ste. 100
Rochester, Minnesota 55904
Phone: (507)288-1122
Fax: (507)282-8960

SCORE Office (Brainerd)
Brainerd Chamber of Commerce

St. Cloud, Minnesota 56301
Phone: (612)255-4955
Fax: (612)255-4957

SCORE Office (Central Area)
4191 2nd St. S
St. Cloud, Minnesota 56301-3600
Phone: (612)255-4955

SCORE Office (St. Paul)
St. Paul Chamber of Commerce
55 5th St. E, No. 101
St. Paul, Minnesota 55101-1713
Phone: (612)223-5010

SCORE Office (Winona)
Box 870
Winona, Minnesota 55987
Phone: (507)452-2272
Fax: (507)454-8814

SCORE Office (Worthington)
Worthington Chamber of Commerce
1121 3rd Ave.
Worthington, Minnesota 56187
Phone: (507)372-2919
Fax: (507)372-2827

Mississippi

SCORE Office (Delta)
Greenville Chamber of Commerce
915 Washington Ave.
PO Box 933
Greenville, Mississippi 38701
Phone: (601)378-3141
Fax: (601)378-3143

SCORE Office (Gulfcoast)
c/o Small Business Administration
Hancock Plz., Ste. 1001
Gulfport, Mississippi 39501-7758
Phone: (601)863-4449

SCORE Office (Jackson)
1st Jackson Center, Ste. 400
101 W. Capitol St.
Jackson, Mississippi 39201
Phone: (601)965-5533

SCORE Office (Meridian)
5220 16th Ave.
Meridian, Mississippi 39305
Phone: (601)482-4412

Missouri

SCORE Office (Lake Ozark)
University Extension
113 Kansas St.
PO Box 1405
Camdenton, Missouri 65020
Phone: (314)346-2644
Fax: (314)346-2694

Chamber of Commerce (Cape
Girardeau)
c/o Chamber of Commerce
PO Box 98
Cape Girardeau, Missouri 63702-
0098
Phone: (314)335-3312

SCORE Office (Mid-Missouri)
c/o Milo Dahl
1705 Halstead Ct.
Columbia, Missouri 65203
Phone: (314)874-1132

SCORE Office (Ozark-Gateway)
101 E. Washington St.
Cuba, Missouri 65453-1826
Phone: (314)885-4954

SCORE Office (Kansas City)
323 W. 8th St., Ste. 104
Kansas City, Missouri 64105
Phone: (816)374-6675
Fax: (816)374-6759

SCORE Office (Sedalia)
c/o State Fair Community College
Lucas Place
323 W. 8th St., Ste.104
Kansas City, Missouri 64105
Phone: (816)374-6675

SCORE Office (Tri-Lakes)
HCRI Box 85
Lampe, Missouri 65681
Phone: (417)858-6798

SCORE Office (Southeast Missouri)
c/o Carl Trautman
505 Lalor Dr.
Manchester, Missouri 63011
Phone: (314)256-3331

SCORE Office (Mexico)
Mexico Chamber of Commerce
111 N. Washington St.

Mexico, Missouri 65265
Phone: (314)581-2765

SCORE Office (Poplar Bluff Area)
c/o James W. Carson, Chair
Rte. 1, Box 280
Neelyville, Missouri 63954
Phone: (314)785-4727

SCORE Office (St. Joseph)
3418 W. Colony Sq.
St. Joseph, Missouri 64506
Phone: (816)232-9793

SCORE Office (St. Louis)
815 Olive St., Rm. 242
St. Louis, Missouri 63101-1569
Phone: (314)539-6600
Fax: (314)889-7687

SCORE Office (Lewis & Clark)
425 Spencer Rd.
St. Peters, Missouri 63376
Phone: (314)928-2900

SCORE Office (Springfield)
c/o Small Business Administration
620 S. Glenstone, Ste. 110
Springfield, Missouri 65802-3200
Phone: (417)864-7670
Fax: (417)864-4108

Montana

SCORE Office (Billings)
815 S. 27th St.
Billings, Montana 59101
Phone: (406)245-4111

SCORE Office (Bozeman)
1205 E. Main St.
Bozeman, Montana 59715
Phone: (406)586-5421
Fax: (406)586-8286

SCORE Office (Butte)
2950 Harrison Ave.
Butte, Montana 59701
Phone: (406)494-5595

SCORE Office (Great Falls)
815 2nd St. S.
Great Falls, Montana 59405
Phone: (406)761-4434

SCORE Office (Helena)
Federal Bldg.

301 S. Park
Drawer 10054
Helena, Montana 59626-0054
Phone: (406)449-5381
Fax: (406)449-5474

SCORE Office (Kalispell)
2 Main St.
Kalispell, Montana 59901
Phone: (406)756-5271
Fax: (406)752-6665

SCORE Office (Missoula)
802 Normans Ln.
Missoula, Montana 59803
Phone: (406)543-6623

Nebraska

SCORE Office (Columbus)
1823 27th St.
Columbus, Nebraska 68601
Phone: (402)564-2769

SCORE Office (North Platte)
414 E. 16th St.
Cozad, Nebraska 69130
Phone: (308)784-2690

SCORE Office (Fremont)
PO Box 325
Freemont Chamber of Commerce
92 W. 5th St.
Fremont, Nebraska 68025
Phone: (402)721-2641

SCORE Office (Hastings)
Box 42
Kearney, Nebraska 68848
Phone: (308)234-9647

SCORE Office (Lincoln)
8800 East O St.
Lincoln, Nebraska 68520
Phone: (402)437-2409

SCORE Office (Norfolk)
504 Pierce St.
Norfolk, Nebraska 68701
Phone: (402)371-0940

SCORE Office (Nebraska Small
Business Development Center)
11145 Mill Valley Rd.
Omaha, Nebraska 68154
Phone: (402)221-3604

SCORE Office (Panhandle)
11145 Mill Valley Rd.
Omaha, Nebraska 68154
Phone: (402)221-3604

Nevada

SCORE Office (Incline Village)
c/o Incline Village Chamber of
Commerce
969 Tahoe Blvd.
Incline Village, Nevada 89451
Phone: (702)831-7327
Fax: (702)832-1605

SCORE Office (Carson City)
301 E. Stewart
PO Box 7527
Las Vegas, Nevada 89125
Phone: (702)388-6104

SCORE Office (Las Vegas)
301 E. Stewart
Box 7527
Las Vegas, Nevada 89125
Phone: (702)388-6104

SCORE Office (Northern Nevada)
50 S. Virginia St., No. 233
PO Box 3216
Reno, Nevada 89505-3216
Phone: (702)784-5477

New Hampshire

SCORE Office (North Country)
PO Box 34
Berlin, New Hampshire 03570
Phone: (603)752-1090

SCORE Office (Concord)
PO Box 1258
Concord, New Hampshire 03302-1258
Phone: (603)225-7763

SCORE Office (Dover)
299 Central Ave.
Dover, New Hampshire 03820
Phone: (603)742-2218
Fax: (603)749-6317

SCORE Office (Monadnock)
34 Mechanic St.
Keene, New Hampshire 03431-3421
Phone: (603)352-0320

SCORE Office (Lakes Region)
67 Water St., Ste. 105

Laconia, New Hampshire 03246
Phone: (603)524-9168

SCORE Office (Upper Valley)
First New Hampshire Bank Bldg.
316 First
Lebanon, New Hampshire 03766
Phone: (603)448-3491

SCORE Office (Merrimack Valley)
275 Chestnut St., Rm. 618
Manchester, New Hampshire 03103
Phone: (603)666-7561

SCORE Office (Seacoast)
195 Commerce Way, Unit-A
Portsmouth, New Hampshire 03801-
3251
Phone: (603)433-0576

New Jersey

SCORE Office (Chester)
c/o John C. Apelian, Chair
5 Old Mill Rd.
Chester, New Jersey 07930
Phone: (908)879-7080

SCORE Office (Greater Princeton)
4 A George Washington Dr.
Cranbury
New Jersey
08512
Phone: (609)520-1776

SCORE Office (Freehold)
Western Monmouth Chamber of
Commerce
36 W. Main St.
Freehold, New Jersey 07728
Phone: (908)462-3030
Fax: (908)462-2123

SCORE Office (Monmouth)
Brookdale Community College
Career Services
765 Newman Springs Rd.
Lincroft, New Jersey 07738
Phone: (908)224-2573

SCORE Office (Manalapan)
Monmough Library
125 Symmes Dr.
Manalapan, New Jersey 07726
Phone: (908)431-7220

SCORE Office (Jersey City)
2 Gateway Ctr., 4th Fl.
Newark, New Jersey 07102
Phone: (201)645-3982
Fax: (201)645-6265

SCORE Office (Newark)
2 Gateway Center, 4th Fl.
Newark, New Jersey 07102-5553
Phone: (201)645-3982

SCORE Office (Bergen County)
327 E. Ridgewood Ave.
Paramus, New Jersey 07652
Phone: (201)599-6090

SCORE Office (Pennsauken)
United Jersey Bank
4900 Rte. 70
Pennsauken, New Jersey 08109
Phone: (609)486-3421

SCORE Office (Southern New
Jersey)
c/o United Jersey Bank
4900 Rte. 70
Pennsauken, New Jersey 08109
Phone: (609)486-3421

SCORE Office (Shrewsbury)
Monmouth County Library
Hwy. 35
Shrewsbury, New Jersey 07702
Phone: (908)842-5995
Fax: (908)219-6140

SCORE Office (Somerset)
Paritan Valley Community College
PO Box 3300
Somerville, New Jersey 08876
Phone: (908)218-8874

SCORE Office (Ocean County)
33 Washington St.
Toms River, New Jersey 08754
Phone: (908)505-6033

SCORE Office (Wall)
Wall Library
2700 Allaire Rd.
Wall, New Jersey 07719
Phone: (908)449-8877

SCORE Office (Wayne)
2055 Hamburg Tpke.
Wayne, New Jersey 07470
Phone: (201)831-7788
Fax: (201)831-9112

New Mexico

SCORE Office (Albuquerque)
Silver Sq., Ste. 330
625 Silver Ave., SW
Albuquerque, New Mexico 87102
Phone: (505)766-1900

SCORE Office (Las Cruces)
Loretto Towne Center
505 S. Main St., Ste. 125
Las Cruces, New Mexico 88001
Phone: (505)523-5627

SCORE Office (Roswell)
Federal Bldg., Rm. 237
Roswell, New Mexico 88201
Phone: (505)625-2112

SCORE Office (Santa Fe)
Montoya Federal Bldg.
120 Federal Place, Rm. 307
Santa Fe, New Mexico 87501
Phone: (505)988-6302

New York

SCORE Office (Northeast)
Lee O'Brien Office Bldg., Rm. 815
Pearl & Clinton Aves.
Albany,New York12207
Phone: (518)472-6300

SCORE Office (Auburn)
c/o Auburn Chamber of Commerce
30 South St.
PO Box 675
Auburn, New York 13021
Phone: (315)252-7291

SCORE Office (South Tier Binghamton)
Metro Center, 2nd Fl.
49 Court St.
PO Box 995
Binghamton, New York 13902
Phone: (607)772-8860

SCORE Office (Queens County City)
12055 Queens Blvd., Rm. 333
Borough Hall, New York 11424
Phone: (718)263-8961

SCORE Office (Buffalo)
Federal Bldg., Rm. 1311
111 W. Huron St.

Buffalo, New York 14202
Phone: (716)846-4301

SCORE Office (Canandaigua)
Chamber of Commerce Bldg.
113 S. Main St.
Canandaigua, New York 14424
Phone: (716)394-4400
Fax: (716)394-4546

SCORE Office (Chemung)
c/o Small Business Administration, 4th Fl.
333 E. Water St.
Elmira, New York 14901
Phone: (607)734-3358

SCORE Office (Geneva)
Chamber of Commerce Bldg.
PO Box 587
Geneva, New York 14456
Phone: (315)789-1776
Fax: (315)789-3993

SCORE Office (Glens Falls)
Adirondack Region Chamber of Commerce
84 Broad St.
Glens Falls, New York 12801
Phone: (518)798-8463
Fax: (518)745-1433

SCORE Office (Orange County)
Orange County Chamber of Commerce
40 Matthews St.
Goshen, New York 10924
Phone: (914)294-8080
Fax: (914)294-6121

SCORE Office (Huntington Area)
c/o Huntington Chamber of Commerce
151 W. Carver St.
Huntington, New York 11743
Phone: (516)423-6100

SCORE Office (Tompkins County)
c/o Tompkins County Chamber of Commerce
904 E. Shore Dr.
Ithaca, New York 14850
Phone: (607)273-7080

SCORE Office (Long Island City)
120-55 Queens Blvd.

Jamaica, New York 11424
Phone: (718)263-8961
Fax: (718)263-9032

SCORE Office (Chatauqua)
c/o Chatauqua Chamber of Commerce
101 W. 5th St.
Jamestown, New York 14701
Phone: (716)484-1103

SCORE Office (Brookhaven)
Dept. of Economic Development
3233 Rte. 112
Medford, New York 11763
Phone: (516)451-6563

SCORE Office (Melville)
35 Pinelawn Rd., Rm. 207-W
Melville, New York 11747
Phone: (516)454-0771

SCORE Office (Nassau County)
400 County Seat Dr., No. 140
Mineola, New York 11501
Phone: (516)571-3304

SCORE Office (Mount Vernon)
c/o Mount Vernon Chamber of Commerce
4 N. 7th Ave.
Mount Vernon, New York 10550
Phone: (914)667-7500

SCORE Office (New York)
26 Federal Plz., Rm. 3100
New York, New York 10278
Phone: (212)264-4507

SCORE Office (Newburgh)
47 Grand St.
Newburgh, New York 12550
Phone: (914)562-5100

SCORE Office (Owego)
Tioga County Chamber of Commerce
188 Front St.
Owego, New York 13827
Phone: (607)687-2020

SCORE Office (Peekskill)
c/o Peekskill Chamber of Commerce
1 S. Division St.
Peekskill, New York 10566
Phone: (914)737-3600
Fax: (914)737-0541

SCORE Office (Penn Yan)
Penn Yan Chamber of Commerce
2375 Rte. 14A
Penn Yan, New York 14527
Phone: (315)536-3111

SCORE Office (Dutchess)
c/o Chamber of Commerce
110 Main St.
Poughkeepsie, New York 12601
Phone: (914)454-1700

SCORE Office (Rochester)
601 Keating Federal Bldg., Rm. 410
100 State St.
Rochester, New York 14614
Phone: (716)263-6473

SCORE Office (Saranac Lake)
30 Main St.
Saranac Lake, New York 12983
Phone: (315)448-0415

SCORE Office (Suffolk)
286 Main St.
Setauket, New York 11733
Phone: (516)751-3886

SCORE Office (Staten Island)
c/o Staten Island Chamber of
Commerce
130 Bay St.
Staten Island, New York 10301
Phone: (718)727-1221

SCORE Office (Ulster)
Ulster County Community College
Clinton Bldg., Rm. 107
Stone Ridge, New York 12484
Phone: (914)687-5035

SCORE Office (Syracuse)
100 S. Clinton St., Rm. 1073
Syracuse, New York 13260
Phone: (315)448-0422

SCORE Office (Oneida)
SUNY Institute of Technology
PO Box 3050
Utica, New York 13504-3050
Phone: (315)792-7553

SCORE Office (Watertown)
CAPC Office
518 Davidson St.
PO Box 899

Watertown, New York 13601
Phone: (315)788-1200

SCORE Office (Westchester)
350 Main St.
White Plains, New York 10601
Phone: (914)948-3907

SCORE Office (Yonkers)
c/o Yonkers Chamber of Commerce
540 Nepperhan Ave., Ste.200
Yonkers, New York 10701
Phone: (914)963-0332

North Carolina

SCORE Office (Asheville)
Federal Bldg., Rm. 259
151 Patton
Asheville, North Carolina 28801
Phone: (704)271-4786

SCORE Office (Chapel Hill)
c/o Chapel Hill/Carrboro Chamber of
Commerce
104 S. Estes Dr.
PO Box 2897
Chapel Hill, North Carolina 27514
Phone: (919)967-7075

SCORE Office (Coastal Plains)
PO Box 2897
Chapel Hill, North Carolina 27515
Phone: (919)967-7075
Fax: (919)968-6874

SCORE Office (Charlotte)
200 N. College St., Ste. A-2015
Charlotte, North Carolina 28202
Phone: (704)344-6576

SCORE Office (Durham)
411 W. Chapel Hill St.
Durham, North Carolina 27701-3616
Phone: (919)541-2171

SCORE Office (Gastonia)
c/o Gastonia Chamber of Commerce
PO Box 2168
Gastonia, North Carolina 28053
Phone: (704)864-2621
Fax: (704)854-8723

SCORE Office (Greensboro)
400 W. Market St., Ste. 410
Greensboro, North Carolina

27401-2241
Phone: (919)333-5399

SCORE Office (Henderson)
PO Box 917
Henderson, North Carolina 27536
Phone: (919)492-2061
Fax: (919)430-0460

SCORE Office (Hendersonville)
Federal Bldg., Rm. 108
W. 4th Ave. & Church St.
Hendersonville, North Carolina 28792
Phone: (704)693-8702

SCORE Office (Unifour)
c/o Catawba County Chamber of
Commerce
PO Box 1828
Hickory, North Carolina 28603
Phone: (704)328-6111

SCORE Office (High Point)
c/o High Point Chamber of
Commerce
1101 N. Main St.
High Point, North Carolina 27262
Phone: (910)882-8625

SCORE Office (Outer Banks)
c/o Outer Banks Chamber of
Commerce
PO Box 1757
Kill Devil Hills, North Carolina
27948
Phone: (919)441-8144

SCORE Office (Down East)
PO Box 14294
New Bern, North Carolina 28561
Phone: (919)633-6688

SCORE Office (Kinston)
PO Box 14294
New Bern, North Carolina 28561
Phone: (919)633-6688

SCORE Office (Raleigh)
Century Post Office Bldg., Ste. 306
PO Box 406
Raleigh, North Carolina 27602
Phone: (919)856-4739

SCORE Office (Sanford)
Small Business Assistance Center
1801 Nash St.
Sanford, North Carolina 27330

Phone: (919)774-6442
Fax: (919)776-8739

SCORE Office (Sandhills Area)
c/o Sand Area Chamber of Commerce
1480 Hwy. 15-501
PO Box 458
Southern Pines, North Carolina 28387
Phone: (910)692-3926

SCORE Office (Wilmington)
Alton Lennon Federal Bldg.
2 Princess St., Ste. 103
Wilmington, North Carolina 28401-3958
Phone: (919)343-4576

North Dakota

SCORE Office (Bismarck-Mandan)
418 E. Broadway Ave.
PO Box 1912
Bismarck, North Dakota 58501-1912
Phone: (701)250-4303

SCORE Office (Fargo)
657 2nd Ave., Rm. 225
PO Box 3086
Fargo, North Dakota 58108-3083
Phone: (701)239-5677

SCORE Office (Upper Red River)
202 N. 3rd St.
Grand Forks, North Dakota 58203
Phone: (701)772-7271

SCORE Office (Minot)
PO Box 507
Minot, North Dakota 58701-0507
Phone: (701)852-6883

Ohio

SCORE Office (Akron)
c/o Akron Regional Development
Board
One Cascade Plz., 7th Fl.
Akron, Ohio 44308
Phone: (216)379-3163

SCORE Office (Ashland)
Ashland University
Gill Center
47 W. Main St.
Ashland, Ohio 44805
Phone: (419)281-4584

SCORE Office (Canton)
116 Cleveland Ave. NW, Ste. 601
Canton, Ohio 44702-1720
Phone: (216)453-6047

SCORE Office (Chillicothe)
165 S. Paint St.
Chillicothe, Ohio 45601
Phone: (614)772-4530

SCORE Office (Cincinnati)
Ameritrust Bldg., Rm. 850
525 Vine St.
Cincinnati, Ohio 45202
Phone: (513)684-2812

SCORE Office (Cleveland)
Eaton Center, Ste. 620
1100 Superior Ave.
Cleveland, Ohio 44114-2507
Phone: (216)522-4194

SCORE Office (Columbus)
2 Nationwide Plz., Ste. 1400
Columbus, Ohio 43215-2542
Phone: (614)469-2357

SCORE Office (Dayton)
Dayton Federal Bldg., Rm. 505
201 W. Second St.
Dayton, Ohio 45402-1430
Phone: (513)225-2887

SCORE Office (Defiance)
Defiance Chamber of Commerce
615 W. 3rd St.
PO Box 130
Defiance, Ohio 43512
Phone: (419)782-7946

SCORE Office (Findlay)
Findlay Chamber of Commerce
123 E. Main Cross St.
PO Box 923
Findlay, Ohio 45840
Phone: (419)422-3314

SCORE Office (Lima)
147 N. Main St.
Lima, Ohio 45801
Phone: (419)222-6045
Fax: (419)229-0266

SCORE Office (Mansfield)
Mansfield Chamber of Commerce
55 N. Mulberry St.
Mansfield, Ohio 44902
Phone: (419)522-3211

SCORE Office (Marietta)
Marietta College
Thomas Hall
Marietta, Ohio 45750
Phone: (614)373-0268

SCORE Office (Medina)
County Administrative Bldg.
144 N. Broadway
Medina, Ohio 44256
Phone: (216)764-8650

SCORE Office (Licking County)
50 W. Locust St.
Newark, Ohio 43055
Phone: (614)345-7458

SCORE Office (Salem)
2491 State Rte. 45 S
Salem, Ohio 44460
Phone: (216)332-0361

SCORE Office (Tiffin)
Tiffin Chamber of Commerce
62 S. Washington St.
Tiffin, Ohio 44883
Phone: (419)447-4141
Fax: (419)447-5141

SCORE Office (Toledo)
1946 N. 13th St., Rm. 352
Toledo, Ohio 43624
Phone: (419)259-7598

SCORE Office (Wooster)
377 W. Liberty St.
Wooster, Ohio 44691
Phone: (216)262-5735

SCORE Office (Youngstown)
Youngstown University
306 Williamson Hall
Youngstown, Ohio 44555
Phone: (216)746-2687

Oklahoma

SCORE Office (Anadarko)
PO Box 366
Anadarko, Oklahoma 73005
Phone: (405)247-6651

SCORE Office (Ardmore)
PO Box 1585
Ardmore, Oklahoma 73402
Phone: (405)223-7765

SCORE Office (Northeast Oklahoma)
Bank of Oklahoma Bldg.
210 S. Main
Grove, Oklahoma 74344
Phone: (918)786-4729

SCORE Office (Lawton)
Federal Bldg., Rm. 107
431 East Ave.
Lawton, Oklahoma 73501
Phone: (405)353-8726

SCORE Office (Oklahoma City)
c/o SBA, Oklahoma Tower Bldg.
210 Park Ave., No. 1300
Oklahoma City, Oklahoma 73102
Phone: (405)231-5163

SCORE Office (Stillwater)
Stillwater Chamber of Commerce
439 S. Main
Stillwater, Oklahoma 74074
Phone: (405)372-5573
Fax: (405)372-4316

SCORE Office (Tulsa)
Tulsa Chamber of Commerce
616 S. Boston, Ste. 406
Tulsa, Oklahoma 74119
Phone: (918)581-7462

Oregon

SCORE Office (Bend)
c/o Bend Chamber of Commerce
63085 N. Hwy. 97
Bend, Oregon 97701
Phone: (503)382-3221

SCORE Office (Willamette)
1401 Willamette St.
PO Box 1107
Eugene, Oregon 97401-4003
Phone: (503)484-5485

SCORE Office (Florence)
c/o Lane Community College, Chuck
Temple
3149 Oak St.
Florence, Oregon 97439
Phone: (503)997-8444
Fax: (503)997-8448

SCORE Office (Southern Oregon)
132 W. Main St.
Medford, Oregon 97501
Phone: (503)776-4220

SCORE Office (Portland)
222 SW Columbia, Ste. 500
Portland, Oregon 97201
Phone: (503)326-3441

SCORE Office (Salem)
PO Box 4024
Salem, Oregon 97302-1024
Phone: (503)370-2896

Pennsylvania

SCORE Office (Altoona-Blair)
c/o Altoona-Blair Chamber of
Commerce
1212 12th Ave.
Altoona, Pennsylvania 16601-3493
Phone: (814)943-8151

SCORE Office (Lehigh Valley)
Lehigh University
Rauch Bldg. 37
621 Taylor St.
Bethlehem, Pennsylvania 18015
Phone: (610)758-4496

SCORE Office (Butler County)
100 N. Main St.
PO Box 1082
Butler, Pennsylvania 16003
Phone: (412)283-2222
Fax: (412)283-0224

SCORE Office (Cumberland Valley)
Chambersburg Chamber of
Commerce
75 S. 2nd St.
Chambersburg, Pennsylvania 17201
Phone: (717)264-4496

SCORE Office (Monroe County-
Stroudsburg)
556 Main St.
East Stroudsburg, Pennsylvania
18301
Phone: (717)421-4433

SCORE Office (Erie)
120 W. 9th St.
Erie, Pennsylvania 16501
Phone: (814)871-5650

SCORE Office (Bucks County)
c/o Bucks County Chamber of
Commerce
409 Hood Blvd.

Fairless Hills, Pennsylvania 19030
Phone: (215)943-8850

SCORE Office (Hanover)
146 Broadway
Hanover, Pennsylvania 17331
Phone: (717)637-6130
Fax: (717)637-9127

SCORE Office (Harrisburg)
100 Chestnut, Ste. 309
Harrisburg, Pennsylvania 17101
Phone: (717)782-3874

SCORE Office (Montgomery County)
Baederwood Shopping Center
1653 The Fairways, Ste. 204
Jenkintown, Pennsylvania 19046
Phone: (215)885-3027

SCORE Office (Kittanning)
c/o Kittanning Chamber of Commerce
2 Butler Rd.
Kittanning, Pennsylvania 16201
Phone: (412)543-1305
Fax: (412)543-6206

SCORE Office (Lancaster)
118 W. Chestnut St.
Lancaster, Pennsylvania 17603
Phone: (717)397-3092

SCORE Office (Westmoreland
County)
St. Vincent College
Latrobe, Pennsylvania 15650
Phone: (412)539-7505

SCORE Office (Lebanon)
252 N. 8th St.
PO Box 899
Lebanon, Pennsylvania 17042-0899
Phone: (717)273-3727
Fax: (717)273-7940

SCORE Office (Lewistown)
Lewistown Chamber of Commerce
3 W. Monument Sq., Ste. 204
Lewistown, Pennsylvania 17044
Phone: (717)248-6713
Fax: (717)248-6714

SCORE Office (Delaware County)
Delaware County Chamber of
Commerce
602 E. Baltimore Pike
Media, Pennsylvania 19063

Phone: (610)565-3677
Fax: (610)565-1606

SCORE Office (Milton Area)
112 S. Front St.
Milton, Pennsylvania 17847
Phone: (717)742-7341
Fax: (717)792-2008

SCORE Office (Mon-Valley)
435 Donner Ave.
Monessen, Pennsylvania 15062
Phone: (412)684-4277

SCORE Office (Monroeville)
William Penn Plaza
2790 Mosside Blvd., Ste. 295
Monroeville, Pennsylvania 15146
Phone: (412)856-0622
Fax: (412)856-1030

SCORE Office (Airport Area)
Chamber of Commerce
986 Brodhead Rd.
Moon Twp, Pennsylvania 15108-2398
Phone: (412)264-6270
Fax: (412)264-1575

SCORE Office (Northeast)
8601 E. Roosevelt Blvd.
Philadelphia, Pennsylvania 19152
Phone: (215)332-3400
Fax: (215)332-6050

SCORE Office (Philadelphia)
3535 Market St., Rm. 4480
Philadelphia, Pennsylvania 19104
Phone: (215)596-5077

SCORE Office (Pittsburgh)
960 Penn Ave., 5th Fl.
Pittsburgh, Pennsylvania 15222
Phone: (412)644-5447

SCORE Office (Tri-County)
238 High St.
Pottstown, Pennsylvania 19464
Phone: (610)327-2673

SCORE Office (Reading)
c/o Reading Chamber of Commerce
645 Penn St.
Reading, Pennsylvania 19601
Phone: (610)376-6766

SCORE Office (Scranton)
Federal Bldg., Rm. 104

Washington Ave. & Linden
Scranton, Pennsylvania 18503
Phone: (717)347-4611

SCORE Office (Central
Pennsylvania)
200 Innovation Blvd., Ste. 242-B
State College, Pennsylvania 16803
Phone: (814)234-9415

SCORE Office (Uniontown)
Federal Bldg.
Pittsburg St.
PO Box 2065 DTS
Uniontown, Pennsylvania 15401
Phone: (412)437-4222

SCORE Office (Warren County)
Warren County Chamber of
Commerce
315 2nd Ave.
PO Box 942
Warren, Pennsylvania 16365
Phone: (814)723-9017

SCORE Office (Waynesboro)
323 E. Main St.
Waynesboro, Pennsylvania 17268
Phone: (717)762-7123
Fax: (717)962-7124

SCORE Office (Chester County)
Government Service Center, Ste. 281
601 Westtown Rd.
West Chester, Pennsylvania 19382-
4538
Phone: (610)344-6910

SCORE Office (Wilkes-Barre)
20 N. Pennsylvania Ave.
Wilkes Barre, Pennsylvania 18702
Phone: (717)826-6502

SCORE Office (North Central
Pennsylvania)
240 W. 3rd St., Rm. 304
PO Box 725
Williamsport, Pennsylvania 17703
Phone: (717)322-3720

SCORE Office (York)
Cyber Center
1600 Pennsylvania Ave.
York, Pennsylvania 17404
Phone: (717)845-8830

Puerto Rico

SCORE Office (Puerto Rico & Virgin
Islands)
Citibank Towers Plaza, 2nd Fl.
252 Ponce de Leon Ave.
San Juan, Puerto Rico 00918-2041
Phone: (809)766-5001

Rhode Island

SCORE Office (Barrington)
Barrington Public Library
281 County Rd.
Barrington, Rhode Island 02806
Phone: (401)247-1920
Fax: (401)247-3763

SCORE Office (Woonsocket)
640 Washington Hwy.
Lincoln, Rhode Island 02865
Phone: (401)334-1000
Fax: (401)334-1009

SCORE Office (Wickford)
8045 Post Rd.
North Kingstown, Rhode Island
02852
Phone: (401)295-5566
Fax: (401)295-8987

SCORE Office (J.G.E. Knight)
380 Westminster St.
Providence, Rhode Island 02903
Phone: (401)528-4571

SCORE Office (Warwick)
3288 Post Rd.
Warwick, Rhode Island 02886
Phone: (401)732-1100
Fax: (401)732-1101

SCORE Office (Westerly)
74 Post Rd.
Westerly, Rhode Island 02891
Phone: (401)596-7761
Free: (800)732-7636
Fax: (401)596-2190

South Carolina

SCORE Office (Aiken)
Aiken Chamber of Commerce
P.O. Box 892
Aiken, South Carolina 29802
Phone: (803)641-1111

Free: (800)542-4536
Fax: (803)641-4174

SCORE Office (Anderson)
Tri-County Technical College
Anderson Mall
3130 N. Main St.
Anderson, South Carolina 29621
Phone: (864)224-0453

SCORE Office (Coastal)
284 King St.
Charleston, South Carolina 29401
Phone: (803)727-4778

SCORE Office (Midlands)
Strom Thurmond Bldg., Rm. 358
1835 Assembly St.
Columbia, South Carolina 29201
Phone: (803)765-5131

SCORE Office (Piedmont)
Federal Bldg., Rm. B-02
300 E. Washington St.
Greenville, South Carolina 29601
Phone: (803)271-3638

SCORE Office (Greenwood)
Piedmont Technical College
PO Drawer 1467
Greenwood, South Carolina 29648
Phone: (864)223-8357

SCORE Office (Hilton Head)
Hilton Head Chamber of Commerce
PO Box 5647
Hilton Head Island, South Carolina
29938
Phone: (803)785-3673
Fax: (803)785-7110

SCORE Office (Grand Strand)
48th Executive Ct., Ste. 211
1109 48th Ave. N
Myrtle Beach, South Carolina 29577
Phone: (803)449-8538

SCORE Office (Spartanburg)
c/o Vernon Wyant Chamber of
Commerce
P.O. Box 1636
Spartanburg, South Carolina 29304
Phone: (864)594-5000
Fax: (864)594-5055

South Dakota

SCORE Office (Rapid City)
444 Mount Rushmore Rd., No. 209
Rapid City, South Dakota 57701
Phone: (605)394-5311

SCORE Office (Sioux Falls)
First Financial Center, No. 200
110 S. Phillips Ave.
Sioux Falls, South Dakota 57102-
1109
Phone: (605)330-4231

Tennessee

SCORE Office (Chattanooga)
Federal Bldg., Rm. 26
900 Georgia Ave.
Chattanooga, Tennessee 37402
Phone: (423)752-5190

SCORE Office (Cleveland)
P.O. Box 2275
Cleveland, Tennessee 37320
Phone: (423)472-6587
Fax: (423)472-2019

SCORE Office (Upper Cumberland
Center)
1225 S. Willow Ave.
Cookeville, Tennessee 38501
Phone: (615)432-4111
Fax: (615)432-6010

SCORE Office (Unicoi County)
c/o Chamber of Commerce
PO Box 713
Erwin, Tennessee 37650
Phone: (423)743-3000
Fax: (423)743-0942

SCORE Office (Greeneville)
115 Academy St.
Greeneville, Tennessee 37743
Phone: (423)638-4111
Fax: (423)638-5345

SCORE Office (Jackson)
c/o Jackson Chamber of Commerce
197 Auditorium St.
PO Box 1904
Jackson, Tennessee 38302
Phone: (901)423-2200

SCORE Office (Northeast Tennessee)
c/o Chamber of Commerce
2710 S. Roan St.
Johnson City, Tennessee 37601
Phone: (423)929-7686
Fax: (423)461-8052

SCORE Office (Kingsport)
c/o Kingsport Chamber of Commerce
151 E. Main St.
Kingsport, Tennessee 37662
Phone: (423)392-8805

SCORE Office (Greater Knoxville)
Farragot Bldg., Ste. 224
530 S. Gay St.
Knoxville, Tennessee 37902
Phone: (423)545-4203

SCORE Office (Maryville)
Blount County Chamber of
Commerce
201 S. Washington St.
Maryville, Tennessee 37804-5728
Phone: (423)983-2241
Free: (800)525-6834
Fax: (423)984-1386

SCORE Office (Memphis)
Federal Bldg., Ste. 148
167 N. Main St.
Memphis, Tennessee 38103
Phone: (901)544-3588

SCORE Office (Nashville)
50 Vantage Way, Ste. 201
Nashville, Tennessee 37228-1500
Phone: (615)736-7621

Texas

SCORE Office (Abilene)
2106 Federal Post Office and Court
Bldg.
Abilene, Texas 79601
Phone: (915)677-1857

SCORE Office (Austin)
300 E. 8th St., Rm. 572
Austin, Texas 78701
Phone: (512)482-5112

SCORE Office (Golden Triangle)
c/o Community Bank
700 Calder, Ste. 101
Beaumont, Texas 77701
Phone: (409)838-6581

SCORE Office (Brownsville)
3505 Boca Chica Blvd., Ste. 305
Brownsville, Texas 78521
Phone: (210)541-4508

SCORE Office (Brazos Valley)
Victoria Bank & Trust
3000 Briarcrest, Ste. 302
Bryan, Texas 77802
Phone: (409)776-8876

SCORE Office (Cleburne)
Watergarden Pl., 9th Fl., Ste. 400
Cleburne, Texas 76031
Phone: (817)871-6002

SCORE Office (Corpus Christi)
c/o Robert Martens
606 N. Carancahua, Ste. 1200
Corpus Christi, Texas 78476
Phone: (512)888-3306
Fax: (512)888-3418

SCORE Office (Dallas)
17218 Preston Road, No. 3202
Dallas, Texas 75252
Phone: (214)733-0189

SCORE Office (El Paso)
10737 Gateway W, Ste. 320
El Paso, Texas 79935
Phone: (915)540-5155

SCORE Office (Bedford)
100 E. 15th St., Ste. 400
Fort Worth, Texas 76102
Phone: (817)871-6002

SCORE Office (Fort Worth)
100 E. 15th St., No. 24
Fort Worth, Texas 76102
Phone: (817)871-6002

SCORE Office (Garland)
2734 W. Kingsley Rd.
Garland, Texas 75041
Phone: (214)271-9224

SCORE Office (Granbury Chamber
of Commerce)
416 S. Morgan
Granbury, Texas 76048
Phone: (817)573-1622
Fax: (817)573-0805

SCORE Office (Lower Rio Grande
Valley)
222 E. Van Buren, Ste. 500

Harlingen, Texas 78550
Phone: (210)427-8533

SCORE Office (Houston)
9301 Southwest Fwy., Ste. 550
Houston, Texas 77074
Phone: (713)773-6565

SCORE Office (Irving)
c/o Irving Chamber of Commerce
3333 N. MacArthur Blvd., Ste. 100
Irving, Texas 75062
Phone: (214)252-8484
Fax: (214)252-6710

SCORE Office (Lubbock)
1611 10th St., Ste. 200
Lubbock, Texas 79401
Phone: (806)743-7462

SCORE Office (Midland)
Post Office Annex
200 E. Wall St., Rm. P121
Midland, Texas 79701
Phone: (915)687-2649

SCORE Office (Orange)
c/o Orange Chamber of Commerce
1012 Green Ave.
Orange, Texas 77630-5620
Phone: (409)883-3536
Free: (800)528-4906
Fax: (409)886-3247

SCORE Office (Plano)
c/o Plano Chamber of Commerce
1200 E. 15th St.
P.O. Drawer 940287
Plano, Texas 75094-0287
Phone: (214)424-7547
Fax: (214)422-5182

SCORE Office (Port Arthur)
c/o Port Arthur Chamber of
Commerce
4749 Twin City Hwy., Ste. 300
Port Arthur, Texas 77642
Phone: (409)963-1107
Fax: (409)963-3322

SCORE Office (Richardson)
c/o Richardson Chamber of
Commerce
411 Belle Grove
Richardson, Texas 75080
Phone: (214)234-4141

Free: (800)777-8001
Fax: (214)680-9103

SCORE Office (San Antonio)
c/o SBA, Federal Bldg., Rm. A527
727 E. Durango
San Antonio, Texas 78206
Phone: (210)229-5931

SCORE Office (Texarkana State
College)
819 State Line Ave.
PO Box 1468
Texarkana, Texas 75501
Phone: (903)792-7191

SCORE Office (East Texas)
1530 SW Loop 323, Ste. 100
Tyler, Texas 75701
Phone: (903)510-2975

SCORE Office (Waco)
Business Resource Center
4601 N. 19th St.
Waco, Texas 76708
Phone: (817)754-8898

SCORE Office (Wichita Falls)
Hamilton Bldg.
PO Box 1860
Wichita Falls, Texas 76307
Phone: (817)766-1602

Utah

SCORE Office (Ogden)
324 25th St., Ste. 6104
Ogden, Utah 84401
Phone: (801)625-5712

SCORE Office (Central Utah)
Old County Court House
51 S. University Ave.
Provo, Utah 84601
Phone: (801)379-2444

SCORE Office (Southern Utah)
c/o Dixie College Small Business
Development Center
225 South 700 East
St. George, Utah 84770
Phone: (801)673-4811

SCORE Office (Salt Lake)
125 S. State St., Rm. 2237
Salt Lake City, Utah 84138
Phone: (801)524-3211

Vermont

SCORE Office (Champlain Valley)
Winston Prouty Federal Bldg.
11 Lincoln St., Room 106
Essex Junction, Vermont 05452
Phone: (802)951-6762

SCORE Office (Montpelier)
c/o U.S. Small Business
Administration
87 State St., Rm. 205
PO Box 605
Montpelier, Vermont 05601
Phone: (802)828-4422

SCORE Office (Marble Valley)
Rutland Industrial Development Corp.
256 N. Main St.
Rutland, Vermont 05701-2413
Phone: (802)773-9147

SCORE Office (Northeast Kingdom)
c/o NCIC
20 Main St.
PO Box 904
St. Johnsbury, Vermont 05819
Phone: (802)748-5101

Virgin Islands

SCORE Office (St. Croix)
United Plaza Shopping Center
PO Box 4010, Christiansted
St. Croix, Virgin Islands 00822
Phone: (809)778-5380

SCORE Office (St. Thomas-St. John)
Federal Bldg., Rm. 21
Veterans Dr.
St. Thomas, Virgin Islands 00801
Phone: (809)774-8530

Virginia

SCORE Office (Arlington)
2009 N. 14th St., Ste. 111
Arlington, Virginia 22201
Phone: 703525-2400

SCORE Office (Blacksburg)
141 Jackson St.
Blacksburg, Virginia 24060
Phone: (540)552-4061

SCORE Office (Bristol)
20 Volunteer Pkwy.

PO Box 519
Bristol, Virginia 24203
Phone: (540)968-4399

SCORE Office (Central Virginia)
918 Emmet St. N, Ste. 200
Charlottesville, Virginia 22903-4878
Phone: (804)295-6712

SCORE Office (Alleghany Satellite)
c/o Chamber of Commerce
241 W. Main St.
Covington, Virginia 24426
Phone: (540)962-2178
Fax: (540)962-2179

SCORE Office (Central Fairfax)
3975 University Dr., Ste. 350
Fairfax, Virginia 22030
Phone: (703)591-2450

SCORE Office (Falls Church)
P.O. Box 491
Falls Church, Virginia 22040
Phone: (703)532-1050
Fax: (703)237-7904

SCORE Office (Glenns)
c/o Rappahannock Community
College
Glenns Campus
Box 287
Glenns, Virginia 23149
Phone: (804)693-9650

SCORE Office (Peninsula)
c/o Peninsula Chamber of Commerce
6 Manhattan Sq.
PO Box 7269
Hampton, Virginia 23666
Phone: (804)766-2000

SCORE Office (Tri-Cities)
c/o Chamber of Commerce
108 N. Main St.
Hopewell, Virginia 23860
Phone: (804)458-5536

SCORE Office (Lynchburg)
Federal Bldg.
1100 Main St.
Lynchburg, Virginia 24504-1714
Phone: (804)846-3235

SCORE Office (Danville)
c/o Martinsville Chamber of
Commerce

115 Broad St.
PO Box 709
Martinsville, Virginia 24112-0709
Phone: (540)632-6401

SCORE Office (Eastern Shore)
c/o Eastern Shore Chamber of
Commerce
Federal Bldg.
200 Grandby St.
Norfolk, Virginia 23510
Phone: (804)441-3733

SCORE Office (Norfolk)
Federal Bldg., Rm. 737
200 Granby St.
Norfolk, Virginia 23510
Phone: (804)441-3733

SCORE Office (Virginia Beach)
Virginia Beach Office of Hampton
Roads
Chamber of Commerce
200 Grandby St., Rm 737
Norfolk, Virginia 23510
Phone: (804)441-3733

SCORE Office (Greater Prince
William)
Prince William Chamber of
Commerce
4320 Ridgewood Center Dr.
Prince William, Virginia 22192
Phone: (703)590-5000

SCORE Office (Radford)
Radford Chamber of Commerce
1126 Norwood St.
Radford, Virginia 24141
Phone: (540)639-2202

SCORE Office (Richmond)
Dale Bldg., Ste. 200
1504 Santa Rosa Rd.
Richmond, Virginia 23229
Phone: (804)771-2400

SCORE Office (Roanoke)
Federal Bldg.
PO Box 1366, Rm. 716
Roanoke, Virginia 24007
Phone: (540)857-2834

SCORE Office (Fairfax)
8391 Old Courthouse Rd., Ste. 300
Vienna, Virginia 22182
Phone: (703)749-0400

SCORE Office (Greater Vienna)
513 Maple Ave. West
Vienna, Virginia 22180
Phone: (703)281-1333
Fax: (703)242-1482

SCORE Office (Shenandoah Valley)
c/o Waynesboro Chamber of
Commerce
301 W. Main St.
Waynesboro, Virginia 22980
Phone: (540)949-8203

SCORE Office (Williamsburg)
c/o Williamsburg Chamber of
Commerce
201 Penniman Rd.
Williamsburg, Virginia 23185
Phone: (804)229-6511

SCORE Office (Northern Virginia)
c/o Winchester-Frederick Chamber of
Commerce
1360 S. Pleasant Valley Rd.
Winchester, Virginia 22601
Phone: (540)662-4118

Washington

SCORE Office (Gray's Harbor)
c/o Gray's Harbor Chamber of
Commerce
506 Duffy St.
Aberdeen, Washington 98520
Phone: (360)532-1924
Fax: (360)533-7945

SCORE Office (Bellingham)
Fourth Corner, Economic
Development Group
PO Box 2803
1203 Cornwall Ave.
Bellingham, Washington 98227
Phone: (360)676-4255

SCORE Office (Everett)
Everett Public Library
2702 Hoyt Ave.
Everett, Washington 98201-3556
Phone: (206)259-8000

SCORE Office (Gig Harbor)
c/o Gig Harbor Chamber of
Commerce
3125 Judson St.

Gig Harbor, Washington 98335
Phone: (206)851-6865

SCORE Office (Kennewick)
Kennewick Chamber of Commerce
PO Box 6986
Kennewick, Washington 99336
Phone: (509)736-0510

SCORE Office (Puyallup)
Puyallup Chamber of Commerce
322 2nd St. SW
PO Box 1298
Puyallup, Washington 98371
Phone: (206)845-6755
Fax: (206)848-6164

SCORE Office (Seattle)
1200 6th Ave., Ste. 1700
Seattle, Washington 98174
Phone: (206)553-7311

SCORE Office (Spokane)
601 1st Ave. W, 10th Fl.
Spokane, Washington 99204-0317
Phone: (509)353-2820

SCORE Office (Clover Park)
PO Box 1933
Tacoma, Washington 98401-1933
Phone: (206)627-2175

SCORE Office (Tacoma)
950 Pacific Ave., No. 300
Tacoma, Washington 98402
Phone: (206)627-2175

SCORE Office (Fort Vancouver)
1200 Fort Vancouver Way
Box 8900
Vancouver, Washington 98668
Phone: (360)699-3241

SCORE Office (Walla Walla)
Walla Walla Small Business Cebter
500 Tausick Way
Walla Walla, Washington 99362
Phone: (509)527-4681

SCORE Office (Mid-Columbia)
c/o Greater Yakima Chamber of
Commerce
PO Box 1490
Yakima, Washington 98907
Phone: (509)248-2021

West Virginia

SCORE Office (Charleston)
1116 Smith St.
Charleston, West Virginia 25301
Phone: (304)347-5463

SCORE Office (Virginia Street)
1116 Smith St., Ste. 302
Charleston, West Virginia 25301
Phone: (304)347-5463

SCORE Office (Marion County)
PO Box 208
Fairmont, West Virginia 26555-0208
Phone: (304)363-0486

SCORE Office (Upper Monongahela
Valley)
c/o WZHTC
200 Fairmont Ave., Ste. 100
Fairmont, West Virginia 26554
Phone: (304)363-0486

SCORE Office (Huntington)
1101 6th Ave., Ste. 220
Huntington, West Virginia 25701-
2309
Phone: (304)523-4092

SCORE Office (Wheeling)
1310 Market St.
Wheeling, West Virginia 26003
Phone: (304)233-2575

Wisconsin

SCORE Office (Fox Cities)
227 S. Walnut St.
Box 1855
Appleton, Wisconsin 54915
Phone: (414)734-7101

SCORE Office (Beloit)
136 W. Grand Ave., Ste. 100
PO Box 717
Beloit, Wisconsin 53511
Phone: (608)365-8835
Fax: (608)365-9170

SCORE Office (Eau Claire)
Federal Bldg., Rm. B11
510 S. Barstow St.
Eau Claire, Wisconsin 54701
Phone: (715)834-1573

SCORE Office (Fond Du Lac)
c/o Fond Du Lac Chamber of
Commerce
207 N. Main St.
Fond Du Lac, Wisconsin 54935
Phone: (414)921-9500
Fax: (414)921-9559

SCORE Office (Green Bay)
835 Potts Ave.
Green Bay, Wisconsin 54305
Phone: (414)496-8930

SCORE Office (Janesville)
20 S. Main St., Ste. 11
PO Box 8008
Janesville, Wisconsin 53547
Phone: (608)757-3160
Fax: (608)757-3170

SCORE Office (La Crosse)
712 Main St.
PO Box 219
La Crosse, Wisconsin 54602-0219
Phone: (608)784-4880

SCORE Office (Madison)
4406 Somerset Lake
Madison, Wisconsin 53711
Phone: (608)831-5464

SCORE Office (Manitowoc)
Manitowoc Chamber of Commerce
1515 Memorial Dr.
PO Box 903
Manitowoc, Wisconsin 54221-0903
Phone: (414)684-5575
Fax: (414)684-1915

SCORE Office (Middleton)
c/o M&I Bank
7448 Hubbard Ave.
Middleton, Wisconsin 53562
Phone: (608)831-5464

SCORE Office (Milwaukee)
310 W. Wisconsin Ave., Ste. 425
Milwaukee, Wisconsin 53203
Phone: (414)297-3942

SCORE Office (Central Wisconsin)
c/o Chapter Chairperson
1224 Lindbergh Ave.
Stevens Point, Wisconsin54481
Phone: (715)344-7729

SCORE Office (Superior)
305 Harborview Pkwy.
Superior, Wisconsin 54880
Phone: (715)394-7716

SCORE Office (Waukesha)
c/o Waukesha Chamber of Commerce
223 Wisconsin Ave.
Waukesha, Wisconsin 53186-4926
Phone: (414)542-4249

SCORE Office (Wausau)
300 3rd St.
PO Box 6190
Wausau, Wisconsin 54402-6190
Phone: (715)845-6231

SCORE Office (Wisconsin Rapids)
2240 Kingston Rd.
Wisconsin Rapids, Wisconsin 54494
Phone: (715)423-1830

Wyoming

SCORE Office (Casper)
Federal Bldg., No. 2215
100 East B St.
Casper, Wyoming 82602
Phone: (307)261-6529

VENTURE CAPITAL & FINANCING COMPANIES

*This section contains a listing of financing
and loan companies in the United States
and Canada. These listings are arranged
alphabetically by country, state/territory/
province, then by city, then by
organization name.*

CANADA

Manitoba

Manitoba Industry, Trade and
Tourism
Small Business Services
Entrepreneurial Development
Business Start Program
155 Carlton St., 5th Fl.,Rm. 525
Winnipeg, Manitoba R3C 3H8
Phone: (204)945-7719
Free: (800)282-8069

Fax: (204)945-2804
A matching loan guarantee program
that will promote the success of new
business start-ups by ensuring that
entrepreneurs have a comprehensive
business plan, by offering business
training and counseling, and by
providing access to funding up to
$10,000 via a loan guarantee through
a number of existing financial
institutions.

Ontario

Industry and Science Canada
Small Business Loans Administration
Branch
235 Queen St., 8th Fl., E.
Ottawa, Ontario K1A 0H5
Phone: (613)954-5540
Fax: (613)952-0290

Quebec

Societe de Developpement Industriel
du Quebec
Small Business Revival Program
1126, Chemin Saint-Louis, 5th Fl.
Bureau 500
Sillery, Quebec G1S 1E5
Phone: (418)643-5172
Free: (800)461-AIDE
Fax: (418)528-2063
Allows businesses facing temporary
difficulties to obtain financial
assistance aimed at reinforcing their
financial structures.

Saskatchewan

Saskatchewan Department of
Economic Development
Investment Programs Branch
Labour-Sponsored Venture Capital
Program
1919 Saskatchewan Dr., 5th Fl.
Regina, Saskatchewan S4P 3V7
Phone: (306)787-2252
Fax: (306)787-3872
Promotes the formation of venture
capital corporations by employees of
a small business, to provide equity
capital for the expansion of existing
facilities or establishment of new

businesses. Federal and provincial tax credits are available to the investor.

UNITED STATES

Alabama

Alabama Small Business Investment Co.
1732 5th Ave. N
Birmingham, Alabama 35203
Phone: (205)324-5231
Fax: (205)324-5234
A minority enterprise small business investment company. Diversified industry preference.

Jefferson County Community Development
Planning and Community Development
805 N. 22nd St.
Birmingham, Alabama 35203
Phone: (205)325-5761
Fax: (205)325-5095
Provides loans for purchasing real estate, construction, working capital, or machinery and equipment.

FJC Growth Capital Corp.
200 W. Court Sq., Ste. 750
Huntsville. Alabama 35801
Phone: (205)922-2918
Fax: (205)922-2909
A minority enterprise small business investment company. Diversified industry preference.

Hickory Venture Capital Corp.
200 W. Side Sq., Ste.100
Huntsville, Alabama 35801
Phone: (205)539-1931
Fax: (205)539-5130
A small business investment corporation. Prefers to invest in later-stage companies. Will not consider oil and gas, or real estate investments.

Alabama Capital Corp.
16 Midtown Park E.
Mobile, Alabama 36606
Phone: (334)476-0700
Fax: (334)476-0026
David C. DeLaney, President
Preferred Investment Size: $400,000.

Investment Policies: Asset based loans with equity. Investment Types: Seed, early, expansion, later stages. Industry Preferences: Diversified. Geographic Preferences: Southeast.

First SBIC of Alabama
16 Midtown Park E.
Mobile, Alabama 36606
Phone: (334)476-0700
Fax: (334)476-0026
David C. DeLaney, President
Preferred Investment Size: $400,000.
Investment Policies: Asset based Loans with equity. Investment Types: Seed, early, expansion, later stages. Industry Preferences: Diversified. Geographic Preferences: Southeast.

Southern Development Council
E-mail: sdc@sdcinc.org
4101 C Wall St.
Montgomery, Alabama 36106
Phone: (334)244-1801
Fax: (334)244-1421
Statewide nonprofit financial packaging corporation. Helps small businesses arrange financing.

Alaska

Alaska Department of Commerce and Economic Development (Anchorage)
Industrial Development and Export Authority
480 W. Tudor Rd.
Anchorage, Alaska 99503-6690
Phone: (907)269-3000
Fax: (907)269-3044
Assists businesses in securing long-term financing for capital investments, such as the acquisition of equipment or the construction of a new plant, at moderate interest rates.

Alaska Department of Commerce and Economic Development (Anchorage)
Division of Investments
E-mail:
investments@commerce.state.ak.us
3601 C St., Ste. 724
Anchorage, Alaska 99503
Phone: (907)269-8150
Fax: (907)269-8147

Offers a program that assists purchasers to assume existing small business loans.

Calista Corp.
601 W. 5th Ave., Ste. 200
Anchorage, Alaska 99501-2225
Phone: (907)279-5516
Fax: (907)272-5060
A minority enterprise small business investment corporation. No industry preference.

Alaska Department of Commerce and Economic Development (Juneau)
Division of Investments
E-mail:
investments@commerce.state.ak.us
PO Box 34159
Juneau, Alaska 99803-4159
Phone: (907)465-2510
Free: (800)478-LOAN
Fax: (907)465-2103
Offers a program that assists purchasers to assume existing small business loans.

Alaska Department of Natural Resources
Division of Agriculture
Agricultural Revolving Loan Fund
PO Box 949
Palmer, Alaska 99645-0949
Phone: (907)745-7200
Free: (800)770-3276
Fax: (907)745-7112
Provides loans for farm development, general farm operations, chattel, and land clearing. Resident farmers, homesteaders, partnerships, and corporations are eligible.

Arizona

First Interstate Equity Corp.
100 W. Washington St.
Phoenix, Arizona 85003
Phone: (602)528-6447
Fax: (602)440-1320
A small business investment company. Diversified industry preference.

Rocky Mountain Equity Corp.
2525 E. Camelback Rd., Ste. 275

Phoenix, Arizona 85016
Phone: (602)955-6100
Fax: (602)956-5909
A small business investment
corporation. No industry preference.

Sundance Venture Partners, L.P.
(Phoenix)
400 E.Van Buren, Ste. 750
Phoenix, Arizona 85004
Phone: (602)259-3441
Fax: (602)259-1450
A small business investment
company.

Arizona Growth Partners
E-mail: jock@valleyventures.com
6155 N. Scottsdale Rd., Ste. 100
Scottsdale, Arizona 85250
Phone: (602)661-6600
Fax: (602)661-6262
Venture capital firm. Industry
preferences include high technology,
medical, biotechnology, and computer
industries.

First Commerce & Loan LP
5620 N. Kolb, No. 260
Tucson, Arizona 85715
Phone: (520)298-2500
Fax: (520)745-6112
A small business investment
company. Diversified industry
preference.

Arkansas

Southern Ventures, Inc.
605 Main St., Ste. 202
Arkadelphia, Arkansas 71923
Phone: (501)246-9627
Fax: (501)246-2182
A small business investment
company. Diversified industry
preference.

Arkansas Development Finance
Authority
PO Box 8023
Little Rock, Arkansas 72203-8023
Phone: (501)682-5900
Fax: (501)682-5859
Provides bond financing to small
borrowers, who may otherwise be
excluded from the bond market due to

high costs, by using umbrella bond
issues. Can provide interim financing
for approved projects awaiting a bond
issuance.

Capital Management Services, Inc.
1910 N. Grant St., Ste.200
Little Rock, Arkansas 72207-4427
Phone: (501)664-8613
A minority enterprise small business
investment corporation. No industry
preference.

Small Business Investment Capital,
Inc.
12103 Interstate 30
P.O. Box 3627
Little Rock, Arkansas 72203
Phone: 501455-6599
Fax: 501455-6556
Charles E. Toland, President
Preferred Investment Size: Up to
$230,000. Investment Policies: Loans.
Investment Types: Start-ups and debt
consolidation. Industry Preferences:
Supermarkets. Geographic
Preferences: Arkansas, Oklahoma,
Texas, Louisiana.

California

Calsafe Capital Corp.
245 E. Main St., Ste. 107
Alhambra, California 91801
Phone: (818)289-3400
Fax: (818)300-8025
A minority enterprise small business
investment company. Diversified
industry preference.

Ally Finance Corp.
9100 Wilshire Blvd., Ste. 408
Beverly Hills, California 90212
Phone: (310)550-8100
Fax: (310)550-6136
A small business investment
corporation. No industry preference.

Developers Equity Capital Corp.
447 S. Robertson Blvd. SE 101
Beverly Hills, California 90211
Phone: (310)550-7552
A small business investment
corporation. Real estate preferred.

Comdisco Venture Group (Corte
Madera)
770 Tamalais Dr., Ste. 300
Corte Madera, California 94925-1737
Phone: (415)927-6777
Fax: (415)927-6767
Prefers start-up businesses in fields of
semiconductors, computer hardware
and software, computer services and
systems, telecommunications, and
medical and biotechnology.
Investments range from $500,000 to
$5 million.

Domain Associates
650 Town Center Dr., Ste. 1830
Costa Mesa, California 92626
Phone: (714)434-6227
Fax: (714)434-6088
Venture capital firm providing early
stage financing. Areas of interest
include life sciences and
biotechnology companies
(biopharmaceuticals, medical devices,
diagnostics, and new materials).

Fairfield Venture Partners (Costa
Mesa)
650 Town Center Dr., Ste. 810
Costa Mesa, California 92626
Phone: (714)754-5717
Fax: (714)754-6802

First SBIC of California (Costa Mesa)
3029 Harbor Blvd.
Costa Mesa, California 92626
Phone: (714)668-6099
Fax: (714)668-6099
A small business investment
corporation and venture capital
company. No industry preference.

Pearl Capital, Inc.
575 Anton Blvd., Ste. 300
Costa Mesa, California 92626
Phone: (714)432-6301
Fax: (714)497-2560
Venture capital firm providing late
stage and mezzanine investments of
$1 million to $10 million. Prefers
investments of $2 million. Areas of
interest include diversified industries
and computer technology.

Westar Capital (Costa Mesa)
950 S. Coast Dr., Ste. 165
Costa Mesa, California 92626
Phone: (714)434-5160
Fax: (714)434-5166
Venture capital firm providing
management financing and corporate
buyouts. Areas of interest include
information, computer and business
services, health care, food processing,
and defense/aerospace.

Fulcrum Venture Capital Corp.
300 Corp. Pl.,Suite 380
Culver City, California 90230
Phone: (310)645-1271
Fax: (310)645-1272
A minority enterprise small business
investment corporation. No industry
preference.

Bay Partners
10600 N. De Anza Blvd., Ste. 100
Cupertino, California 95014
Phone: (408)725-2444
Fax: (408)446-4502
Venture capital supplier. Provides
start-up financing primarily to West
Coast technology companies that have
highly qualified management teams.
Initial investments range from
$100,000 to $800,000. Where large
investments are required, the
company will act as lead investor to
bring in additional qualified venture
investors.

El Dorado Ventures (Cupertino)
E-mail: garyk@eldoradoventures.com
20300 Stevens Creek Blvd., Ste. 395
Cupertino, California 95014
Phone: (408)725-2474
Fax: (408)252-2762

Grace Ventures Corp./Horn Venture
Partners
20300 Stevens Creek Blvd., Ste. 330
Cupertino, California 95014
Phone: (408)725-0774
Fax: (408)725-0327
Areas of interest include information
technology, life sciences, specialty
retail and consumer products,
restaurant, and biotechnology
industries.

Novus Ventures, L.P.
20111 Stevens Creek Blvd., Ste. 130
Cupertino, California 95014
Phone: (408)252-3900
Fax: (408)252-1713
Daniel D. Tompkins, Manager
Preferred Investment Size: $400,000
to $1 Million. Investment Policies:
Convertible debt, Convertible stock.
Industry Preferences: Information
technology. Geographic Preferences:
Western U.S.

Sundance Venture Partners, L.P.
10600 N. DeAnza Blvd., Ste. 215
Cupertino, California 95014
Phone: (408)257-8100
Fax: (408)257-8111
A small business investment
company. Diversified industry
preference.

Chemical Venture Partners (Los
Angeles)
840 Apollo St., Ste. 223 Chase
Capitol
El Segundo, California 90245
Phone: (310)335-1955
Fax: (310)335-1965
Venture capital firm providing later
stage financing. Areas of interest
include health, environmental,
service, distribution, manufacturing,
information services, and education.
Exclusions are real estate and high
technology.

Pacific Mezzanine Fund, L.P.
2200 Powell St., Ste. 1250
Emeryville, California 94608
Phone: (510)595-9800
Fax: (510)595-9801
David C. Woodward, General Partner
Preferred Investment Size: $2 TO $5
Million. Investment Policies: Loans
with equity features. Investment
Types: Expansion, later stage.
Industry Preferences: Diversified.
Geographic Preferences: Western US.

BankAmerica Ventures (Foster City)
950 Tower Ln., Ste. 700
Foster City, California 94404
Phone: (415)378-6000

Fax: (415)378-6040
Robert L. Boswell, Senior Vice
President

First American Capital Funding, Inc.
10840 Warner Ave., Ste. 202
Fountain Valley, California 92708
Phone: (714)965-7190
Fax: (714)965-7193
A minority enterprise small business
investment corporation. No industry
preference.

Opportunity Capital Corp.
2201 Walnut Ave.,Ste. 210
Fremont, California 94538-2261
Phone: (510)795-7000
Fax: (510)494-5439
A minority enterprise small business
investment corporation. No industry
preference.

Opportunity Capital Partners II, LP
2201 Walnut Ave., Ste. 210
Fremont, California 94538
Phone: (510)795-7000
Fax: (510)494-5439
A minority enterprise small business
investment company. Diversified
industry preference.

R and D Funding Corp.
440 Mission Ct., Ste. 250
Fremont, California 94539
Phone: (510)656-1949
Fax: (510)656-1949
Venture capital firm. Invests in high-
growth businesses. Direct investment
in research and development.

San Joaquin Business Investment
Group, Inc.
1900 Mariposa Mall, Ste. 100
Fresno, California 93721
Phone: (209)233-3580
Fax: (209)233-3709
A minority enterprise small business
investment company. Diversified
industry preference.

Magna Pacific Investments
330 N. Brand Blvd., Ste. 670
Glendale, California 91203
Phone: (818)547-0809
Fax: (818)547-9303

A minority enterprise small business investment company. Diversified industry preference.

Asian American Capital Corp.
1251 W. Tennyson Rd., Ste. 4
Hayward, California 94544-4423
Phone: (510)887-6888
A minority enterprise small business investment corporation. Diversified industry preferences.

Brentwood Venture Partners (Irvine)
1920 Main St., Ste. 820
Irvine, California 92614-7227
Phone: (714)251-1010
Fax: (714)251-1011
Prefers to invest in the electronics and health care industries.

Crosspoint Venture Partners (Irvine)
E-mail: roxie@crosspointvc.com
18552 MacArthur, Ste. 400
Irvine, California 92612-1220
Phone: (714)852-1611
Fax: (714)852-9804
Venture capital firm investing in medical, software, and telecommunications.

DSV Partners
E-mail: jbergman@packbell.net
1920 Main St., Ste. 820
Irvine, California 92614-7227
Phone: (714)475-4242
Fax: (714)475-1950
Venture capital firm. Prefers to invest in software, medical, biotechnical, environmental, and other high-growth technology companies.

Ventana Growth Fund L.P. (Irvine)
18881 Von Karman Ave., Ste. 350, Tower 17
Irvine, California 92715
Phone: (714)476-2204
Fax: (714)752-0223

South Bay Capital Corporation
5325 E. Pacific Coast Hwy.
Long Beach, California 90804
Phone: (310)597-3285
Fax: (310)498-7167
John Wang, Manager

Aspen Ventures West II, L.P.
E-mail: twhalen@aspenventures.com
1000 Fremont Ave., Ste. V
Los Altos, California 94024
Phone: (415)917-5670
Fax: (415)917-5677
Alexander Cilento, Mgr.
David Crocket, Mgr.
Preferred Investment Size: $500,000 to $2,5 million. Investment Policies: Equity. Investment Types: Early stage. Industry Preferences: Information technology. Geographic Preferences: Western U.S.

AVI Capital, L.P.
E-mail: vc@avicapital.com
1 1st St., Ste. 12
Los Altos, California 94022
Phone: (415)949-9862
Fax: (415)949-8510
P. Wolken, Mgr.
B. Weinman, Mgr.
Preferred Investment Size: $1,000,000. Investment Policies: Equity Only. Investment Types: Seed, early stage. Industry Preferences: High technology and electronic deals only. Geographic Preferences: West coast, California.

Crosspoint Venture Partners (Los Altos)
1 1st St., Ste. 2
Los Altos, California 94022
Phone: (415)948-8300
Fax: (415)948-6172
Venture capital partnership. Seeks to invest start-up capital in unique products, services, and/or market opportunities in high-technology and biotechnology industries located in the western United States.

HMS Group
1 1st St., Ste. 16
Los Altos, California 94022
Phone: (415)917-0390
Fax: (415)917-0394
Prefers communications industries.

MBW Management, Inc. (Los Altos)
350 2nd St., Ste. 4
Los Altos, California 94022

Phone: (415)941-2392
Fax: (415)941-2865

BankAmerica Capital Corp. (Costa Mesa)
PO Box 60049
Los Angeles, California 90060-0049
Phone: (714)973-8495
Venture capital firm preferring investments of $1 million- $3 million. Diversified industry preference.

Best Finance Corp.
4929 W. Wilshire Blvd., Ste. 407
Los Angeles, California 90010
Phone: (213)937-1636
Fax: (213)937-6393
Vincent Lee, General Manager
Preferred Investment Size: $50,000. Investment Policies: Loans and/or equity. Investment Types: Purchase, seed, expansion. Industry Preferences: Diversified. Geographic Preferences: California.

Brentwood Associates (Los Angeles)
11150 Santa Monica Blvd., Ste. 1200
Los Angeles, California 90025-3314
Phone: (310)477-6611
Fax: (310)477-1011
Venture capital supplier. Provides start-up and expansion financing to technology-based enterprises specializing in computing and data processing, electronics, communications, materials, energy, industrial automation, and bioengineering and medical equipment. Investments generally range from $1 million to $3 million.

BT Capital Corp. (Los Angeles)
300 S. Grand Ave.
Los Angeles, California 90071
Phone: (213)620-8430
A small business investment company.

Charterway Investment Corp.
One Wilshire Bldg., No.1600
Los Angeles, California 90017-3317
Phone: (213)689-9107
Fax: (213)890-1968
A minority enterprise small business investment corporation. No industry preference.

Far East Capital Corp.
977 N. Broadway, Ste.401
Los Angeles, California 90012
Phone: (213)687-1361
Fax: (213)626-7497
A minority enterprise small business
investment company. Diversified
industry preference.

Kline Hawkes California SBIC, LP
11726 San Vicente Blvd., Ste. 300
Los Angeles, California 90049
Phone: (310)442-4700
Fax: (310)442-4707
Frank R. Kline, Manager

Peregrine Ventures
12400 Wilshire Blvd Ste. 240
Los Angeles, California 90025
Phone: (310)458-1441
Fax: (310)394-0771
Venture capital firm providing start-
up, first stage, and leveraged buyout
financing. Areas of interest include
communications and health.

Riordan Lewis & Haden
300 S. Grand Ave., 29th Fl.
Los Angeles, California 90071
Phone: (213)229-8500
Fax: (213)229-8597
Venture capital firm providing all
types of financing, including
management buyouts and turnarounds. Areas of interest include
food and service.

The Seideler Companies, Inc.
515 S. Figueroa St., 11th Fl.
Los Angeles, California 90071-3396
Phone: (213)624-4232
Fax: (213)623-1131

Union Venture Corp.
445 S. Figueroa St.
Los Angeles, California 90071
Phone: (213)236-5658
Fax: (213)688-0101
A small business investment
company. Diversified industry
preference.

Advanced Technology Ventures
(Menlo Park)
485 Ramona St.,Ste. 200

Menlo Park, California 94028-8140
Phone: (415)321-8601
Fax: (415)321-0934

Bessemer Venture Partners (Menlo
Park)
3000 Sand Hill Rd., Bldg. 3, Ste. 225
Menlo Park, California 94025
Phone: (415)854-2200
Fax: (415)854-7415

Brentwood Associates (Menlo Park)
3000 Sandhill Rd., Ste. 260
Menlo Park, California 94025-7020
Phone: (415)854-7691
Fax: (415)854-9513

Canaan Partners
2884 Sand Hill Rd., Ste. 115
Menlo Park, California 94025-7022
Phone: (415)854-8092
Fax: (415)854-8127
Venture capital firm providing start-
up, second and third stage, and buyout
financing. Areas of interest include
information industry products and
services, medical technology, and
health care services.

Comdisco Venture Group (Menlo
Park)
3000 Sand Hill Rd., Bldg. 1, Ste. 155
Menlo Park, California 94025-7141
Phone: (415)854-9484
Fax: (415)854-4026
Prefers start-up businesses in fields of
semiconductors, computer hardware
and software, computer services and
systems, telecommunications, and
medical and biotechnology.
Investments range from $500,000 to
$5 million.

Glenwood Management
3000 Sand Hill Rd., Bldg. 4, Ste. 230
Menlo Park, California 94025
Phone: (415)854-8070
Fax: (415)854-4961
Venture capital supplier. Areas of
interest include high technology and
biomedical industries.

Institutional Venture Partners
3000 Sand Hill Rd., Bldg. 2, Ste. 290
Menlo Park, California 94025

Phone: (415)854-0132
Fax: (415)854-5762
Venture capital fund. Invests in early
stage ventures with significant market
potential in the computer, information
sciences, communications, and life
sciences fields.

Interwest Partners (Menlo Park)
3000 Sand Hill Rd., Bldg. 3, Ste. 255
Menlo Park, California 94025
Phone: (415)854-8585
Fax: (415)854-4706
Venture capital fund. Both high-tech
and low- or non- technology
companies are considered. No oil,
gas, real estate, or construction
projects.

Kleiner Perkins Caufield & Byers
(Menlo Park)
2750 Sand Hill Rd.
Menlo Park, California 94025
Phone: (415)233-2750
Fax: (415)233-0300
Provides seed, start-up, second and
third-round, and bridge financing to
companies on the West Coast.
Preferred industries of investment
include electronics, computers,
software, telecommunications,
biotechnology, medical devices, and
pharmaceuticals.

Matrix Partners
2500 Sand Hill Rd., Ste. 113
Menlo Park, California 94025-7016
Phone: (415)854-3131
Fax: (415)854-3296
Private venture capital partnership.
Investments range from $500,000 to
$1 million.

Mayfield Fund
2800 Sand Hill Rd., Ste. 250
Menlo Park, California 94025
Phone: (415)854-5560
Fax: (415)854-5712
Venture capital partnership. Prefers
high-technology and biomedical
industries.

McCown De Leeuw and Co. (Menlo
Park)
3000 Sand Hill Rd., Bldg. 3, Ste. 290

Menlo Park, California 94025
Phone: (415)854-6000
Fax: (415)854-0853
A venture capital firm. Preferences include the mortgage servicing, building materials, printing, and office products industries.

Menlo Ventures
3000 Sand Hill Rd., Bldg. 4, Ste. 100
Menlo Park, California 94025
Phone: (415)854-8540
Fax: (415)854-7059
Venture capital supplier. Provides start-up and expansion financing to companies with experienced management teams, distinctive product lines, and large growing markets. Primary interest is in technology-oriented, service, consumer products, and distribution companies. Investments range from $500,000 to $3 million; also provides capital for leveraged buy outs.

Merrill Pickard Anderson & Eyre I
2480 Sand Hill Rd., Ste. 200
Menlo Park, California 94025
Phone: (415)854-8600
Fax: (415)854-0345
Steven Merrill, President

New Enterprise Associates (Menlo Park)
2490 Sand Hill Road
Menlo Park, California 94025
Phone: (415)854-9499
Fax: (415)854-9397
Venture capital supplier.

New Enterprise Associates (San Francisco)
2490 Sand Hill Road
Menlo Park, California 94025
Phone: (415)854-9499
Fax: (415)854-9397
Venture capital supplier. Concentrates in technology-based industries that have the potential for product innovation, rapid growth, and high profit margins.

Paragon Venture Partners
3000 Sand Hill Rd., Bldg. 1, Ste. 275
Menlo Park, California 94025

Phone: (415)854-8000
Fax: (415)854-7260
Venture capital firm. Areas of interest include high technology and life sciences with an emphasis on data communications, networking, software, medical devices, biotechnology, and health care services industries.

Pathfinder Venture Capital Funds (Menlo Park)
3000 Sand Hill Rd., Bldg. 1, Ste. 290
Menlo Park, California 94025
Phone: (415)854-0650
Fax: (415)854-9010
Venture capital supplier. Provides start-up and early- stage financing to emerging companies in the medical, computer, pharmaceuticals, and data communications industries. Emphasis is on companies with proprietary technology or market positions and with substantial potential for revenue growth.

Ritter Partners
3000 Sandhill Rd. Bldg.1, Ste. 190
Menlo Park, California 94025
Phone: (415)854-1555
Fax: (415)854-5015
William C. Edwards, President

Sequoia Capital
3000 Sand Hill Rd., Bldg. 4, Ste. 280
Menlo Park, California 94025
Phone: (415)854-3927
Fax: (415)854-2977
Private venture capital partnership with $300 million under management. Provides financing for all stages of development of well-managed companies with exceptional growth prospects in fast-growth industries. Past investments have been made in computers and peripherals, communications, health care, biotechnology, and medical instruments and devices. Investments range from $350,000 for early stage companies to $4 million for late stage accelerates.

Sierra Ventures
3000 Sand Hill Rd., Bldg. 4, Ste. 210

Menlo Park, California 94025
Phone: (415)854-1000
Fax: (415)854-5593
Venture capital partnership.

Sigma Partners
2884 Sand Hill Rd., Ste. 121
Menlo Park, California 94025-7022
Phone: (415)854-1300
Fax: (415)854-1323
Independent venture capital partnership. Prefers to invest in the following areas: communcations, computer hardware, computer software, manufacturing, medical equipment, and semiconductor capital equipment. Avoids investing in construction, hotels, leasing, motion pictures, and natural resources. Minimum initial commitment is $500,000.

Sprout Group (Menlo Park)
3000 Sand Hill Rd., Bldg. 4, Ste. 270
Menlo Park, California 94025-7114
Phone: (415)854-1550
Fax: (415)854-8779

Technology Venture Investors
2480 Sand Hill Rd., Ste. 101
Menlo Park, California 94025
Phone: (415)854-7472
Fax: (415)854-4187
Private venture capital partnership. Primary interest is in technology companies with minimum investment of $1 million.

U.S. Venture Partners
2180 Sand Hill Rd., Ste. 300
Menlo Park, California 94025
Phone: (415)854-9080
Fax: (415)854-3018
Venture capital partnership. Prefers the specialty retail, consumer products, technology, and biomedical industries.

USVP-Schlein Marketing Fund
2180 Sand Hill Rd., Ste. 300
Menlo Park, California 94025
Phone: (415)854-9080
Fax: (415)854-3018
Venture capital fund. Prefers specialty retailing/consumer products companies.

Hall, Morris & Drufva II, L.P.
26161 Lapaz Rd., Ste. E
Mission Viejo, California 92691
Phone: (714)707-5096
Fax: (714)707-5121
A small business investment
corporation. No industry preference.
Provides capital for small and
medium-sized companies through
participation in private placements of
subordinated debt, preferred, and
common stock. Offers growth-
acquisition and later-stage venture
capital.

ABC Capital Corp.
917 Waittier Blvd.
Montebello, California 90640
Phone: (213)725-7890
Fax: (213)725-7115
A minority enterprise small business
investment corporation. No industry
preference.

Allied Business Investors, Inc.
301 W. Valley Blvd. SE 208
Monterey Park, California 91754
Phone: (818)289-0186
Fax: (818)289-2369
Jack Hong, President
Preferred Investment Size: $50,000.
Investment Policies: Loans only.
Investment Types: Early stage.
Industry Preferences: Diversified.
Geographic Preferences: Los Angeles.

LaiLai Capital Corp.
223 E. Garvey Ave., Ste. 228
Monterey Park, California 91754
Phone: (818)288-0704
Fax: (818)288-4101
A minority enterprise small business
investment company. Diversified
industry preference.

Myriad Capital, Inc.
701 S. Atlantic Blvd., Ste. 302
Monterey Park, California 91754-
3242
Phone: (818)570-4548
Fax: (818)570-9570
A minority enterprise small business
investment corporation. Prefers
investing in production and
manufacturing industries.

Enterprise Partners
5000 Birch St., Ste. 6200
Newport Beach, California 92660
Phone: (714)833 3650
Fax: (714)833-3652
Venture capital fund. Prefers to invest
in medical or high- technology
industries in California.

Marwit Capital Corp.
180 Newport Center Dr., Ste. 200
Newport Beach, California 92660
Phone: (714)640-6234
Fax: (714)720-8077
A small business investment
corporation. Provides financing for
leveraged buyouts, mergers,
acquisitions, and expansion stages.
Investments are in the $100,000 to $4
million range. Does not provide
financing for start-ups or real estate
ventures.

Inman and Bowman
4 Orinda Way, Bldg. D, Ste. 150
Orinda, California 94563
Phone: (510)253-1611
Fax: (510)253-9037

Asset Management Co.
2275 E. Bayshore, Ste. 150
Palo Alto, California 94303
Phone: (415)494-7400
Fax: (415)856-1826
Venture capital firm. High-technology
industries preferred.

BankAmerica Ventures (Palo Alto)
5 Palo Alto Sq., Ste. 938
Palo Alto, California 94306
Phone: (415)424-8011
Fax: (415)424-6830

Campbell Venture Management
375 California St.
Palo Alto, California 94308
Phone: (415)853-0766
Fax: (415)857-0303

Citicorp Venture Capital, Ltd. (Palo
Alto)
2 Embarcadero Pl.
2200 Geny Rd., Ste. 203
Palo Alto, California 94303
Phone: (415)424-8000

A small business investment
company.

Greylock Management Corp. (Palo
Alto)
755 Page Mill Rd., Ste. A-100
Palo Alto, California 94304-1018
Phone: (415)493-5525
Fax: (415)493-5575
Venture capital firm providing all
stages of financing. Areas of interest
include computer software,
communications, health,
biotechnology, publishing, and
specialty retail.

MK Global Ventures
2471 E. Bayshore Rd., Ste. 520
Palo Alto, California 94303
Phone: (415)424-0151
Fax: (415)494-2753

Norwest Venture Capital (Menlo
Park)
245 Iytton Ave., Ste. 250
Palo Alto, California 94301
Phone: (415)854-6366
Fax: (415)321-8010
A small business investment
corporation. No industry preference.

Oak Investment Partners (Menlo
Park)
525 University Avenue, Ste. 1300
Palo Alto, California 94301
Phone: (415)614-3700
Fax: (415)328-6345
Small business investment
corporation. Areas of interest include
communications, computer hardware
and software, high technology,
manufacturing, medical equipment
and instrumentation, pharmaceuticals,
and retail.

Patricof & Co. Ventures, Inc. (Palo
Alto)
1 Embarcadero Pl.
2100 Geng Rd., Ste. 150
Palo Alto, California 94303
Phone: (415)494-9944
Fax: (415)494-6751
Venture capital firm providing equity
investments, diversified by markets
and stage of company. Prefers to fund
growth.

Summit Partners (Newport Beach)
499 Hamilton Ave., Ste. 200
Palo Alto, California 94301
Phone: (415)321-1166
Fax: (415)321-1188
Venture capital firm providing
investments in the $2 million-$20
million range. Areas of interest
include technology, health care, and
financial services.

Sutter Hill Ventures
755 Page Mill Rd., Ste. A-200
Palo Alto, California 94304-1005
Phone: (415)493-5600
Fax: (415)858-1854
Venture capital partnership providing
start-up financing for high technology
businesses.

TA Associates (Palo Alto)
435 Tasso St.
Palo Alto, California 94301
Phone: (415)328-1210
Fax: (415)326-4933
Private venture capital firm. Prefers
technology companies and leveraged
buy outs. Provides from $1 to $20
million in investments.

Venrock Associates
755 Page Mill, A-230
Palo Alto, California 94304
Phone: (415)493-5577
Fax: (415)493-6443
Private venture capital supplier.
Prefers high-technology start-up
equity investments.

BankAmerica Ventures (Pasadena)
155 N. Lake Ave., Ste. 1010
Pasadena, California 91109
Phone: (818)304-3451
Fax: (818)440-9931

First SBIC of California (Pasadena)
155 N. Lake Ave., Ste. 1010
Pasadena, California 91109
Phone: (818)304-3451
Fax: (818)440-9931
A small business investment
company.

The Money Store Investment Corp.
3301 "C" St., Ste. 100 M

Sacramento, California 95816
Phone: (916)446-5000
Free: (800)639-1102
Fax: (916)443-2399
Non-bank lender providing start-up
and expansion financing.

AMF Financial, Inc.
4330 La Jolla Village Dr., Ste. 110
San Diego, California 92122-1233
Phone: (619)546-0167
Fax: (619)455-0868
A small business investment
company. Diversified industry
preference.

Forward Ventures
10975 Torreyana Rd., No. 230
San Diego, California 92121
Phone: (619)677-6077
Fax: (619)452-8799
Venture capital firm preferring
investments of $100,000- $500,000.
Areas of interest include
biotechnology and health care.

Idanta Partners Ltd.
4660 La Jolla Village Dr., Ste. 850
San Diego, California 92122-4606
Phone: (619)452-9690
Fax: (619)452-2013
Venture capital partnership. No
industry preferences. Minimum
investment is $500,000.

Sorrento Growth Partners I, L.P.
4225 Executive Sq., Ste. 1450
San Diego, California 92137
Phone: (619)452-6400
Fax: (619)452-7607
Robert Jaffe, Manager
Preferred Investment Size: $750,000
TO $2 Million. Investment Policies:
Equity only. Investment Types: Seed,
early, expansion, later stages. Industry
Preferences: Medicine, health,
communications, electronics, special
retail. Geographic Preferences:
Southern California.

Accel Partners (San Francisco)
E-mail: www.accel.com
1 Embarcadero Center, Ste. 3820
San Francisco, California 94111
Phone: (415)989-5656

Fax: (415)989-5554
Venture capital firm providing start-
up financing. Areas of interest include
health care, information technology,
software, and telecommunications.

American Realty and Construction
1489 Webster St., Ste. 218
San Francisco, California 94115-3767
Phone: (415)928-6600
Fax: (415)928-6363
A minority enterprise small business
investment corporation. No industry
preference.

BANEXI Corp.
555 California St., Ste. 2600
San Francisco, California 94104
Phone: (415)693-3345
Free: (800)766-3863
Fax: (415)433-7326
Venture capital firm preferring late
stage investments. Areas of interest
include biotechnology, health care
products/services, industrial and
environmental services, electronic
technology and information services,
communications, business services,
and specialty retailing.

Bentley Capital
592 Vallejo St. Ste. 2
San Francisco, California 94133
Phone: (415)362-2868
Fax: (415)398-8209
A minority enterprise small business
investment company. Diversified
industry preference.

Bryan and Edwards Partnership (San
Francisco)
600 Montgomery St., 35th Fl.
San Francisco, California 94111-2854
Phone: (415)421-9990
Fax: (415)421-0471
A small business investment
corporation. No industry preference.

Burr, Egan, Deleage, and Co. (San
Francisco)
1 Embarcadero Center, Ste. 4050
San Francisco, California 94111-3729
Phone: (415)362-4022
Fax: (415)362-6178

Private venture capital supplier. Invests start-up, expansion, and acquisitions capital nationwide. Principal concerns are strength of the management team; large, rapidly expanding markets; and unique products for services. Past investments have been made in the fields of biotechnology and pharmaceuticals, cable TV, chemicals/plastics, communications, software, computer systems and peripherals, distributorships, radio common carriers, electronics and electrical components, environmental control, health services, medical devices and instrumentation, and radio and cellular telecommunications. Primarily interested in medical, electronics, and media industries.

Dillon Read Venture Capital
555 California St., No. 4360
San Francisco, California 94104-1714
Phone: (415)296-7900
Fax: (415)296-8956
A venture capital firm. Provides early-stage financing to companies in the biomedical field and the information systems industry.

Dominion Ventures, Inc.
44 Montgomery St., Ste. 4200
San Francisco, California 94104
Phone: (415)362-4890
Fax: (415)394-9245
Venture capital firm providing seed, start-up, second and third stage, and buyout financing. Areas of interest include biotechnology, health care, telecommunications, software, and financial services.

First Century Partners (San Bruno)
E-mail: sagegiven@aol.com
101 California St., Ste. 3160
San Francisco, California 94111
Phone: (415)433-4200
Fax: (415)433-4250
Venture capital firm. Health care, software, technology- based service, and specialty retailing industries preferred.

G C and H Partners
1 Maritime Plz., 20th Fl.
San Francisco, California 94111
Phone: (415)693-2000
Fax: (415)951-3699
A small business investment corporation. No industry preference.

Hambrecht and Quist (San Francisco)
1 Bush St.
San Francisco, California 94104
Phone: (415)439-3300
Free: (800)227-3958
Fax: (415)439-3621
Prefers to invest in computer tehnology, environmental technology, and biotechnology. Investments range from $500,000 to $5,000,000.

Heller First Capital Corp.
650 California St., 23rd Fl.
San Francisco, California 94108
Phone: (415)274-5700
Fax: (415)274-5744
Non-bank lender providing start-up and expansion financing.

Jafco America Ventures, Inc. (San Francisco)
555 California St., Ste. 4380
San Francisco, California 94104
Phone: (415)788-0706
Fax: (415)788-0709
Venture capital firm. Provides middle- to later-stage investments. Avoids investments in real estate, natural resources, entertainment, motion pictures, oil and gas, construction, and non-technical industries.

Jupiter Partners
600 Montgomery St., 35th Fl.
San Francisco, California 94111
Phone: (415)421-9990
Fax: (415)421-0471
A small business investment company. Prefers to invest in electronic manufacturing industry.

Montgomery Securities
600 Montgomery St., 21st Fl.
San Francisco, California 94111-2702
Phone: (415)627-2454
Fax: (415)249-5516

Private venture capital and investment banking firm. Diversified, but will not invest in real estate or energy- related industries. Involved in both start-up and later-stage financing.

Morgan Stanley Venture Capital Fund L.P.
555 California St., Ste. 2200
San Francisco, California 94104
Phone: (415)576-2345
Fax: (415)576-2099
Venture capital firm providing second and third stage and buyout financing. Areas of interest include information technology and health care products/ services.

Positive Enterprises, Inc.
1489 Webster St., Ste. 228
San Francisco, California 94115
Phone: (415)885-6600
Fax: (415)928-6363
A minority enterprise small business investment company. Diversified industry preference.

Quest Ventures (San Francisco)
E-mail: ruby@questventures.com
126 S. Park
San Francisco, California 94107
Phone: (415)546-7118
Fax: (415)243-8514
Independent venture capital partnership. Diversified industry preference.

Robertson-Stephens Co.
E-mail: 800emailol
555 California St., Ste. 2600
San Francisco, California 94104
Phone: (415)781-9700
Fax: (415)781-0278
Investment banking firm. Considers investments in any attractive merging- growth area, including product and service companies. Key preferences include health care, hazardous waste services and technology, biotechnology, software, and information services. Maximum investment is $5 million.

VenAd Administrative Services
E-mail: vallee@eurolink.com

657 Mission Street Ste. 601
San Francisco, California 94105
Phone: (415)543-4448
Fax: (415)541-7775
Private venture capital supplier.
Provides all stages of financing.

VK Capital Co.
600 California St., Ste.1700
San Francisco, California 94108
Phone: (415)391-5600
Fax: (415)397-2744
A small business investment
company. Diversified industry
preference.

Volpe, Welty and Co.
1 Maritime Plz., 11th Fl.
San Francisco, California 94111
Phone: (415)956-8120
Fax: (415)986-6754
Prefers investing with companies
involved in entertainment, multimedia, computer-aided software
engineering, gaming, software tools,
biotechnology, and health care
industries.

Walden Group of Venture Capital
Funds
750 Battery St., Ste. 700
San Francisco, California 94111
Phone: (415)391-7225
Fax: (415)391-7262
Venture capital firm providing seed,
start-up, and second and third stage
financing. Areas of interest include
high technology, consumer products,
health-related industries, hardware,
software, EDP, environmental,
communications, and education.

Weiss, Peck and Greer Venture
Partners L.P. (San Francisco)
555 California St., Ste. 4760
San Francisco, California 94104
Phone: (415)622-6864
Fax: (415)989-5108

Dougery & Wilder (San Mateo)
155 Bovet Rd., Ste. 350
San Mateo, California 94402-3113
Phone: (415)358-8701
Fax: (415)358-8706

Venture capital supplier. Areas of
interest include computers systems
and software, communications, and
medical/biotechnology industries.

Drysdale Enterprises
177 Bovet Rd., Ste. 600
San Mateo, California 94402
Phone: (415)341-6336
Fax: (415)341-1329
Venture capital firm preferring
investments of $250,000-$2 million.
Areas of interest include food
processing, health care, and
communications.

Technology Funding
2000 Alameda de las Pulgas, Ste. 250
San Mateo, California 94403
Phone: (415)345-2200
Free: (800)821-5323
Fax: (415)341-1400
Small business investment
corporation. Provides primarily late
first-stage and early second-stage
equity financing. Also offers secured
debt with equity participation to
venture capital backed companies.
Investments range from $500,000 to
$1 million.

Trinity Ventures Ltd.
E-mail: trinityvc@aol.com
155 Bovet Rd., Ste. 660
San Mateo, California 94402
Phone: (415)358-9700
Fax: (415)358-9785
Private venture capital firm investing
in computer software, consumer
products, and health care industries.

Phoenix Growth Capital Corp.
2401 Kerner Blvd.
San Rafael, California 94901
Phone: (415)485-4655
Free: (800)227-2626
Fax: (415)485-4663
Small business investment
corporation providing start-up, second
and third stage, and buyout financing.
Areas of interest include secured debt
for high technology, biotechnology,
computers and peripherals, and
service industries. (All must be equity
venture capital based.)

InterVen Partners (Santa Monica)
301 Arizona Ave., No. 306
Santa Monica, California 90401-1305
Phone: (310)587-3550
Fax: (310)587-3440
Venture capital fund. Diversified
industry preferences; geographic
preference is the West Coast.

InterVen II L.P. (Portland, OR)
301 Arizona Ave.,Ste 306
Santa Monica, California 90401
Phone: (310)587-3550
Fax: (310)587-3440
A small business investment
corporation. Currently making only
follow-on investments in existing
portfolio companies.

DSC Ventures II, LP
12050 Saratoga Ave. Ste.,B
Saratoga, California 95070
Phone: (408)252-3800
Fax: (408)252-0757
A small business investment
company. Diversified industry
preference.

Western General Capital Corp.
13701 Riverside Dr., Ste. 610
Sherman Oaks, California 91423
Phone: (818)986-5038
Fax: (818)905-9220
A minority enterprise small business
investment company. Diversified
industry preference.

Astar Capital Corp.
9537 E. Gidley St.
Temple City, California 91780
Phone: (818)350-1211
Fax: (818)350-0868
George Hsu, President

Spectra Enterprise Associates
PO Box 7688
Thousand Oaks, California 91359-
7688
Phone: (818)865-0213
Fax: (818)865-1309
Venture capital partnership. Areas of
interest include information,
computer, semiconductor, software,
life sciences, and wireless industries.

National Investment Management,
Inc.
E-mail: Robins621@ad.com
2601 Airport Drive., Ste.210
Torrance, California 90505
Phone: (310)784-7600
Fax: (310)784-7605
Venture capital firm providing
leveraged buyout financing. Areas of
interest include general
manufacturing and distribution.

Round Table Capital Corp.
2175 N. California Blvd., Ste. 400
Walnut Creek, California 94596
Phone: (510)274-1700
Fax: (510)974-3978
A small business investment
corporation. No industry preference.

Colorado

Hill, Carman, and Washing
885 Arapahoe
Boulder, Colorado 80302
Phone: (303)442-5151
Fax: (303)442-8525

Opus Capital
1113 Spruce St., Ste. 406
Boulder, Colorado 80302
Phone: (303)443-1023
Fax: (303)443-0986

Capital Health Management
2084 S. Milwaukee St.
Denver, Colorado 80210
Phone: (303)692-8600
Fax: (303)692-9656

The Centennial Funds
1428 15th St.
Denver, Colorado 80202
Phone: (303)405-7500
Fax: (303)405-7575
Venture capital fund. Prefers to invest
in early stage companies in the Rocky
Mountain region.

Colorado Housing and Finance
Authority
1981 Blake St.
Denver, Colorado 80202-1272
Phone: (303)297-2432
Fax: (303)297-2615

Operates financing programs for
small and minority businesses.

Colorado Office of Business
Development
1625 Broadway, Ste. 1710
Denver, Colorado 80202
Phone: (303)892-3840
Fax: (303)892-3848
Provides loans to new and expanding
businesses.

UBD Capital, Inc.
1700 Broadway
Denver, Colorado 80274
Phone: (303)863-6329
A small business investment
company. Diversified industry
preference.

Columbine Ventures
5460 S. Quebec St., Ste. 270
Englewood, Colorado 80111-1917
Phone: (303)694-3222
Fax: (303)694-9007
Venture capital firm interested in
biotechnology, medical, computer,
electronics, and advanced materials
industries.

Connecticut

AB SBIC, Inc.
275 School House Rd.
Cheshire, Connecticut 06410
Phone: (203)272-0203
Fax: (203)272-9978
A small business investment
company. Prefers to invest in grocery
stores.

Financial Opportunities, Inc.
1 Vision Dr.
Enfield, Connecticut 06082
Phone: (203)741-4444
Fax: (860)741-4494
A small business investment
corporation. Prefers full franchise
convenience stores.

Consumer Venture Partners
3 Pickwick Plz.
Greenwich, Connecticut 06830
Phone: (203)629-8800
Fax: (203)629-2019

Prefers consumer and expansion-stage
investments.

First New England Capital, LP
100 Pearl St.
Hartford, Connecticut 06103
Phone: (203)293-3333
Fax: (203)549-2528
A small business investment
company. Diversified industry
preference.

FRE Capital Partners, LP
36 Grove St.
New Canaan, Connecticut 06840
Phone: (203)966-2800
Fax: (203)966-3109
A small business investment
company. Diversified industry
preference.

RFE Investment Partners V, L.P.
36 Grove St.
New Canaan, Connecticut 06840
Phone: (203)966-2800
Fax: (203)966-3109
James A. Parsons, General Partner
Preferred Investment Size: $5 - $9
Million. Investment Policies: Prefer
equity investments. Investment
Types: Later stage, expansion,
acquisitions. Industry Preferences:
Manufacturing & services.
Geographic Preferences: National,
eastern U.S.

The Vista Group
36 Grove St.
New Canaan, Connecticut 06840
Phone: (203)972-3400
Fax: (203)966-0844
Venture capital supplier. Provides
start-up and second- stage financing
to technology-related businesses that
seek to become major participants in
high-growth markets of at least $100
million in annual sales. Areas of
investment interest include
information systems,
communications, computer
peripherals, medical products and
services, retailing, agrigenetics,
biotechnology, low technology, no
technology, instrumentation, and
genetic engineering.

All State Venture Capital Corp.
The Bishop House
32 Elm St.
PO Box 1629
New Haven, Connecticut 06506
Phone: (203)787-5029
Fax: (203)785-0018
A small business investment
company. Diversified industry
preference.

Nova Tech-Eicon
142 Temple St., 2nd Fl.
New Haven, Connecticut 06510
Phone: (203)789-1260
Fax: (203)789-8261

DCS Growth Fund (Old Greenwich)
PO Box 740
Old Greenwich, Connecticut 06870-
0740
Phone: (203)637-1704
Fax: (203)637-1705

Canaan Partners
105 Rowayton Ave.
Rowayton, Connecticut 06853
Phone: (203)855-0400
Fax: (203)854-9117
Venture capital supplier.

First Connecticut SBIC
1000 Bridgeport St.
Shelton, Connecticut 06484
Phone: (203)366-4726
Free: (800)401-3222
Fax: (203)944-5405
A small business investment
corporation.

Marcon Capital Corp.
10 John St.
Southport, Connecticut 06490-1437
Phone: (203)259-7233
Fax: (203)259-9428
A small business investment
corporation; secured lending
preferred.

Central Texas SBI Corporation
1 Canterbury Green
201 Broad St., 2nd Fl.
Stamford, Connecticut 06901
Phone: (203)352-4056
Fax: (203)352-4184
David E. Erb, Contact Person

James B. Kobak and Co.
2701 Summer St., Ste. 200
Stamford, Connecticut 06905
Phone: (203)363-2221
Fax: (203)363-2218
Venture capital supplier and
consultant. Provides assistance to new
ventures in the communications field
through conceptualization, planning,
organization, raising money, and
control of actual operations. Special
interest is in magazine publishing.

Saugatuck Capital Co.
1 Canterbury Green
Stamford, Connecticut 06901
Phone: (203)348-6669
Fax: (203)324-6995
Private investment partnership. Seeks
to invest in various industries not
dependent on technology, including
health care, telecommunications,
insurance, financial services,
manufacturing, and consumer
products. Prefers leveraged buy out
situations, but will consider start-up
financing. Investments range from $3
to $5 million.

Schroder Ventures
1055 Washington Blvd. 5th Fl.
Stamford, Connecticut 06901
Phone: (203)324-7700
Fax: (203)324-3636

TSG Ventures, Inc.
177 Broad St.,12th Fl.
Stamford, Connecticut 06901
Phone: (203)406-1500
Fax: (203)406-1590
A minority enterprise small business
investment company. Diversified
industry preference.

J. H. Whitney and Co. (New York)
177 Broad St.
Stamford, Connecticut 06901
Phone: (203)973-1400
Fax: (203)973-1422

Xerox Venture Capital (Stamford)
E-mail: xerox.com
Headquarters
800 Long Ridge Rd.
Stamford, Connecticut 06904

Phone: (203)968-3000
Venture capital subsidiary of
operating company. Prefers to invest
in document processing industries.

The SBIC of Connecticut, Inc.
2 Corpoate Rd., Ste. 203
Trumbull, Connecticut 06611
Phone: (203)261-0011
Fax: (203)459-1563
A small business investment
corporation. No industry preference.

Capital Resource Company of
Connecticut, LP
2558 Albany Ave.
West Hartford, Connecticut 06117
Phone: (203)236-4336
Fax: (860)232-8161
A small business investment
corporation. No industry preference.

Marketcorp Venture Associates
285 Riverside Ave.
Westport, Connecticut 06880
Phone: (203)222-1000
Free: (800)243-5077
Fax: (203)222-5829
Venture capital firm. Prefers to invest
in consumer-market businesses,
including the packaged goods,
specialty retailing, communications,
and consumer electronics industries.

Oak Investment Partners (Westport)
1 Gorham Island
Westport, Connecticut 06880
Phone: (203)226-8346
Fax: (203)227-0372

Oxford Bioscience Partners
315 Post Rd. W.
Westport, Connecticut 06880
Phone: (203)341-3300
Fax: (203)341-3309
Independent venture capital
partnership. Areas of interest include
biotechnology, medical devices/
services, and health care services.
Initial investments range from
$500,000 to $1.5 million; up to $3
million over several later rounds of
financing.

Prince Ventures (Westport)
25 Ford Rd.

Westport, Connecticut 06880
Phone: (203)227-8332
Fax: (203)226-5302
Provides early stage financing for medical and life sciences ventures.

Delaware

Delaware Economic Development Authority
99 Kings Hwy.
PO Box 1401
Dover, Delaware 19903-1401
Phone: (302)739-4271
Free: (800)441-8846
Fax: (302)739-5749
Provides financing to new and expanding businesses at interest rates below the prime rate by issuing industrial revenue bonds (IRBs). Manufacturing and agricultural projects are eligible.

PNC Capital Corp.
300 Delaware Ave., Ste. 304
Wilmington, Delaware 19801
Phone: (302)427-5895
Gary J. Zentner, President
Preferred Investment Size: $2 to $8 million. Investment Policies: Loans and/or equity. Investment Types: Expansion, later stage. Industry Preferences: No real estate or tax-oriented investments. Geographic Preferences: Northeast.

District of Columbia

Allied Capital Commercial Corp.
1666 K St. N.W.,9th Fl.
Washington, District of Columbia 20006
Phone: (202)331-1112
Fax: (202)659-2053
Real estate investment trust managed by Allied Capital Advisers, Inc. Investments range from $500,000 to $7.5 million. Prefers to purchase small business loans secured by real estate that are owner-operated or small business controlled. Areas of property interest include convenience stores, hotel/motel establishments, offices, medical facilities and nursing homes, industrial and retail properties, service stations, RV and mobile home parks, office condiminiums, mini-storage facilities, and restaurants.

Allied Capital Corp.
1666 K St. N.W., 9th Fl.
Washington, District of Columbia 20006
Phone: (202)331-1112
Fax: (202)659-2053
Venture capital fund managed by Allied Capital Advisers, Inc. Investments range from $500,000 to $6 million. Prefers later-stage companies that have been in business for at least one year, but gives consideration to early-stage companies and turnaround situations. Geographical preferences include the Northeast, Mid-Atlantic, and Southeast. Areas of interest include communications, computer hardware and software, consumer products, educational products, electronics, environmental, energy, franchising, industrial products and equipment, manufacturing, media, medical/health, publishing, recreation/tourism, restaurant, retail, service, transportation, and wholesale distribution industries.

Allied Capital Corp. II
1666 K St. N.W.,9th Fl.
Washington, District of Columbia 20006
Phone: (202)331-1112
Fax: (202)659-2053
Venture capital fund managed by Allied Capital Advisers, Inc. Investments range from $500,000 to $1 million. Prefers later-stage companies that have been in business for at least one year, but gives consideration to early-stage companies and turnaround situations. Geographical preferences include the Northeast, Mid-Atlantic, and Southeast. Areas of interest include communications, computer hardware and software, consumer products, educational products, electronics, environmental, energy, franchising, industrial products and equipment, manufacturing, media, medical/health, publishing, recreation/tourism, restaurant, retail, service, transportation, and wholesale distribution industries.

Allied Capital Lending Corp.
1666 K St. N.W.,9th Fl.
Washington, District of Columbia 20006
Phone: (202)331-1112
Fax: (202)659-2053
Mangement investment company managed by Allied Capital Advisers, Inc. Investments range from $200,000 to $1 million. Prefers to provide small, privately owned businesses with SBA-guaranteed loans. Areas of interest include manufacturing, hotel/motel, consumer products, retail shops/convenience stores, service stations, laundries and dry cleaning, home furnishings, printing, real estate, recreation/tourism, restaurant, and service industries.

Allied Financial Corp.
1666 K St. N.W.,9th Fl.
Washington, District of Columbia 20006-2804
Phone: (202)331-1112
Fax: (202)659-2053
A minority enterprise small business investment corporation. Diversified industry preference, excluding start-ups, turnarounds, real estate development, natural resources, and foreign companies.

Broadcast Capital, Inc.
1771 N St. NW
Washington, District of Columbia 20036
Phone: (202)429-5393
Fax: (202)775-2991
A minority enterprise small business investment corporation. Invests only in radio and TV stations. Investments lie in the $300,000-$400,000 range.

Fulcrum Venture Capital Corp
2021 K St. NW, Ste. 210
Washington, District of Columbia 20006
Phone: (202)785-4253

Helio Capital, Inc.
666 11th St., NW, Ste. 900
Washington, District of Columbia
20001
Phone: (202)272-3617
Fax: (202)504-2247
A minority enterprise small business
investment corporation. No industry
preference.

Minority Broadcast Investment Corp.
1001 Connecticut NW, Ste. 622
Washington, District of Columbia
20036-2506
Phone: (202)293-1166
Fax: (202)872-1669
A minority enterprise small business
investment corporation.
Communications industry preferred.

Florida

North American Fund, II
312 SE 17th St., Ste.300
Fort Lauderdale, Florida 33316
Phone: (954)463-0681
Fax: (954)527-0904
A small business investment
corporation. No industry preference.
Prefers controlling interest
investments and acquisitions of
established businesses with a history
of profitability.

Quantum Capital Partners, Ltd.
4400 NE 25th Ave.
Fort Lauderdale, Florida 33308
Phone: (305)776-1133
Fax: (305)938-9406
A small business investment
company. Diversified industry
preference.

Pro-Med Investment Corp. (North
Miami Beach)
Presidential Circle
4000 Hollywood Blvd., Ste.435 S.
Hollywood, Florida 33021-6754
Phone: (305)966-8868
Free: (800)954-3617
Fax: (305)969-3223
A minority enterprise small business
investment company.

Venture First Associates
1901 S. Harbor City Blvd., Ste. 501
Melbourne, Florida 32901
Phone: (407)952-7750
Fax: (407)952-5787
Venture capital firm providing seed,
start-up and first stage financing.
Areas of interest include health care,
advanced chemicals, computer
software and hardware, industrial
equipment, electronics, and
communications.

BAC Investment Corp.
6600 NW 27th Ave.
Miami, Florida 33147
Phone: (305)693-5919
Fax: (305)693-7450
A minority enterprise small business
investment company. Diversified
industry preference.

J and D Capital Corp.
12747 Biscayne Blvd.
North Miami, Florida 33181
Phone: (305)893-0303
Fax: (305)891-2338
A small business investment
corporation. No industry preference.

PMC Investment Corp.
AmeriFirst Bank Bldg., 2nd Fl. S
18301 Biscayne Blvd.
North Miami Beach, Florida 33160
Phone: (305)933-5858
Fax: (305)933-9410

Western Financial Capital Corp.
(North Miami Beach)
AmeriFirst Bank Bldg., 2nd Fl. S
18301 Biscayne Blvd.
North Miami Beach, Florida 33160
Phone: (305)933-5858
Fax: (305)933-9410
A small business investment
company.

Florida High Technology and
Industry Council
Collins Bldg.
107 W. Gaines St., Rm. 315
Tallahassee, Florida 32399-2000
Phone: (904)487-3136
Fax: (904)487-3014
Provides financing for research and
development for high-tech businesses.

Florida Capital Ventures, Ltd.
880 Riverside Plz.
100 W. Kennedy Blvd.
Tampa, Florida 33602
Phone: (813)229-2294
Fax: (813)229-2028
A small business investment
company. Diversified industry
preference.

Market Capital Corp.
1102 N. 28th St.
PO Box 31667
Tampa, Florida 33605
Phone: (813)247-1357
Fax: (813)248-9106
A small business investment
corporation. Grocery industry
preferred.

South Atlantic Venture Fund
E-mail: venture@mindspring.com
614 W. Bay St.
Tampa, Florida 33606-2704
Phone: (813)253-2500
Fax: (813)253-2360
A minority enterprise small business
investment corporation. Provides
expansion capital for privately owned,
rapidly growing companies located in
the southeastern United States and
Texas. Prefers to invest in
communications, computer services,
consumer, electronic components and
instrumentation, medical/health-
related services, medical products,
finance, and insurance industries. Will
not consider real estate or oil and gas
investments.

Allied Financial Services Corp. (Vero
Beach)
Executive Office Center, Ste. 300
2770 N. Indian River Blvd.
Vero Beach, Florida 32960
Phone: (407)778-5556
Fax: (407)569-9303
A minority enterprise small business
investment company.

Georgia

Advanced Technology Development
Fund
1000 Abernathy Rd., Ste. 1420

Atlanta, Georgia 30328
Phone: (770)668-2333
Fax: (770)668-2330
Venture capital firm providing start-up, first stage, second stage expansion, purchase or secondary positions, and buyout or acquisition financing. Areas of interest include information processing, health care and specialized mobile radio.

Arete Ventures, Inc./Utech Venture Capital Funds
115 Perimeter Center Pl. NE, No. 1140
Atlanta, Georgia 30346-1282
Phone: (404)399-1660
Venture capital firm providing start-up, first stage, second stage expansion and late stage expansion financing. Areas of interest include utility-related industries.

Cordova Capital Partners, L.P.
3350 Cumberland Cir., Ste. 970
Atlanta, Georgia 30339
Phone: (770)951-1542
Fax: (770)955-7610
Paul DiBella, Manager
Ralph Wright, Manager
Preferred Investment Size: $1 to $3 million. Investment Policies: Equity and/or debt. Investment Types: Early stage, expansion, later stage. Industry Preferences: Diversified. Geographic Preferences: Southeast.

Cravey, Green & Wahlen, Inc./CGW Southeast Partners
12 Piedmont Center, Ste. 210
Atlanta, Georgia 30305-4805
Phone: (404)816-3255
Free: (800)249-6669
Fax: (404)816-3258
Venture capital firm providing buyout or acquisition financing. Areas of interest include manufacturing, distribution, and service industries. Does not provide start-up financing or investments in high technology and medical industries.

EGL Holdings, Inc.
6600 Peachtree-Dunwoody Rd.
300 Embassy Row, Ste. 630

Atlanta, Georgia 30328
Phone: (770)399-5633
Fax: (770)393-4825
Venture capital firm providing late stage expansion, purchase or secondary positions, and buyout or acquisition financing. Areas of interest include information technology, medical/health care, industrial automation, electronic components and instrumentation for venture capital deals, and all industries for buyouts.

Equity South
1790 The Lenox Bldg.
3399 Peachtree Rd., Ste. 1790
Atlanta, Georgia 30326
Phone: (404)237-6222
Fax: (404)261-1578
Venture capital firm providing second stage expansion, late stage expansion, purchase or secondary positions, and buyout or acquisition financing.

Georgia Department of Community Affairs
Community and Economic Development Division
60 Executive Park South NE
Atlanta, Georgia 30329-2231
Phone: (404)679-4940
Fax: (404)679-0669
Provides assistance in applying for state and federal grants.

Georgia Department of Community Affairs
Government Information Division
1200 Equitable Bldg.
100 Peachtree St. NW
Atlanta, Georgia 30303
Phone: (404)656-5526
Fax: (404)656-9792
Central source for information on Georgia's people, economy, and local governments, including information on federal and state funding sources.

Green Capital Investors L.P.
3343 Peachtree Rd., Ste. 1420
Atlanta, Georgia 30326
Phone: (404)261-1187
Fax: (404)266-8677

Venture capital firm providing purchase or secondary positions and buyout or acquisition financing.

Noro-Moseley Partners
E-mail: nmp@mindspring.com
4200 Northside Pky., Bldg. 9
Atlanta, Georgia 30327
Phone: (404)233-1966
Fax: (404)239-9280
Venture capital partnership. Prefers to invest in private, diversified small and medium-sized growth companies located in the southeastern United States.

Premier HealthCare
3414 Peachtree Rd., Ste. 238
Atlanta, Georgia 30326
Phone: (404)816-0049
Fax: (404)816-0248
Venture capital firm providing start-up, first stage, second stage expansion, late stage expansion, purchase or secondary positions, and buyout or acquisition financing. Areas of interest include health care.

Renaissance Capital Corp.
34 Peachtree St. NW, Ste. 2230
Atlanta, Georgia 30303
Phone: (404)658-9061
Fax: (404)658-9064
A minority enterprise small business investment company. Diversified industry preference.

River Capital, Inc.
1360 Peachtree St. NE, Ste. 1430
Atlanta, Georgia 30309
Phone: (404)873-2166
Fax: (404)873-2158
Venture capital firm providing second stage expansion, late stage expansion, purchase or secondary positions, and buyout or acquisition financing. Areas of interest include light manufacturing and distribution companies with annual revenues exceeding $20 million.

Seaboard Management Corp.
3400 Peachtree Rd. NE, Ste. 741
Atlanta, Georgia 30326
Phone: (404)239-6270

Fax: (404)239-6284
Venture capital firm providing first stage and second stage expansion financing. Areas of interest include manufacturing and telecommunications.

Greater Washington Investments, Inc. (Rockville)
105 13th St.
Columbus, Georgia 31901
Phone: (706)641-3140
Fax: (706)641-3159
Haywood Miller, Manager
Preferred Investment Size: $1,000,000. Investment Policies: Subordinated debt with warrant. Investment Types: Expansion, later stage. Industry Preferences: Diversified. Geographic Preferences: National.

First Growth Capital, Inc.
Best Western Plz.
I-75 Georgia 42N Exit 63
Forsyth, Georgia 31029
Phone: (912)994-9260
Free: (800)447-3241
Fax: (912)994-9260
A minority enterprise small business investment company. Diversified industry preference.

North Riverside Capital Corp.
50 Technology Pk./Atlanta
Norcross, Georgia 30092
Phone: (770)446-5556
Fax: (770)446-8627
A small business investment corporation. No industry preference.

Hawaii

Bancorp Hawaii SBIC
130 Merchant St.
Honolulu, Hawaii 96813
Phone: (808)521-6411
Fax: (808)537-8557
A small business investment corporation. No industry preference.

Hawaii Agriculture Department
PO Box 22159
Honolulu, Hawaii 96823-2159
Phone: (808)973-9600

Fax: (808)973-9613
Provides information and advice in such areas as marketing, production, and labeling. Administers loan programs, including the New Farmer Loan Program, the Emergency Loan Program, and the Aquaculture Loan Program.

Hawaii Department of Business, Economic Development, and Tourism
Financial Assistance Branch
1 Capital District Bldg.
250 S. Hotel St., Ste. 503
PO Box 2359
Honolulu, Hawaii 96804
Phone: (808)586-2576
Fax: (808)587-3832
Provides loans to small businesses, including the Hawaii Capital Loan Program and the Hawaii Innovation Development Loan Program.

Pacific Venture Capital Ltd.
222 S. Vineyard St., No. PH-1
Honolulu, Hawaii 96813-2445
Phone: (808)521-6502
Free: (800)455-1888
Fax: (808)521-6541
A minority enterprise small business investment corporation.

Illinois

ABN AMRO Capital (USA) Inc.
135 S. La Salle St.
Chicago, Illinois 60603-4105
Phone: (312)904-6445
Joseph Rizzi, Chairman

Alpha Capital Venture Partners
E-mail: acpltd@aol.com
3 1st National Plz.-Ste. 1400
Chicago, Illinois 60602
Phone: (312)214-3440
Fax: (312)214-3376
A small business investment corporation providing expansion or later stage financing in the Midwest. No industry preference; however, no real estate, oil and gas, or start-up ventures are considered.

Ameritech Development Corp.
225 W. Randolph, 18th C Fl.

Chicago, Illinois 60606
Phone: (312)750-5000
Fax: (312)609-0244
Venture capital supplier. Prefers to invest in telecommunications and information services.

Batterson, Johnson and Wang
Venture Partners
E-mail: bvp@vcapital.com
303 W. Madison St., Ste. 1110
Chicago, Illinois 60606-3300
Phone: (312)269-0300
Fax: (312)269-0021

William Blair and Co. (Chicago)
222 W. Adams St.
Chicago, Illinois 60606-5312
Phone: (312)364-8250
Fax: (312)236-1042
A small business investment corporation. Areas of interest include cable, media, communications, consumer products, retail, health care services, technology and information services, and other service industries.

Brinson Partners, Inc.
209 S. LaSalle, 12th Fl.
Chicago, Illinois 60604-1295
Phone: (312)220-7100
Fax: (312)220-7199

Business Ventures, Inc.
20 N. Wacker Dr., Ste. 1741
Chicago, Illinois 60606-2904
Phone: (312)346-1580
Fax: (312)346-6693
A small business investment corporation. No industry preference; considers only ventures in the Chicago area.

Capital Health Venture Partners
20 N. Wacker Dr. Ste. 2200
Chicago, Illinois 60606
Phone: (312)781-1910
Fax: (312)726-2290
Investments limited to early stage medical, biotech, and health care related companies.

The Combined Fund, Inc.
7936 S. Cottage Grove
Chicago, Illinois 60619

Phone: (773)371-7030
Fax: (773)371-7035
A minority enterprise small business investment company. Diversified industry preference.

Continental Illinois Venture Corp.
231 S. LaSalle St.
Chicago, Illinois 60697
Phone: (312)828-8023
Fax: (312)987-0763
A small business investment corporation. Provides start-up and early stage financing to growth-oriented companies with capable management teams, proprietary products, and expanding markets.

Essex Venture Partners
E-mail: sbila@aol.com
190 S. LaSalle St., Ste. 2800
Chicago, Illinois 60603
Phone: (312)444-6040
Fax: (312)444-6034
Prefers to invest in health care companies.

First Analysis Corp.
E-mail: bmaxwell@facvc.com
c/o Bret Maxwell
233 S. Wacker Dr., Ste. 9500
Chicago, Illinois 60606
Phone: (312)258-1400
Free: (800)866-3272
Fax: (312)258-0334
Small business investment corporation providing first and second stage, mezzanine, and leveraged buyout financing in the $100,000 to $3 million range. Will act as deal originator or investor in deals created by others. Areas of interest include environmental, infrastructure, special chemicals/materials, repetitive revenue service, telecommunications, software, consumer/specialty retail, and health care companies.

First Capital Corp. of Chicago
3 1st National Plz., Ste. 1330
Chicago, Illinois 60602
Phone: (312)732-5400
Fax: (312)732-4098
A small business investment corporation. No industry preference.

First Chicago Venture Capital
3 1st National Plz., Ste. 1330
Chicago, Illinois 60602
Phone: (312)732-5400
Fax: (312)732-4098
Venture capital supplier. Invests a minimum of $1 million in early stage situations to a maximum of $25 million in mature growth or buy out situations. Emphasis is placed on a strong management team and unique market opportunity.

Frontenac Co.
135 S. LaSalle St., Ste.3800
Chicago, Illinois 60603
Phone: (312)368-0044
Fax: (312)368-9520
A small business investment corporation. No industry preference.

Golder, Thoma, Cressey, Rauner, Inc.
6100 Sears Tower
233 S. Wacker
Chicago, Illinois 60606
Phone: (312)382-2200
Fax: (312)382-2201
Private venture capital firm. Diversified industry preference, but does not invest in high technology or real estate industries.

Heller Equity Capital Corp.
500 W. Monroe St.
Chicago, Illinois 60661
Phone: (312)441-7200
Fax: (312)441-7378
A small business investment company. Diversified industry preference.

IEG Venture Management, Inc.
70 West Madison, Ste. 1400
Chicago, Illinois 60602
Phone: (312)644-0890
Fax: (312)454-0369
Venture capital supplier. Provides start-up financing primarily to technology-based companies located in the Midwest.

Illinois Development Finance Authority
Sears Tower
233 S. Wacker Dr., Ste. 5310

Chicago, Illinois 60606
Phone: (312)793-5586
Fax: (312)793-6347
Provides bond, venture capital, and direct loan programs.

Mesirow Capital Partners SBIC, Ltd.
350 N. Clark St., 3rd Fl.
Chicago, Illinois 60610
Phone: (312)595-6000
Fax: (312)595-6035
A small business investment corporation providing later stage growth financing and acquisition financing of non-high- technology companies. Does not provide start-up and turnaround financing.

The Neighborhood Fund, Inc.
25 E. Washington Blvd., Ste. 2015
Chicago, Illinois 60602
Phone: (312)726-6084
Fax: (312)726-0167
Derrick Collins, President
Preferred Investment Size: $100,000 to $300,000. Investment Policies: Equity and loans. Industry Preferences: Manufacturing, technology, product based. Geographic Preferences: Midwest.

Peterson Finance and Investment Co.
3300 W. Peterson Ave., Ste. A
Chicago, Illinois 60659
Phone: (312)539-0502
Fax: (312)267-8846
A minority enterprise small business investment company. Diversified industry preference.

Polestar Capital, Inc.
180 N. Michigan Ave., Ste. 1905
Chicago, Illinois 60601
Phone: (312)984-9875
Fax: (312)984-9877
Wallace Lennox, President
Preferred Investment Size: $350,000 to $700,000. Investment Policies: Primarily equity. Investment Types: Early to later stages.

Prince Ventures (Chicago)
10 S. Wacker Dr., Ste. 2575
Chicago, Illinois 60606-7407
Phone: (312)454-1408
Fax: (312)454-9125

Shorebank Capital Inc.
7936 S. Cottage Grove
Chicago, Illinois 60619
Phone: (312)371-7030
Fax: (312)371-7035
A minority enterprise small business
investment corporation providing
second stage, buyout, and acquisition
financing to companies in the
Midwest. Diversified industry
preference.

Walnut Capital Corp. (Chicago)
2 N. LaSalle St., Ste.2410
Chicago, Illinois 60602
Phone: (312)269-0126
Fax: (312)346-2231
A small business investment
corporation. Diversified industry
preference.

Wind Point Partners (Chicago)
676 N. Michigan Ave., No. 3300
Chicago, Illinois 60611-2804
Phone: (312)649-4000
Fax: (312)649-9644

Marquette Venture Partners
520 Lake Cook Rd., Ste. 450
Deerfield, Illinois 60015
Phone: 847940-1700
Fax: 847940-1724

Seidman, Fisher and Co.
1603 Orrington Ave. Ste. 2050
Evanston, Illinois 60201-5910
Phone: (708)492-1812
Fax: (708)864-9692
Private venture capital supplier.

The Cerulean Fund
E-mail: walnet@aol.com
1701 E. Lake Ave., Ste. 170
Glenview, Illinois 60025
Phone: (847)657-8002
Fax: (847)657-8168
Providers of equity investment.

Tower Ventures, Inc.
Sears Tower, BSC 23-27
3333 Beverly Holtman St., Ste.
AC254A
Hoffman Estates, Illinois 60179
Phone: (847)286-0571
Fax: (847)906-0164

A minority enterprise small business
investment company. Diversified
industry preference.

Allstate Venture Capital
3075 Sanders Rd., Ste. G5D
Northbrook, Illinois 60062-7127
Phone: (847)402-5681
Fax: (847)402-0880
Venture capital supplier. Investments
are not limited to particular industries
or geographical locations. Interest is
in unique products or services that
address large potential markets and
offer great economic benefits;
strength of management team is also
important. Investments range from
$500,000 to $5 million.

Caterpillar Venture Capital, Inc.
100 NE Adams St.
Peoria, Illinois 61629
Phone: (309)675-1000
Fax: (309)675-4457
Venture capital subsidiary of
operating firm.

Cilcorp Ventures, Inc.
300 Hamilton Blvd., Ste. 300
Peoria, Illinois 61602
Phone: (309)675-8850
Fax: (309)0675-8800
Invests in environmental services
only.

Comdisco Venture Group (Rosemont)
6111 N. River Rd.
Rosemont, Illinois 60018
Phone: (847)698-3000
Free: (800)321-1111
Fax: (847)518-5440
Venture capital subsidiary of
operating firm.

Indiana

Cambridge Ventures, LP
8440 Woodfield Crossing, No. 315
Indianapolis, Indiana 46240
Phone: (317)469-9704
Fax: (317)469-3926
A small business investment
company. Diversified industry
preference.

Circle Ventures, Inc.
26 N. Arsenal Ave.
Indianapolis, Indiana 46201-3808
Phone: (317)636-7242
Fax: (317)637-7581
A small business investment
corporation. Prefers second- stage,
leveraged buy out, and growth
financings. Geographical preference
is Indianapolis.

Heritage Venture Partners
135 N. Pennsylvania St., Ste. 2380
Indianapolis, Indiana 46204
Phone: (317)635-5696
Fax: (317)635-5699
Venture capital fund. Prefers radio
broadcast properties in mid-sized
radio markets wherein major
universities are located.

Indiana Business Modernization and
Technology Corp.
1 N. Capitol Ave., Ste. 925
Indianapolis, Indiana 46204
Phone: (317)635-3058
Free: (800)877-5182
Fax: (317)231-7095
Invests in and counsels applied
research ventures.

Indiana Development Finance
Authority
1 N. Capitol Ave., Ste. 320
Indianapolis, Indiana 46204
Phone: (317)233-4332
Fax: (317)232-6786
Administers the Ag Finance, Export
Finance, Loan Guarantee, and
Industrial Development Bond
Financing Programs.

First Source Capital Corp.
PO Box 1602
South Bend, Indiana 46634
Phone: (219)235-2180
Fax: (219)235-2227
A small business investment
corporation. No industry preference.

Thomas Lowe Ventures
3600 McGill St., Ste. 300
PO Box 3688
South Bend, Indiana 46628
Phone: (219)232-0300

Fax: (219)232-0500
Venture capital firm preferring to invest in the toy industry.

Iowa

Allsop Venture Partners (Cedar Rapids)
2750 1st Ave. NE, Ste. 210
Cedar Rapids, Iowa 52402
Phone: (319)363-8971
Fax: (319)363-9519

InvestAmerica Venture Group, Inc. (Cedar Rapids)
101 2nd St. SE, Ste. 800
Cedar Rapids, Iowa 52401
Phone: (319)363-8249
Fax: (319)363-9683
A small business investment corporation. Invests in later stage manufacturing and service businesses.

MorAmerica Capital Corp. (Cedar Rapids)
101 2nd St. SE, Ste. 800
Cedar Rapids, Iowa 52401
Phone: (319)363-8249
Fax: (319)363-9683
A small business investment company. Diversified industry preference.

Iowa Department of Economic Development
Iowa Seed Capitol Corp.
200 E. Grand Ave., Ste. 130
Des Moines, Iowa 50309
Phone: (515)242-4860
Fax: (515)242-4722
Provides risk capital to ventures that have new-job potential in Iowa. Profits are reinvested in other Iowa businesses and products.

Iowa Department of Economic Development
International Division
Export Finance Program
200 E. Grand Ave.
Des Moines, Iowa 50309
Phone: (515)242-4742
Fax: (515)242-4918

Provides funding to qualified exporters of Iowa- manufactured and processed products.

Iowa Department of Economic Development
Iowa New Jobs Training Program
150 Des Moines St.
Des Moines, Iowa 50309
Phone: (515)281-9028
Fax: (515)281-9033
Reimburses new or expanding companies for up to 50 percent of new employees' salaries and benefits for up to one year of on- the-job training. Coordinated through the state's 15 community colleges.

Iowa Department of Economic Development
Bureau of Business Finance
Self-Employment Loan Program
Iowa Dept. of Economic Development
200 E. Grand Ave.
Des Moines, Iowa 50309
Phone: (515)242-4793
Fax: (515)242-4749
Provides low-interest loans for low-income entrepreneurs who are expanding or starting a new business.

Iowa Department of Economic Development
Division of Financial Assistance
Community Development Block Grants
200 E. Grand Ave.
Des Moines, Iowa 50309
Phone: (515)242-4825
Fax: (515)242-4809
Bestows grants from the U.S. Department of Housing and Urban Development to help finance community improvements and job-generating expansions. Funds are primarily awarded on a competitive basis.

Iowa Finance Authority
100 E. Grand Ave., Ste. 250
Des Moines, Iowa 50309
Phone: (515)242-4990
Fax: (515)242-4957

Provides loans to new and expanding small businesses. Funds may be used to purchase land, construction, building improvements, or equipment; loans cannot be used for working capital, inventory, or operations.

Kansas

Allsop Venture Partners (Overland Park)
6602 W. 131st. St.
Overland Park, Kansas 66209
Phone: (913)338-0820
Fax: (913)681-5535

Kansas Venture Capital, Inc. (Overland Park)
6700 Antioch Plz., Ste. 460
Overland Park, Kansas 66204-1200
Phone: (913)262-7117
Fax: (913)262-3509
A small business investment corporation. Prefers to invest in wholesale or distribution, high technology, and service businesses.

Kansas City Equity Partners
4200 Somerset Dr., Ste. 101
Prairie Village, Kansas 66208
Phone: (913)960-1771
Fax: (913)649-2125
Paul H. Henson, Manager
Preferred Investment Size: $500,000 to $2 million. Investment Policies: Equity. Investment Types: Seed, early stage, expansion. Industry Preferences: Diversified. Geographic Preferences: Midwest.

Kansas Development Finance Authority
700 SW Jackson
Jayhawk Tower, Ste. 1000
Topeka, Kansas 66603
Phone: (913)296-6747
Fax: (913)296-6810
Dedicated to improving access to capital financing to business enterprises through the issurance of bonds.

Kansas Housing and Commerce Department
Division of Community Development

700 SW Harrison, Ste. 1300
Topeka, Kansas 66603-3712
Phone: (913)296-3485
Fax: (913)296-0186
Administers Community
Development Block Grants and the
enterprise zone program, in which
businesses receive tax credits and
exemptions for locating in targeted
areas.

Kentucky

Kentucky Cabinet for Economic
Development
Commonwealth Small Business
Development Corp.
2300 Capitol Plaza Tower
Frankfort, Kentucky 40601
Phone: (502)564-4320
Fax: (502)564-3256
Provides loans of up to 40 percent of
the costs of expansion to qualified
small businesses unable to obtain
financing without government aid.

Kentucky Cabinet for Economic
Development
Financial Incentives Department
Capitol Plaza Tower
500 Mero St., 24th Fl.
Frankfort, Kentucky 40601
Phone: (502)564-4554
Fax: (502)564-7697
Provides loans to supplement private
financing. Offers two major
programs: issuance of industrial
revenue bonds; and second mortgage
loans to private firms in participation
with other lenders. Also has a Crafts
Guaranteed Loan Program providing
loans up to $20,000 to qualified
craftspersons, and a Commonwealth
Venture Capital Program,
encouraging the establishment or
expansion of small business and
industry.

Mountain Ventures, Inc.
362 Old Whitley Rd.
PO Box 1738
London, Kentucky 40743-1738
Phone: (606)864-5175
Fax: (606)864-5194

A small business investment
corporation. No industry preference;
geographic area limited to southeast
Kentucky.

Equal Opportunity Finance, Inc.
420 S. Hurstbourne Pky., Ste. 201
Louisville, Kentucky 40222-8002
Phone: (502)423-1943
Fax: (502)423-1945
A minority enterprise small business
investment corporation. No industry
preference; geographic areas limited
to Indiana, Kentucky, Ohio, and West
Virginia.

Louisiana

Bank One Equity Investors, Inc.
451 Florida St.
Baton Rouge, Louisiana 70801
Phone: (504)332-4421
Fax: (504)332-7377
A small business investment
corporation. No industry preference.

Louisiana Department of Economic
Development
E-mail:
marketing@mail.lded.state.la.us
PO Box 94185
Baton Rouge, Louisiana 70804-9185
Phone: (504)342-3000
Fax: (504)342-5389

S.C.D.F. Investment Corp., Inc.
PO Box 3885
Lafayette, Louisiana 70502
Phone: (318)232-7672
Fax: (318)232-5094
A minority enterprise small business
investment corporation. No industry
preference.

First Commerce Capital, Inc.
201 St. Charles Ave., 16th Fl.
PO Box 60279
New Orleans, Louisiana 70170
Phone: (504)623-1600
Fax: (504)623-1779
William Harper, Manager
Preferred Investment Size: $1 to $2
million. Investment Policies: Loans,
equity. Investment Types: Later stage,
acquisition, buyouts. Industry

Preferences: Manufacturing
healthcare, retail, wholesale/
distribution. Geographic Preferences:
Gulf South region.

Maine

Finance Authority of Maine
E-mail: info@samemaine.com
83 Western Ave.
PO Box 949
Augusta, Maine 04332-0949
Phone: (207)623-3263
Fax: (800)623-0095
Assists business development and job
creation through direct loans, loan
guarantee programs, and project
grants.

Maine Capital Corp.
E-mail: info@norhtatlantacapital.com
70 Center St.
Portland, Maine 04101
Phone: (207)772-1001
Fax: (207)772-3257
A small business investment
corporation. No industry preference.

Maryland

ABS Ventures Limited Partnerships
(Baltimore)
135 S. St.
Baltimore, Maryland 21202
Phone: (410)727-1700
Free: (800)638-2596
Fax: (410)234-3699
Invests in the computer software,
health care, and biotechnology
industries.

American Security Capital Corp., Inc.
100 S. Charles St., 8th Fl.
Baltimore, Maryland 21201
Phone: (410)547-4205
Fax: (410)547-4990
A small business investment
company. Diversified industry
preference.

Anthem Capital, L.P.
16 S. Calvert St., Ste. 800
Baltimore, Maryland 21202
Phone: (410)625-1510

Fax: (410)625-1735
William M. Gust, II, Manager

Broventure Capital Management
16 W. Madison St.
Baltimore, Maryland 21201
Phone: (410)727-4520
Fax: (410)727-1436
Venture capital partnership. Provides start-up capital to early stage companies, expansion capital to companies experiencing rapid growth, and capital for acquisitions. Initial investments range from $400,000 to $750,000.

Maryland Department of Business and Economic Development
Financing Programs Division
217 E. Redwood St.,10th Fl.
Baltimore, Maryland 21202-3316
Phone: (410)767-0095
Free: (800)333-6995
Fax: (410)333-1836
Provides short-term financing for government contracts and long-term financing for equipment and working capital. Also operates a surety bond guarantee program for small businesses and an equity participation investment program for potential minority franchises.

Maryland Department of Economic and Employment Development
Financing Programs Division
Community Financing Group
111 N. Utah St.
Baltimore, Maryland 21201-3316
Phone: (410)333-4304
Fax: (410)333-6931

Maryland Department of Economic and Employment Development
Financing Programs Division
Industrial Development Financing Authority
217 E. Redwood St.
Baltimore, Maryland 21202-3316
Phone: (410)767-6300
Fax: (410)333-6911
Insures up to 80 percent of loans or obligations. Also provides tax-exempt revenue bonds for the financing of fixed assets.

New Enterprise Associates
(Baltimore)
1119 St. Paul St.
Baltimore, Maryland 21202
Phone: (410)244-0115
Fax: (410)752-7721
Private free-standing venture capital partnership providing seed and start-up financing. Prefers information technology and medical and life science industries.

T. Rowe Price
100 E. Pratt St.
Baltimore, Maryland 21202
Phone: (410)345-2000
Free: (800)638-7890
Fax: (410)345-2394
Venture capital supplier. Offers specialized investment services to meet the needs of companies in various stages of growth.

Triad Investor's Corp.
300 E. Joppa, Ste. 1111
Baltimore, Maryland 21286
Phone: (410)828-6497
Fax: (410)337-7312
Venture capital firm providing seed and early stage financing. Areas of interest include communications, computer- related, medical/health-related, genetic engineering, and electronic components and instrumentation industries.

Calvert Social Venture Partners
7201 Wisconsin Ave., Ste. 310
Bethesda, Maryland 20814
Phone: (301)718-4272
Fax: (301)656-4421
Private venture capital partnership focusing on Mid- Atlantic companies involved in socially or environmentally beneficial products or services.

Security Financial and Investment Corp.
7720 Wisconsin Ave., Ste. 207
Bethesda, Maryland 20814
Phone: (301)951-4288
Fax: (301)951-9282
A minority enterprise small business investment corporation. No industry preference.

Greater Washington Investments, Inc.
(Chevy Chase)
5454 Wisconsin Ave.
Chevy Chase, Maryland 20815
Phone: (301)656-0626
Fax: (301)656-4053
A small business investment company. Diversified industry preference.

Jupiter National, Inc.
5454 Wisconsin Ave.
Chevy Chase, Maryland 20815
Phone: (301)656-0626
Fax: (301)656-4053
A small business investment corporation. Prefers low to medium technology and subordinated debt investments.

Syncom Capital Corp.
8401 Coalville Rd.-Ste. 300
Silver Spring, Maryland 20910
Phone: (301)608-3203
Fax: (301)608-3307
A minority enterprise small business investment corporation. Areas of interest include telecommunications and media.

Grotech Capital Group
9690 Deereco Rd.,Ste. 800
Timonium, Maryland 21093
Phone: (410)560-2000
Fax: (410)560-1910

Massachusetts

Advent Atlantic Capital Co. LP
75 State St., Ste. 2500
Boston, Massachusetts 02109
Phone: (617)345-7200
Fax: (617)345-7201
Venture capital fund.
Communications industry preferred.

Advent V Capital Co.
75 State St., Ste. 2500
Boston, Massachusetts 02109
Phone: (617)345-7200
Fax: (617)345-7201
Venture capital fund.
Communications industry preferred.

Advent IV Capital Co.
75 State St., Ste. 2500

Boston, Massachusetts 02109
Phone: (617)345-7200
Fax: (617)345-7201
Venture capital fund.
Communications industry preferred.

Advent Industrial Capital Co. LP
75 State St., Ste. 2500
Boston, Massachusetts 02109
Phone: (617)345-7200
Fax: (617)345-7201
Venture capital fund.
Communications industry preferred.

Advent International Corp.
101 Federal St.
Boston, Massachusetts 02110
Phone: (617)951-9400
Fax: (617)951-0566
Venture capital firm. Invests in all
stages, from start-up technology-
based companies to well-established
companies in rapid growth or mature
industries; no retail clothing or real
estate.

American Research and Development
45 Milk St., 4th. Fl.
Boston, Massachusetts 02109
Phone: (617)423-7500
Fax: (617)423-9655
Independent private venture capital
partnership. All stages of financing;
no minimum or maximum
investment.

Aspen Ventures (Boston)
1 Post Office Square, Ste. 3320
Boston, Massachusetts 02109
Phone: (617)426-2151
Fax: (617)426-2181
Venture capital supplier. Provides
start-up and early stage financing to
companies in high-growth industries
such as biotechnology,
communications, electronics, and
health care.

Atlas Venture
222 Berkeley
Boston, Massachusetts 02116
Phone: (617)859-9290
Fax: (617)859-9292

Bain Capital Fund (Boston)
2 Copley Pl.

Boston, Massachusetts 02116
Phone: (617)572-3000
Fax: (617)572-3274
Private venture capital firm. No
industry preference, but avoids
investing in high-tech industries.
Minimum investment is $500,000.

BancBoston Ventures, Inc.
100 Federal St., 32nd Floor
PO Box 2016
Boston, Massachusetts 02110
Phone: (617)434-2442
Fax: (617)434-1153
A small business investment
corporation. Minimum investment is
$1 million.

Battery Ventures (Boston)
200 Portland St.
Boston, Massachusetts 02114
Phone: (617)367-1011
Fax: (617)367-1070
Venture capital firm providing
financing to early and emerging
software and communications
companies. Average investments are
from $1 million to $5 million.

Boston Capital Ventures
E-mail: info@bcv.com
Old City Hall
45 School St.
Boston, Massachusetts 02108
Phone: (617)227-6550
Fax: (617)227-3847
Venture capital firm.

Burr, Egan, Deleage, and Co.
(Boston)
1 Post Office Sq., Ste. 3800
Boston, Massachusetts 02109
Phone: (617)482-8020
Free: (800)756-2877
Fax: (617)482-1944
Private venture capital supplier.
Invests start-up, expansion, and
acquisitions capital nationwide.
Principal concerns are strength of the
management team; large, rapidly
expanding markets; and unique
products or services. Past investments
have been made in the fields of
electronics, health, and
communications. Investments range
from $750,000 to $5 million.

Chestnut Street Partners, Inc.
75 State St., Ste. 2500
Boston, Massachusetts 02109
Phone: (617)345-7220
Fax: (617)345-7201
A small business investment
company. Diversified industry
preference.

Claflin Capital Management, Inc.
E-mail: ccmbost@001.com
77 Franklin St.
Boston, Massachusetts 02110
Phone: (617)426-6505
Fax: (617)482-0016
Private venture capital firm investing
its own capital. No industry
preference but prefers early stage
companies.

Commonwealth Enterprise Fund, Inc.
10 Post Office Sq., Ste. 1090
Boston, Massachusetts 02109
Phone: (617)482-1881
Fax: (617)482-7129
A minority enterprise small business
investment corporation. No industry
preference, but clients must be located
in Massachusetts.

Copley Venture Partners
600 Atlantic Ave., 13th Fl.
Boston, Massachusetts 02210
Phone: (617)722-6030
Fax: (617)523-7739

Eastech Management Co.
45 Milk St.,4th. Floor
Boston, Massachusetts 02109
Phone: (617)423-7500
Fax: (617)423-9655
Private venture capital supplier.
Provides start-up and first- and
second-stage financing to companies
in the following industries:
communications, computer-related
electronic components and
instrumentation, and industrial
products and equipment. Will not
consider real estate, agriculture,
forestry, fishing, finance and
insurance, transportation, oil and gas,
publishing, entertainment, natural
resources, or retail.

Fidelity Venture Associates, Inc.
Fidelity Investments
82 Devonshire St., Mail Zone R25C
Boston, Massachusetts 02109
Phone: (617)563-7000
Fax: (617)728-6755
Privately-held investment
management firm providing financing
to young companies at various stages
of development. Areas of interest
include financial services, publishing,
specialty retailing, health care,
transportation, computer systems and
software, and telecommunications
industries.

Greylock Management Corp.
(Boston)
1 Federal St., 26th Fl.
Boston, Massachusetts 02110
Phone: (617)423-5525
Fax: (617)482-0059
Private venture capital partnership.
Minimum investment of $250,000;
preferred investment size of over $1
million. Will function either as deal
originator or investor in deals created
by others.

John Hancock Venture Partners, Inc.
1 Financial Center, 44th Fl.
Boston, Massachusetts 02111
Phone: (617)348-3707
Fax: (617)350-0305
Venture capital supplier. Diversified
investments.

Harvard Management Co., Inc.
600 Atlantic Ave.
Boston, Massachusetts 02210
Phone: (617)523-4400
Free: (800)723-0044
Fax: (617)523-1283
Diversified venture capital firm.
Minimum investment is $1 million.

Highland Capital Partners
2 International Pl.
Boston, Massachusetts 02110
Phone: (617)330-8765
Fax: (617)531-1550
Industry preferences include health
care, software, and
telecommunications.

Liberty Ventures Corp.
E-mail: @1liberty.com
1 Liberty Sq.
Boston, Massachusetts 02109
Phone: (617)423-1765
Free: (800)423-1766
Fax: (617)338-4362
Venture capital partnership. Provides
start-up, early stage, and expansion
financing to companies that are
pioneering applications of proven
technology; also will consider
nontechnology-based companies with
strong management teams and plans
for expansion. Investments range
from $500,000 to $1 million, with a
$6 million maximum.

Massachusetts Business Development
Corp.
50 Milk St., 16th Fl.
Boston, Massachusetts 02109
Phone: (617)350-8877
Fax: (617)350-0052
Provides assistance to businesses and
individuals attempting to utilize
federal, state, and local loan finance
programs.

Massachusetts Community
Development Finance Corp.
10 Post Office Sq., Ste. 1090
Boston, Massachusetts 02109
Phone: (617)482-9141
Fax: (617)482-7129
Provides financing for small
businesses and for commercial,
industrial, and residential business
developments through community
development corporations (CDCs) in
depressed areas of Massachusetts.
Three investment programs are
offered: the Venture Capital
Investment Program, the Community
Development Program, and the Small
Loan Guarantee Program.

Massachusetts Industrial Finance
Agency
75 Federal St., 10th Fl.
Boston, Massachusetts 02110
Phone: (617)451-2477
Free: (800)445-8030
Fax: (617)451-3429

Promotes expansion, renovation, and
modernization of small businesses
through the use of investment
incentives.

Massachusetts Minority Enterprise
Investment Corp.
50 Milk St., 16th St.
Boston, Massachusetts 02109
Phone: (617)350-8877
Fax: (617)350-0052
Minority enterprise small business
investment corporation. Involved with
community development. Loans range
from $25,000 to $250,000.

Massachusetts Technology
Development Corp. (MTDC)
148 State St., 9th Fl.
Boston, Massachusetts 02109-2506
Phone: (617)723-4920
Fax: (617)723-5983
Makes investments in start-up or early
stage expansion technology-based
businesses within the Commonwealth
of Massachusetts only.

MC PARTNERS
75 State St.,Ste. 2500
Boston, Massachusetts 02109
Phone: (617)345-7200
Fax: (617)345-7201
Venture capital fund.
Communications industry preferred.

Mezzanine Capital Corp.
75 State St., Ste. 2500
Boston, Massachusetts 02109
Phone: (617)345-7200
Fax: (617)345-7201
A small business investment
company. Diversified industry
preference.

Northeast Small Business Investment
Corp.
130 New Market Square
Boston, Massachusetts 02118
Phone: (617)445-2100
Fax: (617)442-1013
A small business investment
corporation. No industry preference.

P. R. Venture Partners, L.P.
100 Federal St., 37th Fl.
Boston, Massachusetts 02110

Phone: (617)357-9600
Fax: (617)357-9601
Venture capital firm providing early stage financing. Areas of interest include health care, information, and food.

Pioneer Ventures LP
60 State St.
Boston, Massachusetts 02109
Phone: (617)742-7825
Fax: (617)742-7315
A small business investment company. Diversified industry preference.

Private Equity Management
60 State St., Ste. 6620
Boston, Massachusetts 02109
Phone: (617)345-9440
Fax: (617)345-9878

Summit Partners
600 Atlantic Ave., 28th Fl.
Boston, Massachusetts 02210-2227
Phone: (617)742-5500
Fax: (617)824-1100
Venture capital firm. Prefers to invest in emerging, profitable, growth companies in the electronic technology, environmental services, and health care industries. Investments range from $1 million to $4 million.

TA Associates (Boston)
125 High St., Ste. 2500
Boston, Massachusetts 02110-2720
Phone: (617)338-0800
Fax: (617)574-6728
Private venture capital partnership. Technology companies, media communications companies, and leveraged buy outs preferred. Will provide from $1 million to $20 million in investments.

Transportation Capital Corp. (Boston)
45 Newbury St., Rm. 207
Boston, Massachusetts 02116
Phone: (617)536-0344
Fax: (617)536-5750
A minority enterprise small business investment corporation. Specializes in taxicabs and taxicab medallion loans.

TVM Techno Venture Management
101 Arch St., Ste. 1950
Boston, Massachusetts 02110
Phone: (617)345-9320
Free: (800)345-2093
Fax: (617)345-9377
Venture capital firm providing early stage financing. Areas of interest include high technology such as software, communications, medical, and biotechnology industries. Preferred investment size is $1 million.

UST Capital Corp.
40 Court St.
Boston, Massachusetts 02108
Phone: (617)726-7000
Free: (800)441-8782
Fax: (617)726-7369
A small business investment company. Diversified industry preference.

Venture Capital Fund of New England II
160 Federal St., 23rd Fl.
Boston, Massachusetts 02110
Phone: (617)439-4646
Fax: (617)439-4652
Venture capital fund. Prefers New England high-technology companies that have a commercial prototype or initial product sales. Will provide up to $500,000 in first-round financing.

First Capital Corp. of Chicago (Boston)
Bank Of Boston
1380 Massachusetts Ave.
Cambridge, Massachusetts 02138-3822
Phone: (617)434-2500
Fax: (617)434-2506
A small business investment company.

MDT Advisers, Inc.
125 Cambridge Park Dr.
Cambridge, Massachusetts 02140
Phone: (617)234-2200
Fax: (617)234-2210

Zero Stage Capital Co., Inc. (State College)
101 Main St., 17th Fl.

Cambridge, Massachusetts 02142
Phone: (617)876-5355
Fax: (617)876-1248
Venture capital firm. Industry preferences include high- technology start-up companies located in the northeastern U.S.

Zero Stage Capital V, L.P. (Cambridge)
E-mail: zerostage@aol.com
Kendall Sq.
1010 Main St., 17th Fl.
Cambridge, Massachusetts 02142
Phone: (617)876-5355
Fax: (617)876-1248
Paul Kelley, Manager
Preferred Investment Size: $50,000 to $500,000. Investment Types: Equity, debit with equity features. Industry Preferences: Biotech, computer hardware and software, energy. Geographic Preferences: Northeast.

Boston College Capital Formation Service
96 College Rd.
Rahner House
Chestnut Hill, Massachusetts 02167
Phone: (617)552-4091
Fax: (617)552-2730

Capital Formation Service
Boston College
96 College Rd., Rahner House
Chestnut Hill, Massachusetts 02167
Phone: (617)552-4091
Fax: (617)552-2730
Provides assistance to clients requiring financing from nonconventional sources, such as quasi-public financing programs; state, federal, and local programs; venture capital; and private investors.

Seacoast Capital Partners, L.P.
E-mail: scpltd.com
55 Ferncroft Rd.
Danvers, Massachusetts 01923
Phone: (508)777-3866
Fax: (508)750-1301
Eben Moulton, Manager
Preferred Investment Size: $1 to $6 million. Investment Policies: Loans and equity investments. Investment

Types: Expansion, later stage.
Industry Preferences: Diversified.
Geographic Preferences: National.

Argonauts MESBIC Corp.
929 Worcester Rd.
Framingham, Massachusetts 01701
Phone: (617)697-0501
A minority enterprise small business
investment company. Diversified
industry preference.

Applied Technology Partners
1 Cranberry Hill
Lexington, Massachusetts 02173-
7397
Phone: (617)862-8622
Fax: (617)862-8367
Venture capital firm providing early
stage investment. Areas of interest
include hardware technologies,
electronics, software,
communications, and information
services.

Venture Founders Corp.
1 Cranberry Hill
Lexington, Massachusetts 02173
Phone: (617)862-8622
Fax: (617)862-8367
Venture capital fund. Preferred
geographical area is the New England
states. Required initial investment
size is between $50,000 and
$400,000.

Business Achievement Corp.
1172 Beacon St.
Newton, Massachusetts 02161
Phone: (617)965-0550
Fax: (617)969-2671
A small business investment
corporation. No industry preference.

Comdisco Venture Group (Newton)
1 Newton Executive Park
2221 Washington 3rd Fl.
Newton Lower Falls, Massachusetts
02162-1417
Phone: (617)244-6622
Free: (800)321-1111
Fax: (617)630-5599

New England MESBIC Inc.
530 Turnpike St.

North Andover, Massachusetts
01845-5812
Phone: (508)688-4326

Analog Devices, Inc.
1 Technology Way
PO Box 9106
Norwood, Massachusetts 02062-9106
Phone: (617)329-4700
Free: (800)262-5643
Fax: (617)326-8703
Venture capital supplier. Prefers to
invest in industries involved in analog
devices.

ABS Ventures Limited Partnerships
(Boston)
404 Wymin St. Ste. 365
Waltham, Massachusetts 02154
Phone: (617)290-0004
Fax: (617)290-0999

Advanced Technology Ventures
(Boston)
281 Winter St., Ste. 350
Waltham, Massachusetts 02154-8713
Phone: (617)290-0707
Fax: (617)684-0045
Private venture capital firm. Prefers
early stage financing in high-
technology industries.

Charles River Ventures
1000 Winter St., Ste. 3300
Waltham, Massachusetts 02154
Phone: (617)487-7060
Fax: (617)487-7065
Venture capital partnership providing
early stage financing. Areas of
interest include communications,
software, environmental, and
specialty financial service industries.

Hambro International Equity Partners
(Boston)
404 Wyman, Ste. 365
Waltham, Massachusetts 02154
Phone: (617)523-7767
Fax: (617)290-0999
Private venture firm. Seeks to invest
in software, electronics and
instrumentation, biotechnology,
retailing, direct marketing of
consumer goods, and environmental
industries.

Matrix Partners III
1000 Winter St.,Ste.4500
Waltham, Massachusetts 02154
Phone: (617)890-2244
Fax: (617)890-2288
Private venture capital partnership.
Industry preference includes high
technology, communications, and
software.

Ampersand Ventures
E-mail: bjt@ampersandventures.com
55 William St., Ste. 240
Wellesley, Massachusetts 02181
Phone: (617)239-0700
Free: (800)239-0706
Fax: (617)239-0824
Venture capital supplier. Provides
start-up and early stage financing to
technology-based companies.
Investments range from $500,000 to
$1 million.

Geneva Middle Market Investors,
L.P.
70 Walnut St.
Wellesley, Massachusetts 02181
Phone: (617)239-8230
Fax: (617)239-8064
James J. Goodman, Manager

Northwest Venture Partners
40 William St., Ste. 305
Wellesley, Massachusetts 02181
Phone: (617)237-5870
Fax: (617)237-6270

Bessemer Venture Partners
(Wellesley Hills)
83 Walnut St.
Wellesley Hills, Massachusetts 02181
Phone: (617)237-6050
Fax: (617)235-7068

Palmer Partners L.P.
300 Unicorn Park Dr.
Woburn, Massachusetts 01801
Phone: (617)933-5445
Fax: (617)933-0698
Venture capital partnership. Provides
early stage, commercialization, and
second and third stage financing. No
industry preference, but does not
invest in real estate or biotechnology
industries.

ORGANIZATIONS, AGENCIES, & CONSULTANTS

Michigan

White Pines Capital Corp.
2929 Plymouth Rd., Ste. 210
Ann Arbor, Michigan 48105
Phone: (313)747-9401
Fax: (313)747-9704
A small business investment
company. Diversified industry
preference.

Dearborn Capital Corp.
PO Box 1729
Dearborn, Michigan
48126-2729
Phone: (313)337-8577
Fax: (313)248-1252
A minority enterprise small business
investment corporation. Loans to
minority-owned, operated, and
controlled suppliers to Ford Motor
Company, Dearborn Capital
Corporation's parent.

Motor Enterprises, Inc.
3044 W. Grand Blvd.
Detroit, Michigan
48202
Phone: (313)556-4273
Fax: (313)974-4854
A minority enterprise small business
investment corporation. Prefers
automotive-related industries.

Metro-Detroit Investment Co.
30777 Northwestern Hwy., Ste. 300
Farmington Hills, Michigan 48334-
2549
Phone: (810)851-6300
Fax: (810)851-9551
A minority enterprise small business
investment corporation. Food store
industry preferred.

Demery Seed Capital Fund
3707 W. Maple Rd.
Franklin, Michigan 48025
Phone: (810)433-1722
Fax: (810)644-4526
Invests in start-up companies in
Michigan.

The Capital Fund
6412 Centurion Dr., Ste. 150
Lansing, Michigan 48917

Phone: (517)323-7772
Fax: (517)323-1999
A small business investment
company. Provides expansion
financing.

State Treasurer's Office
Alternative Investments Division
PO Box 15128
Lansing, Michigan 48901
Phone: (517)373-4330
Fax: (517)335-3668

Minnesota

Ceridian Corp.
8100 34th Ave. S
Bloomington, Minnesota 55425-1640
Phone: (612)853-8100

Altair Ventures, Inc.
7550 France Ave. S, Ste. 201
Minneapolis, Minnesota 55435
Phone: (612)449-0250
Fax: (612)896-4909
Venture capital firm providing
acquisitions and leveraged buyout
financing. Diversified industry
preference.

Artesian Capital Limited Partnership
E-mail: artesian2@aol.com
Foshay Tower
821 Marquette Ave., Ste. 1700
Minneapolis, Minnesota 55402-2905
Phone: (612)334-5600
Fax: (612)334-5600
Venture capital firm providing seed
and start-up financing in the upper
Midwest. Areas of interest include
medical, communications, and
environmental industries.

Capital Dimensions Ventures Fund,
Inc.
2 Appletree Sq., Ste. 335
Minneapolis, Minnesota 55425
Phone: (612)854-3007
A minority enterprise small business
investment corporation. No industry
preference.

Cherry Tree Investment Co.
1400 Northland Plz.
3800 W. 80th St., Ste. 1400

Minneapolis, Minnesota 55431
Phone: (612)893-9012
Fax: (612)893-9036
Venture capital supplier. Provides
start-up and early stage financing.
Fields of interest include information/
software, retail, education, and
publishing industries located in the
Midwest. There are no minimum or
maximum investment limitations.

Coral Group, Inc.
60 S. 6th St., Ste. 35 10
Minneapolis, Minnesota 55402
Phone: (612)335-8666
Fax: (612)335-8668
Venture capital firm providing all
types of financing. Areas of interest
include communications, computer
products, electronics, medical/health,
genetic engineering, industrial
products, transportation and
diversified.

Crawford Capital Corp.
1150 Interchange Tower
600 S. Hwy. 169
Minneapolis, Minnesota 55426
Phone: (612)544-2221
Fax: (612)544-5885
Venture capital firm providing
financing for firm's own venture fund
limited partnerships. Areas of interest
include medical, software, and
technology industries.

FBS SBIC, Ltd. Partnership
1st Bank Place
601 2nd Ave. S., 16th Fl.
Minneapolis, Minnesota 55402
Phone: (612)973-0988
Fax: (612)973-0203
Richard Rinkoff, Manager
Investment Policies: Loans, loans
with warrants. Investment Types:
Expansion, early stage. Industry
Preferences: Diversified. Geographic
Preferences: National.

Milestone Growth Fund, Inc.
401 2nd Ave. S., Ste. 1032
Minneapolis, Minnesota 55401
Phone: (612)338-0090
Fax: (612)338-1172

Minority enterprise small business investment corporation providing financing for expansion of existing companies. Diversified industry preference.

Norwest Equity Partners IV
2800 Piper Jaffray Tower
222 S. 9th St.
Minneapolis, Minnesota 55402-3388
Phone: (612)667-1667
Fax: (612)667-1660
Small business investment company. Invests in all industries except real estate.

Norwest Equity Partners V, L.P.
2800 Piper Jaffrey Tower
222 S. 9th St.
Minneapolis, Minnesota 55402
Phone: (612)667-1667
Fax: (612)667-1660
John F. Whaley, Manager
Preferred Investment Size: $3 to $15 million. Investment Policies: Equity. Investment Types: Start-up, expansion, later stage. Industry Preferences: Diversified. Geographic Preferences: National.

Oak Investment Partners
(Minneapolis)
4550 Norwest Center
90 S. 7th St., Ste. 4550
Minneapolis, Minnesota 55402
Phone: (612)339-9322
Fax: (612)337-8017
Prefers to invest in retail industries.

Pathfinder Venture Capital Funds
(Minneapolis)
7300 Metro Blvd., Ste. 585
Minneapolis, Minnesota 55439
Phone: (612)835-1121
Fax: (612)835-8389
Venture capital supplier providing early stage financing. Areas of interest include medical, pharmaceutical, and health care service; and computer and computer-related industries in the Upper Midwest and West.

Peterson-Spencer-Fansler Co.
Foshay Tower

821 Marquette, Ste. 1900
Minneapolis, Minnesota 55402
Phone: (612)904-2305
Fax: (612)205-0912
Venture capital firm providing seed, research and development, start-up, first stage, and bridge financing. Areas of interest include medical technology and health care service industries.

Piper Jaffray Ventures, Inc.
Piper Jaffray Tower
222 S. 9th St.
Minneapolis, Minnesota 55402
Phone: (612)342-6000
Fax: (612)337-8017

University Technology Center, Inc.
E-mail: utec@pro-ns.net
1313 5th St. SE
Minneapolis, Minnesota 55414
Phone: (612)379-3800
Fax: (612)379-3875
Venture capital firm providing start-up, first stage, initial expansion and acquisition financing. Areas of interest include environment, consumer products, industrial products, transportation and diversified industry.

Wellspring Corp.
4530 IDS Center
Minneapolis, Minnesota 55402
Phone: (612)338-0704
Fax: (612)338-0744
Venture capital firm providing acquisition and leveraged buyout financing. Areas of interest include marine transportation equipment and weighing and measuring equipment manufacturing.

Food Fund
5720 Smatana Dr., Ste. 300
Minnetonka, Minnesota 55343
Phone: (612)939-3944
Fax: (612)939-8106
Venture capital firm providing expansion, management buyouts, early stage and acquisition financing. Areas of interest include food products, food equipment, food packaging, and food distribution.

Medical Innovation Partners, Inc.
Opus Center, Ste. 421
9900 Bren Rd. E
Minnetonka, Minnesota 55343
Phone: (612)931-0154
Fax: (612)931-0003

St. Paul Growth Ventures
E-mail: spence_morley@usa.net
1450 Energy Park Dr., Ste. 110-D
St. Paul, Minnesota 55108-1013
Phone: (612)641-1667
Fax: (612)641-1147
Venture capital firm providing early stage ventures, product development, product launch and early organizational development. Prefers software companies in the Minneapolis/St. Paul area.

Quest Venture Partners
730 E. Lake St.
Wayzata, Minnesota 55391-1769
Phone: (612)473-8367
Fax: (612)473-4702
Venture capital firm providing second stage and bridge financing. Areas of interest include communications, computer products and medical/health care.

Threshold Ventures, Inc.
15500 Wayzata Blvd., Ste.819
Wayzata, Minnesota 55391-1418
Phone: (612)473-2051
A small business investment corporation. No industry preference.

Mississippi

Sun-Delta Capital Access Center, Inc.
E-mail: deltafdn@tednfo.com
819 Main St.
Greenville, Mississippi 38701
Phone: (601)335-5291
Fax: (601)335-5295
A minority enterprise small business investment corporation. No industry preference.

Mississippi Department of Economic and Community Development
Mississippi Business Finance Corp.
1200 Walter Sillers Bldg.
PO Box 849

Jackson, Mississippi 39205
Phone: (601)359-3552
Fax: (601)359-2832
Administers the SBA(503) Loan and
the Mississippi Small Business Loan
Guarantee.

Vicksburg SBIC
PO Box 821568
Vicksburg, Mississippi 39182
Phone: (601)636-4762
Fax: (601)636-9476
A small business investment
corporation. No industry preference.

Missouri

Bankers Capital Corp.
3100 Gillham Rd.
Kansas City, Missouri 64109
Phone: (816)531-1600
Fax: (816)531-1334
A small business investment
corporation. No industry preference.

Capital for Business, Inc. (Kansas
City)
1000 Walnut St., 18th Fl.
Kansas City, Missouri 64106-2123
Phone: (816)234-2357
Fax: (816)234-2333
A small business investment
corporation. No industry preference.

CFB Venture Fund II, Inc.
1000 Walnut St., 18th Fl.
Kansas City, Missouri 64106
Phone: (816)234-2357
Fax: (816)234-2333
A small business investment
company. Diversified industry
preference.

InvestAmerica Venture Group, Inc.
(Kansas City)
Commerce Tower Bldg.
911 Main St., Ste. 2424
Kansas City, Missouri 64105
Phone: (816)842-0114
Fax: (816)471-7339
A small business investment
corporation. No industry preference.

MorAmerica Capital Corp. (Kansas
City)
911 Main St., Ste. 2424

Kansas City, Missouri 64105
Phone: (816)842-0114
Fax: (816)471-7339
A small business investment
company.

United Missouri Capital Corp.
PO Box 419226
Kansas City, Missouri 64141
Phone: (816)860-7914
Fax: (816)860-7143
A small business investment
corporation. No industry preference.

Midland Bank
740 NW Blue Pkwy.
Lees Summit, Missouri 64086-5713
Phone: (816)524-8000
Fax: (816)525-8624
A small business investment
company. Diversified industry
preference.

Allsop Venture Partners (St. Louis)
55 W. Port Plz., Ste. 575
St. Louis, Missouri 63146
Phone: (314)434-1688
Fax: (314)434-6560

Capital for Business, Inc. (St. Louis)
11 S. Meramec, Ste. 1430
St. Louis, Missouri 63105
Phone: (314)746-7427
Fax: (314)746-8739
A small business investment
corporation. Focuses primarily on
later-stage expansion and acquisition
in the manufacturing and distribution
industries.

CFB Venture Fund I, Inc.
11 S. Meramec, Ste. 1436
St. Louis, Missouri 63105
Phone: (314)746-7427
Fax: (314)746-8739
A small business investment
company. Diversified industry
preference.

Gateway Associates L.P.
8000 Maryland Ave., Ste. 1190
St. Louis, Missouri 63105
Phone: (314)721-5707
Fax: (314)721-5135

ITT Small Business Finance Corp.
635 Maryville Center Dr., Ste. 120

St. Louis, Missouri 63141
Phone: (314)205-3500
Free: (800)447-2025
Fax: (314)205-3699
Non-bank lender providing start-up
and expansion financing.

Montana

Montana Board of Investments
Office of Development Finance
Capitol Sta.
555 Fuller Ave.
Helena, Montana 59620-0125
Phone: (406)444-0001
Fax: (406)449-6579
Provides investments to businesses
that will bring long- term benefits to
the Montana economy.

Montana Department of Commerce
Economic Development Division
Finance Technical Assistance
1424 9th Ave.
Helena, Montana 59620-0401
Phone: (406)444-4780
Fax: (406)444-1872
Provides financial analysis, financial
planning, loan packaging, industrial
revenue bonding, state and private
capital sources, and business tax
incentives.

Nebraska

Nebraska Investment Finance
Authority
1230 "O" St., Ste. 200
Lincoln, Nebraska 68508
Phone: (402)434-3900
Free: (800)204-6432
Fax: (402)434-3921
Provides lower cost financing for
manufacturing facilities, certain farm
property, and health care and
residential development. Also
established a Small Industrial
Development Bond Program to help
small Nebraska-based companies
(those with fewer than 100 employees
or less than $2.5 million in gross
salaries).

United Financial Resources Corp.
PO Box 1131

Omaha, Nebraska 68101
Phone: (402)339-7300
Fax: (402)339-9226
A small business investment
corporation. Only interests include the
grocery industry.

Nevada

Nevada Department of Business and
Industry
Bond Division
1665 Hot Springs Rd., Ste. 165
Carson City, Nevada 89710
Phone: (702)687-4250
Fax: (702)687-4266
Issues up to $100 million in bonds to
fund venture capital projects in
Nevada; helps companies expand or
build new facilities through the use of
tax-exempt financing.

Atlanta Investment Co., Inc.
601 Fairview Blvd.
Incline Village, Nevada 89451
Phone: (702)833-1836
Fax: (702)833-1890
L. Mark Newman, Chairman of the
Board
Preferred Investment Size:
$2,000,000. Investment Policies:
Equity. Investment Types: Expansion,
later stage. Industry Preferences:
Technology. Geographic Preferences:
National.

New Hampshire

Business Finance Authority of the
State of New Hampshire
E-mail: bfa@enterwebb.com
4 Park St., Ste. 302
Concord, New Hampshire 03301-6313
Phone: (603)271-2391
Fax: (603)271-2396
Works to foster economic
development and promote the creation
of employment in the state of New
Hampshire. Provides guarantees on
loans to businesses made by banks
and local development organizations;
guarantees on portions of loans
guaranteed in part by the U.S. Small
Business Administration; cash

reserves on loans made by state banks
to businesses with annual revenues
less than or equal to $5,000,000; and
opportunities for local development
organizations to acquire additional
funds for the purpose of promoting
and developing business within the
state.

New Jersey

MidMark Capital, L.P.
E-mail: midmcat@aol.com
(midmcat@aol.com)
466 Southern Blvd.
Chatham, New Jersey 07928
Phone: (201)822-2999
Fax: (201)822-8911
Denis Newman, Manager
Preferred Investment Size:
$5,000,000. Investment Policies:
Equity. Investment Types: Expansion,
later stage. Industry Preferences:
Diversified, communication,
manufacturing, retail/service.
Geographic Preferences: East,
midwest.

Transpac Capital Corp.
1037 Rte. 46 E
Clifton, New Jersey 07013
Phone: (201)470-8855
Fax: (201)470-8827
A minority enterprise small business
investment company. Diversified
industry preference.

Monmouth Capital Corp.
125 Wyckoff Rd.
Midland National Bank Bldg.
PO Box 335
Eatontown, New Jersey 07724
Phone: (908)542-4927
Fax: (908)542-1106
A small business investment
corporation. No industry preference.

Capital Circulation Corp.
2035 Lemoine Ave., 2nd Fl.
Fort Lee, New Jersey 07024
Phone: (201)947-8637
Fax: (201)585-1965
A minority enterprise small business
investment company. Diversified
industry preference.

Japanese American Capital Corp.
716 Jersey Ave.
Jersey City, New Jersey 07310-1306
Phone: (201)798-5000
Fax: (201)798-4362

Taroco Capital Corp.
716 Jersey Ave.
Jersey City, New Jersey 07310-1306
Phone: (201)798-5000
Fax: (201)798-4322
A minority enterprise small business
investment corporation. Focuses on
Chinese-Americans.

Edison Venture Fund
997 Lenox Dr., Ste. 3
Lawrenceville, New Jersey 08648
Phone: (609)896-1900
Fax: (609)896-0066
Private venture capital firm. No
industry preference.

Tappan Zee Capital Corp. (New
Jersey)
201 Lower Notch Rd.
PO Box 416
Little Falls, New Jersey 07424
Phone: (201)256-8280
Fax: (201)256-2841
A small business investment
company. Diversified industry
preference.

CIT Group/Venture Capital, Inc.
650 CIT Dr.
Livingston, New Jersey 07039
Phone: (201)740-5429
Fax: (201)740-5555
A small business investment
company. Diversified industry
preference.

ESLO Capital Corp.
212 Wright St.
Newark, New Jersey 07114
Phone: (201)242-4488
Fax: (201)643-6062
Leo Katz, President
Preferred Investment Size: $100,000.
Investment Policies: Loans.
Investment Types: Start-ups, early
stage. Industry Preferences: Business
services, manufacturing. Geographic
Preferences: Northeast.

Rutgers Minority Investment Co.
180 University Ave., 3rd Fl.
Newark, New Jersey 07102-1803
Phone: (201)648-5627
Fax: (201)648-1175
A minority enterprise small business
investment corporation. No industry
preference.

Accel Partners (Princeton)
1 Palmer Sq.
Princeton, New Jersey 08542
Phone: (609)683-4500
Fax: (609)683-0384
Venture capital firm.
Telecommunications, software, and
health care industries preferred.

Carnegie Hill Co.
202 Carnegie Center, Ste. 103
Princeton, New Jersey 08540
Phone: (609)520-0500
Fax: (609)520-1160

Domain Associates
1 Palmer Sq.
Princeton, New Jersey 08542
Phone: (609)683-4500
Fax: (609)683-0384

DSV Partners (Princeton)
221 Nassau St.
Princeton, New Jersey 08542
Phone: (609)924-6420
Fax: (609)683-0174
Provides financing for the growth of
companies in the biotechnology/
health care, environmental, and
software industries. Also provides
capital to facilitate consolidation of
fragmented industries.

First Century Partners (New York)
1 Palmer Sq. Ste. 425
Princeton, New Jersey 08542
Phone: (609)683-8848
Fax: (609)683-8123
Private venture capital firm.
Minimum investment is $1.5 million.
Prefers specialty retailing and
consumer products industries.

Johnston Associates, Inc.
E-mail: jai181@aol.com
181 Cherry Valley Rd.

Princeton, New Jersey 08540
Phone: (609)924-3131
Fax: (609)683-7524
Venture capital supplier providing
seed and start-up financing. Areas of
interest include pharmaceutical
research, biotechnology, and
bioremediation of toxic waste.

Bishop Capital, L.P.
500 Morris Ave.
Springfield, New Jersey 07081
Phone: (201)376-0345
Fax: (201)376-6527
A small business investment
company. Diversified industry
preference.

BCI Advisors, Inc.
Glenpointe Center W., 2nd Fl.
Teaneck, New Jersey 07666
Phone: (201)836-3900
Fax: (201)836-6368
Venture capital firm providing
mezzanine financing for growth
companies with revenues of $25
million to $200 million. Diversified
industry preference.

Demuth, Folger and Terhune
300 Frank W. Burr, 5th Floor
Teaneck, New Jersey 07666
Phone: (201)836-6000
Fax: (201)836-5666
Venture capital firm with preferences
for technology, services, and health
care investments.

DFW Capital Partners, L.P.
Glenpointe Center E., 5th Fl.
300 Frank W. Burr Blvd.
Teaneck, New Jersey 07666
Phone: (201)836-2233
Fax: (201)836-5666
Donald F. DeMuth, Manager
Preferred Investment Size:
$4,000,000. Investment Policies:
Equity. Investment Types: Early
through later stage. Industry
Preferences: Healthcare, services,
diversified. Geographic Preferences:
National.

New Jersey Commission on Science
and Technology
E-mail: njcst@njcst.gov
28 W. State St., CN 832
Trenton, New Jersey 08625-0832
Phone: (609)984-1671
Fax: (609)292-5920
Awards bridge grants to small
companies that have received seed
money under the Federal State
Business Innovation Research
programs and works to improve the
scientific and technical research
capabilities within the state. Also
provides management and technical
assistance and other services to small,
technology- oriented companies.

New Jersey Department of
Agriculture
Division of Rural Resources
John Fitch Plz., CN 330
Trenton, New Jersey 08625
Phone: (609)292-5532
Fax: (609)633-7229
Fosters the agricutural economic
development of rural areas of the state
through financial assistance for
farmers and agribusinesses.

New Jersey Economic Development
Authority
CN90
Trenton, New Jersey 08625-0990
Phone: (609)292-1800
Fax: (609)292-0368
Arranges low-interest, long-term
financing for manufacturing facilities,
land acquisition, and business
equipment and machinery purchases.
Also issues taxable bonds to provide
financing for manufacturing,
distribution, warehousing, research,
commercial, office, and service uses.

Edelson Technology Partners
Whiteweld Ctr 300 Tice Blvd
Woodcliff Lake, New Jersey 07675
Phone: (201)930-9898
Fax: (201)930-8899
Venture capital partnership interested
in high technology investment,
including medical, biotechnology, and
computer industries.

New Mexico

Albuquerque Investment Co.
P.O. Box 487
Albuquerque, New Mexico 87103-3132
Phone: (505)247-0145
Fax: (505)843-6912
A small business investment corporation. No industry preference.

Associated Southwest Investors, Inc.
1650 University N.E., Ste.200
Albuquerque, New Mexico 87102
Phone: (505)247-4050
Fax: (505)247-4050
A minority enterprise small business investment corporation. No industry preference.

Industrial Development Corp. of Lea County
E-mail: edclea@leaconet.com
PO Box 1376
Hobbs, New Mexico 88240
Phone: (505)397-2039
Free: (800)443-2236
Fax: (505)392-2300
Certified development company.

Ads Capital Corp.
142 Lincoln Ave., Ste. 500
Santa Fe, New Mexico 87501
Phone: (505)983-1769
Fax: (505)983-2887
Venture capital supplier. Prefers to invest in manufacturing or distribution companies.

New Mexico Economic Development Department
Technology Enterprise Division
1100 St. Francis Dr.
Santa Fe, New Mexico 87503
Phone: (505)827-0265
Fax: (505)827-0588
Provides state funds to advanced-technology business ventures that are close to the commerical stage.

New Mexico Economic Development Department
Economic Development Division
1100 St. Francis Dr.
Santa Fe, New Mexico 87503
Phone: (505)827-0300

Free: (800)374-3061
Fax: (505)827-0328
Provides start-up or expansion loans for businesses that are established in or are new to New Mexico.

New Mexico Labor Department
Job Training Division
Aspen Plz.
1596 Pacheco St.
PO Box 4218
Santa Fe, New Mexico 87502
Phone: (505)827-6827
Fax: (505)827-6812
Provides new and expanding industries with state-sponsored funds to train a New Mexican workforce.

New York

Fleet Bank
69 St.
Albany, New York 12207
Phone: (518)447-4115
Fax: (518)447-4043
Venture capital supplier. No industry preference. Typical investment is between $500,000 and $1 million.

NYBDC Capital Corp.
41 State St.
PO Box 738
Albany, New York 12201
Phone: (518)463-2268
Fax: (518)463-0240
A small business investment corporation.

Vega Capital Corp.
80 Business Park Dr., Ste. 201
Armonk, New York 10504-1701
Phone: (914)273-1025
Fax: (914)273-1028
A small business investment corporation. Diversified industry preferences.

Triad Capital Corp. of New York
960 Southern Blvd.
Bronx, New York 10459-3402
Phone: (718)589-5000
Fax: (718)589-4744
A minority enterprise small business investment corporation. No industry preference.

First New York Management Co.
1 Metrotech Center N, 11th Fl.
Brooklyn, New York 11201
Phone: (718)797-5990
Fax: (718)722-3533
A small business investment corporation. No industry preference.

M & T Capital Corporation
1 Fountain Plz., 3rd Fl.
Buffalo, New York 14203-1495
Phone: (716)848-3800
Fax: (716)848-3150
A small business investment corporation providing equity financing for small to mid-size companies for expansion activities, acquisitions, recapitalizations, and buyouts. Initial investments range from $500,000 - $2 million. Prefers businesses located in the Northeast and Midwest.

Rand SBIC, Inc.
1300 Rand Bldg.
Buffalo, New York 14203
Phone: (716)853-0802
Fax: (716)854-8480
A small business investment corporation. Prefers to invest in communications, computer-related, consumer, distributor, and electronic components and instrumentation industries.

Fifty-Third Street Ventures, L.P.
155 Main St.
Cold Spring, New York 10516
Phone: (914)265-4244
Fax: (914)265-4158
A small business investment company. Diversified industry preference.

Tessler and Cloherty, Inc.
155 Main St.
Cold Spring, New York 10516
Phone: (914)265-4244
Fax: (914)265-4158
A small business investment corporation. No industry preference.

Esquire Capital Corp.
69 Veterans Memorial Hwy.
Commack, New York 11725

Phone: (516)462-6946
Fax: (516)864-8152
A minority enterprise small business investment company. Diversified industry preference.

Pan Pac Capital Corp.
121 E. Industry Ct.
Deer Park, New York 11729
Phone: (516)586-7653
Fax: (516)586-7505
A minority enterprise small business investment corporation. No industry preference.

First County Capital, Inc.
135-14 Northern Blvd., 2nd Fl.
Flushing, New York 11354
Phone: (718)461-1778
Fax: (718)461-1835
A minority enterprise small business investment company. Diversified industry preference.

Flushing Capital Corp.
39-06 Union St., Rm.202
Flushing, New York 11354
Phone: (718)886-5866
Fax: (718)939-7761
A minority enterprise small business investment company. Diversified industry preference.

Sterling Commercial Capital, Inc.
175 Great Neck Rd., Ste. 408
Great Neck, New York 11021
Phone: (516)482-7374
Fax: (516)487-0781
A small business investment company. Diversified industry preference.

CEDC Inc.
134 Jackson St.
Hempstead, New York 11550-2418
Phone: (516)292-9710
Fax: (516)292-3176

Situation Ventures Corp.
56-20 59th St.
Maspeth, New York 11378
Phone: (718)894-2000
Fax: (718)326-4642
Sam Hollander, President
Preferred Investment Size: $100,000.
Investment Policies: Loans and/or

equity. Industry Preferences: Manufacturing, service, retail. Geographic Preferences: New York metro area.

KOCO Capital Co., L.P.
111 Radio Cir.
Mount Kisco, New York 10549
Phone: (914)242-2324
Fax: (914)241-7476
Albert Pastino, President
Preferred Investment Size: $2 to $3 million. Investment Policies: Equity and debt with warrants. Investment Types: Expansion. Industry Preferences: Healthcare, media, basic manufacturing. Geographic Preferences: Mid-Atlantic.

Tappan Zee Capital Corp. (New York)
120 N. Main St.
New City, New York 10956
Phone: (914)634-8890
A small business investment company.

Argentum Capital Partners, LP
405 Lexington Ave., 54th Fl.
New York, New York 10174
Phone: (212)949-8272
Fax: (212)949-8294
A small business investment company. Diversified industry preference.

ASEA—Harvest Partners II
767 3rd Ave.
New York, New York 10017
Phone: (212)838-7776
Fax: (212)593-0734
A small business investment corporation. No industry preference.

Asian American Capital Corp.
62 White St.
New York, New York 10013
Phone: (212)315-2600
Howard H. Lin, President

Barclays Capital Investors Corp.
222 Broadway,11th Fl.
New York, New York 10038
Phone: (212)412-3937
Fax: (212)412-7600

A small business investment company. Diversified industry preference.

Bradford Ventures Ltd.
1212 Avenue of the Americas, Ste.1802
New York, New York 10036
Phone: (212)221-4620
Fax: (212)764-3467
Venture capital firm. No industry preference.

BT Capital Corp.
130 Liberty St., M S 2255
New York, New York 10006
Phone: (212)250-8082
Fax: (212)250-7651
A small business investment corporation. No industry preference.

The Business Loan Center
919 3rd Ave., 17th Fl.
New York, New York 10022-1902
Phone: (212)751-5626
Fax: (212)751-9345
A small business loan company.

Capital Investors and Management Corp.
210 Canal St., Ste. 611
New York, New York 10013-4155
Phone: (212)964-2480
Fax: (212)349-9160
A minority enterprise small business investment corporation. No industry preference.

CB Investors, Inc.
560 Lexington Ave.,20th Fl.
New York, New York 10022
Phone: (212)207-6119
Fax: (212)207-6095
A small business investment company. Diversified industry preference.

CBIC Woody Gundy Ventures, Inc.
425 Lexington Ave., 5th Fl.
New York, New York 10017
Phone: (212)856-3713
Fax: (212)697-1554
A small business investment company. Diversified industry preference.

Chase Capital Partners
380 Madison Ave., 12th Fl.
New York, New York 10017-2070
Phone: (212)622-3100
Fax: (212)622-3101
A small business investment
corporation. Areas of interest include
health care, specialty retail, media and
telecommunications, natural
resources, consumer products, and
environmental industries. Also invests
in leveraged buy-outs and growth
equity.

Chase Manhattan Capital Corp.
1 Chase Plz., 8th Fl.
New York, New York 10081
Phone: (212)935-9935
Fax: (212)552-1159
A small business investment
corporation. No industry preference.

Citicorp Venture Capital Ltd. (New
York City)
399 Park Ave., 14th Fl./Zone 4
New York, New York 10043
Phone: (212)559-1127
Fax: (212)888-2940
A small business investment
corporation. Invests in the fields of
information processing and
telecommunications, transportation
and energy, and health care; provides
financing to companies in all stages of
development. Also provides capital
for leveraged buy out situations.

CMNY Capital II, LP
135 E. 57th St., 26th Fl.
New York, New York 10022
Phone: (212)909-8432
Fax: (212)980-2630
A small business investment
company. Diversified industry
preference.

Concord Partners
535 Madison Ave.
New York, New York 10022
Phone: (212)906-7108
Fax: (212)888-0649
Venture capital partnership.
Diversified in terms of stage of
development, industry classification,

and geographic location. Areas of
special interest include computer
software, electronics, environmental
services, biopharmaceuticals, health
care, and oil and gas.

Creditanstalt SBIC
245 Park Ave., 27th Fl.
New York, New York 10167
Phone: (212)856-1248
Fax: (212)856-1699
Dennis O'Dowd, President

CW Group
1041 3rd Ave.
New York, New York 10021
Phone: (212)308-5266
Fax: (212)644-0354
Venture capital supplier. Interest is in
the health care field, including
diagnostic and therapeutic products,
services, and biotechnology. Invests
in companies at developing and early
stages.

DAEDHIE
1261 Broadway, Rm. 405
New York, New York 10001
Phone: (212)684-6411
Fax: (212)684-6474
A minority enterprise small business
investment company. Diversified
industry preference.

DNC Capital Group
55 5th Ave., 15th Fl.
New York, New York 10003
Phone: (212)206-6041
Fax: (212)727-0563
Small business investment
corporation interested in financing
acquisitions in the real estate industry.

East Coast Venture Capital, Inc.
313 W. 53rd St., 3rd Fl.
New York, New York 10019
Phone: (212)245-6460
Fax: (212)265-2962
A minority enterprise small business
investment company. Diversified
industry preference.

Edwards Capital Co.
205 E. 42nd
New York, New York 10016

Phone: (212)682-3300
Fax: (212)983-0351
A small business investment
corporation. Transportation industry
preferred.

Elf Aquitain, Inc.
280 Park Ave., 36th Fl. W
New York, New York 10017-1216
Phone: (212)922-3000
Free: (800)922-0027
Fax: (212)922-3001

Elk Associates Funding Corp.
747 3rd Ave., 4th Fl.
New York, New York 10017
Phone: (212)421-2111
Fax: (212)421-3488
A minority enterprise small business
investment corporation.
Transportation industry preferred.

Elron Technologies, Inc.
850 3rd Ave., 10th Fl.
New York, New York 10022
Phone: (212)935-3110
Fax: (212)935-3882
Venture capital supplier. Provides
incubation and start-up financing to
high-technology companies.

Empire State Capital Corp.
170 Broadway, Ste. 1200
New York, New York 10038
Phone: (212)513-1799
Free: (800)569-9630
Fax: (212)513-1892
A minority enterprise small business
investment company. Diversified
industry preference.

Eos Partners SBIC, L.P.
320 Park Ave., 22nd Fl.
New York, New York 10022
Phone: (212)832-5814
Fax: (212)832-5805
Marc H. Michel, Manager
Preferred Investment Size: $1 - $3
MILLION. Investment Policies:
Equity and equity-oriented Debt.
Investment Types: Expansion, later
stage. Industry Preferences:
Diversified, telecommunications,
info-processing, data services.
Geographic Preferences: National.

Euclid Partners Corp.
50 Rockefeller Plz., Ste. 1022
New York, New York 10020
Phone: (212)489-1770
Fax: (212)757-1686
Venture capital firm. Prefers early
stage health care and information
processing industries.

Exeter Venture Lenders, L.P.
10 E. 53rd St.
New York, New York 10022
Phone: (212)872-1170
Fax: (212)872-1198
Keith Fox, Manager
Preferred Investment Size:
$3,000,000. Investment Policies:
Loans and equity investments.
Investment Types: Expansion, later
stage. Industry Preferences:
Diversified. Geographic Preferences:
National.

Exim Capital Corp.
241 5th Ave., 3rd Fl.
New York, New York 10016-8703
Phone: (212)683-3375
Fax: (212)689-4118
A minority enterprise small business
investment corporation. No industry
preference.

Fair Capital Corp.
212 Canal St., Ste. 611
New York, New York 10013
Phone: (212)964-2480
Fax: (212)349-9160
A minority enterprise small business
investment corporation. No industry
preference.

First Boston Corp.
11 Madison Ave.
New York, New York 10010
Phone: (212)909-2000
Investment banker. Provides
financing to the oil and gas pipeline,
hydroelectric, medical technology,
consumer products, electronics,
aerospace, and telecommunications
industries. Supplies capital for
leveraged buy outs.

First Wall Street SBIC, LP
26 Broadway, Ste. 2310

New York, New York 10004
Phone: (212)742-3770
Fax: (212)742-3776
A small business investment
company. Diversified industry
preference.

Franklin Corp.
450 Park Ave.
G.M. Bldg., 10th Fl.
New York, New York 10022
Phone: (212)486-2323
Fax: (212)755-5451
A small business investment
corporation. No industry preference;
no start-ups.

Fredericks Michael and Co.
2 Wall St., 4th Fl.
New York, New York 10005
Phone: (212)732-1600
Fax: (212)732-1872
Private venture capital supplier.
Provides start-up and early stage
financing, and supplies capital for buy
outs and acquisitions.

Fresh Start Venture Capital Corp.
313 W. 53rd St., 3rd Fl.
New York, New York 10019
Phone: (212)265-2249
Fax: (212)265-2962
A minority enterprise small business
investment corporation. No industry
preference.

Furman Selz SBIC, L.P.
230 Park Ave.
New York, New York 10169
Phone: (212)309-8200
Brian Friedman, Manager
Preferred Investment Size: $2 to $6
million. Investment Policies: Equity.
Investment Types: Expansion, later
stage, no start-ups. Industry
Preferences: Diversified. Geographic
Preferences: National.

Hambro International Equity Partners
(New York)
650 Madison Ave., 21st Floor
New York, New York 10022
Phone: (212)223-7400
Fax: (212)223-0305

Venture capital supplier. Seeks to
invest in mature companies as well as
in high-technology areas from start-
ups to leveraged buy outs.

Hanam Capital Corp.
38 W.32nd St.,Rm.1512
New York, New York 10001
Phone: (212)564-5225
Fax: (212)564-5307
A minority enterprise small business
investment company. Diversified
industry preference.

Harvest Partners, Inc. (New York)
767 3rd Ave.
New York, New York 10017
Phone: (212)838-7776
Fax: (212)593-0734
Private venture capital supplier.
Prefers to invest in high-technology,
growth-oriented companies with
proprietary technology, large market
potential, and strong management
teams.

Holding Capital Group, Inc.
685 5th Ave., 14th Fl.
New York, New York 10022
Phone: (212)486-6670
Fax: (212)486-0843
A small business investment
corporation. No industry preference.
Prefers to purchase well-managed
middle market companies with a
minimum of $1 million cash flow.

IBJS Capital Corp.
1 State St., 8th Fl.
New York, New York 10004
Phone: (212)858-2000
Fax: (212)425-0542
A small business investment
company. Diversified industry
preference.

InterEquity Capital Partners, L.P.
220 5th Ave., 17th Fl.
New York, New York 10001
Phone: (212)779-2022
Fax: (212)779-2103
A small business investment
company. Diversified industry
preference.

Investor International (U.S.), Inc.
320 Park Ave., 33 Fl 10022
New York, New York 10019
Phone: (212)508-0900
Fax: (212)957-0901

Jafco America Ventures, Inc. (New York)
2 World Financial Center, Bldg. B, 17th Fl.
225 Liberty St.
New York, New York 10281-1196
Phone: (212)667-9001
Fax: (212)667-1004
Venture capital firm. Provides middle- to later-stage financing to technology-oriented companies.

Jardine Capital Corp.
105 Lafayette St., Unit 204
New York, New York 10013
Phone: (212)941-0993
Fax: (212)941-0998
Lawrence Wong, President
Preferred Investment Size: $360,000. Investment Policies: Loans and/or equity. Investment Types: Expansion. Industry Preferences: Diversified. Geographic Preferences: North/South.

Josephberg, Grosz and Co., Inc.
420 Lexington, Ste. 2635
New York, New York 10017
Phone: (212)370-4564
Fax: (212)397-5832
Venture capital firm. Invests in companies having a minimum of $2.5 million in sales, significant growth potential, and a strong management base.

J.P. Morgan Investment Corp.
60 Wall St.
New York, New York 10260
Phone: (212)483-2323
A small business investment company. Diversified industry preference.

Kwiat Capital Corp.
579 5th Ave.
New York, New York 10017
Phone: (212)223-1111
Fax: (212)223-2796

A small business investment corporation. No industry preference.

Lambda Fund Management, Inc.
115 E. 69th
New York, New York 10021
Phone: (212)794-6060
Fax: (212)794-6169
Venture capital partnership.

Lawrence, Tyrrell, Ortale, and Smith (New York)
515 Madison Ave., 29th Fl.
New York, New York 10022
Phone: (212)826-9080
Fax: (212)759-2561
Venture capital firm. Prefers to invest in health care, software, and fragmented industries that grow by acquisition.

McCown, De Leeuw and Co. (New York)
101 E. 52nd St., 31st Fl.
New York, New York 10022-6018
Phone: (212)355-5500
Fax: (212)355-6283

Medallion Funding Corp.
205 E. 42nd St., Ste. 2020
New York, New York 10017-5706
Phone: (212)682-3300
Fax: (212)983-0351
A minority enterprise small business investment corporation. Transportation industry preferred.

Mercury Capital, L.P.
650 Madison Ave., Ste. 2600
New York, New York 10022
Phone: (212)838-0888
Fax: (212)838-7598
David W. Elenowitz, Manager

Monsey Capital Corp.
9 E. 40th St., 4th Fl.
New York, New York 10016
Phone: (212)689-2700
Fax: (212)683-7300
A minority enterprise small business investment corporation. No industry preference.

Morgan Stanley Venture Capital (New York)
c/o M. Fazle Husain

1251 Avenue of the Americas, 33rd Fl.
New York, New York 10020
Phone: (212)703-6981
Free: (800)223-2440
Fax: (212)703-8957
Venture capital firm providing later stage financing. Areas of interest include high technology and health care.

NatWest USA Capital Corp.
175 Water St., 27th Fl.
New York, New York 10038
Phone: (212)602-4000
Fax: (212)602-3393
A small business investment company. Diversified industry preference.

Nazem and Co.
645 Madison Ave., 12th Fl.
New York, New York 10022
Phone: (212)371-7900
Fax: (212)371-2150
Venture capital fund. Electronics and medical industries preferred. Will provide seed and first- and second-round financing.

Needham Capital SBIC, L.P.
445 Park Ave.
New York, New York 10022
Phone: (212)705-0291
Fax: (212)371-8418
John Michaelson, Manager
Preferred Investment Size: $500,000 TO $1 Million. Investment Policies: Equity. Industry Preferences: Technology. Geographic Preferences: National.

New York State Urban Development Corp.
633 3rd Ave.
New York, New York 10017
Phone: (212)803-3100
Participates in a broad range of initiatives. Addresses the needs of the state in six areas, including downtown development, industrial development, minority business development, university research and development, and planning and special projects.

Norwood Venture Corp.
1430 Broadway, Ste. 1607
New York, New York 10018
Phone: (212)869-5075
Fax: (212)869-5331
A small business investment
company. Diversified industry
preference.

Paribas Principal, Inc.
787 7th Ave., 33rd Fl.
New York, New York 10019
Phone: (212)841-2000
Fax: (212)841-2146
A small business investment
company. Diversified industry
preference.

Patricof & Co. Ventures, Inc. (New
York)
445 Park Ave., 11th Fl.
New York, New York 10022
Phone: (212)753-6300
Fax: (212)319-6155
Venture capital firm.

Pierre Funding Corp.
805 3rd Ave., 6th Fl.
New York, New York 10022
Phone: (212)888-1515
Fax: (212)688-4252
A minority enterprise small business
investment corporation. No industry
preference.

Prospect Street NYC Discovery Fund,
L.P.
250 Park Ave., 17th Fl.
New York, New York 10177
Phone: (212)490-0480
Fax: (212)490-1566
Richard E. Omohundro, CEO

Prudential Equity Investors
717 5th Ave., Ste. 1100
New York, New York 10022
Phone: (212)753-0901
Fax: (212)826-6798
Venture capital fund. Specialty
retailing, medical and health services,
communications, and technology
companies preferred. Will provide $3
to $7 million in equity financing for
later-stage growth companies.

Pyramid Ventures, Inc.
130 Liberty St., 25th Fl.
New York, New York 10006
Phone: (212)250-9571
Fax: (212)250-7651
A small business investment
company. Diversified industry
preference.

Questech Capital Corp.
600 Madison Ave., 21st Fl.
New York, New York 10022
Phone: (954)583-2960
A small business investment
corporation. No industry preference.

R and R Financial Corp.
1370 Broadway
New York, New York 10018
Phone: (212)356-1400
Free: (800)999-4800
Fax: (212)356-0900
A small business investment
corporation. No industry preference.

Rothschild Ventures, Inc.
1251 Avenue of the Americas
New York, New York 10020
Phone: (212)403-3500
Free: (800)753-5151
Fax: (212)403-3501
Private venture capital firm. Prefers
seed and all later-stage financing.

767 Limited Partnership
767 3rd Ave.
New York, New York 10017
Phone: (212)838-7776
Fax: (212)593-0734
A small business investment
corporation. No industry preference.

Sixty Wall Street SBIC Fund, L.P.
60 Wall St.
New York, New York 10260
Phone: (212)648-7778
Fax: (212)648-5032
David Cromwell
Seth Cunningham

Spectra International Management
Group
140 E. 44th St.
Box 776
New York, New York 10017

Phone: (212)986-6030
Fax: (212)986-8770
Venture capital firm providing all
stages of financing. Areas of interest
include all industries, excluding oil
and gas.

Sprout Group (New York City)
277 Park Ave., 21st Fl.
New York, New York 10172
Phone: (212)892-3600
Fax: (212)892-3444
Venture capital supplier.

TCW Capital
200 Park Ave., Ste. 2200
New York, New York 10166
Phone: (212)297-4055
Fax: (212)297-4025
Venture capital fund. Companies with
sales of $25 to $100 million preferred.
Will provide up to $20 million in
later-stage financing for
recapitalizations, restructuring
management buy outs, and general
corporate purposes.

399 Venture Partners
399 Park Ave., 14th Fl./ Zone 4
New York, New York 10043
Phone: (212)559-1127
Fax: (212)888-2940
A small business investment
company. Diversified industry
preference.

Transportation Capital Corp. (New
York)
315 Park Ave. S, 10th Fl.
New York, New York 10010
Phone: (212)598-3225
Fax: (212)598-3102
A minority enterprise small business
investment company. Diversified
industry preference.

Trusty Capital, Inc.
350 5th Ave., Ste. 2026
New York, New York 10118
Phone: (212)629-3011
Fax: (212)629-3019
A minority enterprise small business
investment company. Diversified
industry preference.

UBS Partners, Inc.
299 Park Ave., 33rd Fl.
New York, New York 10171
Phone: (212)821-6490
Fax: (212)593-4257
Justin S. Maccarone, President

United Capital Investment Corp.
60 E. 42nd St., Ste. 1515
New York, New York 10165
Phone: (212)682-7210
Fax: (212)573-6352
A minority enterprise small business
investment company. Diversified
industry preference.

Venture Capital Fund of America,
Inc.
509 Madison Ave., Ste. 812
New York, New York 10022
Phone: (212)838-5577
Fax: (212)838-7614

Venture Opportunities Corp.
158 E. 59th St., 16th Fl.
New York, New York 10022-1304
Phone: (212)832-3737
Fax: (212)980-6603
A minority enterprise small business
investment corporation. Areas of
interest include radio, cable,
television, telecommunications, real
estate development, medical
consumer products, and service and
manufacturing businesses. Second- or
third-stage for expansion, mergers, or
acquisitions. No start-up or seed
capital investments.

Warburg Pincus Ventures, Inc.
466 Lexington Ave., 10th Fl.
New York, New York 10017-3147
Phone: (212)878-0600
Free: (800)888-3697
Fax: (212)878-9351
Venture capital firm providing all
stages of financing. Areas of interest
include all industries, excluding
gaming, real estate, and investments
in South Africa.

Weiss, Peck and Greer Venture
Partners L.P. (New York)
1 New York Plz.
New York, New York 10004

Phone: (212)908-9500
Fax: (212)908-9652

Welsh, Carson, Anderson, & Stowe
200 Liberty Ste. 3601
New York, New York 10281
Phone: (212)945-2000
Fax: (212)945-2016
Venture capital partnership.

Wolfensohn Partners, L.P. (New
York)
5990 Madison Ave., 32nd Fl.
New York, New York 10022
Phone: (212)894-8121
Fax: (212)446-1307

International Paper Capital
Formation, Inc. (Purchase)
2 Manhattanville Rd.
Purchase, New York 10577-2196
Phone: (914)397-1500
Fax: (914)397-1909
A minority enterprise small business
investment company.

Genesee Funding, Inc.
100 Corporate Woods, Ste. 300
Rochester, New York 14623
Phone: (716)272-2332
Free: (800)933-7739
Fax: (716)272-2396
A small business investment
company. Diversified industry
preference.

Ibero-American Investors Corp.
104 Scio St.
Rochester, New York 14604-2552
Phone: (716)262-3440
Fax: (716)262-3441
A minority enterprise small business
investment corporation. No industry
preference.

Square Deal Venture Capital Corp.
766 N. Main St.
Spring Valley, New York 10977-1903
Phone: (914)354-4100
A minority enterprise small business
investment company. Diversified
industry preference.

Northwood Ventures
485 Underhill Blvd., Ste. 205
Syosset, New York 11791

Phone: (516)364-5544
Fax: (516)364-0879
Venture capital firm providing
leveraged buyout financing, between
$500,000 - $1 million. Diversified
industry preference.

TLC Funding Corp.
660 White Plains Rd.
Tarrytown, New York 10591
Phone: (914)332-5200
Fax: (914)332-5660
A small business investment
corporation. No industry preference.

Bessemer Venture Partners
(Westbury)
1025 Old Country Rd., Ste. 205
Westbury, New York 11590
Phone: (516)997-2300
Fax: (516)997-2371
Venture capital partnership. No
industry preference.

Winfield Capital Corp.
237 Mamaroneck Ave.
White Plains, New York 10605
Phone: (914)949-2600
Fax: (914)949-7195
A small business investment
corporation. No industry preference.

North Carolina

First Union Capital Partners, Inc.
1 1st Union Center, 18th Fl.
301 S. College St.
Charlotte, North Carolina 28288-0732
Phone: (704)374-6487
Fax: (704)374-6711
A small business investment
company. Diversified industry
preference.

Kitty Hawk Capital Ltd.
2700 Coltsgate Rd., Ste. 202
Charlotte, North Carolina 28211
Phone: (704)362-3909
Fax: (704)362-2774
Venture capital firm. Geographical
preference is the southeast.
Investment policy is liberal, but does
not invest in real estate, natural
resources, and single store retail

businesses and does not provide
invention development financing.

NationsBanc Capital Corp.
100 N. Tryon St., 10th Fl.
Charlotte, North Carolina 28255
Phone: (704)386-8063
Fax: (704)386-6432
Walter W. Walker, Jr., President
Preferred Investment Size: $3 to $25
million. Investment Policies: Equity,
sub debt with warrants. Investment
Types: Later stage, expansion.
Industry Preferences: Diversified.
Geographic Preferences: National.

Southeastern Publishing Ventures Inc.
528 E. Blvd.
Charlotte, North Carolina 28203
Phone: (704)373-0051
Fax: (704)343-0170
Private venture capital firm.
Diversified industry preference.

Center for Community Self-Help
North Carolina's Development Bank
PO Box 3619
301 W. Maine St.
Durham, North Carolina 27701
Phone: (919)956-4400
Free: (800)476-7428
Fax: (919)956-4600
Statewide, private-sector financial
institution providing technical
assistance and financing to small
businesses, non- profit organizations,
and low-income homebuyers in North
Carolina.

Atlantic Venture Partners (Winston
Salem)
380 Knollwood St., No. 410
Winston Salem, North Carolina
27103
Phone: (910)721-1800
Fax: (910)748-1208
Private venture capital partnership.
Prefers to invest in manufacturing,
distribution, and service industries.

North Dakota

Bank of North Dakota
Small Business Loan Program
700 E. Main Ave.

Box 5509
Bismarck, North Dakota 58506-5504
Phone: (701)328-5600
Free: (800)472-2166
Fax: (701)328-5632
Assists new and existing businesses in
securing competitive financing with
reasonable terms and conditions.

Fargo Cass County Economic
Development Corp.
E-mail: info@fedc.com
406 Main Ave., Ste. 404
Fargo, North Dakota 58103
Phone: (701)237-6132
Fax: (701)293-7819
Certified development company that
lends to small and medium-sized
businesses at fixed rates.

North Dakota SBIC, L.P.
406 Main Ave., Ste. 404
Fargo, North Dakota 58103
Phone: (701)298-0003
Fax: (701)293-7819
David R. Schroeder, Manager

North Dakota Small Business Loan
Services
406 Main Ave., Ste.417
Fargo, North Dakota 58103
Phone: (701)235-7885
Fax: (701)235-6706
Administers the 504 Loan Program.

Ohio

River Capital Corp. (Cleveland)
2544 Chamberlain Rd.
Akron, Ohio 44333
Phone: (216)781-3655
Fax: (216)781-2821
A small business investment
corporation. No industry preference.

River Cities Capital Fund L.P.
221 E. 4th St., Ste. 2250
Cincinnati, Ohio 45202
Phone: (513)621-9700
Fax: (513)579-8939
R. Glen Mayfield, Manager
Preferred Investment Size: $750,000
TO $1.5 MILLION. Investment
Policies: Equity investments.
Investment Types: Early stage,

expansion, later stage. Industry
Preferences: Diversified. Geographic
Preferences: Ohio, Kentucky, Indiana.

Brantley Venture Partners, L.P.
20600 Chagrin Blvd., Ste. 1150
Cleveland, Ohio 44122
Phone: (216)283-4800
Fax: (216)283-5324
Venture capital firm. Areas of interest
include computer and electronics,
medical/health care, biotechnology,
computer software,
telecommunications, traditional
manufacturing, information
processing, and environmental
industries.

Clarion Capital Corp.
Ohio Savings Plz., Ste. 510
1801 E. 9th St.
Cleveland, Ohio 44114
Phone: (216)687-1096
Fax: (216)694-3545
Small business investment
corporation. Interested in
manufacturing, computer software,
natural resources/natural gas, and
health care.

Gries Investment Co.
1801 E. 9th St.,Ste. 1600
Cleveland, Ohio 44114-3110
Phone: (216)861-1146
Fax: (216)861-0106
A small business investment
corporation. No industry preference.

Key Equity Capital Corp.
127 Public Sq., 6th Fl.
Cleveland, Ohio 44114
Phone: (216)689-5776
Fax: (216)689-3204
Raymond Lancaster, President
Preferred Investment Size:
$2.000,000. Investment Policies:
Willing to make equity investments.
Industry Preferences: Diversified.
Geographic Preferences: National.

Morgenthaler Ventures
629 Euclid Ave.,Ste. 1700
Cleveland, Ohio 44111
Phone: (216)621-3070
Fax: (216)621-2817

Private venture capital firm providing start-up and later- stage financing to all types of business in North America; prefers not to invest in real estate and oil and gas.

National City Capital Corp.
1965 E. 6th St.
Cleveland, Ohio 44114
Phone: (216)575-2491
Fax: (216)575-9965
A small business investment corporation. Provides equity for expansion programs, recapitalizations, acquisitions, and management buyouts. Seeks investment opportunities ranging from $1 million to $5 million. Diversified industry preference.

Primus Venture Partners
1 Cleveland Center, Ste. 2700
1375 E. 9th St.
Cleveland, Ohio 44114
Phone: (216)621-2185
Fax: (216)621-4543
Venture capital partnership. Provides seed, early stage, and expansion financing to companies located in Ohio and the Midwest. Does not engage in gas, oil, or real estate investments.

Society Venture Capital Corp.
127 Public Sq. 6th Fl.
Cleveland, Ohio 44114
Phone: (216)689-5776
Fax: (216)689-3204
A small business investment corporation. Prefers to invest in manufacturing and service industries.

Tomlinson Industries
13700 Broadway Ave.
Cleveland, Ohio 44125-1992
Phone: (216)587-3400
Free: (800)526-9634
Fax: (216)587-0733
A small business investment corporation. Miniature supermarket industry preferred.

Banc One Capital Partners Corp.
(Columbus)
150 E. Gay St.

Columbus, Ohio 43215
Phone: (614)217-1100
Free: (800)837-5100
A small business investment corporation. No industry preference.

Scientific Advances, Inc.
601 W. 5th Ave.
Columbus, Ohio 43201
Phone: (614)424-7005
Fax: (614)424-4874
Venture capital partnership interested in natural gas related industries.

Center City MESBIC, Inc.
8 N. Maine St.
Miami Valley Tur, Ste.1400
Dayton, Ohio 45402
Phone: (513)461-6164
Fax: (513)937-7035
A minority enterprise small business investment corporation. Diversified industries.

Seed One
Park Pl.
10 W. Streetsboro St.
Hudson, Ohio 44236
Phone: (216)650-2338
Fax: (216)650-4946
Private venture capital firm. No industry preference. Equity financing only.

Fifth Third Bank of Northwestern Ohio, N.A.
606 Madison Ave.
Toledo, Ohio 43604
Phone: (419)259-7141
Fax: (419)259-7134
A small business investment corporation. No industry preference.

Lubrizol Performance Products Co.
29400 Lakeland Blvd.
Wickliffe, Ohio 44092
Phone: (216)943-4200
Fax: (216)943-5337
Venture capital supplier. Provides seed capital and later- stage expansion financing to emerging companies in the biological, chemical, and material sciences whose technology is applicable to and related to the

production and marketing of specialty and fine chemicals.

Cactus Capital Co.
6660 High St., Office 1-B
Worthington, Ohio 43085
Phone: (614)436-4060
Fax: (614)436-4060
A minority enterprise small business investment company. Diversified industry preference.

Oklahoma

Southwestern Oklahoma Development Authority
PO Box 569
Burns Flat, Oklahoma 73624
Phone: (405)562-4884
Free: (800)627-4882
Fax: (405)562-4880

Langston University
Minority Business Assistance Center
Hwy. 33 E.
PO Box 667
Langston, Oklahoma 73050
Phone: (405)466-3256
Free: (800)879-6552
Fax: (405)466-2909

BancFirst Investment Corp.
1101 N. Broadway
Oklahoma City, Oklahoma 73102
Phone: (405)270-1000
Fax: (405)270-1089
T. Kent Faison, Manager
Preferred Investment Size: Up to $500,000. Investment Policies: Loans and/or equity. Investment Types: Early stage, expansion. Industry Preferences: Diversified. Geographic Preferences: Oklahoma.

Oklahoma Department of Commerce
Business Development Division
PO Box 26980
Oklahoma City, Oklahoma 73126-0980
Phone: (405)815-6552
Fax: (405)815-5142
Helps companies gain access to capital needed for growth. Provides financial specialists to help businesses analyze their financing needs and to

work closely with local economic development staff to help package proposals for their companies. Also responsible for assisting in the development of new loan and investment programs.

Oklahoma Development Finance
Authority
301 NW 63rd St., Ste. 225
Oklahoma City, Oklahoma 73116
Phone: (405)848-9761
Fax: (405)848-3314
Issues tax-exempt industrial development bonds for manufacturing firms.

Oklahoma Industrial Finance
Authority
301 NW 63rd., Ste. 225
Oklahoma City, Oklahoma 73116-7904
Phone: (405)842-1145
Fax: (405)848-3314
Provides financing for manufacturing projects involving the purchase of land, buildings, and stationary equipment.

Oklahoma State Treasurer's Office
Agriculture/Small Business Linked
Deposit Programs
217 State Capitol
Oklahoma City, Oklahoma 73105
Phone: (405)521-3191
Fax: (405)521-4994
Provides reduced loan rates for Oklahoma's farming, ranching, and small business communities.

Rees/Source Ventures, Inc.
3001 United Founders Blvd.
Oklahoma City, Oklahoma 73112
Phone: (405)843-8049
Fax: (405)843-8048
Venture capital firm providing seed, start-up, first- stage, and second-stage financing. Prefers to make investments in the $250,000 to $500,000 range to companies within a three- mile radius of Oklahoma City. Areas of interest include recreation and leisure, environmental products and services, packaging machinery and materials, energy-related

technologies, printing and publishing, manufacturing and automation, information processing and software, and specialty chemicals industries. Will not consider the following industries: oil, gas, or mineral exploration; real estate; motion pictures; and consulting services.

Alliance Business Investment Co.
(Tulsa)
320 South Boston Ste.1000
Tulsa, Oklahoma 74103-3703
Phone: (918)584-3581
Fax: (918)582-3403
A small business investment corporation. Provides later- stage financing for basic industries.

Davis Venture Partners (Tulsa)
320 S. Boston Ste.,1000
Tulsa, Oklahoma 74103-3703
Phone: (918)584-7272
Fax: (918)582-3403
Venture capital firm. Provides later-stage financing for basic industries.

Rubottom, Dudash and Associates,
Inc.
4870 S. Lewis, Ste. 180
Tulsa, Oklahoma 74105
Phone: (918)742-3031
Management and investment consultants. Emphasis on retail, wholesale, and light fabrication.

Oregon

Olympic Venture Partners II (Lake
Oswego)
340 Oswego Pointe Dr., No. 200
Lake Oswego, Oregon 97034-3230
Phone: (503)697-8766
Fax: (503)697-8863
Invests in early stage high technology, biotechnology, and communications businesses.

Orien Ventures
300 Oswego Pointe Dr., Ste. 100
Lake Oswego, Oregon 97034
Phone: (503)699-1680
Fax: (503)699-1681
Venture capital firm interested in all types of investment.

Northern Pacific Capital Corp.
PO Box 1658
Portland, Oregon 97205
Phone: (503)241-1255
Fax: (503)299-6653
A small business investment company. Diversified industry preference.

Northwest Capital Network
PO Box 6650
Portland, Oregon 97228-6650
Phone: (503)796-3321
Fax: (503)280-6080
Nonprofit business/investor referral service that brings together entrepreneurs requiring capital with investors seeking specific venture opportunities, through means of a confidential database of investment opportunity profiles and investment interest profiles.

Oregon Resource and Technology
Development Fund
4370 NE Halsey
Portland, Oregon 97213
Phone: (503)282-4462
Fax: (503)282-2976
Provides investment capital for early stage business finance and applied research and development projects that leads to commercially viable products.

Shaw Venture Partners
400 SW 6th Ave., Ste. 1100
Portland, Oregon 97204-1636
Phone: (503)228-4884
Fax: (503)227-2471
Small business investment corporation interested in computers, retail, medical/biotechnology, consumer products and international trade investment.

U.S. Bancorp Capital Corp.
P.O. Box 4412
Portland, Oregon 97208
Phone: (503)275-6111
Fax: (503)275-7565
A small business investment company. Diversified industry preference.

Oregon Economic Development
Department
Business Finance Section
SBA Loans Program
775 Summer St. NE
Salem, Oregon 97310
Phone: (503)986-0160
Free: (800)233-3306
Fax: (503)581-5115
A state-wide company providing
Small Business Administration 504
and 7(A) financing to eligible small
businesses; works closely with local
certified development companies.

Oregon Economic Development
Department
Business Finance Section
Oregon Business Development Fund
775 Summer St. NE
Salem, Oregon 97310
Phone: (503)986-0160
Fax: (503)581-5115
Structures and issues loans to
manufacturing, processing, and
tourism-related small businesses.

Tektronix Development Co.
PO Box 1000, Mail Sta. 63-862
Wilsonville, Oregon 97070
Phone: (503)685-4233
Fax: (503)685-3754
Venture capital firm interested in high
tech, opto electronics and
measurement systems investment.

Pennsylvania

NEPA Venture Fund LP
125 Goodman Dr.
Bethlehem, Pennsylvania 18015
Phone: (610)865-6550
Private venture capital partnership
providing seed and start-up financing.

Erie SBIC
32 W. 8th St., Ste. 615
Erie, Pennsylvania 16501
Phone: (814)453-7964
A small business investment
corporation. No industry preference.
Prefers investments ranging from
$100,000 - $200,000.

Pennsylvania Department of
Commerce
Governor's Response Team
439 Forum Bldg.
Harrisburg, Pennsylvania 17120
Phone: (717)787-8199
Fax: (717)772-5419
Works with individual companies to
find buildings or sites for start-up or
expansion projects; contacts
manufacturers to make them aware of
financial and technical assistance
available, to assist with difficulties,
and to learn of future plans for
expansions or cutbacks.

Pennsylvania Department of
Commerce
Bureau of Bonds
Employee Ownership Assistance
Program
E-mail: abrennan@doc.state.pa.us
Office of Program Management
466 Forum Bldg.
Harrisburg, Pennsylvania 17120
Phone: (717)783-1109
Fax: (717)234-4560
Preserves existing jobs and creates
new jobs by assisting and promoting
employee ownership in existing
enterprises which are experiencing
layoffs or would otherwise close.

Pennsylvania Department of
Commerce
Bureau of Bonds
Revenue Bond and Mortgage
Program
E-mail: abrennan@doc.state.pa.us
466 Forum Bldg.
Harrisburg, Pennsylvania 17120
Phone: (717)783-1109
Fax: (717)234-4560
Financing for projects approved
through the Program are borrowed
from private sources, and can be used
to acquire land, buildings, machinery,
and equipment. Borrowers must
create a minimum number of new
jobs within three years of the loan's
closing.

Pennsylvania Department of Energy
Energy Development Authority

P.O. Box 8772 13th Fl.
Rachael Carson State Official
Harrisburg, Pennsylvania 17105-8772
Phone: (717)783-9981
Fax: (717)783-2703
Finances research and development of
energy technology projects.

Enterprise Venture Capital Corp. of
Pennsylvania
111 Market St.
Johnstown, Pennsylvania 15901
Phone: (814)535-7597
Fax: (814)535-8677
A small business investment
corporation. No industry preference.
Geographic preference is two-hour
driving radius of Johnstown,
Pennsylvania.

Foster Management Co.
1018 W. 9th Ave.
King of Prussia, Pennsylvania 19406
Phone: (610)992-7650
Fax: (610)992-3390
Private venture capital supplier. Not
restricted to specific industries or
geographic locations; diversified with
investments in the health care,
transportation, broadcasting,
communications, energy, and home
furnishings industries. Investments
range from $2 million to $15 million.

CIP Capital, LP
20 Valley Stream Pky., Ste.265
Malvern, Pennsylvania 19355
Phone: (610)695-8380
Fax: (215)695-8388
A small business investment
company. Diversified industry
preference.

Core States Enterprise Fund
1345 Chestnut St., F.C. 1-8-12-1
Philadelphia, Pennsylvania 19107
Phone: (215)973-6519
Fax: (215)973-6900
Venture capital supplier. Invests with
any industry except real estate or
construction. Minimum investment is
$1 million.

Fidelcor Capital Corp.
Fidelity Bldg., 11th Fl.

123 S. Broad St.
Philadelphia, Pennsylvania 19109
Phone: (215)985-3722
Fax: (215)985-7282
A small business investment
company. Diversified industry
preference.

Ben Franklin Technology Center of
Southeastern Pennsylvania
University City Science Center
3624 Market St.
Philadelphia, Pennsylvania 19104
Phone: (215)382-0380
Fax: (215)387-6050
Public venture capital fund interested
in technology industries.

Genesis Seed Fund
c/o Howard, Lawson and Co.
2 Penn Center Plz.
Philadelphia, Pennsylvania 19102
Phone: (215)988-0010
Fax: (215)568-0029
Venture capital fund.

Keystone Venture Capital
Management Co.
1601 Market St.,Ste.2500
Philadelphia, Pennsylvania 19103
Phone: (215)241-1200
Fax: (215)241-1211
Private venture capital partnership.
Provides later-stage investments in
the telecommunications, health care,
manufacturing, media, software, and
franchise industries, primarily in the
mid-Atlantic states.

Penn Janney Fund, Inc.
1801 Market St.
Philadelphia, Pennsylvania 19103
Phone: (215)665-6193
Fax: (215)665-6197
Private venture capital limited
partnership.

Philadelphia Ventures
200 S. Broad St., 8th Fl.
Philadelphia, Pennsylvania 19102
Phone: (215)732-4445
Fax: (215)732-4644
A small business investment
corporation. Provides financing to
companies offering products or

services based on technology or other
proprietary capabilities. Industries of
particular interest are information
processing equipment and services,
medical products and services, data
communications, and industrial
automation.

PNC Corporate Finance
(Philadelphia)
1600 Market St., 21st Fl.
Philadelphia, Pennsylvania 19103
Phone: (215)585-6282
Fax: (215)585-5525
Small business investment company.

Fostin Capital Corp.
681 Andersen Dr.
Pittsburgh, Pennsylvania 15220
Phone: (412)928-1400
Fax: (412)928-9635
Venture capital corporation.

Loyalhanna Venture Fund
PO Box 81927
Pittsburgh, Pennsylvania 15217
Phone: (412)687-9027
Fax: (412)681-0960
Venture capital firm. No industry
preference.

PNC Capital Corp. (Pittsburgh)
1 PNC Plaza, 19th Fl.
249 5th Ave.
Pittsburgh, Pennsylvania 15222
Phone: (412)762-7035
Fax: (412)762-6233
A small business investment
corporation. Prefers to invest in later-
stage and leveraged buy out
situations. Will not consider real
estate, coal, or gas ventures.

APA/Fostin Pennsylvania Venture
Capital Fund
100 Matsonford Rd., Bldg. 5, Ste. 470
Radnor, Pennsylvania 19087
Phone: (610)687-3030
Fax: (610)687-8520
Private venture capital limited
partnership providing mid- and later
stage financing.

Meridian Venture Partners (Radnor)
The Fidelity Court Bldg., Ste. 140
259 Radnor-Chester Rd.

Radnor, Pennsylvania 19087
Phone: (610)254-2999
Fax: (610)254-2996
Venture capital firm.

Patricof & Co. Ventures, Inc.
(Radnor)
100 Matsonford Rd., Bldg. 5, Ste. 470
Radnor, Pennsylvania 19087
Phone: (610)687-3030
Fax: (610)687-8520
Venture capital firm providing mid-
to later stage financing.

Meridian Capital Corp. (Reading)
600 Penn St.
Reading, Pennsylvania 19602
Phone: (610)655-1437
Fax: (215)655-1908
Small business investment
corporation.

TDH Small Business Investment Co.
1 Rosemont Business Campus, Ste.
301
919 Conestoga Rd.
Rosemont, Pennsylvania 19010
Phone: (610)526-9970
Fax: (610)526-9971
Private venture capital fund. No
industry preferences.

BankAmerica Ventures (Washington)
PO Box 512
Washington, Pennsylvania 15301
Phone: (412)223-0707
Fax: (412)546-8021
Daniel A. Dye, Contact

First SBIC of California
(Washington)
PO Box 512
Washington, Pennsylvania 15301
Phone: (412)223-0707
Fax: (412)223-8290
A small business investment
company.

S. R. One Ltd.
565 E. Swedesford Rd., Ste. 315
Wayne, Pennsylvania 19087
Phone: (610)293-3400
Fax: (610)293-3419

Sandhurst Co. LP
351 E. Constoga Rd.

Wayne, Pennsylvania 19087
Phone: (610)254-8900
Fax: (610)254-8958
Private venture capital fund.

Technology Leaders LP
800 The Safeguard Bldg.
435 Devon Park Dr.
Wayne, Pennsylvania 19087
Phone: (610)293-0600
Fax: (610)293-0601
Private venture capital fund. Areas of
interest include biotechnology, health
care, information services, and high
technology industries.

Hillman Medical Ventures, Inc.
(Berwyn)
100 Front St., Ste. 1350
West Conshohocken, Pennsylvania
19428
Phone: (610)940-0300
Fax: (610)940-0301
Venture capital firm that invests in
early-stage medical technology
companies.

Puerto Rico

North America Investment Corp.
P.O. Box 191831
San Juan, Puerto Rico 00919-1813
Phone: (809)754-6177
Fax: (809)754-6181
A minority enterprise small business
investment corporation. Diversified
industry preference.

Rhode Island

Domestic Capital Corp.
815 Reservoir Ave.
Cranston, Rhode Island 02910
Phone: (401)946-3310
Fax: (401)943-6708
A small business investment
corporation. No industry preference.

Fairway Capital Corp.
285 Governor St.
Providence, Rhode Island 02906
Phone: (401)454-7500
Fax: (401)455-3636

A small business investment
company. Diversified industry
preference.

Fleet Equity Partners (Providence)
111 Westminster St., 4th Fl.
Providence, Rhode Island 02903
Phone: (401)278-6770
Fax: (401)278-6387
Venture capital firm specializing in
acquisitions and recapitalizations.

Fleet Venture Resources, Inc.
E-mail: fep@fleet.com
111 Westminster St., 4th Fl.
Providence, Rhode Island 02903
Phone: (401)278-6770
Fax: (401)278-6387
Robert M. Van Degna, President
Preferred Investment Size: $5 to $125
million. Investment Policies: Equity.
Investment Types: Leverage buyouts,
expansion. Industry Preferences:
Media/communications, healthcare,
printing, manufacturing. Geographic
Preferences: National.

Moneta Capital Corp.
285 Governor St.
Providence, Rhode Island 02906-4314
Phone: (401)454-7500
Fax: (401)455-3636
A small business investment
corporation. No industry preference.

NYSTRS/NV Capital, Limited
Partnership
111 Westminster St.
Providence, Rhode Island 02903
Phone: (401)276-5597
Fax: (401)278-6387
A small business investment
company. Diversified industry
preference.

Rhode Island Department of
Economic Development
Rhode Island Partnership for Science
and Technology
1 W. Exchange
Providence, Rhode Island 02903
Phone: (401)277-2601
Fax: (401)277-2102
Offers grants to businesses for applied
research with a potential for profitable

commercialization. Research must be
conducted in conjunction with
universities, colleges, or hospitals.
Also has a program which provides
consulting services and grants to
applicants of the Federal Small
Business Innovation Research
Program.

Rhode Island Department of
Economic Development
Rhode Island Port Operations
Division
1 W. Exchange
Providence, Rhode Island 02903
Phone: (401)277-2601
Fax: (401)277-2102
Provides financing through tax-
exempt revenue bonds.

Rhode Island Department of
Economic Development
Ocean State Business Development
Authority
1 W. Exchange
Providence, Rhode Island 02903
Phone: (401)277-2601
Fax: (401)277-2102
Private, nonprofit corporation
certified by the Small Business
Administration to administer the
SBA(504) loan program.

Rhode Island Department of
Economic Development
Rhode Island Industrial-Recreational
Building Authority
1 W. Exchange
Providence, Rhode Island 02903
Phone: (401)277-2601
Fax: (401)277-2102
Issues mortgage insurance on
financing obtained through other
financial institutions.

Rhode Island Office of the General
Treasurer
Business Investment Fund
E-mail:
treasurea@treasurea.state.ri.us
40 Fountain St., 8th Fl.
Providence, Rhode Island 02903-1855
Phone: (401)277-2287
Free: (800)752-8088

Fax: (401)277-6141
Provides fixed-rate loans in cooperation with the U.S. Small Business Administration and local banks.

Richmond Square Capital Corp.
1 Richmond Sq.
Providence, Rhode Island 02906
Phone: (401)521-3000
Fax: (401)751-8997
A small business investment company. Diversified industry preference.

Wallace Capital Corp.
170 Westminster St., Ste.1200
Providence, Rhode Island 02903
Phone: (401)273-9191
Fax: (401)273-9648
A small business investment company. Diversified industry preference.

South Carolina

Charleston Capital Corp.
111 Church St.
PO Box 328
Charleston, South Carolina 29402
Phone: (803)723-6464
Fax: (803)723-1228
Small business investment corporation preferring secured loans. Assists the southeastern U.S. only.

Lowcountry Investment Corp.
4401 Piggly Wiggly Dr.
PO Box 18047
Charleston, South Carolina 29405
Phone: (803)554-9880
Fax: (803)745-2730
A small business investment corporation. Diversified industry preference.

Floco Investment Co., Inc.
PO Box 1629
Lake City, South Carolina 29560
Phone: (803)389-2731
Fax: (803)389-4199
A small business investment corporation. Invests only in grocery stores.

South Dakota

South Dakota Department of Agriculture
Office of Rural Development
Agricultural Loan Participation Program
Foss Bldg.
523 E. Capitol
Pierre, South Dakota 57501-3182
Phone: (605)773-3375
Free: (800)228-5254
Fax: (605)773-5926
Provides loans, administered and serviced through local lenders, that are intended to supplement existing credit.

South Dakota Development Corp.
SBA 504 Loan Program
711 E. Wells Ave.
Pierre, South Dakota 57501-3369
Free: (800)872-6190
Fax: (605)773-3256
Offers subordinated mortgage financing to healthy and expanding small businesses.

South Dakota Governor's Office of Economic Development
Revolving Economic Development and Initiative Fund
711 E. Wells Ave.
Pierre, South Dakota 57501-3369
Free: (800)872-6190
Provides low-interst revolving loans for the creation of primary jobs, capital investment, and the diversification of the state's economy. Costs eligible for participation include land and the associated site improvements; construction, acquistion, and renovation of buildings; fees, services and other costs associated with construction; the purchase and installation of machinery and equipment; and trade receivables, inventory, and work-in-progress inventory.

South Dakota Governor's Office of Economic Development
Economic Development Finance Authority

711 E. Wells Ave.
Pierre, South Dakota 57501-3369
Free: (800)872-6190
Fax: (605)773-3256
Pools tax-exempt or taxable development bonds to construct any site, structure, facility, service, or utility for the storage, distribution, or manufacture of industrial, agricultural, or nonagricultural products, machinery, or equipment.

Tennessee

Valley Capital Corp.
100 W. Martin Luther King Blvd.
Ste. 212
Chattanooga, Tennessee 37402
Phone: (423)265-1557
Fax: (423)265-1588
A minority enterprise small business investment corporation. Diversified industry preferences. Limited to the Southeast, preferably four-hour driving radius.

Franklin Venture Capital, Inc.
237 2nd Ave. S
Franklin, Tennessee 37064
Phone: (615)791-9462
Fax: (615)791-9636
A small business investment corporation. Prefers to invest in the health care and biotechnology industries.

Chickasaw Capital Corp.
6200 Poplar Ave.
PO Box 387
Memphis, Tennessee 38147
Phone: (901)383-6000
Fax: (901)383-6141
A minority enterprise small business investment corporation. No industry preference.

Flemming Companies
1991 Corporate Ave.
Memphis, Tennessee 38132
Phone: (901)395-8000
Fax: (901)395-8586
A small business investment corporation.

Gulf Pacific
5100 Poplar Ave., No. 427
Memphis, Tennessee 38137-0401
Phone: (901)767-3400
Free: (800)456-1867
Fax: (901)680-7033
A minority enterprise small business
investment corporation.

International Paper Capital
Formation, Inc.
6400 Poplar Ave.
Tower 2, 4th Fl., Rm. 130
Memphis, Tennessee 38197
Phone: (901)763-6217
Fax: (901)763-6076
A minority enterprise small business
investment corporation. Diversified
industry preference. Involvement
includes expansion, refinancing, and
acquisitions, but no start-up projects.
Requires a minimum investment of
$50,000 to $300,000.

Union Platters
158 Madison Ave.
Memphis, Tennessee 38103-0708
Phone: (901)578-2405
Free: (800)821-9979
A small business investment
corporation.

West Tennessee Venture Capital
Corp.
Tennessee Valley Center for Minority
Economics Dev.
5 N. 3rd St., Ste. 2000
Memphis, Tennessee 38103-2610
Phone: (901)523-1884
Fax: (901)527-6091
A minority enterprise small business
investment corporation.

L.P. Equitas
2000 Glen Echo Rd., Ste 100
PO Box 158838
Nashville, Tennessee 37215
Phone: (615)383-8673
Fax: (615)383-8693
D. Shannon LeRoy, President

Massey Burch Investment Group
310 25th Ave. N, Ste. 103
Nashville, Tennessee 37203
Phone: (615)329-9448

Fax: (615)329-9237
Venture capital firm providing
investments ranging from $1 to $3
million. Areas of interest include
health care services, information
services, environmental services,
privatization, systems integration, and
telecommunications.

Sirrom Capital, LP
500 Church St., Ste. 200
Nashville, Tennessee 37219
Phone: (615)256-0701
Fax: (615)726-1208
A small business investment
company. Diversified industry
preference.

Tennessee Department of Economic
and Community Development
Grants Program Management Section
Rachel Jackson Bldg., 6th Fl.
320 6th Ave. N.
Nashville, Tennessee 37243-0405
Phone: (615)741-6201
Free: (800)342-8470
Fax: (615)741-5070
Administers grant money for the
community development block grant
program, the Appalachian Regional
Commission, and the Economic
Development Administration.

Tennessee Equity Capital Corp.
1102 Stonewall Jackson Ct.
Nashville, Tennessee 37220-1705
A minority enterprise small business
investment corporation.

Texas

Austin Ventures L.P.
114 W. 7th St., STe. 1300
Austin, Texas 78701
Phone: (512)479-0055
Fax: (512)476-3952
Administers investments through two
funds, Austin Ventures L.P. and Rust
Ventures L.P., in the $1 million to $4
million range. Prefers to invest in
start-up/emerging growth companies
located in the southwest, and in
special situations such as buy outs,
acquisitions, and mature companies.

No geographic limitations are placed
on later-stage investments. Past
investments have been made in
media, data communications,
telecommunications, software,
environmental services, and general
manufacturing.

Forum Financial
600 Congress Ave., No. 1630
Austin, Texas 78701-3236
Phone: (512)476-7800
Fax: (512)476-3850
Venture capital firm providing second
stage, acquisitions and leveraged
buyout financing. Areas of interest
include mining, oil and gas, real estate
development, and project financing.

Huber Capital Ventures
11917 Oak Knoll, Ste. G
Austin, Texas 78759
Phone: (512)258-8668
Fax: (512)258-9091
Venture capital firm providing short-
term working capital funding for
specific projects. Areas of interest
include small capitalization
companies in manufacturing,
wholesaling, and technical services.

Texas Department of Commerce
Finance Office
PO Box 12728
Austin, Texas 78711
Phone: (512)936-0281
Fax: (512)936-0520
Administers several programs that
benefit small businesses, including
those authorized under the Industrial
Development Corporation Act of
1979 and the Rural Development Act,
as well as the state industrial revenue
bond program.

Triad Ventures Ltd.
E-mail: cole.amf@myriad.net
8911 Capital of Texas Hwy., Ste.
3320
Austin, Texas 78759
Phone: (512)343-8087
Fax: (512)342-1993
Venture capital firm providing second
stage, acquisitions, mezzanine and

leveraged buyout financing. Areas of interest include Texas-based companies.

Alliance Enterprise Corp. (Dallas)
12655 N. Central Expy., Ste 710
Dallas, Texas 75243
Phone: (972)991-1597
Fax: (972)991-1647
A minority enterprise small business investment company. Diversified industry preference.

AMT Capital, Ltd.
8204 Elmbrook Dr., Ste. 101
Dallas, Texas 75247
Phone: (214)905-9760
Fax: (214)905-9761
Tom H. Delimitros, CGP
Preferred Investment Size: $200,000 to $500,000. Investment Policies: Loan or equity. Investment Types: Early stage, expansion. Industry Preferences: Advanced materials & products. Geographic Preferences: National.

Banc One Capital Corp. (Dallas)
300 Crescent Ct., Ste. 1600
Dallas, Texas 75201
Phone: (214)979-4375
Fax: (214)979-4355
A small business investment corporation. Specializes in later-stage investments for traditional businesses with revenues in excess of $15 million annually. Areas of interest include manufacturing, distribution, and health care industries.

Capital Southwest Corp.
12900 Preston Rd., Ste. 700
Dallas, Texas 75230
Phone: (214)233-8242
Fax: (214)233-7362
Venture capital firm. Provides first stage and expansion financing. Diversified industry preferences.

Citicorp Venture Capital, Ltd. (Dallas)
2001 Ross Ave.
1400 Tramalcrowe Center
Dallas, Texas 75201
Phone: (214)953-3800

Fax: (214)953-1495
A small business investment company.

Davis Venture Partners (Dallas)
2121 San Jacinto St., Ste. 975
Dallas, Texas 75201
Phone: (214)954-1822
Fax: (214)969-0256
Venture capital firm interested in diversified industries, excluding oil, gas, and real estate.

Diamond A. Ford Corp.
200 Crescent Court, Ste. 1350
Dallas, Texas 75201
Phone: (214)871-5177
Fax: (214)871-5199
A small business investment company. Diversified industry preference.

Erickson Capital Group, Inc.
5950 Berkshire Lane, Ste. 1100
Dallas, Texas 75225
Phone: (214)365-6060
Fax: (214)365-6001
Venture capital firm providing seed, start-up, first and second stage, and expansion financing. Areas of interest include health care.

Gaekeke Landers
4131 N. Central Expy., Ste. 900
Dallas, Texas 75204
Phone: (214)528-8883
Fax: (214)528-8058
Venture capital firm providing acquisition, start-up, and leverage equity financing. Areas of interest include real estate.

Hook Partners
13760 Noel Rd., Ste. 805
Dallas, Texas 75240-4360
Phone: (214)991-5457
Fax: (214)991-5458
Venture capital firm providing seed, start-up and first stage financing. Areas of interest include high technology industries.

Interwest Partners (Dallas)
2 Galleria Tower
13455 Noel Rd., Ste. 1670

Dallas, Texas 75240
Phone: (214)392-7279
Fax: (214)490-6348

Kahala Investments, Inc.
8214 Westchester Dr., Ste. 715
Dallas, Texas 75225
Phone: (214)987-0077
Venture capital firm providing financing for all stages including expansion capital, leveraged buyouts, and management buyouts. Areas of interest include a wide variety of industries.

Mapleleaf Capital, Ltd.
3 Forest Plz., Ste.935
12221 Merit Dr.
Dallas, Texas 75251
Phone: (214)239-5650
Fax: (214)701-0024
A small business investment company. Diversified industry preference.

May Financial Corp.
8333 Douglas Ave., Ste. 400
Lock Box 82
Dallas, Texas 75225
Phone: (214)987-5200
Free: (800)767-4397
Fax: (214)987-1994
Brokerage firm working with a venture capital firm. Prefers food, oil and gas, and electronics industries.

Merchant Banking Group Ltd.
700 N. Pearl, Ste. 1910 NT, LB 321
Dallas, Texas 75201
Phone: (214)777-6466
Fax: (214)777-6475
Venture capital firm providing leveraged buyout financing. Areas of interest include basic manufacturing and distribution.

MESBIC Ventures, Inc.
12655 N. Central Expy., Ste. 710
Dallas, Texas 75243
Phone: (972)991-1597
Fax: (972)991-1647
Donald R. Lawhorne, President
Preferred Investment Size: Up to $1,000,000. Investment Policies: Loans and/or equity. Investment

Types: early stage, expansion, later stage. Industry Preferences: Diversified. Geographic Preferences: Mostly Southwest.

MSI Capital Corp.
6500 Greenville Ave., Ste. 720
Dallas, Texas 75206-1012
Phone: (214)265-1801
Fax: (214)265-1804
No industry preference.

Nations Bank Venture Capital
901 Maine St., 64th Fl.
Dallas, Texas 75202-2911
Phone: (214)508-0988
Fax: (214)508-0604
A small business investment company. Diversified industry preference.

NationsBank Capital Corp.
NationBank Plz., Ste. 71
901 Main St.
Dallas, Texas 75202
Phone: (214)508-6262
Fax: (214)508-5060
Venture capital firm providing second stage, mezzanine and leveraged buyout financing. Areas of interest include communications, medical, environmental, specialty retail, transportation and energy services.

NCNB Texas Venture Group, Inc.
1401 Elm St., Ste. 4764
Dallas, Texas 75202
Phone: (214)508-6262
Venture capital firm providing expansion and leveraged buyout financing. Areas of interest include medical products and services, energy service, environmental, specialty retail, transportation, general manufacturing, and communications.

North Texas MESBIC, Inc.
12770 Coit Rd., Ste.240
Dallas, Texas 75251
Phone: (214)991-8060
Fax: (214)991-8061
A minority enterprise small business investment company. Diversified industry preference.

Phillips-Smith Specialty Retail Group
E-mail: pssrg@aol.com
5080 Spectrum Dr., Ste. 700 W
Dallas, Texas 75248
Phone: (214)387-0725
Fax: (214)458-2560
Prefers specialty retail industry investments, including the restaurant industry.

PMC Capital, Inc.
Attn: Andy Rosemore
17290 Preston Rd., 3rd Fl.
Dallas, Texas 75252-5618
Phone: (214)380-0044
Free: (800)486-3223
Fax: (214)380-1371
A small business investment corporation, minority enterprise small business investment corporation, and SBA guaranteed lender. No industry preferred.

Pro-Med Investment Corp.
17290 Preston Rd., Ste. 300
Dallas, Texas 75252
Phone: (214)380-0044
Fax: (214)380-1371
A minority enterprise small business investment company. Diversified industry preference.

Sevin Rosen Funds
13455 Noel Rd., Ste. 1670
Dallas, Texas 75240
Phone: (214)702-1100
Fax: (214)702-1103
Venture capital firm providing start-up and first stage financing. Industry preferences include information sciences and electronic sciences.

Southwest Enterprise Associates
14457 Gillis Rd.
Dallas, Texas 75244
Phone: (214)450-3894
Fax: (214)450-3899
Venture capital supplier. Concentrates on technology-based industries that have the potential for product innovation, rapid growth, and high profit margins. Investments range from $250,000 to $1.5 million. Past investments have been made in the

following industries: computer software, medical and life sciences, computers and peripherals, communications, semiconductors, and defense electronics. Management must demonstrate intimate nowledge of its marketplace and have a well-defined strategy for achieving strong market penetration.

Stratford Capital Partners, L.P.
200 Crescent Ct., Ste. 1650
Dallas, Texas 75201
Phone: (214)740-7377
Fax: (214)740-7340
Michael D. Brown, President
Preferred Investment Size: $3 to $9 million. Investment Policies: Equity, sub debt with equity. Investment Types: Expansion, later stage, acquisition. Industry Preferences: Manufacturing, distribution, diversified. Geographic Preferences: National.

Sullivan Enterprises
9130 Markville Dr.
PO Box 743803
Dallas, Texas 75374-3803
Phone: (214)414-5690
Venture capital firm providing refinancings and expansion, mezzanine, and leveraged buyouts financing. Areas of interest include manufacturing, service, retailing, wholesale and distribution.

Sunwestern Capital Corp.
12221 Merit Dr., Ste. 1300
Dallas, Texas 75251-2248
Phone: (214)239-5650
Fax: (214)701-0024
Small business investment corporation providing start-up, first stage, second stage, third stage and leveraged buyout financing. Areas of interest include computer peripherals, software, information services, biotechnology and telecommunications.

Tower Ventures, Inc.
12655 N. Central Expy., Ste. 710
Dallas, Texas 75243

Phone: (972)391-1597
Fax: (972)991-1647
Donald R. Lawhorne, President
Preferred Investment Size: Up to
$500,000. Investment Policies: Loans
and/or equity. Investment Types:
Early stage, expansion, later stage.

Western Financial Capital Corp.
17290 Preston Rd., Ste. 300
Dallas, Texas 75252
Phone: (214)380-0044
Fax: (214)380-1371
A small business investment
company. Provides financing to the
medical industry.

Wingate Partners
750 N. St. Paul St., Ste. 1200
Dallas, Texas 75201
Phone: (214)720-1313
Fax: (214)871-8799
Venture capital firm providing mature
stage financing. Areas of interest
include manufacturing and
distribution.

HCT Capital Corp.
4916 Camp Bowie Blvd., Ste. 200
Fort Worth, Texas 76107
Phone: (817)763-8706
Fax: (817)377-8049
A small business investment
company. Diversified industry
preference.

SBIC Partners, L.P.
201 Main St., Ste. 2302
Fort Worth, Texas 76102
Phone: (817)729-3222
Fax: (817)729-3226
Gregory Forrest, Manager
Jeffrey Brown, Manager
Preferred Investment Size: $2 to $5
million. Investment Policies: Equity.
Investment Types: Expansion, later
stage. Industry Preferences:
Diversified. Geographic Preferences:
National.

Acorn Ventures, Inc.
520 Post Oak Blvd., Ste. 130
Houston, Texas 77027
Phone: (713)622-9595
Fax: (713)622-9595
No industry preference.

Alliance Business Investment Co.
(Houston)
1221 McKinney Ste.3100
Houston, Texas 77010
Phone: (713)659-3131
Fax: (713)659-8070
A small business investment
corporation.

Aspen Capital Ltd.
55 Waugh, Ste. 710
Houston, Texas 77007
Phone: (713)880-4494
A small business investment
corporation. No industry preference.

The Catalyst Fund, Ltd.
3 Riverway, Ste. 770
Houston, Texas 77056
Phone: (713)623-8133
Fax: (713)623-0473
A small business investment
company. Diversified industry
preference.

Charter Venture Group, Inc.
2600 Citadel Plaza Dr., Ste. 600
PO Box 4525
Houston, Texas 77210-4525
Phone: (713)622-7500
Fax: (713)552-8446
A small business investment
corporation. No industry preference.

Chen's Financial Group, Inc.
10101 Southwest Fwy., Ste. 370
Houston, Texas 77074
Phone: (713)772-8868
Fax: (713)772-2168
A minority enterprise small business
investment corporation. Areas of
interest include real estate, franchise
restaurants, banking, and import/
export industries.

Criterion Ventures
1330 Post Oak Blvd., Ste. 1525
Houston, Texas 77056
Phone: (713)627-9200
Fax: (713)627-9292
Venture capital fund. Raises venture
capital. Interested in companies
headquartered in the Sunbelt region.
Areas of interest include
telecommunications, biomedical, and
specialty retail.

Cureton & Co., Inc.
1100 Louisiana, Ste. 3250
Houston, Texas 77002
Phone: (713)658-9806
Fax: (713)658-0476
Prefers oilfield service,
environmental, electronics,
manufacturing, and distribution.

Energy Assets, Inc.
700 Louisiana, Ste. 5000
Houston, Texas 77002
Phone: (713)236-9999
Free: (800)933-5508
A small business investment
corporation. Specializes in oil and gas
energy industries.

High Technology Associates
1775 St. James Pl., Ste. 105
Houston, Texas 77056
Phone: (713)963-9300
Fax: (713)963-8341
Venture capital firm providing second
stage and expansion financing. Areas
of interest include biotechnology,
chemicals, food processing and food
processing machinery. Particularly
interested in companies willing to
establish operations in the Northern
Netherlands.

Houston Partners, SBIC
401 Louisiana, 8th Fl.
Houston, Texas 77002
Phone: (713)222-8600
Fax: (713)222-8932
A small business investment
company. Diversified industry
preference.

MESBIC Financial Corp. of Houston
9130 North Fwy., Ste. 203
Houston, Texas 77037
Phone: (281)447-3000
Fax: (281)447-4222
Atillio Galli, President
Preferred Investment Size: $100,000
to $1 million. Investment Policies:
Loans and equity investments.
Investment Types: Consolidated debt
& preferred stock with warrants.
Industry Preferences: Diversified - no
real estate or gas and oil. Geographic
Preferences: Houston.

Payne Webber, Inc.
700 Louisiana St., Ste.3800
Houston, Texas 77002
Phone: (713)236-3180
Fax: (713)236-3133

Penzoil
PO Box 2967
Houston, Texas 77252
Phone: (713)546-8910
Fax: (713)546-4154
A small business investment
company. Diversified industry
preference.

Southern Orient Capital Corp.
2419 Fannin, Ste. 200
Houston, Texas 77002-9181
Phone: (713)225-3369
A minority enterprise small business
investment corporation. No industry
preference.

Tenneco Ventures, Inc.
PO Box 2511
Houston, Texas 77252
Phone: (713)757-8229
Fax: (713)651-1666
Venture capital supplier. Provides
financing to small, early stage growth
companies. Areas of interest include
energy- related technologies, factory
automation, biotechnology, and health
care services. Prefers to invest in
Texas-based companies, but will
consider investments elsewhere
within the United States. Investments
range from $250,000 to $1 million;
will commit additional funds over
several rounds of financing, and will
work with other investors to provide
larger financing.

Texas Commerce Investment Group
PO Box 2558
Houston, Texas 77252-8032
Phone: (713)216-4553
A small business investment
corporation. No industry preference.

UNCO Ventures, Inc.
520 Post Oak Blvd., Ste. 130
Houston, Texas 77027
Phone: (713)622-9595
Fax: (713)622-9007

A small business investment
company. Diversified industry
preference.

United Oriental Capital Corp.
908 Town and Country Blvd., Ste.
310
Houston, Texas 77024-2207
Phone: (713)461-3909
Fax: (713)465-7559
A minority enterprise small business
investment corporation. No industry
preference.

Ventex Partners, Ltd.
1001 Fannin St., Ste. 1095
Houston, Texas 77002
Phone: (713)659-7860
Fax: (713)659-7855
A small business investment
partnership providing later stage
financing.

Capital Marketing Corp.
P.O. Box 1177
Keller, Texas 76244
Phone: (817)431-5767
A small business investment
corporation.

First Capital Group of Texas
E-mail: jpb@texas.net
PO Box 15616
San Antonio, Texas 78212-8816
Phone: (210)736-4233
Fax: (210)736-5449
A small business investment
corporation. No industry preference,
but does not invest in oil, gas, and real
estate industries.

Southwest Venture Partnerships
16414 St. Pedro, Ste. 345
San Antonio, Texas 78232
Phone: (210)402-1200
Free: (800)725-0867
Fax: (210)402-1221
Venture capital partnership. Invests in
maturing companies located primarily
in the southwest. Average investment
is $1 million.

Norwest Bank & Trust
1 O'Connor Plz.
Victoria, Texas 77902

Phone: (512)573-5151
Fax: (512)574-5236
A small business investment
company. Diversified industry
preference.

Woodlands Venture Partners L.P.
2170 Buckthorne Pl., Ste. 170
The Woodlands, Texas 77380
Phone: (713)367-9999
Fax: (713)298-1295
Venture capital firm providing start-
up, first stage, second stage and seed
financing. Areas of interest include
medical/biotechnology only.

Utah

Deseret Certified Development Corp.
(Midvale)
E-mail: deseretcdc@aol.com
7050 Union Park Center, No. 570
Midvale, Utah 84047
Phone: (801)566-1163
Fax: (801)566-1532
Maintains an SBA(504) loan
program, designed for community
development and job creation, and an
intermediary loan program, through
Farmer's Home Administration.

Deseret Certified Development Corp.
(Orem)
228 N. Orem Blvd.
Orem, Utah 84057-5011
Phone: (801)221-7772
Fax: (801)221-7775
Maintains an SBA(504) loan
program, designed for community
development and job creation, and an
intermediary loan program, through
Farmer's Home Administration.

First Security Business Investment
Corp.
79 S. Main St., Ste. 800
Salt Lake City, Utah 84111
Phone: (801)246-5737
Fax: (801)246-5424
Louis D. Alder, Manager
Preferred Investment Size: $500,000
to $1 million. Investment Policies:
Loans and/or equity. Investment
Types: Expansion, later stage.

Industry Preferences: Diversified. Geographic Preferences: West/ midwest.

Utah Technology Finance Corp.
177 E., 100 S.
Salt Lake City, Utah 84111
Phone: (801)364-4346
Fax: (801)364-4361
Assists the start-up and growth of emerging technology- based businesses and products.

Utah Ventures
423 Wakara Way, Ste. 206
Salt Lake City, Utah 84108
Phone: (801)583-5922
Fax: (801)583-4105
Invests in the life sciences at an early stage.

Wasatch Venture Corp.
1 S. Main St., Ste. 1000
Salt Lake City, Utah 84133
Phone: (801)524-8939
Fax: (801)524-8941
W. David Hemingway, Manager
Preferred Investment Size: $500,000.
Investment Policies: Equity and debt.
Investment Types: Early stage.
Industry Preferences: High technology. Geographic Preferences: West, midwest, Rocky.

Vermont

Queneska Capital Corp.
123 Church St.
Burlington, Vermont 05401
Phone: (802)865-1806
Fax: (802)865-1891
A small business investment company. Diversified industry preference.

Vermont Economic Development Authority
58 E. State St.
Montpelier, Vermont 05602
Phone: (802)828-5627
Fax: (802)828-5474
Several financial programs to assist small and medium- sized manufacturing firms in the state.

Vermont Economic Development Authority
Vermont Job Start
58 E. State St.
Montpelier, Vermont 05602
Phone: (802)828-5627
Fax: (802)828-5474
A state-funded economic opportunity program aimed at increasing self-employment by low-income Vermonters.

Green Mountain Capital, L.P.
RR 1 Box 1503
Waterbury, Vermont 05676
Phone: (802)244-8981
Fax: (802)244-8990
A small business investment company. Diversified industry preference.

Virgin Islands

Tri-Island Economic Development Council, Inc.
PO Box 838
St. Thomas, Virgin Islands 00804-0838
Phone: (809)774-7215
Provides counseling, information, referrals, and management and technical assistance to help strengthen existing businesses and expand the rate of development of new businesses.

Virginia

Metropolitan Capital Corp.
2550 Huntington Ave.
Alexandria, Virginia 22303
Phone: (703)550-0747
A small business investment corporation. Equity or loans with equity features. Does not invest in retail or real estate.

Continental SBIC
4141 N. Henderson Rd., Ste. 8
Arlington, Virginia 22203
Phone: (703)527-5200
Fax: (703)527-3700
A minority enterprise small business investment company. Diversified industry preference.

East West United Investment Co. (Falls Church)
200 Park Ave.
Falls Church, Virginia 22046-3107
Phone: (703)536-0268
Fax: (703)536-0619
A minority enterprise small business investment company. Diversified industry preference.

Rural America Fund, Inc.
Attenton: Richard Balman
2201 Cooperative Way
Herndon, Virginia 22071
Phone: (703)709-6750
Fax: (703)709-6774
A small business investment company. Diversified industry preference.

East West United Investment Co. (Mc Lean)
1568 Spring Hill Rd., Ste. 100
McLean, Virginia 22102
Phone: (703)442-0150
Fax: (703)442-0156
Dung Bui, President

Ewing, Monroe & Co.
E-mail: emcompany@aol.com
901 E. Cary St., Ste. 1410
Richmond, Virginia 23219
Phone: (804)780-1900
Fax: (804)780-1901
A small business investment corporation. No industry preference.

Virginia Small Business Financing Authority
PO Box 446
Richmond, Virginia 23218-0446
Phone: (804)371-8254
Fax: (804)225-3384
Assists small businesses in obtaining financing for development and expansion.

Walnut Capital Corp. (Vienna)
8000 Towers Crescent Dr., Ste.1070
Vienna, Virginia 22182-2700
Phone: (703)448-3771
Fax: (703)448-7751
A small business investment corporation. No industry preference.

Washington

Cable and Howse Ventures (Bellevue)
777 108th Ave. NE, Ste. 2300
Bellevue, Washington 98004
Phone: (206)646-3030
Fax: (206)646-3041
Venture capital investor. Provides
start-up and early stage financing to
enterprises in the western United
States, although a national perspective
is maintained. Interests lie in
proprietary or patentable technology.
Investments range from $50,000 to $2
million.

Pacific Northwest Partners SBIC, L.P.
E-mail: pnwp@msn.com
Ste. 800, City Center Bellevue
500 - 108th Ave., NE
Bellevue, Washington 98004
Phone: (206)646-7357
Fax: (206)646-7356
Theodore M Wight, Manager
Preferred Investment Size:
$1,000,000. Investment Policies:
Private equity investments.
Investment Types: Seed Through later
stage. Industry Preferences:
Diversified, retail, healthcare,
technology. Geographic Preferences:
Pacific Northwest.

Materia Venture Associates, L.P.
E-mail: materiaventure@msn.com
3435 Carillon Pointe
Kirkland, Washington 98033
Phone: (206)822-4100
Fax: (206)827-4086
Prefers investing in advanced
materials and related technologies.

Olympic Venture Partners (Kirkland)
E-mail: info@ovp.com
2420 Carillon Pt.
Kirkland, Washington 98033-7353
Phone: (206)889-9192
Fax: (206)889-0152
Prefers to fund early stage,
technology companies in the West.

Washington Department of
Community, Trade and Economic
Development
Development Loan Fund

906 Columbia St. SW
PO Box 48300
Olympia, Washington 98504-8300
Phone: (360)753-5630
Fax: (360)586-2424
Provides capital for businesses in
distressed areas to create new jobs,
particularly for low and moderate
income persons.

Washington Department of
Community, Trade and Economic
Development
Community Development Finance
(CDF) Program
900 Columbia St. SW
PO Box 48300
Olympia, Washington 98504-8300
Phone: (360)753-7426
Fax: (360)586-3582
Helps businesses and industries
secure needed financing by
combining private financial loans
with federal and state loans.

The Phoenix Partners
E-mail: dionnsto@interserv.com
1000 2nd Ave., Ste. 3600
Seattle, Washington 98104
Phone: (206)624-8968
Fax: (206)624-1907
Prefers to invest in companies
involved in biotechnology, health
care, medical devices, computer
software, semiconductors, and
telecommunications.

Washington Department of
Community, Trade and Economic
Development
Industrial Revenue Bonds
2001 6th Ave., Ste. 2600
Seattle, Washington 98121
Phone: (206)464-7143
Fax: (360)464-7222
Issued to finance the acquisition,
construction, enlargement, or
improvement of industrial
development facilities.

West Virginia

Anker Capital Corp.
E-mail: south-venture@citynet.com
208 Capital St., Ste. 300

Charleston, West Virginia 25301
Phone: (304)344-1794
Fax: (304)344-1798
Thomas Loehr, Manager
Preferred Investment Size: $500,000.
Investment Policies: Combination of
debt and equity. Investment Types:
Expansion, early stage, spin-off.
Industry Preferences: Wood products,
computer industry, manufacturing.
Geographic Preferences: West
Virginia, Ohio, Pennsylvania,
Virginia, Maryland.

Shenandoah Venture Capital L.P.
E-mail: south-venture@citynet.com
208 Capital St., Ste. 300
Charleston, West Virginia 25301
Phone: (304)344-1796
Fax: (304)344-1798
Thomas E. Loehr, President

West Virginia Development Office
West Virginia SBA
State Capitol Complex, Bldg 6, Rm.
525
1018 Kanawha Blvd.,Ste. 501
Charleston, West Virginia 25305
Phone: (304)558-3650
Fax: (304)558-0206
Provides long-term, fixed-rate loans
for small and medium- sized firms.

West Virginia Development Office
West Virginia Economic
Development Authority
1018 Kanawha Blvd., E., Ste. 501
Charleston, West Virginia 25301-
2827
Phone: (304)558-3650
Fax: (304)558-0206
Provides low-interest loans for land or
building acquisition, building
construction, and equipment
purchases.

WestVen Ltd. Partnership
208 Capitol St., Ste. 300
Charleston, West Virginia 25301
Phone: (304)344-1794
Fax: (304)344-1798
Thomas E. Loehr, President
Preferred Investment Size: $500,000.
Investment Policies: Combination of
debt and equity. Investment Types:

Expansion, early stage, spin-off.
Industry Preferences: Wood products,
computer industry, manufacturing.
Geographic Preferences: West
Virginia, Ohio, Pennsylvania,
Virginia, Maryland.

Wisconsin

Impact Seven, Inc.
E-mail: impact@win.bright.net
651 Darvfield
Almena, Wisconsin 54805
Phone: (715)357-3334
Fax: (715)357-6233
Provides equity investment.

Polaris Capital Corp.
2525 N. 124th St., Ste.200
Brookfield, Wisconsin 53005-4614
Phone: (414)789-5780
Fax: (414)789-5799
A small business investment
corporation. Prefers equity- type
investments of up to $500,000,
expansion stage companies, seasoned
companies, and management buyouts.
Diversified industry preference,
including industrial, electronic
products/equipment, and consumer
and business products/services in
Wisconsin and northern Illinois.

Madison Development Corp.
550 W. Washington Ave.
Madison, Wisconsin 53703
Phone: (608)256-2799
Fax: (608)256-1560
Provides loans of up to $150,000 to
eligible businesses in Dane County
for working capital, inventory,
equipment, leasehold improvements,
and business real estate.

Venture Investors of Wisconsin, Inc.
(Madison)
E-mail: viw@macc.wisc.edu
565 Science Dr., Ste. A
Madison, Wisconsin 53711
Phone: (608)233-3070
Fax: (608)238-5120
Venture capital firm providing early-
stage financing to Wisconsin-based
companies with strong management
teams. Areas of interest include

biotechnology, software, analytical
instruments, medical products,
consumer products, and publishing
industries.

Venture Investors of Wisconsin, Inc.
(Milwaukee)
E-mail: viw@macc.wisc.edu
565 Science Dr.,Ste.A
Madison, Wisconsin 53711
Phone: (414)298-3070
Fax: (608)238-5120
Providers of equity financing.

Wisconsin Business Development
Finance Corp.
E-mail: wbdfc@waun.tdsnet.com
PO Box 2717
Madison, Wisconsin 53701
Phone: (608)258-8830
Fax: (608)258-1664
Provides small business financing for
the purchase of land, buildings,
machinery, equipment, and the
construction and moderization of
facilities.

Wisconsin Department of
Development
Wisconsin Development Fund
123 W. Washington Ave.
PO Box 7970
Madison, Wisconsin 53707
Phone: (608)266-2742
Free: (800)HELP-BUS
Fax: (608)264-6151

Wisconsin Housing and Economic
Development Authority
Venture Capital Fund
Economic Development Analyst
1 S. Pinckney St., No. 500
PO Box 1728
Madison, Wisconsin 53701
Phone: (608)266-7884
Free: (800)334-6873
Fax: (608)267-1099
Invests in new and existing businesses
that are developing new products.

Wisconsin Innovation Network
Foundation
PO Box 71
Madison, Wisconsin 53701-0071
Phone: (608)256-8348

Fax: (608)256-0333
Seeks to join people with marketing
and sales ideas to those willing to
finance them. Acts as a resource
center for financing information;
offers networking opportunities for
business professionals, entrepreneurs,
and small business owners at regular
monthly meetings.

Capital Investment, Inc. (Mequon)
1009 W. Glen Oaks Ln., Ste. 103
Mequon, Wisconsin 53092
Phone: (414)241-0303
Fax: (414)241-8451
James R. Sanger, President
Preferred Investment Size: $500,000
to $1 million. Investment Policies:
Subordinated debt with warrant.
Investment Types: Expansion, later
stage. Industry Preferences:
Manufacturing and value-added
distributors. Geographic Preferences:
Midwest, national.

Banc One Venture Corp. (Milwaukee)
111 E. Wisconsin Ave.
Milwaukee, Wisconsin 53202
Phone: (414)765-3278
H. Wayne Foreman, President
Preferred Investment Size: $1 to $10
million. Investment Types: Later
stage, expansion, LBO, MBO.
Industry Preferences: Publishing,
distribution, manufacturing, mail-
order. Geographic Preferences:
Natinal.

Capital Investments, Inc.
(Milwaukee)
700 N. Water St., Ste. 325
Milwaukee, Wisconsin 53202
Phone: (414)278-7744
Free: (800)345-6462
Fax: (414)278-8403
A small business investment
corporation. Prefers later- stage
companies located in the Midwest,
involved in manufacturing and
specialty distribution.

Future Value Venture, Inc.
330 E. Kilbourn Ave., Ste.711
Milwaukee, Wisconsin 53202
Phone: (414)278-0377

Fax: (414)278-7321
A minority enterprise small business investment corporation. Diversified industry preference. Minimum initial investment is $100,000.

Horizon Partners, Ltd.
225 E. Mason St., Ste. 600
Milwaukee, Wisconsin 53202
Phone: (414)271-2200
Fax: (414)271-4016
Providers of equity financing for low-to-medium technology industries.

InvestAmerica Venture Group, Inc.
(Milwaukee)
600 E. Mason St., Ste.304
Milwaukee, Wisconsin 53202
Phone: (414)276-3839
Fax: (414)276-1885
A small business investment corporation. Prefers later- stage and acquisition financings of $1,000,000 to $3,000,000 with equity participation. Will not consider real estate investments.

Lubar and Co., Inc.
777 E. Wisconsin, Ste. 3380
Milwaukee, Wisconsin 53202
Phone: (414)291-9000
Fax: (414)291-9061
Private investment and management firm.

M & I Ventures Corp.
770 N. Water St.
Milwaukee, Wisconsin 53202
Phone: (414)765-7700
Free: (800)342-2265
Fax: (414)765-7850
A small business investment corporation. Areas of interest include manufacturing, technology, electronics, health care, publishing, and communications industries. Average investment is from $1 million to $3 million.

MorAmerican Capital Corp.
(Milwaukee)
600 E. Mason St.,Ste. 304
Milwaukee, Wisconsin 53202
Phone: (414)276-3839
Fax: (414)276-1885

A small business investment company.

Wisconsin Venture Capital Fund
777 E. Wisconsin Ave., Ste. 3380
Milwaukee, Wisconsin 53202
Phone: (414)291-9000
Fax: (414)291-9061

WITECH Corp., Inc.
1000 N. Water, Ste. 1805
PO Box 2949
Milwaukee, Wisconsin 53202
Phone: (414)347-1550
Fax: (414)221-4990
Venture capital firm.

Wind Point Partners (Racine)
420 3 Mile, Apt. B4
Racine, Wisconsin 53402
Phone: (414)639-3113
Fax: (414)639-3417
Venture capital firm.

Bando-McGlocklin SBIC
W239 N. 1700 Busse Rd.
Waukesha, Wisconsin 53188
Phone: (414)523-4300
Fax: (414)523-4193
George Schonath, Chief Executive Officer
Preferred Investment Size: $3,000,000. Investment Policies: Loans. Investment Types: Early stage, expansion, later stage. Industry Preferences: Diversified. Geographic Preferences: Midwest.

Wyoming

Frontier Certified Development Co.
PO Box 3599
Casper, Wyoming 82602
Phone: (307)234-5351
Free: (800)934-5351
Fax: (307)234-0501
Created by the Wyoming Industrial Development Corporation to provide expansion financing for Wyoming business.

Wyoming Industrial Development Corp.
PO Box 3599
Casper, Wyoming 82602

Phone: (307)234-5351
Free: (800)934-5351
Fax: (307)234-0501
Administers SBA 7(A) and SBA(502) programs. Purchases the guaranteed portion of U.S. Small Business Administration and Farmers Home Administration Loans to small businesses to pool into a common fund that enables small businesses to obtain loans at more reasonable rates and terms.

Wyoming Department of Commerce
Economic and Community Development Division
New Business Retention and Financing
Barrett Bldg.
6109 Yellowstone
Cheyenne, Wyoming 82002
Phone: (307)777-6418
Fax: (307)777-6005

Appendix C - Glossary of Small Business Terms

Glossary of Small Business Terms

Absolute liability
Liability that is incurred due to product defects or negligent actions. Manufacturers or retail establishments are held responsible, even though the defect or action may not have been intentional or negligent.

ACE
See Active Corps of Executives

Accident and health benefits
Benefits offered to employees and their families in order to offset the costs associated with accidental death, accidental injury, or sickness.

Account statement
A record of transactions, including payments, new debt, and deposits, incurred during a defined period of time.

Accounting system
System capturing the costs of all employees and/or machinery included in business expenses.

Accounts payable
See Trade credit

Accounts receivable
Unpaid accounts which arise from unsettled claims and transactions from the sale of a company's products or services to its customers.

Active Corps of Executives (ACE)
(See also Service Corps of Retired Executives)
A group of volunteers for a management assistance program of the U.S. Small Business Administration; volunteers provide one-on-one counseling and teach workshops and seminars for small firms.

ADA
See Americans with Disabilities Act

Adaptation
The process whereby an invention is modified to meet the needs of users.

Adaptive engineering
The process whereby an invention is modified to meet the manufacturing and commercial requirements of a targeted market.

Adverse selection
The tendency for higher-risk individuals to purchase health care and more comprehensive plans, resulting in increased costs.

Advertising
A marketing tool used to capture public attention and influence purchasing decisions for a product or service. Utilizes various forms of media to generate consumer response, such as flyers, magazines, newspapers, radio, and television.

Age discrimination
The denial of the rights and privileges of employment based solely on the age of an individual.

Agency costs
Costs incurred to insure that the lender or investor maintains control over assets while allowing the borrower or entrepreneur to use them. Monitoring and information costs are the two major types of agency costs.

Agribusiness
The production and sale of commodities and products from the commercial farming industry.

America Online
(See also Prodigy)
An online service which is accessible by computer modem. The service features Internet access, bulletin boards, online periodicals, electronic mail, and other services for subscribers.

Americans with Disabilities Act (ADA)
Law designed to ensure equal access and opportunity to handicapped persons.

Annual report
(See also Securities and Exchange Commission)
Yearly financial report prepared by a business that adheres to the requirements set forth by the Securities and Exchange Commission (SEC).

Antitrust immunity
(See also Collective ratemaking)
Exemption from prosecution under antitrust laws. In the transportation industry, firms with antitrust immunity are

permitted—under certain conditions—to set schedules and sometimes prices for the public benefit.

Applied research
Scientific study targeted for use in a product or process.

Asians
A minority category used by the U.S. Bureau of the Census to represent a diverse group that includes Aleuts, Eskimos, American Indians, Asian Indians, Chinese, Japanese, Koreans, Vietnamese, Filipinos, Hawaiians, and other Pacific Islanders.

Assets
Anything of value owned by a company.

Audit
The verification of accounting records and business procedures conducted by an outside accounting service.

Average cost
Total production costs divided by the quantity produced.

Balance Sheet
A financial statement listing the total assets and liabilities of a company at a given time.

Bankruptcy
(See also Chapter 7 of the 1978 Bankruptcy Act; Chapter 11 of the 1978 Bankruptcy Act)
The condition in which a business cannot meet its debt obligations and petitions a federal district court either for reorganization of its debts (Chapter 11) or for liquidation of its assets (Chapter 7).

Basic research
Theoretical scientific exploration not targeted to application.

Basket clause
A provision specifying the amount of public pension funds that may be placed in investments not included on a state's legal list (see separate citation).

BBS
See Bulletin Board Service

BDC
See Business development corporation

Benefit
Various services, such health care, flextime, day care, insurance, and vacation, offered to employees as part of a hiring package. Typically subsidized in whole or in part by the business.

BIDCO
See Business and industrial development company

Billing cycle
A system designed to evenly distribute customer billing throughout the month, preventing clerical backlogs.

Birth
See Business birth

Blue chip security
A low-risk, low-yield security representing an interest in a very stable company.

Blue sky laws
A general term that denotes various states' laws regulating securities.

Bond
(See also General obligation bond; Taxable bonds; Treasury bonds)
A written instrument executed by a bidder or contractor (the principal) and a second party (the surety or sureties) to assure fulfillment of the principal's obligations to a third party (the obligee or government) identified in the bond. If the principal's obligations are not met, the bond assures payment to the extent stipulated of any loss sustained by the obligee.

Bonding requirements
Terms contained in a bond (see separate citation).

Bonus
An amount of money paid to an employee as a reward for achieving certain business goals or objectives.

Brainstorming
A group session where employees contribute their ideas for solving a problem or meeting a company objective without fear of retribution or ridicule.

Brand name
The part of a brand, trademark, or service mark that can be spoken. It can be a word, letter, or group of words or letters.

Bridge financing
A short-term loan made in expectation of intermediate-term or long-term financing. Can be used when a company plans to go public in the near future.

Broker
One who matches resources available for innovation with those who need them.

Budget

An estimate of the spending necessary to complete a project or offer a service in comparison to cash-on-hand and expected earnings for the coming year, with an emphasis on cost control.

Bulletin Board Service (BBS)

An online service enabling users to communicate with each other about specific topics.

Business birth

The formation of a new establishment or enterprise. The appearance of a new establishment or enterprise in the Small Business Data Base (see separate citation).

Business conditions

Outside factors that can affect the financial performance of a business.

Business contractions

The number of establishments that have decreased in employment during a specified time.

Business cycle

A period of economic recession and recovery. These cycles vary in duration.

Business death

The voluntary or involuntary closure of a firm or establishment. The disappearance of an establishment or enterprise from the Small Business Data Base (see separate citation).

Business development corporation (BDC)

A business financing agency, usually composed of the financial institutions in an area or state, organized to assist in financing businesses unable to obtain assistance through normal channels; the risk is spread among various members of the business development corporation, and interest rates may vary somewhat from those charged by member institutions. A venture capital firm in which shares of ownership are publicly held and to which the Investment Act of 1940 applies.

Business dissolution

For enumeration purposes, the absence of a business that was present in the prior time period from any current record.

Business entry

See Business birth

Business ethics

Moral values and principles espoused by members of the business community as a guide to fair and honest business practices.

Business exit

See Business death

Business expansions

The number of establishments that added employees during a specified time.

Business failure

Closure of a business causing a loss to at least one creditor.

Business format franchising

(See also Franchising)

The purchase of the name, trademark, and an ongoing business plan of the parent corporation or franchisor by the franchisee.

Business and industrial development company (BIDCO)

A private, for-profit financing corporation chartered by the state to provide both equity and long-term debt capital to small business owners (see separate citations for equity and debt capital).

Business license

A legal authorization issued by municipal and state governments and required for business operations.

Business name

(See also Business license; Trademark)

Enterprises must register their business names with local governments usually on a "doing business as" (DBA) form. (This name is sometimes referred to as a "fictional name.") The procedure is part of the business licensing process and prevents any other business from using that same name for a similar business in the same locality.

Business norms

See Financial ratios

Business permit

See Business license

Business plan

A document that spells out a company's expected course of action for a specified period, usually including a detailed listing and analysis of risks and uncertainties. For the small business, it should examine the proposed products, the market, the industry, the management policies, the marketing policies, production needs, and financial needs. Frequently, it is used as a prospectus for potential investors and lenders.

Business proposal

See Business plan

Business service firm

An establishment primarily engaged in rendering services to other business organizations on a fee or contract basis.

Business start

For enumeration purposes, a business with a name or similar designation that did not exist in a prior time period.

Cafeteria plan

See Flexible benefit plan

Capacity

Level of a firm's, industry's, or nation's output corresponding to full practical utilization of available resources.

Capital

Assets less liabilities, representing the ownership interest in a business. A stock of accumulated goods, especially at a specified time and in contrast to income received during a specified time period. Accumulated goods devoted to production. Accumulated possessions calculated to bring income.

Capital expenditure

Expenses incurred by a business for improvements that will depreciate over time.

Capital gain

The monetary difference between the purchase price and the selling price of capital. Capital gains are taxed at a rate of 28% by the federal government.

Capital intensity

(See also Debt capital; Equity midrisk venture capital; Informal capital; Internal capital; Owner's capital; Secondhand capital; Seed capital; Venture capital)
The relative importance of capital in the production process, usually expressed as the ratio of capital to labor but also sometimes as the ratio of capital to output.

Capital resource

The equipment, facilities and labor used to create products and services.

Caribbean Basin Initiative

An interdisciplinary program to support commerce among the businesses in the nations of the Caribbean Basin and the United States. Agencies involved include: the Agency for International Development, the U.S. Small Business Administration, the International Trade Administration of the U.S. Department of Commerce, and various private sector groups.

Catastrophic care

Medical and other services for acute and long-term illnesses that cost more than insurance coverage limits or that cost the amount most families may be expected to pay with their own resources.

CDC

See Certified development corporation

CD-ROM

Compact disc with read-only memory used to store large amounts of digitized data.

Certified development corporation (CDC)

A local area or statewide corporation or authority (for profit or nonprofit) that packages U.S. Small Business Administration (SBA), bank, state, and/or private money into financial assistance for existing business capital improvements. The SBA holds the second lien on its maximum share of 40 percent involvement. Each state has at least one certified development corporation. This program is called the SBA 504 Program.

Certified lenders

Banks that participate in the SBA guaranteed loan program (see separate citation). Such banks must have a good track record with the U.S. Small Business Administration (SBA) and must agree to certain conditions set forth by the agency. In return, the SBA agrees to process any guaranteed loan application within three business days.

Champion

An advocate for the development of an innovation.

Channel of distribution

The means used to transport merchandise from the manufacturer to the consumer.

Chapter 7 of the 1978 Bankruptcy Act

Provides for a court-appointed trustee who is responsible for liquidating a company's assets in order to settle outstanding debts.

Chapter 11 of the 1978 Bankruptcy Act

Allows the business owners to retain control of the company while working with their creditors to reorganize their finances and establish better business practices to prevent liquidation of assets.

Closely held corporation

A corporation in which the shares are held by a few

persons, usually officers, employees, or others close to the management; these shares are rarely offered to the public.

Code of Federal Regulations

Codification of general and permanent rules of the federal government published in the Federal Register.

Code sharing

See Computer code sharing

Coinsurance

(See also Cost sharing)

Upon meeting the deductible payment, health insurance participants may be required to make additional health care cost-sharing payments. Coinsurance is a payment of a fixed percentage of the cost of each service; copayment is usually a fixed amount to be paid with each service.

Collateral

Securities, evidence of deposit, or other property pledged by a borrower to secure repayment of a loan.

Collective ratemaking

(See also Antitrust immunity)

The establishment of uniform charges for services by a group of businesses in the same industry.

Commercial insurance plan

See Underwriting

Commercial loans

Short-term renewable loans used to finance specific capital needs of a business.

Commercialization

The final stage of the innovation process, including production and distribution.

Common stock

The most frequently used instrument for purchasing ownership in private or public companies. Common stock generally carries the right to vote on certain corporate actions and may pay dividends, although it rarely does in venture investments. In liquidation, common stockholders are the last to share in the proceeds from the sale of a corporation's assets; bondholders and preferred shareholders have priority. Common stock is often used in first-round start-up financing.

Community development corporation

A corporation established to develop economic programs for a community and, in most cases, to provide financial support for such development.

Competitor

A business whose product or service is marketed for the same purpose/use and to the same consumer group as the product or service of another.

Computer code sharing

An arrangement whereby flights of a regional airline are identified by the two-letter code of a major carrier in the computer reservation system to help direct passengers to new regional carriers.

Consignment

A merchandising agreement, usually referring to second-hand shops, where the dealer pays the owner of an item a percentage of the profit when the item is sold.

Consortium

A coalition of organizations such as banks and corporations for ventures requiring large capital resources.

Consultant

An individual that is paid by a business to provide advice and expertise in a particular area.

Consumer price index

A measure of the fluctuation in prices between two points in time.

Consumer research

Research conducted by a business to obtain information about existing or potential consumer markets.

Continuation coverage

Health coverage offered for a specified period of time to employees who leave their jobs and to their widows, divorced spouses, or dependents.

Contractions

See Business contractions

Convertible preferred stock

A class of stock that pays a reasonable dividend and is convertible into common stock (see separate citation). Generally the convertible feature may only be exercised after being held for a stated period of time. This arrangement is usually considered second-round financing when a company needs equity to maintain its cash flow.

Convertible securities

A feature of certain bonds, debentures, or preferred stocks that allows them to be exchanged by the owner for another class of securities at a future date and in accordance with any other terms of the issue.

Copayment

See Coinsurance

Copyright

A legal form of protection available to creators and authors to safeguard their works from unlawful use or claim of ownership by others. Copyrights may be acquired for works of art, sculpture, music, and published or unpublished manuscripts. All copyrights should be registered at the Copyright Office of the Library of Congress.

Corporate financial ratios

(See also Industry financial ratios)

The relationship between key figures found in a company's financial statement expressed as a numeric value. Used to evaluate risk and company performance. Also known as Financial averages, Operating ratios, and Business ratios.

Corporation

A legal entity, chartered by a state or the federal government, recognized as a separate entity having its own rights, privileges, and liabilities distinct from those of its members.

Cost containment

Actions taken by employers and insurers to curtail rising health care costs; for example, increasing employee cost sharing (see separate citation), requiring second opinions, or preadmission screening.

Cost sharing

The requirement that health care consumers contribute to their own medical care costs through deductibles and coinsurance (see separate citations). Cost sharing does not include the amounts paid in premiums. It is used to control utilization of services; for example, requiring a fixed amount to be paid with each health care service.

Cottage industry

(See also Home-based business)

Businesses based in the home in which the family members are the labor force and family-owned equipment is used to process the goods.

Credit Rating

A letter or number calculated by an organization (such as Dun & Bradstreet) to represent the ability and disposition of a business to meet its financial obligations.

Customer service

Various techniques used to ensure the satisfaction of a customer.

Cyclical peak

The upper turning point in a business cycle.

Cyclical trough

The lower turning point in a business cycle.

DBA

See Business name

Death

See Business death

Debenture

A certificate given as acknowledgment of a debt (see separate citation) secured by the general credit of the issuing corporation. A bond, usually without security, issued by a corporation and sometimes convertible to common stock.

Debt

(See also Long-term debt; Mid-term debt; Securitized debt; Short-term debt)

Something owed by one person to another. Financing in which a company receives capital that must be repaid; no ownership is transferred.

Debt capital

Business financing that normally requires periodic interest payments and repayment of the principal within a specified time.

Debt financing

See Debt capital

Debt securities

Loans such as bonds and notes that provide a specified rate of return for a specified period of time.

Deductible

A set amount that an individual must pay before any benefits are received.

Demand shock absorbers

A term used to describe the role that some small firms play by expanding their output levels to accommodate a transient surge in demand.

Demographics

Statistics on various markets, including age, income, and education, used to target specific products or services to appropriate consumer groups.

Demonstration

Showing that a product or process has been modified sufficiently to meet the needs of users.

Deregulation

The lifting of government restrictions; for example, the lifting of government restrictions on the entry of new businesses, the expansion of services, and the setting of prices in particular industries.

Desktop Publishing

Using personal computers and specialized software to produce camera-ready copy for publications.

Disaster loans

Various types of physical and economic assistance available to individuals and businesses through the U.S. Small Business Administration (SBA). This is the only SBA loan program available for residential purposes.

Discrimination

The denial of the rights and privileges of employment based on factors such as age, race, religion, or gender.

Diseconomies of scale

The condition in which the costs of production increase faster than the volume of production.

Dissolution

See Business dissolution

Distribution

Delivering a product or process to the user.

Distributor

One who delivers merchandise to the user.

Diversified company

A company whose products and services are used by several different markets.

Doing business as (DBA)

See Business name

Dow Jones

An information services company that publishes the Wall Street Journal and other sources of financial information.

Dow Jones Industrial Average

An indicator of stock market performance.

Earned income

A tax term that refers to wages and salaries earned by the recipient, as opposed to monies earned through interest and dividends.

Economic efficiency

The use of productive resources to the fullest practical

extent in the provision of the set of goods and services that is most preferred by purchasers in the economy.

Economic indicators

Statistics used to express the state of the economy. These include the length of the average work week, the rate of unemployment, and stock prices.

Economically disadvantaged

See Socially and economically disadvantaged

Economies of scale

See Scale economies

EEOC

See Equal Employment Opportunity Commission

8(a) Program

A program authorized by the Small Business Act that directs federal contracts to small businesses owned and operated by socially and economically disadvantaged individuals.

Electronic mail (e-mail)

The electronic transmission of mail via phone lines.

E-mail

See Electronic mail

Employee leasing.

A contract by which employers arrange to have their workers hired by a leasing company and then leased back to them for a management fee. The leasing company typically assumes the administrative burden of payroll and provides a benefit package to the workers.

Employee tenure

The length of time an employee works for a particular employer.

Employer identification number

The business equivalent of a social security number. Assigned by the U.S. Internal Revenue Service.

Enterprise

An aggregation of all establishments owned by a parent company. An enterprise may consist of a single, independent establishment or include subsidiaries and other branches under the same ownership and control.

Enterprise zone

A designated area, usually found in inner cities and other areas with significant unemployment, where businesses receive tax credits and other incentives to entice them to establish operations there.

Entrepreneur
A person who takes the risk of organizing and operating a new business venture.

Entry
See Business entry

Equal Employment Opportunity Commission (EEOC)
A federal agency that ensures nondiscrimination in the hiring and firing practices of a business.

Equal opportunity employer
An employer who adheres to the standards set by the Equal Employment Opportunity Commission (see separate citation).

Equity
(See also Common Stock; Equity midrisk venture capital)
The ownership interest. Financing in which partial or total ownership of a company is surrendered in exchange for capital. An investor's financial return comes from dividend payments and from growth in the net worth of the business.

Equity capital
See Equity; Equity midrisk venture capital

Equity financing
See Equity; Equity midrisk venture capital

Equity midrisk venture capital
An unsecured investment in a company. Usually a purchase of ownership interest in a company that occurs in the later stages of a company's development.

Equity partnership
A limited partnership arrangement for providing start-up and seed capital to businesses.

Equity securities
See Equity

Equity-type
Debt financing subordinated to conventional debt.

Establishment
A single-location business unit that may be independent (a single-establishment enterprise) or owned by a parent enterprise.

Establishment and Enterprise Microdata File
See U.S. Establishment and Enterprise Microdata File

Establishment birth
See Business birth

Establishment Longitudinal Microdata File
See U.S. Establishment Longitudinal Microdata File

Ethics
See Business ethics

Evaluation
Determining the potential success of translating an invention into a product or process.

Exit
See Business exit

Experience rating
See Underwriting

Export
A product sold outside of the country.

Export license
A general or specific license granted by the U.S. Department of Commerce required of anyone wishing to export goods. Some restricted articles need approval from the U.S. Departments of State, Defense, or Energy.

Failure
See Business failure

Fair share agreement
(See also Franchising)
An agreement reached between a franchisor and a minority business organization to extend business ownership to minorities by either reducing the amount of capital required or by setting aside certain marketing areas for minority business owners.

Feasibility study
A study to determine the likelihood that a proposed product or development will fulfill the objectives of a particular investor.

Federal Trade Commission (FTC)
Federal agency that promotes free enterprise and competition within the U.S.

Federal Trade Mark Act of 1946
See Lanham Act

Fictional name
See Business name

Fiduciary

An individual or group that hold assets in trust for a beneficiary.

Financial analysis

The techniques used to determine money needs in a business. Techniques include ratio analysis, calculation of return on investment, guides for measuring profitability, and break-even analysis to determine ultimate success.

Financial intermediary

A financial institution that acts as the intermediary between borrowers and lenders. Banks, savings and loan associations, finance companies, and venture capital companies are major financial intermediaries in the United States.

Financial ratios

See Corporate financial ratios; Industry financial ratios

Financial statement

A written record of business finances, including balance sheets and profit and loss statements.

Financing

See First-stage financing; Second-stage financing; Third-stage financing

First-stage financing

(See also Second-stage financing; Third-stage financing) Financing provided to companies that have expended their initial capital, and require funds to start full-scale manufacturing and sales. Also known as First-round financing.

Fiscal year

Any twelve-month period used by businesses for accounting purposes.

504 Program

See Certified development corporation

Flexible benefit plan

A plan that offers a choice among cash and/or qualified benefits such as group term life insurance, accident and health insurance, group legal services, dependent care assistance, and vacations.

FOB

See Free on board

Format franchising

See Business format franchising; Franchising

401(k) plan

A financial plan where employees contribute a percentage of their earnings to a fund that is invested in stocks, bonds, or money markets for the purpose of saving money for retirement.

Four Ps

Marketing terms referring to Product, Price, Place, and Promotion.

Franchising

A form of licensing by which the owner—the franchisor—distributes or markets a product, method, or service through affiliated dealers called franchisees. The product, method, or service being marketed is identified by a brand name, and the franchisor maintains control over the marketing methods employed. The franchisee is often given exclusive access to a defined geographic area.

Free on board (FOB)

A pricing term indicating that the quoted price includes the cost of loading goods into transport vessels at a specified place.

Frictional unemployment

See Unemployment

FTC

See Federal Trade Commission

Fulfillment

The systems necessary for accurate delivery of an ordered item, including subscriptions and direct marketing.

Full-time workers

Generally, those who work a regular schedule of more than 35 hours per week.

Garment registration number

A number that must appear on every garment sold in the U.S. to indicate the manufacturer of the garment, which may or may not be the same as the label under which the garment is sold. The U.S. Federal Trade Commission assigns and regulates garment registration numbers.

Gatekeeper

A key contact point for entry into a network.

GDP

See Gross domestic product

General obligation bond

A municipal bond secured by the taxing power of the municipality. The Tax Reform Act of 1986 limits the purposes for which such bonds may be issued and establishes volume limits on the extent of their issuance.

GNP
See Gross national product

Good Housekeeping Seal
Seal appearing on products that signifies the fulfillment of the standards set by the Good Housekeeping Institute to protect consumer interests.

Goods sector
All businesses producing tangible goods, including agriculture, mining, construction, and manufacturing businesses.

GPO
See Gross product originating

Gross domestic product (GDP)
The part of the nation's gross national product (see separate citation) generated by private business using resources from within the country.

Gross national product (GNP)
The most comprehensive single measure of aggregate economic output. Represents the market value of the total output of goods and services produced by a nation's economy.

Gross product originating (GPO)
A measure of business output estimated from the income or production side using employee compensation, profit income, net interest, capital consumption, and indirect business taxes.

HAL
See Handicapped assistance loan program

Handicapped assistance loan program (HAL)
Low-interest direct loan program through the U.S. Small Business Administration (SBA) for handicapped persons. The SBA requires that these persons demonstrate that their disability is such that it is impossible for them to secure employment, thus making it necessary to go into their own business to make a living.

Health maintenance organization (HMO)
Organization of physicians and other health care professionals that provides health services to subscribers and their dependents on a prepaid basis.

Health provider
An individual or institution that gives medical care. Under Medicare, an institutional provider is a hospital, skilled nursing facility, home health agency, or provider of certain physical therapy services.

Hispanic
A person of Cuban, Mexican, Puerto Rican, Latin American (Central or South American), European Spanish, or other Spanish-speaking origin or ancestry.

HMO
See Health maintenance organization

Home-based business
(See also Cottage industry)
A business with an operating address that is also a residential address (usually the residential address of the proprietor).

Hub-and-spoke system
A system in which flights of an airline from many different cities (the spokes) converge at a single airport (the hub). After allowing passengers sufficient time to make connections, planes then depart for different cities.

Human Resources Management
A business program designed to oversee recruiting, pay, benefits, and other issues related to the company's work force, including planning to determine the optimal use of labor to increase production, thereby increasing profit.

Idea
An original concept for a new product or process.

Import
Products produced outside the country in which they are consumed.

Income
Money or its equivalent, earned or accrued, resulting from the sale of goods and services.

Income statement
A financial statement that lists the profits and losses of a company at a given time.

Incorporation
The filing of a certificate of incorporation with a state's secretary of state, thereby limiting the business owner's liability.

Incubator
A facility designed to encourage entrepreneurship and minimize obstacles to new business formation and growth, particularly for high-technology firms, by housing a number of fledgling enterprises that share an array of services, such as meeting areas, secretarial services, accounting, research library, on-site financial and management counseling, and word processing facilities.

Independent contractor
An individual considered self-employed (see separate citation) and responsible for paying Social Security taxes and income taxes on earnings.

Indirect health coverage
Health insurance obtained through another individual's health care plan; for example, a spouse's employer-sponsored plan.

Industrial development authority
The financial arm of a state or other political subdivision established for the purpose of financing economic development in an area, usually through loans to nonprofit organizations, which in turn provide facilities for manufacturing and other industrial operations.

Industry financial ratios
(See also Corporate financial ratios)
Corporate financial ratios averaged for a specified industry. These are used for comparison purposes and reveal industry trends and identify differences between the performance of a specific company and the performance of its industry. Also known as Industrial averages, Industry ratios, Financial averages, and Business or Industrial norms.

Inflation
Increases in volume of currency and credit, generally resulting in a sharp and continuing rise in price levels.

Informal capital
Financing from informal, unorganized sources; includes informal debt capital such as trade credit or loans from friends and relatives and equity capital from informal investors.

Initial public offering (IPO)
A corporation's first offering of stock to the public.

Innovation
The introduction of a new idea into the marketplace in the form of a new product or service or an improvement in organization or process.

Intellectual property
Any idea or work that can be considered proprietary in nature and is thus protected from infringement by others.

Internal capital
Debt or equity financing obtained from the owner or through retained business earnings.

Internet
A government-designed computer network that contains large amounts of information and is accessible through various vendors for a fee.

Intrapreneurship
The state of employing entrepreneurial principles to nonentrepreneurial situations.

Invention
The tangible form of a technological idea, which could include a laboratory prototype, drawings, formulas, etc.

IPO
See Initial public offering

Job description
The duties and responsibilities required in a particular position.

Job tenure
A period of time during which an individual is continuously employed in the same job.

Joint marketing agreements
Agreements between regional and major airlines, often involving the coordination of flight schedules, fares, and baggage transfer. These agreements help regional carriers operate at lower cost.

Joint venture
Venture in which two or more people combine efforts in a particular business enterprise, usually a single transaction or a limited activity, and agree to share the profits and losses jointly or in proportion to their contributions.

Keogh plan
Designed for self-employed persons and unincorporated businesses as a tax-deferred pension account.

Labor force
Civilians considered eligible for employment who are also willing and able to work.

Labor force participation rate
The civilian labor force as a percentage of the civilian population.

Labor intensity
(See also Capital intensity)
The relative importance of labor in the production process, usually measured as the capital-labor ratio; i.e., the ratio of units of capital (typically, dollars of tangible assets) to the number of employees. The higher the capital-labor ratio exhibited by a firm or industry, the lower the capital intensity of that firm or industry is said to be.

Labor surplus area

An area in which there exists a high unemployment rate. In procurement (see separate citation), extra points are given to firms in counties that are designated a labor surplus area; this information is requested on procurement bid sheets.

Labor union

An organization of similarly-skilled workers who collectively bargain with management over the conditions of employment.

Laboratory prototype

See Prototype

LAN

See Local Area Network

Lanham Act

Refers to the Federal Trade Mark Act of 1946. Protects registered trademarks, trade names, and other service marks used in commerce.

Large business-dominated industry

Industry in which a minimum of 60 percent of employment or sales is in firms with more than 500 workers.

LBO

See Leveraged buy-out

Leader pricing

A reduction in the price of a good or service in order to generate more sales of that good or service.

Legal list

A list of securities selected by a state in which certain institutions and fiduciaries (such as pension funds, insurance companies, and banks) may invest. Securities not on the list are not eligible for investment. Legal lists typically restrict investments to high quality securities meeting certain specifications. Generally, investment is limited to U.S. securities and investment-grade blue chip securities (see separate citation).

Leveraged buy-out (LBO)

The purchase of a business or a division of a corporation through a highly leveraged financing package.

Liability

An obligation or duty to perform a service or an act. Also defined as money owed.

License

(See also Business license)

A legal agreement granting to another the right to use a technological innovation.

Limited partnerships

See Venture capital limited partnerships

Liquidity

The ability to convert a security into cash promptly.

Loans

See Commercial loans; Disaster loans; SBA direct loans; SBA guaranteed loans; SBA special lending institution categories

Local Area Network (LAN)

Computer networks contained within a single building or small area; used to facilitate the sharing of information.

Local development corporation

An organization, usually made up of local citizens of a community, designed to improve the economy of the area by inducing business and industry to locate and expand there. A local development corporation establishes a capability to finance local growth.

Long-haul rates

Rates charged by a transporter in which the distance traveled is more than 800 miles.

Long-term debt

An obligation that matures in a period that exceeds five years.

Low-grade bond

A corporate bond that is rated below investment grade by the major rating agencies (Standard and Poor's, Moody's).

Macro-efficiency

(See also Economic efficiency)

Efficiency as it pertains to the operation of markets and market systems.

Managed care

A cost-effective health care program initiated by employers whereby low-cost health care is made available to the employees in return for exclusive patronage to program doctors.

Management and technical assistance

A term used by many programs to mean business (as opposed to technological) assistance.

Management Assistance Programs

See SBA Management Assistance Programs

Mandated benefits

Specific treatments, providers, or individuals required by law to be included in commercial health plans.

Market evaluation

The use of market information to determine the sales potential of a specific product or process.

Market failure

The situation in which the workings of a competitive market do not produce the best results from the point of view of the entire society.

Market information

Data of any type that can be used for market evaluation, which could include demographic data, technology forecasting, regulatory changes, etc.

Market research

A systematic collection, analysis, and reporting of data about the market and its preferences, opinions, trends, and plans; used for corporate decision-making.

Market share

In a particular market, the percentage of sales of a specific product.

Marketing

Promotion of goods or services through various media.

Master Establishment List (MEL)

A list of firms in the United States developed by the U.S. Small Business Administration; firms can be selected by industry, region, state, standard metropolitan statistical area (see separate citation), county, and zip code.

Maturity

(See also Term)

The date upon which the principal or stated value of a bond or other indebtedness becomes due and payable.

Medicaid (Title XIX)

A federally aided, state-operated and administered program that provides medical benefits for certain low-income persons in need of health and medical care who are eligible for one of the government's welfare cash payment programs, including the aged, the blind, the disabled, and members of families with dependent children where one parent is absent, incapacitated, or unemployed.

Medicare (Title XVIII)

A nationwide health insurance program for disabled and aged persons. Health insurance is available to insured persons without regard to income. Monies from payroll taxes cover hospital insurance and monies from general revenues and beneficiary premiums pay for supplementary medical insurance.

MEL

See Master Establishment List

MESBIC

See Minority enterprise small business investment corporation

MET

See Multiple employer trust

Metropolitan statistical area (MSA)

A means used by the government to define large population centers that may transverse different governmental jurisdictions. For example, the Washington, D.C. MSA includes the District of Columbia and contiguous parts of Maryland and Virginia because all of these geopolitical areas comprise one population and economic operating unit.

Mezzanine financing

See Third-stage financing

Micro-efficiency

(See also Economic efficiency)

Efficiency as it pertains to the operation of individual firms.

Microdata

Information on the characteristics of an individual business firm.

Mid-term debt

An obligation that matures within one to five years.

Midrisk venture capital

See Equity midrisk venture capital

Minimum premium plan

A combination approach to funding an insurance plan aimed primarily at premium tax savings. The employer self-funds a fixed percentage of estimated monthly claims and the insurance company insures the excess.

Minimum wage

The lowest hourly wage allowed by the federal government.

Minority Business Development Agency

Contracts with private firms throughout the nation to

sponsor Minority Business Development Centers which provide minority firms with advice and technical assistance on a fee basis.

Minority Enterprise Small Business Investment Corporation (MESBIC)

A federally funded private venture capital firm licensed by the U.S. Small Business Administration to provide capital to minority-owned businesses (see separate citation).

Minority-owned business

Businesses owned by those who are socially or economically disadvantaged (see separate citation).

Mom and Pop business

A small store or enterprise having limited capital, principally employing family members.

Moonlighter

A wage-and-salary worker with a side business.

MSA

See Metropolitan statistical area

Multi-employer plan

A health plan to which more than one employer is required to contribute and that may be maintained through a collective bargaining agreement and required to meet standards prescribed by the U.S. Department of Labor.

Multi-level marketing

A system of selling in which you sign up other people to assist you and they, in turn, recruit others to help them. Some entrepreneurs have built successful companies on this concept because the main focus of their activities is their product and product sales.

Multimedia

The use of several types of media to promote a product or service. Also, refers to the use of several different types of media (sight, sound, pictures, text) in a CD-ROM (see separate citation) product.

Multiple employer trust (MET)

A self-funded benefit plan generally geared toward small employers sharing a common interest.

NAFTA

See North American Free Trade Agreement

NASDAQ

See National Association of Securities Dealers Automated Quotations

National Association of Securities Dealers Automated Quotations

Provides price quotes on over-the-counter securities as well as securities listed on the New York Stock Exchange.

National income

Aggregate earnings of labor and property arising from the production of goods and services in a nation's economy.

Net assets

See Net worth

Net income

The amount remaining from earnings and profits after all expenses and costs have been met or deducted. Also known as Net earnings.

Net profit

Money earned after production and overhead expenses (see separate citations) have been deducted.

Net worth

(See also Capital)

The difference between a company's total assets and its total liabilities.

Network

A chain of interconnected individuals or organizations sharing information and/or services.

New York Stock Exchange (NYSE)

The oldest stock exchange in the U.S. Allows for trading in stocks, bonds, warrants, options, and rights that meet listing requirements.

Niche

A career or business for which a person is well-suited. Also, a product which fulfills one need of a particular market segment, often with little or no competition.

Nodes

One workstation in a network, either local area or wide area (see separate citations).

Nonbank bank

A bank that either accepts deposits or makes loans, but not both. Used to create many new branch banks.

Noncompetitive awards

A method of contracting whereby the federal government negotiates with only one contractor to supply a product or service.

Nonmember bank
A state-regulated bank that does not belong to the federal bank system.

Nonprofit
An organization that has no shareholders, does not distribute profits, and is without federal and state tax liabilities.

Norms
See Financial ratios

North American Free Trade Agreement (NAFTA)
Passed in 1993, NAFTA eliminates trade barriers among businesses in the U.S., Canada, and Mexico.

NYSE
See New York Stock Exchange

Occupational Safety & Health Administration (OSHA)
Federal agency that regulates health and safety standards within the workplace.

Optimal firm size
The business size at which the production cost per unit of output (average cost) is, in the long run, at its minimum.

Organizational chart
A hierarchical chart tracking the chain of command within an organization.

OSHA
See Occupational Safety & Health Administration

Overhead
Expenses, such as employee benefits and building utilities, incurred by a business that are unrelated to the actual product or service sold.

Owner's capital
Debt or equity funds provided by the owner(s) of a business; sources of owner's capital are personal savings, sales of assets, or loans from financial institutions.

P & L
See Profit and loss statement

Part-time workers
Normally, those who work less than 35 hours per week. The Tax Reform Act indicated that part-time workers who work less than 17.5 hours per week may be excluded from health plans for purposes of complying with federal nondiscrimination rules.

Part-year workers
Those who work less than 50 weeks per year.

Partnership
Two or more parties who enter into a legal relationship to conduct business for profit. Defined by the U.S. Internal Revenue Code as joint ventures, syndicates, groups, pools, and other associations of two or more persons organized for profit that are not specifically classified in the IRS code as corporations or proprietorships.

Patent
A grant made by the government assuring an inventor the sole right to make, use, and sell an invention for a period of 17 years.

PC
See Professional corporation

Peak
See Cyclical peak

Pension
A series of payments made monthly, semiannually, annually, or at other specified intervals during the lifetime of the pensioner for distribution upon retirement. The term is sometimes used to denote the portion of the retirement allowance financed by the employer's contributions.

Pension fund
A fund established to provide for the payment of pension benefits; the collective contributions made by all of the parties to the pension plan.

Performance appraisal
An established set of objective criteria, based on job description and requirements, that is used to evaluate the performance of an employee in a specific job.

Permit
See Business license

Plan
See Business plan

Pooling
An arrangement for employers to achieve efficiencies and lower health costs by joining together to purchase group health insurance or self-insurance.

PPO
See Preferred provider organization

Preferred lenders program
See SBA special lending institution categories

Preferred provider organization (PPO)

A contractual arrangement with a health care services organization that agrees to discount its health care rates in return for faster payment and/or a patient base.

Premiums

The amount of money paid to an insurer for health insurance under a policy. The premium is generally paid periodically (e.g., monthly), and often is split between the employer and the employee. Unlike deductibles and coinsurance or copayments, premiums are paid for coverage whether or not benefits are actually used.

Prime-age workers

Employees 25 to 54 years of age.

Prime contract

A contract awarded directly by the U.S. Federal Government.

Private company

See Closely held corporation

Private placement

A method of raising capital by offering for sale an investment or business to a small group of investors (generally avoiding registration with the Securities and Exchange Commission or state securities registration agencies). Also known as Private financing or Private offering.

Pro forma

The use of hypothetical figures in financial statements to represent future expenditures, debts, and other potential financial expenses.

Proactive

Taking the initiative to solve problems and anticipate future events before they happen, instead of reacting to an already existing problem or waiting for a difficult situation to occur.

Procurement

(See also 8(a) Program; Small business set asides)

A contract from an agency of the federal government for goods or services from a small business.

Prodigy

(See also America Online)

An online service which is accessible by computer modem. The service features Internet access, bulletin boards, online periodicals, electronic mail, and other services for subscribers.

Product development

The stage of the innovation process where research is translated into a product or process through evaluation, adaptation, and demonstration.

Product franchising

An arrangement for a franchisee to use the name and to produce the product line of the franchisor or parent corporation.

Production

The manufacture of a product.

Production prototype

See Prototype

Productivity

A measurement of the number of goods produced during a specific amount of time.

Professional corporation (PC)

Organized by members of a profession such as medicine, dentistry, or law for the purpose of conducting their professional activities as a corporation. Liability of a member or shareholder is limited in the same manner as in a business corporation.

Profit and loss statement (P & L)

The summary of the incomes (total revenues) and costs of a company's operation during a specific period of time. Also known as Income and expense statement.

Proposal

See Business plan

Proprietorship

The most common legal form of business ownership; about 85 percent of all small businesses are proprietorships. The liability of the owner is unlimited in this form of ownership.

Prospective payment system

A cost-containment measure included in the Social Security Amendments of 1983 whereby Medicare payments to hospitals are based on established prices, rather than on cost reimbursement.

Prototype

A model that demonstrates the validity of the concept of an invention (laboratory prototype); a model that meets the needs of the manufacturing process and the user (production prototype).

Prudent investor rule or standard

A legal doctrine that requires fiduciaries to make investments using the prudence, diligence, and intelligence that would be used by a prudent person in making similar investments. Because fiduciaries make investments on behalf of third-party beneficiaries, the standard results in very conservative investments. Until recently, most state regulations required the fiduciary to apply this standard to each investment. Newer, more progressive regulations permit fiduciaries to apply this standard to the portfolio taken as a whole, thereby allowing a fiduciary to balance a portfolio with higher-yield, higher-risk investments. In states with more progressive regulations, practically every type of security is eligible for inclusion in the portfolio of investments made by a fiduciary, provided that the portfolio investments, in their totality, are those of a prudent person.

Public equity markets

Organized markets for trading in equity shares such as common stocks, preferred stocks, and warrants. Includes markets for both regularly traded and nonregularly traded securities.

Public offering

General solicitation for participation in an investment opportunity. Interstate public offerings are supervised by the U.S. Securities and Exchange Commission (see separate citation).

Quality control

The process by which a product is checked and tested to ensure consistent standards of high quality.

Rate of return

(See also Yield)

The yield obtained on a security or other investment based on its purchase price or its current market price. The total rate of return is current income plus or minus capital appreciation or depreciation.

Real property

Includes the land and all that is contained on it.

Realignment

See Resource realignment

Recession

Contraction of economic activity occurring between the peak and trough (see separate citations) of a business cycle.

Regulated market

A market in which the government controls the forces of supply and demand, such as who may enter and what price may be charged.

Regulation D

A vehicle by which small businesses make small offerings and private placements of securities with limited disclosure requirements. It was designed to ease the burdens imposed on small businesses utilizing this method of capital formation.

Regulatory Flexibility Act

An act requiring federal agencies to evaluate the impact of their regulations on small businesses before the regulations are issued and to consider less burdensome alternatives.

Research

The initial stage of the innovation process, which includes idea generation and invention.

Research and development financing

A tax-advantaged partnership set up to finance product development for start-ups as well as more mature companies.

Resource mobility

The ease with which labor and capital move from firm to firm or from industry to industry.

Resource realignment

The adjustment of productive resources to interindustry changes in demand.

Resources

The sources of support or help in the innovation process, including sources of financing, technical evaluation, market evaluation, management and business assistance, etc.

Retained business earnings

Business profits that are retained by the business rather than being distributed to the shareholders as dividends.

Revolving credit

An agreement with a lending institution for an amount of money, which cannot exceed a set maximum, over a specified period of time. Each time the borrower repays a portion of the loan, the amount of the repayment may be borrowed yet again.

Risk capital

See Venture capital

Risk management

The act of identifying potential sources of financial loss and taking action to minimize their negative impact.

Routing

The sequence of steps necessary to complete a product during production.

S corporations

See Sub chapter S corporations

SBA

See Small Business Administration

SBA direct loans

Loans made directly by the U.S. Small Business Administration (SBA); monies come from funds appropriated specifically for this purpose. In general, SBA direct loans carry interest rates slightly lower than those in the private financial markets and are available only to applicants unable to secure private financing or an SBA guaranteed loan.

SBA 504 Program

See Certified development corporation

SBA guaranteed loans

Loans made by lending institutions in which the U.S. Small Business Administration (SBA) will pay a prior agreed-upon percentage of the outstanding principal in the event the borrower of the loan defaults. The terms of the loan and the interest rate are negotiated between the borrower and the lending institution, within set parameters.

SBA loans

See Disaster loans; SBA direct loans; SBA guaranteed loans; SBA special lending institution categories

SBA Management Assistance Programs

(See also Active Corps of Executives; Service Corps of Retired Executives; Small business institutes program)
Classes, workshops, counseling, and publications offered by the U.S. Small Business Administration.

SBA special lending institution categories.

U.S. Small Business Administration (SBA) loan program in which the SBA promises certified banks a 72-hour turnaround period in giving its approval for a loan, and in which preferred lenders in a pilot program are allowed to write SBA loans without seeking prior SBA approval.

SBDB

See Small Business Data Base

SBDC

See Small business development centers

SBI

See Small business institutes program

SBIC

See Small business investment corporation

SBIR Program

See Small Business Innovation Development Act of 1982

Scale economies

The decline of the production cost per unit of output (average cost) as the volume of output increases.

Scale efficiency

The reduction in unit cost available to a firm when producing at a higher output volume.

SCORE

See Service Corps of Retired Executives

SEC

See Securities and Exchange Commission

SECA

See Self-Employment Contributions Act

Second-stage financing

(See also First-stage financing; Third-stage financing)
Working capital for the initial expansion of a company that is producing, shipping, and has growing accounts receivable and inventories. Also known as Second-round financing.

Secondary market

A market established for the purchase and sale of outstanding securities following their initial distribution.

Secondary worker

Any worker in a family other than the person who is the primary source of income for the family.

Secondhand capital

Previously used and subsequently resold capital equipment (e.g., buildings and machinery).

Securities and Exchange Commission (SEC)

Federal agency charged with regulating the trade of securities to prevent unethical practices in the investor market.

Securitized debt

A marketing technique that converts long-term loans to marketable securities.

Seed capital

Venture financing provided in the early stages of the

innovation process, usually during product development.

Self-employed person

One who works for a profit or fees in his or her own business, profession, or trade, or who operates a farm.

Self-Employment Contributions Act (SECA)

Federal law that governs the self-employment tax (see separate citation).

Self-employment income

Income covered by Social Security if a business earns a net income of at least $400.00 during the year. Taxes are paid on earnings that exceed $400.00.

Self-employment retirement plan

See Keogh plan

Self-employment tax

Required tax imposed on self-employed individuals for the provision of Social Security and Medicare. The tax must be paid quarterly with estimated income tax statements.

Self-funding

A health benefit plan in which a firm uses its own funds to pay claims, rather than transferring the financial risks of paying claims to an outside insurer in exchange for premium payments.

Service Corps of Retired Executives (SCORE)

(See also Active Corps of Executives)

Volunteers for the SBA Management Assistance Program who provide one-on-one counseling and teach workshops and seminars for small firms.

Service firm

See Business service firm

Service sector

Broadly defined, all U.S. industries that produce intangibles, including the five major industry divisions of transportation, communications, and utilities; wholesale trade; retail trade; finance, insurance, and real estate; and services.

Set asides

See Small business set asides

Short-haul service

A type of transportation service in which the transporter supplies service between cities where the maximum distance is no more than 200 miles.

Short-term debt

An obligation that matures in one year.

SIC codes

See Standard Industrial Classification codes

Single-establishment enterprise

See Establishment

Small business

An enterprise that is independently owned and operated, is not dominant in its field, and employs fewer than 500 people. For SBA purposes, the U.S. Small Business Administration (SBA) considers various other factors (such as gross annual sales) in determining size of a business.

Small Business Administration (SBA)

An independent federal agency that provides assistance with loans, management, and advocating interests before other federal agencies.

Small Business Data Base

(See also U.S. Establishment and Enterprise Microdata File; U.S. Establishment Longitudinal Microdata File)

A collection of microdata (see separate citation) files on individual firms developed and maintained by the U.S. Small Business Administration.

Small business development centers (SBDC)

Centers that provide support services to small businesses, such as individual counseling, SBA advice, seminars and conferences, and other learning center activities. Most services are free of charge, or available at minimal cost.

Small business development corporation

See Certified development corporation

Small business-dominated industry

Industry in which a minimum of 60 percent of employment or sales is in firms with fewer than 500 employees.

Small Business Innovation Development Act of 1982

Federal statute requiring federal agencies with large extramural research and development budgets to allocate a certain percentage of these funds to small research and development firms. The program, called the Small Business Innovation Research (SBIR) Program, is designed to stimulate technological innovation and make greater use of small businesses in meeting national innovation needs.

Small business institutes (SBI) program

Cooperative arrangements made by U.S. Small Business Administration district offices and local colleges and universities to provide small business firms with graduate students to counsel them without charge.

Small business investment corporation (SBIC)
A privately owned company licensed and funded through the U.S. Small Business Administration and private sector sources to provide equity or debt capital to small businesses.

Small business set asides
Procurement (see separate citation) opportunities required by law to be on all contracts under $10,000 or a certain percentage of an agency's total procurement expenditure.

Smaller firms
For U.S. Department of Commerce purposes, those firms not included in the Fortune 1000.

SMSA
See Metropolitan statistical area

Socially and economically disadvantaged
Individuals who have been subjected to racial or ethnic prejudice or cultural bias without regard to their qualities as individuals, and whose abilities to compete are impaired because of diminished opportunities to obtain capital and credit.

Sole proprietorship
An unincorporated, one-owner business, farm, or professional practice.

Special lending institution categories
See SBA special lending institution categories

Standard Industrial Classification (SIC) codes
Four-digit codes established by the U.S. Federal Government to categorize businesses by type of economic activity; the first two digits correspond to major groups such as construction and manufacturing, while the last two digits correspond to subgroups such as home construction or highway construction.

Standard metropolitan statistical area (SMSA)
See Metropolitan statistical area

Start-up
A new business, at the earliest stages of development and financing.

Start-up costs
Costs incurred before a business can commence operations.

Start-up financing
Financing provided to companies that have either completed product development and initial marketing or have been in business for less than one year but have not yet sold their product commercially.

Stock
(See also Common stock; Convertible preferred stock)
A certificate of equity ownership in a business.

Stop-loss coverage
Insurance for a self-insured plan that reimburses the company for any losses it might incur in its health claims beyond a specified amount.

Strategic planning
Projected growth and development of a business to establish a guiding direction for the future. Also used to determine which market segments to explore for optimal sales of products or services.

Structural unemployment
See Unemployment

Sub chapter S corporations
Corporations that are considered noncorporate for tax purposes but legally remain corporations.

Subcontract
A contract between a prime contractor and a subcontractor, or between subcontractors, to furnish supplies or services for performance of a prime contract (see separate citation) or a subcontract.

Surety bonds
Bonds providing reimbursement to an individual, company, or the government if a firm fails to complete a contract. The U.S. Small Business Administration guarantees surety bonds in a program much like the SBA guaranteed loan program (see separate citation).

Swing loan
See Bridge financing

Target market
The clients or customers sought for a business' product or service.

Targeted Jobs Tax Credit
Federal legislation enacted in 1978 that provides a tax credit to an employer who hires structurally unemployed individuals.

Tax number
(See also Employer identification number)
A number assigned to a business by a state revenue department that enables the business to buy goods without paying sales tax.

Taxable bonds
An interest-bearing certificate of public or private indebt-

edness. Bonds are issued by public agencies to finance economic development.

Technical assistance
See Management and technical assistance

Technical evaluation
Assessment of technological feasibility.

Technology
The method in which a firm combines and utilizes labor and capital resources to produce goods or services; the application of science for commercial or industrial purposes.

Technology transfer
The movement of information about a technology or intellectual property from one party to another for use.

Tenure
See Employee tenure

Term
(See also Maturity)
The length of time for which a loan is made.

Terms of a note
The conditions or limits of a note; includes the interest rate per annum, the due date, and transferability and convertibility features, if any.

Third-party administrator
An outside company responsible for handling claims and performing administrative tasks associated with health insurance plan maintenance.

Third-stage financing
(See also First-stage financing; Second-stage financing)
Financing provided for the major expansion of a company whose sales volume is increasing and that is breaking even or profitable. These funds are used for further plant expansion, marketing, working capital, or development of an improved product. Also known as Third-round or Mezzanine financing.

Time deposit
A bank deposit that cannot be withdrawn before a specified future time.

Time management
Skills and scheduling techniques used to maximize productivity.

Trade credit
Credit extended by suppliers of raw materials or finished products. In an accounting statement, trade credit is referred to as "accounts payable."

Trade name
The name under which a company conducts business, or by which its business, goods, or services are identified. It may or may not be registered as a trademark.

Trade periodical
A publication with a specific focus on one or more aspects of business and industry.

Trade secret
Competitive advantage gained by a business through the use of a unique manufacturing process or formula.

Trade show
An exhibition of goods or services used in a particular industry. Typically held inexhibition centers where exhibitors rent space to display their merchandise.

Trademark
A graphic symbol, device, or slogan that identifies a business. A business has property rights to its trademark from the inception of its use, but it is still prudent to register all trademarks with the Trademark Office of the U.S. Department of Commerce.

Translation
See Product development

Treasury bills
Investment tender issued by the Federal Reserve Bank in amounts of $10,000 that mature in 91 to 182 days.

Treasury bonds
Long-term notes with maturity dates of not less than seven and not more than twenty-five years.

Treasury notes
Short-term notes maturing in less than seven years.

Trend
A statistical measurement used to track changes that occur over time.

Trough
See Cyclical trough

UCC
See Uniform Commercial Code

UL
See Underwriters Laboratories

Underwriters Laboratories (UL)

One of several private firms that tests products and processes to determine their safety. Although various firms can provide this kind of testing service, many local and insurance codes specify UL certification.

Underwriting

A process by which an insurer determines whether or not and on what basis it will accept an application for insurance. In an experience-rated plan, premiums are based on a firm's or group's past claims; factors other than prior claims are used for community-rated or manually rated plans.

Unfair competition

Refers to business practices, usually unethical, such as using unlicensed products, pirating merchandise, or misleading the public through false advertising, which give the offending business an unequitable advantage over others.

Unfunded accrued liability

The excess of total liabilities, both present and prospective, over present and prospective assets.

Unemployment

The joblessness of individuals who are willing to work, who are legally and physically able to work, and who are seeking work. Unemployment may represent the temporary joblessness of a worker between jobs (frictional unemployment) or the joblessness of a worker whose skills are not suitable for jobs available in the labor market (structural unemployment).

Uniform Commercial Code (UCC)

A code of laws governing commercial transactions across the U.S., except Louisiana. Their purpose is to bring uniformity to financial transactions.

Uniform product code (UPC symbol)

A computer-readable label comprised of ten digits and stripes that encodes what a product is and how much it costs. The first five digits are assigned by the Uniform Product Code Council, and the last five digits by the individual manufacturer.

Unit cost

See Average cost

UPC symbol

See Uniform product code

U.S. Establishment and Enterprise Microdata (USEEM) File

A cross-sectional database containing information on employment, sales, and location for individual enterprises and establishments with employees that have a Dun & Bradstreet credit rating.

U.S. Establishment Longitudinal Microdata (USELM) File

A database containing longitudinally linked sample microdata on establishments drawn from the U.S. Establishment and Enterprise Microdata file (see separate citation).

U.S. Small Business Administration 504 Program

See Certified development corporation

USEEM

See U.S. Establishment and Enterprise Microdata File

USELM

See U.S. Establishment Longitudinal Microdata File

VCN

See Venture capital network

Venture capital

(See also Equity; Equity midrisk venture capital)
Money used to support new or unusual business ventures that exhibit above-average growth rates, significant potential for market expansion, and are in need of additional financing to sustain growth or further research and development; equity or equity-type financing traditionally provided at the commercialization stage, increasingly available prior to commercialization.

Venture capital company

A company organized to provide seed capital to a business in its formation stage, or in its first or second stage of expansion. Funding is obtained through public or private pension funds, commercial banks and bank holding companies, small business investment corporations licensed by the U.S. Small Business Administration, private venture capital firms, insurance companies, investment management companies, bank trust departments, industrial companies seeking to diversify their investment, and investment bankers acting as intermediaries for other investors or directly investing on their own behalf.

Venture capital limited partnerships

Designed for business development, these partnerships are an institutional mechanism for providing capital for young, technology-oriented businesses. The investors' money is pooled and invested in money market assets until venture investments have been selected. The general partners are experienced investment managers who select and invest the equity and debt securities of firms with high growth potential and the ability to go public in the near future.

Venture capital network (VCN)

A computer database that matches investors with entrepreneurs.

WAN

See Wide Area Network

Wide Area Network (WAN)

Computer networks linking systems throughout a state or around the world in order to facilitate the sharing of information.

Withholding

Federal, state, social security, and unemployment taxes withheld by the employer from employees' wages; employers are liable for these taxes and the corporate umbrella and bankruptcy will not exonerate an employer from paying back payroll withholding. Employers should escrow these funds in a separate account and disperse them quarterly to withholding authorities.

Workers' compensation

A state-mandated form of insurance covering workers injured in job-related accidents. In some states, the state is the insurer; in other states, insurance must be acquired from commercial insurance firms. Insurance rates are based on a number of factors, including salaries, firm history, and risk of occupation.

Working capital

Refers to a firm's short-term investment of current assets, including cash, short-term securities, accounts receivable, and inventories.

Yield

(See also Rate of return)

The rate of income returned on an investment, expressed as a percentage. Income yield is obtained by dividing the current dollar income by the current market price of the security. Net yield or yield to maturity is the current income yield minus any premium above par or plus any discount from par in purchase price, with the adjustment spread over the period from the date of purchase to the date of maturity.

Appendix D - Bibliography

Bibliography

Bibliography citations are listed alphabetically by title under appropriate subject subheadings, which also appear alphabetically (in bold).

Accounting/Budgets and Budgeting

"Account Yourself" in *Business Start-Ups.* (Vol. 7, No. 8, August 1995, p. 79).

"Accountant Wanted" in *Business Start-Ups.* (October 1994, pp. 20-23). By Gloria Gibbs Marullo.

"Audit Tip Sheet" in *Inc.* (Vol. 16, No. 4, April 1994, p. 118). By Jill Andresky Fraser.

"Balancing Act" *Entrepreneur.* (Vol. 23, No. 3, March 1995, pp. 56, 58- 59, 61). By Bob Weinstein.

"Before You File" in *Income Opportunities.* (Vol. 32, No. 1, January 1997, pp. 27-30). By Janine S. Pouliot.

"Bill Auditing" in *Small Business Opportunities.* (Vol. 8, No. 2, March 1996, p. 20). By Terry Schwartz.

"Bill of Wrongs" in *Entrepreneur.* (Vol. 23, No. 5, May 1995, pp. 166, 168, 170-171). By David R. Honodel.

"Bookkeeper in a Box" in *Inc. Technology.* (Vol. 15, No. 13, p. 98). By Phaedra Hise.

"Count on It" in *Hispanic Business.* (Vol. 18, No. 6, June 1996, p. 122). By Rick Mendosa.

"Count On It" in *Entrepreneur.* (Vol. 23, No. 8, August 1995, pp. 30, 32- 33). By Cheryl J. Goldberg.

"Counting On Profit" in *Small Business Opportunities.* (Vol. 7, No. 3, May 1995, pp. 42-43, 82). By Martin Waterman.

"Database Husbandry" in *Inc. Technology.* (Vol. 16, No. 13, p. 100). By Phaedra Hise.

"Dream Accountant" in *Income Opportunities.* (Vol. 30, No. 1, January 1995, pp. 108, 110). By Peg Byron.

"Firing Line" in *Entrepreneur.* (Vol. 23, No. 12, November 1995, pp. 56, 59). By David R. Evanson.

"For the Record" in *Business Start-Ups.* (Vol. 7, No. 5, May 1995, pp. 78, 80-81). By Cynthia E. Griffin.

"Going It Alone" in *Newsweek.* (April 1996, pp. 50-51). By Ellyn E. Spragins and Steve Rhodes.

"How to Survive an IRS Audit" in *Nation's Business.* (Vol. 82, No. 4, April 1994, pp. 42-43). By Joan C. Szabo.

"Hunting for an Accountant" in *Pennsylvania CPA Journal.* (Vol. 63, No. 4, Summer 1993, pp. 10-13). By Gerald J. Rosenthal.

"It Adds Up" in *Income Opportunities.* (Vol. 31, No. 1, January 1996, pp. 32, 34, 38). By Debra D'Agostino.

"Ledger-Demain" in *Inc.* (Vol. 18, No. 9, June 1996, pp. 87-88). By Ellen DePasquale.

"Let's Get Fiscal" in *Entrepreneur.* (June 1995, pp. 68, 70-71). By Bob Weinstein.

"No Accounting for Success" in *Inc.* (Vol. 18, No. 8, June 1996, p. 2526). By Norm Brodsky.

"Non-Taxing Matters" in *Inc.* (Vol. 19, No. 4, March 1997, pp. 90-92). By Ellen DePasquale.

"On the Books" in *Income Opportunities.* (Vol. 32, No. 1, January 1997, pp. 38, 40, 42). By Mike Hogan.

"Second Time Around" in *Business Start-Ups.* (Vol. 8, No. 11, November 1996, pp. 74-75). By Lisa Pelec Hyde.

"Small Business Controller" in *Management Accounting.* (Vol. 76, No. 5, November 1994, pp. 38-41). By Bonnie D. Labrack.

"Step 5: Plan a Realistic Budget" in *Business Start-Ups.* (Vol. 8, No. 9, September 1996, pp. 80, 82). By Kylo-Patrick Hart.

"To the Rescue" in *Business Start-Ups.* (Vol. 7, No. 5, May 1995, pp. 68, 70-71). By Sue Clayton.

"Tracking Your Mileage" in Business Start-Ups. (Vol. 8, No. 12, December 1996, pp. 76, 78). By Gloria Gibbs Marullo.

"Will Banking Go Virtual?" in *Inc.* (Vol. 18, No. 13, September 1996, pp. 49-52). By Jill Andresky Fraser.

"Winning Numbers" in *Inc.* (Vol. 18, No. 13, September 1996, pp. 84-87). By Ellen DePasquale.

"You May Need the 'C' in CPA" in *Inc.* (Vol. 16, No. 9, September 1994, p. 126). By Jill Andresky Fraser.

Bagel Shop

"Bagel Shop Bakes Way into Hearts of Customers" in

Denver Business Journal. (Vol. 46, No. 1, September 16, 1994, p. 22). Denver, Colorado, American City Business Journals.

"Bagels" in *Entrepreneur.* (September 1993, pp. 188, 190-191). Irvine, California, Entrepreneur, Inc. Editor, Gayle Sato Stodder.

"Brownie-Baking Business Is a Sweet Deal for Owners" in *The Business Journal.* (Vol. 14, No. 15, February 11, 1994, p. 26). Sacramento, California, Sacramento Business Journal. Editor, Teena Chadwell.

"Brownie Points" in *Income Opportunities.* (Vol. 31, No. 9, September 1996, pp. 96, 98, 100). New York, New York, IO Publications Inc. Editor, Amy H. Berger.

"Business for Sale" in *Inc.* (Vol. 18, No. 14, October 1996, p. 112). Boston, Massachusetts, Goldhirsh Group, Inc. Editor, Jill Andresky Fraser.

"Competition Rising for Bread-Makers" in *Crain's Small Business.* (Vol. 5, No. 4, April 1997, p. 8). Detroit, Michigan, Crain Communications Inc. Editor, Jeffrey McCracken.

"Directory of Food Industry Resources" in *Income Opportunities.* (Vol. 31, No. 8, August 1996, pp. 26-27). New York, New York, IO Publications Inc. Editor, Stephanie Jeffrey.

"Easy as Pie" in *Houston Business Journal.* (Vol. 23, No. 37, January 31, 1994, p. 17). Houston, Texas, American City Business Journals, John Beddow Corp.

"Entrepreneurial Superstars" in *Entrepreneur.* (April 1997, pp. 108-139). Irvine, California, Entrepreneur Media Inc. Editor, Debra Phillips and others.

"Entrepreneurs Across America" in *Entrepreneur.* (Vol. 24, No. 4, April 1996, pp. 100-104, 106-108, 110-112, 114- 116, 118, 120-123). Irvine, California, Entrepreneur Media, Inc. Editor, Janean Chum, Debra Phillips, Cynthia E. Griffin, Heather Page, Lynn Beresford, Holly Celeste Fisk, and Charlotte Mulbern.

"Fresh & Hot" in *Entrepreneur.* (December 1996, p. 156). Irvine, California, Entrepreneur Media Inc. Editor, Karen Axelton.

"From Banker to Baker" in *Small Business Opportunities.* (Vol. 6, No. 6, November 1994, pp. 58-63). New York, New York, Harris Publications, Inc. Editor, Geri Anderson.

"Frugal Baker's Biz is Finally Taking Off" in *Crain's Small Business.* (June 1996, p. 9). Detroit, Michigan, Crain Communications Inc. Editor, Michelle Krebs.

"Growing on Scones Alone" in *Crain's Detroit Business.*

(Vol. 12, No. 48, Nov. 25-Dec. 1, 1996, pp. 3, 41). Detroit, Michigan, Crain Communications Inc. Editor, Marsha Stopa.

"Jammin'" in *Income Opportunities.* (Vol. 30, No. 6, June 1995, pp. 64, 66). New York, New York, IO Publications, Inc. Editor, Stephanie Jeffrey.

"Minding the Store" in *Inc.* (Vol. 15, No. 11, November 1993, pp. 66-69, 71, 74-75). Boston, Massachusetts, Goldhirsh Group, Inc. Editor, Leslie Brokaw.

"On the Rise" in *Entrepreneur.* (Vol. 23, No. 5, May 1995, pp. 196, 198). Irvine, California, Entrepreneur Media, Inc. Editor, Gayle Sato Stodder.

"Persuading the Persuader" in *Crain's Small Business.* (December 1996, pp. 4, 6). Detroit, Michigan, Crain Communications Inc. Editor, Jeffrey McCracken.

"Pinning Hopes on Pastries" in *Crain's Detroit Business.* (Vol. 12, No. 47, November 1996, pp. 3, 34). Detroit, Michigan, Crain Communications Inc. Editor, Marsha Stopa.

"Say When" in *Inc.* (Vol. 17, No. 2, February 1995, pp. 19-20). Boston, Massachusetts, Goldhirsh Group, Inc. Editor, Steven L. Marks.

"The Service Boom" in *Small Business Opportunities.* (Vol. 9, No. 3, May 1997, pp. 22-41). New York, New York, Harris Publications, Inc.

"Suddenly, Last Summer" in *Entrepreneur.* (Vol. 22, No. 13, December 1994, p. 14) . Irvine, California, Entrepreneur Media, Inc. Editor, Karen Zehring Davis.

"Super Bakery, Inc." in *Planning Review.* (Vol. 22, No. 1, January/February 1994, pp. 8-17). Chicago, Illinois, The Planning Forum. Editor, Bruce L. Darling.

"A Sweet Deal" in *Black Enterprise.* (Vol. 25, No. 2, September 1994, pp. 30-32). New York, New York, Earl G. Graves Publishing Co. Inc. Editor, Ann Brown.

"Taking the Cake" in *Business Start-Ups.* (October 1994, p. 87). Irvine, California, Entrepreneur Media Inc.

"Warning Signs" in *Black Enterprise.* (Vol. 27, No. 4, November 1996, pp. 89-94). New York, New York, Earl G. Graves Publishing Co. Inc. Editor, Tonia L. Shakespeare.

Business Growth and Statistics

"10 Tips for Success" in *Business Start-Ups.* (Vol. 8, No. 8, August 1996, pp. 74-75). Irvine, California: Entrepreneur Media Inc. By Kelli Reyes.

"24th Annual Report on Black Business" in *Black Enterprise*. (Vol. 26 No. 11, June 1996, pp. 103-139). New York, New York: Earl G. Graves Publishing Co. Inc. By Derek T. Dingle.

"1996 May Be Best Year for Those Seeking Loans" in *Washington Business Journal: Small Business Resource Guide*. (May 1996, p. 16). Arlington, Virginia: American City Business Journals. By Melissa Wuestenberg.

"After the Storm" in *Forbes*. (July 95, pp. 65-66). New York, New York: Forbes Inc. By Gary Samuels.

"The Age of the Gazelle" in *Inc*. (Vol. 18, No. 7, May 1996, p. 44). Boston, Massachusetts: Goldhirsh Group, Inc. By John Case.

"And Still We Rise" in *Black Enterprise*. (Vol. 26, No. 9, April 1996, p. 18). New York, New York: Earl G. Graves Publishing Co. Inc. By Cliff Hocker.

"Are You Ready to Go Public?" in *Nation's Business*. (Vol. 83, No. 1, January 1995, pp. 30-32). Washington, District of Columbia: U.S. Chamber of Commerce. By Roberta Maynard.

"At the Brink" in *Inc*. (Vol. 17, No. 16, November 1995, pp. 21- 22). Boston, Massachusetts: Goldhirsh Group, Inc. By Rick McCloskey.

"Battling to Be the Big Cheese" in *Income Opportunities*. (Vol. 32, No. 1, January 1997, pp. 14-17, 80). New York, New York: IO Publications Inc. By Constance Gustke.

"Best of the Best" in *Entrepreneur*. (March 1997, pp. 136, 138-139). Irvine, California: Entrepreneur Media Inc.

"Branching Out" in *Nation's Business*. (Vol. 82, No. 11, November 1994, p. 53). Washington, District of Columbia: U.S. Chamber of Commerce. By Roberta Maynard.

"Brave New World" in *Income Opportunities*. (Vol. 30, No. 4, April 1995, pp. 30-32, 34-36, 38, 40, 42, 44). New York, New York: IO Publications, Inc. By Dale D. Buss.

"Breaking New Ground" in *Income Opportunities*. (Vol. 31, No. 6, June 1996, pp. 22-25, 64). New York, New York: IO Publications Inc. By Ed Klimuska.

"Brighter Days" in *Entrepreneur*. (Vol. 23, No. 7, July 1995, p. 16). Irvine, California: Entrepreneur Media, Inc. By Janean Chun.

"Bringing Up Business" in *Entrepreneur*. (vol. 23, No. 1, January 1995, pp. 124-128). Irvine, California: Entrepreneur Media, Inc. By Erika Kotite.

"Building Companies to Last" in *Inc*. (Special Issue: The State of Small Business, February 1996, pp. 83-84, 87-88). Boston, Massachusetts: Goldhirsh Group, Inc. By James C. Collins.

"Business Finally Invests Some Trust in Bank Lending" in *Crain's Small Business*. (October 1995, p. 8). Detroit, Michigan: Crain Communications, Inc. By Jeffrey McCracken.

"Business and Gravy" in *The Red Herring*. (March 1997, pp. 50-51). San Francisco, California: Herring Communications Inc. By Luc Hatlestad.

"Business Must Refocus Once It Outgrows Entrepreneur's Control" in *Crain's Small Business*. (October 1995, p. 16). Detroit, Michigan: Crain Communications, Inc. By Jon Greenawalt.

"California, Here We Come!" in *Hispanic Business*. (Vol. 18, No. 5, May 1996, pp. 33-36, 38-39, 42, 44). Santa Barbara, California: Hispanic Business Inc. By Rick Mendoza.

"Capital Steps" in *Inc*. (Vol. 18, No. 2, February 1996, pp. 42-44, 47). Boston, Massachusetts: Goldhirsh Group, Inc. By Jill Andresky Fraser.

"A Cautionary Tale" in *Feminist Bookstore News*. (Vol. 19, No. 4, November/December 1996, pp. 21-23). San Francisco, California: Feminist Bookstore News. By Carol Seajay.

"The Computer in the Dell" in *Business Start-Ups*. (Vol. 8, No. 6, June 1996, pp. 22-27). Irvine, California: Entrepreneur Media Inc. By Bob Weinstein.

"Crafts Course" in *Entrepreneur*. (June 1995, pp. 178-180). Irvine, California: Entrepreneur Media Inc. By Gayle Sato Stodder.

"Crain's Small Business Index" in *Crain's Small Business*. (Vol. 4, No. 11, November 1996, p. 5). Detroit, Michigan: Crain Communications Inc.

"Demographica" in *Crain's Small Business*. (Vol. 4, No. 11, November 1996, p. 22). Detroit, Michigan: Crain Communications Inc.

"The Economics of Progress" in *Hispanic Business*. (Vol. 18 No. 9, September 1996, pp. 28-30, 32). Santa Barbara, California: Hispanic Business Inc. By J. Antonio Villamil.

"Entrepreneurs Collide: Will Zoning Take Town Downhill?" in *Inc*. (Vol. 19, No. 5, April 1997, p. 32). Boston, Massachusetts: Goldhirsh Group, Inc. By Joshua Macht.

"The Fast-Growing 100" in *Hispanic Business*. (Vol. 18, No. 7/8, July/August 1996, pp. 40, 42, 44). Santa Barbara, California: Hispanic Business Inc. By Maria Zate.

"Fast Track" in *Entrepreneur*. (February 1997, p. 22).

Irvine, California: Entrepreneur Media Inc.

"The Fast Trackers" in *Working Woman*. (March 1995, pp. 44-48, 86). New York, New York: Working Woman, Inc. By Louise Washer.

"A Field Guide to Your Local Economy" in *Inc*. (Special Issue: The State of Small Business, February 1996, pp. 51-54). Boston, Massachusetts: Goldhirsh Group, Inc. By Joel Garreau.

"Financial Ratios in Large Public and Small Private Firms" in *Journal of Small Business Management*. (Vol. 30, No. 3, July 1992, p. 35). Morgantown, West Virginia: West Virginia University. By Jerome Osteryoung and Richard L. Constand and Donald Nast.

"Forging New Frontiers " in *Black Enterprise*. (Vol. 26, No. 10, May 1996, pp. 70-72, 74, 76, 78). New York, New York: Earl G. Graves Publishing Co. Inc. By Marjorie Whigham-Desir.

"Fueling the Growth of Black Companies" in *Black Enterprise*. (Vol. 25, No. 4, November 1994, pp. 158-159, 162, 164). New York, New York: Earl G. Graves Publishing Co. Inc. By Gracian Mack.

"Get Rich in 1997" in *Small Business Opportunities*. (Vol. 9, No. 1, January 1997, pp. 22-24, 26, 28, 30, 34). New York, New York: Harris Publications, Inc.

"Growing Companies Gain from University Relationships" in *Income Opportunities*. (Vol. 30, No. 4, April 1995, p. 3). New York, New York: IO Publications, Inc. By Patricia Hamilton.

"Growing with the Flow" in *Inc*. (Vol. 16, No. 11, 1994, pp. 88-90). Boston, Massachusetts: Goldhirsh Group, Inc. By Martha E. Mangelsdorf.

"Growing Pains" in *Business Start-Ups*. (Vol. 9, No. 5, May 1997, pp. 8, 10, 12). Irvine, California: Entrepreneur Media Inc. By Carolyn Campbell.

"Growing Pains" in *Entrepreneur*. (November, 1996, pp. 214, 216-217). Irvine, California: Entrepreneur Media Inc. By Charlotte Mulhern.

"Growing Up" in *Entrepreneur*. (July 1996, pp. 124-128). Irvine, California: Entrepreneur Media Inc. By Lynn Beresford.

"A Growing Year for Small Business" in *Income Opportunities*. (Vol. 30, No. 10, October 1995, p. 3). New York, New York: IO Publications, Inc. By Heath F. Eiden.

"Growing Your Consulting Business" in *Black Enterprise*. (Vol. 25, No. 4, November 1994, pp. 108-116). New York, New York: Earl G. Graves Publishing Co. Inc. By Margie Markarian.

"Growth in a Developing Market" in *Inc. 500*. (Vol. 16, No. 11, 1994, pp. 92, 94, 96, 98-99). Boston, Massachusetts: Goldhirsch Group, Inc. By Martha E. Mangelsdorf.

"Growth Happens" in *Inc*. (Vol. 19, No. 3, March 1997, pp. 68-70, 72-74). Boston, Massachusetts: Goldhirsh Group, Inc. By Robert A. Mamis.

"Growth Moderates Leading into Election" in *Crain's Small Business*. (Vol. 4, No. 11, November 1996, p. 5). Detroit, Michigan: Crain Communications Inc. By David Sowerby.

"A Guide May Be Needed to Set Up Shop On-Line" in *Crain's Detroit Business*. (Vol. 11, No. 29, July 1995, p. 11). Detroit, Michigan: Crain Communications Inc.

"Hitting the Wall" in *Inc*. (Vol. 17, No. 10, July 1995, pp. 21-22). Boston, Massachusetts: Goldhirsh Group, Inc. By James L. Bildner.

"The Hottest Industries for New Business Opportunities" in *Black Enterprise*. (Vol. 25, No. 8, March 1995). New York, New York: Earl G. Graves Publishing Co. Inc. By Carolyn M. Brown, Yolanda Gault, Lloyd Gite, Adrienne Harris, Eric Houston, Dasha Jones and Valencia Roner.

"How the Census Bureau Devalues Black Businesses" in *Black Enterprise*. (Vol. 26 No. 11, June 1996, pp. 223-228). New York, New York: Earl G. Graves Publishing Co. Inc. By Margaret C. Simms.

"The Inc. 500: 15th Annual List" in *Inc*. (October 1996, pp. 15-16). Boston, Massachusetts: Goldhirsh Group, Inc. By Joshua Hyatt.

"Incubation Period" in *Income Opportunities*. (Vol. 32, No. 1, January 1997, pp. 20-24, 64). New York, New York: IO Publications Inc. By Dale D. Buss.

"Index" in *Crain's Detroit Business*. (Vol. 5, No. 1, January 1997, p. 22). Detroit, Michigan: Crain Communications Inc. By David Sowerby.

"Is Bigger Better?" in *Working Woman*. (March 1995, pp. 39-40, 42, 90). New York, New York: Working Woman, Inc. By Louise Washer.

"Is Black Business Paving the Way?" in *Black Enterprise*. (Vol. 26 No. 11, June 1996, pp. 194-202, 206). New York, New York: Earl G. Graves Publishing Co. Inc. By Eric L. Smith.

"It Cuts Both Ways" in *Crain's Detroit Business*. (Vol. 10, No. 41, October 10-16, 1994, p. 9). Detroit, Michigan: Crain's Communications, Inc. By Marilyn Sambrano.

"The Knockout Lesson" in *Inc*. (Vol. 17, No. 8, June 1995, pp. 21-22). Boston, Massachusetts: Goldhirsh Group, Inc.

By Amy Miller.

"L.A. Quakes in the Shadow of Beautiful Downtown Burbank" in *Inc.* (Vol. 18, No. 18, December 1997, p. 28). Boston, Massachusetts: Goldhirsh Group, Inc. By Joel Kotkin.

"Looking for Customers? Pick on Someone Your Own Size" in *Inc.* (Vol. 19, No. 3, March 1997, p. 22). Boston, Massachusetts: Goldhirsh Group, Inc. By Jerry Useem.

"Making a Move" in *Hispanic Business.* (Vol. 18, No. 9, September 1996, pp. 42-43). Santa Barbara, California: Hispanic Business Inc. By Maria Zate.

"Marketing by Mail" in *Black Enterprise.* (Vol. 26 No. 11, June 1996, pp. 275-282). New York, New York: Earl G. Graves Publishing Co. Inc. By Robert W. Bly.

"Masters of Flexibility" in *Hispanic Business.* (Vol. 18, No. 6, June 1996, pp. 62, 64, 66, 68, 70). Santa Barbara, California: Hispanic Business Inc. By Maria Zate.

"Mighty Morphing" in *Entrepreneur.* (November, 1996, p. 16). Irvine, California: Entrepreneur Media Inc. By Cynthia E. Griffin.

"A Million and Counting" in *Hispanic Business.* (Vol. 18, No. 7/8, July/August 1996, p. 10). Santa Barbara, California: Hispanic Business Inc. By Rick Mendosa.

"Mistakes Your Growing Company Needs To Avoid" in *Money Money Guide Supplement.* (1994, pp. 76-81). New York, New York: Time, Inc. By Mary Rowland.

"The 'Net Investor Link" in *Hispanic Business.* (Vol. 18, No. 7/8, July/August 1996, p. 84). Santa Barbara, California: Hispanic Business Inc. By Rick Mendosa.

"Networking Works" in *Business Start-Ups.* (Vol. 7, No. 10, October 1995, p. 10). Irvine, California: Entrepreneur Media Inc. By Leann Anderson.

"Never Too Small to Manage" in *Inc.* (Vol. 19, No. 2, February 1997, pp. 56-58, 61). Boston, Massachusetts: Goldhirsh Group, Inc. By David Whitford.

"A New Loan Option to Bank, Venture Capital" in *Crain's Small Business.* (February 1996, pp. 9-10). Detroit, Michigan: Crain Communications, Inc. By Jeffrey McCracken.

"Niches That Need Filling" in *Hispanic Business.* (Vol. 19, No. 1, January 1997, pp. 18, 20-22). Santa Barbara, California: Hispanic Business Inc.

"On Their Own" in *Wall Street Journal Special Reports: Small Business (Special Edition).* (May 23, 1996, p. R20). New York, New York: Wall Street Journal: Dow Jones & Co., Inc. By Jeffrey A. Tannenbaum.

"One-Hit Wonders" in *Entrepreneur.* (Vol. 23, No. 1, January 1995, pp. 258-260, 262, 264). Irvine, California: Entrepreneur Media, Inc. By Mark Henricks.

"The 100 Fastest-Growing Companies: Under Control" in *Hispanic Business.* (Vol. 17, No. 8, August 1995, p. 22). Santa Barbara, California: Hispanic Business Inc. By Maria Zate.

"Out of the Ashes" in *Entrepreneur.* (November 1996, pp. 66, 68). Irvine, California: Entrepreneur Media Inc. By Cynthia E. Griffin.

"Part 1: Peos for Ceos" in *Corporate Detroit.* (Vol. 13, No. 12, December 1995, pp. 23, 64). Detroit, Michigan: Corporate Detroit, Inc. By Steven R. Light.

"Paying for Growth" in *Inc.* (Vol. 18, No. 14, October 1996, pp. 29-30). Boston, Massachusetts: Goldhirsh Group, Inc. By Norm Brodsky.

"Peer Review" in *Entrepreneur.* (July 1996, p. 18). Irvine, California: Entrepreneur Media Inc. By L.B.

"Promotion Commotion" in *Small Business Opportunities.* (Vol. 8, No. 5, September 1996, p. 56). New York, New York: Harris Publications, Inc. By Susan Froetschel.

"Right from the Start" in *Small Business Opportunities.* (Vol. 9, No. 3, May 1997, pp. 20, 42). New York, New York: Harris Publications, Inc. By Dr. Sandy Weinberg.

"Sales Through Superior Service" in *Business Start-Ups.* (Vol. 8, No. 8, August 1996, pp. 70-71). Irvine, California: Entrepreneur Media Inc. By Donna Clapp.

"The Six Secrets of Strategic Growth" in *Working Woman.* (March 1995, pp. 50-51,78). New York, New York: Working Woman, Inc. By Rhonda M. Abrams.

"Small Biz Can Give Input, Vital Data Via Web Site" in *Crain's Small Business.* (March 1996, p. 3). Detroit, Michigan: Crain Communications, Inc. By Jeffrey McCracken.

"Small Businesses are Thriving" in *Income Opportunities.* (Vol. 30, No. 1, January 1995, p. 2). New York, New York: IO Publications, Inc. By Eric Barnes.

"Small Is Beautiful! Big Is Best!" in *Inc.* (Special Issue: The State of Small Business, February 1996, pp. 39-44, 46, 48-49). Boston, Massachusetts: Goldhirsh Group, Inc. By George Gendron.

"Small Talk" in *Wall Street Journal Special Reports: Small Business (Special Edition).* (May 23, 1996, p. R28). New York, New York: Wall Street Journal: Dow Jones & Co., Inc. By Stephanie N. Mehta.

"Small World" in *Entrepreneur.* (Vol. 23, No. 8, August

1995, p. 17). Irvine, California: Entrepreneur Media, Inc. By Heather Page.

"Something Borrowed" in *Entrepreneur.* (February 1997, p. 26). Irvine, California: Entrepreneur Media Inc.

"Sounding Board" in *Income Opportunities.* (Vol. 30, No. 6, June 1995, pp. 114, 116). New York, New York: IO Publications, Inc. By Richard J. Maturi.

"A Sporting Chance" in *Detroit Free Press.* (January 1997, pp. 1e-2e). Detroit, Michigan: Knight-Ridder, Inc. By Molly Brauer.

"Stage Right" in *Entrepreneur.* (April 1997, pp. 71-73). Irvine, California: Entrepreneur Media Inc. By Mark Henricks.

"The Startling Truth About Growth Companies" in *Inc.* (Vol. 18, No. 7, May 1996, pp. 84-86, 88, 90-92). Boston, Massachusetts: Goldhirsh Group, Inc. By Martha E. Mangelsdorf.

"A Strategy For Growth" in *Black Enterprise.* (Vol. 25, No. 4, November 1994). New York, New York: Earl G. Graves Publishing Co. Inc. By Joan Delaney.

"Striking the Faustian Bargain" in *Corporate Detroit.* (Vol. 12, No. 11, November 1994, pp. 38-39). Detroit, Michigan: Corporate Detroit, Inc. By Gary Hoffman.

"The Survival Factor" in *Hispanic Business.* (Vol. 17, No. 8, August 1995, pp. 44-46). Santa Barbara, California: Hispanic Business Inc. By Rick Mendosa.

"A Sweet Deal" in *Black Enterprise.* (Vol. 25, No. 2, September 1994, pp. 30-32). New York, New York: Earl G. Graves Publishing Co. Inc. By Ann Brown.

"There Are No Simple Businesses Anymore" in *Inc.* (Special Issue: The State of Small Business, February 1996, pp. 66-79). Boston, Massachusetts: Goldhirsh Group, Inc. By Edward O. Welles.

"Think Small" in *Entrepreneur.* (May 1996, p. 86). Irvine, California: Entrepreneur Media Inc. By Jay Conrad Levinson.

"To Advance, Try a Retreat" in *Crain's Small Business.* (January 1996, p. 17). Detroit, Michigan: Crain Communications, Inc. By Jim Brady.

"U.S. Business Data Worst in World—And Getting Worse" in *Inc.* (Vol. 18, No. 14, October 1996, p. 26). Boston, Massachusetts: Goldhirsh Group, Inc. By Jerry Useem.

"Where the Money Is" in *Hispanic Business.* (Vol. 19, No. 2, February 1997, p. 60). Santa Barbara, California: Hispanic Business Inc. By Jonathan J. Higuera.

"Who Needs Growth?" in *Inc.* (Vol. 18, No. 14, October 1996, p. 90). Boston, Massachusetts: Goldhirsh Group, Inc. By Susan Greco.

"Who's On-Line?" in *Inc.* (Vol. 19, No. 4, March 1997, pp. 34-39). Boston, Massachusetts: Goldhirsh Group, Inc. By Dan Kennedy.

"Women Putting Themselves on Local Biz Map" in *Crain's Detroit Business.* (Vol. 12, No. 13, March 1996, p. 9). Detroit, Michigan: Crain Communications Inc. By Karen Eness Pope.

"The Wonderland Economy" in *Inc.* (Special Issue: The State of Small Business, February 1996, pp. 14-16, 18-20, 23-24, 26-27, 29). Boston, Massachusetts: Goldhirsh Group, Inc. By John Case.

Business Plans

"3 Factors Help Make a Strategy Successful" in *Crain's Detroit Business.* (Vol. 5, No. 1, January 1997, p. 19). Detroit, Michigan: Crain Communications Inc. By Jim Brady.

"Best Laid Plans" in *Business Start-Ups.* (Vol. 7, No. 11, November 1995, p. 7). Irvine, California: Entrepreneur Media Inc. By Lynn Norquist.

"The Best Laid Plans" in *Entrepreneurial Woman.* (September 1990, pp. 74-79). Irvine, California: Entrepreneur, Inc. By Edward C. Rybka.

"Building a Better Business Plan" in *Home Office-Computing.* (February 1990, p. 30). New York, New York: Scholastic, Inc. By Charles H. Gajeway.

"Business Busters" in *Black Enterprise.* (Vol. 23, No. 4, November 1992, pp. 75-85). New York, New York: Earl G. Graves Publishing Co. Inc. By Caryne Brown.

"Business Plan" in *Business Start-Ups.* (Vol. 7, No. 12, December 1995, pp. 8, 10-11). Irvine, California: Entrepreneur Media Inc. By Charles Fuller.

"A Business-Plan Outline" in *Crain's Small Business.* (December 1995, p. 11). Detroit, Michigan: Crain Communications, Inc. By Jeffrey McCracken.

"Business-Plan Software Streamlines Process" in *Crain's Detroit Business.* (Vol. 5, No. 1, January 1997, p. 17). Detroit, Michigan: Crain Communications Inc. By Len Strazewski.

"Business Plan Stumbling Blocks" in *Working Woman.* (October 1994, pp. 45-48). New York, New York: Working Woman, Inc. By Rhonda M. Abrams.

"Change of Plans" in *Business Start-Ups.* (Vol. 7, No. 6,

June 1995, p. 9). Irvine, California: Entrepreneur Media Inc. By Erika Kotite.

"Change of Plans" in *Entrepreneur*. (May 1996, p. 30). Irvine, California: Entrepreneur Media Inc.

"College Pals Won't Tamper with Success" in *Crain's Small Business*. (Vol. 4, No. 11, November 1996, p. 21). Detroit, Michigan: Crain Communications Inc. By Jeffrey McCracken.

"The Complete New-Business Survival Guide" in *Inc*. (Vol. 14, No. 7, July 1992, pp. 48-66). Boston, Massachusetts: Goldhirsh Group, Inc. By Susan Greco.

"Credibility Gap" in *Income Opportunities*. (Vol. 32, No. 4, April 1997, pp. 42, 44). New York, New York: IO Publications Inc. By Dorothy Elizabeth Brooks.

"Decide Where to Go Before Drawing a Map" in *Crain's Small Business*. (Vol. 5, No. 4, April 1997, p. 22). Detroit, Michigan: Crain Communications Inc. By Jim Brady.

"Do Business Plans Matter?" in *Inc*. (Vol. 18, No. 2, February 1996, p. 21). Boston, Massachusetts: Goldhirsh Group, Inc. By Mary Baechler.

"Do You Have a Plan?" in *In Business*. (April 1990, pp. 12-14). Emmaus, Pennsylvania: J.G. Press, Inc. By David M. Freedman.

"The Do's and Don'ts of Writing A Winning Business Plan" in *Black Enterprise*. (Vol. 26, No. 9, April 1996, pp. 114-116, 120, 122). New York, New York: Earl G. Graves Publishing Co. Inc. By Carolyn M. Brown.

"Entrepreneur Had Better Know Where All the Money's Going" in *Crain's Detroit Business*. (Vol. 5, No. 1, January 1997, p. 15). Detroit, Michigan: Crain Communications Inc. By Jerry Balan.

"Entrepreneurs Collide: Will Zoning Take Town Downhill?" in *Inc*. (Vol. 19, No. 5, April 1997, p. 32). Boston, Massachusetts: Goldhirsh Group, Inc. By Joshua Macht.

"Exit Gracefully" in *Income Opportunities*. (Vol. 31, No. 11, November 1996, pp. 32, 34, 36). New York, New York: IO Publications Inc. By Dorothy Elizabeth Brooks.

"Facing an Uphill Battle" in *Black Enterprise*. (Vol. 22, No. 4, November 1991, pp. 51-57). New York, New York: Earl G. Graves Publishing Co. Inc. By Kevin D. Thompson.

"A Factor Analytic Study of the Perceived Causes of Small Business Failure" in *Journal of Small Business Management*. (Vol. 31, No. 4, October 1993, pp. 18-31). Morgantown, West Virginia: West Virginia University. By LuAnn Ricketts Gaskill and Howard E. Van Auken and Ronald A. Manning.

"Financial Ratios in Large Public and Small Private Firms" in *Journal of Small Business Management*. (Vol. 30, No. 3, July 1992, p. 35). Morgantown, West Virginia: West Virginia University. By Jerome Osteryoung and Richard L. Constand and Donald Nast.

"Finding Your Niche" in *Business Start-Ups*. (Vol. 9, No. 4, April 1997, pp. 72, 74). Irvine, California: Entrepreneur Media Inc. By Carla Goodman.

"Fools Rush In? The Institutional Context of Industry Creation" in *Academy of Management Review*. (Vol. 19, No. 4, October 1994, p. 645). Ada, Ohio: Academy of Management. By Howard E. Aldrich and Marlene C. Fiol.

"Fyi" in *Income Opportunities*. (Vol. 32, No. 1, January 1997). New York, New York: IO Publications Inc.

"Game Plan" in *Entrepreneur*. (Vol. 23, No. 8, August 1995, pp. 38-41). Irvine, California: Entrepreneur Media, Inc. By David R. Evanson.

"Garbarge In, Garbage Out" in *Inc*. (Vol. 18 , No. 11, August 1996, pp. 41-44). Boston, Massachusetts: Goldhirsh Group, Inc. By Brian McWilliams.

"How to Determine Your Debt Comfort Zone" in *Crain's Small Business*. (Vol. 4, No. 10, October 1996, p. 21). Detroit, Michigan: Crain Communications Inc. By Kevin Reitzloff.

"How to Get Biz Beyond the Start-Up Stage" in *Crain's Small Business*. (June 1996, p. 8). Detroit, Michigan: Crain Communications Inc. By Lawrence Gardner.

"How To Start an Inc. 500 Company" in *Inc. 500*. (Vol. 16, No. 11, 1994, pp. 51-52, 54, 57-58, 60, 63-65). Boston, Massachusetts: Goldhirsch Group, Inc. By Leslie Brokaw.

"How to Write a Business Plan" in *Nation's Business*. (Vol. 81, No. 2, February 1993, pp. 29-30). Washington, District of Columbia: U.S. Chamber of Commerce. By J. Tol Broome, Jr.

"It's All In The Plan" in *Small Business Reports*. (Vol. 19, No. 6, June 1994, pp. 38-43). New York, New York: Faulkner & Gray, Inc. By Alan W. Jackson.

"It's a Plan" in *Entrepreneur*. (June 1995, pp. 28, 30-31). Irvine, California: Entrepreneur Media Inc. By Cheryl J. Goldberg.

"Key Ingredient in Recipe: The Right People" in *Crain's Small Business*. (Vol. 4, No. 11, November 1996, p. 23). Detroit, Michigan: Crain Communications Inc. By Jim Brady.

"Keys to Success? For Starters, Here Are 15" in

Contractor. (Vol. 41, No. 11, November 1994, p. 12). Des Plaines, Illinois: Cahners Publishing Co. By Jeff Ferenc.

"Line Forms Even Before Zone Capital Shop Opens" in *Crain's Detroit Business.* (Vol. 12, No. 46, November 1996, pp. 16-17). Detroit, Michigan: Crain Communications Inc. By Shekini Gilliam.

"Many Stop at Oakland's Shop for Business Info" in *Crain's Detroit Business.* (Vol. 12, No. 46, November 1996, p. 17). Detroit, Michigan: Crain Communications Inc. By Shekini Gilliam.

"Mapping Your Route" in *Business Start-Ups.* (Vol. 8, No. 12, December 1996, pp. 40, 42-44). Irvine, California: Entrepreneur Media Inc. By Lynn H. Colwell.

"The Money Is Out There...How To Get It" in *Agency Sales Magazine.* (Vol. 24, No. 2, February 1994, pp. 15-17). Laguna Hills, California: Manufacturers' Agents National Association. By Jeff Fromberg.

"The Numbers Speak Volumes" in *Small Business Reports.* (Vol. 19, No. 7, July 1994, pp. 39-43). New York, New York: Faulkner & Gray, Inc. By Lamont Change.

"Obstacle Course" in *Income Opportunities.* (Vol. 31, No. 11, November 1996, pp. 27-30, 96). New York, New York: IO Publications Inc. By Dale D. Buss.

"Opening a New Store...Reasonable Goals and Careful Planning" in *Stores.* (Vol. 76, No. 10, October 1994, pp. 101-102). Washington, New York: National Retail Federation. By Bill Pearson.

"Plan of Action" in *Income Opportunities.* (Vol. 30, No. 7, July 1995, pp. 96, 98, 100). New York, New York: IO Publications, Inc. By Toni Reinhold.

"Plan of Attack" in *Inc.* (Vol. 18, No. 1, January 1996, pp. 41-44). Boston, Massachusetts: Goldhirsh Group, Inc. By Martha E. Mangelsdorf.

"Plan Can Help Put the Success in Succession" in *Crain's Small Business.* (June 1996, p. 13). Detroit, Michigan: Crain Communications Inc. By Don Clayton.

"Plan Of Attack" in *Entrepreneur.* (Vol. 23, No. 8, August 1995, pp. 150, 152-157). Irvine, California: Entrepreneur Media, Inc. Excerpted from *The Entrepreneur Magazine Small Business Advisor: The One-Stop Information Source for Starting, Managing, and Growing a Small Business* by The Entrepreneur Magazine Group.

"Planning for Projects" in *Income Opportunities.* (Vol. 29, No. 7, July 1994, p. 44). New York, New York: IO Publications Inc. By Carol More.

"Planning for Success" in *Business Start-Ups.* (Vol. 8, No. 3, March 1996, pp. 50, 52-53). Irvine, California:

Entrepreneur Media Inc. By Lynn L. Norquist.

"Poor Planning Plagues Small Business" in *Income Opportunities.* (Vol. 30, No. 4, April 1995, p. 2). New York, New York: IO Publications, Inc. By Patricia Hamilton.

"Prepare for Frustration You'll Create Exhilaration" in *Crain's Small Business.* (Vol. 4, No. 10, October 1996, p. 19). Detroit, Michigan: Crain Communications Inc. By Jim Brady.

"Putting It Together" in *Business Start-Ups.* (Vol. 8, No. 9, September 1996, pp. 12, 14). Irvine, California: Entrepreneur Media Inc. By Ellen DePasquale.

"Right Adds Might When You Write Proposal" in *Crain's Small Business.* (June 1996, p. 16). Detroit, Michigan: Crain Communications Inc. By Jim Brady.

"Savvy Partners Weren't Taken to Cleaners" in *Crain's Small Business.* (Vol. 4, No. 9, September 1996, pp. 9, 10). Detroit, Michigan: Crain Communications Inc. By Tim Moran.

"SCORE Points to Success" in *Black Enterprise.* (Vol. 25, No. 6, January 1995, p. 38). New York, New York: Earl G. Graves Publishing Co. Inc. By Christina F. Watts.

"The Seven Traps of Strategic Planning" in *Inc.* (Vol. 18, No. 16, November 1996, pp. 99, 101, 103). Boston, Massachusetts: Goldhirsh Group, Inc. By Joseph C. Picken and Gregory G. Dess.

"Split Decisions" in *Income Opportunities.* (Vol. 31, No. 9, September 1996, pp. 34, 36, 38). New York, New York: IO Publications Inc. By Diane M. Calabrese.

"Start with Strategic Fundamentals" in *Crain's Small Business.* (September 1995, p. 9). Detroit, Michigan: Crain Communications, Inc. By Jim Brady.

"Staying Alive " in *Black Enterprise.* (Vol. 25, No. 4, November 1994, pp. 90-92, 95-96). New York, New York: Earl G. Graves Publishing Co. Inc. By Rhonda Reynolds.

"Step 6: Compose a Winning Business Plan" in *Business Start-Ups.* (Vol. 8, No. 10, October 1996, pp. 68, 70). Irvine, California: Entrepreneur Media Inc. By Kylo-Patrick Hart.

"Surviving the Holidays" in *Hispanic Business.* (Vol. 18, No. 11, November 1996, pp. 60, 62). Santa Barbara, California: Hispanic Business Inc. By Graham Witherall.

"Ten Steps to Creating Your Business Plan" in *Income Opportunities.* (December/January 1991, pp. 55-56). New York, New York: IO Publications, Inc. By Ruth Anne King.

"When Your Banker Says No" in *Income Opportunities.* (Vol. 30, No. 11, November 1995, pp. 24-28). New York, New York: IO Publications, Inc. By Randall Kirkpatrick.

"Where's Your Plan" in *Hispanic Business.* (Vol. 20, No. 3, March 1997, p. 46). Santa Barbara, California: Hispanic Business Inc. By Rick Mendosa.

"Why My Business Failed" in *Black Enterprise.* (Vol. 24, No. 11, June 1994, pp. 236-242). New York, New York: Earl G. Graves Publishing Co. Inc. By Charles Jamison.

"Working Capital Woes" in *Black Enterprise.* (Vol. 26 No. 11, June 1996, p. 48). New York, New York: Earl G. Graves Publishing Co. Inc. By Carolyn M. Brown.

Business Vision/Goals

"3 Factors Help Make a Strategy Successful" in *Crain's Detroit Business.* (Vol. 5, No. 1, January 1997, p. 19). Detroit, Michigan: Crain Communications Inc. By Jim Brady.

"Above and Beyond" in *Entrepreneur.* (February 1997, pp. 84-86). Irvine, California: Entrepreneur Media Inc. By Robert McGarvey.

"Act of Courage" in *Business Start-Ups.* (Vol. 8, No. 6, June 1996, pp. 14, 16). Irvine, California: Entrepreneur Media Inc. By Carolyn Z. Lawrence.

"Added Attraction " in *Entrepreneur: Buyer's Guide to Franchise and Business Opportunities.* (Vol. 22, No. 11, 1995, pp. 36, 38-40). Irvine, California: Entrepreneur Media, Inc. By Guen Sublette.

"The Affair" in *Inc.* (Vol. 18, No. 16, November 1996, pp. 35, 37). Boston, Massachusetts: Goldhirsh Group, Inc. By Ichak Adizes.

"The Art (& Smarts) of the Deal" in *Corporate Detroit.* (Vol. 13, No. 12, December 1995, p. 49). Detroit, Michigan: Corporate Detroit, Inc. By Charles Rothstein.

"Asking for Directions" in *Business Start-Ups.* (Vol. 8, No. 2, December 1996, pp. 16, 18-19). Irvine, California: Entrepreneur Media Inc. By Johanna S. Billings.

"Back To The Future" in *Entrepreneur.* (Vol. 23, No. 1, January 1995, pp. 238-242, 245). Irvine, California: Entrepreneur Media, Inc. By Robert McGarvey.

"The Best Of Times" in *Entrepreneur.* (Vol. 24, No. 4, April 1996, pp. 139-142). Irvine, California: Entrepreneur Media, Inc. By Mark Henricks.

"Bright Ideas" in *Business Start-Ups.* (Vol. 7, No. 8, August 1995, pp. 50, 52-54, 57). Irvine, California: Entrepreneur Media Inc. By Bob Weinstein.

"Building Companies to Last" in *Inc.* (Special Issue: The State of Small Business, February 1996, pp. 83-84, 87-88). Boston, Massachusetts: Goldhirsh Group, Inc. By James C. Collins.

"Business Brainstorms" in *Business Start-Ups.* (Vol. 9, No. 3, March 1997, pp. 8, 10). Irvine, California: Entrepreneur Media Inc. By Carolyn Campbell.

"Business Must Refocus Once It Outgrows Entrepreneur's Control" in *Crain's Small Business.* (October 1995, p. 16). Detroit, Michigan: Crain Communications, Inc. By Jon Greenawalt.

"Businesses Needn't Be Related to Construction" in *Crain's Small Business.* (Vol. 5, No. 3, March 1997, p. 11). Detroit, Michigan: Crain Communications Inc. By Jeffrey McCracken.

"By the Book" in *Entrepreneur.* (June 1995, pp. 141-145). Irvine, California: Entrepreneur Media Inc. By Jane Easter Bahls.

"Choose Your Vehicle" in *Business Start-Ups.* (Vol. 8, No. 12, December 1996, pp. 24, 26-27). Irvine, California: Entrepreneur Media Inc. By Lin Grensing-Pophal.

"Creativity at the Edge of Chaos" in *Working Woman.* (February 1997, pp. 47-51, 53). New York, New York: MacDonald Communications Corporation. By Joseph Marshall.

"Destination Success" in *Business Start-Ups.* (Vol. 8, No. 12, December 1996, p. 50). Irvine, California: Entrepreneur Media Inc. By Carla Goodman.

"Everything According to Plan" in *INC.* (Vol. 17, No. 3, March 1995, pp. 79-85). Boston, Massachusetts: Goldhirsch Group, Inc. By Jay Finegan.

"Fools Rush In? The Institutional Context of Industry Creation" in *Academy of Management Review.* (Vol. 19, No. 4, October 1994, p. 645). Ada, Ohio: Academy of Management. By Howard E. Aldrich and Marlene C. Fiol.

"Forging New Frontiers " in *Black Enterprise.* (Vol. 26, No. 10, May 1996, pp. 70-72, 74, 76, 78). New York, New York: Earl G. Graves Publishing Co. Inc. By Marjorie Whigham-Desir.

"Fueling Up" in *Business Start-Ups.* (Vol. 8, No. 12, December 1996, pp. 46, 48). Irvine, California: Entrepreneur Media Inc. By Carla Goodman.

"Going It Alone" in *Newsweek.* (April 1996, pp. 50-51). New York, New York: Newsweek, Inc. By Ellyn E. Spragins and Steve Rhodes.

"Ground Zero" in *Entrepreneur.* (December 1996, p. 18). Irvine, California: Entrepreneur Media Inc. By Janean

Chun.

"Growing Strong" in *Income Opportunities*. (Vol. 31, No. 6, June 1996, pp. 30, 32, 34). New York, New York: IO Publications Inc. By Dorothy Elizabeth Brooks.

"High-Technology Horizon" in *Corporate Detroit*. (Vol. 14, No. 4, April 1996, pp. 27-29). Detroit, Michigan: Corporate Detroit, Inc. By Kevin J. Lamiman.

"The Inc. 500: 15th Annual List" in *Inc*. (October 1996, pp. 15-16). Boston, Massachusetts: Goldhirsh Group, Inc. By Joshua Hyatt.

"Independents Need a 'Big Picture' Person" in *Crain's Small Business*. (Vol. 5, No. 2, February 1997, p. 22). Detroit, Michigan: Crain Communications Inc. By Jim Brady.

"Inventor's Workshop" in *Business Start-Ups*. (October 1994, pp. 26-29). Irvine, California: Entrepreneur Media Inc. By Jacquelyn Lynn Denali.

"Journey of a Thousand Miles" in *Business Start-Ups*. (Vol. 8, No. 12, December 1996, p. 4). Irvine, California: Entrepreneur Media Inc. By Carolyn Z. Lawrence.

"Just a Suggestion" in *Entrepreneur*. (December 1996, p. 40). Irvine, California: Entrepreneur Media Inc. By Jacquelyn Lynn.

"Just Their Luck" in *Entrepreneur*. (Vol. 23, No. 2, February 1995, pp. 120, 122-25). Irvine, California: Entrepreneur Media, Inc. By Gayle Sato Stodder.

"Laying out Firm's Vision Isn't Mission Impossible" in *Crain's Small Business*. (Vol. 5, No. 4, April 1997, p. 11). Detroit, Michigan: Crain Communications Inc. By Lawrence Gardner.

"Like Pulling Teeth" in *Hispanic Business*. (Vol. 18, No. 6, June 1996, pp. 138, 140). Santa Barbara, California: Hispanic Business Inc. By Graham Witherall.

"Marketing on a Shoestring" in *Small Business Opportunities*. (Vol. 8, No. 6, November 1996, pp. 22-24, 26, 28, 30, 32, 34). New York, New York: Harris Publications, Inc. By Jeanie Crane.

"Measuring Up" in *Entrepreneur*. (November, 1996 pp. 168-173). Irvine, California: Entrepreneur Media Inc. By Robert McGarvey.

"Motivating Statistics" in *Business Start-Ups*. (Vol. 8, No. 8, August 1996, p. 4). Irvine, California: Entrepreneur Media Inc. By Karin Moeller.

"A Nation of Owners" in *Inc*. (Special Issue: The State of Small Business, February 1996, pp. 89-91). Boston, Massachusetts: Goldhirsh Group, Inc. By William Bridges.

"The Not-Too-Distant Future" in *Business Start-Ups*. (Vol. 9, No. 1, January 1997, pp. 36, 38, 40-42). Irvine, California: Entrepreneur Media Inc. By Kris Neri.

"Opening a New Store...Reasonable Goals and Careful Planning" in *Stores*. (Vol. 76, No. 10, October 1994, pp. 101-102). Washington, New York: National Retail Federation. By Bill Pearson.

"Q & A" in *Performance*. (September 1995, pp. 12-16). New York, New York: Bill Communications, Inc.

"Say When" in *Inc*. (Vol. 17, No. 2, February 1995, pp. 19-20). Boston, Massachusetts: Goldhirsh Group, Inc. By Steven L. Marks.

"Seize the Day" in *Income Opportunities*. (Vol. 32, No. 1, January 1997, pp. 32, 34, 36, 66). New York, New York: IO Publications Inc. By Dorothy Elizabeth Brooks.

"Small Like Me" in *Wall Street Journal Special Reports: Small Business (Special Edition)*. (May 23, 1996, p. R31). New York, New York: Wall Street Journal: Dow Jones & Co., Inc. By John Buskin.

"Small Talk" in *Wall Street Journal Special Reports: Small Business (Special Edition)*. (May 23, 1996, p. R28). New York, New York: Wall Street Journal: Dow Jones & Co., Inc. By Stephanie N. Mehta.

"Sounding Board" in *Income Opportunities*. (Vol. 30, No. 6, June 1995, pp. 114, 116). New York, New York: IO Publications, Inc. By Richard J. Maturi.

"Start Your Engines" in *Business Start-Ups*. (Vol. 8, No. 12, December 1996, pp. 6, 9). Irvine, California: Entrepreneur Media Inc. By Kylo-Patrick Hart.

"Staying Alive" in *Entrepreneur*. (Vol. 23, No. 3, March 1995, pp. 114-118). Irvine, California: Entrepreneur Media, Inc. By Robert McGarvey.

"Steps to Analyze and Control Your Cash" in *Crain's Small Business*. (Vol. 5, No. 3, March 1997, p. 8). Detroit, Michigan: Crain Communications Inc. By Lawrence Gardner.

"Tapping Creativity" in *Exhibitor Times*. (Vol. 4, No. 2, February 1996, pp. 40-43). Scottsdale, Arizona: Virgo Publishing, Inc. By Lorraine Denham and Heather Ransford.

"Think About Where You Want to Go, How to Get There" in *Crain's Small Business*. (Vol. 4, No. 9, September 1996, p. 18). Detroit, Michigan: Crain Communications Inc. By Jim Brady.

"Time to Make '97's Business Resolutions" in *Crain's Detroit Business*. (Vol. 5, No. 1, January 1997, p. 22). Detroit, Michigan: Crain Communications Inc. By David

Sowerby.

"Tomorrow Land" in *Entrepreneur.* (Vol. 24, No. 2, February 1996, pp. 135-138). Irvine, California: Entrepreneur Media, Inc. By Robert McGarvey.

"Turn It On" in *Entrepreneur.* (November, 1996 pp. 154-158, 161). Irvine, California: Entrepreneur Media Inc. By Robert McGarvey.

"What Does Business Really Want from Governments?" in *Inc.* (Special Issue: The State of Small Business, February 1996, pp. 92-103). Boston, Massachusetts: Goldhirsh Group, Inc. By Tom Richman.

"When Slow and Steady Wins the Race" in *Inc.* (Vol. 18, No. 17, November 1996, pp. 72-73, 76). Boston, Massachusetts: Goldhirsh Group, Inc. By Jeffrey Zygmont.

"With Luck, This Biz Will Go Down the Toilet" in *Inc.* (Vol. 19, No. 5, April 1997, p. 21). Boston, Massachusetts: Goldhirsh Group, Inc. By Phaedra Hise.

Car Wash

"Carwash Investment Information" in *Professional Carwashing and Detailing.* (December 1989, pp. 8-20). Latham, New York, National Trade Publications, Inc.

"Cleaning Up Off the Field" in *Forbes.* (Vol. 154, No. 3, August 1, 1994, p. 16). New York, New York, Forbes, Inc. Editor, William M. Stern.

"For Busy Execs, Mobile Car Wash Is Just the Ticket" in *Memphis Business Journal.* (Vol. 16, No. 8, July 4, 1994, p. 12). Memphis, Tennessee, Mid-South Communications, Inc. Editor, David Yawn.

"Keeping the `Pride and Joy' Clean Remains Prominent on DIY Activity" in *Aftermarket Business.* (Vol. 104, No. 8, August 1, 1994, p. 34). Cleveland, Ohio, Adbanstar Communications, Inc.

"Making Car Washes Pay: Is the Climate Right?" in *National Petroleum News.* (Vol. 86, No. 5, May 1994, pp. 50-54). Elk Grove Village, Illinois, Hunter Publishing Limited Partnership.

"Minnesota Operator Cleans Up with Car Wash" in *National Petroleum News.* (Vol. 86, No. 5, May 1994, p. 52). Elk Grove Village, Illinois, Hunter Publishing Limited Partnership.

"Waxing Customer Service and Cars" in *Management Review.* (Vol. 83, No. 7, July 1994, pp. 25-28). New York, New York, American Management Association. Editor, Jo-Ann Johnston.

Consultants

"Advice-For-Hire Not Just for Big Businesses" in *Crain's Small Business.* (June 1996, p. 10). Detroit, Michigan: Crain Communications Inc. By Fred Leeb and Eric Weiss.

"Advisory Advice" in *Small Business Opportunities.* (Vol. 6, No. 5, September 1994, p. 18). New York, New York: Harris Publications, Inc. By Steve Veltkamp.

"All for One" in *Crain's Small Business.* (Vol. 4, No. 10, October 1996, p. 1). Detroit, Michigan: Crain Communications Inc. By Kimberly Lifton.

"A Climate for Investment" in *Hispanic Business.* (Vol. 15, No. 11, November 1994, pp. 58-60). Santa Barbara, California: Hispanic Business, Inc. By Christopher Boyd.

"An Evaluation of SBI Marketing Consulting" in *Journal of Small Business Management.* (Vol. 30, No. 4, October 1992, pp. 62-71). Morgantown, West Virginia: West Virginia University. By Art Weinstein, J.A.F. Nicholls and Bruce Seaton.

"Fast Forward, Garbage Guru" in *Working Woman.* (January 1997, p. 18). New York, New York: MacDonald Communications Corporation. By Kambiz Foroohar.

"Fast Forward, Up & Comers" in *Working Woman.* (January 1997, p. 20). New York, New York: MacDonald Communications Corporation. By K.F.

"Finding a Lawyer for Your Business" in *Nation's Business.* (Vol. 82, No. 4, April 1994, pp. 34-35). Washington, District of Columbia: U.S. Chamber of Commerce. By Kenneth A. Ehrman.

"For Sale: Management Expertise from Small Companies" in *Inc.* (Vol. 19, No. 2, March 1997, p. 26). Boston, Massachusetts: Goldhirsh Group, Inc. By Jerry Useem.

"Get Rich in '95" in *Small Business Opportunities.* (Vol. 7, No. 1, January 1995, pp. 20, 22, 24, 26, 28, 30, 32, 34, 36, 38-40, 42-45). New York, New York: Harris Publications, Inc. By Cheryl Rogers, et al.

"Good Advice" in *Income Opportunities.* (Vol. 30, No. 4, April 1995, pp. 116-117). New York, New York: IO Publications, Inc. By Richard J. Maturi.

"How To Pick a Consultant" in *Small Business Reports.* (Vol. 19, No. 1, January 1994, p. 9). New York, New York: Faulkner & Gray, Inc. By Alan W. Jackson.

"An Insurance Consultant May Benefit Your Bottom Line" in *Air Conditioning, Heating & Refrigeration News.* (Vol. 193, No. 5, October 3, 1994, p. 22). Troy, Michigan: Business News Publishing Company. By Joseph Arkin.

"Keep 'em Coming Back for More" in *Business Start-Ups.*

(Vol. 9, No. 1, January 1997, pp. 70, 72). Irvine, California: Entrepreneur Media Inc. By Carla Goodman.

"Legal Aid" in *Business Start-Ups.* (Vol. 7, No. 2, February 1995, pp. 78, 80-81). Irvine, California: Entrepreneur Media Inc. By Sue Clayton.

"Never Too Small to Manage" in *Inc.* (Vol. 19, No. 2, February 1997, pp. 56-58, 61). Boston, Massachusetts: Goldhirsh Group, Inc. By David Whitford.

"No-cost (and Low-cost) Consulting" in *Occupational Hazards.* (Vol. 57, No. 1, January 1995, pp. 59-63). Cleveland, Ohio: Penton Publishing. By Mark S. Kuhar.

"One Stop Capital Shop Not Quite Ready" in *Crain's Detroit Business.* (Vol. 11, No. 24, June 12-18, 1996, p. 12). Detroit, Michigan: Crain Communications Inc. By Michael Goodin.

"Pieces of Advice" in *Inc.* (Vol. 17, No. 6, May 1995, pp. 57-60, 62). Boston, Massachusetts: Goldhirsh Group, Inc.

"Southfield Company Handles Botsford Data" in *Crain's Detroit Business.* (Vol. 13, No. 8, February/March 1997, p. 16). Detroit, Michigan: Crain Communications Inc. By David Barkholz.

"Spend Your Consulting Dollars Wisely" in *Marketing News.* (Vol. 28, No. 18, August 29, 1994, p. 15). Chicago, Illinois: American Marketing Association By Vicki Clift.

"What to Consider When Seeking Outside Advice" in *Crain's Small Business.* (Vol. 4, No. 10, October 1996, pp. 12-13). Detroit, Michigan: Crain Communications Inc. By Lawrence Gardner.

Entrepreneurship on the Web

"Alternative Investments" in *Black Enterprise.* (Vol. 27, No. 3, October 1996, p. 50). New York, New York: Earl G. Graves Publishing Co. Inc. By Glenn Jeffers.

"Big Blue Horizons" in *Hispanic Business.* (Vol. 18, No. 6, June 1996, p. 126). Santa Barbara, California: Hispanic Business Inc. By Rick Mendosa.

"Big Deal" in *The Red Herring.* (September 1996, pp. 51-52, 54, 56). San Francisco, California: Herring Communications Inc. By Andrew P. Madden.

"The Birth of a Web Page "Empire"" in *Feminist Bookstore News.* (Vol. 19, No. 5, January/February 1997, pp. 25-28). San Francisco, California: Feminist Bookstore News. By Lee Anne Phillips.

"Buy Local Focus of State Program" in *Entrepreneur.* (Vol. 22, No. 13, December 1994, p. 18). Irvine, California: Entrepreneur Media, Inc. By Cynthia E.

Griffin.

"Calling All Cybercustomers!" in *Independent Business.* (Vol. 8, No. 1, Jan./Feb. 1997, p. 46). Thousands Oaks, California: Group IV Communications Inc. By Eric J. Adams.

"Don't Get Trapped" in *Hispanic Business.* (Vol. 19, No. 1, January 1997, p. 46). Santa Barbara, California: Hispanic Business Inc. By Rick Mendosa.

"Drag and Click" in *Crain's Small Business.* (Vol. 5, No. 2, February 1997, p. 3). Detroit, Michigan: Crain Communications Inc. By Jeffrey McCracken.

"The E-Mail Edge" in *Income Opportunities.* (Vol. 31, No. 9, October 1996, pp. 48, 50, 52,). New York, New York: IO Publications Inc. By Laura Klepacki.

"Easy E-Marketing" in *Independent Business.* (Vol. 8, No. 1, Jan./Feb. 1997, p. 40). Thousands Oaks, California: Group IV Communications Inc. By Pam Froman.

"Entrepreneurial Spirit Awards" in *Hispanic Business.* (Vol. 18, No. 12, December 1996, pp. 26, 28, 30, 34, 36, 38). Santa Barbara, California: Hispanic Business Inc. By Maria Zate.

"Getting Caught in the Web of On-Line Information" in *Exhibitor Times.* (Vol. 4, No. 1, January 1996, pp. 38-39). Scottsdale, Arizona: Virgo Publishing, Inc. By Valerie A.M. Demetros.

"Getting the Most from the Web" in *Crain's Small Business.* (July 1996, p. 8). Detroit, Michigan: Crain Communications Inc. By Jeffrey McCracken.

"He Wants PC Users to Face the Music" in *Crain's Small Business.* (Vol. 5, No. 3, March 1997, p. 15). Detroit, Michigan: Crain Communications Inc. By Jeffrey McCracken.

"The High-Tech 50" in *Hispanic Business.* (Vol. 18, No. 7/8, July/August 1996, p. 36). Santa Barbara, California: Hispanic Business Inc. By Maria Zate.

"Home Sweet Home" in *Independent Business.* (Vol. 8, No. 1, Jan./Feb. 1997, pp. 30-32). Thousands Oaks, California: Group IV Communications Inc. By Kirk Kirksey.

"Hot Opportunity of the Month" in *Income Opportunities.* (Vol. 31, No. 5, May 1996, p. 6). New York, New York: IO Publications Inc. By Stephanie Jeffrey.

"How Do You Say Apple?" in *Hispanic Business.* (Vol. 19, No. 1, January 1997, p. 47). Santa Barbara, California: Hispanic Business Inc. By Rick Mendosa.

"Idea Man" in *Hits.* (Winter 1997, pp. 18-22). San

Francisco, California: Herring Communications, Inc. By Alex Gove.

"Information Superhighway May Be a Dead End" in *Crain's Small Business*. (June 1996, p. 12). Detroit, Michigan: Crain Communications Inc. By Scott Segal.

"Internet Resources" in *Small Business Opportunities*. (Vol. 9, No. 3, May 1997, pp. 54, 56). New York, New York: Harris Publications, Inc. By Lin Grensing-Pophal.

"Marketing 101" in *Entrepreneur*. (March 1997, pp. 112-117). Irvine, California: Entrepreneur Media Inc. By Robert McGarvey.

"The Message is the Medium" in *Performance*. (September 1995). New York, New York: Bill Communications, Inc. By Ross Weiland.

"Net Income" in *Crain's Small Business*. (July 1996, p. 1). Detroit, Michigan: Crain Communications Inc. By Jeffrey McCracken.

"Net Profits" in *Working Woman*. (June 1996, pp. 44-49, 70,72). New York, New York: MacDonald Communications Corporation. By Gloria Brame.

"Net Rewards" in *Entrepreneur*. (March 1997, pp. 144, 146). Irvine, California: Entrepreneur Media Inc. By Heather Page.

"Net Working" in *Crain's Detroit Business*. (Vol. 13, No. 3, January 1997, p. 8). Detroit, Michigan: Crain Communications Inc. By Art Dridgeforth, Jr.

"Nothing but Net" in *Inc*. (Vol. 18, No. 18, December 1997, pp. 43-44). Boston, Massachusetts: Goldhirsh Group, Inc.

"Online Advice" in *Independent Business*. (Vol. 8, No. 1, Jan./Feb. 1997, p. 16). Thousands Oaks, California: Group IV Communications Inc. By Maryann Hammers.

"PR Firm Takes Press-Release Production Online" in *Crain's Detroit Business*. (Vol. 12 No. 38, September 1996, p. 14). Detroit, Michigan: Crain Communications Inc. By Arthur Bridgeforth, Jr.

"Q & A" in *Performance*. (September 1995, pp. 12-16). New York, New York: Bill Communications, Inc.

"Real Law in a Virtual World" in *Black Enterprise*. (Vol. 27, No. 5, December 1996, p. 44). New York, New York: Earl G. Graves Publishing Co. Inc. By Tariq K. Muhammad.

"Rev It Up" in *Entrepreneur*. (March 1997, pp. 50, 52-53). Irvine, California: Entrepreneur Media Inc. By Cheryl J. Goldberg.

"Safety Net" in *Entrepreneur*. (February 1997, pp. 82-84).

Irvine, California: Entrepreneur Media Inc. By Steven C. Bahls and Jane Easter Bahls.

"Short Cut to a Job" in *Hispanic Business*. (Vol. 19, No. 2, February 1997, p. 64). Santa Barbara, California: Hispanic Business Inc. By Claudia Armann.

"Sites to Surf" in *Income Opportunities*. (Vol. 31, No. 5, May 1996, pp. 44, 46). New York, New York: IO Publications Inc. By Debra D'Agostino.

"Surf's Up" in *Small Business Opportunities*. (Vol. 9, No. 1, January 1997, p. 10). New York, New York: Harris Publications, Inc. By Lin Grensing-Pophal.

"Take in the Sites" in *Independent Business*. (Vol. 8, No. 1, Jan./Feb. 1997, p. 20). Thousands Oaks, California: Group IV Communications Inc. By Rick Mendosa.

"To Website or Not to Website" in *Feminist Bookstore News*. (Vol. 19, No. 5, January/February 1997, pp. 29-36). San Francisco, California: Feminist Bookstore News. By Carol Seajay.

"Toy Story" in *Entrepreneur*. (February 1997, p. 38). Irvine, California: Entrepreneur Media Inc. By Lynn Beresford.

"Tradeport an Excellent Source of Trade Information and Leads" in *Hispanic Business*. (Vol. 18, No. 6, June 1996, p. 126). Santa Barbara, California: Hispanic Business Inc. By Rick Mendosa.

"Translating the Web" in *Hits*. (Winter 1997, pp. 12-13). San Francisco, California: Herring Communications, Inc. By Nikki C. Goth.

"Way of the Web?" in *Hispanic Business*. (Vol. 18, No. 10, October 1996, p. 88). Santa Barbara, California: Hispanic Business Inc. By Rick Mendosa.

"Web Fever!" in *Independent Business*. (Vol. 8, No. 1, Jan./Feb. 1997, pp. 36-39). Thousands Oaks, California: Group IV Communications Inc. By Eric J. Adams.

"Wired Kingdom" in *Inc*. (Vol. 19, No. 4, March 1997, p. 112). Boston, Massachusetts: Goldhirsh Group, Inc.

"Your Hassle-Free Web Site" in *Independent Business*. (Vol. 8, No. 1, Jan./Feb. 1997, p. 18). Thousands Oaks, California: Group IV Communications Inc. By Maryann Hammers.

Gift Store

"Albert Maslia: A Social Expression Genius" in *GSB: Gift and Stationery Business*. (March 1991, pp. 34-36). New York, New York, Gralla Publications. Editor, Maria Sagurton.

"The Birth of a Business" in *Working Woman Magazine.* (December 1989, pp. 45-53). New York, New York, Lang Communications. Editor, Louise Washer.

"Cash in on Country" in *Small Business Opportunities.* (Vol. 9, No. 3, May 1997, pp. 66-67). New York, New York, Harris Publications, Inc. Editor, Geri Anderson.

"Consumers Are Starting to Notice Stationery Brands" in *Discount Store News.* (Vol. 33, No. 20, October 17, 1994, p. 43). New York, New York, Lebhar-Friedman, Inc.

"Finding Your Niche" in *Business Start-Ups.* (Vol. 9, No. 4, April 1997, pp. 72, 74). Irvine, California, Entrepreneur Media Inc. Editor, Carla Goodman.

"Gift Keeps on Giving" in *Small Business Opportunities.* (Vol. 9, No. 1, January 1997, pp. 56, 58). New York, New York, Harris Publications, Inc. Editor, Marie Sherlock.

"Local Color" in *Business Start-Ups.* (Vol. 7, No. 3, March 1995, p. 120). Irvine, California, Entrepreneur Media Inc. Editor, Guen Sublette.

"The Queen of Hearts" in *Entrepreneur.* (April 1988, pp. 105-107). Irvine, California, Entrepreneur, Inc.

"Retailing's Entrepreneurs of the Year" in *Chain Store Age Executive.* (Vol. 70, No. 12, December 1994, pp. 33-68). New York, New York, Lebhar-Friedman, Inc.

"Reviving the Dying Store" in *Direct Marketing.* (Vol. 56, No. 7, November 1993, pp. 20-21). Long Island, New York, Hoke Communications. Editor, Murray Raphel.

"Taking the Cake" in *Business Start-Ups.* (October 1994, p. 87). Irvine, California, Entrepreneur Media Inc.

"This Card Shop Is a Labor of Love" in *Greetings Magazine.* (August 1991, pp. 8-9). New York, New York, Mackay Publishing Corp.

"Unforgettable" in *Business Start-Ups.* (Vol. 7, No. 3, March 1995, p. 8). Irvine, California, Entrepreneur Media Inc. Editor, Cynthia E. Griffin.

"A Winning Season" in *Business Start-Ups.* (Vol. 8, No. 7, July 1996, pp. 4547, 49-50). Irvine, California, Entrepreneur Media Inc. Editor, Carla Goodman.

High-Tech Business

"Ace in the Hole" in *Entrepreneur.* (May 1997, pp. 69-71). Irvine, California: Entrepreneur Media Inc. By David R. Evanson.

"Attracting Advertisers" in *Hits.* (Fall 1996, p. 68). San Francisco, California: Herring Communications, Inc.

"Business and Gravy" in *The Red Herring.* (March 1997, pp. 50-51). San Francisco, California: Herring Communications Inc. By Luc Hatlestad.

"Bytes Can Bite Back" in *Crain's Small Business* Office Tech '96 Supplement. (Vol. 4, No. 11, November 1996, p. T-19). Detroit, Michigan: Crain Communications Inc. By Claudia Rast and Marc Bergsman.

"Cashing in on the Web" in *Hits.* (Fall 1996, p. 66). San Francisco, California: Herring Communications, Inc.

"Changing the Future of Business" in *Black Enterprise.* (Vol. 27, No. 8, March 1997, pp. 80-84). New York, New York: Earl G. Graves Publishing Co. Inc. By Marvin V. Greene.

"College Pals Won't Tamper with Success" in *Crain's Small Business.* (Vol. 4, No. 11, November 1996, p. 21). Detroit, Michigan: Crain Communications Inc. By Jeffrey McCracken.

"Computer Resale Shops Offer Buyers Alternative" in *Crain's Detroit Business.* (Vol. 11, No. 14, April 1995, p. 11). Detroit, Michigan: Crain Communications Inc. By Michael Maurer.

"Customize Customers" in *Crain's Small Business* Office Tech '96 Supplement. (Vol. 4, No. 11, November 1996, p. T-7). Detroit, Michigan: Crain Communications Inc. By Arthur Bridgeforth, Jr.

"Digital Commerce" in *The Red Herring.* (February 1997, pp. 46, 4850). San Francisco, California: Herring Communications Inc. By Alex Gove.

"Don't Hold Your Breath" in *The Red Herring.* (February 1997, p. 84). San Francisco, California: Herring Communications Inc. By Andrew P. Madden.

"E-Male Dominates?" in *Crain's Small Business* Office Tech '96 Supplement. (Vol. 4, No. 11, November 1996, p. T-4). Detroit, Michigan: Crain Communications Inc. By Shekini Gilliam.

"An Entrepreneur Cries for Help" in *Crain's Detroit Business.* (Vol. 5, No. 1, January 1997, p. 4). Detroit, Michigan: Crain Communications Inc. By Jeffrey McCracken.

"Entrepreneurial Superstars" in *Entrepreneur.* (April 1997, pp. 108-139). Irvine, California: Entrepreneur Media Inc. By Debra Phillips and others.

"Even Old Machines Can Thrive in High-Tech World" in *Crain's Small Business.* (June 1996, p. 6). Detroit, Michigan: Crain Communications Inc. By Dave Guilford.

"Friendship Begets 11-Years Partnership" in *Crain's Small Business.* (Vol. 5, No. 4, April 1997, p. 23). Detroit, Michigan: Crain Communications Inc. By Jeffrey

McCracken.

"The Future of Your Business" in *Business Start-Ups*. (Vol. 9, No. 4, April 1997, pp. 26-32). Irvine, California: Entrepreneur Media Inc. By Kylo-Patrick Hart.

"Going Public Proved a Rich Experience for Technology Entrepreneurs in '96" in *Wall Street Journal*. (Vol. Ic, No. 22, 09/31/97, p. B1). New York, New York: Wall Street Journal: Dow Jones & Co., Inc. By Michael Selz.

"Growth Squeezes Collectibles Shop" in *Crain's Small Business*. (Vol. 4, No. 10, October 1996, p. 4). Detroit, Michigan: Crain Communications Inc. By Jeffrey McCracken.

"A Guide May Be Needed to Set Up Shop On-Line" in *Crain's Detroit Business*. (Vol. 11, No. 29, July 1995, p. 11). Detroit, Michigan: Crain Communications Inc.

"Hacker Attackers" in *Crain's Small Business* Office Tech '96 Supplement. (Vol. 4, No. 11, November 1996, p. T-6). Detroit, Michigan: Crain Communications Inc. By Arthur Bridgeforth, Jr.

"High-Tech Firm Discovers Lease-To-Buy is Way to Go" in *Crain's Small Business*. (Vol. 5, No. 4, April 1997, p. 10). Detroit, Michigan: Crain Communications Inc. By Tim Moran.

"High-Tech Hoods" in *Inc*. (Vol. 19, No. 4, March 1997, pp. 48-51). Boston, Massachusetts: Goldhirsh Group, Inc. By Sarah Schafer.

"His Customers' Plea Became New Calling" in *Crain's Small Business*. (July 1996, p. 15). Detroit, Michigan: Crain Communications Inc. By Jeffrey McCracken.

"Instant Ally" in *Business Start-Ups*. (Vol. 8, No. 7, July 1996, pp. 12, 14). Irvine, California: Entrepreneur Media Inc. By Pamela Palmer.

"Investors Bet on Cyberspace Path to Terra Firm Travel" in *Wall Street Journal*. (Vol. Ic, No. 9, January 14, 1997, p. B2). New York, New York: Wall Street Journal: Dow Jones & Co., Inc. By Michael Selz.

"Marketing Online" in *Black Enterprise*. (Vol. 27, No. 2, September 1996, pp. 85-88). New York, New York: Earl G. Graves Publishing Co. Inc. By Tariq K. Muhammand.

"New York" in *Hispanic Business*. (Vol. 17, No. 5, May 1995, p. 36). Santa Barbara, California: Hispanic Business Inc. By Yvonne Conde.

"No Line Online, but Use with Caution" in *Crain's Small Business*. (Vol. 4, No. 11, November 1996, p. 10). Detroit, Michigan: Crain Communications Inc. By Jeff Pace.

"Not Everyone's On-Line" in *Crain's Detroit Business*. (Vol. 11, No. 29, July 1995, p. 10). Detroit, Michigan: Crain Communications Inc. By Michael Maurer.

"On-Line Upstarts Tap Big Media Companies for Funds" in *Wall Street Journal*. (Vol. Ic, No. 19, February 10, 1997, p. B2). New York, New York: Wall Street Journal: Dow Jones & Co., Inc. By Stephanie N. Metha.

"Online Salesperson" in *Crain's Small Business* Office Tech '96 Supplement. (Vol. 4, No. 11, November 1996, p. T-3). Detroit, Michigan: Crain Communications Inc.

"Safeguarding Your Network" in *Black Enterprise*. (Vol. 27, No. 3, October 1996, pp. 48-50). New York, New York: Earl G. Graves Publishing Co. Inc. By Joyce E. Davis.

"Small Access Providers Weave Some Tangled Routes to the Web" in *Detroit Free Press*. (March 24, pp. 10f-11f, 14f). Detroit, Michigan: Knight-Ridder, Inc. By Mike Brennan.

"Surf's Up!" in *Hits*. (Fall 1996, pp. 9, 11). San Francisco, California: Herring Communications, Inc. By Anthony B. Perkins.

"Taking It to The Street" in *Hits*. (Spring 1997, pp. 16-20). San Francisco, California: Herring Communications, Inc. By Anne T. Linsmayer.

"Tech Trash" in *Crain's Detroit Business*. (Vol. 11, No. 29, July 1995, p. 8). Detroit, Michigan: Crain Communications Inc. By Mary Dempsey.

"Using Technology to Enhance Your Business" in *Black Enterprise*. (Vol. 27, No. 8, March 1997, pp. 64-72). New York, New York: Earl G. Graves Publishing Co. Inc.

"Was That Cybernet Inc. or Interweb Co.?" in *Wall Street Journal*. (Vol. Ic, No. 5, January 8, 1997, pp. B1-B2). New York, New York: Wall Street Journal: Dow Jones & Co., Inc. By Rodney Ho.

"What the Doctor Ordered" in *Crain's Detroit Business*. (Vol. 13, No. 15, April 1997, p. 9). Detroit, Michigan: Crain Communications Inc. By David Barkholz.

"Wired for Success" in *Black Enterprise*. (Vol. 27, No. 8, March 1997, pp. 75-80). New York, New York: Earl G. Graves Publishing Co. Inc. By Tariq K. Muhammad.

Home-Based Business

"Advantage: Home" in *Business Start-Ups*. (Vol. 8, No. 6, June 1996, pp. 84, 86). Irvine, California: Entrepreneur Media Inc. By Janie Sullivan.

"Alone Behind the Desk" in *Business Start-Ups*. (Vol. 9,

No. 4, April 1997, pp. 8, 10). Irvine, California: Entrepreneur Media Inc. By Carolyn Campbell.

"Attention Getters" in *Entrepreneur*. (Vol 23, No. 1, January 1995, pp. 76, 78). Irvine, California: Entrepreneur Media, Inc. By Debra Phillips.

"Beat the January Blues" in *Business Start-Ups*. (Vol. 8, No. 1, January 1996, pp. 18-19). Irvine, California: Entrepreneur Media Inc.

"The Big Sell" in *Entrepreneur*. (December 1996, pp. 61-62). Irvine, California: Entrepreneur Media Inc. By Cynthia E. Griffin.

"Bottled Profits" in *Income Opportunities*. (Vol. 31, No. 6, June 1996, pp. 96, 94). New York, New York: IO Publications Inc. By Amy H. Berger.

"Broadcast News" in *Business Start-Ups*. (Vol. 7, No. 6, June 1995, p. 16). Irvine, California: Entrepreneur Media Inc. By Cynthia E. Griffin.

"Bucks in Buttons" in *Small Business Opportunities*. (Vol. 9, No. 1, January 1997, p. 48). New York, New York: Harris Publications, Inc. By Carla Goodman.

"Building the Perfect Home Office" in *Black Enterprise*. (Vol. 27, No. 8, March 1997, pp. 36-37). New York, New York: Earl G. Graves Publishing Co. Inc. By Rafiki Cai.

"Buying Wisely for Your Office" in *Black Enterprise*. (Vol. 27, No. 9, April 1997, pp. 35-36). New York, New York: Earl G. Graves Publishing Co. Inc. By Tariq K. Muhammad.

"Catering Requirements" in *Black Enterprise*. (Vol. 27, No. 8, March 1997, p. 30). New York, New York: Earl G. Graves Publishing Co. Inc. By Sheryl E. Huggins.

"A Clothes Call" in *Income Opportunities*. (Vol. 32, No. 4, April 1997, p. 12). New York, New York: IO Publications Inc. By Lana Sanderson.

"Collectibles Search" in *Business Start-Ups*. (Vol. 8, No. 7, July 1996, p. 32). Irvine, California: Entrepreneur Media Inc. By Guen Sublette.

"Combat Zone" in *Entrepreneur*. (Vol. 22, No. 9, September 1994, p. 100). Irvine, California: Entrepreneur Media, Inc. By Janean Huber.

"Community Centered" in *Business Start-Ups*. (Vol. 8, No. 6, June 1996, pp. 68, 70-71). Irvine, California: Entrepreneur Media Inc. By Deborah Richman.

"Conference Call" in *Entrepreneur*. (Vol. 23, No. 12, November 1995, pp. 48, 50). Irvine, California: Entrepreneur Media, Inc. By Cynthia E. Griffin.

"Congressman Plans Bill to Aid Home-Based Businesses" in *Wall Street Journal*. (Vol. Ic, No. 16, January 23, 1997, p. B2). New York, New York: Wall Street Journal: Dow Jones & Co., Inc. By Rodney Ho.

"Cost Controls" in *Income Opportunities*. (Vol. 30, No. 5, May 1995, p. 8). New York, New York: IO Publications, Inc. By Lana Sanderson.

"Couple to Relocate Sanit-Air for Sanity" in *Crain's Small Business*. (Vol. 4, No. 11, November 1996, p. 21). Detroit, Michigan: Crain Communications Inc. By Jeffrey McCracken.

"Day-Care Dollars" in *Small Business Opportunities*. (Vol. 9, No. 3, May 1997, pp. 94-95). New York, New York: Harris Publications, Inc. By Marie Sherlock.

"A Delicate Balance" in *Business Start-Ups*. (Vol. 8, No. 9, September 1996, pp. 8, 10). Irvine, California: Entrepreneur Media Inc. By Ken Ohlson.

"Doing Your Home Work" in *Income Opportunities*. (Vol. 32, No. 4, April 1997, pp. 24-27). New York, New York: IO Publications Inc.

"Don't Get Zoned Out" in *Income Opportunities*. (Vol. 31, No. 9, September 1996, pp. 21-23). New York, New York: IO Publications Inc. By Eric Barnes.

"Eleven Businesses You Can Run From Home" in *Homebased Business*. (Winter 1990, pp. 29-32). Irvine, California: Entrepreneur, Inc. By Frances Huffman.

"Entrepreneur Hails Power of Marketing" in *Crain's Small Business*. (June 1996, p. 23). Detroit, Michigan: Crain Communications Inc. By Jeffrey McCracken.

"Everything You Need to Know to Start Your Business at Home" in *Business Start-Ups*. (Vol. 8, No. 6, June 1996, pp. 28, 30, 32, 34-36). Irvine, California: Entrepreneur Media Inc. By Karin Moeller.

"Fast Forward, Up & Comers" in *Working Woman*. (January 1997, p. 20). New York, New York: MacDonald Communications Corporation. By K.F.

"Fast-Growing Trends" in *Business Start-Ups*. (Vol. 9, No. 2, February 1997, pp. 42, 44, 46). Irvine, California: Entrepreneur Media Inc. By Carla Goodman.

"Fed Funds" in *Entrepreneur*. (Vol. 23, No. 8, August 1995, pp. 50, 52- 53). Irvine, California: Entrepreneur Media, Inc. By Cynthia E. Griffin.

"Finding the Perfect Job" in *Crain's Detroit Business*. (Vol. 11, No. 34, August 1995, p. 15). Detroit, Michigan: Crain Communications Inc. By Steve Raphael.

"A Fine Mess" in *Income Opportunities*. (Vol. 31, No. 4, April 1996, p. 10). New York, New York: IO Publications,

Inc. By Lana Sanderson.

"First Things First" in *Business Start-Ups.* (Vol. 8, No. 8, August 1996, pp. 8, 10). Irvine, California: Entrepreneur Media Inc. By Carolyn Campbell.

"Get It Together" in *Business Start-Ups.* (Vol. 7, No. 8, August 1995, p. 14). Irvine, California: Entrepreneur Media Inc.

"Getting Connected" in *Entrepreneur.* (Vol. 24, No. 2, February 1996, pp. 48, 50-51). Irvine, California: Entrepreneur Media, Inc. By Cynthia E. Griffin.

"Giving Thanks" in *Business Start-Ups.* (Vol. 8, No. 11, November 1996, pp. 8, 10). Irvine, California: Entrepreneur Media Inc. By Julie Bawden Davis.

"Greener Pastures" in *Income Opportunities.* (Vol. 30, No. 9, September 1995, pp. 24-27, 106). New York, New York: IO Publications, Inc. By Meg North.

"Growing Pains" in *Business Start-Ups.* (Vol. 9, No. 5, May 1997, pp. 8, 10, 12). Irvine, California: Entrepreneur Media Inc. By Carolyn Campbell.

"Heading Home" in *Income Opportunities.* (Vol. 32, No. 4, April 1997, pp. 46, 49-50). New York, New York: IO Publications Inc. By Robert L. Perry.

"Hello, World" in *Income Opportunities.* (Vol. 30, No. 4, April 1995, p. 8). New York, New York: IO Publications, Inc. By Lana Sanderson.

"Help Wanted" in *Entrepreneur.* (May 1996, pp. 55-57). Irvine, California: Entrepreneur Media Inc.

"He's Right at Home in Chili and Shuttles" in *Crain's Small Business.* (June 1996, p. 23). Detroit, Michigan: Crain Communications Inc. By Jeffrey McCracken.

"High-Tech Know-How" in *Small Business Opportunities.* (Vol. 8, No. 3, May 1996, pp. 62, 64, 106). New York, New York: Harris Publications, Inc. By Jeff Berner.

"Hints from the Pros: Try This At Home" in *Business Start-Ups.* (Vol. 7, No. 6, June 1995, p. 16). Irvine, California: Entrepreneur Media Inc. By Eileen Glick, president of the Home-based Business Administration, offers tips for running a home-based business.

"Holiday Helpers" in *Business Start-Ups.* (Vol. 7, No. 11, November 1995, pp. 14, 16). Irvine, California: Entrepreneur Media Inc.

"Home Alone" in *Small Business Opportunities.* (Vol. 6, No. 5, September 1994, p. 50). New York, New York: Harris Publications, Inc. By Robin Montgomery.

"Home Alone: Small Business Strategies" in *Working Woman.* (Vol. 18, No. 3, March 1993, pp. 45-50). New York, New York: Working Woman, Inc. By Louise Washer.

"Home-based Business Opportunity" in *Business Start-Ups.* (Vol. 6, No. 9, September 1994, p. 33). Irvine, California: Entrepreneur Media, Inc.

"Home-Based Franchises" in *Income Opportunities.* (Mid-March 1990, pp. 51-52). New York, New York: IO Publications, Inc. By Lynie Arden.

"Home-Based Riches!" in *Small Business Opportunities.* (Vol. 8, No. 2, March 1996, pp. 22-24, 26, 28, 30, 32, 34, 82, 102, 122). New York, New York: Harris Publications, Inc.

"Home Business Start-Up Basics" in *Income Opportunities.* (Mid-September 1990, pp. 54-56). New York, New York: IO Publications, Inc. By Mildred Jailer.

"Home Grown" in *Business Start-Ups.* (Vol. 7, No. 3, March 1995, pp. 36-47). Irvine, California: Entrepreneur Media Inc. By Guen Sublette.

"Home Is Where the Business Is" in *Black Enterprise.* (Vol. 25, No. 4, November 1994, pp. 128-138). New York, New York: Earl G. Graves Publishing Co. Inc. By Christina F. Watts.

"Home Run" in *Business Start-Ups.* (Vol. 7, No. 10, October 1995, p. 72). Irvine, California: Entrepreneur Media Inc. By Nancy L. Scarlato.

"Home Runs" in *Entrepreneur.* (Vol. 22, No. 13, December 1994, p. 63). Irvine, California: Entrepreneur Media, Inc. By Janean Huber.

"Home Safe" in *Income Opportunities.* (Vol. 32, No. 2, February 1997, pp. 38, 40, 42). New York, New York: IO Publications Inc. By Janine S. Pouliot.

"Home is Where the Customer Is" in *Sales & Marketing Management.* (Vol. 144, No. 9, August 1992, p. 54). New York, New York: Bill Communications. By Betsy Wiesendanger.

"Home Working: Here To Stay" in *Income Opportunities.* (Vol. 31, No. 2, February 1996, p. 4). New York, New York: IO Publications, Inc. By Michele Marrinan.

"Homebased 400 Business Opportunity" in *Business Start-Ups.* (Vol. 8, No. 9, September 1996, pp. 31-61). Irvine, California: Entrepreneur Media Inc. By Stephanie Osowski.

"Homebased Business Insurance" in *Business Start-Ups.* (Vol. 8, No. 7, July 1996, pp. 16, 18-21). Irvine, California: Entrepreneur Media Inc. By Dennis Whittington.

"The Homebased Psyche" in *Entrepreneur.* (March 1990, pp. 76-81). Irvine, California: Entrepreneur, Inc. By Christine Forbes.

"House Hunting" in *Entrepreneur.* (Vol. 23, No. 4, April 1995, pp. 84, 86-87). Irvine, California: Entrepreneur Media, Inc. By Cynthia E. Griffin.

"House Rules" in *Entrepreneur.* (Vol. 23, No. 7, July 1995, pp. 46, 48-49). Irvine, California: Entrepreneur Media, Inc. By Cynthia E. Griffin.

"How to Succeed in 4 Easy Steps" in *Inc.* (Vol. 17, No. 10, July 1995, pp. 30-32, 34, 36-40, 42). Boston, Massachusetts: Goldhirsh Group, Inc. By Bo Burlingham.

"How To Start an Inc. 500 Company" in *Inc. 500.* (Vol. 16, No. 11, 1994, pp. 51-52, 54, 57-58, 60, 63-65). Boston, Massachusetts: Goldhirsch Group, Inc. By Leslie Brokaw.

"The Hype About Home Businesses" in *Inc.* (Vol. 18, No. 7, May 1996, p. 58). Boston, Massachusetts: Goldhirsh Group, Inc. By John Case.

"In The Cards" in *Income Opportunities.* (Vol. 31, No. 2, February 1996, p. 10). New York, New York: IO Publications, Inc. By Lana Sanderson.

"Insurance: Easy Rider" in *Business Start-Ups.* (Vol. 7, No. 6, June 1995, p. 18). Irvine, California: Entrepreneur Media Inc. By Janean Huber.

"Interior Design" in *Business Start-Ups.* (Vol. 7, No. 7, July 1995, p. 18). Irvine, California: Entrepreneur Media Inc. By Wendy Neuman.

"Is the Price Right?" in *Income Opportunities.* (Vol. 29, No. 9, September 1994, pp. 102-104). New York, New York: IO Publications Inc. By Jo Frohbieter-Mueller.

"Item-Of-The-Month Club" in *Business Start-Ups.* (Vol. 8, No. 7, July 1996, p. 29). Irvine, California: Entrepreneur Media Inc. By Guen Sublette.

"Just a Mailbox Away" in *Black Enterprise.* (Vol. 27, No. 3, October 1996, p. 34). New York, New York: Earl G. Graves Publishing Co. Inc. By Robyn Clarke.

"Keep in Touch" in *Business Start-Ups.* (Vol. 8, No. 5, May 1996, pp. 8, 10). Irvine, California: Entrepreneur Media Inc. By Carla Goodman.

"Keep Your Firm From Zoning Out" in *Black Enterprise.* (Vol. 26, No. 8, March 1996, p. 29). New York, New York: Earl G. Graves Publishing Co. Inc. By Carolyn M. Brown.

"The Kiddie Zone" in *Income Opportunities.* (Vol. 30, No. 10, October 1995, pp. 32, 34, 36). New York, New York: IO Publications, Inc. By Pamela Rohland.

"Kids Underfoot" in *Business Start-Ups.* (Vol. 8, No. 1, January 1996, p. 16). Irvine, California: Entrepreneur Media Inc. By Johanna S. Billings.

"Love Bytes" in *Income Opportunities.* (Vol. 30, No. 7, July 1995, p. 8). New York, New York: IO Publications, Inc. By Lana Sanderson.

"Make the Guidelines Clear When Home, Office Overlap" in *Crain's Small Business.* (December 1996, pp. 10-11). Detroit, Michigan: Crain Communications Inc. By Jeffrey McCracken.

"Making It Big" in *Business Start-Ups.* (Vol. 7, No. 10, October 1995, p. 16). Irvine, California: Entrepreneur Media Inc.

"Marketing Magic" in *Business Start-Ups.* (Vol. 7, No. 9, September 1995, pp. 12, 14). Irvine, California: Entrepreneur Media Inc. By Sue Clayton.

"Medical Transcription" in *Business Start-Ups.* (Vol. 9, No. 1, January 1997, p. 30). Irvine, California: Entrepreneur Media Inc. By Karin Moeller.

"Meeting of the Minds" in *Entrepreneur.* (August 1996, p. 55). Irvine, California: Entrepreneur Media Inc. By Cynthia E. Griffin.

"Minimize Your Exposure" in *Hispanic Business.* (Vol. 18, No. 11, November 1996, p. 58). Santa Barbara, California: Hispanic Business Inc. By Rick Mendosa.

"Mixed Signals" in *Income Opportunities.* (Vol. 30, No. 10, October 1995, p. 10). New York, New York: IO Publications, Inc. By Lana Sanderson.

"Money from Home" in *Income Opportunities.* (Vol. 29, No. 11, November 1994, pp. 28-34). New York, New York: IO Publications Inc. By Robert L. Perry.

"Moving Day" in *Income Opportunities.* (Vol. 30, No. 11, November 1995, p. 10). New York, New York: IO Publications, Inc. By Lana Sanderson.

"Moving Out" in *Income Opportunities.* (Vol. 32, No. 4, April 1997, pp. 1418, 88). New York, New York: IO Publications Inc. By Dale D. Buss.

"Name That Business" in *Business Start-Ups.* (Vol. 8, No. 4, April 1996, pp. 18, 20). Irvine, California: Entrepreneur Media Inc. By Sue Clayton.

"Name Your Price" in *Entrepreneur.* (Vol. 24, No. 4, April 1996, p. 52). Irvine, California: Entrepreneur Media, Inc. By Cynthia E. Griffin.

"Necessary Ingredients" in *Entrepreneur.* (Vol. 23, No. 5, May 1995, pp. 62, 64-65). Irvine, California: Entrepreneur Media, Inc. By Cynthia E. Griffin.

"Networking from Home" in *Business Start-Ups.* (Vol. 7, No. 11, November 1995, p. 14). Irvine, California: Entrepreneur Media Inc. By Sue Clayton.

"A New Resolve" in *Income Opportunities.* (Vol. 31, No. 1, January 1996, p. 10). New York, New York: IO Publications, Inc. By Lana Sanderson.

"No Place Like Home" in *Black Enterprise.* (Vol. 25, No. 8, March 1995, p. 39). New York, New York: Earl G. Graves Publishing Co. Inc. By Nadirah Z. Sabir.

"No Place Like Home" in *Hispanic Business.* (Vol. 16, No. 9, September 1994, pp. 50, 52). Santa Barbara, California: Hispanic Business, Inc. By Maria Zate.

"Noise Pollution" in *Income Opportunities.* (Vol. 31, No. 6, June 1996, p. 10). New York, New York: IO Publications Inc. By Lana Sanderson.

"Northern Exposure" in *Entrepreneur.* (Vol. 23, No. 2, February 1995, pp. 80, 82). Irvine, California: Entrepreneur Media, Inc. By Debra Phillips.

"Not-So-Impossible Dream" in *Small Business Opportunities.* (Vol. 8, No. 6, November 1996, pp. 92, 110). New York, New York: Harris Publications, Inc. By Lin Grensing-Pophal.

"On Her Soapbox" in *Income Opportunities.* (Vol. 32, No. 2, 1997, pp. 88, 90, 92). New York, New York: IO Publications Inc. By Laurel Berger.

"On Location" in *Entrepreneur.* (Vol. 23, No. 3, March 1995, pp. 86, 89). Irvine, California: Entrepreneur Media, Inc. By Debra Phillips.

"On The Home Front" in *Income Opportunities.* (Vol. 31, No. 4, April 1996, pp. 54-60, 62, 64-65, 72). New York, New York: IO Publications, Inc. By Robert L. Perry.

"One Hundred One Home Business Money Makers" in *Income Opportunities.* (Mid-March 1993, pp. 35-38, 50, 52, 54, 56, 58, 60-65). New York, New York: IO Publications, Inc.

"Order from Chaos" in *Small Business Opportunities.* (Vol. 9, No. 2, March 1997, pp. 12, 146). New York, New York: Harris Publications, Inc. By Marie Sherlock.

"Out of the Ashes" in *Entrepreneur.* (November 1996, pp. 66, 68). Irvine, California: Entrepreneur Media Inc. By Cynthia E. Griffin.

"Parental Advice" in *Business Start-Ups.* (Vol. 7, No. 11, November 1995, p. 17). Irvine, California: Entrepreneur Media Inc.

"Plan Healthy Schedule for Work at Home" in *Crain's Small Business.* (January 1996, p. 4). Detroit, Michigan: Crain Communications, Inc. By Frank Provenzano.

"Pressing Matters" in *Income Opportunities.* (Vol. 31, No. 9, October 1996, pp. 94, 96). New York, New York: IO Publications Inc. By Kendra Russell.

"The Quiet Revolution" in *Entrepreneur.* (September 1993, pp. 77-81). Irvine, California: Entrepreneur, Inc. By Janean Huber.

"Real Money Starts Here" in *Crain's Detroit Business.* (Vol. 10, No. 41, October 10-16, 1994, pp. 1, 26). Detroit, Michigan: Crain's Communications, Inc. By Michael Maurer.

"Resume Writing" in *Business Start-Ups.* (Vol. 8, No. 7, July 1996, p. 28). Irvine, California: Entrepreneur Media Inc. By Guen Sublette.

"The Right Connection" in *Income Opportunities.* (Vol. 29, No. 9, September 1994, pp. 30-31). New York, New York: IO Publications Inc. By John T. Cleland.

"Right Moves" in *Business Start-Ups.* (Vol. 7, No. 10, October 1995, p. 14). Irvine, California: Entrepreneur Media Inc. By Sue Clayton.

"Rule of Engagement" in *Business Start-Ups.* (Vol. 8, No. 7, July 1996, pp. 8, 10). Irvine, California: Entrepreneur Media Inc. By Janie Sullivan.

"Safe and Sound" in *Business Start-Ups.* (Vol. 8, No. 10, October 1996, pp. 8, 10). Irvine, California: Entrepreneur Media Inc. By Julie Bawden Davis.

"Self Worth" in *Income Opportunities.* (Vol. 30, No. 9, September 1995, p. 10). New York, New York: IO Publications, Inc. By Lana Sanderson.

"Sending Workers Home—To Work" in *Independent Business.* (Vol. 7, No. 4, July/Aug. 1996, pp. 20-22). Thousands Oaks, California: Group IV Communications Inc. By Verna Gates.

"Separation Anxiety" in *Business Start-Ups.* (Vol. 9, No. 1, January 1997, pp. 8, 10). Irvine, California: Entrepreneur Media Inc. By Carolyn Campbell.

"The Service Boom" in *Small Business Opportunities.* (Vol. 9, No. 3, May 1997, pp. 22-41). New York, New York: Harris Publications, Inc.

"Setting Up at Home" in *Black Enterprise.* (Vol. 24, No. 12, July 1994, pp. 36-38). New York, New York: Earl G. Graves Publishing Co. Inc. By Rhonda Reynolds.

"Shattering the Myth" in *Income Opportunities.* (Vol. 29, No. 7, July 1994, p. 34). New York, New York: IO Publications Inc. By Jo Frohbieter-Mueller.

"Shoestring Start-Ups" in *Income Opportunities.* (Vol. 31,

No. 2, February 1996, pp. 22-25, 72, 74, 80-81, 88, 90). New York, New York: IO Publications, Inc. By Lori Schwind Murray.

"Shoestring Start-Ups" in *Income Opportunities*. (Vol. 30, No. 1, January 1995, pp. 34-44). New York, New York: IO Publications, Inc. By Lori Schwind Murray.

"Shoestring Start-Ups" in *Income Opportunities*. (Vol. 32, No. 4, April 1997, pp. 20-23, 76, 82, 84, 86). New York, New York: IO Publications Inc. By Lori Schwind Murray.

"Silver Lining" in *Entrepreneur*. (June 1995, pp. 52, 54-55). Irvine, California: Entrepreneur Media Inc. By Cynthia E. Griffin.

"Solid Foundations" in *Black Enterprise*. (Vol. 27, No. 7, February 1997, p. 38). New York, New York: Earl G. Graves Publishing Co. Inc. By Denolyn Carroll.

"The Stamp of Success" in *Income Opportunities*. (Vol. 30, No. 5, May 1995, pp. 35-36, 94, 102). New York, New York: IO Publications, Inc. By Amy H. Berger.

"Start a Home Business With $500—Or Less" in *Woman's Day*. (October 2, 1990, pp. 34-38). New York, New York: Hachette Magazine, Inc. By Robin Warshaw.

"Start-Up Chasers Track New-Biz Storm" in *Inc.* (Vol. 19, No. 5, April 1997, p. 22). Boston, Massachusetts: Goldhirsh Group, Inc. By Jerry Useem.

"Staying Sane" in *Business Start-Ups*. (Vol. 7, No. 10, October 1995, pp. 14, 16). Irvine, California: Entrepreneur Media Inc.

"Step 2: Do Your Homework" in *Business Start-Ups*. (Vol. 8, No. 6, June 1996, pp. 8, 10). Irvine, California: Entrepreneur Media Inc. By Kylo-Patrick Hart.

"Sun Block" in *Income Opportunities*. (Vol. 30, No. 6, June 1995, p. 8). New York, New York: IO Publications, Inc. By Lana Sanderson.

"Taking Stock" in *Income Opportunities*. (Vol. 31, No. 3, March 1996, p. 10). New York, New York: IO Publications, Inc. By Lana Sanderson.

"Tech Tools: No Mixed Signals" in *Business Start-Ups*. (Vol. 7, No. 6, June 1995, p. 19). Irvine, California: Entrepreneur Media Inc. By Irene Bennet.

"Technical Difficulties" in *Income Opportunities*. (Vol. 31, No. 8, August 1996, p. 12). New York, New York: IO Publications Inc. By Lana Sanderson.

"Ten Easy-to-Start Home Businesses" in *Income Opportunities*. (December 1993, pp. 51-56, 91, 93-95, 97). New York, New York: IO Publications, Inc. By Tyler G. Hiccks.

"The Top. 10 Home-Based Businesses to Start Now!" in *Small Business Opportunities*. (March 1994, pp. 22-39). New York, New York: Harris Publications, Inc.

"Tough Calls" in *Income Opportunities*. (Vol. 31, No. 11, November 1996, p. 12). New York, New York: IO Publications Inc. By Lana Sanderson.

"12-Step Program" in *Business Start-Ups*. (Vol. 7, No. 7, July 1995, p. 20). Irvine, California: Entrepreneur Media Inc.

"Twenty-Five Best Home-Based Businesses to Start Right Now" in *Income Opportunities*. (Mid-March 1990, pp. 47-50). New York, New York: IO Publications, Inc. By Stephen Wagner.

"United We Stand" in *Business Start-Ups*. (Vol. 7, No. 8, August 1995, pp. 14-15). Irvine, California: Entrepreneur Media Inc.

"An Untapped Market: The Home-Based Business" in *Direct Marketing*. (April 1991, pp. 37-38). Garden City, New York: Hoke Communications, Inc. By David L. Biddulph.

"Video Ventures" in *Small Business Opportunities*. (Vol. 6, No. 5, September 1994, p. 68). New York, New York: Harris Publications, Inc.

"When Mom Works at Home" in *Money*. (Vol. 23, No. 10, October 1994, pp. 126-136). New York, New York: Time Inc. By Lani Luciano.

"Work, Suite Work" in *Crain's Small Business* Office Tech '96 Supplement. (Vol. 4, No. 11, November 1996, p. T-9). Detroit, Michigan: Crain Communications Inc. By Regina Baraban.

"Working Around the Family" in *Income Opportunities*. (October 1993, pp. 60-61, 90). New York, New York: IO Publications, Inc. By Joan Wester Anderson.

"The Year of Living Dangerously" in *Business Start-Ups*. (Vol. 7, No. 6, June 1995, pp. 74, 76-77). Irvine, California: Entrepreneur Media Inc. By Jeannie Pearce.

"Your Home Business: A Winning Game Plan" in *Changing Times*. (February 1991, pp. 63-65). Washington, District of Columbia: Kiplinger Washington Editors, Inc. By Ronaleen R. Roha.

Incubators

"Al Geiger Aiming to Help Small Businesses Grow" in *The Business Journal*. (Vol. 11, No. 26, September 19, 1994, p. 16). Sacramento, California: Sacramento Business Journal. By Ray Dussault.

"Alphabet Soup" in *Inc.* (Vol. 16, No. 12, November 1994, pp. 31-32). Boston, Massachusetts: Goldhirsh Group, Inc. By Heather E. Stone.

"Birth of a Business" in *Hispanic Business.* (Vol. 18, No. 9, September 1996, p. 10). Santa Barbara, California: Hispanic Business Inc. By Rick Mendosa. Northern California business incubator program helps small Hispanic owned businesses. Cities with incubator programs willingly take this risk in order to assist in economic development.

"Blastoff" in *Forbes.* (Vol. 154, No. 5, August 29, 1994, p. 154). New York, New York: Forbes, Inc. By James M. Clash.

"A Boost for Start-Ups" in *Nation's Business.* (Vol. 80, No. 8, August 1992, p. 40). Washington, District of Columbia: U.S. Chamber of Commerce. By Bradford McKee.

"Business Incubation" in *California Business.* (Vol. 29, No. 5, September 1994, p. 10). Burlingame, California. By Claudia Viek.

"Cash Infusion to Incubator Nurtures Small Businesses" in *The Business Journal Serving Greater Sacramento.* (Vol. 11, No. 18, July 25, 1994, p. 2). Sacramento, California: Sacramento Business Journal. By Mike McCarthy.

"Company Coach" in *The Kansas City Business Journal.* (Vol. 12, No. 17, January 14, 1994, p. 3). Kansas City, Missouri: American City Business Journals, Inc. By Barry Henderson.

"Fledgling Business Incubator Hatches 13 New Enterprises" in *The Business Journal.* (Vol. 12, No. 31, October 31, 1994, p. 13). Sacramento, California: Sacramento Business Journal. By Michele Hostetler.

"Growing Places" in *Entrepreneur.* (Vol. 23, No. 2, February 1995, pp. 108, 110-113). Irvine, California: Entrepreneur Media, Inc. By Cynthia E. Griffin.

"Hatching a Business" in *Small Business Opportunities.* (Vol. 8, No. 5, September 1996, pp. 78, 80). New York, New York: Harris Publications, Inc. By Mary Ann McLaughlin.

"Hatching a New Venture" in *EDN.* (Vol. 39, No. 17, August 18, 1994, p. 51). Newton, Massachusetts: Cahners Publishing Co.

"How to Hatch New Businesses" in *D & B Reports.* (Vol. 39, No. 4, July/August 1991, pp. 54-55). New York, New York: Dun & Bradstreet. By Bill Hogan.

"Incubator Boosts LI's High Tech" in *Long Island Business News.* (No. 6, February 7, 1994, p. 3T).

Ronkonkoma, New York: Long Island Commercial Review, Inc. By Christopher Hord.

"Incubator Roundup" in *Entrepreneur.* (Vol. 23, No. 11, October 1995, p. 188). Irvine, California: Entrepreneur Media, Inc. By Cynthia E. Griffin.

"Incubators Nurture Start-Up Firms: Do Incubators Really Work?" in *Computerworld.* (Vol. 25, No. 37, September 16, 1991, pp. 105, 112). Framingham, Massachusetts: Computerworld, Inc. By Johanna Ambrosio.

"New Product Incubator: Pilot Plant Helps Processors Develop New Products" in *Dairy Foods.* (Vol. 95, No. 9, September 1994, p. 139). Des Plaines, Illinois: Cahners Publishing Co.

"Tech Incubator Growing Up" in *Denver Business Journal.* (Vol. 46, No. 15, December 23, 1994, p. 1B). Denver, Colorado: American City Business Journals By Tom Locke.

"Trapped in the Nest? Start-Up Firms Try to Fly" in *Baltimore Business Journal.* (Vol. 12, No. 9, July 22, 1994, p. 1). Baltimore, Maryland: American City Business Journals, Inc. By Greg Abel.

"VC Incubators Are Hatching New Companies Again" in *Electronic Business Buyer.* (Vol. 20, No. 1, January 1994, p. 90). Newton, Massachusetts: Cahners Publishing Co. By Stephen W. Quickel.

"What the Incubators Have Hatched" in *Planning.* (Vol. 58, No. 5, May 1992, pp. 28-30). Chicago, Illinois: American Planning Association. By Richard Steffens.

"Where Dreams Get Hope" in *Crain's Detroit Business.* (Vol. 12, No. 16, April 1996, pp. 3, 26). Detroit, Michigan: Crain Communications Inc. By Robert Akeny.

"Yellow Brick Road Winds into Florida" in *Orlando Business Journal.* (Vol. 10, No. 35, February 4, 1994, p. 16). Orlando, Florida: American City Business Journals. By Danialle Weaver.

Manufacturing Business

"1996 Small Business Entrepreneurs of the Year" in *Black Enterprise.* (Vol. 27, No. 4, November 1996, pp. 75-77). New York, New York: Earl G. Graves Publishing Co. Inc. By Robyn Clarke.

"Anasteel & Supply Co." in *Hispanic Business.* (Vol. 18, No. 6, June 1996, p. 106). Santa Barbara, California: Hispanic Business Inc. By Graham Witherall.

"Beyond Latin America" in *Hispanic Business.* (Vol. 18, No. 11, November 1996, pp. 34, 36, 38, 40-41). Santa

Barbara, California: Hispanic Business Inc. By Joel Russell.

"Chain Reaction" in *Income Opportunities*. (Vol. 30, No. 1, January 1995, pp. 26-28, 30, 33). New York, New York: IO Publications, Inc. By Dale D. Buss.

"Clothes Make the Man" in *Business Start-Ups*. (Vol. 7, No. 7, July 1995, pp. 62, 64, 66). Irvine, California: Entrepreneur Media Inc. By Pamala Rohland.

"Crash Course" in *Inc.* (Vol. 17, No. 2, February 1995, pp. 54-56, 59-63). Boston, Massachusetts: Goldhirsh Group, Inc. By Robert A. Mamis.

"Doing Business in South Africa" in *Black Enterprise*. (Vol. 25, No. 10, May 1995, pp. 58-62, 67-68). New York, New York: Earl G. Graves Publishing Co. Inc. By Frank McCoy.

"Entrepreneurial Superstars" in *Entrepreneur*. (April 1997, pp. 108-139). Irvine, California: Entrepreneur Media Inc. By Debra Phillips and others.

"Entrepreneurs Across America" in Entrepreneur. (Vol. 24, No. 4, April 1996, pp. 100-104, 106-108, 110-112, 114-116, 118, 120-123). Irvine, California: Entrepreneur Media, Inc. By Janean Chum, Debra Phillips, Cynthia E. Griffin, Heather Page, Lynn Beresford, Holly Celeste Fisk, and Charlotte Mulbern.

"Legends" in *Small Business Opportunities*. (Vol. 7, No. 1, January 1995, pp. 46, 48). New York, New York: Harris Publications, Inc.

"Make Your Service Fail-Safe" in *Sloan Management Review*. (Vol. 35, No. 3, Spring 1994, pp. 35-44). Cambridge, Massachusetts: Massachusetts Institute of Technology, Sloan School of Management. By Richard B. Chase and Douglas M. Stewart.

"Metallurgical Urge Beats Martial Plan" in *Crain's Small Business*. (July 1996, p. 15). Detroit, Michigan: Crain Communications Inc. By Jeffrey McCracken.

"New York" in *Hispanic Business*. (Vol. 17, No. 5, May 1995, p. 36). Santa Barbara, California: Hispanic Business Inc. By Yvonne Conde.

"Outsourcery" in *Inc.* (Vol. 19, No. 5, April 1997, pp. 54-56, 58, 60). Boston, Massachusetts: Goldhirsh Group, Inc. By Edward O. Welles.

"Pricing by the Numbers" in *Inc. Technology*. (Vol. 16, No. 13, p. 101). Boston, Massachusetts: Goldhirsh Group, Inc. By Phaedra Hise.

"A Profitable Feast" in *Business Start-Ups*. (Vol. 8, No. 6, June 1996, pp. 60, 62-66). Irvine, California: Entrepreneur Media Inc. By Sandra Mardenfeld.

"Prototyping Firm 'can Hardly Keep Up' with Work" in *Crain's Detroit Business*. (Vol. 13, No. 6, February 1997, p. 31). Detroit, Michigan: Crain Communications Inc. By Arthur Bridgeforth Jr.

"Rainbow's Good Luck" in *Crain's Detroit Business*. (Vol. 13, No. 13, March/April 1997, pp. 3, 14). Detroit, Michigan: Crain Communications Inc. By Matt Roush.

"Running out of Time" in *Inc.* (Vol. 19, No. 2, February 1997, pp. 63-64, 68, 72-73). Boston, Massachusetts: Goldhirsh Group, Inc. By John Grossmann.

"Shady Business" in *Small Business Opportunities*. (Vol. 6, No. 5, September 1994, p. 40). New York, New York: Harris Publications, Inc. By Robin Montgomery.

"Sole Survivor" in *Inc.* (Vol. 16, No. 6, June 1994, pp. 50-60). Boston, Massachusetts: Goldhirsh Group, Inc. By John Case.

"Stamp out Bad Checks" in *Black Enterprise*. (Vol. 27, No. 3, October 1996, p. 36). New York, New York: Earl G. Graves Publishing Co. Inc. By Ann L. Brown

"This Big One Didn't Get Away" in *Crain's Detroit Business*. (Vol. 12, No. 35, Aug. 26-Sept. 1, 1996, pp. 3, 26). Detroit, Michigan: Crain Communications Inc. By Joseph Serwach.

Metal Shop

"Cheap Funding For Free Enterprise" in *Journal of European Business*. (Vol. 5, No. 4, March/April 1994, pp. 8- 12). New York, New York, Faulkner & Gray, Inc. Editor, Sam Lambroza.

"Even Old Machines Can Thrive in High-Tech World" in *Crain's Small Business*. (June 1996, p. 6). Detroit, Michigan, Crain Communications Inc. Editor, Dave Guilford.

"Industrial Innovation Among Small and Medium-Sized Firms" in *Growth & Change*. (Vol. 25, No. 2, Spring 1994, pp. 145-163). Lexington, Kentucky, University of Kentucky. Editor, Alan D. MacPherson.

"It Cuts Both Ways" in *Crain's Detroit Business*. (Vol. 10, No. 41, October 10-16, 1994, p. 9). Detroit, Michigan, Crain's Communications, Inc. Editor, Marilyn Sambrano.

"Just-In-Time" in *Industrial Management*. (Vol. 36, No. 4, July/August 1994, pp. 23-26). Norcross, Georgia, Institute of Industrial Engineers. Editor, Vidyaranya B. Gargeya and Johnathan B. Thompson.

"Making a Difference" in *Forbes*. (Vol. 153, No. 10, May 9, 1994, pp. 164-165). New York, New York, Forbes, Inc.

Editor, Gail Buchalter.

"Manufacturing: Smaller is Better, Nimbler, Cheaper" in *Nation's Business.* (Vol. 82, No. 4, April 1994, pp. 49-50). Washington, District of Columbia, U.S. Chamber of Commerce. Editor, John S. DeMott.

"Micro Factories Aid Competition" in *American Metal Market.* (Vol. 96, No. 54, March 18, 1988, p. 14). New York, New York, Capital Cities - ABC, Inc., Diversified Publishing Group. Editor, D. Bruce Merrifield.

"Tool Company: Just Grow with It" in *Crain's Small Business.* (December 1995, pp. 25-26). Detroit, Michigan, Crain Communications, Inc. Editor, Jeffrey McCracken.

Nontraditional Financing

"Angels in Cyberspace" in *Hispanic Business.* (Vol. 20, No. 3, March 1997, pp. 38, 40). Santa Barbara, California: Hispanic Business Inc. By Rick Mendosa.

"A Capital Idea Helps Nurture Small Firms in Wayne County" in *Crain's Small Business.* (October 1995, p. 21). Detroit, Michigan: Crain Communications, Inc. By Pam Woodside.

"Cards May Be Ticket to Survive Cash-Flow Crunch" in *Crain's Small Business.* (March 1996, p. 14). Detroit, Michigan: Crain Communications, Inc. By Lawrence Gardner.

"Found Money" in *Entrepreneur.* (Vol. 23, No. 4, April 1995, pp. 108-110, 112-115). Irvine, California: Entrepreneur Media, Inc. By David R. Evanson.

"Franchises That Offer Creative Financing" in *Business Start-Ups.* (Vol. 8, No. 9, September 1996, pp. 62, 64, 67-68). Irvine, California: Entrepreneur Media Inc. By Andrew A. Caffey.

"Get Cash Now!" in *Success.* (Vol. 38, No. 10, December 1991, pp. 26-32). New York, New York: Lang Communications. By Ronit Addis Rose.

"Going Public on Main Street, Not Wall Street" in *Working Woman.* (June 1996, p. 11). New York, New York: MacDonald Communications Corporation. By Kerry Hannon.

"Hatching Uncle Sam's Entrepreneurs" in *Management Today.* (November 1993, pp. 54-56). London: Haymarket Management Magazines By John Thackray.

"How to Obtain Export Capital" in *Nation's Business.* (Vol. 82, No. 5, May 1994, p. 24). Washington, District of Columbia: U.S. Chamber of Commerce

"Kid Venture Capital" in *Black Enterprise.* (Vol. 25, No.

5, December 1994, p. 34). New York, New York: Earl G. Graves Publishing Co. Inc. By Tonia L. Shakespeare.

"LEAF Me a Loan" in *Business Start-Ups.* (Vol. 8, No. 1, January 1996, pp. 74-75). Irvine, California: Entrepreneur Media Inc.

"Leasing Lessons" in *Business Start-Ups.* (Vol. 8, No. 2, February 1996, p. 72). Irvine, California: Entrepreneur Media Inc. By Eric J. Adams.

"Look at Every Option—And Beyond" in *Nation's Business.* (Vol. 79, No. 7, July 1991, p. 9). Washington, District of Columbia: U.S. Chamber of Commerce. By Thomas Hierl.

"Money Hunting" in *Hispanic Business.* (Vol. 19, No. 1, January 1997, pp. 28, 30). Santa Barbara, California: Hispanic Business Inc. By Joel Russell.

"The Money Is Out There...How To Get It" in *Agency Sales Magazine.* (Vol. 24, No. 2, February 1994, pp. 15-17). Laguna Hills, California: Manufacturers' Agents National Association. By Jeff Fromberg.

"A New Loan Option to Bank, Venture Capital" in *Crain's Small Business.* (February 1996, pp. 9-10). Detroit, Michigan: Crain Communications, Inc. By Jeffrey McCracken.

"19 Sources of Capital for Your Start-Up" in *Income Opportunities.* (Vol. 31, No. 2, February 1996, pp. 26-30). New York, New York: IO Publications, Inc. By Terri Cullen.

"Northern Exposure" in *Entrepreneur.* (Vol. 23, No. 5, May 1995, p. 15). Irvine, California: Entrepreneur Media, Inc. By Cynthia E. Griffin.

"The Numbers Speak Volumes" in *Small Business Reports.* (Vol. 19, No. 7, July 1994, pp. 39-43). New York, New York: Faulkner & Gray, Inc. By Lamont Change.

"Options, Discounts Are in the Cards" in *Crain's Small Business.* (Vol. 5, No. 4, April 1997, pp. 1, 20). Detroit, Michigan: Crain Communications Inc. By Jeffrey McCracken.

"Peer Power" in *Entrepreneur.* (Vol. 23, No. 4, April 1995, p. 15). Irvine, California: Entrepreneur Media, Inc. By Heather Page.

"Plastic Surgery" in *Crain's Small Business.* (Vol. 5, No. 4, April 1997, pp. 1, 20,-21). Detroit, Michigan: Crain Communications Inc. By Jeffrey McCracken.

"Play Misty for Me" in *Business Start-Ups.* (Vol. 7, No. 9, September 1995, p. 114). Irvine, California: Entrepreneur Media Inc. By Eric J. Adams.

"Program Gives Small Businesses a Financial Boost" in *Entrepreneur.* (Vol. 32, No. 7, July 1995, p. 17). Irvine, California: Entrepreneur Media, Inc. By Cynthia E. Griffin.

"Saving on Next-Day Delivery" in *Black Enterprise.* (Vol. 27, No. 5, December 1996, p. 36). New York, New York: Earl G. Graves Publishing Co. Inc. By Ann Brown.

"The Secrets of Bootstrapping" in *Inc.* (Vol. 13, No. 9, September 1991, pp. 52-70). Boston, Massachusetts: Goldhirsh Group, Inc. By Robert A. Mamis.

"The Six Best Ways to Raise Cash" in *Money Money Guide Supplement.* (Vol. , No. , 1994, pp. 34-39). New York, New York: Time, Inc. By Vanessa O'Connell.

"Small Loans, Big Dreams" in *Working Woman.* (Vol. 20, No. 2, February 1995, pp. 46-49, 72-73, 77). New York, New York: Working Woman, Inc. By Elizabeth Kadetsky.

"Stocking Up" in *Entrepreneur.* (April 1997, pp. 58, 60-61). Irvine, California: Entrepreneur Media Inc. By David R. Evanson.

"Treasure Hunt" in *Business Start-Ups.* (Vol. 7, No. 7, July 1995, 56-58, 60-61). Irvine, California: Entrepreneur Media Inc. By Gloria Gibbs Marullo.

"Where Are All the Wanda Buffets?" in *Money.* (Vol. 23, No. 11, November 1994, pp. 116-117). New York, New York: Time Inc. By Nancy J. Perry.

"Where to Look for Money Now" in *Working Woman.* (Vol. 19, No. 10, October 1994, pp. 56-62). New York, New York: Working Woman, Inc. By Ilyce R. Glink.

Office Furniture Retailer

"An Ageless Craft" in *Income Opportunities.* (Vol. 30, No. 6, June 1995, pp. 68, 70-71). New York, New York, IO Publications, Inc. Editor, Amy H. Berger.

"The Art of Making Old Things New: Furniture Magic" in *Income Opportunities.* (May 1994, pp. 46, 48). New York, New York, IO Publications, Inc.Editor, Mildred Jailer.

"Chairwoman of the Board" in *Small Business Opportunities.* (Vol. 8, No. 3, May 1996, pp. 86, 88). New York, New York, Harris Publications, Inc. Editor, Geri Anderson.

"Cleaning Up" in *Business Start-Ups.* (Vol. 7, No. 8, August 1995, pp. 26-31, 33). Irvine, California, Entrepreneur Media Inc. Editor, Glen Webber and Lynn Norquist.

"Couldn't Stand the Heat, So They Got into Kitchens" in *Crain's Small Business.* (November 1994, p. 21). Detroit, Michigan, Crain's Communications, Inc. Editor, Jeffery McCracken.

"Fix-it Shop Profits" in *Small Business Opportunities.* (Vol. 6, No. 6, November 1994, pp. 38, 40- 41). New York, New York, Harris Publications, Inc. Editor, Robin Montgomery.

"New & Noteworthy" in *Income Opportunities.* (Vol. 29, No. 9, September 1994, pp. 40-46). New York, New York, IO Publications Inc. Editor, Robert L. Perry.

"A Re-Engineered Life" in *Business Start-Ups.* (Vol. 7, No. 6, June 1995, p. 116). Irvine, California, Entrepreneur Media Inc. Editor, Carl Bryant.

"Remanufacturing an Idea on No Money" in *Crain's Small Business.* (December 1995, pp. 22-23). Detroit, Michigan, Crain Communications, Inc. Editor, Michelle Krebs.

"Three Cheers for Chair Repair" in *Income Opportunities.* (September 1992, pp. 59, 74, 76, 78, 85). New York, New York, IO Publications, Inc. Editor, B. Jack Gebhardt.

"Wood Work" in *Small Business Opportunities.* (Vol. 8, No. 5, September 1996, p. 72). New York, New York, Harris Publications, Inc.

Restaurant/Microbrewery

"A&W Plants Roots as Growing Fast-Food Chain" in *Crain's Detroit Business.* (Vol. 13, No. 6, February 1997, pp. 3, 32). Detroit, Michigan, Crain Communications Inc. Editor, Marsha Stopa.

"Affordable Fast Food" in *Income Opportunities.* (Vol. 29, No. 8, August 1994, pp. 22, 24, 26, 28, 30-31). New York, New York, IO Publications Inc. Editor, Robert L. Perry.

"Area Code Cafe Dials into Customer Connections" in *Nation's Restaurant News.* (Vol. 28, No. 34, August 29, 1994, p. 12). New York, New York, Lebhar-Friedman, Inc. Editor, Peter O. Keegan.

"Arresting Success" in *Small Business Opportunities.* (Vol. 6, No. 6, November 1994, p. 68). New York, New York, Harris Publications, Inc.

"At Lagerheads" in *Inc.* (Vol. 16, No. 3, March 1994, p. 36). Boston, Massachusetts, Goldhirsh Group, Inc. Editor, Alessandra Bianchi.

"Beer" in *Entrepreneur.* (February 1994, pp. 168, 170-171). Irvine, California, Entrepreneur, Inc. Editor, Gayle Sato Stodder.

"Best Bets" in *Entrepreneur.* (December 1996, pp. 108-112). Irvine, California, Entrepreneur Media Inc. Editor,

Lynn Bersford and Heather Page.

"Bit O' the Green" in *Entrepreneur.* (March 1997, p. 156). Irvine, California, Entrepreneur Media Inc. Editor, C.M.

"Biz Men Put Their Bucks on the Block" in *Crain's Small Business.* (Vol. 5, No. 4, April 1997, pp. 16-17, 19). Detroit, Michigan, Crain Communications Inc. Editor, Jeffrey McCracken.

"A Brew Apart" in *Inc.* (Vol. 18, No. 3, March 1996, pp. 62-64, 67-69). Boston, Massachusetts, Goldhirsh Group, Inc. Editor, Christopher Caggiano.

"Brew Pubs Are Hoppin'" in *New Business Opportunities.* (December 1989, pp. 26-31). Irvine, California, Entrepreneur, Inc. Editor, Kevin McLaughlin.

"Brewed to Perfection" in *Income Opportunities.* (Vol. 31, No. 9, September 1996, pp. 14-18). New York, New York, IO Publications Inc. Editor, Pamela Rohland.

"Brewing Success" in *Crain's Detroit Business.* (Vol. 12, No. 35, Aug. 26-Sept. 1, 1996, p. 9). Detroit, Michigan, Crain Communications Inc. Editor, Tim Moran.

"Business du Jour" in *Entrepreneurial Woman.* (March/April 1990, pp. 73-77). Irvine, California, Entrepreneur, Inc. Editor, Erika Kotite.

"Cider Makers Hope to Reprise Success of Microbrewers" in *Wall Street Journal.* (Vol. lxxviii, No. 12, October 26, 1996, pp. B1-B2). New York, New York, Wall Street Journal, Dow Jones & Co., Inc. Editor, Stephanie N. Mehta.

"Could Drive You to Drink" in *Crain's Small Business.* (December 1996, pp. 8-9). Detroit, Michigan, Crain Communications Inc. Editor, Jeffrey McCracken.

"Counter Culture" in *Entrepreneur.* (November 1996, pp. 110, 112-113). Irvine, California, Entrepreneur Media Inc. Editor, Gayle Sato Stodder.

"Delicious Success" in *Selling Power.* (Vol. 16, No. 3, April 1996, pp. 65-66, 68). Fredericksburg, Virginia, Selling Power, Inc. Editor, Malcolm Fleschner.

"Directory of Food Industry Resources" in *Income Opportunities.* (Vol. 31, No. 8, August 1996, pp. 26-27). New York, New York, IO Publications Inc. Editor, Stephanie Jeffrey.

"Double Take" in *Income Opportunities.* (Vol. 31, No. 5, May 1996, pp. 92, 94). New York, New York, IO Publications Inc. Editor, Maria Garcia.

"Dreams That Were Brought Up in a Barn" in *Crain's Small Business.* (December 1995, p. 15). Detroit, Michigan, Crain Communications, Inc. Editor, Jeffrey McCracken.

"Eating, Drinking Places Among Most Appetizing" in *Crain's Small Business.* (October 1995, p. 13). Detroit, Michigan, Crain Communications, Inc. Editor, Jeffrey McCracken.

"An Enterprise on Tap" in *Nation's Business.* (Vol. 82, No. 7, July 1994, p. 17). Washington, District of Columbia, U.S. Chamber of Commerce. Editor, Rosalind Resnick.

"Entrepreneurial Spirit Awards" in *Hispanic Business.* (Vol. 18, No. 12, December 1996, pp. 26, 28, 30, 34, 36, 38). Santa Barbara, California, Hispanic Business Inc. Editor, Maria Zate.

"Entrepreneurial Superstars" in *Entrepreneur.* (April 1997, pp. 108-139). Irvine, California, Entrepreneur Media Inc. Editor, Debra Phillips and others.

"Fast Cash in Fast Food" in *Small Business Opportunities.* (Vol. 6, No. 5, September 1994, p. 46). New York, New York, Harris Publications, Inc.

"Fast-Food Operator Braces for Price War" in *Detroit Free Press.* (February 28, pp. 1e-2e). Detroit, Michigan, Knight-Ridder, Inc. Editor, Vintage Foster.

"Finding Your Niche" in *Small Business Reports.* (Vol. 19, No. 1, January 1994, p. 22). New York, New York, Faulkner & Gray, Inc. Editor, Jenny C. McCune.

"For Restaurateurs, Excellence Is Merely First Course" in *Crain's Small Business.* (October 1995, p. 6). Detroit, Michigan, Crain Communications, Inc. Editor, Dave Guilford.

"From Beer to Eternity" in *Business Start-Ups.* (Vol. 9, No. 2, February 1997, pp. 36, 38-40). Irvine, California, Entrepreneur Media Inc. Editor, Bob Weinstein.

"Gatzaros' Projects" in *Crain's Detroit Business.* (Vol. 11, No. 9, February 27-March 5, 1995, pp. 38-39). Detroit, Michigan, Crain's Communications, Inc. Editor, Michael Goodin.

"A Glass of Handmade" in *Atlantic Monthly.* (November 1987, pp. 75-80). New York, New York, Atlantic Monthly.

"Go for It" in *Black Enterprise.* (Vol. 27, No. 7, February 1997, pp. 72-73). New York, New York, Earl G. Graves Publishing Co. Inc. Editor, Cassandra Hayes.

"Good for the Soul" in *Entrepreneur.* (April 1997, p. 16). Irvine, California, Entrepreneur Media Inc. Editor, J.C.

"Heady Brews: Amber Waves of Gain" in *Venture.* (January 1988, pp. 58-61). New York, New York, Venture

Magazine, Inc.

"High Spirits" in *Entrepreneur*. (July 1996, p. 26). Irvine, California, Entrepreneur Media Inc.

"Hot Plates" in *Entrepreneur*. (June 1995, p. 20). Irvine, California, Entrepreneur Media Inc.

"House Special" in *Entrepreneur*. (May 1996, p. 38). Irvine, California, Entrepreneur Media Inc.

"It's Going to Be a Cold One" in *Crain's Detroit Business*. (Vol. 12, No. 52, December 1996, pp. 3, 14). Detroit, Michigan, Crain Communications Inc. Editor, Marsha Stopa.

"Jammin'" in *Income Opportunities*. (Vol. 30, No. 6, June 1995, pp. 64, 66). New York, New York, IO Publications, Inc. Editor, Stephanie Jeffrey.

"Just Imagine!" in *Direct Marketing*. (Vol. 56, No. 12, April 1994, pp. 38-40). Long Island, New York, Hoke Communications. Editor, Ray Jutkins.

"Little Giants" in *Beverage World*. (Vol. 113, No. 1581, December 1994, pp. 26-35). Great Neck, New York, Keller International Publishing Corporation. Editor, Greg W. Prince.

"Local Pubs Go for the Gusto of Brewing" in *USA Today*. (January 24, 1989). Arlington, Virginia, Gannett Co., Inc.

"A Matter of Taste" in *Income Opportunities*. (Vol. 30, No. 8, August 1995, pp. 22-24, 68-70). New York, New York, IO Publications, Inc. Editor, Meg North.

"Mo' Better Zanzibar Blue" in *Black Enterprise*. (Vol. 27, No. 5, December 1996, pp. 106-114). New York, New York, Earl G. Graves Publishing Co. Inc. Editor, Caroline V. Clarke.

"Net Worth" in *Entrepreneur*. (December 1996, pp. 64, 66-67). Irvine, California, Entrepreneur Media Inc. Editor, David R. Evanson.

"New Venture Flying High" in *Black Enterprise*. (Vol. 27, No. 2, September 1996, p. 20). New York, New York, Earl G. Graves Publishing Co. Inc. Editor, Paula M. White.

"No Hang-Out Booths Here" in *Restaurant Hospitality*. (Vol. 75, No. 12, December 1991, pp. 122-128). Cleveland, Ohio, Penton Publishing. Editor, David Farkas.

"No More Singing the Blues" in *Black Enterprise*. (Vol. 27, No. 3, October 1996, p. 22). New York, New York, Earl G. Graves Publishing Co. Inc. Editor, Erin Aubrey.

"Opportunity Watch" in *Entrepreneur*. (Vol. 22, No. 9, September 1994, p. 216). Irvine, California, Entrepreneur Media, Inc. Editor, Laura Radloff.

"Plucking for Profits" in *Black Enterprise*. (Vol. 27, No. 9,

April 1997, p. 2830). New York, New York, Earl G. Graves Publishing Co. Inc. Editor, Scott Wade.

"Propitious Returns" in *Beverage World*. (Vol. 114, No. 1583, January 1995, pp. 38-47). Great Neck, New York, Keller International Publishing Corporation. Editor, Larry Jabbonsky.

"Pub Grub" in *Income Opportunities*. (Vol. 29, No. 8, August 1994, p. 127). New York, New York, IO Publications Inc. Editor, Bryce Webster.

"Raw Food Revolution" in *Black Enterprise*. (Vol. 25, No. 6, January 1995, p. 32). New York, New York, Earl G. Graves Publishing Co. Inc. Editor, Tonia L. Shakespeare.

"Reversal of Fortune" in *Income Opportunities*. (Vol. 30, No. 2, February 1995, pp. 54-55, 58-62). New York, New York, IO Publications Inc. Editor, Edmond M. Rosenthal.

"Roadkill Restaurateur" in *Crain's Detroit Business*. (Vol. 11, No. 9, February 27-March 5, 1995, pp. 3, 26). Detroit, Michigan, Crain's Communications, Inc. Editor, Marsha Stopa.

"The Six Best Ways to Raise Cash" in *Money Money Guide Supplement*. (Vol. , No. , 1994, pp. 34-39). New York, New York, Time, Inc. Editor, Vanessa O'Connell.

"Standing Room Only" in *Entrepreneur*. (July 1996, p. 17). Irvine, California, Entrepreneur Media Inc. Editor, L.B.

"Star Search" in *Entrepreneur*. (Vol.23, No. 8, August 1995, p. 12). Irvine, California, Entrepreneur Media, Inc. Editor, Janean Chun.

"Start-Up: Microbrewery" in *Entrepreneur*. (June 1992, pp. 134-138). Irvine, California, Entrepreneur, Inc. Editor, Angela LoSasso.

"Stocking Up" in *Business Start-Ups*. (Vol. 8, No. 12, 1997, pp. 14-15). Irvine, California, Entrepreneur Media Inc. Editor, Glen Weisman.

"Strange Brew" in *Income Opportunities*. (Vol. 29, No. 8, August 1994, pp. 68, 70-72, 74). New York, New York, IO Publications Inc. Editor, Bryce Webster.

"Top of the Hops" in *Entrepreneur*. (May 1996, p. 16). Irvine, California, Entrepreneur Media Inc. Editor, H.P.

"Turnaround Tactic" in *Independent Business*. (Vol. 7, No. 2, March/April 1996, p. 48). Thousand Oaks, California, Group IV Communications Inc.

"Turning the Tables" in *Entrepreneur*. (Vol. 23, No. 7, July 1995, pp. 18-19). Irvine, California, Entrepreneur Media, Inc. Editor, Debra Phillips.

"Warning Signs" in *Black Enterprise*. (Vol. 27, No. 4,

November 1996, pp. 89-94). New York, New York, Earl G. Graves Publishing Co. Inc. Editor, Tonia L. Shakespeare.

"What Color Is Yours? Red Tape Comes in a Lot of Different Shades" in *Restaurant Business*. (Vol. 93, No. 12, August 10, 1994, p. 78). New York, New York, Bill Communications, Inc.

"What's Haute" in *Entrepreneur*. (January 1991, pp. 278-286). Irvine, California, Entrepreneur, Inc. Editor, Gayle Sato.

"What's Hoppin'" in *Entrepreneurial Woman*. (December 1990, pp. 61-63). Irvine, California, Entrepreneur, Inc. Editor, Gayle Sato Stodder.

"What's New" in *Entrepreneur*. (July 1996, p. 206). Irvine, California, Entrepreneur Media Inc.

"Will Diners Want a Lotta Ja Da?" in *Crain's Detroit Business*. (Vol. 12, No. 45, November 1996, pp. 3, 22). Detroit, Michigan, Crain Communications Inc. Editor, Tenisha Mercer.

"Worshiping a Dream" in *Crain's Detroit Business*. (Vol. 12, No. 39, September 1996, p. 8). Detroit, Michigan, Crain Communications Inc. Editor, Matt Roush.

"You're Only as Good as Your Last Meal" in *Venture*. (February 1988, pp. 55-58). New York, New York, Venture Magazine, Inc.

Retailing

"Achieving Success Through a Smaller Market" in *Washington Business Journal: Small Business Resource Guide*. (May 1996, p. 18). Arlington, Virginia, American City Business Journals. Editor, Bill Murray.

"Amid the Large Retailers, You Can Find Your Niche" in *Crain's Small Business*. (June 1996, p. 19). Detroit, Michigan, Crain Communications Inc. Editor, Linda Wasche.

"Business Etiquette Overseas" in *Black Enterprise*. (Vol. 26, No. 3, October 1995, pp. 142-143). New York, New York, Earl G. Graves Publishing Co. Inc. Editor, Marjorie Whigham-Desir.

"Caught Re-Handed" in *Black Enterprise*. (Vol. 26, No. 10, May 1996, p. 21). New York, New York, Earl G. Graves Publishing Co. Inc. Editor, Eric L. Smith.

"Competing with the Giants" in *Sporting Goods Business*. (Vol. 27, No. 2, February 1994, pp. 78-81). New York, New York, Miller Freeman Inc. Editor, Stephanie Barlow.

"Designing for Empowerment" in *Chain Store Age Executive*. (Vol. 71, No. 1, January 199, p. 131). New York, New York, Lebhar-Friedman, Inc. Editor, Marianne Wilson.

"Digital Commerce" in *The Red Herring*. (February 1997, pp. 46, 4850).San Francisco, California, Herring Communications Inc. Editor, Alex Gove.

"Don't Hold Your Breath" in *The Red Herring*. (February 1997, p. 84).San Francisco, California, Herring Communications Inc. Editor, Andrew P. Madden.

"Finding and Helping the Mom-and-Pops" in *Chain Store Age Executive*. (Vol. 70, No. 10, October 1994, p. 104). New York, New York, Lebhar-Friedman, Inc. Editor, Thomas B. McKee.

"From Toilets to Toys: First Franchisee Plunges In" in *Crain's Detroit Business*. (Vol. 12, No. 44, Oct. 28- Nov. 3, 1996, p. 13). Detroit, Michigan, Crain Communications Inc. Editor, Matt Roush.

"The Future of Bankcard Authorization" in *Chain Store Age Executive*. (Vol. 69, No. 10, October 1993, pp. 85-85). New York, New York, Lebhar-Friedman, Inc.

"Getting Carded" in *Entrepreneur*. (Vol. 23, No. 3, March 1995, p. 22). Irvine, California, Entrepreneur Media, Inc. Editor, Janean Huber and Debra Phillips.

"G.I. Joe's Fill a New Niche" in *Discount Merchandiser*. (Vol. 34, No. 7, July 1994, pp. 34-38). New York, New York, Schwartz Publications. Editor, Jerry Minkoff.

"Give 'Em Credit" in *Entrepreneur*. (Vol. 23, No. 12, November 1995, p. 28). Irvine, California, Entrepreneur Media, Inc. Editor, David R. Evanson.

"Hitching Your Wagon to a Retailing Star" in *Nation's Business*. (Vol. 82, No. 11, November 1994, pp. 33-38). Washington, District of Columbia, U.S. Chamber of Commerce. Editor, Dale D. Buss.

"Home Is Where the Business Is" in *Black Enterprise*. (Vol. 25, No. 4, November 1994, pp. 128-138). New York, New York, Earl G. Graves Publishing Co. Inc. Editor, Christina F. Watts.

"How to Hit the Target with Local Advertising" in *Shooting Industry*. (Vol. 39, No. 6, June 1994, p. 26). San Diego, California, Publishers' Development Corp. Editor, Carolee Boyles-Sprenkel.

"In the Know" in *Entrepreneur*. (Vol. 23, No. 4, April 1995, pp. 62-63). Irvine, California, Entrepreneur Media, Inc. Editor, Gayle Sato Stodder.

"In the Shadow of Wal-Mart" in *Management Review*. (Vol. 83, No. 12, December 1994, pp. 10-16). New York, New York, American Management Association. Editor,

Jenny C. McCune.

"An Independent Point of View" in *Stores*. (Vol. 76, No. 3, March 1994, pp. 57-58). Washington, New York, National Retail Federation. Editor, Bill Pearson.

"Independent Specialty Stores...End of an Era?" in *Stores*. (Vol. 76, No. 2, February 1994, pp. 59-60). Washington, New York, National Retail Federation. Editor, Bill Pearson.

"Just Imagine!" in *Direct Marketing*. (Vol. 56, No. 12, April 1994, pp. 38-40). Long Island, New York, Hoke Communications. Editor, Ray Jutkins.

"The Lure of Mail Order" in *Direct Marketing*. (Vol. 57, No. 6, March 1994, pp. 42-44). Long Island, New York, Hoke Communications. Editor, Pete Hoke.

"Manufacturers, Distributors and Retailers Team Up with Co-op Advertising" in *Shooting Industry*. (Vol. 39, No. 8, August 1994, p. 26). San Diego, California, Publishers' Development Corp. Editor, Carolee Boyles-Sprenkel.

"Never Fear" in *Entrepreneur*<<(Vol. 23, No. 5, May 1995, p. 14). Irvine, California, Entrepreneur Media, Inc. Editor, Janean Huber.

"New Markets Open With Move from Funky to Chic" in *Packaging*. (Vol. 39, No. 5, May 1994, p. 26). Des Plaines, Illinois, Cahners Publishing Co. Editor, Greg Erickson.

"Not Everyone's On-Line" in *Crain's Detroit Business*. (Vol. 11, No. 29, July 1995, p. 10). Detroit, Michigan, Crain Communications Inc. Editor, Michael Maurer.

"Opening a New Store...Reasonable Goals and Careful Planning" in *Stores*. (Vol. 76, No. 10, October 1994, pp. 101-102). Washington, New York, National Retail Federation. Editor, Bill Pearson.

"Outsourcery" in *Inc*. (Vol. 19, No. 5, April 1997, pp. 54-56, 58, 60). Boston, Massachusetts, Goldhirsh Group, Inc. Editor, Edward O. Welles.

"Price Advertising - The Winner by Default" in *Stores*. (Vol. 77, No. 1, January 1995, pp. 173-174). Washington, New York, National Retail Federation. Editor, Bill Pearson.

"The Price Is Right" in *Small Business Reports*. (Vol. 19, No. 6, June 1994, pp. 9-13). New York, New York, Faulkner & Gray, Inc. Editor, Robert J. Calvin.

"Profits By Designs" in *Business Start-Ups*. (Vol. 7, No. 11, November 1995, p. 6). Irvine, California, Entrepreneur Media Inc. Editor, Lynn Norquist.

"Progress is No Big Deal" in *Crain's Detroit Business*. (Vol. 12, No. 13, March 1996, pp. 14-15). Detroit,

Michigan, Crain Communications Inc. Editor, Michelle Krebs.

"Rags to Riches" in *Forbes*. (Vol. 153, No. 7, March 28, 1994, p. 108). New York, New York, Forbes, Inc. Editor, Damon Darlin.

"Retail Survival Strategies" in *Independent Business*. (Vol. 7, No. 5, Sept./Oct. 1996, p. 15). Thousands Oaks, California, Group IV Communications Inc. Editor, Maryann Hammers.

"Retailers Share Strategies for Competing with Superstore Giants" in *Pet Product News*. (Vol. 48, No. 3, March 1994, p. 23). Los Angeles, California, Fancy Publications. Editor, Liz Swain.

"Retailing. 2000" in *Chain Store Age Executive*. (Vol. 70, No. 4, April 1994, p. 58). New York, New York, Lebhar-Friedman, Inc. Editor, Thom Blischok.

"Reviving the Dying Store" in *Direct Marketing*. (Vol. 56, No. 7, November 1993, pp. 20-21). Long Island, New York, Hoke Communications. Editor, Murray Raphel.

"Shopping Spree" in *Income Opportunities*. (Vol. 31, No. 11, November 1996, pp. 68, 70, 72, 74-76, 78). New York, New York, IO Publications Inc. Editor, Robert L. Perry.

"Small Retailers Struggling for Survival" in *Income Opportunities*. (Vol. 30, No. 4, April 1995, pp. 2-3). New York, New York, IO Publications, Inc. Editor, Patricia Hamilton.

"Talking Shop" in *Entrepreneur*. (Vol. 23, No. 7, July 1995, p. 13). Irvine, California, Entrepreneur Media, Inc. Editor, Lynn Beresford.

"Ties That Bind Large and Small" in *Nation's Business*. (Vol. 80, No. 2, February 1992, pp. 24-26). Washington, District of Columbia, U.S. Chamber of Commerce. Editor, Bradford McKee.

"Visual Aid" in *Entrepreneur*. (March 1996, p. 38). Irvine, California, Entrepreneur Media Inc.

"What Truly Deters Check Fraud?" in *Banking Journal*. (Vol. 87, No. 2, February 1995, pp. 74-78). New York, New York, Simmons-Boardman Publishing Corporation. Editor, Penny Lunt.

"Where the Shoppers Are" in *Inc*. (Vol. 17, No. 6, May 1995, p. 133). Boston, Massachusetts, Goldhirsh Group, Inc. Editor, Susan Greco.

"Where's the Retail Direct Mail Revolution?" in *Direct Marketing*. (Vol. 55, No. 7, November 1992, pp. 23-26). Long Island, New York, Hoke Communications. Editor, Murray Raphel.

"Who Speaks for the Small Retailer?" in *Direct Marketing*. (Vol. 57, No. 7, November 1994, pp. 30-32). Long Island, New York, Hoke Communications. Editor, Murray Raphel.

"Window Shopping" in *Entrepreneur*. (Vol. 23, No. 5, May 1995, p. 26).Irvine, California, Entrepreneur Media, Inc. Editor, Heather Page.

"You Sell Merchandise, But Customer Buys Service" in *Crain's Small Business*. (March 1996, p. 18). Detroit, Michigan, Crain Communications, Inc. Editor, Ken Guoin.

Small Business Development

"1996 May Be Best Year for Those Seeking Loans" in *Washington Business Journal: Small Business Resource Guide*. (May 1996, p. 16). Arlington, Virginia: American City Business Journals. By Melissa Wuestenberg.

"A&W Plants Roots as Growing Fast-Food Chain" in *Crain's Detroit Business*. (Vol. 13, No. 6, February 1997, pp. 3, 32). Detroit, Michigan: Crain Communications Inc. By Marsha Stopa.

"Achieving Success Through a Smaller Market" in *Washington Business Journal: Small Business Resource Guide*. (May 1996, p. 18). Arlington, Virginia: American City Business Journals. By Bill Murray.

"After the Covers: What Are They Up to Now?" in *Chain Store Age Executive*. (Vol. 70, No. 7, July 1994, pp. 19-33). New York, New York: Lebhar-Friedman, Inc.

"The Age of the Gazelle" in *Inc*. (Vol. 18, No. 7, May 1996, p. 44). Boston, Massachusetts: Goldhirsh Group, Inc. By John Case.

"All Season Woman" in *Small Business Opportunities*. (Vol. 9, No. 3, May 1997, pp. 58, 60, 72). New York, New York: Harris Publications, Inc. By Diane Morelli.

"Alphabet Soup" in *Inc*. (Vol. 16, No. 12, November 1994, pp. 31-32). Boston, Massachusetts: Goldhirsh Group, Inc. By Heather E. Stone.

"Answers to Your Small-Business Questions" in *Business Start-Ups*. (Vol. 8, No. 7, July 1996, p. 6). Irvine, California: Entrepreneur Media Inc. By Haidee Jezek.

"Answers to Your Small Business Questions" in *Business Start-Ups*. (Vol. 8, No. 6, June 1996, p. 6). Irvine, California: Entrepreneur Media Inc. By Lynn L. Norquist.

"Are You Online Yet?" in *Black Enterprise*. (Vol. 25, No. 9, April 1995, p. 41). New York, New York: Earl G. Graves Publishing Co., Inc. By Valencia Roner and Matthew S. Scott.

"Ask the Experts" in *Income Opportunities*. (Vol. 32 , No. 3, March 1997, pp. 56, 58, 60). New York, New York: IO Publications Inc.

"Automatic Venture" in *Small Business Opportunities*. (Vol. 9, No. 1, January 1997, pp. 50, 52). New York, New York: Harris Publications, Inc.

"Bankruptcies Rise 25%" in *Crain's Detroit Business*. (Vol. 13, No. 6, February 1997, pp. 1, 32). Detroit, Michigan: Crain Communications Inc. By Tenisha Mercer.

"Barden Trump Card: Experience" in *Crain's Detroit Business*. (Vol. 13, No. 6, February 1997, pp. 1, 22). Detroit, Michigan: Crain Communications Inc. By Robert Ankeny.

"Betting on the Future" in *D&B Reports*. (Vol. 40, No. 6, Nov./Dec. 1992, p. 44). New York, New York: Dun & Bradstreet. By Robert J. Klein.

"Beyond Latin America" in *Hispanic Business*. (Vol. 18, No. 11, November 1996, pp. 34, 36, 38, 40-41). Santa Barbara, California: Hispanic Business Inc. By Joel Russell.

"Big Ideas for Your Small Business" in *Changing Times*. (November 1989, pp. 57-60). Washington, District of Columbia: Kiplinger Washington Editors, Inc.

"Bottling Success" in *Hispanic Business*. (Vol. 18, No. 7/8, July/August 1996, p. 78). Santa Barbara, California: Hispanic Business Inc. By Maria Zate.

"Bright Ideas" in *Business Start-Ups*. (Vol. 7, No. 8, August 1995, pp. 50, 52-54, 57). Irvine, California: Entrepreneur Media Inc. By Bob Weinstein.

"Bucks in Buttons" in *Small Business Opportunities*. (Vol. 9, No. 1, January 1997, p. 48). New York, New York: Harris Publications, Inc. By Carla Goodman.

"Building a Better Burger" in *Business Start-Ups*. (Vol. 8, No. 3, March 1996, pp. 21-22, 24-25). Irvine, California: Entrepreneur Media Inc. By Bob Weinstein.

"Building a Business Framework" in *Hispanic Business*. (Vol. 18, No. 11, November 1996, p. 24). Santa Barbara, California: Hispanic Business Inc.

"Building the Perfect Home Office" in *Black Enterprise*. (Vol. 27, No. 8, March 1997, pp. 36-37). New York, New York: Earl G. Graves Publishing Co. Inc. By Rafiki Cai.

"Business Balloons" in *Small Business Opportunities*. (Vol. 9, No. 1, January 1997, p. 76). New York, New York: Harris Publications, Inc. By Vicki Cromwell-Slakey.

"A Call of Arms for Black Business" in *Black Enterprise*.

(Vol. 27, No. 4, November 1996, pp. 79-86). New York, New York: Earl G. Graves Publishing Co. Inc. By Carolyn M. Brown and Tonia L. Shakespeare.

"Capture the Future" in *Success*. (Vol. 40, No. 10, December 1993, pp. 63-70). New York, New York: Lang Communications. By Katherine Callan.

"Carving a Niche" in *Small Business Opportunities*. (Vol. 8, No. 6, November 1996, p. 50). New York, New York: Harris Publications, Inc. By Carla Goodman.

"A Checklist for Starting a Business" in *Crain's Small Business*. (December 1995, p. 30). Detroit, Michigan: Crain Communications, Inc.

"Cleaning Up" in *Small Business Opportunities*. (Vol. 9, No. 3, May 1997, p. 62). New York, New York: Harris Publications, Inc. By Carla Godman.

"Coffee Cola Talk" in *Small Business Opportunities*. (Vol. 9, No. 2, March 1997, pp. 44, 100). New York, New York: Harris Publications, Inc. By Anne Hart.

"Consumer Report" in *Entrepreneur*. (May 1997, pp. 125-130). Irvine, California: Entrepreneur Media Inc. By Gayle Sato Stodder.

"Contacts for Contracts" in *Hispanic Business*. (Vol. 18, No. 7/8, July/August 1996, p. 58). Santa Barbara, California: Hispanic Business Inc. By Claudia Armann.

"Could You Succeed in Small Business" in *Business Horizons*. (September/October 1989, pp. 65-69). Bloomington, Indiana: Indiana University

"Crafting a Business" in *Entrepreneur*. (March 1997, pp. 58, 60-61). Irvine, California: Entrepreneur Media Inc. By Cynthia E. Griffin.

"Crafty Biz" in *Small Business Opportunities*. (Vol. 9, No. 2, March 1997, pp. 54, 88). New York, New York: Harris Publications, Inc. By Carla Goodman.

"Credibility Gap" in *Income Opportunities*. (Vol. 32, No. 4, April 1997, pp. 42, 44). New York, New York: IO Publications Inc. By Dorothy Elizabeth Brooks.

"Cubs Send Minor-League Owners to the Showers" in *Inc*. (Vol. 19, No. 5, April 1997, p. 24). Boston, Massachusetts: Goldhirsh Group, Inc. By Phaedra Hise.

"Cycle of Success" in *Small Business Opportunities*. (Vol. 9, No. 2, March 1997, pp. 86, 88). New York, New York: Harris Publications, Inc. By Stan Roberts.

"Dare to Be Different" in *Entrepreneur*. (Vol. 23, No. 4, April 1995, pp. 122, 124-127). Irvine, California: Entrepreneur Media, Inc. By Gayle Sato Stodder.

"The Deal Maker" in *Inc*. (Vol. 15, No. 13, December

1993, pp. 129-130). Boston, Massachusetts: Goldhirsh Group, Inc. By Phaedra Hise.

"Developer Eyes 65-Acre Site in Sterling Heights" in *Crain's Detroit Business*. (Vol. 13, No. 6, February 1997, p. 3). Detroit, Michigan: Crain Communications Inc. By Tenisha Mercer.

"Eco-Preneuring" in *Small Business Opportunities*. (Vol. 9, No. 2, March 1997, pp. 70, 72). New York, New York: Harris Publications, Inc. By Geri Anderson.

"Entrepreneurial Fables" in *Entrepreneur*. (Vol. 23, No. 8, August 1995, pp. 120, 122-124, 127). Irvine, California: Entrepreneur Media, Inc. By Gayle Sato Stodder.

"Entrepreneurial Spirit Awards" in *Hispanic Business*. (Vol. 18, No. 12, December 1996, pp. 26, 28, 30, 34, 36, 38). Santa Barbara, California: Hispanic Business Inc. By Maria Zate.

"Entrepreneurs Collide: Will Zoning Take Town Downhill?" in *Inc*. (Vol. 19, No. 5, April 1997, p. 32). Boston, Massachusetts: Goldhirsh Group, Inc. By Joshua Macht.

"Entrepreneurship: The Role of the Individual in Small Business Development" in *IBAR*. (Vol. 15, 1994, pp. 62-75). By Stan Cromie.

"Essential Books for Start-ups" in *Working Woman*. (February 1995, p. 54). New York, New York: Working Woman, Inc. By Jane Applegate.

"Every Day's a Holiday" in *Small Business Opportunities*. (Vol. 9, No. 1, January 1997, pp. 70, 72, 114). New York, New York: Harris Publications, Inc. By Anne Hart.

"Experience" in *Business Start-Ups*. (Vol. 7, No. 12, December 1995, p. 20). Irvine, California: Entrepreneur Media Inc. By Jacquelyn Lynn.

"Fifteen Start-Up Mistakes" in *Business Start-Ups*. (Vol. 7, No. 12, December 1995, p. 22). Irvine, California: Entrepreneur Media Inc. By Mel Mandell.

"Finding Your Niche" in *Business Start-Ups*. (Vol. 9, No. 4, April 1997, pp. 72, 74). Irvine, California: Entrepreneur Media Inc. By Carla Goodman.

"Focus on: Small Business" in *Journal of Accountancy*. (Vol. 177, No. 5, May 1994, p. 41). Jersey City, New Jersey: American Institute of Certified Public Accountants. By Jacqueline L. Babicky and Larry Field and Norman C. Pricher.

"Food for Thought" in *Small Business Opportunities*. (Vol. 9, No. 2, March 1997, pp. 78, 80). New York, New York: Harris Publications, Inc. By Cheryl Rodgers.

"Fools Rush In? The Institutional Context of Industry Creation" in *Academy of Management Review*. (Vol. 19, No. 4, October 1994, p. 645). Ada, Ohio: Academy of Management. By Howard E. Aldrich and Marlene C. Fiol.

"Get on the Peace Train" in *Small Business Opportunities*. (Vol. 9, No. 1, January 1997, p. 86). New York, New York: Harris Publications, Inc. By Carla Goodman.

"Get Rich in 1997" in *Small Business Opportunities*. (Vol. 9, No. 1, January 1997, pp. 22-24, 26, 28, 30, 34). New York, New York: Harris Publications, Inc.

"Get into Show Business" in *Small Business Opportunities*. (Vol. 9, No. 1, January 1997, pp. 104, 114). New York, New York: Harris Publications, Inc. By Anne Hart.

"Gift Keeps on Giving" in *Small Business Opportunities*. (Vol. 9, No. 1, January 1997, pp. 56, 58). New York, New York: Harris Publications, Inc. By Marie Sherlock.

"Go West for Success" in *Small Business Opportunities*. (Vol. 9, No. 2, March 1997, p. 118). New York, New York: Harris Publications, Inc. By Carla Goodman.

"Going It Alone" in *Newsweek*. (April 1996, pp. 50-51). New York, New York: Newsweek, Inc. By Ellyn E. Spragins and Steve Rhodes.

"Going Solo" in *Income Opportunities*. (Vol. 30, No. 11, November 1995, pp. 30, 32, 34). New York, New York: IO Publications, Inc. By Pamela Rohland.

"Grounds for Success" in *Small Business Opportunities*. (Vol. 9, No. 2, March 1997, p. 62). New York, New York: Harris Publications, Inc. By Carla Goodman.

"Grounds for Success" in *Small Business Opportunities*. (Vol. 9, No. 1, January 1997, p. 54). New York, New York: Harris Publications, Inc. By Carla Goodman.

"Group Therapy" in *Crain's Small Business*. (September 1995, pp. 1, 12-13). Detroit, Michigan: Crain Communications, Inc. By Kimberly Lifton.

"Group's Plan is to Make Knowledge Accessible" in *Washington Business Journal: Small Business Resource Guide*. (May 1996, pp. 4, 13). Arlington, Virginia: American City Business Journals. By Lakhinder J.S. Vohra.

"Growing a Business" in *Small Business Opportunities*. (Vol. 9, No. 3, May 1997, pp. 48, 104, 122). New York, New York: Harris Publications, Inc. By Anne Hart.

"Help Getting Started" in *Business Start-Ups*. (Vol. 7, No. 12, December 1995, pp. 28-29). Irvine, California: Entrepreneur Media Inc. By Sue Clayton.

"Helping Biz Cope" in *Small Business Opportunities*. (Vol. 9, No. 1, January 1997, p. 98). New York, New York: Harris Publications, Inc. By Annette Wood.

"Holograms Are Solid Success" in *Small Business Opportunities*. (Vol. 9, No. 2, March 1997, pp. 126-127). New York, New York: Harris Publications, Inc. By Anne Hart.

"Hot Areas for Small Business" in *Black Enterprise*. (Vol. 24, No. 4, November 1993, p. 54). New York, New York: Earl G. Graves Publishing Co. Inc.

"The Hottest Entrepreneurs in America" in *Inc*. (Vol. 14, No. 13, December 1992, pp. 88-103). Boston, Massachusetts: Goldhirsh Group, Inc. By Martha E. Mangelsdorf.

"How to Make Your Ex-Boss Your Client" in *Black Enterprise*. (Vol. 24, No. 9, April 1994, pp. 92-96). New York, New York: Earl G. Graves Publishing Co. Inc. By Caryne Brown.

"How to Succeed in. 4 Easy Steps" in *Inc*. (Vol. 17, No. 10, July 1995, pp. 30-32, 34, 36-40, 42). Boston, Massachusetts: Goldhirsh Group, Inc. By Bo Burlingham.

"Improving Your Luck" in *Inc*. (Vol. 19, No. 5, April 1997, pp. 35-36). Boston, Massachusetts: Goldhirsh Group, Inc. By Norm Brodsky.

"In the Zone" in *Entrepreneur*. (May 1996, pp. 116, 118-121). Irvine, California: Entrepreneur Media Inc. By Cynthia E. Griffin.

"Is the Price Right?" in *Income Opportunities*. (Vol. 29, No. 9, September 1994, pp. 102-104). New York, New York: IO Publications Inc. By Jo Frohbieter-Mueller.

"Jimmy's Top Ten List" in *Business Start-Ups*. (Vol. 7, No. 8, August 1995, p. 7). Irvine, California: Entrepreneur Media Inc.

"Keeping Small Businesses Healthy" in *Franchising World*. (Vol. 27, No. 1, January/February 1995, pp. 56-57). Washington, District of Columbia: International Franchise Association. By Cindy Murphy.

"Keys to Success? For Starters, Here Are 15" in *Contractor*. (Vol. 41, No. 11, November 1994, p. 12). Des Plaines, Illinois: Cahners Publishing Co. By Jeff Ferenc.

"Know It All" in *Entrepreneur*. (March 1997, p. 28). Irvine, California: Entrepreneur Media Inc.

"Knowledge" in *Business Start-Ups*. (Vol. 7, No. 12, December 1995, p. 38). Irvine, California: Entrepreneur Media Inc. By Carolyn Lawrence.

"Leading the Charge" in *Hispanic Business*. (Vol. 18, No.

5, May 1996, pp. 26-28, 30). Santa Barbara, California: Hispanic Business Inc. By Maria Zate.

"Leaving Home" in *Inc.* (Vol. 18, No. 18, December 1997, p. 127). Boston, Massachusetts: Goldhirsh Group, Inc. By Christopher Caggiano.

"Looking for Customers? Pick on Someone Your Own Size" in *Inc.* (Vol. 19, No. 3, March 1997, p. 22). Boston, Massachusetts: Goldhirsh Group, Inc. By Jerry Useem.

"Lost Dollars" in *Black Enterprise.* (Vol. 27, No. 4, November 1996, p. 34). New York, New York: Earl G. Graves Publishing Co. Inc. By Sheryl E. Huggins.

"Magic Carpet Ride" in *Small Business Opportunities.* (Vol. 9, No. 2, March 1997, pp. 104-105). New York, New York: Harris Publications, Inc.

"Mail-Order Biz Sells 300 Products Made from Recycled Goods." in *Small Business Opportunities.* (Vol. 9, No. 1, January 1997, p. 46). New York, New York: Harris Publications, Inc. By Geri Anderson.

"Make Your Pitch" in *Independent Business.* (Vol. 7, No. 4, July/Aug. 1996, pp. 14-15). Thousands Oaks, California: Group IV Communications Inc.

"Making a Hopp to Top Agency" in *Crain's Detroit Business.* (Vol. 13, No. 6, February 1997, pp. 3, 26). Detroit, Michigan: Crain Communications Inc. By Jean Halliday.

"Mapping Your Route" in *Business Start-Ups.* (Vol. 8, No. 12, December 1996, pp. 40, 42-44). Irvine, California: Entrepreneur Media Inc. By Lynn H. Colwell.

"Mentoring Helps Grow Emerging Businesses" in *Puget Sound Business Journal.* (Vol. 12, No. 18, September 23, 1991, p. 24). Seattle, Washington: Scripps Howard Business Publications. By Linda Lang.

"Mind Power" in *Entrepreneur.* (Vol. 23, No. 5, May 1995, pp. 100, 102-106). Irvine, California: Entrepreneur Media, Inc. By Robert McGarvey.

"Mini Storage Maxi Profit" in *Small Business Opportunities.* (Vol. 9, No. 1, January 1997, p. 84). New York, New York: Harris Publications, Inc. By Stan Roberts.

"Minority Banks Are on the Rise" in *Hispanic Business.* (Vol. 18, No. 5, May 1996, p. 15). Santa Barbara, California: Hispanic Business Inc. By Joel Russell.

"Money in Marble" in *Small Business Opportunities.* (Vol. 9, No. 2, March 1997, pp. 48, 50). New York, New York: Harris Publications, Inc. By Geri Anderson.

"More Power to You" in *Entrepreneur.* (March 1997, p.

10). Irvine, California: Entrepreneur Media Inc. By Janean Chun.

"Moving Out" in *Income Opportunities.* (Vol. 32, No. 4, April 1997, pp. 1418, 88). New York, New York: IO Publications Inc. By Dale D. Buss.

"Murder, She Sold" in *Small Business Opportunities.* (Vol. 9, No. 2, March 1997, pp. 64, 66). New York, New York: Harris Publications, Inc. By Mary Ann McLaughlin.

"My Company is Small. How Can I Attract My First Big Client?" in *Inc.* (Vol. 18, No. 18, December 1997, p. 120). Boston, Massachusetts: Goldhirsh Group, Inc. By Christopher Caggiano.

"Myth of the Gunslinger" in *Success.* (Vol. 41, No. 2, March 1994, pp. 34-40). New York, New York: Lang Communications. By Ingrid Abramovitch.

"Never Too Small to Manage" in *Inc.* (Vol. 19, No. 2, February 1997, pp. 56-58, 61). Boston, Massachusetts: Goldhirsh Group, Inc. By David Whitford.

"New Beginnings" in *Business Start-Ups.* (Vol. 8, No. 1, January 1996, p. 96). Irvine, California: Entrepreneur Media Inc. By Joann K. Jones.

"1995 Small Business Tax Guide" in *Income Opportunities.* (Vol. 30, No. 1, January 1995, pp. 48-60). New York, New York: IO Publications, Inc. By Randall Kirkpatrick and Meg North.

"No Biz Like Shoe Biz" in *Small Business Opportunities.* (Vol. 9, No. 1, January 1997, pp. 80, 82). New York, New York: Harris Publications, Inc. By Dorothy Elizabeth Brooks.

"An Olympic-Sized Letdown" in *Inc.* (Vol. 19, No. 2, February 1997, p. 21). Boston, Massachusetts: Goldhirsh Group, Inc. By Michael E. Kanell.

"On a Mission to Demystify" in *Hispanic Business.* (Vol. 17, No. 5, May 1995, p. 42). Santa Barbara, California: Hispanic Business Inc. By Rick Mendosa.

"On Their Own" in *Wall Street Journal Special Reports: Small Business (Special Edition).* (May 23, 1996, p. R20). New York, New York: Wall Street Journal: Dow Jones & Co., Inc. By Jeffrey A. Tannenbaum.

"On Your Mark..." in *Business Start-Ups.* (Vol. 7, No. 2, February 1995, pp. 37-44). Irvine, California: Entrepreneur Media Inc. By Gustav Berle and Jacquelyn Lynn.

"Out of the Blue" in *Inc.* (Vol. 17, No. 10, July 1995, pp. 68-72). Boston, Massachusetts: Goldhirsh Group, Inc. By Tom Ehrenfeld.

"Out on a Limb and on Their Own" in *Nation's Business.* (Vol. 82, No. 3, March 1994, pp. 33-34). Washington, District of Columbia: U.S. Chamber of Commerce. By John S. DeMott.

"A Perfect Fit" in *Business Start-Ups.* (Vol. 7, No. 9, September 1995, pp. 78, 80-81). Irvine, California: Entrepreneur Media Inc. By Jacquelyn Lynn.

"The Platinum 200" in *Income Opportunities.* (Vol. 32 , No. 3, March 1997, pp. 13-15). New York, New York: IO Publications Inc. By Robert L. Perry.

"Power Play" in *Entrepreneur.* (March 1997, pp. 104, 106-105). Irvine, California: Entrepreneur Media Inc. By Tomima Edmark.

"Prepare for Frustration You'll Create Exhilaration" in *Crain's Small Business.* (Vol. 4, No. 10, October 1996, p. 19). Detroit, Michigan: Crain Communications Inc. By Jim Brady.

"Profits by the Book" in *Small Business Opportunities.* (Vol. 9, No. 2, March 1997, p. 114). New York, New York: Harris Publications, Inc. By Anne Hart.

"Profits in Ponds" in *Small Business Opportunities.* (Vol. 8, No. 5, September 1996, pp. 60, 62, 64, 66). New York, New York: Harris Publications, Inc.

"Quitting" in *Business Start-Ups.* (Vol. 7, No. 12, December 1995, pp. 60-61). Irvine, California: Entrepreneur Media Inc. By Sue Clayton.

"Replace Yourself" in *Inc.* (Vol. 18, No. 18, December 1997, pp. 125-126). Boston, Massachusetts: Goldhirsh Group, Inc. By Susan Greco.

"Restless Youth" in *Wall Street Journal Special Reports: Small Business (Special Edition).* (May 23, 1996, pp. R18-R19). New York, New York : Wall Street Journal: Dow Jones & Co., Inc. By Roger Ricklefs.

"The Right Mix" in *Hispanic Business.* (Vol. 18, No. 12, December 1996, pp. 22-24). Santa Barbara, California: Hispanic Business Inc. By Maria Zate.

"Right from the Start" in *Small Business Opportunities.* (Vol. 9, No. 3, May 1997, pp. 20, 42). New York, New York: Harris Publications, Inc. By Dr. Sandy Weinberg.

"Rudy Alvarado, Ceo" in *Hispanic Business.* (Vol. 18, No. 7/8, July/August 1996, p. 32). Santa Barbara, California: Hispanic Business Inc. By Maria Zate.

"Run Your Company Smarter" in *Money.* (Vol. 23, No. 11, November 1994, pp. 136-140). New York, New York: Time Inc. By Marlys J. Harris.

"Running out of Time" in *Inc.* (Vol. 19, No. 2, February 1997, pp. 63-64, 68, 72-73). Boston, Massachusetts: Goldhirsh Group, Inc. By John Grossmann.

"Sanchez: a Victory of Her Own" in *Hispanic Business.* (Vol. 19, No. 4, April 1997, pp. 16, 18). Santa Barbara, California: Hispanic Business Inc. By Rick Mendosa.

"Saucy Success" in *Black Enterprise.* (Vol. 27, No. 7, February 1997, p. 36). New York, New York: Earl G. Graves Publishing Co. Inc. By Ann Brown.

"Say When" in *Inc.* . (Vol. 17, No. 2, February 1995, pp. 19-20). Boston, Massachusetts: Goldhirsh Group, Inc. By Steven L. Marks.

"Saying Goodbye to Corporate America" in *Black Enterprise.* (Vol. 22, No. 11, June 1992, pp. 312-318). New York, New York: Earl G. Graves Publishing Co. Inc. By Shawn Kennedy.

"SCORE Points to Success" in *Black Enterprise.* (Vol. 25, No. 6, January 1995, p. 38). New York, New York: Earl G. Graves Publishing Co. Inc. By Christina F. Watts.

"Search for Tomorrow" in *Entrepreneur.* (May 1997, pp. 112, 144, 116122). Irvine, California: Entrepreneur Media Inc. By Genion Chan.

"Seat-Of-The-Pants Strategy Won't Keep You Growing" in *Crain's Small Business.* (Vol. 4, No. 10, October 1996, pp. 8-9). Detroit, Michigan: Crain Communications Inc. By Tim Bannister.

"Senate Classifies Workers" in *Income Opportunities.* (Vol. 31, No. 6, June 1996, p. 5). New York, New York: IO Publications Inc. By Michele Marrinan.

"Sending Workers Home—To Work" in *Independent Business.* (Vol. 7, No. 4, July/Aug. 1996, pp. 20-22). Thousands Oaks, California: Group IV Communications Inc. By Verna Gates.

"Service Sector is a Good Franchise Bet" in *Washington Business Journal: Small Business Resource Guide.* (May 1996, pp. 8, 10). Arlington, Virginia: American City Business Journals. By Lakhinder J.S. Vohra.

"Setting an Agenda" in *Hispanic Business.* (Vol. 18, No. 11, November 1996, pp. 18, 22). Santa Barbara, California: Hispanic Business Inc.

"Setting Up Shop (in SOHO)" in *Working Woman.* (October 1994, pp. 65-69). New York, New York: Working Woman, Inc. By Jeff Ubois.

"The Seven Traps of Strategic Planning" in *Inc.* (Vol. 18, No. 16, November 1996, pp. 99, 101, 103). Boston, Massachusetts: Goldhirsh Group, Inc. By Joseph C. Picken and Gregory G. Dess.

"Silver Lining" in *Entrepreneur.* (June 1995, pp. 52, 54-55). Irvine, California: Entrepreneur Media Inc. By Cynthia E. Griffin.

"Small Business A to Z" in *Business Start-Ups.* (Vol. 8, No. 7, July 1996, p. 4). Irvine, California: Entrepreneur Media Inc. By Karin Moeller.

"Small Business Committed to Workplace Safety" in *Independent Business.* (Vol. 8, No. 2, Mar./Apr. 1997, p. 54). Thousands Oaks, California: Group IV Communications Inc.

"Small Like Me" in *Wall Street Journal Special Reports: Small Business (Special Edition).* (May 23, 1996, p. R31). New York, New York: Wall Street Journal: Dow Jones & Co., Inc. By John Buskin.

"So Long to Sarseps" in *Hispanic Business.* (Vol. 18, No. 11, November 1996, p. 12). Santa Barbara, California: Hispanic Business Inc. By Rick Mendosa.

"Solid Foundations" in *Black Enterprise.* (Vol. 27, No. 7, February 1997, p. 38). New York, New York: Earl G. Graves Publishing Co. Inc. By Denolyn Carroll.

"Something Borrowed" in *Entrepreneur.* (February 1997, p. 26). Irvine, California: Entrepreneur Media Inc.

"A Sporting Chance" in *Detroit Free Press.* (January 1997, pp. 1e-2e). Detroit, Michigan: Knight-Ridder, Inc. By Molly Brauer.

"Start with Strategic Fundamentals" in *Crain's Small Business.* (September 1995, p. 9). Detroit, Michigan: Crain Communications, Inc. By Jim Brady.

"Starting an Appraisal Firm" in *Real Estate Appraiser.* (Vol. 58, No. 1, April 1992, pp. 16-20). Chicago, Illinois: Appraisal Institute. By Terrence L. Love.

"Starting Over" in *Business Start-Ups.* (Vol. 7, No. 8, August 1995, p. 6). Irvine, California: Entrepreneur Media Inc. By Lynn H. Colwell.

"Starting on a Shoestring" in *New Business Opportunities.* (March 1990, pp. 26-28). Irvine, California: Entrepreneur, Inc.

"Step 2: Do Your Homework" in *Business Start-Ups.* (Vol. 8, No. 6, June 1996, pp. 8, 10). Irvine, California: Entrepreneur Media Inc. By Kylo-Patrick Hart.

"Steps to Start a Business" in *Washington Business Journal: Small Business Resource Guide.* (May 1996, p. 4). Arlington, Virginia: American City Business Journals.

"Success Secrets" in *Small Business Opportunities.* (Vol. 9, No. 2, March 1997, p. 84). New York, New York: Harris Publications, Inc. By Carla Goodman.

"Support System" in *Entrepreneur.* (Vol. 23, No. 4, April 1995, pp. 136-142). Irvine, California: Entrepreneur Media, Inc. By Bob Weinstein.

"The Takeover" in *Inc.* (Vol. 19, No. 5, April 1997, pp. 72-75, 78, 80-82). Boston, Massachusetts: Goldhirsh Group, Inc. By Stephanie Gruner.

"Taking a Stand" in *Hispanic Business.* (Vol. 18, No. 11, November 1996, pp. 26,28, 30). Santa Barbara, California: Hispanic Business Inc.

"Talking Business with Ron Dubren, Inventor of Tickle Me Elmo" in *Income Opportunities.* (Vol. 32, No. 4, April 1997, pp. 28-32). New York, New York: IO Publications Inc. By Stephanie Jeffrey.

"The 10 Best Businesses to Start in 1996" in *Income Opportunities.* (Vol. 31, No. 1, January 1996, pp. 12-16, 72, 79-80). New York, New York: IO Publications, Inc. By Jack Rosenberger.

"The Three Criteria for a Successful New Business" in *Inc.* (Vol. 18, No. 5, April 1996, pp. 21-22). Boston, Massachusetts: Goldhirsh Group, Inc. By Norm Brodsky.

"Tips from the Experts" in *Washington Business Journal: Small Business Resource Guide.* (May 1996, p. 5). Arlington, Virginia: American City Business Journals.

"The Truth About Start-Ups" in *Inc.* (Vol. 17, No. 2, February 1995, pp. 23-24). Boston, Massachusetts: Goldhirsh Group, Inc. By Paul Reynolds.

"Tune in & Start Up" in *Business Start-Ups.* (Vol. 8, No. 7, July 1996, p. 4). Irvine, California: Entrepreneur Media Inc. By Karin Moeller.

"The 12 Biggest Mistakes Made By New Businesses" in *Income Opportunities.* (Vol. 31, No. 4, April 1996, pp. 18-21). New York, New York: IO Publications, Inc. By Pamela Rohland.

"Use Your Head" in *Business Start-Ups.* (Vol. 7, No. 7, July 1995, pp. 44, 46-49). Irvine, California: Entrepreneur Media Inc. By Bob Weinstein.

"Using Technology to Enhance Your Business" in *Black Enterprise.* (Vol. 27, No. 8, March 1997, pp. 64-72). New York, New York: Earl G. Graves Publishing Co. Inc.

"Video Offers a Way of Life Beyond the Minimum Wage" in *Crain's Small Business.* (June 1996, p. 2). Detroit, Michigan: Crain Communications Inc. By Jeffrey McCracken.

"The Virtue of Necessity" in *Inc. 2.* (Vol. 18, No. 18, December 1997, pp. 80, 82, 85, 88, 93). Boston, Massachusetts: Goldhirsh Group, Inc. By Jerry Useem.

"What to Do with a Lousy Business" in *Management Review*. (Vol. 83, No. 6, June 1994, pp. 40-43). New York, New York: American Management Association. By Dan Thomas.

"What's the Big Idea?" in *Small Business Opportunities*. (Vol. 7, No. 5, September 1995, p. 17). New York, New York: Harris Publications, Inc. By Carla Goodman.

"Where Dreams Get Hope" in *Crain's Detroit Business*. (Vol. 12, No. 16, April 1996, pp. 3, 26). Detroit, Michigan: Crain Communications Inc. By Robert Akeny.

"Who Needs Growth?" in *Inc*. (Vol. 18, No. 14, October 1996, p. 90). Boston, Massachusetts: Goldhirsh Group, Inc. By Susan Greco.

"Wired for Success" in *Black Enterprise*. (Vol. 27, No. 8, March 1997, pp. 75-80). New York, New York: Earl G. Graves Publishing Co. Inc. By Tariq K. Muhammad.

"With Luck, This Biz Will Go Down the Toilet" in *Inc*. (Vol. 19, No. 5, April 1997, p. 21). Boston, Massachusetts: Goldhirsh Group, Inc. By Phaedra Hise.

"The Wrong Question" in *INC*. (Vol. 17, No. 3, March 1995, p. 27). Boston, Massachusetts: Goldhirsch Group, Inc. By Henry Kressel and Bruce Guile.

"The Year of Living Dangerously" in *Business Start-Ups*. (Vol. 7, No. 6, June 1995, pp. 74, 76-77). Irvine, California: Entrepreneur Media Inc. By Jeannie Pearce.

"Year One" in *Business Start-Ups*. (Vol. 7, No. 12, December 1995, pp. 76-77). Irvine, California: Entrepreneur Media Inc. By Jacquelyn Lynn.

"Yes, You Can Create Your Own Job" in *Public Relations Journal*. (Vol. 50, No. 6, June/July 1994, pp. 18-20). New York, New York: Public Relations Society of America, Inc. By Betty Hall.

"Your Path to Success" in *Hispanic Business*. (Vol. 19, No. 1, January 1997, p. 27). Santa Barbara, California: Hispanic Business Inc.

Venture/Capital Funding

"20 Best Mutual Funds" in *Inc*. (Vol. 18, No. 12, September 1996, pp. 5254, 56, 58). Boston, Massachusetts: Goldhirsh Group, Inc. By Jill Andresky Fraser.

"Alternative Funding" in *Black Enterprise*. (Vol. 26, No. 12, July 1996, p. 30). New York, New York: Earl G. Graves Publishing Co. Inc. By Kenneth Gay.

"Angel Networks" in *Black Enterprise*. (Vol. 25, No. 12, July 1995, p. 38). New York, New York: Earl G. Graves Publishing Co. Inc.By Carolyn M. Brown.

"The Art of the Deal" in *The Red Herring*. (May 1996, p. 21). San Francisco, California: Herring Communications Inc. By Alex Gove.

"Balancing Act" in *Entrepreneur*. (Vol. 24, No. 2, February 1996, pp. 52, 54-55). Irvine, California: Entrepreneur Media, Inc. By David R. Evanson.

"Bank On It!" in *Entrepreneur*. (May 1993, pp. 85-88). Irvine, California: Entrepreneur, Inc. By Elizabeth Wallace.

"Banks Open Their Wallets for Women" in *Income Opportunities*. (Vol. 32, No. 1, January 1997, p. 10). New York, New York: IO Publications Inc. By Michele Marrinan.

"A Bike Shop in Harlem: Part VIII of a Special Series" in *Income Opportunities*. (Vol. 30, No. 5, May 1995, pp. 58, 60, 62-63, 66). New York, New York: IO Publications, Inc. By Maureen Nevin Duffy.

"Blue-Ribbon Fair Presentations" in *Inc*. (Vol. 18, No. 11, August 1996, p. 95). Boston, Massachusetts: Goldhirsh Group, Inc. By Jill Andresky Fraser.

"Booming Venture-Capital Firms Tap Trainees for Major Projects" in *Wall Street Journal*. (Vol. Ic, No. 14, January 21, 1997, p. B2). New York, New York: Wall Street Journal: Dow Jones & Co., Inc. By Stephanie N. Metha.

"Borrowing Against Collateral You May Not Know You Have" in *Money*. (Vol. 23, No. 11, November 1994, pp. 114-116). New York, New York: Time Inc. By Nancy J. Perry.

"Breaking the Bank" in *Entrepreneur*. (May 1993, pp. 78, 80-82). Irvine, California: Entrepreneur, Inc. By Stephanie Barlow.

"Breaking the Bank" in *Entrepreneurial Woman*. (November 1990, pp. 60-63). Irvine, California: Entrepreneur, Inc. By Kim Remesch.

"Business Owners Dip into Capital" in *Black Enterprise*. (Vol. 26, No. 9, April 1996, p. 29). New York, New York: Earl G. Graves Publishing Co. Inc. By Carolyn M. Brown.

"Calculated Risk" in *Business Start-Ups*. (Vol. 8, No. 1, January 1996, pp. 75-76). Irvine, California: Entrepreneur Media Inc. By Steve Marshall Cohen.

"Capital Questions" in *Entrepreneur*. (March 1997, pp. 62, 64-65). Irvine, California: Entrepreneur Media Inc. By David R. Evanson.

"Capitalists on a Mission" in *Black Enterprise*. (Vol. 25, No. 4, November 1994, pp. 166-167, 170-171). New York,

New York: Earl G. Graves Publishing Co. Inc. By Mark Lowery.

"The Card File" in *Business Start-Ups*. (Vol. 7, No. 11, November 1995, p. 98). Irvine, California: Entrepreneur Media Inc. By Karin Moeller.

"Charge It" in *Business Start-Ups*. (Vol. 8, No. 1, January 1996, pp. 62-63). Irvine, California: Entrepreneur Media Inc. By Gerri Detweiler.

"Club Benefits" in *Entrepreneur*. (May 1996, pp. 58, 60-61). Irvine, California: Entrepreneur Media Inc. By David R. Evanson.

"Criteria Used by Venture Capitalists" in *International Small Business Journal*. (Vol. 13, No. 1, October/December 1994, pp. 26-37). Cheshire: Woodcock Publications Ltd. By Russell M. Knight.

"Dialing For Dollars" in *Entrepreneur*. (Vol. 23, o. 12, November 1995, pp. 52, 54-55). Irvine, California: Entrepreneur Media, Inc. By David R. Evanson.

"Doll-Makers Worked Around Obstacles" in *Crain's Small Business*. (December 1995, pp. 13-14). Detroit, Michigan: Crain Communications, Inc. By Jeffrey McCracken.

"Dollars and Sense" in *Entrepreneur*. (July 1996, pp. 62, 64-65). Irvine, California: Entrepreneur Media Inc. By David R. Evanson.

"Factors to Consider" in *Small Business Opportunities*. (Vol. 7, No. 3, May 1995, pp. 20, 74). New York, New York: Harris Publications, Inc. By Robert Kassebaum.

"A Fair to Remember" in *Entrepreneur*. (Vol. 23, No. 2, February 1995, pp. 38-39). Irvine, California: Entrepreneur Media, Inc. By Davis R. Evanson.

"Fatal Flaws" in *Entrepreneur*. (November, 1996 pp. 70, 73). Irvine, California: Entrepreneur Media Inc. By David R. Evanson.

"Finance for Small and Medium-Sized Enterprises" in *International Journal of Bank Marketing*. (Vol. 12, No. 6, 1994, pp. 3-9). W. Yorks: M C B University Press Ltd. By Pamela Edwards, Peter Turnbull.

"Financial Management 101" in *Inc*. (Vol. 18, No. 8, June 1996, p. 120). Boston, Massachusetts: Goldhirsh Group, Inc. By Jill Andresky Fraser.

"Financing Your Franchise" in *Business Start-Ups*. (Vol. 8, No. 1, January 1996, pp. 68, 70-71). Irvine, California: Entrepreneur Media Inc. By Jacquelyn Lynn.

"Find Financing" in *Income Opportunities*. (December/January 1991, p. 57). New York, New York: IO Publications, Inc. By D. Frederick Riggs.

"For What It's Worth" in *Entrepreneur*. (Vol. 23, No. 5, May 1995, pp. 40-41). Irvine, California: Entrepreneur Media, Inc. By David R. Evanson.

"Foreign Power" in *Entrepreneur*. (February 1997, pp. 68, 70-71). Irvine, California: Entrepreneur Media Inc. By David R. Evanson.

"Found Money" in *Business Start-Ups*. (Vol. 8, No. 6, June 1996, pp. 18, 20). Irvine, California: Entrepreneur Media Inc. By Carla Goodman.

"Fueling Up" in *Business Start-Ups*. (Vol. 8, No. 12, December 1996, pp. 46, 48). Irvine, California: Entrepreneur Media Inc. By Carla Goodman.

"Get Cash Now!" in *Success*. (Vol. 38, No. 10, December 1991, pp. 26-32). New York, New York: Lang Communications. By Ronit Addis Rose.

"Going for Broke" in *Inc. Magazine*. (September 1990, pp. 34-44). Boston, Massachusetts: Goldhirsh Group, Inc.

"Good Luck" in *Entrepreneur*. (March 1996, pp. 59-61). Irvine, California: Entrepreneur Media Inc. By David R. Evanson.

"Hatching Uncle Sam's Entrepreneurs" in *Management Today*. (November 1993, pp. 54-56). London: Haymarket Management Magazines. By John Thackray.

"Heaven Cent" in Entrepreneur. (Vol. 24, No. 2, February 1996, p. 29). Irvine, California: Entrepreneur Media, Inc. By Cynthia E. Griffin.

"How to Finance Anything" in *Inc. Magazine*. (February 1993, pp. 54, 56-58, 62, 64, 66, 68). Boston, Massachusetts: Goldhirsh Group, Inc. By Bruce G. Posner.

"How to Obtain Export Capital" in *Nation's Business*. (Vol. 82, No. 5, May 1994, p. 24). Washington, District of Columbia: U.S. Chamber of Commerce

"Inatome Made It, Now He Wants To Help Others" in *Crain's Small Business*. (March 1996, p. 11). Detroit, Michigan: Crain Communications, Inc. By Jeffrey McCracken.

"Investors Bet on Cyberspace Path to Terra Firm Travel" in *Wall Street Journal*. (Vol. Ic, No. 9, January 14, 1997, p. B2). New York, New York: Wall Street Journal: Dow Jones & Co., Inc. By Michael Selz.

"Investors Look for Businesses Likely to Hit a Home Run'" in *Crain's Small Business*. (March 1996, p. 11). Detroit, Michigan: Crain Communications, Inc. By Jeffrey McCracken.

"An Investor's View" in *In Business*. (January/February

1990, pp. 32-33). Emmaus, Pennsylvania: J.G. Press, Inc. By Abbie C. Page.

"It's Who You Know" in *Entrepreneur*. (Vol. 23, No. 11, October 1995, pp. 48, 51). Irvine, California: Entrepreneur Media, Inc. By David R. Evanson.

"Job One: Find Money" in *Success Magazine*. (Vol. 41, No. 10, December 1994, pp. 23-33). New York, New York: Lang Communications. By Jenny C. McCune.

"Keep Your Eye on the Angels" in *Inc*. (Vol. 18, No. 7, May 1996, p. 22). Boston, Massachusetts: Goldhirsh Group, Inc.

"Kid Venture Capital" in *Black Enterprise*. (Vol. 25, No. 5, December 1994, p. 34). New York, New York: Earl G. Graves Publishing Co. Inc. By Tonia L. Shakespeare.

"Listing Your Company on a Stock Exchange" in *D & B Reports*. (Vol. 40, No. 2, March/April 1992, pp. 62-63). New York, New York: Dun & Bradstreet. By Mark Stevens.

"Look at Every Option—And Beyond" in *Nation's Business*. (Vol. 79, No. 7, July 1991, p. 9). Washington, District of Columbia: U.S. Chamber of Commerce. By Thomas Hierl.

"Making a Statement" in *Entrepreneur*. (Vol. 23, No. 7, July 1995, pp. 34-37). Irvine, California: Entrepreneur Media, Inc. By David R. Evanson.

"A Match Made in Fiber Optics" in *Hispanic Business*. (Vol. 16, No. 9, September 1994, pp. 24, 26). Santa Barbara, California: Hispanic Business, Inc. By Rick Mendosa.

"Money" in *Business Start-Ups*. (Vol. 7, No. 12, December 1995, pp. 50-51). Irvine, California: Entrepreneur Media Inc. By Nancy Scarlato.

"Money Chain" in *Wall Street Journal Special Reports: Small Business (Special Edition)*. (May 23, 1996, p. R12). New York, New York: Wall Street Journal: Dow Jones & Co., Inc. By Jeffrey A. Tannebaum.

"Money Guide" in *Crain's Small Business*. (Vol. 3, No. 1, January 1995, pp. 4-6). Detroit, Michigan: Crain's Communications, Inc. By Dorothy Heyart and Gail Popyk.

"Money Hunting" in *Hispanic Business*. (Vol. 19, No. 1, January 1997, pp. 28, 30). Santa Barbara, California: Hispanic Business Inc. By Joel Russell.

"The Money Is Out There...How To Get It" in *Agency Sales Magazine*. (Vol. 24, No. 2, February 1994, pp. 15-17). Laguna Hills, California: Manufacturers' Agents National Association. By Jeff Fromberg.

"Money Now" in *Success*. (December 1990, pp. 29-36). Harlan, Iowa: Success Magazine Co. By Ronit Addis Rose.

"Name Your Price" in *Business Start-Ups*. (Vol. 7, No. 11, November 1995, pp. 96-97). Irvine, California: Entrepreneur Media Inc. By Steve Marshall Cohen.

"New Enterprise Forum" in *Crain's Small Business*. (December 1995, p. 31). Detroit, Michigan: Crain Communications, Inc.

"A New Way to Get Funding for Your Business" in *Successful Opportunities*. (April 1990, pp. 36-38). San Diego, California: National Publications, Inc. By David Brainer.

"Nothing Ventured" in *Crain's Small Business*. (March 1996, pp. 1, 10). Detroit, Michigan: Crain Communications, Inc. By Jeffrey McCracken.

"Nothing Ventured, Nothing Gained" in *Entrepreneur*. (Vol. 23, No. 4, April 1995, p. 110). Irvine, California: Entrepreneur Media, Inc. By David R. Evanson.

"The Numbers Speak Volumes" in *Small Business Reports*. (Vol. 19, No. 7, July 1994, pp. 39-43). New York, New York: Faulkner & Gray, Inc. By Lamont Change.

"On the Grow" in *Entrepreneur*. (May 1997, p. 34). Irvine, California: Entrepreneur Media Inc. By Michael Stout.

"Peer Review" in *Entrepreneur*. (July 1996, p. 18). Irvine, California: Entrepreneur Media Inc. By L.B.

"Quick Fix" in *Income Opportunities*. (Vol. 30, No. 3, March 1995, pp. 88, 90). New York, New York: IO Publications Inc. By Peg Byron.

"Raising Money From Your Bank" in *In Business*. (April 1990, pp. 21-23). Emmaus, Pennsylvania: J.G. Press, Inc. By Allen C. Finley and Robert W. Pricer.

"Report Seeks to Show How State Should Venture Forth" in *Crain's Small Business*. (March 1996, p. 13). Detroit, Michigan: Crain Communications, Inc. By Jeffrey McCracken.

"Reservations Accepted" in *Entrepreneur*. (Vol. 23, No. 3, March 1995, pp. 46-47). Irvine, California: Entrepreneur Media, Inc. By David R. Evanson.

"SBA Lends a Hand" in *New Business Opportunities*. (April 1990, pp. 10-15). Irvine, California: Entrepreneur, Inc. By Iris Lorenz-Fife.

"Scoring Points" in *Entrepreneur*. (June 1995, pp. 38-41). Irvine, California: Entrepreneur Media Inc. By David R. Evanson.

"The Secrets of Bootstrapping" in *Inc*. (Vol. 13, No. 9,

September 1991, pp. 52-70). Boston, Massachusetts: Goldhirsh Group, Inc. By Robert A. Mamis.

"Show Me the Money" in *Inc.* (Vol. 19, No. 3, March 1997, pp. 110, 112). Boston, Massachusetts: Goldhirsh Group, Inc. By Jill Andresky Fraser.

"Show and Tell" in *Entrepreneur.* (March 1996, p. 28). Irvine, California: Entrepreneur Media Inc.

"The Six Best Ways to Raise Cash" in *Money Money Guide Supplement.* (Vol. , No. , 1994, pp. 34-39). New York, New York: Time, Inc. By Vanessa O'Connell.

"Small Offerings" in *Entrepreneur.* (Vol. 23, No. 1, January 1995, pp. 40-41). Irvine, California: Entrepreneur Media, Inc. By David R. Evanson.

"Something Ventured" in *Entrepreneur.* (Vol. 23, No. 11, October 1995, p. 24). Irvine, California: Entrepreneur Media, Inc. By David R. Evanson.

"Start-up Funding: Consider the Sources" in *Inc.* (Vol. 6, No. 8, August 1994, p. 32). Boston, Massachusetts: Goldhirsh Group, Inc. By Martha E. Mangelsdorf.

"Step 9: Generate Start-Up Capital" in *Business Start-Ups.* <Vol. 9, No. 2, February 1997, pp. 64, 66). Irvine, California: Entrepreneur Media Inc. By Kylo-Patrick Hart.

"Three Sources to Finance a Small Business" in *Crain's Small Business.* (December 1995, p. 15). Detroit, Michigan: Crain Communications, Inc. By Jeffrey McCracken.

"Turning to the Government" in *Practical Accountant.* (Vol. 27, No. 6, June 1994, pp. 37-44). New York, New York: Faulkner and Gray, Inc. By John Cosgriff and Leonard Sliwoski.

"Under Inspection" in *Entrepreneur.* (December 1996, p. 19). Irvine, California: Entrepreneur Media Inc. By Karen Axelton.

"Venture Capital" in *Business Start-Ups.* (Vol. 7, No. 12, December 1995, p. 70). Irvine, California: Entrepreneur Media Inc. By Nancy Scarlato.

"Venture Capital Raised by Companies Was a Record $10.1 Billion in 1996" in *Wall Street Journal.* (Vol. Ic, No. 25, Feb. 5, 1997, p. B2). New York, New York: Wall Street Journal: Dow Jones & Co., Inc. By Stephanie N. Mehta.

"Venture Capitalists Step Up Role in Ipos" in *Wall Street Journal.* (Vol. Ic, No. 4, January 7, 1997, p. B2). New York, New York: Wall Street Journal: Dow Jones & Co., Inc. By Stephanie N. Mehta.

"Wanted: Innovative Ideas" in *Black Enterprise.* (Vol. 27, No. 4, November 1996, p. 27). New York, New York: Earl G. Graves Publishing Co. Inc. By Glenn Jeffers.

"Where Are All the Wanda Buffets?" in *Money.* (Vol. 23, No. 11, November 1994, pp. 116-117). New York, New York: Time Inc. By Nancy J. Perry.

"Where to Look for Money Now" in *Working Woman.* (Vol. 19, No. 10, October 1994, pp. 56-62). New York, New York: Working Woman, Inc. By Ilyce R. Glink.

"You Can Bank on It" in *Business Start-Ups.* (Vol. 8, No. 8, August 1996, pp. 56, 58, 60-61). Irvine, California: Entrepreneur Media Inc. By Jacquelyn Lynn.

"You Can't Start Too Soon" in *Inc.* (Vol. 17, No. 6, May 1995, p. 144). Boston, Massachusetts: Goldhirsh Group, Inc. By Susan Greco.